THE 21ST CENTURY COOKBOOK

FLORENCE H. ALDRICH
and
MARILYN D. PATRICK

 ERMINE PUBLISHERS, INC., Hollywood, California

COPYRIGHT © 1978 by Florence H. Aldrich and Marilyn D. Patrick in the United States of America.

Library of Congress Catalog Card No. 77-80981
ISBN 0-89343-026-9

Editorial Assistance: B. J. Warren

Ermine Publishers, Inc.
6253 Hollywood Blvd., Suite 312
Hollywood, California 90028
213/461-3256

WITH MUCH AFFECTION TO
BYRON AND PETER
FLORENCE H. ALDRICH

FOR MY HEALTHY, DYNAMIC
AND LUMINOUS FAMILY
MARILYN D. PATRICK

ACKNOWLEDGEMENTS

My sincere thanks and appreciation to the following generous people who contributed so much to this book:

Mr. Leland J. "Butch" Simas, Simas Sporting Goods Store, Santa Maria, California, member of Santa Maria Elks Lodge No. 1538, for the material for the Santa Maria style Barbecue; Dr. Robert J. Hammond, M.D. for his valuable advice and suggestion to add potassium to the recipe components; Dr. and Mrs. Donald E. Reiner, specialists in nutrition, for their professional opinions; Mrs. Pat Porter, Dietician, formerly of the Marian Hospital, Santa Maria, California, for her advice and contributions titled Food Components and What They Do for You, and Best Sources of Food Essentials (see Appendices Four and Five); Mrs. Mary Middlecamp, Dietician, formerly of Marian Hospital, for her advice on sources of nutrition; Miss Cecelia Negus, Dietician, Dietary Consultant for Valley Community Hospital, Santa Maria, California for her advice, particularly on the cholesterol content of foods; Mrs. G. T. Pinckard, science-fiction author and high school teacher of creative writing, for her professional advice; Mr. John Reese, author of many books of western stories, for his professional advice; Miss Cynthia Garner, teacher and summer school principal, Ventura, California, who contributed recipes in "My Cook Book" — 1776-1976, a student-parent project of the Blanche Reynolds Summer School; Mrs. John Abst, Scottsdale, Arizona, and Mrs. W. N. Vaughan, Lompoc, California for contributions of their own special recipes, and to Rev. and Mrs. Ron France, of the First Christian Church of Santa Maria, and Mr. and Mrs. L. Gorka, proprietors of The Book Harbor, Santa Maria, for their continuing encouragement.

....

CONTENTS

FORWARD

THE 21ST CENTURY COOKBOOK

There are no diets in this book. It is a cookbook for people on regular diets but the recipes have been calculated to show the composition of their ingredients to help those who are on low-sodium, low-cholesterol and reducing diets.

Gram weights of foods, calories, milligrams of sodium and potassium are shown in figures; protein, fat, carbohydrates, cholesterol, saturated and unsaturated fatty acids, calcium and iron are letter coded, as follows:

F = fair content
G = good content
H = high content
L = low content
n/a = no information was available
--- = there were no measureable amounts present, OR zero content

At the top of most of the calculated recipes, you will find the averages for each serving, or whatever the item happens to be. For example: Hot cross buns will show the average weight in grams of each, average number of calories in each; also the average number of milligrams of sodium and potassium. If eggs are called for in the recipes, or other ingredients that have a cholesterol content, the average milligrams of cholesterol is also shown, and the computation of the cholesterol is given in a paragraph below the method for the recipe, along with the authority for those figures. (Vitamins are shown in the body of the recipe).

However, a food that is low is sodium or cholesterol may not appear on your diet list for some other reason, so please check with your doctor. Show him this book, if you wish, because there might be foods that you could add to your diet. This book is not intended to show you what you may or may not have. No book can do this — not even a diet book. Your own physician is the only one who can help you because he knows you and he knows your problems.

USING THE FOOD LISTS

To assist in planning nutritious meals, and to further help those on diets, each chapter in this book is headed by food lists titled "Nutrition at Your Fingertips." They are also calculated by components and are more extensive because there are many foods not mentioned in the recipes that appear on these lists. Headings and abbreviations are explained below.

GRAM WTS. — Gram weights of the foods listed

VITAMINS — Not abbreviated

CAL — Calories (food energy)

SOD — Sodium, not shown in milligrams

PRO — Protein, expressed in letters

FAT — Not abbreviated, expressed in letters

CARB — Carbohydrates, expressed in letters

CHOL — Cholesterol, expressed in letters but show in milligrams in the "Average" section at the top of each recipe.

FATTY ACIDS . . . .

SAT — Saturated fatty acids, expressed in letters

UNSAT — Unstaurated fatty acids, expressed in letters

CALC — Calcium, expressed in letters

IRON — Not abbreviated, expressed in letters

POTSM — Potassium, shown in milligrams

Information for the food lists was obtained from "COMPOSITION OF FOODS," U.S.D.A. Agriculture Handbook No. 8, and "NUTRITIVE VALUE OF FOODS," U.S.D.A. Home and U.S.D.A. Home and Garden Bulletin No. 72.

The following abbreviations are used only in the 'Ingredients' portion of each individual recipe.

tsp — teaspoon

tblspn — tablespoon

cp — cup

lb — pounds

. . . .

II

APPENDIX ONE

EQUIVALENTS OF FOOD BY WEIGHT AND VOLUME

Food	Weight	Volume
Beans, dried:		
white	1 pound equals	about 2 cups uncooked, 6 cups cooked.
kidney	1 pound equals	2-2/3 cups uncooked. 6-1/4 cups cooked.
lima	1 pound equals	3 cups uncooked; 6-1/2 to 7 cups cooked.
Beans, fresh:		
string, wax or snap	1 pound equals	4 cups uncooked, 3 cups cooked.
lima	1 pound equals	2/3 cup, shelled
Beef, raw, ground	1 pound equals	about 2 cups cooked.
Beets, fresh	1 pound equals	2 cups cooked, 3 to 4 servings.
Beet sugar (see sugar)		
Blackberries, fresh	1 pound equals	6 cups
Black raspberries, fresh	1 pound equals	3-1/2 cups
Blueberries, fresh	1 pound equals	3-1/2 cups
Bran	10 ounce package	6 cups (1 cup weighs about 1-2/3 ounce.)
Breadcrumbs, fresh	1 pound equals	9 cups
dry	1 pound	3-1/2 to 4 cups
Bread (loaves)		
white	1 pound equals	18 slices (soft crumb type)
		22 slices (soft crumb type)
		20 slices (firm crumb type)
	1-1/2 pound equals	24 slices (soft crumb type)
		28 slices (soft crumb type)
	2 pounds equals	34 slices (firm crumb type)
	3 pounds equals	39 to 40 slices (restaurant)
whole wheat	1 pound equals	16 slices (soft crumb type)
	1 pound equals	18 slices (firm crumb type)
rye (restaurant)	2 pounds equals	30 to 32 slices
Broccoli	1 pound equals	about 2 cups
Brussel sprouts	1-1/4 pounds equals	1 quart box
Butter	1 pound equals	2 cups (48 to 60 pats)
	1 ounce equals	2 tablespoons
Cabbage, raw	1 pound equals	1-1/3 quarts shredded coarse
		2-1/2 cups shredded fine
Cane sugar (see sugar)		
Carrots	3 ounces equals	2/3 cup sliced, uncooked
	1 pound equals	3 cups diced, raw, or 2 cups cooked.
Celery	1 pound equals	4 cups coarsely cut or 3 cups finely cut, or 2 cups cooked, diced.
Celery seed	1 ounce equals	6 tablespoons (finely ground)
Cheese, cheddar	1 pound equals	5 cups grated
Cheese, grated	1 ounce equals	1/3 cup
Cherries, candied	1 pound equals	about 120 cherries
Maraschino	32 ounces equals	60 to 70 cherries

EQUIVALENTS OF FOOD BY WEIGHT AND VOLUME

Food	Weight	Volume
Chocolate	1 pound equals	16 squares
	6 ounces equals	1 cup (1 package) semi-sweet chocolate pieces
	2 ounces, melted, unsweetened equals	1 cup grated or 2 squares
	1 ounce equals	1 square, or 1/4 cup cocoa (1 square grated equals 5 tablespoons)

(See substitution for chocolate under cocoa.)

Food	Weight	Volume
Cinnamon	1 ounce equals	4 to 4-1/2 tablespoons
Cloves	1 ounce equals	4 to 4-1/2 tablespoons
Cocoa	1 pound equals	4-1/2 cups

3 tablespoons cocoa, plus 2/3 tablespoon margarine or other sortening, may be substituted for 1 ounce (2 square) of chocolate.

Food	Weight	Volume
Coconut (shredded)	1 pound equals	6 cups
Coffee	1 pound equals	5 cups
Cornmeal, White or Yellow		
Uncooked	1 pound equals	3 cups; 1 cup uncooked equals 4 cups cooked.
Cooked	1 pound equals	about 2-1/2 quarts
Cornstarch	1 pound equals	3 cups
	3 grams equals	1 teaspoon
	9 grams equals	1 tablespoon

NOTE: To substitute cornstarch for flour, use half as much cornstarch as flour given in the recipe.

To substitute cornstarch for eggs in custards, use 1/2 tablespoon cornstarch for each egg omitted.

Food	Weight	Volume
Crabmeat (see Shellfish)		
Crackers		
Graham	1 pound equals	about 40
Oyster	1 pound equals	450 to 500
Saltines	1 pound equals	about 125
Soda	1 pound equals	70 to 90
Cranberries, fresh	1 pound equals	about 4 cups
Cream of tartar	1 ounce equals	3 tablespoons
Cream, whipping, 40%	8 ounces equals	2 cups whipped
Cucumber	12 ounces equals	about 2 cups sliced, or 1-1/2 cups diced.
Currants, dried	1 pound equals	about 2-2/3 to 3-1/2 cups
Dates	1 pound equals	50 to 60
	10 ounce package equals	about 2 cups cut up

EQUIVALENTS OF FOOD BY WEIGHT AND VOLUME

Food	Weight	Volume
Eggs		
Whites	8 ounces equals	8 to 11 (1 cup)
Whole (shelled)	8 ounces equals	4 to 6 (1 cup)
Yolks	8 ounces equals	12 to 14 (1 cup)
NOTE:	In custards, 2 egg yolks to 1 cup milk may be used instead of 1 whole egg.	
Figs:		
Dried	1 pound equals	about 20; cut up and about 2-2/3 cups.
Pressed	1 pound equals	25 to 30
Filberts (Hazelnuts)	1 pound unshelled equals	1-1/3 cups shelled
Flour:		
Graham	1 pound equals	about 4-1/2 cups
White all-purpose or bread flour (sifted)	1 pound equals	about 4 cups, or
	1 ounce equals	4 tablespoons
Cake of pastry	1 pound equals	about 4-1/2 cups
Rye	1 pound equals	about 4-1/4 cups
NOTE:	To substitute all-purpose flour for cake flour, subtract 2 tablespoons all-purpose flour from the amount to be used in a recipe, and add 1-1/2 tablespoons cornstarch for each cup.	
Ginger	1 pound equals	4-1/2 cups
	1 ounce equals	3 tablespoons
Grapes:		
Seedless	1 pound equals	2 cups
Other (halved and seeded)	1 pound equals	about 2-1/4 cups
Honey	12 fluid ounces equals	1 cup, or 8 tablespoons
	1-1/2 fluid ounces equals	1 tablespoon
Lard	1 pound equals	2 cups
Lemons	1 pound equals	3 to 5 lemons
	8 fluid ounces equals	about 1 cup (4 juicy lemons)
NOTE:	1 medium lemon will yield about 1-1/2 teaspoons of grated peel, or about 3 tablespoons juice.	
Lobster	1, 2-1/2 or 3 pounds equals	2 cups cooked meat
Macaroni	1 pound dry equals	about 4 cups; 7 to 8 cups cooked.
	8 ounces equals	2-1/2 cups; 4 to 5 cups cooked.
Mace	1 ounce equals	about 4 tablespoons

EQUIVALENTS OF FOOD BY WEIGHT AND VOLUME

Food	Weight	Volume
Margarine	1 pound equals	2 cups (4 sticks)
	1/2 pound equals	1 cup (2 sticks)
	1/4 pound equals	1/2 cup (1 stick)
	1/8 pound equals	1/4 cup (1/2 stick)
	1 ounce equals	2 tablespoons
	5 grams equals	1 teaspoon (1/3 tablespoon) also about 1 tablespoon melted.
Marshmallows	1 pound	about 60
Milk:		
Condensed (sweetened)	7-1/2 fluid ounces equals	2/3 cup
Evaporated	5-1/3 fluid ounces equals	2/3 cup
Fresh	32 fluid ounces equals	1 quart of 4 cups or 2 pints.
Mustard:		
dry	1 ounce equals	14 teaspoons
seed	1 ounce equals	2-1/2 tablespoons
Noodles	8 ounces equals	2-1/2 cups uncooked, 4 to 5 cups cooked.
Nutmeats	1/4 pound equals	1 cup chopped
Nutmeg, ground	1 ounce equals	about 11 teaspoons, 1 whole nutmeg yields about 2-3/4 tablespoons grated.
Oats, dry (rolled)	1 pound equals	about 5-1/2 cups
	1 ounce equals	1-3 cup
cooked	1 pound equals	2-1/2 quarts
Oatmeal, dry	1 pound equals	about 2-2/3 cups; cooked. 2-1/2 quarts.
Onions, dry	1 pount equals	about 4, 2-1/2" dia.; or 3 cups chopped
Parsnips, fresh	1 pound equals	2-1/2 cups cooked, sliced
Peaches:		
fresh	1 pound equals	2-1/2 cups sliced
dried	5-1/2 pounds fresh equals	1 pound dried
Peanut butter	1 pound equals	1-3/4 cups
Peanuts, shelled, raw	1 pound equals	about 2-2/3 cups, depending upon type.
Peas, fresh shelled	1 pound equals	1 cup
split, yellow or green	1 pound equals	2 cups cooked, 12 servings
Pecans (shelled)	1 pound equals	3 to 4 cups
Pepper:		
Whole, black	1 ounce equals	4 tablespoons
Ground, black	1 ounce equals	4-1/2 tablespoons
Ground, white	1 ounce equals	12 teaspoons
Pickles:		
chopped	1 pound equals	3 cups
whole, 3"	1 pound equals	16 pickles
whole, 2"	1 pound equals	22 pickles

EQUIVALENTS OF FOOD BY WEIGHT AND VOLUME

Food	Weight	Volume
Popcorn, uncooked	8 ounces equals	5 cups popped corn
Potatoes	1 pound equals	about 3 medium; 2-1/2 cups cooked, diced, or 2-1/4 cups mashed.
Prunes	1 pound equals	4 cups cooked, drained, unpitted; 2 cups pitted. 20 50 80; average 40 to 60.
Raisins:		
with seeds	15 ounce package equals	3-1/2 cups
seedless	15 ounce package equals	about 3 cups
Raspberries, fresh	1 pound equals	about 3-1/2 cups
Rhubarb, fresh	1 pound equals	2 cups sauce
Rice, polished	1 pound equals	2 cups uncooked, 6 cups cooked.
Salt	4 grams equals	1 teaspoon
Sauerkraut	10 pounds equals	6 to 7 quarts
Shellfish (crab or shrimp)	1 pound equals	2 cups cooked meat
Shortening (see butter, lard or margarine)		
Shrimp (see shellfish)		
Spaghetti, broken	1 pound equals	5 cups uncooked; 11 cups cooked.
	8 ounces equals	2-1/2 cups uncooked; 5-1/2 cups cooked.
Spinach, fresh	1 pound equals	1-1/2 to 2-1/2 cups cooked
Strawberries	1 pound equals	about 3-1/2 cups depending upon size.
String beans (see Beans, fresh)		
Sugar:		
Brown	1 pound equals	2-1/2 to 2-3/4 cups. depending upon moisture
Granulated	1 pound equals	about 2-1/4 cups
Cubes or loaf	1 pound equals	50 to 70
Powdered (Confectioner's)	1 pound equals	about 3 cups
Sweet potatoes	1-1/4 pounds equals	4 medium or 2-3/4 cups mashed
Tapioca	1 pound equals	2-1/2 cups
NOTE:	1 cup pearl tapioca is equal to 3/4 cup quick-cooking type.	
Quick-cooking type	6 ounces equals	1 cup
Tea, dry	1 pound equals	6-1/2 cups
Thyme, finely ground	1 ounce equals	averages 8 tablespoons
Tomatoes, raw	1 pound equals	4 small
Turnips	1 pound equals	about 4 or 2 cups cooked, diced.
Vanilla	1 fluid ounce	2 tablespoons; 6 teaspoons
Walnuts:		
shelled	1 pound equals	about 4 cups
unshelled	1 pound equals	about 2 cups nutmeats
Water	236 grams equals	1 cup
Watercress, fresh	1 ounce equals	1-1/3 cups pressed into measuring cup.
Yeast:		
Compressed	5 grams equals	1 cake
Dry, active	7 grams equals	1 package

. . . .

APPENDIX TWO

FOOD COMPONENTS AND WHAT THEY DO FOR YOU

Your body is your most precious asset. It's priceless. It's unique to you alone. To keep it in good condition, its demands are great. It must be washed, combed, manicured and pedicured, and sunned, loved, dressed, shaved and exercised. But more importantly, it must be fed.

To function properly, to grow and to maintain good health, the body also needs calcium, copper, manganese, fats, iodine, iron, potassium, phosphorous, protein, sugars, starches and vitamins. All of these materials are found in the foods we eat. Their functions and where they're found are shown below:

CALCIUM	—	for bones, teeth, glands, nerves and muscles. It's present in almonds, beans, cheese, egg yolk, dates and figs, green vegetables and tops, milk, olives, pecans, dried peas, and all sea foods.
COPPER AND MANGANESE	—	with IRON, to help make blood. It's found in almonds and pecans, peas and beans, dried lentils, dates, huckleberries, oatmeal, oysters, shrimp, turnip tops, and whole wheat.
FATS	—	for heat, energy, and padding for nerves and muscles. It's in avocados, butter, cheese, cream, lard, oils, salad dressings, some desserts, some breads, rolls, pies, cookies, some cakes, fish, meats, poultry, egg yolks, peanut butter, chocolate, olives and margarine.
IODINE	—	for the functioning of the thyroid gland. It's contained in cod-liver oil, iodized salt, salt-water fish and sea food.
IRON	—	with copper and manganese to make blood. It's found in almonds, beans, currants, egg yolks, green vegetables and tops, dates, avocados, liver (calves, chicken, lamb), oysters, dried peas, lentils, prunes, raisins, and fresh meats.
PHOSPHOROUS	—	for bones, teeth, glands, nerves and muscles. It's found in cashew nuts, peanuts pecans, walnuts, almonds, beans, cheese, lima beans, liver, lentils, chocolate, egg yolks, unrefined grains, all salt-water fish, all meats, poultry, and dried beans.
PROTEIN	—	makes flesh and blood. It's present in all grains, fish, poultry, meat, game, sea food, nuts, cheese, milk, eggs, beans, peas, corn, some rolls, some breads, and zweibach.
STARCHES AND SUGARS	—	for heat, energy, and fat. Needed for the proper functioning of the liver, and digestion of fat. Starches are found in arrowroot, Jersualem artichokes, beans, corn, cornstarch, dried peas, grains, lentils, flour, potatoes, okra, pumpkin, winter squash, nuts, rice, yams, and tapioca. Sugar is found in all sugars, molasses, sirups, honey, dried fruits, sweet chocolate, candies, sorghum, jams, jellies, preserves and beets.

. . . .

BEST SOURCES OF FOOD ESSENTIALS

VITAMIN A	—	Butter fat
		Cod liver oil, and other fish oils
		Egg yolk, milk, cream and cheese
		Green leafy vegetables
		Yellow vegetables
		Fruit
		Liver
		Yellow cornmeal and foods made from it.
Functions	—	Vitamin A promotes the growth of bones, teeth and muscles; helps the body resist infectious diseases; prevents certain eye diseases and helps keep the skin soft and smooth.

THE B GROUP

VITAMIN B1 (Thiamin)	—	Wheat Germ
		Whole cereals
		Brewer's Yeast
		Legumes
		Pork
		Milk
		Eggs
Functions	—	see below
VITAMIN B2 (Riboflavin)	—	Liver
		Lean meat
		Milk
		Green leafy vegetables
		Eggs
		Brewer's Yeast
Nicotinic Acid (Niacin)	—	Yeast
		Liver, chicken, fish
		Wheat Germ
		Lean meat
		Fresh vegetables
		Fruits
Functions	—	The B Vitamins help prevent fatigue, promote growth, stimulate the appetite, protect nerve and brain tissue and function.

VITAMIN C (Ascorbic Acid)	—	Citrus fruits particularly; also other fruits
		Liver (beef, calves, chicken, hog, lamb)
		Vegetables
Functions	—	Vitamin C is needed for youthful vigor; it promotes growth, strengthens small blood vessels, prevents scurvy, protects jawbones and teeth, the health of gums and skin, and improves resistance to certain infections.

VITAMIN D	—	Fish liver oils
		Fortified milk, cereals and margarine
Functions	—	known as the sunshine vitamin because it is stored when the body is exposed to the sun, Vitamin D prevents rickets, promotes calcification of teeth and bones, good growth and healthy nerves.

BEST SOURCES OF FOOD ESSENTIALS

VITAMIN E	—	Wheat Germ
		Egg Yolks
		Legumes
		Leafy vegetables
		Nuts
		Margarine
		Vegetable oils
Functions	—	Prevents the oxidation of unsaturated fats, particularly, and other fats.

VITAMIN K	—	Tomatoes
		Egg yolks
		Soybean oil
		Leafy vegetables, such as carrot tops, kale, spinach
		Seaweed
		Cabbage, cauliflower
Functions	—	Essential for the promotion of blood clotting and the prevention of hemorrhage. Deficiencies are rare in normal adults.

VITAMIN P	—	a crystalline fraction of fruit juices
Function	—	used to treat certain conditions involving hemorrhage of the skin.

FOODS HIGHEST IN SODIUM (salt)
Breads and some prepared cereals
Meat extracts
Cheese, salted butter
Endive, olives, spinach, beets, celery and watercress
Dried lima beans
Egg white
Condiments, corned, pickled or salted foods
All brined foods
Gelatin

FOODS LOWEST IN SODIUM (salt)
Cereal and flour
Meat
Fruits
Squash, potatoes, tomatoes parsnips, and lettuce.
Honey and Maple sirup
Unsalted butter

FOODS HIGHEST IN CHOLESTEROL
Liver, kidney, brains
Sweetbreads
Egg yolds
Butter, suet, lard
Fish and poultry
Oysters

FOODS LOWEST IN CHOLESTEROL
Breadstuffs
Egg whites
Cereals
Fruits
Nuts
Sugars and sirups
Vegetables and vegetable oils

BEST SOURCES OF FOOD ESSENTIALS

FOODS HIGHEST IN CALCIUM
Milk
Cheese
Almonds, Brazil nuts
Legumes
Molasses
Leafy vegetables

FOODS LOWEST IN CALCIUM
Cereal
Egg white
Meats
Fish
Other fruits and vegetables
Sugar

FOODS HIGHEST IN IRON
Liver, kidney
Egg yolks
Molasses
Legumes
Dried fruits
Muscular meats
Whole grain cereals
Oysters
Nuts

FOODS LOWEST IN IRON
Vegetables, other than greens
Most fruits
Refined cereals
Other meats
Milk
Cheese
Egg whites

FOODS HIGHEST IN OXALIC ACID
Beets and beet greens
Cocoa
Currants
Figs, dried
Pears
Peppers
Potatoes
Raspberries
Rhubarb
Spinach
Strawberries

FOODS LOWEST IN OXALIC ACID
Apples
Brussel sprouts
Cauliflower
Celery
Kale
Lettuce
Melons
Onions
Summer squash

FOODS HIGHEST IN PHOSPHOROUS
Fish
Legumes
Milk, cheese, eggs
Meats and glandular meats
Small amount in vegetables and fruits
Whole grain cereals

FOODS LOWEST IN PHOSPHOROUS
Egg white
Most fruits and vegetables
Refined cereals
Sugars

FOODS HIGHEST IN POTASSIUM
Fish
Legumes
Meat extracts
Meat and glandular meats
Nuts
Most vegetables and fruits

FOODS LOWEST IN POTASSIUM
Butter
Cheese
Eggs
Milk
Refined cereals

BEST SOURCES OF FOOD ESSENTIALS

FOODS HIGHEST IN IODINE
Salt-water fish
Shell Fish
Iodized salt
Eggs
Mushrooms
Leafy Vegetables

NEUTRAL ASH FOODS
Butter, cream, lard, sugar,
tapioca, salad oils.

ACID ASH FOODS
Breads, cereals, eggs
and meats.

ALKALINE ASH FOODS
Most fruits and vegetables,
except cranberries, rhubarb,
plums and prunes.

A POSTSCRIPT ON VITAMINS

Vitamins are perishable. They are easily destroyed by cooking, and by the lapse of time in getting foods from the producer to the consumer. That is the reason vegetables should be cooked in as little water as possible, and the water saved for use in gravies, soups and stews, because these liquids contain vitamins that are lost when drained off.

. . . .

APPENDIX FOUR

SURE YOU CAN EAT BREAKFAST

It's a well known fact that breakfast is the most important meal of the day because our bodies haven't been fed for a period of ten or twelve hours (since the night before) and the food from breakfast acts to refuel our energy reserves. It's also a well known fact that many people skip breakfast for various reasons: some prefer to sleep a little longer; others hope to control their weight; some admit to such hectic, disorganized mornings before rushing off to work that eating is an impossibility.

Perhaps the following suggestions may help. A lot can be done the night before; it's only a matter of getting into the routine of doing them.

1. For perked coffee, fix the automatic pot the night before — water and all. Plug it in before you get dressed in the morning. It'll be ready by the time you are.

2. For instant coffee, put out the spoons, cups and the jar of coffee. Fill the teakettle (or pan) with water. Put the kettle or pan on the stove over the burner. In the morning, the water can be heating on low while you dress.

3. Squeeze the orange juice, or fix the frozen juice the night before. Put the container in the refrigerator. Shake it in the morning and it's all set to pour.
    a. For a nice change of pace, try concord grape juice, or cranberry juice cocktail.
    b. Or fix oranges or grapefruit the night before. Cut them in half and put them on a plate cut sides up. Cover with foil or plastic wrap, then refrigerate. They'll stay as fresh as first cut.

4. Dried appricots, prunes, or other fruit can be prepared on weekends and stored in glass jars in the refrigerator. If jars should not have tops, cut circles of foil and secure them with tape or rubber bands.

5. Put the toaster out the night before. Near it, place a knife with which to spread the margarine or butter that is ready beside it in the morning, spread the toast over a paper towel; it'll save time cleaning up the crumbs — just gather up the towel and throw it away.
    a. If you keep the bread in the refrigerator (which prevents it from molding at a slower rate than bread kept in a cannister at room temperature) put the number of slices you'll need for breakfast in a plastic bag handy to the toaster.
       Coffee keeps fresher in the refrigerator, too!

6. Dry cereal can be set out in bowls the night before and covered with a napkin.
    a. Or sweet rolls, placed in a plastic bag.
    b. Frozen waffles, or French toast, take only a moment to prepare. If you want hot sirup, place the bottle in a deep saucepan and pour enough water until about a third of the bottle is submerged. While you're getting dressed in the morning, turn the heat on low. BE SURE TO LOOSEN THE BOTTLE CAP FIRST Or pour the sirup directly into the saucepan and turn the heat on very low.

7. The table or breakfast bar can be set at night.

. . . .

EIGHT BREAKFAST SUGGESTIONS WITH CALORIES

(Servings are for one person)

No. 1.	Calories	No. 2.	Calories
Stewed prunes, 3	50	1/2 cup strawberries	25
2 scrambled eggs with	150	1 teaspoon powdered sugar	10
2 tablespoons 2% low-fat milk	20	2 links pork sausage	125
1 slice whole wheat toast	65	1 poached egg	75
with 1 tablespoon margarine	100	1 slice whole wheat toast with margarine	165
Total	385	Total	400
No. 3.		No. 4.	
1/2 cup concord grape juice	80	1/2 cup fresh blueberries	40
2 bran muffins	200	1/2 cup hot oatmeal	65
2 teaspoons margarine	67	1/2 cup 2% low-fat milk	73
1 tablespoon strawberry jam	50	1 slice cinnamon toast	232
Total	397	Total	410
No. 5.		No. 6.	
1/2 grapefruit	50	Sliced orange, 2-5/8" in diameter	65
1/ teaspoon sugar	8	3/4 cup cream of wheat	100
3 strips crisp bacon	130	with 1/8 cup raisins	60
1 egg fried in 2 teaspoon margarine	100	1/2 cup 2% low-fat milk	73
1 slice white toast, buttered	115	1 teaspoons sugar	32
Total	403	Total	330
No. 7.		No. 8. *	
1/2 banana, sliced	50	3 ozs. cranberry juice	55
1 cup cornflakes	100	1 ham waffle with 2 ounces of ham	345
1/2 cup 2% low-fat milk	73	2 tablespoons maple sirup	120
2 teaspoons sugar	32	1 teaspoon margarine	33
1 toasted English muffin	150 (est)		
2 teaspoons margarine	67		
Total	472	Total	553

* Instead of maple sirup, use 1 tablespoon powdered sugar, calories:62. and change total calories to 495 instead of 553.

. . . .

VITAMIN INFORMATION

Vitamin	Name	Need In Human Nutrition	U. S. RDA	Deficiency Disease
A *	Retinol	Essential for growth and maintenance of body tissue, strong bones and teeth, and good eyesight. (Helps to form and maintain healthy function of eyes, skin, hair, teeth, gums, various glands and mucous membranes. Also involved in fat metabolism.†)	5,000 I. U., for adults and children four or more years of age, except pregnant and lactating women for whom the RDA is 8,000 I. U.	Xeropthalmia; Night Blindness
B Complex	Thiamine (B1)	Essential for utilization of carbohydrates in energy production. Promotes healthy central nervous system and mental atitude, and improvement of food assimilation and digestion.	1.5 mg.	Beriberi
B Complex	Riboflavin (B2)	Essential for good vision and healthy skin, nails and hair Functions with other substances to breakdown and utilize carbohydrates, fats and proteins.	1.7 mg.	Ariboflavinosis —lesions of the mouth, lips, skin and genitalia.
B Complex	Niacin (Niacinamide or Nicotinic Acid)	Essential for healthy brain functions, nervous system, and skin. Important in tissue respiration. Essential for synthesis of sex hormones.	20 mg.	Pellagra.
B * Complex	Cobalamin Cyanocobalamin (B12)	Essential for maintenance of healthy nervous system, and for utilization of carbohydrates, fats and proteins.	6 mcg.	Perniciousanemia; brain
B Complex	Para-Aminobenzoic Acid (PABA)	Helps to form folic acid, and in utilization of proteins.	Not established	Depression; headache; eczema.
B Complex	Folacin, or Folic Acid	Essential for division of body cells, for production of nucleic acids (RNA and DNA) and for utilization of sugar and amino acids.	0.4 mg. (400 mcg.)	Anemia
B Complex	Inositol	Combines with choline to form lecithin, which in turn metabolizes fats and cholesterol. Important for healthy hair.	Not established.	Eczema

Subclinical Symptoms	Natural/Food Source	Antagonists	Toxicity Level
Eyes—Inability to adjust to darkness; dry and inflamed eyeball; sties. Face and/or Skin Blemishes—rough, dry, prematurely aged skin. General—Loss of smell; loss of appetite; frequent fatigue; diarrhea.	Fish liver oil; carrots; green and yellow vegetables; liver; whole milk and dairy products; egg yolk, yellow fruits.	Excessive consumption of alcoholic beverages; mineral oil; cortisone (and other drugs); polyunsaturated fatty acids with carotene (unless anti-oxidants are present).	More than 50,000 I. U. daily could produce some toxic effects.
Muscles—Cramps; general weakness; tenderness in calf. General—Loss of appetite; fatigue; loss of weight; burning sensation in soles of feet.	Brewer's yeast; wheat germ; brain; liver.	Cooking heat, air, water caffeine; food processing techniques; sulfa drugs; sleeping pills; estrogen; alcohol.	No known toxic effects.
Eyes—burning sensation; bloodshot.	Milk; liver; enriched cereals; brewer's yeast; leafy green vegetables; fish; eggs.	Water; cooking; sunlight food processing techniques sulfa drugs; sleeping pills; estrogen; alcohol.	No known toxic effects.
Nervous System—hostility; suspicion; insomnia; loss of memory; irritability; anxiety. General—abdominal pain; burning sensation in tongue; dry and scaly patches of skin.	Liver; brewer's yeast; kidney; wheat germ; whole grains; fish eggs; lean meat; nuts.	Water; food processing techniques; sulfa drugs; sleeping pills; estrogen; alcohol.	Nontoxic, except some side effects may result from more than 100 mg. daily.
Nervousness; heart palpitations; inflamed tongue.	Liver; kidney; milk and dairy products; some types of meat.	Water; sunlight; acids; alkalis; food processing techniques; sulfa drugs; sleeping pills, estrogen; alcohol.	No known toxic effects.
Fatigue; irritability; constipation; nervousness; graying hair.	Liver; kidney; whole grains	Water; food processing techniques; sulfa drugs; sleeping pills; estrogen; alcohol.	No known toxic effects.
Gastrointestinal disorders.	Liver; Tortula yeast; green vegetables.	Water; food processing techniques; sulfa drugs; sleeping pills, estrogen; alcohol; sunlight.	No known toxic effects.
Loss of hair; constipation.	Liver; brewer's yeast, whole grains; wheat germ; unrefined molasses; corn; citrus.	Water; food processing techniques, sulfa drugs; sleeping pills; estrogen; alcohol.	No known toxic effects.

Vitamin	Name	Need In Human Nutrition	U. S. RDA	Deficiency Disease
B * Complex	Choline	Combines with inositol to form lecithin, which in turn metabolizes fat and cholesterol. Essential for healthy liver and kidneys.	Not established.	Kidney damage.
B Complex	Pantothenic Acid; Panthenol; Calcium Pantothenate.	Essential for conversion of fat and sugar to energy, for use of PABA and choline, and vital to proper function of adrenal glands.	10 mg.	Hypoglycemia; other blood disorders; duodenal ulcers; skin disorders.
B * Complex	Pyridoxine (B6)	Essential for metabolism of amino acids. Aids in blood building, utilization of fats, and normal functioning of brain, nervous system and muscles.	2 mg.	Anemia
B Complex	Biotin (Also called Coenzyme R or Vitamin H)	Essential for utilization of proteins, carbohydrates and fats, and for healthy hair and skin. Aids in the maintenance of the thyroid and adrenal glands, reproductive tract, and the nervous system.	0.3 mg. (300 mcg.)	Dermatitis; depression; anemia; anorexia.
C*	Ascorbic Acid	Principal function is to maintain collagen, which is necessary for the connective tissue that holds body cells together. It is involved in wound healing, the formation of red blood cells and believed to be involved in disease resistance.	60 mg.	Scurvy
D *	Calciferol	Essential for utilization of calcium and phosphorus. Necessary for strong teeth and bones.	400 I. U.	Rickets; osteomalacia; senile osteoporosis.
E *	Tocopherol	Protects from oxidation Vitamin A, selenium, two sulphur amino acids, polyunsaturated fatty acids, and some Vitamin C. †	30 I. U.	Kidney and liver damage; anemia*

XX

Subclinical Symptoms	Natural/Food Source	Antagonists	Toxicity Level
Deteriorating kidneys, abnormally high blood pressure	Brewer's yeast; liver; kidney; wheat germ; egg yolk	Water; food processing techniques; sulfa drugs; sleeping pills; estrogen; alcohol.	No known toxic effects
Restlessness; vomiting, abdominal pains; muscle cramps; burning sensation in feet	Whole grains; wheat germ; bran; kidney; liver; heart? green vegetables; brewer's yeast.	Heat; cooking; canning; caffeine; food processing techniques; sulfa drugs; sleeping pills; estrogen; alcohol.	No known toxic effects
Loss of hair; water retention during pregnancy; nervous system disorder; cracks around mouth and eyes; increase in urination.	Brewer's yeast; wheat bran; rice bran; wheat germ; liver; kidney; heart; blackstrap molasses; milk; eggs; cabbage; beef.	Canning; long storage; roasting or stewing (meat); water; food processing techniques; sulfa drugs; sleeping pills, estrogen; alcohol.	No known toxic effects
Mental depression; dry, peeling skin; muscular pains; poor appetite; lack of energy.	Brewer's yeast; egg yolk; liver; milk; kidney.	Water; food processing techniques; sulfa drugs; sleeping pills; estrogen; alcohol.	No known toxic effects
Slow wound healing; loss of appetite; bleeding gums; muscular weakness; shortness of breath.	Fresh fruits and vegetables	Heat; light; oxygen; water Much Vitamin C is destroyed when vegetables are over washed or cooked, and when fruit is overwashed.	No known toxic effect. Although not proven, excessive use of Vitamin C has been associated with kidney stones in some persons, and has a diuretic and/or laxative effect on some people.
Weakening bones, including teeth; weakening muscles.	Fish liver oils, milk and dairy products: sunlight	Mineral Oil	25,000 I.U. daily over a long period of time could produce a toxic effect in adults.
Muscle degeneration; enlarged prostate; red blood cell damage.	Vegetable oils; whole raw seeds and nuts; soybeans.	Food processing techniques; heat; freezing temperatures; oxygen; iron; mineral oil.	Nontoxic, except for persons with high blood pressure or chronic rheumatic heart disease.

Vitamin	Name	Need In Human Nutrition	U. S. RDA	Deficiency Disease
K *	Menadione	Essential for formation of pro-thrombin, a bloodclotting chemical. Important to proper liver function and longevity.	Not established.	Celiac disease; sprue; colitis; hemorrhage.
P *	Bioflavonoids	Essential for proper use of Vitamin C.	Not established.	Combined with Vitamin C, rheumatism and rheumatic fever.

* See Miscellaneous Notes on the following page.

Subclinical Symptoms	Natural/Food Source	Antagonists	Toxicity Level
Diarrhea; bleeding nose.	Yogurt; egg yolk; saf-flower oil; fish liver oils; kelp; alfalfa; leafy green vegetables.	Aspirin; x-rays and radiation; frozen foods; industrial air pollution.	Natural Vitamin K is considered non-toxic but more than 500 mcg. per day of synthetic Vitamin K is not recommended.
High tendency to bleed easily.	White pigments of citrus fruits; rutin.	Same as Vitamin C.	No known toxicity.

Miscellaneous Notes

A Retinol

The human body—except for diabetics and persons with impaired thyroid functions—has the ability to convert a certain portion of carotene obtained from foods into Vitamin A.

† Information provided by the Vitamin Information Bureau, Inc., Chicago, Illinois

B Cobalamin

Cobalamin, or Vitamin B12 is the only vitamin that contains a mineral, cobalt.

B Choline

Can be synthesized in the human liver.

B Biotin

Can be produced in the human body by the intestinal microflora.

C Ascorbic Acid

Claims as to the beneficial effect of Vitamin C have been made by a number of scientists, among them Nobel Prize winner Dr. Linus Pauling. Among the beneficial effects are increased resistance to disease, particularly the common cold, less tooth decay and possible use as a general antiviral agent.

D Calciferol

Ultraviolet rays of the sun activate the cholesterol present in the skin, converting it to Vitamin D.

E Tocopherol

If taking vitamin and mineral supplements, Vitamin E should be taken at least two hours before or after a person takes an iron supplement.

† Nutritionists, doctors and Federal government scientists disagree as to the exact metabolic function of Vitamin E, and therefore, its deficiency diseases as well. The need listed here, however, is generally agreed to by those involved with nutrition research.

K Menadione

The abundance of Vitamin K in most diets generally precludes the need to supplement food with this vitamin. Vitamin K deficiency is rare, except for newborn babies.

. . . .

BREADS, BISCUITS, ROLLS and OTHER GRAIN PRODUCTS

Breads, Biscuits, Rolls and Other Grain Products

F=Fair; G=Good; H=High; L=Low; t or T = trace; n/a = no information available;   dashes = zero or unmeasurable

GRAM WT.	FOOD	VITAMINS	CAL	(mg) SOD	PRO	FAT	CARB	CHOL	FATTY ACIDS SAT	UNSAT	CALC	IRON	(mg) POTSM
55	BAGEL 3" diameter, made with egg, 1	A B1 B2	165	n/a	F	L	G	---	---	---	L	F	n/a
55	BAGEL 3" diameter, made with water, 1	B1 B2	165	n/a	F	L	G	---	---	---	L	F	n/a
200	BARLEY pearled, light, uncooked 1 cup	B1 B2	700	6	L	L	H	---	---	---	L	F	320
	BISCUITS baking powder, baked from home recipe, made with												
39	Enriched, pre-sifted flour (see recipe) 1 biscuit	A B1 B2 C	112	273		(See recipe for values)							43
100	Unenriched flour, based on biscuits made with baking powder and vegetable fat.	A B1 B2 C	369	626	L	F	G	---	---	---	G	F	117
100	Self-rising, enriched flour	A B1 B2 C	372	660	L	F	G	---	---	---	H	F	64
100	BISCUIT DOUGH commercial with enriched flour chilled in cans	A^t B1 B2	277	868	L	L	G	---	---	---	F	F	65
100	frozen	A^t B1 B2 C^t	327	910	L	F	G	---	---	---	F	F	86
100	BISCUIT DOUGH commercial with biscuits baked from mix made with milk	A^t B1 B2 C^t	325	973	L	L	G	--------n/a---------			F	F	116
42	BOSTON BROWN BREAD 1 slice	A B1 B2 C	88	87		(see recipe for values)							168
	BRAN FLAKES												
35	40%, added thiamine and iron, 1 cp	B1 B2	105	324	F	L	H	---	---	---	F	F	---
50	with raisins, added thiamine and iron, 1 cp	A^t B1 B2	145	400	F	L	H	---	---	---	F	F	---
	CRACKED WHEAT BREAD												
	1 slice	A^t B1 B2 C^t	65	158	F	L	G	---	---	---	G	F	34
454	1 pound loaf	A^t B1 B2 C^t	1190	2860	F	L	G	n/a	L	L	G	F	608

Breads, Biscuits, Rolls and Other Grain Products

F=Fair; G=Good; H=High; L=Low; t or T = trace; n/a = no information available; dashes = zero or unmeasurable

GRAM WT.	FOOD	VITAMINS	CAL	(mg) SOD	PRO	FAT	CARB	CHOL	FATTY ACIDS SAT	UNSAT	CALC	IRON	(mg) POTSM
454	FRENCH OR VIENNA BREAD 1 pound loaf, enriched or unenriched	A^t B1 B2 C^t	1315	2633	L	L	G	n/a	L	L	L	L	409
454	ITALIAN BREAD Enriched or unenriched, 1 pound loaf	B1 B2	1250	2656	L	L	G	n/a	L	L	L	L	337
454	RAISIN BREAD 1 pound loaf	A^t B1 B2 C^t	1190	1657	L	L	G	n/a	L	L	F	F	1058
25	1 slice (18 per loaf) (Also see recipe in this book)	A^t B1 B2 C^t	65	91	L	L	G	---	---	---	F	F	58
454	RYE BREAD American, light (1/3 rye, 2/3 wheat) 1 pound loaf	B1 B2	1100	2656	L	L	G	---	---	---	F	F	658
25	1 slice (18 per loaf) (also see recipe in this book)	B1 B2	60	145	L	L	G	---	---	---	F	F	36
454	PUMPERNICKEL 1 pound loaf	B1 B2	1115	2583	L	L	G	n/a	n/a	n/a	F	F	2061
100	SALT-RISING BREAD	A B1 B2 C^t	267	265	L	L	G	n/a	n/a	n/a	L	L	304
	SOURDOUGH BREAD see recipe												
25	WHITE BREAD soft-crumb type 1 slice (18 per loaf)	A^t B1 B2 C^t	70	127	L	L	G	---	---	---	F	F	n/a
20	1 slice (22 per loaf)	A^t B1 B2 C^t	55	101	L	L	G	---	---	---	F	F	n/a
28	1 slice (24 per loaf)	A^t B1 B2 C^t	75	142	L	L	G	---	---	---	F	F	n/a
24	1 slice (28 per loaf) firm-crumb type 1 pound loaf	A^t B1 B2 C^t	65	122	L	L	G	---	---	---	F	F	n/a
23	1 slice (20 per loaf)	A^t B1 B2 C^t	65	107	F	L	G	---	---	---	F	F	n/a

NUTRITION AT YOUR FINGERTIPS

Breads, Biscuits, Rolls and Other Grain Products

F=Fair; G=Good; H=High; L=Low; t or T = trace; n/a = no information available; dashes = zero or unmeasurable

GRAM WT.	FOOD	VITAMINS	CAL	(mg) SOD	PRO	FAT	CARB	CHOL	FATTY ACIDS SAT	UNSAT	CALC	IRON	(mg) POTSM
27	1 slice (34 per loaf) 2 Pound loaf	A^t B1 B2 C^t	75	137	F	L	G	---	---	---	F	F	n/a
	WHOLE-WHEAT BREAD soft-crumb type; 1 pound loaf												
28	1 slice (16 per loaf) firm-crumb type; 1 pound loaf	A^t B1 B2 C^t	65	148	F	L	G	---	---	---	F	F	n/a
25	1 slice (18 per loaf)	A^t B1 B2 C^t	60	132	F	L	G	---	---	---	F	F	n/a
100	BREADCRUMBS Dry, grated 1 cup	A^t B1 B2 C^t	390	736	F	L	G	---	---	---	G	F	152
	BREAD STICKS See Salt Sticks												
	BREAD STUFFING prepared from mix												
100	Dry, crumbly, prepared with water and table fat	A B1 B2 C^t	358	896	L	F	F	---	---	---	F	F	90
100	Moist, prepared with egg, water and table fat (Also see recipes in this book)	A B1 B2 C^t	208	504	L	F	F	n/a	n/a	n/a	L	F	58
	BREAKFAST CEREALS See Bran Corn, Farina, Oats, Rice & Wheat												
	BUCKWHEAT whole grain flour												
100	whole grain	B1	335	---	F	L	H	---	---	---	G	G	448
100	dark flour	B1 B2	333	---	F	L	H	---	---	---	L	F	---
100	light flour	B1 B2	349	---	L	L	H	---	---	---	L	F	320
	BUCKWHEAT PANCAKE MIX see pancakes												
135	*BULGUR Canned, seasoned 1 cup	B1 B2	245	621	L	L	F	---	---	---	L	F	112

*(NOTE: Processed, partially debranned, whole-kernel wheat with chicken fat, chicken stock base, dehydrated onion flakes, salt, monosodium glutamate, and herbs.)

Breads, Biscuits, Rolls and Other Grain Products

F=Fair; G=Good; H=High; L=Low; t or T = trace; n/a = no information available; dashes = zero or unmeasurable

GRAM WT.	FOOD	VITAMINS	CAL	(mg) SOD	PRO	FAT	CARB	CHOL	FATTY ACIDS SAT	FATTY ACIDS UNSAT	CALC	IRON	(mg) POTSM
	CORN BREAD baked from home recipes												
100	Southern style, made with whole-ground cornmeal*	A B1 B2 C	207	628	L	L	F	n/a	n/a	n/a	G	F	157
100	Degermed cornmeal, enriched (white*)	A B1 B2 C	224	591	L	L	F	n/a	n/a	n/a	G	F	157
	(*See corn bread recipes in this chapter which show cholesterol and fatty acids)												
100	Johnnycake(northern style) made with enriched, yellow degermed cornmeal	A B1 B2 C	267	690	L	L	G	n/a	n/a	n/a	G	F	188
100	Corn pone, made with white, whole-ground cornmeal	A^t B1 B2	204	396	L	L	F	n/a	n/a	n/a	F	F	61
100	Spoonbread, made with white whole-ground cornmeal	A B1 B2 C^t	195	482	L	F	F	n/a	n/a	n/a	G	F	132
100	Baked from mix: made with fresh eggs and milk	A B1 B2 C^t	233	744	L	L	F	n/a	n/a	n/a	F	F	127
	CORN FLAKES see corn products												
100	Corn Flour	A** B1 B2	368	(1)	L	L	H	---	---	---	L	F	------
	(**Vitamin A based on yellow varieties; white varieties have only a trace of cryptoxanthin and carotenes, the pigments in corn that have biological activity) (Figure in parenthesis denote values imputed, usually from another form of the food or from a similar food - per U.S.D.A. Handbook No. 8, Composition of Foods)												
100	CORN FRITTERS	A$^+$ B1 B2 C	377	477	L	F	F	---	---	---	F	F	133
	NOTE: vitamin A is based on fritters made with yellow sweet corn. White corn value is 230 Int'l units per 100 grams. (Also see recipe in this chapter)												
245	CORN (hominy) GRITS degermed cooked, enriched, unenriched, 1 cup	A^{++} B1 B2	125	502	L	L	F	---	---	---	L	L	27
	++ Vitamin A based on yellow varieties, white varieties contain only a trace of cryptoxanthin and carotene												
	CORNMEAL												
122	Whole-ground, unbolted, dry 1 cup	A B1 B2	435	1	L	L	G	---	---	---	L	F	346
122	Bolted, nearly whole-grain, dry 1 cup	A B1 B2	440	1	L	L	G	---	---	---	L	F	303

Breads, Biscuits, Rolls and Other Grain Products

F=Fair; G=Good; H=High; L=Low; t or T = trace; n/a = no information available;   dashes = zero or unmeasurable

GRAM WT.	FOOD	VITAMINS	CAL	(mg) SOD	PRO	FAT	CARB	CHOL	FATTY ACIDS SAT	UNSAT	CALC	IRON	(mg) POTSM
138	Degermed, enriched dry form, 1 cup	A B1 B2	500	1	L	L	G	---	---	---	L	F	166
240	cooked, 1 cup	A B1 B2	120	264	L	L	F	---	---	---	L	L	38
138	Degermed, unenriched Dry form, 1 cup	A B1 B2	500	1	L	L	H	---	---	---	L	F	166
240	Cooked, 1 cup	A B1 B2	120	264	L	L	F	---	---	---	L	L	38
100	Self-rising Whole-ground with soft wheat flour added	A B1 B2	347	1380	L	L	H	---	---	---	H	F	212
100	without wheat flour added	A B1 B2	347	1380	L	L	H	---	---	---	H	F	234
	degermed, with or without wheat flour added	A B1 B2	348	1380	L	L	H	---	---	---	H	F	111
	CORN MUFFINS see muffins, corn												
	CORN PRODUCTS used mainly as ready-to-eat breakfast cereals corn flakes with added nutrients												
25	Plain, 1 cup	B1 B2	100	251	L	L	H	---	---	---	L	F	30
40	Sugar-coated, 1 cup	B1 B2	155	310	L	L	H	---	---	---	L	F	---
100	puffed with added nutrients	B1 B2	399	1060	L	L	H	---	---	---	L	G	---
100	presweetened, nutrients added	B1 B2	379	300	L	L	H	---	---	---	L	F	---
100	cocoa flavored, added nutrients	B1 B2	390	850	L	L	H	---	---	---	L	G	---
100	fruit flavored, added nutrients	B1 B2 C	395	600	L	L	H	---	---	---	L	G	---
100	corn shredded, added nutrients	B1 B2	389	988	L	L	H	---	---	---	L	F	---
100	Corn, rice and wheat flakes mixed, with added nutrients	B1	389	950	L	L	H	---	---	---	L	F	---
100	Corn, flaked with protein concentrate (casein), and other added nutrients	B1 B2 C	378	1100	F	L	G	---	---	---	H	H	---

Breads, Biscuits, Rolls and Other Grain Products

F=Fair; G=Good; H=High; L=Low; t or T = trace; n/a = no information available; dashes = zero or unmeasurable

GRAM WT.	FOOD	VITAMINS	CAL	(mg) SOD	PRO	FAT	CARB	CHOL	FATTY ACIDS SAT	UNSAT	CALC	IRON	(mg) POTSM
	CORNSTARCH												
3	1 teaspoon	---	11	---	L	T	H	---	---	---	---	---	---
9	1 tablespoon	---	34	---	L	T	H	---	---	---	---	---	---
100	1 cup	---	362	T	L	T	H	---	---	---	---	---	T
100	COTTONSEED FLOUR 3.57 ozs.	A B1 B2	356	---	H	L	F	---	---	---	H	H	---
	CRACKERS												
100	Animal	A B1 B2 C^t	429	303	F	F	H	n/a	n/a	n/a	F	L	95
100	Butter	A B1 B2	458	1092	F	G	H	n/a	n/a	n/a	G	L	113
100	Cheese Graham	A B1 B2	479	1039	F	G	H	n/a	n/a	n/a	H	L	109
100	Chocolate coated	A B1 B2	475	407	F	G	H	n/a	n/a	n/a	F	F	320
28	Plain, 2-1/2" square, 4	B1 B2	110	188	F	F	H	---	---	---	F	L	384
100	Sugar/honey coated	B1 B2	411	504	F	F	H	n/a	n/a	n/a	F	F	270
11	Saltines, 4	B1 B2^t	50	121	F	F	H	---	---	L	L	F	5
100	Sandwich type (peanut/cheese)	B1 B2	491	992	G	G	G	n/a	n/a	n/a	F	L	226
100	Soda	A B1 B2	439	1100	F	F	H	---	---	---	L	F	120
100	Whole wheat	B1 B2	403	547	F	F	H	n/a	n/a	n/a	L	L	---
	CRACKER MEAL see crackers, soda												
100	CREAM PUFFS custard filling *If whole milk is used, also reflected in the eggs	A B1 B2 C^t	233	83	L	F	G	H*	H*	H*	F	L	121
	DANISH PASTRY see Rolls and Buns.												
	DOUGHNUTS												
32	Cake type, 1	A B1 B2 C^t	125	160	L	F	G	n/a	L	L	L	F	29

Breads, Biscuits, Rolls and Other Grain Products

F=Fair; G=Good; H=High; L=Low; t or T = trace; n/a = no information available; dashes = zero or unmeasurable

GRAM WT.	FOOD	VITAMINS	CAL	(mg) SOD	PRO	FAT	CARB	CHOL	FATTY ACIDS SAT	UNSAT	CALC	IRON	(mg) POTSM
	(Also see recipe in this book for milligrams of cholesterol, average per doughnut.)												
100	Yeast leavened	A B1 B2	414	234	L	F	G	n/a	n/a	n/a	L	F	80
100	ECLAIRS custard filling, chocolate icing	A B1 B2 C^t	239	82	L	F	F	n/a	n/a	n/a	F	L	122
	FARINA enriched												
100	regular, cooked, 1 cup	B1 B2	42	144	L	L	L	---	---	---	L	L	83
245	Quick cooking, cooked, 1 cup	B1 B2	105	466	L	T	F	---	---	---	G	L	221
100	instant cooking, cooked,1 cup	B1 B2	55	188	L	L	F	---	---	---	F	G	83
100	regular, unenriched, cooked	B1 B2	42	133	L	L	F	---	---	---	L	L	9
	FLOUR see corn, rice, rye, soya and wheat												
	GINGERBREAD see cakes, cookies, pies, bakery, Chapter 2												
	GLUTEN FLOUR see wheat flour												
	GRIDDLECAKES see pancakes												
	GRITS see corn (hominy) grits												
	LADYFINGERS see cakes, cookies, pies, bakery, Chapter 2												
	MACARONI cooked enriched												
130	firm stage, 1 cup	B1 B2	190	1	L	L	F	---	---	---	L	F	103
140	tender, 1 cup	B1 B2	155	1	L	L	F	---	---	---	L	L	85
	unenriched												
130	firm stage, 1 cup	B1 B2	190	1	L	L	F	---	---	---	L	L	103
140	tender, 1 cup	B1 B2	155	1	L	L	F	---	---	---	L	L	85

Breads, Biscuits, Rolls and Other Grain Products

F=Fair; G=Good; H=High; L=Low; t or T = trace; n/a = no information available; dashes = zero or unmeasurable

GRAM WT.	FOOD	VITAMINS	CAL	(mg) SOD	PRO	FAT	CARB	CHOL	FATTY ACIDS SAT	UNSAT	CALC	IRON	(mg) POTSM
240	enriched, baked with cheese, canned, 1 cup (Also see recipe in this book for baked macaroni and cheese, Chapter 3, Dairy Products.	A B1 B2 C^t	230	730	L	L	F	n/a	F	L	F	L	288
	MUFFINS: baked from home recipes Plain, made with enriched white flour;												
40	muffin 1, 3" diameter (see recipe Chapter 1)	A B1 B2 C^t	120	176	L	F	G	F	F	L	G	F	50
100	unenriched flour other, made with enriched flour	A B1 B2 C^t	294	441	L	F	G	F	F	L	G	F	125
100	blueberry	A B1 B2 C	281	632	L	L	G	F	F	L	G	G	115
100	bran other made with enriched, de-germed	A B1 B2 C^t	261	448	L	L	G	L	L	L	G	G	431
100	cornmeal	A B1 B2 C^t	314	481	L	L	G	F	F	L	G	F	135
100	whole-ground cornmeal	A B2 B2 C^t	288	495	L	L	G	n/a	n/a	n/a	G	F	132
100	corn muffins made from yellow degermed cornmeal mixes, egg and milk	A B1 B2 C^t	324	479	L	L	G	n/a	n/a	n/a	G	F	110
100	muffins made with cake flour also egg and water	A B1 B2 C^t	297	346	L	L	G	n/a	n/a	n/a	G	F	104
	NOODLES: egg, cooked												
160	enriched, 1 cup	A B1 B2	200	3	L	L	F	---	---	---	L	L	70
160	unenriched, 1 cup	A B1 B2	200	3	L	L	F	---	---	---	L	L	70
	OAT PRODUCTS USED MAINLY AS HOT BREAKFAST CEREALS												
100	oat cereal with toasted wheat germ and soy grits, cooked	B1 B2	62	292	L	L	L	---	---	---	L	F	T
100	oat flakes, maple flavored, instant cooking, cooked (thmeans thiamine only)	B1th	69	107	L	L	L	---	---	---	L	L	---

Breads, Biscuits, Rolls and Other Grain Products

F=Fair; G=Good; H=High; L=Low; t or T = trace; n/a = no information available; dashes = zero or unmeasurable

GRAM WT.	FOOD	VITAMINS	CAL	(mg) SOD	PRO	FAT	CARB	CHOL	FATTY ACIDS SAT	UNSAT	CALC	IRON	(mg) POTSM
100	oat and wheat cereal, cooked	B1 B2	65	168	L	L	L	---	---	---	L	L	---
100	oat granules, maple-flavored quick cooking, cooked	B1 th	60	72	L	L	L	---	---	---	L	L	---
100	oatmeal or rolled oats, cooked	B1 B2	55	218	L	L	L	---	---	---	L	L	61
100	oats, shredded with protein and other added nutrients	B1 B2	379	610	F	L	H	---	---	---	H	H	---
25	oats(with or without corn) puffed with added nutrients,1 cup	B1 B2	100	317	L	L	H	---	---	---	H	H	---
100	oats(with or without corn, wheat) puffed, added nutrients and sugar coated	B1 B2	396	588	L	L	H	---	---	---	F	H	---
100	oats (with soy flour and rice) flaked, added nutrients	B1 B2	397	1200	L	L	H	---	---	---	G	H	---
	PANCAKES: 4" diameter												
27	Wheat, enriched flour, home recipe, 1 pancake	A B1 B2 C^t	60	152	L	L	F	L	T	L	G	F	33
27	buckwheat made from mix with egg, milk, 1 pancake	A B1 B2 C^t	55	125	L	L	F	H	H	T	G	F	66
27	plain or buttermilk made from mix with egg and milk, 1 cake	A B1 B2 C^t	60	125	L	L	F	H	H	T	G	F	42
100	PEANUT FLOUR defatted	B1 B2	371	9	G	L	F	n/a	n/a	n/a	G	G	1186
	POPCORN popped												
6	plain, large kernel, 1 cup	B1^n B2	25	T	F	L	H	---	---	---	L	L	---
9	with oil and salt, 1 cup (B^n means Niacin only)	B1^n B2	40	175	L	F	G	---	---	---	L	F	---
35	sugar coated, 1 cup	B1^n B2	135	T	L	L	H	---	---	---	L	F	---
100	POPOVERS baked from home recipe with enriched flour (*high cholesterol reflected in the eggs) also see Popover recipe in this chapter	A B1 B2 C^t	224	220	L	L	F	H*	H*	L*	F	F	150

Breads, Biscuits, Rolls and Other Grain Products

F=Fair; G=Good; H=High; L=Low; t or T = trace; n/a = no information available; dashes = zero or unmeasurable

GRAM WT.	FOOD	VITAMINS	CAL	(mg) SOD	PRO	FAT	CARB	CHOL	FATTY ACIDS SAT	UNSAT	CALC	IRON	(mg) POTSM
	PRETZELS												
16	dutch, twisted, 1 pretzel	B1 B2^t	60	269**	L	L	G	---	---	---	L	F	21
6	thin, twisted, 1 pretzel	B1^t B2^t	25	101**	L	L	G	---	---	---	L	L	n/a
3	sticks, small, 2-1/4", 10 sticks	B1^t B2^t	10	168**	T	T	G	---	---	---	L	T	n/a
3	sticks, regular 3-1/8", 5 sticks	B1^t B2^t	10	168**	T	T	G	---	---	---	L	T	n/a

**Sodium content is variable. For example, very thin pretzel sticks contain about twice the average amount listed.

GRAM WT.	FOOD	VITAMINS	CAL	(mg) SOD	PRO	FAT	CARB	CHOL	SAT	UNSAT	CALC	IRON	(mg) POTSM
	RICE												
100	brown, cooked	B1 B2	119	282	L	L	F	---	---	---	L	L	70
	white, fully milled or polished enriched, common commercial varieties, all types,												
100	cooked	B1 B2^1	109	374	L	L	F	---	---	---	L	L^1	28

[1] Values for iron, thiamine and niacin are based on the minimum levels of enrichment in standards of identity.

GRAM WT.	FOOD	VITAMINS	CAL	(mg) SOD	PRO	FAT	CARB	CHOL	SAT	UNSAT	CALC	IRON	(mg) POTSM
	long grain;												
100	cooked (parboiled)	B1 B2^1	106	358	L	L	F	---	---	---	L	L	43
100	precooked (instant); ready-to-serve	B1 B2^1	109	273	L	T	F	---	---	---	L	F	T
100	unenriched, common commercial varieties, cooked	B1 B2	109	374	L	L	F	---	---	---	L	L	28
100	rice bran	B1 B2	276	T	F	F	G	n/a	n/a	n/a	F	H	1495
100	hot breakfast cereals, granulated, cooked	B1 B2	50	176	L	T	F	---	---	---	L	L	T
	cold breakfast cereals (ready-to-eat)												
100	rice flakes, added nutrients	B1 B2	390	987	L	L	H	---	---	---	F	F	180
15	puffed rice, added nutrients, no salt, 1 cup	B1 B2	60	T	L	L	H	---	---	---	L	F	15
	puffed, or oven-popped, pre-sweetened;												
100	honey and added nutrients	B1	388	706	L	L	H	---	---	---	F	L	---
100	honey or cocoa, added nutrients including fat	B1 B2	401	358	L	L	H	---	---	---	F	F	61

Breads, Biscuits, Rolls and Other Grain Products

F=Fair; G=Good; H=High; L=Low; t or T = trace; n/a = no information available; dashes = zero or unmeasurable

GRAM WT.	FOOD	VITAMINS	CAL	(mg) SOD	PRO	FAT	CARB	CHOL	FATTY ACIDS SAT	FATTY ACIDS UNSAT	CALC	IRON	(mg) POTSM
100	rice, shredded, added nutrients	B1	392	846	L	L	H	---	---	---	L	F	---
	ROLLS AND BUNS enriched; cloverleaf or pan,												
35	home recipe, 1 roll	A B1 B2 C^t	120	142	L	L	G	n/a	L	L	F	F	41
28	commercial, 1 roll	A^t B1 B2 C^t	85	98	L	L	G	n/a	T	L	F	F	n/a
40	frankfurter, hamburger, 1 roll	A^t B1 B2 C^t	120	202	L	L	G	n/a	L	L	F	L	n/a
50	hard, round or rectangular, 1	A^t B1 B2 C^t	155	313	L	L	L	n/a	T	T	F	F	49
100	pastry, danish	A B1 B2 C^t	422	366	L	F	G	n/a	n/a	n/a	F	L	112
100	sweet rolls	A^t B1 B2 C^t	316	384	L	L	G	n/a	n/a	n/a	F	L	124
100	wholewheat rolls	A^t B1 B2 C^t	257	564	L	L	F	n/a	n/a	n/a	F	F	292
100	brown-n'-serve rolls, baked	A^t B1 B2 C^t	328	562	L	L	F	n/a	n/a	n/a	F	F	100
100	rusks	A B1 B2 C^t	419	246	L	L	G	n/a	n/a	n/a	L	F	161
113	**RYE FLOUR** medium, sifted, 1 cup	B1 B2	397	1	F	L	H	---	---	---	L	F	229
13	**RYE WAFERS** whole-grain, 1-7/8" by 3-1/2", 2 wafers	B1 B2	45	115	F	L	G	---	---	---	F	G	78
	SALT STICKS												
100	regular type	A^t B1 B2 C^t	384	1674	F	L	G	n/a	n/a	n/a	L	L	92
100	vienna bread type	A^t B1 B2 C^t	304	1565	F	L	G	n/a	n/a	n/a	L	L	94
	SHORTBREAD see cookies, Chapter 2												
	SPAGHETTI												
100	cooked firm ("al dente") 8 to 10 minutes	B1 B2	148	1	L	L	F	---	---	---	L	F	79
140	cooked tender - 14 to 20 min. 1 cup	B1 B2	155	1	L	L	F	---	---	---	L	L	85

Breads, Biscuits, Rolls and Other Grain Products

F=Fair; G=Good; H=High; L=Low; t or T = trace; n/a = no information available; dashes = zero or unmeasurable

GRAM WT.	FOOD	VITAMINS	CAL	(mg) SOD	PRO	FAT	CARB	CHOL	FATTY ACIDS SAT	UNSAT	CALC	IRON	(mg) POTSM
	with meat balls and tomato sauce:												
248	home recipe, 1 cup	A B1 B2 C	330	1009	L	L	F	H	H	L	F	F	665
250	canned, 1 cup	A B1 B2 C	260	1220	L	L	F	H	H	L	L	F	245
	with tomato sauce and cheese;												
250	home recipe, 1 cup	A B1 B2 C	260	955	L	L	F	H	H	T	L	L	408
250	canned, 1 cup	A B1 B2 C	190	955	L	L	F	H	H	T	L	F	303
100	SPANISH RICE cooked from home recipe (*cooked with meat; if cooked without meat, values are zero)	A B1 B2 C	87	316	L	L	F	H*	H*	F*	L	L	231
75	WAFFLES with enriched flour 7" diameter, 1 waffle (* Reflected in eggs and milk)	A B1 B2 C^t	210	356	L	L	F	H*	H*	L*	G	F	109
75	made from enriched mix, eggs and milk added, 7" dia., 1	A B1 B2 C^t	205	515	L	L	F	H*	H*	L*	H	F	146
	WHEAT PRODUCTS: used mainly as hot cereals												
100	rolled wheat, cooked	B1 B2	75	295	L	L	F	---	---	---	L	L	84
100	whole-meal, cooked	B1 B2	45	212	L	L	L	---	---	---	L	L	48
100	wheat and malt barley cereal, quick-cooking, cooked	B1th B2	65	72	L	L	F	---	---	---	L	L	T
100	instant-cooking	B1th B2	80	102	L	L	F	---	---	---	L	L	T
	(Also see FARINA)												
	used mainly as ready-to-eat breakfast cereals												
	BRAN: see BRAN FLAKES												

Breads, Biscuits, Rolls and Other Grain Products

F=Fair; G=Good; H=High; L=Low; t or T = trace; n/a = no information available; dashes = zero or unmeasurable

GRAM WT.	FOOD	VITAMINS	CAL	(mg) SOD	PRO	FAT	CARB	CHOL	FATTY ACIDS SAT	UNSAT	CALC	IRON	(mg) POTSM
30	wheat flakes, added nutrients 1 cup	B1 B2	105	310	F	L	G	---	---	---	F	F	---
100	wheat germ, toasted	A B1 B2	391	2	F	F	F	---	---	---	F	G	947
15	puffed wheat, added nutrients 1 cup	B1 B2	55	1	F	L	G	---	---	---	L	F	51
25	shredded wheat, plain, 1 biscuit	B1 B2	90	1	L	L	G	---	---	---	L	F	87
100	wheat and malt barley flakes, nutrients added	B1 B2	392	780	L	L	G	---	---	---	L	F	---
	WHEAT FLOURS:												
120	whole-wheat, from hard wheats, stirred, 1 cup	B1 B2	400	4	F	L	G	---	---	---	F	F	444
	all-purpose or family flour, enriched;												
115	sifted, 1 cup	B1 B2	420	2	F	L	G	---	---	---	L	F	109
125	unsifted, 1 cup	B1 B2	455	2	F	L	G	---	---	---	L	L	n/a
125	self-rising, enriched, 1 cup	B1 B2	440	1349	F	L	G	---	---	---	H	F	113
96	cake or pastry flour, 1 cup	B1 B2	350	2	L	L	G	---	---	---	L	L	91
100	WILD RICE: raw	B1 B2	353	7	F	L	G	---	---	---	L	F	220
100	ZWEIBACH	A B1 B2	423	250	F	L	G	---	---	---	L	L	150

BAKING BREAD

There is nothing as tantalizing as the smell of bread baking, nor the heavenly taste of its warm crust (if you're lucky enough to get it), because homemade bread seems to carry its own magic over all other baked goods. However, as easy as bread is to make, as much care as baking a cake should go into it. Follow the recipe exactly. Use good ingredients, and use level measurements. Unless the all-purpose or general purpose flour is pre-sifted, it should be sifted before measuring.

Level measuring is done by filling the cup, spoon, or other measure to overflowing, then passing a spatula or blade of a knife over the top, scraping off the excess material. This is for measuring dry materials; for liquids, fill the measure with all it will hold.

To measure a half teaspoon or tablespoon of dry material such as flour, sugar, salt, baking powder, etc., dip the spoon into the material. Then owing to the difference in capacity of the tip of the spoon's bowl, after leveling with a knife, divide the material in half lengthwise and push the unneeded half of the material back into the original receptacle. For a quarter measurement, divide the teaspoon or tablespoon of material in half as explained above and then crosswise at the center. Push out the three quarter sections. Of course, the easiest method is to buy a set of standard measuring spoons which come in quarter, half, teaspoon and tablespoon sizes. These are simply dipped into the material and leveled with a knife blade.

Why level? Because most recipes are based on level measurement. If a recipe calls for 1 teaspoon of salt, and a rounded teaspoon is used, as much as 1-1/2 teaspoons of salt may go into the recipe. Too much flour in a bread recipe makes the loaf coarse-textured, dry and smaller in volume, also solid and heavy. Too much soda gives breads and cakes a bad color and a disagreeable flavor.

USE ACCURATE MEASURING EQUIPMENT:

A ONE-CUP MEASURE, with thirds of a cup on one side and fourths of a cup on the other, is one-fourth of a quart, or one-half pint.

A TWO-CUP MEASURE, with thirds of a cup on one side and fourths on the other, is half a quart or one pint. This measure is used for amounts measuring over a cup, such as: 1-1/3, or 1-1/2 or 1-3/4 cups.

A STANDARD TABLESPOON.

A STANDARD TEASPOON.

A SCALE, tested for accuracy.

BREAD PANS. Teflon-coated pans should be greased, the same as bread pans not Teflon-coated. Size of loaf pan will depend upon size of the loaf or loaves to be made. Beginners may find it more feasible to start with a 1-pound loaf recipe (which usually makes two loaves of bread) and, as experience in bread making is gained, 1-1/2 to 2 pound loaves can be made.

YEAST

The best temperature for the development of yeast is from 75 F. to 85 F. If temperature is below 30 F., yeast ceases to grow, and is destroyed when temperature is above 90 F. Yeast should be softened in lukewarm water or liquid.

To determine the freshness of compressed yeast, break the cake apart. If it is brittle and does not stretch, it is probably fresh. It should break with a clean edge and should smell fresh with an odor like cheese. Only fresh yeast should be used in making bread. The advantage of compressed yeast over dry yeast is that it takes less time to work.

Dry yeast is cornmeal and yeast mixed and dried. Dry yeast will live for some time but cannot grow without moisture, therefore it keeps for many weeks. When warmth, food and moisture are added they gradually become active.

Granular yeast is in dry granular form that will keep without refrigeration for several weeks. It should be softened in a little lukewarm water (not milk), for about 5 minutes and it will then act as quickly as compressed yeast. The water used in the softening process should be counted as part of the liquid used in the recipe.

As little as 1/6 of a cake to 2 cakes of yeast may be used to one cup of liquid in bread making. The bread is usually allowed to rise over night if the minimum amount is used, however, if the maximum amount is used, the bread may be finished in three or four hours from the time it was started.

UTENSILS NEEDED FOR BAKING BREAD

2 One pound loaf pans (be sure to grease generously).

3 Mixing bowls; 1 small, 1 medium, and 1 large enough in which to allow bread dough to rise to double in bulk.

1 Teaspoon and 1 tablespoon for measuring.

1 Measuring cup (8 ounces), 1 two cup measuring cup.

1 Wooden mixing spoon, or a large metal spoon heavy enough to stir bread dough.

1 Dinner knife for leveling measurements.

1 Molding board for kneading.

1 Sauce pan, or double boiler, large enough to hold 2 cups liquid.

. . . .

WHITE BREAD — — STANDARD RECIPE FOR TWO ONE—POUND LOAVES

F=Fair; G=Good; H=High; L=Low; t or T = trace; n/a = no information available; dashes = zero or unmeasurable

GRAM WT.	FOOD	VITAMINS	CAL	(mg) SOD	PRO	FAT	CARB	CHOL	FATTY ACIDS SAT	UNSAT	CALC	IRON	(mg) POTSM
26	AVERAGE PER SLICE		67	67									32
	Ingredients:												
492	2 cup 2% low-fat milk, scalded	A B1 B2 C	290	300	H	F	G	L	L	L	H	L	861
24	2 Tblspn granulated sugar	---	96	T	---	---	H	---	---	---	---	T	1
28	2 Tblspn corn oil or margarine	A D	200	279	L	H	L	---	L	H	L	---	6
6	1-1/2 tsp salt	---	---	2355	---	---	---	---	---	---	G	---	---
5	1 cake compressed yeast	A^t B1 B2 C^t	20	1	F	L	F	---	---	---	L	G	31
59	1/4 cp lukewarm water	---	---	---	---	---	---	---	---	---	---	---	---
4	1 Tsp granulated sugar	---	15	T	---	---	H	---	---	---	---	T	---
550	5-1/2 to 6 cp all-purpose flour	B1 B2	2310	11	F	L	G	---	---	---	L	F	523
1168	Recipe total (gms, cal, sod, & potsm)		2931	2946									1422

METHOD FOR BAKING BREAD

A NOTE ABOUT SIFTING AND MEASURING FLOUR   If flour is not presifted, it must be sifted before measuring, otherwise too much flour will be used, and the crumb of the loaf will be heavy. Sifting adds air to the flour which makes a lighter, tastier crumb.

After sifting, caution should be taken when measuring flour. Lightly spoon it into a measuring cup. Do not shake, knock or pack down, then level off with a knife blade.

STEP 1. To allow the scalded milk to cool down to lukewarm, this should be done first. Measure 2 cups of milk in a saucepan, over medium to low heat so the milk will not scorch. (Scalding can also be done in the top of a double boiler over boiling water.) Scalding means heating almost to the boiling point, and one advantage in using a double boiler is that the milk will not boil, but if a saucepan is used, the milk should be watched until scalding takes place. Milk is scalded when a line of bubbles forms around the edge of the pan. When the pan is tipped, the line of milk bubbles adhere to the pan.

STEP 2. Remove pan from the heat (or top of the double boiler from the boiling water), and stir in the 2 tblspns. of sugar, 2 tblspns. margarine, and the 1 -1/2 tsp salt. Mix well then set aside to cool to lukewarm.

STEP 3.   In a small mixing bowl, crumble the yeast, add 1 tsp of sugar and 1/4 cup of lukewarm water. To test the water, drop a little on the inside of the wrist first. If it feels hot, pour a little out and add some cold water, bringing it up to 1/4 cup again. (Water should feel the same temperature as the wrist.) This is very important because, as discussed earlier, heat kills the yeast action and the bread will not rise. Stir the yeast and water mixture and set aside about 5 minutes.

STEP 4.   When milk is lukewarm, pour into a medium-size bowl, add yeast mixture and 3 cups of flour. Beat until smooth, then add enough additional flour to make a soft dough.

STEP 5.   Spread enough remaining flour on the board to prevent dough from sticking to it, then turn dough out in the center of the board.

STEP 6.   First, flour the hands to prevent dough sticking to them while kneading; also, sprinkle a little flour over the dough. Second, fold the dough over on itself, sprinkle a little flour on top, then, with the heels of the hands, push dough away from you, lightly, but using enough pressure so that the top layer of dough will adhere to the lower layer. Turn dough in a quarter circle and repeat the motion, adding flour as needed. Continue turning in quarter circles, folding and kneading, and adding as much remaining flour as necessary until dough is elastic and smooth and does not stick to an unfloured board. (A good test for elasticity is to poke an index finger into the dough, making a hole which should close quickly after pulling the finger out.)

STEP 7.   Using soft margarine, grease a large mixing bowl. This should be of sufficient size to allow the dough to double in bulk. Turn the kneaded dough into the bowl, flip it over so the bottom is on top, which allows some of the grease from the bowl to adhere to it, brush top with a little soft margarine, then cover bowl with a tea towel and set it in a warm place, free of drafts, until double in bulk. If you have a gas stove, take out the top rack in the oven. Set bowl in cold oven toward the back. Close the door. The pilot light will keep the oven warm enough to allow dough to rise. Another warmer area which is also a good place to allow dough to rise, is on top of the refrigerator.

STEP 8.   When the dough is light (doubled in bulk), punch down by folding the edges in and pressing down on the center of the dough, then flip the dough over again so the smooth side is on top. Grease lightly with melted margarine, cover again and let rise until double in bulk. Although it is not necessary, texture of the bread is improved when dough is allowed to rise a second time.

STEP 9.   To shape bread into loaves, turn dough out onto a lightly floured board and divide into two equal portions, then shape into two smooth balls. Cover and let stand 10 or 12 minutes. This rest allows the dough to become less compact and easier to handle. Flatten one of the balls of dough and fold lengthwise, pressing the edges together. Then stretch the dough lengthwise carefully to about three times the length of the bread pan. Then overlap one end, bringing it to the center of dough and then the other end, overlapping it across the center. Press edges together. Dough should be about the size of the bread pan. Grease bread pan generously. Place dough in it seam side down. For a tender crust, brush top of dough with melted margarine; for a hard crust, brush with warm water; and for a glazed or shiney crust, brush with egg white beaten with a little water. Cover pan with a tea towel and let dough rise in a warm place, free of drafts. Do the same with a second ball of dough.

STEP 10.   When bread has risen above the pans about one inch, bake in a preheated, 400 F oven 10 minutes, then reduce heat to 375 F. and bake 35 to 40 minutes longer. Tap top of loaves with the fingertips, if they sound hollow, the bread is done. Turn out on rack at once to allow the air to circulate on all sides of the loaves. As soon as cool, place in plastic bags and seal with a twist. Be sure the loaves are cool or bread will sweat in the bags.

If a darker crust is desired, preheat the oven to 425 F. and bake the bread 35 minutes. This produces a thin, dark brown crust on a 1-pound loaf (containing about 3 cups of flour and 1 cup of liquid). When the temperature is reduced from 400 F. to 375 F., as in Step 10., a lighter, thicker crust is produced. Total baking time should then be 45 to 50 minutes. This method should always be used for breads containing eggs or extra sugar, since these rich breads seem to brown quicker.

Bread can be tested for doneness, if the color is a rich golden brown or if the loaf shrinks from the sides of the pan, or if the loaf sounds hollow when tapped.

SPONGE METHOD OF MAKING BREAD

Add sugar and softened yeast to lukewarm liquid, then stir in half the flour and beat well. Cover and set in a warm place (not warmer than a warm room) until batter is bubbly and light. Add salt, melted margarine and enough additional flour to make a dough which can be kneaded. Turn out onto a floured board and knead until satiny and smooth.

. . ...

APRICOT NUT BREAD

F=Fair; G=Good; H=High; L=Low; t .or T = trace; n/a = no information available;   dashes = zero or unmeasurable

GRAM WT.	FOOD	VITAMINS	CAL	(mg) SOD	PRO	FAT	CARB	CHOL	FATTY ACIDS SAT	UNSAT	CALC	IRON	(mg) POTSM
50	AVERAGE PER SLICE		150	150				15					130
	Ingredients												
150	1 cp dried apricots	A B1 B2 C	390	39	L	L	H	---	---	---	H	H	1469
200	1 cp granulated sugar	---	770	2	L	L	H	---	---	---	---	L	6
28	2 Tblspn corn oil / margarine	A D	200	279	L	H	L	---	L	G	L	---	6
50	1 egg	A B1 B2	75	61	G	G	L	H*	H	L	F	F	65
124	1/2 cp fresh orange juice	A B1 B2 C	55	1	L	L	F	---	---	---	F	L	248
59	1/4 cp water	---	---	---	---	---	---	---	---	---	---	---	---
6	2 tsp baking powder	---	6	630	L	T	H	---	---	---	H	---	---
1	1/4 tsp baking soda	---	1	110	L	T	G	---	---	---	H	---	---
4	1 tsp salt	---	---	1569	---	---	---	---	---	---	G	---	---
54	1/2 cp chopped pecans	A B1 B2 C	370	T	L	H	F	---	---	---	F	F	326
230	2 cp presifted, all purpose flour	B1 B2	840	4	F	L	G	---	---	---	L	F	219
906	Recipe total (gms; cal; sod and potsm mg.)		2707	2695									2339

METHOD

Cut up the apricots and soak in warm water for 30 minutes or until soft, then drain. Mix margarine, sugar and egg together thoroughly. Add orange juice and water, stirring into the sugar mixture until well blended. Sift the flour, baking powder, soda and salt together and add to the first mixture. Add the nuts and apricots. Grease a 9-1/4 x 5-1/4 x 2- 3/4'' loaf pan and line with greased paper. Pour in the batter and let it stand 20 minutes. Then bake at 350 F. 55-65 minutes or until a toothpick inserted in the center comes out clean. Remove bread from the pan and take the paper off immediately, then cool on a rack.

* According to U.S.D.A. Handbook No. 8, pg. 146, item 12, there are 275 milligrams of cholesterol in 50 grams of egg (550 mg in 100 gms). Total milligrams in this recipe equal 275; divided by 18 slices (estimated),   equals 15 milligrams of cholesterol per slice, average. Therefore, high cholesterol is reflected in the egg only, not in the entire recipe.

. . . .

F=Fair; G=Good; H=High; L=Low; t or T = trace; n/a = no information available; dashes = zero or unmeasurable

GRAM WT.	FOOD	VITAMINS	CAL	(mg) SOD	PRO	FAT	CARB	CHOL	FATTY ACIDS SAT	UNSAT	CALC	IRON	(mg) POTSM
								(mgs)*					
75	AVERAGE PER SLICE		174	146				31					139
	Ingredients:												
113	1/2 cp corn oil / margarine	A D	815	1115	L	H	L	---	L	H	L	---	26
200	1 cp granulated sugar	---	770	2	---	---	H	---	---	---	---	L	6
100	2 eggs	A B1 B2	150	122	G	G	L	H*	H	L	F	F	129
525	1 cp mashed bananas (2or3 ripe)	A B1 B2 C	300	5	L	T	G	---	---	---	L	L	1943
230	2 cp presifted flour	B1 B2	840	4	F	L	G	---	---	---	L	F	219
4	1 tsp baking soda	---	3	439	L	T	G	---	---	---	H	---	---
2	1/2 tsp salt	---	---	785	---	---	---	---	---	---	G	---	---
123	1/2 cp buttermilk (from skim)	A B1 B2 C	45	160	H	L	H	---	---	---	F	L	172
60	1/2 cp powdered sugar	---	230	T	---	---	H	---	---	---	---	L	2
1357	Recipe totals (gms; cal; sod. and potsm)		3153	2632									2497

METHOD

Cream shortening and sugar until fluffy. Add the beaten eggs and mashed bananas. Sift the dry ingredients together and add alternately with the buttermilk, beating well after each addition. Turn batter into well greased 9"x 5" bread pan and bake at 350 F. for 1 hour or until a toothpick inserted in the center of the bread comes out clean. While bread is still hot, glaze with a little powdered sugar moistened with 1 teaspoon of water. Spread thinly over the loaf. This bread may be frozen, but do not use the glaze if it is to be put in the freezer. Yield: 1 loaf.

For banana-nut bread, add 3/4 cup chopped pecans or other nuts to be folded into the batter just before baking. Mix thoroughly.

* There are 550 milligrams of cholesterol in 100 grams of egg, per U.S.D.A. Handbook No. 8, Pg. 146, item 12. Dividing 550 by 18 (estimated) slices of banana bread, equals 31 milligrams of cholesterol average per slice.

. . . .

BUTTERMILK YEAST BREAD

F=Fair; G=Good; H=High; L=Low; t or T = trace; n/a = no information available; dashes = zero or unmeasurable

GRAM WT.	FOOD	VITAMINS	CAL	(mg) SOD	PRO	FAT	CARB	CHOL	FATTY ACIDS SAT	UNSAT	CALC	IRON	(mg) POTSM
33	AVERAGE PER SLICE		83	128									26
	Ingredients:												
492	2 cp buttermilk	A B1 B2 C	180	640	H	L	H	---	---	---	F	L	689
150	2/3 cp margarine	A D	1086	1480	L	H	L	---	L	H	F	---.	35
20	5 tsp. salt	---	---	7845	---	---	---	---	---	---	G	---	1
72	6 tblspns sugar	---	276	1	---	---	H	---	---	---	---	L	2
14	2 cakes compressed yeast	A^t B1 B2 C^t	40	2	H	L	H	---------n/a--------			F	G	85
570	2-1/2 cp water	---	---	---	---	---	---	---	---	---	---	---	---
2	1/2 tsp baking soda	---	2	220	-------------------n/a-------------------								
1320	12 cp presifted all-purpose flour	B1 B2	5040	24	F	L	H	---	---	---	L	G	1254
2640	Recipe total (gms; cal; sod. & potsm mg)		6624	10212									2066

METHOD

Scald the buttermilk, then remove from heat and add margarine, salt and sugar. Mix well. Set aside to cool to luke-warm. Dissolve yeast in warm water. Stir before adding to the lukewarm buttermilk mixture. After adding to the buttermilk, transfer mixture to a large mixing bowl. Add the soda to 1 cup of flour and mix well. Stir into the buttermilk. Beat thoroughly, then add the rest of the flour a little at a time, until about 1 - 1/2 cups of flour remain. Spread this on a molding board and knead into the dough for at least 10 minutes until the dough is smooth and satiny. Cover the bowl with a tea towel and let the dough rise about an hour. Then punch down; let it rest about 15 minutes, then shape into loaves and put them into greased bread pans. Cover and let rise until double in bulk. Bake at 400 F. for 35 — 45 minutes. Turn out at once onto a rack to cool. Grease tops. Yield ′ 4 loaves.

. . . .

SOUR MILK CORN BREAD "OR JOHNNYCAKE"

F=Fair; G=Good; H=High; L=Low; t or T = trace; n/a = no information available; dashes = zero or unmeasurable

GRAM WT.	FOOD	VITAMINS	CAL	(mg) SOD	PRO	FAT	CARB	CHOL	FATTY ACIDS SAT	FATTY ACIDS UNSAT	CALC	IRON	(mg) POTSM
91	AVERAGE PER SERVING		161	331				57(mg)					132
	Ingredients:												
276	2 cp yellow cornmeal	A B1 B2	1000	2	L	L	G	--	---	---	L	F	331
6	1 - 1/2 tsp salt	---	---	2355	---	---	---	--	---	---	G	---	---
4	1 tsp baking soda	---	3	439	L	T	G	--	---	---	H	---	---
24	2 tblspn sugar	---	96	T	---	---	H	---	---	---	---	L	1
492	2 cp sour milk, low-fat	A B1 B2 C	290	300	H	F	H	L*	L	L	H	L	861
100	2 eggs, beaten	A B1 B2	150	122	H	H	L	H*	H	L	F	F	129
10	2 tsp margarine, melted	A D	68	94	L	H	T	---	L	H	L	---	---
912	Recipe totals (gms; cal; sod. & potsm.)		1607	3312									1322

METHOD

In a large mixing bowl, sift the cornmeal, salt, baking soda, and sugar together. Add milk, beaten eggs, and melted margarine and beat until smooth. Pour into a greased 8" by 10" pan and bake at 400 F. 30 Minutes or until a toothpick inserted in the center comes out clean. Yield 1 loaf (about 10 servings).

* There are 550 milligrams of cholesterol in 100 grams of whole egg, and 15 milligrams of cholesterol in 492 grams of low-fat milk**, per U.S.D.A. Handbook No. 8, pg. 146, items 12 and 29 respectively, for a total of 565 milligrams of cholesterol; divided by 10 servings equals 57 average milligrams of cholesterol per serving.

** We used values for sweet milk, because there were none for sour milk in U.S.D.A. Handbook No. 8.

. . . .

NEW ORLEANS SWEET MILK CORN BREAD OR JOHNNYCAKE

F=Fair; G=Good; H=High; L=Low; t or T = trace; n/a = no information available; dashes = zero or unmeasurable

GRAM WT.	FOOD	VITAMINS	CAL	(mg) SOD	PRO	FAT	CARB	CHOL	FATTY ACIDS SAT	UNSAT	CALC	IRON	(mg) POTSM
42	AVERAGE EACH PIECE		78	183				18(mg)					60
	Ingredients:												
369	1 - 1/2 cp 2% low-fat milk	A B1 B2 C	218	225	H	F	G	L*	L	L	H	L	646
207	1 - 1/2 cp white cornmeal	A B1 B2	750	2	L	L	G	---	---	---	L	F	248
4	1 tsp salt	---	---	1569	---	---	---	---	---	---	G	---	---
28	2 tblspn margarine	A D	200	279	L	H	T	---	L	H	L	---	6
8	2 - 1/2 tsp baking powder	---	8	788	L	T	H	---	---	---	H	---	---
50	1 egg, separated	A B1 B2	75	61	G	G	L	H*	H	L	F	F	65
666	Recipe totals (gms; cal; sod. & potsm)		1251	2924									965

METHOD

Scald milk, then blend in cornmeal, salt and shortening. Cool. Add baking powder and beaten egg yolk and mix well. Fold in stiffly beaten egg white. Pour into greased 8" x 8" loaf pan and bake at 400 F. for 20 minutes. Yield   1 loaf cut in 16 pieces, 2" x 2" each. If desired, diced bacon may be sprinkled over the top before baking.

* There are 275 milligrams of cholesterol in 50 grams of whole egg, and 11 milligrams of cholesterol in 369 grams of low-fat milk, per U.S.D.A. Handbook No. 8, pg. 146, items 12 and 29 respectively. Total milligrams of cholesterol 286, divided by 16 pieces equals 18 average milligrams of cholesterol per serving.

. . . .

BOSTON BROWN BREAD

F=Fair; G=Good; H=High; L=Low; t or T = trace; n/a = no information available; dashes = zero or unmeasurable

GRAM WT.	FOOD	VITAMINS	CAL	(mg) SOD	PRO	FAT	CARB	CHOL	FATTY ACIDS SAT	FATTY ACIDS UNSAT	CALC	IRON	(mg) POTSM
42	AVERAGE PER SLICE		86	87			---						167
	Ingredients:												
138	1 cp enriched cornmeal	A B1 B2	500	2	L	L	H	---	---	---	L	H	166
102	1 cp rye flour	B1 B2	357	1	F	L	H	---	---	---	F	F	207
129	1 cp graham (whole wheat) flour	B1 B2	470	3	F	L	H	---	---	---	L	F	477
3	3/4 tsp baking soda	---	3	330	L	T	G	---	---	---	H	---	---
4	1 tsp salt	---	---	1569	---	---	---	---	---	---	G	---	T
240	3/4 cp molasses (light)	B1 B2	600	36	---	---	H	---	---	---	H	G	2201
490	2 cp buttermilk (from skim milk) OR sour milk	A B1 B2 C	180	637	L	L	F	---	---	---	F	L	686
165	1 cp seedless raisins	A B1 B2 C	480	45	L	T	H	---	---	---	G	H	1259
1271	Recipe total (gms; cal; sod. & potsm)		2590	2623									4996

METHOD:

Sift all dry ingredients together in a large mixing bowl. (To prevent raisins from sinking to the bottom of the bread, boil them in a little water for 5 minutes, drain well, then mix with flour.) Add the molasses and buttermilk and mix well. Grease molds thoroughly. If regular steam molds are not available, use No. 2 cans. Seal the tops with foil and tie down so they don't come off during steaming. Foil should be greased on the bread side, or, if lids are used, they should also be tied down and greased on the bread side. Place molds in a deep pan then fill with enough boiling water to half way up the molds. (Before tying the foil or lids, check the batter to be sure the cans are not more than 2/3 full.) Steam, tightly covered, for 3 hours, adding water as needed. If tops are still wet, dry in 375 F. oven uncovered. Makes 3 loaves.

. . . .

CRANBERRY FIESTA BREAD

F=Fair; G=Good; H=High; L=Low; t or T = trace; n/a = no information available; dashes = zero or unmeasurable

GRAM WT.	FOOD	VITAMINS	CAL	(mg) SOD	PRO	FAT	CARB	CHOL	FATTY ACIDS SAT	UNSAT	CALC	IRON	(mg) POTSM
55	AVERAGE PER SLICE		149	62				15 (mg)					56
	Ingredients:												
227	2 cp fresh cranberries	A B1 B2 C	104	5	L	L	F	---	---	---	L	L	82
80	3/4 cp pecans, chopped	A B1 B2 C	555	1	L	H	F	---	---	---	F	F	488
28	2 tblspns margarine	A D	200	279	L	H	L	---	L	H	L	---	6
230	2 cp presifted, all-purpose flour	B1 B2	840	4	F	L	G	---	---	---	L	F	219
224	1 cp plus 2 tblspns sugar	---	866	2	---	---	H	---	---	---	---	L	7
5	1 - 3/4 tsp baking powder	---	5	552	L	T	H	---	---	---	H	---	---
2	1/2 tsp baking soda	---	2	220	L	T	G	---	---	---	H	---	------
50	1 egg, well beater	A B1 B2	75	61	G	G	L	H*	H	L	F	F	65
72	1/3 cp fresh orange juice	A B1 B2 C	34	1	L	L	F	---	---	---	F	L	144
59	1/4 cp water	---	---	---	---	---	---	---	---	---	---	---	---
5	1 tsp grated orange rind	A B1 B2 C	n/a	1	L	L	F	---	---	---	F	L	11
982	Recipe Total (gms; cal; sod. & Potsm.)		2681	1125									1022

METHOD

Wash cranberries in a colander under cold, running water for a few minutes. Then pick them over and discard any that are spoiled; also remove any stems. Cut berries in half and set aside. Coarsely cut pecans and add to the cranberries. Melt the margarine over low heat to prevent burning; cool slightly. Sift the flour, salt, soda and baking powder together in a mixing bowl large enough to take the rest of the ingredients. Set aside. In a small bowl, combine the egg (beaten), orange juice and water then stir in the slightly cooled margarine. Make a well in the dry ingredients and add the liquid all at once. Stir only enough to blend and moisten. Add cranberries, nuts and rind and stir just enough to mix. Pour into a 9" x 5" x 3" loaf pan that has been greased only on the bottom. Bake at 350 F. for 1 hour. Test for doneness with a toothpick by inserting it in the center of the bread. If it comes out clean, the bread is ready. Turn bread out on a rack to cool.

* There are 275 milligrams of cholesterol in 50 grams of whole egg, per U.S.D.A. Handbook No. 8, pg. 146, item 12. Divide 275 by 18 slices equals 15 milligrams of cholesterol per slice.

. . . .

JALAPENO CORN BREAD

F=Fair; G=Good; H=High; L=Low; t or T = trace; n/a = no information available;   dashes = zero or unmeasurable

GRAM WT.	FOOD	VITAMINS	CAL	(mg) SOD	PRO	FAT	CARB	CHOL	FATTY ACIDS SAT	FATTY ACIDS UNSAT	CALC	IRON	(mg) POTSM
85	AVERAGE PER SLICE		220	230				28(mg)					88
	Ingredients:												
115	1 cp presifted, all-purpose flour	B1 B2	420	2	F	L	G	---	---	---	L	G	109
138	1 cp yellow cornmeal	A B1 B2	500	1	L	L	G	---	---	---	L	F	166
12	4 tsp baking powder	---	12	1260	L	T	H	---	---	---	H	---	---
2	1/2 tsp salt	---	--	785	---	---	---	---	---	---	G	---	T
50	1 egg	A B1 B2	75	61	G	G	L	H*	H	L	F	F	65
308	1 - 1/4 cp 2% low-fat milk	A B1 B2 C	181	188	H	F	G	L*	L	L	H	L	539
110	1/2 cp salad oil	---	973	---	---	---	H	---	---	T	H	---	---
113	1/4 cp jalapeno chilies, finely chopped	A B1 B2 C	42	---	L	L	L	---	---	---	F	G	---
848	Recipe total (gms; cal; sod. & potsm.)		2203	2297									879

METHOD

In a large mixing bowl, sift the flour, cornmeal, baking powder and salt together, then add the unbeaten egg, milk, salad oil and chilies. Beat until smooth. Bake in a greased 8" square pan, or fill greased muffin tins 2/3 full, for approximately 20 — 25 minutes at 425 F.   Test for doneness by inserting a toothpick in the center of the bread. If no batter sticks to it, the bread is ready.

*   There are 550 milligrams of cholesterol in 100 grams of whole egg and in 308 grams of skim milk, there are 9 milligrams, according to U.S.D.A. Handbook No. 8, pg. 146, items 12 and 29 respectively. In 275 milligrams in this recipe plus 9, there is a total of 284 milligrams of cholesterol. Divide 284 by 10 slices of bread, average milligrams of cholesterol is 28 per slice.

. . . .

MASHED POTATO BREAD

F=Fair; G=Good; H=High; L=Low; t or T = trace; n/a = no information available; dashes = zero or unmeasurable

GRAM WT.	FOOD	VITAMINS	CAL	SOD (mg)	PRO	FAT	CARB	CHOL	FATTY ACIDS SAT	UNSAT	CALC	IRON	POTSM (mg)
31	AVERAGE PER SLICE		55	86				---					39
	Ingredients:												
5	1 cake compressed yeast	A^t B1 B2 C^t	20	1	F	L	F	---	---	---	F	G	31
118	1/2 cp lukewarm water	---	---	---	---	---	---	---	---	---	---	---	---
118	1/2 cp boiling water	---	---	---	---	---	---	---	---	---	---	---	---
5	1 - 1/4 tsp salt	---	---	1962	---	---	---	---	---	---	G	---	T
12	1 tblspn granulated sugar	---	48	T	---	---	H	---	---	---	---	L	---
14	1 tblspn soft margarine	A D	100	139	L	H	T	---	L	H	L	---	3
390	2 cp mashed potato	A B1 B2 C	255	1170	L	L	F	---	---	---	L	L	1018
460	4 cp (approximately) presifted all-purpose flour	B1 B2	1680	8	F	L	G	---	---	---	L	F	437
1122	Recipe total (gms; cal; sod. & potsm.)		2103	3280									1489

METHOD

Crumble yeast in the lukewarm water and set aside. In a large mixing bowl, combine the boiling water, salt, sugar, margarine and mashed potatoes. Mix well. Stir the yeast and water and add to the potato mixture. Add 3 cups flour and blend. Turn dough out onto a floured board and knead in the additional flour. Then follow directions as for white bread, Step 6, at the beginning of this chapter. Yield 2 loaves — about 38 slices.

. . . .

F=Fair; G=Good; H=High; L=Low; t or T = trace; n/a = no information available; dashes = zero or unmeasurable

GRAM WT.	FOOD	VITAMINS	CAL	(mg) SOD	PRO	FAT	CARB	CHOL	FATTY ACIDS SAT	UNSAT	CALC	IRON	(mg) POTSM
34	AVERAGE PER SLICE		110	27				17(mg)					52
	Ingredients:												
403	3 −1/2 cp presifted, all-purpose flour	B1 B2	1470	7	F	L	G	---	---	---	L	F	383
6	2 tsp baking powder	---	6	630	L	T	H	---	---	---	H	---	---
2	1/2 tsp salt	---	---	785	---	---	---	---	---	---	G	---	T
3	1 − 1/2 tsp cinnamon							-n/a-					
1	1/2 tsp ginger							-n/a-					
---	1/4 tsp cloves							-n/a-					
600	3 cp granulated sugar	---	2310	6	---	---	H	---	---	---	---	L	18
220	1 cp cooking oil	---	1945	---	---	H	---	---	T	---	---	---	---
200	4 eggs, unbeaten	A B1 B2	300	244	G	G	L	H*	H	L	F	F	258
79	1/3 cp water	---	---	---	---	---	---	---	---	---	---	---	---
456	2 cp canned pumpkin	A B1 B2 C	150	8	L	L	L	---	---	---	L	L	1094
165	1 cp seedless raisins	A B1 B2 C	480	45	L	T	H	---	---	---	G	H	1259
54	1/2 cp pecans, chopped (Opt.)	A B1 B2 C	370	T	L	H	F	---	---	---	F	F	326
2189	Recipe total (gms; cal; sod. & potsm.)		7031	1725									3338

METHOD

Sift all dry ingredients together. Combine eggs, water, oil, and pumpkin, then stir in dry ingredients just until moistened, but smooth. Flour and grease 4 1−pound coffee cans and fill with the mixture until 1/2 full. Let stand for about 20 minutes. Then bake at 350 F. for approximately 1 hour. To loosen the bread, run a spatula around the inside, then turn out on a rack to cool. Yield   4 1−pound loaves.

*   There are 550 milligrams of cholesterol in 100 grams of whole egg, according to U.S.D.A. Handbook No. 8, pg. 146, item 12. In 200 grams of whole egg, there are 1100 milligrams of cholesterol -- divide by 64 slices of pumpkin bread (16 slices per loaf for 4 loaves) the average milligrams of cholesterol per slice equals 17.

. . . .

EGGLESS RAISIN BREAD

F=Fair; G=Good; H=High; L=Low; t or T = trace; n/a = no information available;   dashes = zero or unmeasurable

GRAM WT.	FOOD	VITAMINS	CAL	(mg) SOD	PRO	FAT	CARB	CHOL	FATTY ACIDS SAT	UNSAT	CALC	IRON	(mg) POTSM
36	AVERAGE PER SLICE NG		90	75				---					67
	Ingredients:												
5	1 cake compressed yeast	A^t B1 B2 C^t	20	1	F	L	F	n/a	n/a	n/a	F	G	31
59	1/4 cp lukewarm water	---	---	---	---	---	---	---	---	---	---	---	---
492	2 cp 2% low-fat milk, scalded	A B1 B2 C	290	300	H	F	G	L*	L	L	H	L	861
28	2 tblspns margarine	A D	200	279	L	H	L	---	L	H	L	---	6
55	1/4 cp brown sugar	B1 B2	205	16	---	---	H	---	---	---	G	G	189
6	1 – 1/2 tsp salt	----	---	2355	---	---	---	---	---	---	G	---	T
690	6 cp presifted, all-purpose flour	B1 B2	2520	12	F	L	G	---	---	---	L	F	656
124	3/4 cp raisins, chopped	A B1 B2 C	360	34	L	T	H	---	---	---	G	H	946
1459	Recipe totals (gms; cal; sod. & potsm.)		3595	2997									2689

METHOD

Use either the "straight dough method" for making bread, or the "sponge method" explained at the beginning of this chapter. Add the raisins with the flour. When loaves are cool, if desired, spread tops with a thin powdered sugar icing Yield 2 loaves (approximately 40 slices).

. . . .

F=Fair; G=Good; H=High; L=Low; t or T = trace; n/a = no information available; dashes = zero or unmeasurable

GRAM WT.	FOOD	VITAMINS	CAL	SOD (mg)	PRO	FAT	CARB	CHOL	FATTY ACIDS SAT	FATTY ACIDS UNSAT	CALC	IRON	POTSM (mg)
71	AVERAGE PER SLICE		184	108				15(mg)					181
	Ingredients:												
586	2 —2/3 cp light brown sugar	B1 B2	2187	176	---	---	H	---	---	---	G	G	2016
220	2 cp raw carrots, shredded	a B1 B2 C	92	103	L	L	L	---	---	---	F	L	750
630	2 — 2/3 cups water	---	---	---	---	---	---	---	---	---	---	---	---
330	2 cp yellow seedless raisins	A B1 B2 C	960	89	L	T	H	---	---	---	G	H	2518
1	1 tsp cinnamon	---	---	---	---	---	---	---	---	---	---	---	-----
113	1/2 cp margarine (1 stick)	A D	815	1115	L	H	L	---	L	H	L	---	26
100	2 large eggs	A B1 B2	150	122	G	G	L	H*	H	L	F	F	129
460	4 cp presift, all-purpose flour	B1 B2	1680	8	F	L	G	---	---	---	L	F	437
11	1 tblspn baking soda	---	9	1317	L	T	G	---	---	---	---	---	---
2	1/2 tsp salt	---	---	785	---	---	---	---	---	---	G	---	T
108	1 cp pecan halves, chopped (Opt.)	A B1 B2 C	740	T	L	H	F	---	---	---	F	F	651
2561	Recipe total (gms; cal; sod. & potsm.)		6633	3715									6527

METHOD

In a large saucepan, mix the brown sugar, shredded raw carrots, water, raisins, cinnamon and margarine. Bring to a boil, cover and simmer gently about 20 minutes. Remove from heat and set aside to cool. Transfer to a medium-size mixing bowl and beat in the eggs, one at a time. Sift flour, soda and salt together, add nuts (optional), stir the flour mixture into the cooled carrot and raisin mixture until batter is free of lumps. Turn dough into two greased, 8" loaf pans, dividing batter evenly between the two pans. Bake at 350 F. 45 minutes, or until a toothpick inserted in the center of the loaves comes out clean. Bread should be moist, and turned out of pans to cool on racks as soon as it is taken from the oven. Yield 2 loaves.

* There are 550 milligrams of cholesterol in 100 grams of whole egg, according to U.S.D.A. Handbook No. 8, pg. 146, item 12. Divide 550 by 36 (approximate number of slices in 2 loaves) equals 15 average milligrams of cholesterol in each slice.

. . . .

RYE BREAD

F=Fair; G=Good; H=High; L=Low; t or T = trace; n/a = no information available; dashes = zero or unmeasurable

GRAM WT.	FOOD	VITAMINS	CAL	(mg) SOD	PRO	FAT	CARB	CHOL	FATTY ACIDS SAT	UNSAT	CALC	IRON	(mg) POTSM
28	AVERAGE PER SLICE		49	97			---						32
	Ingredients:												
54	6 tblspn yellow cornmeal, raw	A B1 B2	196	1	L	L	H	---	---	---	L	H	65
118	1/2 cp cold water	---	---	---	---	---	---	---	---	---	---	---	---
236	1 cp boiling water	---	---	---	---	---	---	---	---	---	---	---	---
8	2 tsp salt	---	---	3142	---	---	---	---	---	---	G	---	T
14	1 tblspn margarine	A D	100	140	T	H	T	---	L	H	L	---	3
5	1 cake compressed yeast	A^t B1 B2 C^t	20	1	F	L	F	------n/a---------			F	G	31
59	1/4 cp lukewarm water	---	---	---	---	---	---	---	---	---	---	---	---
195	1 cp mashed potatoes (low-fat 2% milk added)	A B1 B2 C	125	587	L	L	F	---	---	---	F	L	509
254	2 — 1/2 cp rye flour (sifted)	B1 B2	893	1	F	L	H	---	---	---	F	F	516
172	1 — 1/2 cp white flour (sifted)	B1 B2	630	2	F	L	G	---	---	---	L	F	163
1115	Recipe total (gms; cal; sod. & potsm.)		1964	3874									1287

METHOD

In a medium-size saucepan, mix the cornmeal with cold water, add 1 cup of boiling water and cook 2 minutes, stirring constantly. Remove from heat, add salt and margarine and set aside to cool to lukewarm. Crumble yeast into the 1/4 cup of lukewarm water. As soon as the cornmeal mixture is cooled to lukewarm, transfer to a large mixing bowl then add the softened yeast, the cup of mashed potatoes and stir in well. Next, mix in the rye flour, and 1 cup of white flour. Turn out on a board floured with remaining 1/2 cup of white flour. Knead quickly to a stiff dough. It will be sticky. Handle as rapidly as possible to prevent too much flour from being absorbed. Put dough in a greased bowl, cover and let rise until double in bulk. Divide dough in half and shape into 2 loaves. Place in greased 1-pound bread pans, or shape into round loaves and cover and let rise until double in bulk again. Bake in a preheated over at 375 F. 45 minutes. If desired, carraway seeds may be sprinkled over the tops before baking (about 1 teaspoon per loaf). Cool on racks. Yield 2 loaves.

. . . .

SOURDOUGH BREAD

Although historians on food have advanced many theories as to when and where this bread originated, they have not been able to pinpoint its introduction to America. However, we'd be willing to wager that if the Alaskan and Canadian prospectors were alive today, they'd probably get a lot of feedback from the old range cooks on cattle drives as they bragged about their "original" starter recipes.

Whatever its true source, we're thankful that the methods for making sourdough bread have survived so that we can enjoy them today.

Sourdough bread is made from a mixture called "starter" that is allowed to stand 2 or 3 days until it ferments. This fermented dough gives the bread its sour taste. Recipes for the bread and starter are given on the next few pages.

SOURDOUGH STARTER

F=Fair; G=Good; H=High; L=Low; t or T = trace; n/a = no information available; dashes = zero or unmeasurable

GRAM WT.	FOOD	VITAMINS	CAL	(mg) SOD	PRO	FAT	CARB	CHOL	FATTY ACIDS SAT	UNSAT	CALC	IRON	(mg) POTSM
121	AVERAGE PER CUP		299	2				---					96
	Ingredients:												
7	1 package active dry yeast	A^t B1 B2 C^t	20	4	F	L	F	---	---	---	F	H	140
236	4 cp lukewarm water	---	---	---	---	---	---	---	---	---	---	---	------
24	2 tblspn granulated sugar	---	96	T	---	---	H	---	---	---	---	L	T
460	4 cp presifted, all-purpose flour	B1 B2	1680	8	F	L	G	---	---	---	L	F	437
727	Recipe total (gms; cal; sod. & potsm.)		1796	12									577

METHOD

In a large crockery or glass mixing bowl (DO NOT USE A METAL BOWL) soften yeast in the 4 cups of lukewarm water, Add the sugar and stir in flour gradually, beating until smooth. Cover loosely with cheesecloth or a porous towel and allow to rise until light in a warm place. In about 2 days, the mixture should smell slightly sour. Stir down occasionally. Then store, loosely covered, in the refrigerator. This recipe makes about 6 cups. To keep the starter going, replace each amount of started used for each recipe with equal amounts of flour and water stirred into it. (For example: for each cup of starter used in a receip, replace with 1/2 cup of water and 1/2 cup of flour). Let stand, lightly covered, overnight until it bubbles, then stir down and store, loosely covered, in the refrigerator. The starter becomes more active and sour each time this process is repeated.

. . . .

SOURDOUGH BREAD

F=Fair; G=Good; H=High; L=Low; t or T = trace; n/a = no information available; dashes = zero or unmeasurable

GRAM WT.	FOOD	VITAMINS	CAL	(mg) SOD	PRO	FAT	CARB	CHOL	FATTY ACIDS SAT	UNSAT	CALC	IRON	(mg) POTSM
42	AVERAGE PER SLICE		125	88				---					42
	Ingredients:												
246	1 cp 2% low-fat milk	A B1 B2 C	145	150	H	L	H	L	L	L	H	L	431
67	1/3 cp granulated sugar	---	257	T	---	---	H	---	---	---	---	L	2
75	1/3 cp margarine	A D	534	741	L	H	L	---	L	H	L	---	17
4	1 tsp salt	---	---	1569	---	---	---	---	---	---	G	---	T
7	1 pkg active dry yeast or												
	1 cake compressed yeast	A^t B1 B2 C^t	20	4	H	L	H	---	---	---	F	H	140
30	2 tblspn lukewarm water	---	---	---	---	---	---	---	---	---	---	---	---
182	1 — 1/2 cp sourdough starter	A^t B1 B2 C^t	449	3	F	L	G	---	---	---	F	F	148
575	5 cp all-purpose flour	B1 B2	2100	10	F	L	G	---	---	---	L	F	546
1186	Recipe total (gms; cal; sod. & potsm.)		3505	2477									1284

METHOD

Scald milk; add sugar, margarine and salt. Stir to melt sugar and shortening. Cool to lukewarm. Dissolve yeast in warm water. When scalded milk mixture is lukewarm, add yeast, starter and 2 cups of flour. Mix well. Then add enough flour to make a stiff dough. Turn onto a floured board and knead 5 or 10 minutes, adding only enough flour to keep dough from sticking. (Flour hands, too.) Place dough in a generously greased bowl, that is large enough to allow the dough to rise until double in bulk. Then turn the dough over so that the bottom is on top. This is an easy way to grease the surface. Cover with a tea towel and let rise until dough has doubled in bulk. (Bowl should be set in a warm place out of drafts.) Dough should double its bulk in about 1 — 1/2 hours. Then punch down, cover with a tea towel again and let rise for a second time in a warm place about 1/2 hour. Turn dough onto floured board again; divide into 2 equal parts, shape into balls, cover with a towel and let dough rest 10 minutes. Shape into 2 loaves and put into greased 9'' x 5'' x 3'' bread pans. Let rise until double in bulk (about 1 hour). Bake at 400 F. for 40 minutes. Turn out and cool on a rack.

. . . .

SPOON BREAD

F=Fair; G=Good; H=High; L=Low; t or T = trace; n/a = no information available; dashes = zero or unmeasurable

GRAM WT.	FOOD	VITAMINS	CAL	(mg) SOD	PRO	FAT	CARB	CHOL	FATTY ACIDS SAT	UNSAT	CALC	IRON	(mg) POTSM
124	AVERAGE PER SERVING		124	265				(mgs) 70					92
	Ingredients:												
472	2 cp boiling water	---	---	---	---	---	---	---	---	---	---	---	---
138	1 cp white cornmeal	A B1 B2	500	1	L	L	G	---	---	---	L	F	166
4	1 tsp salt	---	---	1569	---	---	---	---	---	---	G	---	T
28	1 tblspn soft margarine	A D	200	279	L	H	L	---	L	H	L	---	6
246	1 cp 2% low-fat milk	A B1 B2 C	145	150	H	L	H	L	L	L	H	L	431
100	2 eggs, separated	A B1 B2	150	122	G	G	L	H*	H	L	F	F	129
988	Recipe total (gms; cal; sod. & potsm)		995	2121									732

METHOD

In a medium-size bowl mix the cornmeal, margarine, salt and boiling water together and set aside to cool. Add milk and beaten egg yolks and mix well. Fold in stiffly beaten egg whites and pour batter into a greased baking dish. Bake at 400 F. 30 – 40 minutes. Serve from baking dish. Yield 6 to 8 servings.

* There are 550 milligrams of cholesterol in 100 grams of whole egg, and 7 milligrams of cholesterol in 246 grams of fluid skim milk, as calculated from U.S.D.A. Handbook No. 8, pg. 146, items 12 and 29 respectively. Total milligrams in this recipe are 557, divided by 8 servings equal 70 milligrams average cholesterol content per serving.

. . . .

F=Fair; G=Good; H=High; L=Low; t or T = trace; n/a = no information available; dashes = zero or unmeasurable

GRAM WT.	FOOD	VITAMINS	CAL	(mg) SOD	PRO	FAT	CARB	CHOL	FATTY ACIDS SAT	UNSAT	CALC	IRON	(mg) POTSM
44	AVERAGE PER BUN UNFROSTED		130	87				19					79
50	AVERAGE PER BUN FROSTED		152	99				19					81
	Ingredients:												
246	1 cp 2% low-fat milk	A B1 B2 C	145	150	H	L	H	L	L	L	H	L	431
3	3/4 tsp salt	---	---	1178	--	--	---	---	--	---	G	---	T
100	1/2 cp granulated sugar	---	385	1	--	---	H	---	---	---	---	L	3
113	1/2 cp margarine (1 stick)	A D	815	1115	L	H	L	---	L	`H	L	---	26
5	1 cake compressed yeast	A^t B1 B2 C^t	20	1	F	L	F	-------n/a---------			F	G	31
59	1/4 cp lukewarm water	---	---	---	---	---	---	---	--	--	---	---	---
518	4-1/2 cp (approx.) presifted all-purpose flour	B1 B2	1890	9	F	L	G	---	---	---	L	F	492
100	2 eggs	A B1 B2	150	122	G	G	L	H*	H	L	F	F	129
165	1 cp seedless raisins	A B1 B2 C	480	45	L	T	H	---	---	---	G	H	1259
1	1 tsp cinnamon	-------------------------------n/a---------------------------------											
1310	Recipe total (gms; cal; sod. & potsm.		3885	2621									2371

METHOD

Scald the milk. Remove from heat and add the salt, sugar and margarine; stir and set aside to cool to lukewarm. Crumble the yeast into a small bowl, add the lukewarm water and let stand about 5 minutes. When milk mixture is cooled to lukewarm, transfer to a large mixing bowl. Stir the yeast and water then add to the milk. (Be sure the milk is lukewarm because if it is too hot, it will kill the yeast.) Add 2 cups of flour and the eggs. Beat well. Then add the raisins and cinnamon to the remaining flour and stir until well blended. Add to batter and mix thoroughly. Turn the dough out onto a floured board and also sprinkle a little flour over the dough to make it easier to handle. Flour the hands to prevent dough from sticking to them. Then knead until smooth. (Dough should feel elastic.) Place dough in a large mixing bowl, generously greased, and cover with a tea towel. Let rise until double in bulk (about 2 hours) in a warm place away from drafts. Then punch down and turn dough out onto a lightly floured board. Roll to 1" thickness. Cut into rounds (the floured rim of a standard drinking glass will do) and place rounds 2" apart on greased baking sheets. Brush with egg white beaten with 1 tblspn of water (for glaze). Cut a cross on each bun with a sharp knife or razor blade. Allow buns to double in bulk, then bake at 400 F. for about 20 minutes. While still warm, fill the cross with confectioners' frosting. Yield· 30 buns.

*   There are 550 milligrams of cholesterol in 100 grams of whole egg, and 7 milligrams in 246 grams of low-fat milk, per U.S.D.A. Handbook No. 8, pg. 146, items 12 and 29 respectively. Total milligrams of cholesterol (557) is divided by recipe's yield (30 buns) which equals an average of 19 milligrams of cholesterol per bun.

CONFECTIONER'S FROSTING

F=Fair; G=Good; H=High; L=Low; t or T = trace; n/a = no information available;   dashes = zero or unmeasurable

GRAM WT.	FOOD	VITAMINS	CAL	(mg) SOD	PRO	FAT	CARB	CHOL	FATTY ACIDS SAT	UNSAT	CALC	IRON	(mg) POTSM
6	AVERAGE PER BUN		22	10				---					2
	Ingredients:												
120	1 cp powdered sugar	---	460	1	---	---	H	---	---	---	---	L	4
28	2 tblspn soft margarine	A D	200	279	L	H	L	---	L	H	L	---	6
5	1/2 tsp vanilla						-n/a-						
31	2 tblspn low-fat milk (approx)	A B1 B2 C	18	19	H	L	H	L	L	L	G	G	54
184	Recipe total (gms; cal; sod. & potsm)		678	299									64

METHOD

Cream soft margarine and sugar together, pressing out any lumps. Add vanilla and milk and blend until frosting is smooth and light. If more milk is needed, add a few drops at a time until desired consistency is reached.

. . . .

BUTTERMILK BISCUITS

F=Fair; G=Good; H=High; L=Low; t or T = trace; n/a = no information available; dashes = zero or unmeasurable

GRAM WT.	FOOD	VITAMINS	CAL	(mg) SOD	PRO	FAT	CARB	CHOL	FATTY ACIDS SAT	UNSAT	CALC	IRON	(mg) POTSM
45	AVERAGE PER BISCUIT		112	275				---					48
	Ingredients:												
230	2 cp presifted, all-purpose flour	B1 B2	840	4	F	L	G	---	---	---	L	F	219
2	1/2 tsp baking soda	---	2	220	L	T	G		----n/a-----		H	---	---
6	2 tsp baking powder	---	6	630	L	T	H		----n/a-----		H	---	---
4	1 tsp salt	---	---	1569	---	---	---	---	---	---	G	---	T
56	4 tblspn cold margarine	A D	400	558	L	H	L	---	L	H	L	---	13
245	1 cp cold buttermilk	A B1 B2 C	90	319	H	L	H		----n/a-----		F	T	343
543	Recipe total (gms; cal; sod & potsm.)		1338	3300									575

METHOD

Sift flour, baking soda, baking powder and salt together. Cut in the cold margarine then stir in the cold milk until mixture forms a ball of soft dough. Turn out onto a floured board and knead about 30 seconds. Roll until 1/2" thick. Cut with a floured biscuit cutter. Arrange biscuits on a greased cookie sheet close together. Bake at 450 F. 12 – 15 minutes, or until golden brown. Yield   12 Biscuits.

. . . .

PLAIN BAKING POWDER BISCUITS

F=Fair; G=Good; H=High; L=Low; t or T = trace; n/a = no information available; dashes = zero or unmeasurable

GRAM WT.	FOOD	VITAMINS	CAL	(mg) SOD	PRO	FAT	CARB	CHOL	FATTY ACIDS SAT	UNSAT	CALC	IRON	(mg) POTSM
39	AVERAGE PER BISCUIT		112	260				---					43
	Ingredients:												
230	2 cp presifted, all-purpose flour	B1 B2	840	4	F	L	G	---	---	---	L	F	219
9	3 tsp baking powder	---	9	945	L	T	H	---	---	---	H	---	---
4	1 tsp salt	---	---	1569	---	---	---	---	---	---	G	---	T
56	4 tblspn margarine	A D	400	558	L	H	L	---	L	H	L	---	13
164	2/3 cp 2% low-fat milk	A B1 B2 C	96	100	H	L	H	L	L	L	H	L	287
463	Recipe total (gms; cal; sod. & potsm.)		1345	3176									519

METHOD

Sift the flour, baking powder and salt together, then cut in the shortening with a knife or the fingertips, working quickly. Stir in the cold milk until mixture forms a ball of soft dough. Turn onto a lightly floured board and knead about 30 seconds. Pat or roll out with a floured rolling pin until 1/2" thick, handling dough as little as possible. Arrange biscuits on a greased cookie sheet, close together. If desired, brush tops with melted margarine. Bake at 450 F. 12 – 15 minutes or until golden brown. Yield   12 Biscuits.

For drop biscuits, use 1 cup of milk, do not knead and mix batter until as smooth as possible. A teaspoon is used to drop small biscuits onto a greased cookie sheet; a soup spoon makes larger biscuits.

This recipe may also be used to make crusts for meat pies: after kneading the dough, roll out to 1/4" thickness on a floured board to fit the meat pie dish. Carefully fold the dough in half and lift it over the meat-filled dish so that the fold is across the center. Place folded half on the dish, then gently lift folded half over side that isn't covered. Dough should overlap edges to allow fluting. If dough is too wide, trim it with a sharp knife or scissors to within 1/2" of the dish. Then flute the edges all around, using the index finger and thumb, and pressing the crust to the dish to seal. Cut a few 1/2 to 1" openings in the top to allow steam to escape. Follow meat pie directions for baking.

> VARIATIONS :
> 1. SCONES
>   Roll plain dough into 2 circles 1/2" thick. Cut into wedges and bake on a hot griddle, turning to brown both sides. Split scones while hot and spread with margarine.
> 2. CHEESE BISCUITS
>   Add 1/2 cup grated chedder cheese before adding the milk. Then follow regular method.
>   Averages per biscuit will change as follows:
>   Gms: 42; Cal: 126; SOD(mg): 280; CHOL(mg): 3.5;* POTSM(mg): 46

*According to U.S.D.A. Handbook No. 8, pg. 146, item 5, there are 100 milligrams of cholesterol in 100 grams (edible portion) cheddar cheese.

. . . .

F=Fair; G=Good; H=High; L=Low; t or T = trace; n/a = no information available; dashes = zero or unmeasurable

GRAM WT.	FOOD	VITAMINS	CAL	(mg) SOD	PRO	FAT	CARB	CHOL	FATTY ACIDS SAT	UNSAT	CALC	IRON	(mg) POTSM
58	AVERAGE PER MUFFIN		173	255				24(mg)					61
	Ingredients:												
230	2 cp presifted flour	B1 B2	840	4	F	L	G	---	---	---	L	F	219
9	3 tsp baking powder	---	9	945	L	T	H	---	---	---	H	---	---
2	1/2 tsp salt	---	---	785	---	---	---	---	---	---	G	---	T
48	4 tblspn granulated sugar	---	192	1	---	---	H	---	---	---	---	L	1
113	1/2 cp margarine (1 stick)	A D	815	1115	L	H	L	---	L	H	L	---	26
50	1 egg, beaten	A B1 B2	75	61	G	G	L	H*	H	L	F	F	65
246	1 cp 2% low-fat milk	A B1 B2 C	145	150	H	L	H	L*	L	L	H	L	431
698	Recipe total (gms; cal; sod. & potsm.)		2076	3061									742

METHOD

In a medium-size mixing bowl, sift the flour with the baking powder and salt, then set aside. In another medium-size bowl, cream the margarine and sugar together until light and fluffy. In a two-cup measure, beat the egg with a fork, add to the shortening and sugar mixture and a little of the cup of milk. (The milk can be measured in the same cup as the egg was beaten, stirring it around to get all of the egg). Add about 1 cup of flour and blend well, then a little more milk. Continue to add the dry and liquid ingredients until all is used.

Pour the smooth batter into greased muffin pans, filling them 2/3 full. Bake at 375 F. 30 minutes. Test for doneness with a toothpick. If it comes out clean, muffins are ready. Yield   12 muffins.

This recipe also makes 1 loaf of bread.

* The 24 milligrams of cholesterol, average per muffin, is based on 275 milligrams of cholesterol in 50 grams of whole egg, per U.S.D.A. Handbook No. 8, pg. 146, item 12, and 3 milligrams of cholesterol in 100 grams of skim milk, item 29.

. . . .

FRENCH TOAST

F=Fair; G=Good; H=High; L=Low; t or T = trace; n/a = no information available; dashes = zero or unmeasurable

GRAM WT.	NOTE: Averages are without sirup, sugar or margarine added.	VITAMINS	CAL	(mg) SOD	PRO	FAT	CARB	CHOL	FATTY ACIDS SAT	UNSAT	CALC	IRON	(mg) POTSM
196	AVERAGE SERVING (2 Slices)		240	350				141 (mg)					295
192	Ingredients: 8 slices white bread 1/2" thick	A^t B1 B2 C^t	520	976	L	L	G	---	---	---	F	F	190
100	2 eggs	A B1 B2	150	122	G	G	L	H*	H	L	F	F	129
492	2 cp 2% low-fat milk	A D	290	300	H	L	H	L*	L	L	H	L	861
784	Recipe totals (gms; cal; sod. & pots m.)		960	1398									1180

METHOD

Beat the eggs thoroughly; add milk, stir until well blended. Dip both sides of bread in egg milk mixture and sauté in a little hot margarine, in a skillet or griddle, until each side is a delicate brown. Serve hot with hot maple sirup and margarine, or sprinkel confectioners' sugar, or brown sugar, over each slice. Yield 4 Servings

* There are 550 milligrams of cholesterol in 100 grams of whole egg and 15 milligrams of cholesterol in 492 grams of skim milk, total cholesterol, 565 milligrams. Divide 565 by 4 servings equals 141 average milligrams of cholesterol per serving, as calculated from U.S.D.A. Handbook No. 8, pg. 146, items 12 and 29 respectively.

. . . .

GRANNY'S FRIED CORNMEAL MUSH

F=Fair; G=Good; H=High; L=Low; t or T = trace; n/a = no information available; dashes = zero or unmeasurable

GRAM WT.	NOTE: Averages are for plain mush with no sweet topping	VITAMINS	CAL	(mg) SOD	PRO	FAT	CARB	CHOL	FATTY ACIDS SAT	UNSAT	CALC	IRON	(mg) POTSM
22	AVERAGE PER SERVING		25	34				T*(mg)					32
429	Ingredients: 2 cp 2% low-fat milk	A B1 B2 C	290	300	H	F	G	L*	L	L	H	L	861
59	1 cp water	---	---	---	---	---	---	---	---	---	---	---	---
138	1 cp cornmeal	A B1 B2	500	1	L	L	G	---	---	---	L	F	166
2	1/2 tsp salt	---	---	785	---	---	---	---	---	---	G	---	T
691	Recipe totals (gms; cal; sod. & potsm,)		790	1086									1027

METHOD

In a large sauce pan, heat the milk and water to boiling. Mix the cornmeal with 1 cup cold water and stir in the salt, then pour this into the boiling milk and water, stirring constantly to prevent scorching. Cook until thick. Cover and continue cooking until very thick over low heat (about 10 minutes). Pour mush into a shallow, greased 8" x 8" loaf pan, smoothing the surface. Chill for serveral hours or overnight. When cold, cut into 4" x 1/2" slices, dip in flour or cornmeal and fry in fat heated to 365 F. Serve with warm maple sirup, or confectioners' sugar, or honey, or jam or jelly. Yield   16 servings.

METHOD 2

Cut cold must into 1/2" thick slices. Saute in a little melted margarine until both bides are crisp and brown.   Serve with crisp bacon or ham. (Hominy or other cereals may be fried in the same way).

. . . .

MICHIGAN GOLDEN CORN MUFFINS

F=Fair; G=Good; H=High; L=Low; t or T = trace; n/a = no information available; dashes = zero or unmeasurable

GRAM WT.	FOOD	VITAMINS	CAL	(mg) SOD	PRO	FAT	CARB	CHOL	FATTY ACIDS SAT	UNSAT	CALC	IRON	(mg) POTSM
56	AVERAGE PER MUFFIN		145	209				(mgs) 23					66
	Ingredients:												
115	1 cp presifted,all-purpose flour	B1 B2	420	2	F	L	G	---	---	---	L	F	109
138	1 cp yellow cornmeal	A B1 B2	500	1	L	L	G	---	---	---	L	F	166
50	1/4 cp granulated sugar	---	192	T	---	---	H	---	---	---	---	L	2
2	1/2 tsp salt	---	---	785	---	---	---	---	---	---	G	---	T
9	3 tsp baking powder	---	9	945	L	T	F	---	---	---	H	---	---
50	1 egg	A B1 B2	75	61	G	G	T	H*	H	L	F	F	65
246	1 cp 2% low-fat milk	A B1 B2 C	145	150	H	F	G	L*	L	L	H	L	431
56	4 tblspn soft margarine	A D	400	558	L	H	L	---	L	H	L	---	13
666	Recipe total (gms; cal; sod. & potsm.)		1741	2502									786

METHOD

Grease muffin pans. Sift flour with cornmeal, sugar, salt, and baking powder into a medium-size bowl. Add egg, milk and shortening and beat with a rotary beater about 1 minute. Fill muffin pans 2/3 full. Bake at 425 F. 15 — 20 minutes or until a toothpick inserted in the center comes out dry. Yield   12 corn muffins.

. . . .

BRAN MUFFINS WITH RAISINS

F=Fair; G=Good; H=High; L=Low; t or T = trace; n/a = no information available; dashes = zero or unmeasurable

GRAM WT.	FOOD	VITAMINS	CAL	(mg) SOD	PRO	FAT	CARB	CHOL	FATTY ACIDS SAT	UNSAT	CALC	IRON	(mg) POTSM
43	AVERAGE PER MUFFIN		107	218				16(mg)					87
	Ingredients:												
173	1 – 1/2 cp presifted, all-purpose flour	B1 B2	630	3	F	L	G	---	---	---	L	F	164
15	5 tsp baking powder	---	15	1575	L	T	F	---	---	---	H	---	---
54	4 – 1/2 tblspn granulated sugar	---	216	T	---	---	H	---	---	---	---	L	2
3	3/4 tsp salt	---	---	1178	---	---	---	---	---	---	G	---	T
276	1 cp & 2 tblspn 2% low fat milk	A B1 B2 C	163	168	H	L	H	L	L	L	H	L	483
53	1 – 1/2 cp bran cereal	B1 B2	158	490	F	L	H	---	---	---	H	G	---
50	1 egg	A B1 B2	75	61	G	G	T	H*	H	L	F	F	65
2	1/4 tsp cornstarch	---	9	----	L	T	H	---	---	---	---	---	---
42	3 tblspn margarine, melted	A D	300	419	L	H	L	---	L	H	L	---	10
110	3/4 cp seedless raisins	A B1 B2 C	360	34	L	T	H	---	---	---	G	H	839
778	Recipe total (gms; cal; sod. & potsm.)		1926	3928									1563

METHOD   Sift flour, baking powder, sugar and salt together. Add milk to bran cereal. Let stand until very soft. Add beaten egg and cornstarch then fold in melted margarine. Add to flour mixture only until moistened. Fold in raisins. Fill greased muffin pans 2/3 full. Bake at 425 F. about 18 – 20 minutes or until a toothpick inserted in the center comes out clean. Yield   about 18 muffins.

VARIATIONS :

1. For plain muffins, eliminate the raisins.
2. Instead of raisins, add 3/4 cup pitted, chopped dates.
3. Add 3/4 cup chopped nuts to batter.

CALCULATIONS:

1. Without raisins, totals and averages will be:

668	Total for recipe		1566	3894									724
37	Average per muffin		87	216									40

2. With chopped dates:

668	Total (plain muffins)		1566	3894									724
134	add 3/4 cup chopped dates	A B1 B2	368	2	L	L	H	---	---	---	G	H	486
802	Total with dates added		1934	3896									1210
45	Average per muffin with dates		107	216									67

CALCULATIONS:

3. With chopped nuts:

668	Pervious total, plain muffins			1566	3894									724
81	3/4 cup chopped nuts (pecans)	A B1 B2 C		555	T	L	H	F	---	---	---	F	F	488
749	Total with nuts added			2121	3894									1212
42	Average per muffin with nuts			118	216									67

* There are 275 milligrams of cholesterol in 50 grams of whole egg, and 3 milligrams in 100 grams of skim milk per U.S.D.A. Handbook No. 8. pg. 146, items 12 and 29 respectively. Based on these figures, total milligrams of cholesterol in this recipe equals 283 milligrams of cholesterol. Divide 283 milligrams by 18 (yield) equals 16 milligrams of cholesterol per muffin.

. . . .

F=Fair; G=Good; H=High; L=Low; t or T = trace; n/a = no information available; dashes = zero or unmeasurable

GRAM WT.	FOOD	VITAMINS	CAL	(mg) SOD	PRO	FAT	CARB	CHOL	FATTY ACIDS SAT	UNSAT	CALC	IRON	(mg) POTSM
58	AVERAGE PER MUFFIN		145	227				(mg) 23					70
	Ingredients:												
230	2 cp₂ presifted all-purpose flour	B1 B2	840	4	F	L	G	---	---	---	L	F	219
9	3 tsp baking powder	---	9	945	L	T	F	---	---	---	H	---	---
24	2 tblspn granulated sugar	---	96	T	---	---	H	---	---	---	---	L	1
2	1/2 tsp salt	---	---	785	---	---	---	---	---	---	G	---	T
75	1/3 cp margarine	A D	533	740	L	H	L	---	L	H	L	---	17
50	1 egg	A B1 B2	75	61	G	G	L	H*	H	L	F	F	65
307	1 — 1/4 cp 2% low-fat milk	A B1 B2 C	181	187	H	L	H	L	L	L	H	L	537
697	Recipe total (gms; cal; sod. & potsm.)		1734	2722									839

METHOD

Sift flour with baking powder, sugar and salt then cut in shortening until it looks like fine meal. Combine beaten egg and milk and stir into the dry ingredients only until moistened, not until the batter is smooth. Fill greased muffin pans 2/3 full and bake at 425 F. 15 — 20 minutes or until a toothpick inserted in the center of a muffin comes out clean. Yield About 12 medium-size muffins.

VARIATIONS:
1.   Blueberry muffins - Add 2 additional tblspn of sugar to the batter and fold in 1 cup well-drained, canned or fresh (washed and stemmed blueberries).
2.   Date muffins - Add 1 cup of pitted dates, cut up.
3.   Nut muffins - Add 1/2 cp chopped nuts to batter.
4.   Pineapple muffins - Add 1/2 cp flour, 1 tblspn sugar, 2 tblspn shortening and 1 No. 1 can crushed pineapple. Mix and bake as above.
5.   Spice muffins - Add tsp cinnamon, 1/4 tsp nutmeg and 1/8 tsp cloves to flour before sifting with dry ingredients. Sprinkle tops of muffins with plain or colored sugar before baking.
6.   Jelly muffins - Fill muffin pans 1/3 full of batter, add 1 tsp tart jelly, then top with equal amounts of batter.

* There are 275 milligrams of cholesterol in 50 grams of whole egg, and 9 milligrams of cholesterol in 307 grams of 2% milk, total 284 milligrams as calculated from U.S.D.A. Handbook No. 8, pg. 146, items 12 and 29 respectively.   Divide 284 by 12 (yield) equals 23 average number of milligrams of cholesterol per muffin.

. . . .

F=Fair;　G=Good;　H=High;　L=Low;　t' or T = trace;　n/a = no information available;　dashes = zero or unmeasurable

GRAM WT.	FOOD	VITAMINS	CAL	(mg) SOD	PRO	FAT	CARB	CHOL	FATTY ACIDS SAT	UNSAT	CALC	IRON	(mg) POTSM
58	AVERAGE PER POPOVER		94	89				(mg) 69					84
	Ingredients												
115	1 cp presifted, all-purpose flour	B1 B2	420	2	F	L	G	—	—	—	L	F	109
1	1/4 tsp salt	—	—	393	—	—	—	—	—	—	G	—	T
100	2 eggs, beaten	A B1 B2	150	122	G	G	L	H*	H	L	F	F	129
246	1 cp 2% low-fat milk	A B1 B2 C	145	150	H	L	H	L*	L	L	H	L	431
5	1 tsp margarine, melted	A D	34	47	T	H	T	—	L	H	F	—	1
467	RECIPE TOTAL (gms; cal; sod. & potsm)		749	714									670

METHOD

Sift flour and salt together, then stir in the beaten eggs and milk. Melt the teaspoon of margarine in a large metal spoon over a stove burner and add to the mixture. Beat with a rotary or electric mixer until batter is smooth. Grease 8 muffin tins, fill half full of batter and bake at 450 F. about 20 minutes. Reduce temperature to 350 F. and bake 15 minutes longer. Serve hot.

* Total milligrams of cholesterol; 557 milligrams, calculated from U.S.D.A. Handbook No. 8, pg. 146, items 12 and 29 respectively. Divide by 8 popovers equals 69 average milligrams of cholesterol per popover.

. . . .

BASIC ROLLS NO. 1 (WITHOUT EGGS)

F=Fair; G=Good; H=High; L=Low; t or T = trace; n/a = no information available; dashes = zero or unmeasurable

GRAM WT.	FOOD	VITAMINS	CAL	(mg) SOD	PRO	FAT	CARB	CHOL	FATTY ACIDS SAT	UNSAT	CALC	IRON	(mg) POTSM
45	AVERAGE PER ROLL		114	108									52
	Ingredients:												
492	2 cp 2% low-fat milk	A B1 B2 C	290	300	H	L	H	L	L	L	H	L	861
6	1 – 1/2 tsp salt	--	--	2355	--	--	--	--	--	--	G	--	T
48	4 tblspn sugar	--	192	1	--	--	H	--	--	--	--	L	1
56	4 tblspn margarine	A D	400	558	L	H	L	--	L	H	L	--	13
5	1 cake compressed yeast	A^t B1 B2 C^t	20	1	H	L	H	——n/a——			F	G	31
59	1/4 cp lukewarm water	--	--	--	--	--	--	--	--	--	--	--	--
690	6 cp presifted, all-purpose flour	B1 B2	2520	12	F	L	G	--	--	--	L	F	656
1356	Recipe total (gms; cal; sod. & potsm.)		3422	3227									1562

METHOD

Scald milk, remove from heat and stir in the salt, sugar and margarine. Set aside to cool to lukewarm. In a large mixing bowl, crumble yeast in the lukewarm water. Let stand 5 or 6 minutes then stir. As soon as the milk mixture is lukewarm, stir into the yeast and water. Blend well then add 3 cups of flour and beat until smooth. Gradually add about 2 cups additional flour, 1/2 cup at a time, and stir and beat until batter is well blended. Dough will be soft. Spread remaining flour on a board, turn the dough out on it, sprinkle a little flour over it to prevent it from sticking to the hands during the kneading process, then knead as much of the flour into the dough as necessary to make the dough smooth and elastic. Place dough in a greased mixing bowl, brush with a little melted margarine, cover with a tea towel and set in a warm place, free of drafts, until double in bulk. Then punch down, turn dough over, brush the top with a little more melted margarine and again cover with a tea towel. Set in a warm place free of drafts until the dough has doubled in bulk. Shape into rolls. Yield about 30, depending on type of roll as follows:

BUTTER-LEAF ROLLS:

Roll dough as thin as possible; brush with melted margarine. Cut into strips 1 – 1/2" wide and place in piles of 6. Then cut into 1" slices and place in greased muffin pans with longer cut edge down. Let rise until light, then bake at 425 F. about 20 minutes.

CINNAMON ROLLS:

When dough is light, roll 1/4" thick, brush with melted margarine and sprinkle with sugar and cinnamon, also raisins if desired. Roll up like a jelly roll and slice about 1" thick, or if larger rolls are desired, 1 – 1/4" thick. Place on greased cookie sheet (cut side down) about 1" apart. When light, bake at 425 F. about 20 minutes. If desired, rolls may be frosted with thin confectioners' icing, such as used for hot cross buns.

CLOVER-LEAF ROLLS:

When dough is light, break off pieces about the size of large marbles, brush with melted margarine, roll pieces in the ball of the hands until smooth and round. In greased muffin pans, place 3 or 4 balls of dough together (3 larger balls or 4 small). When very light, bake in 425 F. oven about 15 minutes.

CRESCENT ROLLS:

When dough is light, roll out and cut into triangles on a lightly floured board. Brush with melted margarine. Beginning at the long end, roll triangle until small end curves underneath. Place on greased cookie sheets, still with point underneath, and curve the ends toward each other. Let rise until light, then bake at 425 F. 15 – 20 minutes. When nearly done, brush with egg yolk mixed with milk and return to oven to brown.

ENGLISH MUFFINS:

Make a very soft dough. Knead lightly, let rise, punch down and let rise again. Roll 1/4" thick on a lightly floured board. Cut into large circles and let rise until light. Bake on hot, ungreased griddle, turning when one side is brown. When second side is brown, reduce heat and cook more slowly. Baking may be finished in the oven.

PARKERHOUSE ROLLS:

Follow Basic Roll recipe, and when dough is light, roll 1/4" thick, cut with biscuit cutter, brush circle with melted margarine and crease through center of each circle with handle of a dinner knife. Fold each roll over double. Place about 1" apart on greased cookie sheet. Brush with melted margarine. When very light, bake at 425 F. 15 – 20 minutes at 425 F. until golden brown.

PLAIN ROLLS:

When dough is light, cut or tear pieces about the size of a small egg, grease plams and roll as for clover-leaf until smooth. Grease tops; when light bake at 425 F. 15 – 20 minutes. Yield 30.

. . . .

BASIC ROLL RECIPE NO. 2 (WITH EGGS)

F=Fair; G=Good; H=High; L=Low; t or T = trace; n/a = no information available; dashes = zero or unmeasurable

GRAM WT.	FOOD	VITAMINS	CAL	(mg) SOD	PRO	FAT	CARB	CHOL	FATTY ACIDS SAT	UNSAT	CALC	IRON	(mg) POTSM
								(mg)					
48	AVERAGE PER FOLL		132	119				11					36
	Ingredients:												
307	1 – 1/4 cps scalded milk (2%)	A B1 B2 C	181	187	H	L	H	L	L	L	H	L	537
227	1 cp margarine (2 sticks)	A D	1633	2239	L	H	T	---	L	H	L	---	52
100	2 eggs, beaten	A B1 B2	150	122	G	G	L	H*	H	L	F	F	129
200	1 cp granulated sugar	---	770	2	---	---	H	---	---	---	L	---	6
8	2 tsp salt	---	---	3138	---	---	---	---	---	---	G	---	T
295	1 – 1/4 cp cold water	---	---	---	---	---	---	---	---	---	---	---	---
10	2 cakes compressed yeast	A^t B1 B2 C^t	40	2	H	L	H	--------n/a--------			F	G	61
177	3/4 cp lukewarm water	---	---	---	---	---	---	---	---	---	---	---	---
977	about 8 – 1/2 cps presifted, all-purpose flour	B1 B2	3570	17	F	L	G	---	---	---	L	F	928
2301	Recipe total (gms; cal; sod. & potsm)		6344	5707									1713

METHOD

Scald the milk, then add the margarine and blend until melted. Beat eggs, add sugar and salt and stir in the cold water gradually, until mixture is smooth. Set second mixture aside. In another bowl, crumble yeast into the 3/4 cup lukewarm water and, when yeast is liquified, stir to blend. As soon as the milk and margarine have cooled to lukewarm, stir in second mixture, then the yeast and water mixture, beating well after each addition. Proceed as for Basic Roll Recipe No. 1, or store in a greased, covered bowl in the refrigerator until needed. However, it should not be kept longer than 4 days. This recipe makes richer, sweeter rolls than No. 1.

* There are 550 milligrams of cholesterol in 100 grams of whole egg, and 3 milligrams of cholesterol in 100 grams of skim milk, per U.S.D.A. Handbook No. 8, pg. 146, items 12 and 29 respectively. Total milligrams in this recipe 559, divided by 48 rolls equals 11.6 average milligrams of cholesterol per roll.

. . . .

F=Fair; G=Good; H=High; L=Low; t or T = trace; n/a = no information available; dashes = zero or unmeasurable

GRAM WT.	FOOD	VITAMINS	CAL	(mg) SOD	PRO	FAT	CARB	CHOL	FATTY ACIDS SAT	UNSAT	CALC	IRON	(mg) POTSM
54	AVERAGE PER ROLL		161	146				(mg) 46					53
	Ingredients:												
246	1 cp 2% low-fat milk	A B1 B2 C	145	150	H	L	H	L*	L	L	H	L	431
150	2/3 cp margarine	A D	1067	1484	L	H	L	---	L	H	L	---	35
4	1 tsp salt	---	---	1569	---	---	---	---	---	---	G	---	T
100	1/2 cp granulated sugar	---	385	1	---	---	H	---	---	---	---	L	3
10	2 cakes compressed yeast	A^t B1 B2 C^t	40	2	H	L	H	-------n/a-------			F	G	61
59	1/4 cp lukewarm water	---	---	---	---	---	---	---	---	---	---	---	---
200	4 eggs, beaten	A B1 B2	300	244	G	G	L	H*	H	L	F	F	258
518	4–1/2 cp presifted, all-purpose flour	B1 B2	1890	10	F	L	G	---	---	---	L	F	492
5	1 tsp margarine, melted	A D	34	47	L	H	T	---	L	H	L	---	1
1292	Recipe totals (gms; cal; sod. & potsm.)		3861	3507									1281

METHOD

Scald milk, then add margarine, salt and sugar and stir until margarine melts. Set aside to cool to lukewarm. Soften yeast in lukewarm water. When milk mixture is lukewarm, add yeast and water, also well-beaten eggs. Add flour, a little at a time, beating until smooth. Allow to rise in a warm place about 6 hours. Until ready to use, refrigerate, or chill overnight. Form quickly into small balls and place in greased muffin pans. Brush tops with melted margarine and let rise until double in bulk. Bake at 400 F. about 20 minutes. Yield 24.

* There are 550 milligrams of cholesterol in 100 grams of whole egg; in 200 grams, there are 1100 milligrams. In 246 grams of low-fat milk, there are 7 milligrams of cholesterol. Total milligrams in this recipe 1107 as calculated by figures based on information in U.S.D.A. Handbook NO. 8, pg. 146, items 12 and 29 respectively. For average milligrams of cholesterol per roll, divide 1107 by 24 rolls which equals 46.

. . . .

CRULLERS

F=Fair; G=Good; H=High; L=Low; t or T = trace; n/a = no information available; dashes = zero or unmeasurable

GRAM WT.	FOOD	VITAMINS	CAL	(mg) SOD	PRO	FAT	CARB	CHOL	FATTY ACIDS SAT	UNSAT	CALC	IRON	(mg) POTSM
30	AVERAGE PER CRULLER		88	76				(mg) 17					28
	Ingredients:												
57	4 tblspn margarine	A D	400	558	L	H	T	---	L	H	L	---	13
200	1 cp granulated sugar	---	770	2	---	---	H	---	---	---	---	L	6
100	2 eggs, well beaten	A B1 B2	150	122	G	G	L	H*	H	L	F	F	129
11	3 – 1/2 tsp baking powder	---	11	1103	L	T	H	---	---	---	H	---	---
n/a	1/4 tsp nutmeg							-n/a-					
2	1/2 tsp salt	---	---	785	---	---	---	---	---	---	G	---	T
460	4 cp presifted all-purpose flour	B1 B2	1680	8	F	L	G	---	---	---	L	F	437
246	1 cp 2% low-fat milk	A B1 B2 C	145	150	H	L	H	L	L	L	H	L	431
1076	Recipe totals (gms; cal; sod. & potsm.)		3156	2728									1016

METHOD

Cream margarine and sugar together, add eggs and beat until smooth. Sift baking powder, nutmeg and salt with 1 cup of flour and add alternately with milk to the first mixture. Add enough additional flour to make a stiff dough. Toss on floured board, roll 1/2" thick and cut into strips. Twist and fry in deep fat (365 F.). Drain on brown paper (market bags will do) or on absorbent paper towels. While still warm, roll in powdered sugar or granulated sugar, or shake in paper bags, 2 or 3 at a time. Yield   About 36.

* There are 550 milligrams of cholesterol in 100 grams of whole egg, and 7 milligrams of cholesterol in 246 grams of skim milk, according to calculations based on U.S.D.A. Handbook No. 8, pg. 146, items 12 and 29 respectively. Total 557 milligrams of cholesterol in this recipe. Average milligrams of cholesterol for each cruller equals 17.

. . . .

JELLY-FILLED BISMARCKS

F=Fair; G=Good; H=High; L=Low; t or T = trace; n/a = no information available; dashes = zero or unmeasurable

GRAM WT.	FOOD	VITAMINS	CAL	(mg) SOD	PRO	FAT	CARB	CHOL	FATTY ACIDS SAT	UNSAT	CALC	IRON	(mg) POTSM
39	AVERAGE EACH SERVING		103	113				(mg) 15					42
	Ingredients:												
369	1 – 1/2 cp 2% low-fat milk	A B1 B2 C	218	225	H	L	H	L*	L	L	H	L	646
56	4 tblspn margarine	A D	400	558	L	H	L	---	L	H	L	---	13
100	1/2 cp granulated sugar	---	385	2	---	---	H	---	---	---	---	L	3
8	2 tsp salt	---	---	3138	---	---	---	---	---	---	G	---	T
10	2 cakes compressed yeats (or 2 pkgs. dry granular yeast)	A^t B1 B2 C^t	40	2	H	L	H	--------n/a--------			F	G	61
59	1/4 cp lukewarm water	---	---	---	---	---	---	---	---	---	---	---	---
100	2 eggs, beaten	A B1 B2	150	122	G	G	L	H*	H	L	F	F	129
633	5 - 1/2 to 6 cps presifted, all-purpose flour	B1 B2	2310	11	F	L	G	---	---	---	L	F	601
80	4 tblspn raspberry jam	A^t B1 B2 C^t	220	10	T	T	H	---	---	---	F	L	70
1415	Recipe totals (gms; cal; sod. & potsm.)		3723	4068									1523

METHOD

Scald milk, add margarine, sugar and salt, after removing from heat, and stir until well mixed. Pour into a large mixing bowl to cool to lukewarm. Crumble yeast in lukewarm water, and when yeast in liquified, stir to blend. As soon as milk is lukewarm (test by dropping a little on the inside of the wrist . . . it should feel neither hot nor cold to be right temperature) add the yeast and water mixture, then the beaten eggs and 2 – 1/2 cups of flour. Beat until smooth. Add enough remaining flour to make a soft dough, stir until thoroughly mixed. Cover dough and let rise 10 minutes. Turn out onto a floured board and knead until smooth and satiny, using about 1/2 cup of flour for kneading. Place dough in a generously greased bowl, brush with melted margarine and cover with a tea towel. Let rise in a warm place, free of drafts, until double in bulk. This takes about an hour. Punch down and let rise again for about 45 minutes. Roll out on a lightly floured board to 1/4" thickness. Cut into 2-1/2" rounds. (The floured rim of a standard drinking glass in about the right size and makes a good cutter for this purpose). Place 1 teaspoon of raspberry (or other jam) in the center of half the rounds. Moisten the jellied halves around edges with water, then top each with one of the plain rounds and pinch the edges together to prevent jam or jelly from leaking into the fat in which they will be cooked. Let rise, uncovered, until double in bulk (20 to 30 minutes). Fry in deep, hot fat (365 F.) about 2 minutes, turning when underside is brown. As soon as both sides are browned, remove from fat and drain on absorbent paper towels. When slightly cooled, coat with granulated sugar by shaking gently in a paper.

122

JELLY-FILLED BISMARCK (Continued)

bag containing a small amount of sugar. (Note: this dough may be used for any kind of filled doughnut). Yield about 36.

VARIATION: Maple Bars; Roll dough 1/2" thick. Cut into 1" wide strips about 5" long. Let rise until light (about 30 minutes). Fry as for raised doughnuts. While warm ice with a thin frosting made by adding 2 tablespoons water to 1 — 1/2 cups powdered sugar, and 1 teaspoon maple flavoring. Mix until smooth.

* There are 550 milligrams of cholesterol in 100 grams of whole milk and 3 milligrams of cholesterol in 100 grams of skim milk. Total for this recipe 561 milligrams, calculated from U.S.D.A. Handbook No. 8, pg. 146, items 12 and 29 respectively. Average number of milligrams of cholesterol in each bismarck equals 15, calculated by dividing 561 by yield of 36.

. . . .

CAKE DOUGHNUTS

F=Fair; G=Good; H=High; L=Low; t or T = trace; n/a = no information available; dashes = zero or unmeasurable

GRAM WT.	FOOD	VITAMINS	CAL	(mg) SOD	PRO	FAT	CARB	CHOL	FATTY ACIDS SAT	UNSAT	CALC	IRON	(mg) POTSM
43	AVERAGE PER DOUGHNUT		117	131				(mg) 35					43
	Ingredients:												
150	3 eggs	A B1 B2	225	183	G	G	L	H*	H	L	F	F	194
200	1 cp granulated sugar	---	770	2	---	---	H	---	---	---	---	L	6
28	2 tblspn margarine	A D	200	279	L	H	L	---	L	H	L	---	6
9	3 tsp baking powder	---	9	945	L	T	H	--------n/a--------			H	---	---
4	1 tsp salt	---	---	1569	---	---	---	---	---	---	G	---	T
n/a	1/2 tsp nutmeg	--------------------------------n/a--------------------------------											
403	3 - 1/2 cp presifted, all-purpose flour	B1 B2	1470	4	F	L	G	---	---	---	L	F	383
246	1 cp 2% low-fat milk	A B1 B2 C	145	150	H	L	H	L*	L	L	H	1	431
n/a	1/2 tsp lemon flavoring	--------------------------------n/a--------------------------------											
1040	Recipe total (gms; cal; sod. & potsm.)		2819	3132									1020

METHOD

Beat eggs until very light, then beat in sugar and melted margarine. Sift baking powder, salt and nutmeg with 1 — 1/2 cups of flour and stir into the first mixture alternately with milk. Add lemon extract and enough additional flour to make a soft dough. Chill about an hour. On a lightly floured board, roll dough about 3/4" thick. A soft dough makes light, tender doughnuts. Cut with doughnut cutter. Use pancake turner to transfer uncooked doughnuts to hot, deep fat (365 — 370 F.). If no thermometer is available, temperature of fat can be tested by dropping a 1" cube of bread into it. If it browns in 1 minute, it is ready to use.

A WORD OF CAUTION: Because the hot fat boils up when uncooked doughnuts are dropped into it, care should be taken not to fill the pan or skillet with fat too close to the top, otherwise it might run over onto the stove. Also, do not put too many doughnuts into the pan at once because they expand as they cook.

If the fat is the right temperature, doughnuts will brown quickly. Turn doughnuts to brown the other sides then lift out with a slotted spoon and drain on absorbent paper towels.

VARIATIONS : Sugared doughnuts (either granulated or powdered) - as soon as doughnuts have cooled a little, place two or three doughnuts in a plastic bag or brown paper bag, which has either granulated or powdered sugar in it, then twist the top closed, and shake until doughnuts are well coated. Continue coating doughnuts and adding sugar as needed. For cinnamon-sugar doughnuts, mix 2 teaspoons of cinnamon with each 1/2 cup of granulated sugar used, and follow above directions for coating. Doughnuts can also be iced with a thin coating of confectioners' sugar frosting.

CAKE DOUGHNUTS (continued)

* According to U.S.D.A. Handbook No. 8, there are 550 milligrams of cholesterol in 100 grams of whole egg and 3 milligrams of cholesterol in 100 grams of low-fat milk. (Pg. 146, items 12 and 29 respectively.) In this recipe, there are 825 milligrams of cholesterol in 150 grams of egg, and 7 milligrams of cholesterol in the low-fat milk, for a total of 832 milligrams. Divide 832 milligrams by 24 doughnuts (recipe yield) for an average of 35 milligrams of cholesterol per doughnut.

. . . .

HARRIE CARRIE BUTTERMILK DOUGHNUTS

F=Fair; G=Good; H=High; L=Low; t or T = trace; n/a = no information available; dashes = zero or unmeasurable

GRAM WT.	FOOD	VITAMINS	CAL	(mg)* SOD	PRO	FAT	CARB	CHOL	FATTY ACIDS SAT	UNSAT	CALC	IRON	(mg) POTSM
44	AVERAGE PER DOUGHNUT		121	79				(mg) 23					38
	Ingredients:												
460	4 cp presifted, all-purpose flour	B1 B2	1680	8	F	L	G	---	---	---	L	F	427
9	3 tsp baking powder	---	9	945	L	T	H	---	---	---	H	---	---
2	1/2 tsp baking soda	---	2	220	L	T	G	---	---	---	H	---	---
n/a	1 tsp nutmeg						--n/a--						
n/a	1 tsp cinnamon						--n/a--						
n/a	1/8 tsp ground cloves						--n/a--						
100	2 eggs	A B1 B2	150	122	G	G	L	H*	H	L	F	F	129
200	1 cp granulated sugar	---	770	2	---	---	H	---	---	---	---	L	6
28	2 tblspn margarine	A D	200	279	L	H	L	---	L	H	L	---	6
245	1 cp buttermilk (from skim)	A B1 B2 C	90	319	H	L	H	---	---	---	G	L	343
1044	Recipe total (gms; cal; sod. & potsm.)		2901	1895									911

METHOD

Sift flour with baking powder, soda, nutmeg, cinnamon, cloves and salt and sift again. Beat eggs until foamy, add sugar slowly and beat well. Add melted margarine and blend into ingredients until well mixed. Add sifted dry ingredients alternately with buttermilk, beating until batter is smooth, after each addition. Turn onto a lightly floured board and roll out until 1/3" thick. Cut with floured 2-1/2" doughnut cutter. Let stand 5 minutes then drop into deep, hot fat (375 F.). Turn when doughnuts rise to the top of the fat, and turn occasionally as they cook. When golden brown on all sides, remove with a slotted spoon or tongs and drain on several thicknesses of paper towels or brown paper bags. Ice when still warm, or shake to coat in paper or plastic bags in which there is either powdered or granulated sugar. For powdered sugar icing, follow directions on the box but use only half the recipe. Instead of melted chocolate, use cocoa for a change. (See Equivalents for cocoa and chocolate.) Yield 24 doughnuts.

NOTE If fat is too hot, doughnuts will crack; also when too much flour has been added. Dough can be rolled after chilling first which will prevent using too much flour.

DESSERT SUGGESTIONS Split a doughnut or two, cover with strawberries, top with whipped cream or one of the commercial toppings, and sprinkle with chopped walnuts or pecans.

* There are 550 milligrams of cholesterol in 100 grams of whole egg, according to U.S.D.A. Handbook No. 8, pg. 146, item 12, as in this recipe. Dividing 550 milligrams by 24 doughnuts (recipe yield), equals 23 average milligrams of cholesterol per doughnut.

. . . .

RAISED DOUGHNUTS

F=Fair; G=Good; H=High; L=Low; t or T = trace; n/a = no information available;   dashes = zero or unmeasurable

GRAM WT.	FOOD	VITAMINS	CAL	(mg) SOD	PRO	FAT	CARB	CHOL	FATTY ACIDS SAT	UNSAT	CALC	IRON	(mg) POTSM
39	**AVERAGE PER DOUGHNUT**		104	86				(mg) 12					38
	Ingredients:												
5	1 cake compressed yeast	A^t B1 B2 C^t	20	1	H	L	H	-------n/a-------			F	G	31
59	1/4 cp lukewarm water	---	---	---	---	---	---	---	---	---	---	---	---
246	1 cp 2% low-fat milk	A B1 B2 C	145	150	H	L	H	L	L	L	H	L	431
4	1 tsp salt	---	---	1569	---	---	---	---	---	---	G	---	T
150	3/4 cp granulated sugar	---	578	2	---	---	H	---	---	---	---	L	5
28	2 tblspn margarine	A D	200	279	L	H	L	---	L	H	L	---	6
403	3-1/2 to 4 cp sifted flour	B1 B2	1470	7	F	L	G	---	---	---	L	F	383
50	1 egg	A B1 B2	75	61	G	G	L	H*	H	L	F	F	65
n/a	1/2 tsp nutmeg	-----------------------------------n/a-----------------------------------											
945	Recipe total (gms; cal; sod. & potsm.)		2488	2069									921

METHOD

Soften yeast in lukewarm water and set aside. Scald milk and cool to lukewarm, then add salt, sugar and margarine; stir to blend, or add salt, sugar and margarine to the hot milk, if preferred. When milk mixture is lukewarm, add the yeast and water mixture and   1-1/2 cups of flour, stirring until smooth. Allow the sponge to stand in a warm place, free of drafts, until the mixture is so light that the sponge will fall at the slightest touch. (To keep the sponge free of drafts, the bowl can be covered with a cloth.)

As soon as sponge is light, add egg, nutmeg and remainder of the flour, then knead. Dough should be softer than bread dough. Put kneaded dough back in bowl, cover, and set in a warm place to rise. Then place on a lightly floured board and roll 3/4'' thick. Cut with a doughnut cutter and let rise. Fry in deep, hot fat (365 F.) 2 or 3 minutes. When frying, put the raised side of the doughnut down in the fat. The heat will cause the top side to rise by the time the doughnut is ready to turn. Yield   24 doughnuts.

NOTE   Milk is scalded to destroy bacteria and enzymes which might cause injury to the dough during the rising process at room temperature. Scalding means bringing the milk almost to the boiling point. Little bubbles of milk will cling to the pan, all around the edge, when the pan is tipped, which indicates scalding has taken place. Pan in which milk has been scalded will wash easier if milk is transferred to another container (such as a bowl large enough to mix the sponge) as soon as scalding has taken place, then fill pan with cold water immediately.

*   There are 275 milligrams of cholesterol in 1 whole egg and 7 milligrams of cholesterol in 246 grams of low-fat milk, as calculated from U.S.D.A. Handbook No. 8, pg. 146, items 12 and 29 respectively. Divide 282 milligrams of cholesterol by yield of 24 equals 12 average milligrams of cholesterol per doughnut.

. . . .

F=Fair; G=Good; H=High; L=Low; t or T = trace; n/a = no information available; dashes = zero or unmeasurable

GRAM WT.	FOOD	VITAMINS	CAL	(mg) SOD	PRO	FAT	CARB	CHOL	FATTY ACIDS SAT	UNSAT	CALC	IRON	(mg) POTSM
53	AVERAGE PER FLAPJACK		76	46				(mg) 35					66
	Ingredients:												
14	1 tblspn margarine	A D	100	139	L	H	T	---	L	H	L	---	3
12	1 tblspn granulated sugar	---	48	T	---	---	H	---	---	---	---	T	T
100	2 eggs, beaten	A B1 B2	150	122	G	G	L	H*	H	L	F	F	129
173	1-1/2 cp sifted, all-purpose flour	B1 B2	630	3	F	L	G	---	---	---	L	F	164
3	1 tsp baking powder	---	3	315	L	T	H	---	---	---	H	---	---
n/a	1 tsp cinnamon						-n/a-						
300	1 cp apples, chopped	A B1 B2 C	140	3	T	T	F	---	---	---	L	L	330
246	1 cp 2% low-fat milk	A B1 B2 C	145	150	H	L	H	L*	L	L	H	L	431
848	Recipe total (gms; cal; sod. & potsm.)		1216	732									1057

METHOD

Cream margarine and sugar together, add beaten eggs, then flour sifted with baking powder and cinnamon. Stir until smooth, then add the chopped apples (these should be cut quite fine), and milk (slowly), to make a smooth, medium-thick batter. Bake on greased griddle, as for pancakes. Serve with hot maple sirup, or with powdered sugar, or as an accompaniment with pork chops, or hot or cold roast pork, or ham or sausage. (Note instead of fresh apples, canned or cooked apples may be used in the batter). Yield   About 16 flapjacks.

*   There are 550 milligrams of cholesterol in 100 grams of whole egg and 3 milligrams of cholesterol in 100 grams of low-fat milk, according to U.S.D.A. Handbook No. 8, pg. 146, items 12 and 29 respectively. Total of 557 milligrams of cholesterol divided by yield of 16 flapjacks equals 35 average milligrams of cholesterol per flapjack.

. . . .

GRIDDLE CAKES

F=Fair; G=Good; H=High; L=Low; t or T = trace; n/a = no information available; dashes = zero or unmeasurable

GRAM WT.	FOOD	VITAMINS	CAL	(mg) SOD	PRO	FAT	CARB	CHOL	FATTY ACIDS SAT	FATTY ACIDS UNSAT	CALC	IRON	(mg) POTSM
43	AVERAGE PER SERVING		88	167				(mg) 16					58
	Ingredients:												
230	2 cp presifted flour	B1 B2	840	4	F	L	G	---	---	---	L	F	219
9	3 tsp baking powder	---	9	945	L	T	H	---	---	---	H	---	---
3	3/4 tsp salt	---	---	1178	---	---	---	---	---	---	G	---	T
50	1 egg, beaten	A B1 B2	75	61	G	G	L	H*	H	L	F	F	65
431	1-3/4 cp 2% low-fat milk	A B1 B2 C	254	263	H	L	H	L*	L	L	H	L	754
56	1/4 cp margarine, melted	A D	400	558	L	H	L	---	L	H	L	---	13
779	Recipe total (gms; cal; sod. & potsm.)		1578	3009									1051

METHOD

Sift flour with baking powder and salt. Add milk to beaten egg, stir in melted margarine and mix well. (Margarine should be cool before adding to the milk and egg.) Stir into dry ingredients only until flour is moistened. Pour or ladle onto hot, greased griddle, forming medium-size cakes. When bubbles form around the edges of the pancake, turn with a pancake turner and brown the other side. Lift out and stack on hot plates in the over (200 F.) until enough cakes have been made to serve. For thinner pancakes add more milk. Yield 18 Griddle Cakes.

To test if griddle, or heavy frying-pan is hot enough, drop a little water on the heated utensil. If drops scatter, griddle or pan is ready. To keep griddle cakes from sticking, rub a little raw potato on the griddle, or rub with a little cloth bag filled with salt which will prevent smoking and odor. Batter can be prepared the night before if the baking powder is left out and added just before baking in the morning. Griddle cakes will brown more readily if 1 teaspoon of molasses or brown sugar is added to the batter. Another way to keep cakes hot is to wrap them in foil, and place them in a 180 F. oven — or they can be kept hot in the top of a double boiler over boiling water.

Should batter become lumpy, mix with a rotary beater a few minutes.

Although maple sirup is the traditional one to serve with pancakes, there are many delicious fruit sirups on the market which are also good for a change of pace. Powdered, or just plain brown sugar and margarine is preferred by many because it does not soak into the cakes as sirup does and some enjoy this with a sprinkle of cinnamon.

*   There are 275 milligrams of cholesterol in 50 grams of whole egg and 13 milligrams of cholesterol in 431 grams of fluid skim milk, according to U.S.D.A. Handbook No. 8, pg. 146, items 12 and 29 respectively. Total of 288 milligrams of cholesterol divided by yield of 18 griddle cakes equals 16 average milligrams of cholesterol per serving.

. . . .

MAINE FLANNEL CAKES

F=Fair; G=Good; H=High; L=Low; t or T = trace; n/a = no information available; dashes = zero or unmeasurable

GRAM WT.	FOOD	VITAMINS	CAL	(mg) SOD	PRO	FAT	CARB	CHOL	FATTY ACIDS SAT	UNSAT	CALC	IRON	(mg) POTSM
35	AVERAGE PER CAKE		55	124				(mg) 24					50
	Ingredients:												
320	2 cp presifted flour	B1 B2	840	4	F	L	G	---	---	---	L	F	219
4	1 tsp salt	---	---	1569	---	---	---	---	---	---	G	---	T
9	3 tsp baking powder	---	9	945	L	T	H	---	---	---	H	---	---
100	2 eggs, separated	A B1 B2	150	122	G	G	L	H*	H	L	F	F	129
492	2 cp 2% low-fat milk	A B1 B2 C	290	300	H	L	H	L*	L	L	H	L	861
5	1 tsp margarine, melted	A D	34	47	L	H	T	---	L	H	L	---	1
840	Recipe total (gms; cal; sod. & potsm.)		1323	2987									1210

METHOD

Sift flour, salt and baking powder together, then set aside. Separate eggs. Beat yolks, add milk and melted shortening. Beat flour mixture into egg mixture with rotary beater, or slow to medium speed on an electric mixer. Beat egg whites until stiff and fold gently into batter. Bake on hot, greased griddle until both sides are golden brown. Yield   24 cakes.

*   There are 550 milligrams of cholesterol in 100 grams of whole egg and 15 milligrams of cholesterol in 492 grams of low-fat milk,   according to   U.S.D.A. Handbook No. 8, pg. 146, items 12 and 29 respectively.   Total 565 milligrams divided by yield of 24 cakes equals 24 average milligrams of cholesterol per cake.

. . . .

BAKING POWDER BUCKWHEAT CAKES

F=Fair; G=Good; H=High; L=Low; t or T = trace; n/a = no information available;   dashes = zero or unmeasurable

GRAM WT.	FOOD	VITAMINS	CAL	(mg) SOD	PRO	FAT	CARB	CHOL	FATTY ACIDS SAT	UNSAT	CALC	IRON	(mg) POTSM
39	AVERAGE PER CAKE		69	171			(mg) 1						85
	Ingredients:												
147	1-1/2 cp buckwheat flour ur	B1 B2	510	---	L	L	H	---	---	---	L	F	470
56	1/2 cp presifted flour	B1 B2	210	1	F	L	G	---	---	---	L	F	53
15	5 tsp baking powder	---	15	1575	L	T	H	---	---	---	H	---	---
2	1/2 tsp salt	---	---	785	---	---	---	---	---	---	G	---	T
14	1 tblspn margarine	A D	100	139	L	H	T	---	L	H	L	---	3
369	1-1/2 cp 2% low-fat milk lk	A B1 B2 C	218	225	H	L	H	L	L	L	H	L	646
20	1 tblspn molasses	B1 B2	50	3	---	---	H	---	---	---	H	G	184
623	Recipe total (gms; cal; sod. & potsm.)		1103	2728									1356

METHOD

Sift dry ingredients together. Combine melted margarine, milk and molasses then add slowly to the dry mixture. Beat thoroughly. Bake on slightly greased, hot griddle; size of cakes will depend upon how large you want them. Medium-size cakes will take about 3 tablespoons of batter. As soon as cakes are browned on one side, turn over and brown the other side, using a pancake turner. If cakes stick, use a little more grease, applying with a crumpled paper towel by dipping it in oil or grease and rubbing it over the hot griddle quickly. Yield 16 buckwheat cakes.

*   There are 11 milligrams of cholesterol in 369 grams of low-fat milk, per U.S.D.A. Handbook No. 8, pg. 146, item 29, calculation of 3 milligrams of cholesterol per 100 grams.   Divide 11 milligrams by yield of 16 cakes to equal .69 average milligrams of cholesterol per cake, which has been rounded out to one since it is over a half.

. . . .

IOWA CORNMEAL GRIDDLE CAKES

F=Fair; G=Good; H=High; L=Low; t or T = trace; n/a = no information available; dashes = zero or unmeasurable

GRAM WT.	FOOD	VITAMINS	CAL	(mg) SOD	PRO	FAT	CARB	CHOL	FATTY ACIDS SAT	UNSAT	CALC	IRON	(mg) POTSM
37	AVERAGE PER CAKE		49	80				(mg) 15					32
	Ingredients:												
472	2 cp boiling water	---	---	---	---	---	---	---	---	---	---	---	---
138	1 cp cornmeal	A B1 B2	500	1	L	L	G	---	---	---	L	F	166
12	1 tblspn sugar	---	48	T	---	---	H	---	---	---	---	L	T
4	1 tsp salt	---	---	1569	---	---	---	---	---	---	G	---	T
369	1-1/2 cp 2% low-fat milk	A B1 B2 C	218	225	H	L	H	L*	L	L	H	L	646
230	2 cp presifted, all-purpose flour	B1 B2	840	4	F	L	G	---	---	---	L	F	219
9	3 tsp baking powder	---	9	945	L	T	H	---	---	---	H	---	---
100	2 eggs, beaten	A B1 B2	150	122	G	G	L	H*	H	L	F	F	129
1334	Recipe total (gms; cal; sod. & potsm.)		1765	2866									1160

METHOD

Pour boiling water over cornmeal, sugar and salt. Mix well. Let stand until cornmeal swells then stir in milk and let stand until cool. Sift flour and baking powder together and add to cooled ingredients. Fold in beaten eggs. Bake on hot greased griddle, turning to brown each side. Cakes should be small, about 3 inches across, and well cooked. They require longer cooking than wheat cakes. Yield 36 griddle cakes.

*   There are 550 milligrams of cholesterol in 100 grams of whole egg and three milligrams of cholesterol in 100 grams of low-fat milk, as calculated from U.S.D.A. Handbook No. 8, pg. 146, items 12 and 29 respectively. Total 561 milligrams divided by yield of 36 cakes equals 15 average milligrams of cholesterol per cake.

. . . .

JELLY PANCAKES

F=Fair; G=Good; H=High; L=Low; t or T = trace; n/a = no information available; dashes = zero or unmeasurable

GRAM WT.	FOOD	VITAMINS	CAL	(mg) SOD	PRO	FAT	CARB	CHOL	FATTY ACIDS SAT	UNSAT	CALC	IRON	(mg) POTSM
43	AVERAGE PER PANCAKE		65	98				(mg) 69					60
	Ingredients:												
150	3 eggs, separated	A B1 B2	225	183	G	G	L	H*	H	L	F	F	194
4	1 tsp sugar	---	16	T	---	---	H	---	---	---	---	L	T
2	1/2 tsp salt	---	---	785	---	---	---	---	---	---	G	---	T
246	1 cp 2% low-fat milk	A B1 B2 C	145	150	H	L	H	L*	L	L	H	L	431
58	1/2 cp presifted, all-purpose flour	B1 B2	210	1	F	L	G	---	---	---	L	F	55
5	1 tsp margarine	A D	34	47	L	H	T	---	L	H	L	---	1
54	Approximately 3 tblspn jelly	A^t B1 B2 C^t	150	9	T	T	H	---	---	---	F	L	41
519	Recipe total (gms; cal; sod. & potsm.)		780	1175									722

METHOD

Separate eggs. Set the whites aside, then beat the yolks, add sugar, salt and 1/2 cup of milk and blend well. Add flour and melted margarine. Mix until smooth, then add remaining milk. Beat egg whites until stiff, then carefully fold them into the batter. Bake cakes on hot, greased griddle, making cakes larger than usual and very thin. Spread with jelly and roll up while hot. Serve with overlapping edges of cakes on bottom to keep them from unrolling. Sprinkle with confectioners' sugar if desired. Yield About 12 pancakes.

*   There are 550 milligrams of cholesterol in 100 grams of whole egg and 3 milligrams of cholesterol in 100 milligrams of low-fat milk, as calculated from U.S.D.A. Handbook No. 8, pg. 146, items 12 and 29 respectively. Total 832 milligrams divided by yield of 12 pancakes equals 69 average milligrams of cholesterol per cake.

. . . .

ALABAMA CORN FRITTERS

F=Fair; G=Good; H=High; L=Low; t or T = trace; n/a = no information available; dashes = zero or unmeasurable

GRAM WT.	FOOD	VITAMINS	CAL	(mg) SOD	PRO	FAT	CARB	CHOL (mg)*	FATTY ACIDS SAT	UNSAT	CALC	IRON	(mg) POTSM
53	AVERAGE PER FRITTER		75	184				43					58
	Ingredients:												
115	1 cp presifted all-purpose flour	B1 B2	420	2	F	L	G	---	---	---	L	F	109
5	1-1/2 tsp baking powder	---	5	473	L	T	H	---	---	---	H	---	---
4	1 tsp salt	---	---	1569	---	---	---	---	---	---	G	---	T
75	5 tblspn 2T low-fat milk	A B1 B2 C	45	45	H	L	H	L	L	L1	H	L	131
34	2 egg yolks, beaten	A B1 B2	120	18	F	G	T	H	H	L	G	H	33
336	2 cp frozen whole kernel corn	A B1 B2 C	275	4	L	L	F	---	---	---	L	L	326
66	2 egg whites, beaten too stiff peaks	B1 B2	30	96	F	T	L	---	---	---	L	L	92
635	Recipe total (gms; cal; sod. & potsm.)		895	2207									691

METHOD

Sift flour with baking powder and salt and set aside. Combine beaten egg yolks, milk and corn and add to the dry ingredients, mixing only until smooth. Carefully fold in stiffly beaten egg whites. Drop from a spoon into deep, hot fat (370 F.). Cook and turn until fritters are golden brown. Drain on paper towels. Serve with hot maple sirup. Yield 12 fritters.

*   There are 510 milligrams of cholesterol in 34 grams of egg yolk and 2 milligrams of cholesterol in 75 grams of low-fat milk, as calculated from U.S.D.A. Handbook No. 8, pg. 146, items 12 and 29 respectively. Total 512 milligrams of cholesterol divided by yield of 12 fritters equals 43 average milligrams of cholesterol per fritter.

. . . .

F=Fair; G=Good; H=High; L=Low; t or T = trace; n/a = no information available; dashes = zero or unmeasurable

GRAM WT.	FOOD	VITAMINS	CAL	(mg) SOD	PRO	FAT	CARB	CHOL	FATTY ACIDS SAT	UNSAT	CALC	IRON	(mg) POTSM
46	AVERAGE PER FRITTER		75	99				(mg) 23					42
	Ingredients:												
153	1-1/3 cp presifted flour	B1 B2	560	2	F	L	G	---	---	---	L	F	145
1	1/4 tsp salt	---	---	393	---	---	---	---	---	---	G	---	T
6	2 tsp baking powder	---	6	630	L	T	H	---	---	---	H	---	---
24	2 tblspn sugar	---	96	T	---	---	H	---	---	---	---	L	1
50	1 egg	A B1 B2	75	61	G	G	L	H*	H	L	F	F	65
164	2/3 cp 2% low-fat milk	A B1 B2 C	97	100	H	L	H	L*	L	L	H	L	287
150	1 medium Pippin apple	A B1 B2 C	70	2	L	L	F	---	---	---	L	L	165
548	Recipe total (gms; cal; sod. & potsm.)		904	1188									663

METHOD

Sift dry ingredients together, add well-beaten egg, then milk. Mix until smooth. Batter should be thick enough to coat the apple slices. If it is too thin, add a little flour; if too thick, add more milk.   Pare, core and cut the apples into 12 slices. Dip each slice into fritter batter so that each is covered with batter. Fry in deep, hot fat (365 F.) for 2 to 3 minutes, until brown. Serve with hot maple sirup or sprinkle with confectioners' sugar. Yield 12 fritters.

VARIATION   If fresh peaches are used instead of apples, peel the peaches, split in two, remove the pits, sprinkle granulated sugar over them and dip each half in the fritter batter and fry as for apple fritters. Serve with confectioners' sugar or foamy sauce. (Foamy sauce is made by creaming 1/2 cup of soft margarine with 1 cup powdered sugar and 1 well-beaten egg. Add 2 tablespoons hot water and 1 teaspoon vanilla. Heat over hot water, beating continually until the sauce thickens).

*   There are 275 milligrams of cholesterol in 50 grams of whole egg and 5 milligrams of cholesterol in 164 grams of low-fat milk, as calculated from U.S.D.A. Handbook No. 8 pg. 146, items 12 and 29 respectively. Total of 280 milligrams of cholesterol divided by yield of 12 fritters equals 23 average milligrams of cholesterol per fritter.

. . . .

BANANA FRITTERS

GRAM WT.	FOOD	VITAMINS	CAL	(mg) SOD	PRO	FAT	CARB	CHOL	FATTY ACIDS SAT	UNSAT	CALC	IRON	(mg) POTSM
137	AVERAGE PER FRITTER		188	351				(mg) 35					368
	Ingredients:												
144	1-1/4 cp presifted flour	B1 B2	525	2	F	L	G	---	---	---	L	F	137
100	1/2 cp granulated sugar	---	385	1	---	---	H	---	---	---	---	L	3
5	1-1/4 tsp salt	---	---	1962	---	---	---	---	---	---	G	---	T
6	2 tsp baking powder	-- ---	6	630	L	T	H	---	---	---	H	---	---
50	1 egg, well beaten	A B1 B2	75	61	G	G	L	H*	H	L	F	F	65
82	1/3 cp 2% low-fat milk	A B1 B2 C	48	50	H	L	H	L*	L	L	H	L	144
10	2 tsp melted margarine	A D	68	94	L	H	T	---	L	H	L	---	2
700	4 medium-size bananas	A B1 B2 C	400	8	L	T	G	---	---	---	L	---	2590
1097	Recipe Total (gms; cal; sod. & potsm.)		1507	2808									2941

METHOD

Sift 1 cup flour with sugar, salt and baking powder. Mix beaten egg and milk; add to flour mixture gradually, stirring until smooth. Add melted shortening. Peel bananas, cut crosswise into halves or quarters; roll in remaining flour, then dip in batter and fry in deep, hot fat (375 F.) 4 to 6 minutes. This batter is much stiffer than for most fritters and requires longer cooking. Yield 8 fritters.

*   There are 275 milligrams of cholesterol in 50 grams of whole egg and 3 milligrams of cholesterol in 200 grams of low-fat milk, as calculated from U.S.D.A. Handbook No. 8, pg. 146, items 12 and 29 respectively. Total of 277 milligrams of cholesterol divided by yield of 8 fritters equals 35 average milligrams of cholesterol per serving.

. . . .

BUTTERMILK WAFFLES

F=Fair; G=Good; H=High; L=Low; t or T = trace; n/a = no information available;   dashes = zero or unmeasurable

GRAM WT.	FOOD	VITAMINS	CAL	(mg) SOD	PRO	FAT	CARB	CHOL	FATTY ACIDS SAT	UNSAT	CALC	IRON	(mg) POTSM
34	AVERAGE PER WAFFLE		65	130				(mg) 34					40
	Ingredients:												
173	1-1/2 cp presifted, all-purpose flourr	B1 B2	630	3	F	L	G	---	---	---	L	F	164
2	1/2 tsp salt	---	---	785	---	---	---	---	---	---	G	---	T
4	1-1/4 tsp baking powder	---	4	394	L	T	H	---	---	---	H	---	---
2	1/ 2 tsp baking soda	---	2	220	L	T	G	---	---	---	H	---	---
100	2 eggs, separated	A B1 B2	150	122	G	G	L	H*	H	L	F	F	129
245	1 cp buttermilk (from skim)	A B1 B2 C	90	319	H	L	H	------n/a------			G	L	343
24	1-2/3 tblspn margarine	A D	168	231	L	H	L	---	L	H	L	---	6
550	Recipe totals (gms; cal; sod. & potsm.)		1044	2074									642

METHOD

Sift flour, salt, baking powder and soda together. Separate eggs. Beat the yolks, add buttermilk and melted margarine (this should equal 5 tablespoons), add to the flour mixture and beat with a rotary egg beater or electric mixer until batter is smooth. Then fold in stiffly beaten egg whites. Bake in waffle iron, heated according to manufacturer's instructions. Yield   4 full waffles (16 sections).

*   There are 550 milligrams of cholesterol in 100 grams of whole egg according to U.S.D.A. Handbook No. 8, pg. 146, item 12. Total of 550 milligrams of cholesterol divided by yield of 16 sections equals 34 average milligrams of cholesterol per waffle.

. . . .

CAKES, COOKIES, PIES and OTHER BAKERY PRODUCTS

BAKERY — CAKES, COOKIES AND PIES

If you can read a recipe, you can cook anything; it's how you put it all together that makes the difference. A basic recipe, plus little dabs of this and that of your own creation can turn a plain cookie, or cake, or pie into something a cut above the usual.

A good example of that difference is exemplified in everything we cook. Case in point: when baking an apple pie, do you follow the recipe exactly, or do you deviate a bit? Not the measurements, of course - - they're usually set up by experts in their field and shouldn't be tampered with - - I mean, in the addition of a little maple sirup over the apples, and cinnamon and nutmeg. The addition of a little extra spice can turn a bland dessert into something special. Also, for a festive occasion, sprinkle some green and red sugar over the top crust just before putting the pie into the oven.

In other words - - don't be afraid to experiment a little - - you'll find that doing your own thing can really be fun.

. . . .

CAKES, COOKIES, PIES AND OTHER BAKERY PRODUCTS

F=Fair; G=Good; H=High; L=Low; t or T = trace; n/a = no information available; dashes = zero or unmeasurable

GRAM WT.	FOOD	VITAMINS	CAL	(mg) SOD	PRO	FAT	CARB	CHOL	FATTY ACIDS SAT	UNSAT	CALC	IRON	(mg) POTSM
	Cakes baked from home recipes*												
	*Unenriched cake flour used, unless otherwise specified; baking powder with monocalcium phosphate monohydrate, and vegetable fat.												
100	Angelfood	B1 B2	269	283	L	L	H	---	---	---	L	L	60
69	Boston Cream Pie												
	8" pie 1/12 serving	A B1 B2 C^t	210	128	L	L	H	n/a	L	L	G	L	61
100	Caramel:												
	without icing	A B1 B2 C^t	385	305	L	F	H	n/a	L	L	G	F	68
	with caramel icing	A B1 B2 C^t	379	252	L	F	H	n/a	L	L	G	F	64
100	Chocolate Devil's Food:												
	without icing	A B1 B2 C^t	366	294	L	F	H	n/a	L	L	G	L	140
	with chocolate icing	A B1 B2 C^t	369	235	L	F	H	n/a	L	L	G	F	154
	with uncooked, white icing	A B1 B2 C^t	369	234	L	F	H	n/a	L	L	G	L	110
100	Cottage Pudding, made with enriched flour:												
	without sauce	A B1 B2 C^t	344	299	L	F	H	n/a	L	L	G	F	88
	with chocolate sauce	A B1 B2 C^t	318	233	L	L	H	n/a	L	L	G	F	140
	with fruit sauce(strawberry)	A B1 B2 C^t	292	233	L	L	H	n/a	L	L	G	F	93
100	Fruitcake, made with enriched flour:												
	Dark	A B1 B2 C^t	379	158	L	F	H	n/a	T	T	G	F	496
	Light	A B1 B2 C^t	389	193	L	F	H	--------n/a--------			G	F	233
100	Gingerbread, made with enriched flour	A B1 B2 C^t	317	237	L	F	H	n/a	L	L	G	F	454
100	Plain cake or cupcakes:												
	without icing	A B1 B2 C^t	364	300	L	F	H	n/a	L	L	G	L	79
	with chocolate icing	A B1 B2 C^t	368	229	L	F	H	n/a	L	L	G	L	114
	with boiled, white icing	A B1 B2 C^t	352	262	L	F	H	n/a	---	---	G	L	64
	with uncooked, white icing	A B1 B2 C^t	367	227	L	F	H	--------n/a--------			G	L	61
100	Pound cake: (Old fashioned with equal parts flour, sugar, table-fat and eggs)	A B1 B2	473	110	L	G	H	n/a	L	L	L	L	60
	modified	A B1 B2 C^t	411	178	L	G	H	--------n/a--------			F	L	78
100	Sponge cake	A B1 B2 C^t	297	167	L	L	H	--------n/a--------			L	F	87

CAKES, COOKIES, PIES AND OTHER BAKERY PRODUCTS

F=Fair; G=Good; H=High; L=Low; t or T = trace; n/a = no information available; dashes = zero or unmeasurable

GRAM WT.	FOOD	VITAMINS	CAL	(mg) SOD	PRO	FAT	CARB	CHOL	FATTY ACIDS SAT	UNSAT	CALC	IRON	(mg) POTSM
100	White cake:												
	without icing	A B1 B2 C[t]	375	323	L	F	H	n/a	L	L	F	L	76
	with coconut icing	A B1 B2 C[t]	371	257	L	F	H	--------n/a-------			F	L	106
	with uncooked white icing	A B1 B2 C[t]	375	234	L	F	H	n/a	L	L	F	L	58
100	Yellow cake:												
	without icing	A B1 B2 C[t]	363	258	L	F	H	n/a	L	L	F	L	78
	with caramel icing	A B1 B2 C[t]	362	226	L	F	H	n/a	L	L	F	L	73
	with chocolate icing	A B1 B2 C[t]	365	208	L	F	H	n/a	L	L	F	L	108
100	Devil's food cake, frozen, commercial :												
	with chocolate icing	A B1 B2 C[t]	380	420	L	F	H	--------n/a-------			F	L	119
	with whipped-cream filling and chocolate icing	A B1 B2 C[t]	371	190	L	G	H	--------n/a-------			G	L	113
	Cake mixes and cake baked from mixes:												
100	Angelfood cake, made with water and flavorings	B1 B2	259	146	L	L	H	---	---	---	G	L	60
100	Chocolate cake, made with eggs, water and uncooked white icing	A B1 B2 C[t]	346	318	L	L	H	--------n/a-------			F	L	80
100	Coffeecake, made with enriched flour, egg and milk	A B1 B2 C[t]	322	431	L	L	H	--------n/a-------			F	F	109
100	Cupcakes:												
	made with eggs, milk, without icing	A B1 B2 C[t]	350	453	L	L	H	--------n/a-------			H	L	84
	made with eggs, milk, and chocolate icing	A B1 B2 C[t]	358	335	L	L	H	--------n/a-------			H	L	117
100	Devil's Food, made with eggs, water chocolate icing	A B1 B2 C[t]	330	262	L	L	H	--------n/a-------			F	L	130
100	Gingerbread, made with water	A[t] B1 B2 C[t]	276	304	L	L	G	--------n/a-------			G	F	274
100	Honey Spice, made with eggs, water and caramel icing	A B1 B2 C	352	245	L	L	G	--------n/a-------			G	L	82
100	Marble, made with eggs, water, and boiled white icing	A B1 B2 C[t]	331	259	L	L	H	--------n/a-------			G	L	122
100	White, made with water, egg whites, and chocolate icing	A B1 B2 C[t]	351	227	L	L	H	--------n/a-------			G	L	116

CAKES, COOKIES, PIES AND OTHER BAKERY PRODUCTS

F=Fair; G=Good; H=High; L=Low; t or T = trace; n/a = no information available; dashes = zero or unmeasurable

GRAM WT.	FOOD	VITAMINS	CAL	(mg) SOD	PRO	FAT	CARB	CHOL	FATTY ACIDS SAT	UNSAT	CALC	IRON	(mg) POTSM
100	Yellow, made with eggs, water and chocolate icing	A B1 B2 C^t	337	227	L	L	H	-------n/a-------			G	L	109
	CAKE ICINGS												
100	Caramel	A B1 B2 C^t	360	83	L	L	H	---	---	---	H	G	52
100	Chocolate	A B1 B2 C^t	376	61	L	F	H	*	*	*	F	F	195

* If margarine is used instead of butter, cholesterol will be zero (unrestricted). Bitter chocolate has more than twice as much fat content as dry cocoa powder, and is twice as high in saturated fatty acids. However, no information on cholesterol content was available, on either cocoa or chocolate.

GRAM WT.	FOOD	VITAMINS	CAL	(mg) SOD	PRO	FAT	CARB	CHOL	SAT	UNSAT	CALC	IRON	(mg) POTSM
100	Coconut	B1 B2	364	118	L	L	H	---	---	---	L	L	167
100	White												
	Uncooked	A B1^t B2 C^t	376	49	L	---	H	---	---	---	L	T	18
	Boiled	B1^t B2	316	143	L	---	H	---	---	---	L	T	18
	Cake icing mixes:												
100	Chocolate Fudge, made with water and table fat	A B1 B2	378	156	L	F	H	-------n/a-------			L	F	63
100	Creamy Fudge (contains non-fat dry milk): made with water;	A^t B1 B2 C^t	339	232	L	L	H	-------n/a-------			L	F	97
	made with water and table fat	A B1 B2 C^t	383	321	L	F	H	-------n/a-------			L	F	89
	COOKIES												
	(Products are commercial unless otherwise specified).												
100	Assorted, packaged	A B1 B2 C^t	480	365	L	F	G	-------n/a-------			L	L	67
	Brownies with nuts:												
100	baked from home recipe, and enriched flour	A B1 B2 C^t	485	251	L	F	G	n/a	L	L	L	F	190
20	1 brownie	A B1 B2 C^t	95	50	L	F	G	n/a	L	L	L	F	38
	Made from mix: (with water)												
20	1 brownie (with nuts)	A B1 B2 C^t	85	44	L	F	G	-------n/a-------			L	F	36
100	frozen, with chocolate icing	A B1 B2 C^t	419	200	L	F	G	-------n/a-------			L	F	179
100	Butter cookies, thin, rich	A B1 B2	457	418	L	G	H	-------n/a-------			G	L	60
100	Chocolate	A B1 B2 C^t	445	137	L	G	H	-------n/a-------			F	F	128
	Chocolate chip:												
100	baked from home recipe, with enriched flour	A B1 B2 C^t	516	348	L	G	H	n/a	L	L	L	F	117
10	1 cookie	A B1 B2 C^t	50	35	L	G	H	n/a	n/a	T	L	F	12

CAKES, COOKIES, PIES AND OTHER BAKERY PRODUCTS

F=Fair; G=Good; H=High; L=Low; t or T = trace; n/a = no information available; dashes = zero or unmeasurable

GRAM WT.	FOOD	VITAMINS	CAL	(mg) SOD	PRO	FAT	CARB	CHOL	FATTY ACIDS SAT	UNSAT	CALC	IRON	(mg) POTSM
100	Commercial type	A B1 B2 C^t	471	401	L	G	H		------n/a------		L	F	134
10	1 cookie	A B1^t B2^t C^t	50	40	L	G	H		------n/a------		L	L	13
100	Coconut bars	A B1 B2	494	148	L	G	H		------n/a------		F	F	228
100	Fig bars	A B1 B2 C^t	358	252	L	L	H	---	---	---	F	F	198
14	1 fig bar	A B1 B2 C^t	50	35	L	L	H	---	---	---	F	F	28
100	Ginger snaps	A B1 B2 C^t	420	571	L	L	H		------n/a------		G	G	462
100	Ladyfingers	A B1 B2	360	71	L	L	G		------n/a------		L	F	71
100	Macaroons	B1 B2	475	34	L	F	G		------n/a------		L	L	463
100	Marshmallow	A B1 B2 C^t	409	209	L	F	H		------n/a------		L	L	91
100	Molasses	A B1 B2	422	386	L	F	H		------n/a------		F	F	138
100	Oatmeal with raisins	A B1 B2 C^t	451	162	L	F	H		------n/a------		L	G	370
100	Peanut	A B1 B2 C^t	473	173	F	G	H		------n/a------		L	L	175
100	Raisin	A B1 B2 C^t	379	52	L	L	H		------n/a------		F	F	272
	Sandwich Type:												
100	Chocolate or vanilla	B1 B2	495	483	L	F	H		------n/a------		L	L	38
10	1 sandwich-type cookie	B1 B2^t	50	48	L	T	H		------n/a------		L	L	4
100	Shortbread	A B1 B2	498	60	L	F	H		------n/a------		F	L	66
100	Sugar, soft, thick, with enriched flour, baked from home recipe	A B1 B2 C^t	444	318	L	F	H		------n/a------		F	F	76
100	Sugar wafers	A B1 B2	485	189	L	F	H		------n/a------		L	L	60
100	Vanilla Wafers	A B1 B2	462	252	L	F	H	L	L	L	L	L	72
	COOKIE MIXES AND COOKIES BAKED FROM MIXES												
100	Brownies, enriched flour, with nuts and water (complete mix)	A B1 B2	403	218	L	F	G		------n/a------		L	F	180
100	Brownies, incomplete mix, add egg, water and nuts	A B1 B2 C^t	428	166	L	F	G		------n/a------		L	F	168
100	Plain cookies, with unenriched flour, eggs and water	A B1 B2	493	347	L	F	G		------n/a------		F	L	42
100	made with milk	A B1 B2 C^t	490	345	L	F	G		------n/a------		F	L	42
	PIES: Baked, pie crust made with unenriched flour, Pg. 144												

CAKES, COOKIES, PIES AND OTHER BAKERY PRODUCTS

F=Fair; G=Good; H=High; L=Low; t or T = trace; n/a = no information available; dashes = zero or unmeasurable

GRAM WT.	FOOD	VITAMINS	CAL	(mg) SOD	PRO	FAT	CARB	CHOL	FATTY ACIDS SAT	UNSAT	CALC	IRON	(mg) POTSM
135	Apple, 2 crust,1/7 of 9" pie	A B1 B2 C	350	406	L	F	F	n/a	L	L	L	L	108
100	Banana Custard	A B1 B2 C	221	194	L	L	F	n/a	L	L	F	L	203
100	Blackberry	A B1 B2 C	243	268	L	F	G	--------n/a-------			L	L	100
	Boston Cream Pie - See CAKES												
130	Butterscotch, 1 crust, 1 section	A B1 B2 C^t	350	278	L	F	G	n/a	L	L	L	L	124
135	Cherry, 2 crust, 1 section	A B1 B2 C^t	350	410	L	F	G	n/a	L	L	L	L	142
100	Chocolate chiffon	A B1 B2	328	252	L	F	G	--------n/a-------			L	F	110
100	Chocolate Meringue	A B1 B2 C^t	252	256	L	F	G	--------n/a-------			F	L	139
100	Coconut Custard	A B1 B2	235	247	L	L	F	n/a	L	L	F	L	163
130	Custard, 1 crust	A B1 B2	285	373	L	L	F	n/a	L	L	F	L	178
100	Lemon Chiffon	A B1 B2 C	313	261	L	L	F	n/a	L	L	L	L	81
120	Lemon Meringue, 1 crust	A B1 B2 C	305	338	L	L	F	n/a	L	L	L	L	60
135	Mince, 2 crust, 1 section	A^t B1 B2 C	365	605	L	L	F	n/a	L	F	L	L	240
100	Peach	A B1 B2 C	255	268	L	L	F	n/a	L	L	L	L	149
118	Pecan, 1 crust, 1 section	A B1 B2 C^t	490	261	L	F	G	--------n/a-------			L	F	145
100	Pineapple	A B1 B2 C	253	271	L	L	G	n/a	L	L	L	L	72
93	Pineapple Chiffon,1 crust, 1 Sect	A B1 B2 C	265	173	L	L	F	n/a	L	L	L	L	91
100	Pineapple Cream(or custard)	A B1 B2 C	220	186	L	L	F	n/a	L	L	F	L	97
130	Pumpkin, 1 crust, 1 section	A B1 B2 C^t	275	278	L	L	F	n/a	L	L	L	L	208
100	Raisin	A B1 B2 C	270	285	L	L	F	--------n/a-------			L	L	192
100	Rhubarb	A B1 B2 C	253	270	L	L	F	--------n/a-------			F	L	159
100	Strawberry	A B1 B2 C	198	194	L	L	F	--------n/a-------			L	L	120
100	Sweet potato	A B1 B2 C	213	218	L	L	F	--------n/a-------			F	L	163
	Frozen in unbaked form:												
100	Apple:												
	Unbaked	A B1 B2 C	210	177	L	L	F	--------n/a-------			L	L	60
	Baked	A B1 B2 C^t	254	213	L	F	F	--------n/a-------			L	L	72
100	Cherry:												
	Unbaked	A B1 B2 C	256	202	L	F	F	--------n/a-------			L	L	72
	Baked	A B1 B2 C	291	229	L	F	F	--------n/a-------			L	L	82
100	Coconut Custard:												
	Unbaked	A B1 B2 C^t	205	238	L	L	F	--------n/a-------			G	L	157
	Baked	A B1 B2 C^t	249	252	L	L	G	--------n/a-------			G	L	172
100	PIE MIX, coconut custard & pie baked from mix, prepared with egg yolk and milk	A B1 B2 C^t	203	235	L	L	F	--------n/a-------			F	L	154

CAKES, COOKIES, PIES AND OTHER BAKERY PRODUCTS

F=Fair; G=Good; H=High; L=Low; t or T = trace; n/a = no information available; dashes = zero or unmeasurable

GRAM WT.	FOOD	VITAMINS	CAL	(mg) SOD	PRO	FAT	CARB	CHOL	FATTY ACIDS SAT	UNSAT	CALC	IRON	(mg) POTSM
	PIE CRUST or plain pastry made with enriched and unenriched flour:												
100	Unbaked	B1 B2	464	568	L	F	F	--------n/a------			L	F	46
100	Baked	B1 B2	500	611	L	F	F	--------n/a------			L	F	50
	PIE CRUST MIX (including stick form) and pie crust baked from mix:												
100	Pie crust, prepared with water and baked	B1 B2	464	813	L	F	F	--------n/a------			L	L	56
	PIZZA PIE:												
75	with cheese topping 5-1/2" section (1/8 — 14" pie)	A B1 B2 C	185	526	F	L	F	H	H	L	H	F	98
100	with sausage topping	A B1 B2 C	234	729	L	L	F	H	H	T	L	F	168
	POTPIES: See Meat and Poultry List, under beef, chicken and turkey.												

Figures for Nutrition at Your Fingertips were taken from U.S.D.A. Handbook No. 8 and U.S.D.A. Home and Garden Bulletin No. 72. (Recipes in this book are an interesting comparison. Only vegetable shortening and low-fat milk were used.)

PREPARATION OF LAYER—CAKE PANS

Before mixing the cake, it is advisable to prepare the pans. Whether Teflon coated or of other material, pans should be greased with unsalted shortening, unless otherwise specified, which will enable removing the cake easier. Although many people lightly flour their cake pans, I have found that wax paper cut in circles the size of the pans prevents the cake from sticking to the pan. To do this, fold a piece of wax paper in half. This should be large enough so that two circles may be cut at the same time. Put one of the pans on top of the wax paper and trace around it with the point of a paring knife. Then cut around the circle about 1/2" inside the original tracing. By cutting the paper a little shorter than the pan, the paper will not bunch up at the edges. Place the circles as evenly as possible in the greased pans, smooth out with the back of the fingers, pressing out any air bubbles.

REMOVING THE CAKE

Cakes usually shrink a little from the sides of the pans when done, but this doesn't mean the cakes will not stick when being removed, so it is nearly always necessary to run the blunt edge of a dinner knife around the edges carefully before trying to free the cakes for removal. Push the knife slightly against the cake as you run it around the edges of the pan which will free the bottom of the cake and is not covered with wax paper. When this has been done, place cake plate upside down over the cake, centering it. Grasp each side of the cake plate and layer-cake pan together, then quickly turn over. Cake plate should be on the bottom. Tap layer-cake pan lightly, then life. Cake should free itself and fall upside down on the cake plate. If it doesn't, turn over again, and run the knife around the edges of the pan once more.

Cakes will be easier to handle and remove from the pan if allowed to stand about 10 minutes after they have been taken from the oven. They should be placed on racks to allow the air to circulate over and under the pans.

As soon as cakes have been removed from the pans, the wax paper should be taken off, otherwise it will be hard to get off. Start at the outer edge and lift the paper carefully with the point of a paring knife, then peel the paper back all around the edges first, gently working it off to avoid cracking the cake. The second layer will be less tricky to remove if you'll place the wax paper from the first layer onto a dinner plate (flat plate, not one with inundations). Then take the second layer out and place it on top of the wax paper. (Or paper can be placed on top of the second layer, dinner plate placed on top of it, then turned upside down, whichever is easier.) The wax paper will prevent the cake from sticking to the plate when it is removed and placed on top of the iced, first layer. Then remove wax paper from the second layer. Allow cakes to cool thoroughly before icing them.

ICING THE CAKES

The bottom layer of the cake should be iced first. Start at the center and spread frosting outward smoothly, with a dinner knife, until completely covered. Place the flat side of the second layer on top of the iced, flat side of the first layer carefully to avoid cracking it, then ice the top and sides, working from the center out. Rinse knife often in hot, running water to keep icing smooth and free of crumbs.

. . . .

146

ANGLE FOOD CAKE

F=Fair; G=Good; H=High; L=Low; t or T = trace; n/a = no information available; dashes = zero or unmeasurable

GRAM WT.	FOOD	VITAMINS	CAL	(mg) SOD	PRO	FAT	CARB	CHOL	FATTY ACIDS SAT	UNSAT	CALC	IRON	(mg) POTSM
57	AVERAGE PER 2" SLICE		124	125									47
	Ingredients:												
250	1-1/4 cp granulated sugar	---	962	4	---	---	H	---	---	---	---	L	8
96	1 cp sifted cake flour	B1 B2	350	2	F	L	G	---	---	---	L	F	91
330	1 cp egg whites (approx. 10)	B1 B2	150	482	L	T	T	---	---	---	L	T	459
3	1 tsp cream of tartar	---	2	230	T	T	F	-----	-n/a-	-----	---	---	---
2	1/2 tsp salt	---	---	785	--	---	---	---	---	---	G	---	T
n/a	1 tsp vanilla							-n/a-					
n/a	3/4 tsp almond extract							-n/a-					
681	Recipe totals (gms; cal; sod. & potsm.)		1464	1503									558

METHOD

Sift 1/4 cup sugar and flour together 4 times. Beat the egg whites, cream of tartar and salt to a stiff foam. Add the remaining cup of sugar a few tablespoons at a time, beating it in until the mixture holds soft peaks. Add flavorings and blend, then fold in the remaining flour, sifting a little at a time over the egg mixture until thoroughly blended or until no patches of flour remain. Pour mixture into a large ungreased tube pan; cut through the batter with a spatula to remove large air bubbles. Bake at 350 F. 45 – 60 minutes or until done.

After removing from the oven, invert pan and cool about an hour. Then remove cake. Ice with thin confectioners' frosting if desired.

NOTE: Averages will depend on size of pieces served. A 10" tubular cake pan was used for the averages in this recipe.

. . . .

GREEN APPLE CAKE

F=Fair; G=Good; H=High; L=Low; t or T = trace; n/a = no information available; dashes = zero or unmeasurable

GRAM WT.	FOOD	VITAMINS	CAL	(mg) SOD	PRO	FAT	CARB	CHOL	FATTY ACIDS SAT	UNSAT	CALC	IRON	(mg) POTSM
110	AVERAGE EACH SERVING (2" x 3")		205	184				(mg) 31					104
	Ingredients:												
100	2 eggs	A B1 B2	150	122	G	G	L	H*	H	L	F	F	129
400	2 cp granulated sugar	---	1540	2	---	---	H	---	---	---	---	L	12
110	1/2 cp cooking oil	---	---	1945	---	H	---	---	T	H	---	---	---
118	1/2 cp water	---	---	---	---	---	---	---	---	---	---	---	---
n/a	1 tsp vanilla	----------						-n/a-					----------
4	1 tsp baking soda	---	3	439	L	T	G	---	---	---	H	---	---
230	2 cp presifted, all-purpose flour	B1 B2	840	4	F	L	G	---	---	---	L	F	219
n/a	2 tsp cinnamon	----------						-n/a-					----------
2	1/2 tsp salt	---	---	785	---	---	---	---	---	---	G	---	T
108	1 cp pecans, chopped	A B1 B2 C	740	T	L	H	F	---	---	---	F	F	651
908	4 cp diced, pared apples	A B1 B2 C	422	8	L	L	F	---	---	---	L	L	858
1980	Recipe totals (gms; cal; sod. & potsm.)		3695	3305									1869

METHOD

Beat eggs until foamy, then add the sugar (creamed with the oil), and water and vanilla. Sift the soda, flour, cinnamon and salt together, add to the creamed mixture and beat thoroughly. Batter will be thick. Add nuts and apples and mix well. Pour batter into a greased 9" x 13" baking dish or a large angel food cake tubular pan, and bake at 350 F. for 45 — 60 minutes. Frost when cool.

* There are 550 milligrams of cholesterol in 100 grams of whole egg, according to U.S.D.A. Handbook No. 8, pg. 146, item 12. Total 550 milligrams divided by yield of approximately 18 pieces equals 31 average milligrams of cholesterol in each serving.

. . . .

APPLESAUCE CAKE

F=Fair; G=Good; H=High; L=Low; t or T = trace; n/a = no information available; dashes = zero or unmeasurable

GRAM WT.	FOOD	VITAMINS	CAL	(mg) SOD	PRO	FAT	CARB	CHOL	FATTY ACIDS SAT	UNSAT	CALC	IRON	(mg) POTSM
								(mg)					
77	AVERAGE EACH PIECE		209	189				23					47
	Ingredients:												
200	1 cp granulated sugar	---	770	2	---	---	H	---	---	---	---	L	6
113	1/2 cp margarine (1 stick)	A D	815	1115	L	H	L	---	L	G	---	L	26
50	1 egg	A B1 B2	75	61	G	G	L	H*	H	L	F	F	65
8	2 tsp baking soda	---	6	878	L	T	G	---	---	---	H	---	---
192	2 cp cake flour	B1 B2	700	4	F	L	G	---	---	---	L	F	182
---	Dash salt (1/8 tsp)	---	---	197	---	---	---	---	---	---	G	---	---
n/a	1/4 tsp ground cloves	---						-n/a-					
n/a	1/2 tsp cinnamon							-n/a-					
n/a	1/8 tsp allspice							-n/a-					
366	1-1/2 cp unsweetened applesauce	A B1 B2 C	150	7	L	T	F	---	---	---	L	F	285
n/a	1 tsp vanilla							-n/a-					
929	Recipe totals (gms; cal; sod. & potsm.)		2516	2264									564

METHOD

Cream sugar and margarine together. Add unbeaten egg and beat thoroughly. Sift soda, flour, salt and spices together then add to the sugar and egg mixture alternately with the applesauce (cold), beating until smooth after each addition. Add vanilla and blend thoroughly. Bake in lightly greased 8" or 9" loaf pan or tube pan at 350 F. for 45 — 50 minutes or until done. Frost with any desired icing. If raisins and nuts are added to this recipe, add 1 cup of seedless raisins and 1 cup finely chopped nuts to the flour before adding to the sugar and egg mixture.

* There are 275 milligrams of cholesterol in 50 grams of whole egg, as calculated from U.S.D.A. Handbook No. 8, pg. 146, item 12. Total of 275 milligrams of cholesterol divided by 12 pieces equals 23 average milligrams of cholesterol per piece.

. . . .

BANANA CAKE

F=Fair; G=Good; H=High; L=Low; t or T = trace; n/a = no information available; dashes = zero or unmeasurable

GRAM WT.	FOOD	VITAMINS	CAL	SOD (mg)	PRO	FAT	CARB	CHOL (mg)	FATTY ACIDS SAT	UNSAT	CALC	IRON	POTSM (mg)
97	AVERAGE EACH PIECE		230	276				52					164
	Ingredients:												
216	2-1/4 cp sifted cake flour	B1 B2	718	4	F	L	G	---	---	---	L	F	205
334	1-2/3 cp granulated sugar	---	1283	3	---	---	---	---	---	---	---	L	10
4	1-1/4 tsp baking powder	---	4	394	L	T	H	---	---	---	H	---	---
5	1-1/4 tsp baking soda	---	4	549	L	T	G	---	---	---	H	---	---
4	1 tsp salt	---	---	1569	---	---	---	---	---	---	G	---	T
150	2/3 cp margarine	A D	1089	1493	L	H	L	---	L	H	L	---	35
164	2/3 cp buttermilk	A B1 B2 C	60	212	H	L	H	--------n/a--------			G	L	229
150	3 eggs	A B1 B2	225	183	G	G	L	H*	H	L	F	F	194
525	1-1/4 cp mashed bananas (approximately 3 large bananas)	A B1 B2 C	300	5	L	L	G	---	---	---	L	L	1943
1552	Recipe totals (gms; cal; sod. & potsm.)		3683	4412									2616

METHOD

Measure all ingredients into a large mixing bowl. Blend 1/2 minute on low speed. Scrape bowl almost continuously. Beat 3 minutes on high speed, scraping bowl occasionally. Pour batter into 2 greased layer pans, either 8" or 9". Bake at 350 F. for 35 — 40 minutes or until toothpick inserted in center comes out clean. Let cake cool 15 minutes before removing from pans. Frost when cold.

* There are 825 milligrams of cholesterol in 150 grams of whole egg, as calculated from U.S.D.A. Handbook No. 8, pg. 146, item 12.   Dividing 825 milligrams of cholesterol by 16 pieces equals 52 average milligrams of cholesterol per piece.

. . . .

CHOCOLATE CHIP 'N DATE CAKE

F=Fair; G=Good; H=High; L=Low; t or T = trace; n/a = no information available;   dashes = zero or unmeasurable

GRAM WT.	FOOD	VITAMINS	CAL	(mg) SOD	PRO	FAT	CARB	CHOL	FATTY ACIDS SAT	UNSAT	CALC	IRON	(mg) POTSM
56	AVERAGE EACH PIECE		190	119				(mg) 21					108
	Ingredients:												
178	1 cp pitted dates, cut up	A B1 B2 C	490	2	L	L	H	---	---	---	G	H	1153
295	1-1/4 cp boiling water							-n/a-					----
170	3/4 cp softened margarine	A D	1224	1680	L	H	L	---	L	H	L	---	39
200	1 cp granulated sugar	---	770	2	---	---	H	---	---	---	---	L	6
100	2 eggs	A B1 B2	150	122	G	G	L	H*	H	L	F	F	129
173	1-1/2 cp presifted, all-purpose flour	B1 B2	630	3	F	L	G	---	---	---	L	F	164
4	1 tsp baking soda	---	3	439	L	T	G	---	---	---	H	---	---
12	2 tblspn dry cocoa	B1 B2	43	34	L	L	H	-n/a-			L	F	60
2	1/2 tsp salt	---	---	785	---	---	---	---	---	---	G	---	T
110	1/2 cp brown sugar	B1 B2	410	33	---	---	H	---	---	---	G	G	378
170	1 cp chocolate chips (6 oz. bag)	A B1 B2	860	3	L	L	G	n/a	G	F	L	F	553
54	1/2 cp chopped pecans	A B1 B2 C	370	T	L	H	F	---	---	---	F	F	326
1468	Recipe totals (gms; cal; sod. & potsm.)		4950	3103									2808

METHOD

Put the dates in a small bowl and pour the boiling water over them. Stir and set aside to cool. Cream the margarine and sugar together until fluffy then add the eggs and beat thoroughly. Add the cooled dates and water mixture, blending well. Sift the soda, dry cocoa and salt with the flour and add to the first mixture, beating until smooth. Pour batter into greased and lightly floured 13" x 9" pan. Mix the brown sugar, chocolate chips and nuts together and sprinkle over the batter. Bake at 350 F. for 35 — 40 minutes or until done. When cool, frost if desired.

*   There are 550 milligrams of cholesterol in 100 grams of whole egg, according to U.S.D.A. Handbook No. 8, pg. 146, item 12. Total 550 milligrams divided by yield of approximately 26 pieces of cake equals 21 average milligrams of cholesterol per serving.

. . . .

CHOCOLATE LAYER CAKE

F=Fair; G=Good; H=High; L=Low; t or T = trace; n/a = no information available;   dashes = zero or unmeasurable

GRAM WT.	FOOD	VITAMINS	CAL	(mg) SOD	PRO	FAT	CARB	CHOL	FATTY ACIDS SAT	UNSAT	CALC	IRON	(mg) POTSM
76	AVERAGE EACH PIECE		237	175				(mg) 69					124
	Ingredients:												
71	5 tblspn margarine	A D	500	696	L	H	L	---	L	H	L	---	16
250	1-1/4 cp granulated sugar	---	962	2	---	---	H	---	---	---	---	L	8
150	3 eggs	A B1 B2	225	183	G	G	L	H*	H	L	F	F	194
98	3-1/2 squares bitter chocolate	A B1 B2	508	4	F	G	F	n/a	F	F	F	G	813
11	3-1/2 tsp baking powder	---	11	1103	L	T	H	---	---	---	H	---	--
144	1-1/2 cp cake flour	B1 B2	525	3	F	L	G	---	---	---	L	F	137
n/a	1 tsp vanilla	------	------	------	------	------	------	---n/a---	------	------	------	------	------
185	3/4 cp 2% low-fat milk	A B1 B2 C	109	113	H	L	H	L	L	L	H	L	324
909	Recipe totals (gms; cal; sod. & potsm.)		2840	2104									1492

Grease the layer-cake pans and line the bottoms with circles of wax paper. Preheat oven to 350 F.

METHOD

Cream the margarine, add the sugar gradually and beat until light and fluffy. Add the eggs, one at a time, beating after each addition. Melt chocolate over hot water then add to above mixture, blending in well.

Sift baking powder with the flour. Add vanilla to the milk. Add flour mixture alternately with milk to margarine, sugar and eggs, beginning and ending with dry ingredients. After each addition, beat until smooth. Pour batter into pans and bake 25 — 35 minutes or until done. Cool on racks about 15 minutes then remove cake and wax paper. (See paragraph on "Removing the Cake" at the beginning of this chapter). Allow cake to cool thoroughly before frosting.

*   There are 825 milligrams of cholesterol in 150 grams of whole egg and 6 milligrams of cholesterol in 185 grams of low-fat milk, as calculated in U.S.D.A. Handbook No. 8, pg. 146, items 12 and 29 respectively. Total 831 milligrams divided by yield of approximately 12 pieces of cake equals 69 average milligrams of cholesterol in each serving.

. . . .

CINNAMON SUPPER CAKE

F=Fair; G=Good; H=High; L=Low; t or T = trace; n/a = no information available;   dashes = zero or unmeasurable

GRAM WT.	FOOD	VITAMINS	CAL	(mg) SOD	PRO	FAT	CARB	CHOL	FATTY ACIDS SAT	UNSAT	CALC	IRON	(mg) POTSM
67	AVERAGE PER SERVING		218	213				(mg) 35					51
	Ingredients:												
56	4 tblspn margarine	A D	400	558	L	H	L	---	L	H	L	---	13
150	3/4 cp granulated sugar	---	577	2	---	---	H	---	---	---	---	L	5
50	1 egg	A B1 B2	75	61	G	G	L	H*	H	L	F	F	65
n/a	1 tsp vanilla							-n/a-					
123	1/2 cp 2% low-fat milk	A B1 B2 C	73	75	H	L	H	L*	L	L	G	G	215
115	1 cp presifted flour	B1 B2	420	2	F	L	G	---	---	---	L	F	109
5	1-1/2 tsp baking powder	---	5	473	L	T	H	---	---	---	H	---	---
1	1/4 tsp salt	---	---	393	---	---	---	---	---	---	G	---	---
14	1 tblspn margarine	A D	100	139	L	H	T	---	L	H	L	---	3
24	3 tblspn powdered sugar	---	93	T	---	---	H	---	---	---	---	L	1
n/a	1 tsp cinnamon							-n/a-					
538	Recipe totals (gms; cal; sod. & potsm.)		1743	1703									411

METHOD

Preheat oven to 375 F. Cream margarine, add sugar gradually; add beaten egg, and beat mixture until fluffy. Add vanilla to the milk. Sift flour with baking powder and salt, then add milk alternately with flour, ending with dry ingredients. Beat until smooth after each addition. Pour into 9" round layer pan or 8" square pan. Bake for 25 minutes. Remove from oven and spread margarine on top at once. Then sift powdered sugar and cinnamon over entire cake. Serve warm. Yield   approximately 8 servings.

*   There are 275 milligrams of cholesterol in 50 grams of whole egg and 4 milligrams of cholesterol in 123 grams of low-fat milk, as calculated in U.S.D.A. Handbook No. 8, pg. 146, items 12 and 29 respectively. Total 279 milligrams divided by yield of 8 pieces of cake equals 35 average milligrams of cholesterol in each serving.

. . . .

COCOA CAKE

F=Fair; G=Good; H=High; L=Low; t or T = trace; n/a = no information available; dashes = zero or unmeasurable

GRAM WT.	FOOD	VITAMINS	CAL	(mg) SOD	PRO	FAT	CARB	CHOL	FATTY ACIDS SAT	UNSAT	CALC	IRON	(mg) POTSM
72	AVERAGE EACH PIECE		220	154				*					37
	Ingredients:												
48	1/2 cp cocoa	B1 B2	176	136	L	L	H	n/a	L	L	L	F	240
177	3/4 cp boiling water	----------						---n/a---					----
113	1/2 cp margarine (1 stick)	A D	815	1115	L	H	L	--	L	H	L	---	26
400	2 cp granulated sugar	---	1540	4	---	---	H	---	---	---	---	L	12
192	2 cp sifted cake flour	B1 B2	700	4	F	L	G	---	---	---	L	F	182
2	1/2 tsp salt	---	--	785	---	---	---	---	---	---	G	---	T
115	1/2 cp sour cream	A B1 B2 C	243	49	L	G	F	--------n/a---			G	L	n/a
2	1/2 tsp baking soda	---	2	220	L	T	G	---	---	---	H	---	---
n/a	1 tsp vanilla	----------						---n/a---					----
99	3 egg whites	B1 B2	45	144	F	T	L	---	---	---	L	L	138
1148	Recipe totals (gms; cal; sod. & potsm.)		3521	2457									598

METHOD

Mix cocoa in boiling water and stir until smooth. Set aside to cool. Cream margarine and sugar together until light and fluffy then add the cooled cocoa mixture and blend in thoroughly. Sift flour, salt and soda together and add alternately with sour cream to the first mixture. Beat until smooth after each addition. Add vanilla then fold in the stiffly beaten egg whites. Pour batter evenly into layer cake pans and bake at 350 F. 30 minutes or until cake tests for doneness either by inserting a toothpick in the center, and if it comes out clean the cake is done, or by pressing the fingers lightly on the cake; if it springs back, the cake is done. Cool cake on racks about 15 minutes before removing to plates. Frost with 7 minute icing or confectioners' frosting.

* No information was available on cholesterol content of sour cream and cocoa at the time this research was completed.

. . . .

DEVIL'S FOOD CAKE

F=Fair; G=Good; H=High; L=Low; t or T = trace; n/a = no information available; dashes = zero or unmeasurable

GRAM WT.	FOOD	VITAMINS	CAL	(mg) SOD	PRO	FAT	CARB	CHOL	FATTY ACIDS SAT	UNSAT	CALC	IRON	(mg) POTSM
86	AVERAGE EACH PIECE		250	206				(mg) 52					201
	Ingredients:												
216	2-1/4 cp cake flour	B1 B2	788	4	F	L	G	---	---	---	L	F	205
8	2 tsp baking soda	---	6	878	L	T	G	---	---	---	H	---	---
2	1/2 tsp salt	---	---	785	---	---	---	---	---	---	G	---	---
113	1/2 cp margarine (1 stick)	A D	815	1115	L	H	L	---	L	H	L	---	26
454	2-1/2 to 2-3/4 cp brown sugar	B1 B2	1692	136	---	---	H	---	---	---	G	G	1560
150	3 eggs	A B1 B2	225	183	G	G	L	H*	H	L	F	F	194
84	3 oz unsweetened chocolate (1 oz)	A B1 B2	435	33	F	H	G	n/a*	H	L	G	G	1054
123	1/2 cp buttermilk	A B1 B2 C	45	160	H	L	H	---	---	---	F	L	172
n/a	2 tsp vanilla							n/a					
236	1 cp boiling water							n/a					
1386	Recipe totals (gms; cal; sod. & potsm.)		4006	3294									3211

METHOD

Sift flour, soda and salt together. Cream margarine until soft then add brown sugar gradually and continue to cream together until smooth, pressing out any lumps in the brown sugar. Add melted chocolate. (To melt chocolate: 1. Leave squares in their paper covers and place in a small pan and turn heat to low. Chocolate will melt in the paper and can be scraped out of it, or 2. Unwrap the chocolate and melt in a double boiler over boiling water). After melted chocolate has been added and blended into the sugar and margarine mixture, add eggs, one at a time, beating hard after each addition. Sift 1/3 of the flour into the batter and stir in well. Add half of the buttermilk and stir slightly. Repeat, adding flour and buttermilk, ending with the flour. Add flavoring and boiling water. Mix thoroughly. Pour batter into two 9" greased layer-cake pans or a 9" x 13-1/2" cake pan. Bake at 375 F. for 25–35 minutes or until done. Cool on rack about 15 minutes if in layer-cake pans then remove cake from pans. Frost when cold. Yield approximately 16 pieces of cake.

* There is no information available on the cholesterol content of chocolate at this writing, however, there are 825 milligrams of cholesterol in 150 grams of whole egg as calculated from U.S.D.A. Handbook No. 8, pg. 146, item 12. Total 825 milligrams divided by yield of 16 slices of cake equals 52 average milligrams of cholesterol per serving.

. . . .

WHITE LAYER CAKE

F=Fair; G=Good; H=High; L=Low; t or T = trace; n/a = no information available; dashes = zero or unmeasurable

GRAM WT.	FOOD	VITAMINS	CAL	(mg) SOD	PRO	FAT	CARB	CHOL	FATTY ACIDS SAT	UNSAT	CALC	IRON	(mg) POTSM
45	AVERAGE EACH PIECE		152	132				(mg) 35					34
	Ingredients:												
113	1/2 cp margarine (1 stick)	A D	815	1115	L	H	L	---	L	H	L	---	26
200	1 cp granulated sugar	---	770	2	---	---	H	---	---	---	---	L	6
100	2 eggs	A B1 B2	150	122	G	G	L	H*	H	L	F	F	129
8	2-1/2 tsp baking powder	---	8	788	---	---	---	---	---	---	H	---	---
168	1-3/4 cp cake flour	B1 B2	612	4	F	L	G	---	--	---	L	F	160
123	1/2 cp 2% low-fat milk	A B1 B2 C	73	75	H	L	H	L	L	L	H	L	215
n/a	1 tsp vanilla or almond extract	----------						----n/a----					----------
712	Recipe totals (gms; cal; sod. & potsm.)		2428	2106									536

METHOD

Grease two 8" layer cake pans; line bottoms with circles of wax paper. Preheat oven to 350 F.

Cream margarine and sugar together until light and fluffy. Add the eggs, one at a time, beating well after each addition. Sift flour and baking powder together; add vanilla (or almond extract) to the milk, stirring until well mixed. Then, starting with the dry ingredients, add the flour and milk mixtures alternately, ending with the dry ingredients. Beat until smooth. Divide batter evenly in the two pans. Bake 20 — 30 minutes, or until cake tests done. Cool cake on racks 15 minutes then turn out and remove wax paper. Frost when cold.

*   There are 550 milligrams of cholesterol in 100 grams of whole egg and 4 milligrams of cholesterol in 123 grams of low-fat milk, as calculated from U.S.D.A. Handbook No. 8, pg. 146, items 12 and respectively. Total 554 milligrams divided by yield of 16 slices of cake equals 35 average milligrams of cholesterol per serving.

. . . .

FIG—RAISIN CAKE

F=Fair; G=Good; H=High; L=Low; t or T = trace; n/a = no information available; dashes = zero or unmeasurable

GRAM WT.	FOOD	VITAMINS	CAL	(mg) SOD	PRO	FAT	CARB	CHOL	FATTY ACIDS SAT	UNSAT	CALC	IRON	(mg) POTSM
89	AVERAGE EACH PIECE		311	206				(mg) 55					303
	Ingredients:												
227	1 cp margarine, softened	A D	1633	2239	L	H	L	---	L	H	L	---	52
440	2 cp brown sugar	B1 B2	1640	132	---	---	H	---	---	---	G	G	1514
200	4 eggs, beaten	A B1 B2	300	244	G	G	L	H*	H	L	F	F	258
288	3 cp cake flour	B1 B2	1050	6	F	L	G	---	L	---	L	F	274
9	3 tsp baking powder	---	9	945	L	T	H	---	---	---	H	---	---
1	1/4 tsp salt	---	---	393	---	---	---	---	---	---	G	---	T
n/a	1 tsp cinnamon							-n/a-					
n/a	1/2 tsp ground cloves							-n/a-					
n/a	1 tsp nutmeg							-n/a-					
59	1 cp water	---	---	---	---	---	---	---	---	---	---	---	---
227	1/2 lb dried figs, cut fine	A B1 B2	622	77	L	L	H	---	---	---	H	L	1452
330	2 cp seedless raisins, chopped	A B1 B2 C	960	90	L	T	H	---	---	---	G	H	2518
1781	Recipe totals (gms; cal; sod. & potsm.)		6214	4126									6068

METHOD

Cream the softened margarine with the brown sugar gradually. When light and fluffy, add the well-beaten eggs. Sift the dry ingredients together and add alternately with the water to the creamed mixture, beating until smooth. Fold in fruits. Bake in loaf pan 5-1/2" x 10" that has been lightly greased and lined with wax paper, at 300 F. (slow oven) about 2 hours.

*   There are 1100 milligrams of cholesterol in 200 grams of whole egg as calculated from U.S.D.A. Handbook No. 8, pg. 146, item 12. Total 1100 milligrams divided by yield of 20 pieces of cake equals 55 average milligrams of cholesterol per serving.

. . . .

WHITE FRUIT CAKE

F=Fair; G=Good; H=High; L=Low; t or T = trace; n/a = no information available; dashes = zero or unmeasurable

GRAM WT.	• FOOD	VITAMINS	CAL	(mg) SOD	PRO	FAT	CARB	CHOL (mg)	FATTY ACIDS SAT	UNSAT	CALC	IRON	(mg) POTSM
29	AVERAGE EACH PIECE		116	45				14					60
	Ingredients:												
454	4 sticks margarine	A D	3266	4478	L	H	L	---	L	H	L	---	104
600	3 cp granulated sugar	---	2310	3	---	---	H	---	---	---	---	L	18
300	6 eggs, separated	A B1 B2	450	366	G	G	L	H*	H	L	F	F	387
575	5 cp presifted, all-purpose flour	B1 B2	2100	10	F	L	G	---	---	---	L	F	546
454	1 lb white raisins**	A B1 B2 C	1311	122	L	T	H	---	---	---	G	H	3464
	(**Values are for natural, unbleached raisins, as values for white raisins were not available.)												
454	4 cp pecans, coarse pieces	A B1 B2 C	2960	T	L	H	F	---	---	---	F	F	2738
227	1 cp candied cherries, chopped	n/a	770	n/a	L	L	H	---	---	---	---	---	---
227	1 cp candied pineapple, chopped	n/a	717	n/a	L	L	H	---	---	---	---	---	---
84	6 tblspn spiced peach juice	----------						---n/a---					----------
56	2 oz lemon extract	----------						---n/a---					----------
4	(1 tsp baking soda, dissolved	---	3	439	L	T	G	---	---	---	H	---	---
28	in 2 tblspn warm water	---	---	---	---	---	---	---	---	---	---	---	---
3463	Recipe Totals (gms; cal; sod. & potsm.)		13887	5418									7257

METHOD

Cream margarine and sugar together; add egg yolks and beat thoroughly. Coat raisins, nuts and candied fruit with part of the flour (which prevents these ingredients from sinking to the bottom of the cake), and set aside. Add remaining flour to the creamed mixture gradually, beating after each addition.   Then add floured ingredients, spiced peach juice, lemon extract and soda solution, mixing well. Beat egg whites until they peak, fold into batter. Bake at 250 F. about 90 minutes, or until toothpick inserted in center of cakes comes out clean. This recipe will fill 2 angelfood tube pans, or four 5" x 8" loaf pans. Pans should be greased well and lined with brown paper. Makes about 6 pounds of cake.

*   There are 1650 milligrams of cholesterol in 300 grams of whole egg, as calculated from U.S.D.A. Handbook No. 8, pg. 146, item 12. Total 1650 milligrams divided by yield of approximately 120 pieces of cake equals 14 average milligrams of cholesterol per serving.

. . . .

GOLD CAKE

F=Fair; G=Good; H=High; L=Low; t or T = trace; n/a = no information available; dashes = zero or unmeasurable

GRAM WT.	FOOD	VITAMINS	CAL	(mg) SOD	PRO	FAT	CARB	CHOL	FATTY ACIDS SAT	UNSAT	CALC	IRON	(mg) POTSM
65	AVERAGE EACH PIECE		241	201				(mg) 128					46
	Ingredients:												
170	3/4 cp margarine (1-1/2 sticks)	A D	1224	1680	L	H	L	---	L	H	L	---	39
300	1-1/2 cp granulated sugar	---	1155	3	---	---	H	---	---	---	---	L	9
136	8 egg yolks	A B1 B2	480	72	F	G	T	H*	H	T	G	H	133
240	2-1/2 cp sifted cake flour	A B1 B2	875	5	F	L	G	---	---	---	L	F	228
9	3 tsp baking powder	---	9	945	L	T	H	---	---	---	H	---	---
1	1/4 tsp salt	---	---	393	---	---	---	---	---	---	G	---	T
185	3/4 cp 2% low-fat milk	A B1 B2 C	109	113	H	L	H	L*	L	L	H	L	324
n/a	1 tsp vanilla							---n/a---					
1041	Recipe totals (gms; cal; sod. & potsm.)		3852	3211									733

METHOD

Cream margarine and sugar together until light and fluffly; add beaten egg yolks and continue to blend. Sift the baking powder and salt with flour 3 times, then add alternately with the milk to the creamed mixture. Beat until batter is smooth. Pour into lined cake pans and bake at 350 F. 18 – 20 minutes or until a toothpick inserted in the center comes out clean. Allow cake to cool on a rack for 15 minutes before removing from pans. Peel wax paper off very carefully (if pans were prepared in accordance with "Preparation of Layer Cake Pans" as suggested in the first part of this chapter). Frost with your favorite icing.

* There are 2,040 milligrams of cholesterol in 136 grams of egg yolk, calculated from U.S.D.A. Handbook No. 8, pg. 146, item 14 (fresh egg yolk); and 6 milligrams of skim milk, from item 29. Total 2,046 milligrams divided by yield of approximately 16 slices of cake equals 128 average milligrams of cholesterol per serving.

. . . .

GINGERBREAD

F=Fair; G=Good; H=High; L=Low; t or T = trace; n/a = no information available; dashes = zero or unmeasurable

GRAM WT.	FOOD	VITAMINS	CAL	(mg) SOD	PRO	FAT	CARB	CHOL	FATTY ACIDS SAT	UNSAT	CALC	IRON	(mg) POTSM
104	AVERAGE EACH PIECE		290	325				(mg) 34					326
	Ingredients:												
192	2 cp sifted cake flour	B1 B2	700	4	F	L	G	---	---	---	L	F	182
6	2 tsp baking powder	---	6	630	L	T	H	---	---	---	H	---	---
1	1/4 tsp baking soda	---	1	110	L	T	G	---	---	---	H	---	---
n/a	2 tsp ginger							---------n/a---------					
n/a	1 tsp cinnamon							---------n/a---------					
2	1/2 tsp salt	---	---	785	---	---	---	---	---	---	G	---	T
75	1/3 cp margarine	A D	534	740	L	H	L	---	L	H	L	---	17
100	1/2 cp granulated sugar	---	385	1	---	---	H	---	---	---	---	L	3
50	1 egg, beaten	A B1 B2	75	61	F	F	L	H*	H	L	F	F	65
220	2/3 cp molasses	B1 B2	550	33	---	---	H	---	---	---	H	G	2017
185	3/4 cp 2% low-fat sour milk or but-termilk.	A B1 B2 C	68	239	H	L	H	---	---	---	G	L	324
831	Recipe totals (gms; cal; sod. & potsm.)		2319	2603									2608

METHOD

Sift flour with the baking powder, soda, spices and salt 3 times. Cream margarine with sugar until light; add beaten egg and molasses, then add sifted ingredients alternately with milk, beating after each addition until smooth. Pour batter into a greased 8" x 8" pan and bake at 350 F. about 50 minutes, or until a toothpick inserted in the center comes out clean. Yield 8 pieces, size 2" x 4" or 16 pieces size 1" x 4".

* There are 275 milligrams of cholesterol in 50 grams of whole egg, as calculated from U.S.D.A. Handbook No. 8, pg. 146, item 12. Total 275 milligrams divided by yield of 16 or 8 pieces of gingerbread respectively equals 17 average milligrams of cholesterol per serving.

. . . .

JELLY ROLL

F=Fair; G=Good; H=High; L=Low; t or T = trace; n/a = no information available; dashes = zero or unmeasurable

GRAM WT.	FOOD	VITAMINS	CAL	(mg) SOD	PRO	FAT	CARB	CHOL	FATTY ACIDS SAT	UNSAT	CALC	IRON	(mg) POTSM
61	AVERAGE EACH PIECE		164	74				(mg) 115					49
	Ingredients:												
250	5 eggs	A B1 B2	375	305	G	G	L	H*	H	1	F	F	323
133	2/3 cp granulated sugar	---	513	2	---	---	H	---	---	---	---	L	4
1	1/4 tsp salt	---	---	393	---	---	---	---	---	---	G	---	---
48	1/2 cp sifted cake flour	B1 B2	175	1	F	L	G	---	---	---	L	F	46
14	1 tblspn margarine	A D	100	139	L	H	T	---	L	H	L	---	3
n/a	1 tsp almond or vanilla extract							----n/a----					
288	1 cp jelly (or jam)	A^t $B1^t$ B2 C	800	48	L	L	H	---	----	---	L	F	216
734	Recipe totals (gms; cal; sod. & potsm.)		1963	888									592

METHOD

Beat sugar and eggs together until well blended, then heat over hot water until mixture is slightly hot. Remove from heat and beat until mixture holds a slight peak. Combine salt and flour; fold into egg mixture. Melt 1/3 of the margarine in a metal cooking spoon that measures 1 tablespoon. (The melted margarine should equal 1 tablespoon.) Fold melted margarine into the batter, then melt the second third of the margarine and fold into batter. When last of the margarine is melted and folded into the batter, blend in flavoring (extract).

Pour batter into a lightly greased, 10" x 15" jelly roll pan that has been lined with heavy waxed paper which has also been lightly greased. Bake at 350 F. for 15 – 20 minutes, or until done. Turn out quickly onto a waxed paper covered cookie sheet on which confectioners' sugar has been sprinkled and trim the browned edges. Remove the waxed paper from the cake, quickly spread with jelly and roll up. (Jelly should be slightly beaten which makes it easier to apply.) Wrap in waxed paper and cool. Cake can also be rolled up before adding jelly and when cold, unroll, spread with beaten jelly and roll up. Before serving, sieve a little confectioners' sugar over cake.
Yield   1 Jelly Roll.

*   There are 1375 milligrams of cholesterol in 250 grams of whole egg, as calculated in U.S.D.A. Handbook No. 8, pg. 146, item 12. Total 1375 milligrams divided by yield of 12 servings of jelly roll equals 115 average milligrams of cholesterol in each serving.

. . . .

(No eggs, no milk)

F=Fair; G=Good; H=High; L=Low; t or T = trace; n/a = no information available; dashes = zero or unmeasurable

GRAM WT.	FOOD	VITAMINS	CAL	SOD (mg)	PRO	FAT	CARB	CHOL	FATTY ACIDS SAT	FATTY ACIDS UNSAT	CALC	IRON	POTSM (mg)
92	AVERAGE EACH PIECE		239	110									161
	Ingredients:												
165	1 cp seedless raisins	A B1 B2 C	480	45	L	T	H	---	---	---	G	H	1259
236	2 cp water							-n/a-					
28	2 tblspn margarine	A D	200	280	L	H	L	---	L	H	L	---	6
200	1 cp granulated sugar	---	770	2	---	---	H	---	---	---	---	L	6
192	2 cp cake flour	B1 B2	700	4	F	L	G	---	---	---	L	F	182
6	1-1/2 tsp baking soda	---	5	659	L	T	G	---	---	---	H	---	---
n/a	1 tsp cinnamon							-n/a-					
n/a	1 tsp nutmeg							-n/a-					
827	Recipe totals (gms; cal; sod. & potsm.)		2155	990									1453

METHOD

Cook raisins in 2 cups water and simmer until 1 cup of liquid remains. Set aside to cool. Cream shortening with sugar, add raisins and liquid. Sift flour, soda and spices together and add to the first mixture. Beat until thoroughly blended.   Bake in greased 8" square pan at 325 F. 30 — 40 minutes or until cake tests done. Serve plain or glaze while warm with a thin coating of confectioners' icing. Yield   9 individual servings.

. . . .

ORANGE CAKE

F=Fair; G=Good; H=High; L=Low; t or T = trace; n/a = no information available; dashes = zero or unmeasurable

GRAM WT.	FOOD	VITAMINS	CAL	(mg) SOD	PRO	FAT	CARB	CHOL	FATTY ACIDS SAT	UNSAT	CALC	IRON	(mg) POTSM
79	AVERAGE EACH PIECE (UNFROSTED)		245	270				(mg) 52					55
	Ingredients:												
169	3/4 cp margarine (1-1/2 sticks)	A D	1215	1680	L	H	L	---	L	H	L	---	39
300	1-1/2 cp granulated sugar	---	1155	3	---	---	H	---	---	---	---	L	9
150	3 eggs	A B1 B2	225	183	G	G	L	H*	H	L	F	F	194
21	Grated rind of 1 orange	A B1 B2 C	n/a	1	L	L	F	---	---	---	G	L	45
345	3 cp presifted, all-purpose flour	B1 B2	1260	6	F	L	G	---	---	---	L	F	328
12	4 tsp baking powder	---		12	1260	L	T	H	---	---	---	H	---	---
3	3/4 tsp salt	---	---	1178	---	---	---	---	---	---	G	---	T
124	1/2 cp orange juice	A B1 B2 C	55	1	L	L	F	---	---	---	F	L	248
15	1 tblspn lemon juice	A B1 B2 C	4	---	L	T	F	---	---	---	F	L	21
118	1/2 cp water	--------------------------------n/a---------------------------											
1257	Recipe totals (gms; cal; sod. & potsm.)		3926	4312									884

METHOD

Cream margarine and sugar together until fluffy. Add eggs, one at a time, beating after each addition. Add orange rind. Sift dry ingredients together 3 times and add alternately with liquids to the creamed mixture. Line the bottoms of two 9" greased, layer-cake pans with waxed paper. Pour batter in the pans, distributing it evenly. Bake at 350 F. 25 – 30 minutes or until done. Cool on racks 15 minutes. Remove from pans; also remove waxed paper. When cold, frost with orange filling between layers and orange confectioners' icing. (See the following recipes for filling and frosting).   Yield 16 individual servings.

. . . .

ORANGE FILLING

F=Fair; G=Good; H=High; L=Low; t or T = trace; n/a = no information available; dashes = zero or unmeasurable

GRAM WT.	FOOD	VITAMINS	CAL	(mg) SOD	PRO	FAT	CARB	CHOL	FATTY ACIDS SAT	FATTY ACIDS UNSAT	CALC	IRON	(mg) POTSM
21	**AVERAGE EACH PIECE**		38	25				(mg) 34					27
	Ingredients:												
28	2 tblspn softened margarine	A D	200	279	L	H	L	---	l	H	L	---	6
50	1/4 cp granulated sugar	---	192	T	---	---	H	---	---	---	---	L	2
100	2 eggs, beaten	A B1 B2	150	122	G	G	L	H*	H	L	F	F	129
124	1/2 cp orange juice	A B1 B2 C	55	1	L	L	F	---	---	---	F	L	248
14	1 tblspn grated orange rind	A B1 B2 C	n/a	T	L	L	F	---	---	---	G	L	30
15	1 tblspn lemon juice	A B1 B2 C	4	T	L	T	F	---	---	---	F	L	21
331	Recipe totals (gms; cal; sod. & potsm.)		601	402									436

METHOD

Combine all ingredients and mix thoroughly. Cook over hot water, stirring constantly until well thickened. (About 10 minutes). Chill well before spreading on cake.

*   There are 550 milligrams of cholesterol in 100 grams of whole egg, according to U.S.D.A. Handbook No. 8, pg. 146, item 12.   Total 550 milligrams divided by yield of 16 pieces equals 34 average milligrams of cholesterol per serving.

. . . .

ORANGE CONFECTIONERS' FROSTING

F=Fair; G=Good; H=High; L=Low; t or T = trace; n/a = no information available;   dashes = zero or unmeasurable

GRAM WT.	FOOD	VITAMINS	CAL	(mg) SOD	PRO	FAT	CARB	CHOL	FATTY ACIDS SAT	UNSAT	CALC	IRON	(mg) POTSM
22	**AVERAGE EACH PIECE**		83	35									8
	Ingredients:												
240	2 cps confectioners' sugar	---	920	2	---	---	H	---	---	---	---	L	7
56	4 tblspn soft margarine	A D	400	558	L	H	T	---	L	H	L	---	13
21	Grated rind of 1 medium orange	A B1 B2 C	n/a	1	L	L	F	---	---	---	G	L	45
30	2 tblspn orange juice	A B1 B2 C	14	T	L	L	F	---	---	---	F	L	60
5	1 tsp lemon juice	A b1 B2 C	1	---	L	T	F	---	---	---	F	L	7
352	Recipe totals (gms; cal; sod. & potsm.)		1335	561									132

METHOD

In a medium size mixing bowl, press out any lumps in the granulated sugar with a tablespoon, then cream in the softened margarine until fluffy. Add orange rind, orange and lemon juice and mix thoroughly. If frosting is a little too runny to spread, add more powdered sugar; if too dry, add more orange juice, a few drops at a time. This recipe will frost top and sides of a two-layer cake generously. If orange filling is omitted and orange frosting used for entire cake, use a full box of confectioners' sugar and 2 additional tablespoons of softened margarine.

. . . .

CRUSHED PINEAPPLE CAKE

F=Fair; G=Good; H=High; L=Low; t or T = trace; n/a = no information available; dashes = zero or unmeasurable

GRAM WT.	FOOD	VITAMINS	CAL	(mg) SOD	PRO	FAT	CARB	CHOL (mg)	FATTY ACIDS SAT	UNSAT	CALC	IRON	(mg) POTSM
65	AVERAGE PER SERVING		202	124				23					89
	Ingredients:												
113	1 stick softened margarine	A D	815	1115	L	H	L	---	L	H	L	---	26
300	1-1/2 cp granulated sugar	---	1155	3	---	---	H	---	---	---	---	L	9
100	2 eggs	A B1 B2	150	122	G	G	L	H*	H	L	F	F	129
230	2 cps presifted, all-purpose flour	B1 B2	840	4	F	L	G	---	---	---	L	F	219
2	1/2 tsp salt	---	---	785	---	---	---	---	---	---	G	---	T
8	2 tsp baking soda	---	6	878	L	T	G	---	---	---	H	---	
454	1 (16 ōz.) can crushed pineapple undrained	A B1 B2 C	263	5	L	T	F	---	---	---	F	L	440
126	1 cp walnuts, chopped	A B1 B2	790	4	G	G	G	--	--	H	T	G	567
220	1 cp brown sugar	B1 B2	820	66	---	---	H	---	---	---	G	G	757
1553	Recipe totals (gms; cal; sod. & potsm.)		4839	2982									2147

METHOD

Cream margarine and sugar together until light; add eggs and beat until smooth. Sift flour, salt, and soda together then add to the creamed mixture and blend well. Add undrained pineapple and continue to blend until smooth. Pour batter into 9" x 12" x 2" greased pan. Mix the chopped walnuts with the brown sugar and distribute evenly over the batter. Bake at 350 F. about 45 minutes or until a toothpick inserted in the center comes out clean. Frost if desired. Yield about 24 pieces, depending on size.

* There are 550 milligrams of cholesterol in 100 grams of whole egg as calculated from U.S.D.A. Handbook No. 8, pg. 146, item 12. Total 550 milligrams divided by yield of approximately 24 pieces of cake equals 23 average milligrams of cholesterol per serving.

. . . .

PINEAPPLE UPSIDE-DOWN CAKE

F=Fair; G=Good; H=High; L=Low; t or T = trace; n/a = no information available; dashes = zero or unmeasurable

GRAM WT.	FOOD	VITAMINS	CAL	(mg) SOD	PRO	FAT	CARB	CHOL	FATTY ACIDS SAT	UNSAT	CALC	IRON	(mg) POTSM
74	**AVERAGE EACH PIECE**		209	162				(mg) 34					96
	Ingredients:												
56	1/2 stick margarine	A D	400	558	L	H	L	---	L	H	L	---	13
220	1 cp brown sugar, firmly packed	B1 B2	820	66	---	---	H	---	---	---	G	G	757
273	6 small slices pineapple, canned and drained	A B1 B2 C	162	3	T	T	F	---	---	---	L	L	265
30	6 maraschino cherries	---	102	---	L	L	F	---	---	---	---	---	---
144	1-1/2 cp sifted cake flour	B1 B2	525	3	F	L	G	---	---	---	L	F	137
6	2 tsp baking powder	---	6	630	L	T	H	---	---	---	H	---	---
1	1/4 tsp salt	---	---	393	---	---	---	---	---	---	G	---	---
75	5-1/3 tblspn margarine	A D	534	741	L	H	L	---	L	H	L	---	17
150	3/4 cp granulated sugar	---	578	1	---	---	H	---	---	---	---	L	5
100	2 eggs, beaten	A B1 B2	150	122	G	G	L	H*	H	L	F	F	129
123	1/2 cp 2% low-fat milk	A B1 B2 C	73	75	H	L	H	L*	L	L	H	L	215
n/a	1 tsp almond extract	---------						-n/a-					---------
1178	Recipe totals (gms; cal; sod. & potsm.)		3350	2592									1538

METHOD

In a medium to heavy weight frying pan, 10-1/2" in diameter by 2—1/2" deep, melt the margarine slowly to avoid browning. When the shortening is melted, spread the brown sugar evenly in the pan. Place the pineapple slices in a circle around the pan with one in the center. Place a maraschino cherry in the center of each slice.

In a medium size mixing bowl, sift the flour once, measure and sift again with baking powder and salt. Set aside. In a large mixing bowl, cream the 1/3 cup margarine (5-1/3 tablsepoons) with the 3/4 cup granulated sugar gradually until light and fluffy. Add beaten eggs and mix thoroughly. Add some of the flour mixture and half of the milk and beat. Add the almond extract and beat again. Continue adding flour and milk alternately, beating until batter is smooth after each addition, ending with the flour. Pour batter over fruit in pan and bake at 350 F. about an hour, or until done. Remove from oven, place a cake plate upside-down over the cake, and grasping cake plate and pan together, turn right-side up. Pineapple slices and cherries will be on top. Serve warm or cool with either sweetened whipped cream to which a little vanilla has been added, or any non-dairy topping.

NOTE Peaches, cherries, apricots and other fruit can be substituted for pineapple.

* There are 550 milligrams of cholesterol in 100 grams of whole egg, and 4 milligrams of cholesterol in 123 grams of low-fat milk, as calculated from U.S.D.A. Handbook No. 8, pg. 146, items 12 and 29 respectively. Total 554 milligrams divided by yield of 16 pieces of cake equal 34 average milligrams of cholesterol per serving.

. . . .

POUND CAKE

F=Fair; G=Good; H=High; L=Low; t or T = trace; n/a = no information available; dashes = zero or unmeasurable

GRAM WT.	FOOD	VITAMINS	CAL	(mg) SOD	PRO	FAT	CARB	CHOL (mg)	FATTY ACIDS SAT	UNSAT	CALC	IRON	(mg) POTSM
53	AVERAGE EACH PIECE		216	171				73					33
	Ingredients:												
454	4-1/2 cp sifted cake flour	B1 B2	1651	9	F	L	G	---	---	---	L	F	431
2	1/2 tsp salt	---	---	785	---	---	---	---	---	---	G	---	---
n/a	3/4 tsp nutmeg							-n/a-					
454	2 cp margarine (4 sticks)	A D	3266	4477	L	H	L	---	L	H	L	---	104
454	2-1/4 cp granulated sugar	---	1746	5	---	---	H	---	---	---	---	L	14
454	9 eggs, separated	A B1 B2	675	549	G	G	L	H*	H	L	F	F	586
n/a	1 tsp vanilla							-n/a-					
n/a	1 tsp almond							-n/a-					
1818	Recipe totals (gms; cal; sod. & potsm.)		7338	5825									1135

METHOD

Sift flour once, measure, then sift again with salt and nutmeg. Cream margarine and work in the flour until mixture is like meal. Beat egg yolks, sugar and flavorings together until thick and light. Add flour and margarine mixture gradually, beating thoroughly after each addition. Beat hard about 5 minutes. Pour batter into 2 greased and waxed paper lined loaf pans 9" x 5" x 3" and bake at 325 F. for 1 to 1-1/4 hours.

*   There are 2475 milligrams of cholesterol in 454 grams of whole egg, as calculated from U.S.D.A. Handbook No. 8, pg. 146, item 12. Total 2475 milligrams divided by yield of approximately 34 slices of cake equals 73 average milligrams of cholesterol in each piece.

. . . .

F=Fair; G=Good; H=High; L=Low; t or T = trace; n/a = no information available;   dashes = zero or unmeasurable

GRAM WT.	FOOD	VITAMINS	CAL	(mg) SOD	PRO	FAT	CARB	CHOL	FATTY ACIDS SAT	UNSAT	CALC	IRON	(mg) POTSM
43	AVERAGE EACH PIECE		135	84				(mg) 32					71
	Ingredients:												
113	1 stick margarine, softened	A D	815	1115	L	H	T	---	L	H	L	---	26
200	1 cp granulated sugar	---	770	2	---	---	H	---	---	---	---	L	6
150	3 eggs	A B1 B2 C	225	183	G	G	L	H*	H	L	F	F	194
n/a	1 tsp vanilla	--------						---n/a---					
173	1-1/2 cp presifted, all-purpose flour	B1 B2	630	3	F	L	G	---	---	---	L	F	164
4	1 tsp baking soda	---	3	439	L	T	G	---	---	---	H	---	---
n/a	1 tsp cinnamon	--------						---n/a---					
n/a	1/2 tsp cloves	--------						---n/a---					
n/a	1/2 tsp nutmeg	--------						---n/a---					
1	1/4 tsp salt	---	---	393	---	---	---	---	---	---	G	---	---
45	3 tblspn. hot water	---	---	---	---	---	---	---	---	---	---	---	---
45	3 tblspn sour milk	A B1 B2 C	27	27	H	L	H	L	L	L	H	L	79
270	1 cp stewed, unsweetened prunes, well drained	A B1 B2 C	295	11	L	L	G	---	---	---	F	F	883
113	1 cp English walnuts, chopped, (Optional)	A B1 B2 C	738	2	G	G	G	---	---	H	G	G	509
1114	Recipe totals (gms; cal; sod. & potsm.)		3503	2175									1861

METHOD

Cream softened margarine with the sugar gradually until mixture is light and fluffy. Add the eggs and vanilla and beat until smooth. Sift the dry ingredients together and add to the creamed mixture alternately with the hot water and sour milk, beating well after each addition. Stir in pitted and cut up prunes and nuts, chopped as finely as desired. Pour batter into greased and lightly floured 13" x 9" x 2" pan. Bake at 350 F. for 40 minutes or until wooden toothpick inserted in the center comes out clean. Serve plain, or frost if desired.

*   There are 825 milligrams of cholesterol in 150 grams of whole egg as calculated from U.S.D.A. Handbook No. 8, pg. 146, item 12. Total 825 milligrams divided by yield of 26 individual servings of cake equals 32 average milligrams of cholesterol per serving.   No figures available for sour milk. In 45 grams sweet milk there is one milligram of cholesterol.

. . . .

F=Fair; G=Good; H=High; L=Low; t or T = trace; n/a = no information available; dashes = zero or unmeasurable

GRAM WT.	FOOD	VITAMINS	CAL	(mg) SOD	PRO	FAT	CARB	CHOL	FATTY ACIDS SAT	UNSAT	CALC	IRON	(mg) POTSM
71	AVERAGE EACH PIECE		242	148				(mg) 52					120
	Ingredients:												
113	1/2 cp soft margarine (1 stick)	A D	815	1115	L	H	L	---	L	G	L	---	26
440	2 cp brown sugar	B1 B2	1640	132	---	---	H	---	---	---	G	G	1514
150	3 eggs, separated	A B1 B2	225	183	G	G	L	H*	H	L	F	F	194
192	2 cp sifted cake flour	B1 B2	700	4	F	L	G	---	---	---	L	F	182
1	1/4 tsp salt	---	---	393	---	---	---	---	---	---	G	---	---
4	1 tsp baking soda	---	3	439	L	T	G	---	---	---	H	---	---
n/a	2 tsp cinnamon							-n/a-					
n/a	1 tsp cloves							-n/a-					
n/a	1/2 tsp nutmeg							-n/a-					
230	1 cp thick sour cream	A B1 B2 C	485	96	L	H	L	n/a	H	L	H	L	n/a
1130	Recipe totals (gms; cal; sod. & potsm.)		3868	2362									1916

METHOD

Cream margarine, add sugar gradually and cream together until light and fluffy. Beat in the egg yolks. Sift dry ingredients together 3 times then add alternately with sour cream to first mixture. Beat well after each addition. Fold in stiffly beaten egg whites. Pour into lightly greased, 9" square cake pan lined with waxed paper. Bake at 350 F. about 50 minutes. Yield about 16 pieces.

NOTE   1 cup of raisins may be added with the flour (before mixing with the creamed mixture), if desired. Values for raisins in the recipe are as follows:

165	1 cp raisins pressed down	A B1 B2 C	480	45	L	T	H	---	---	---	G	H	1259

*   There are 825 milligrams of cholesterol in 150 grams of whole egg as calculated from U.S.D.A. Handbook No. 8, pg. 146, item 12. Total 825 milligrams divided by 16 pieces of cake equals 52 average milligrams of cholesterol per serving.

. . . .

SPONGE CAKE

F=Fair; G=Good; H=High; L=Low; t or T = trace; n/a = no information available; dashes = zero or unmeasurable

GRAM WT.	FOOD	VITAMINS	CAL	(mg) SOD	PRO	FAT	CARB	CHOL	FATTY ACIDS SAT	UNSAT	CALC	IRON	(mg) POTSM
48	AVERAGE EACH PIECE		125	59				(mg) 115					38
	Ingredients:												
96	1 cp sifted cake flour	B1 B2	350	2	F	L	G	---	---	---	L	F	91
1	1/4 tsp salt	---	---	393	---	---	---	---	---	---	G	---	---
4	Grated rind of lemon (3/4 tsp)	A B1 B2 C	---	T	L	L	F	---	---	---	F	L	6
23	1-1/2 tblspn lemon juice	A B1 B2 C	6	---	L	T	F	---	---	---	F	L	32
250	5 eggs, separated	A B1 B2	375	306	G	G	L	H*	H	L	F	F	323
200	1 cp granulated sugar	---	770	1	---	---	H	---	---	---	---	L	6
574	Recipe totals (gms; cal; sod. & potsm.)		1501	702									458

METHOD

Sift flour and salt together 4 times; add lemon rind and juice to beaten egg yolks and beat until light and thick. Beat egg whites until stiff but not dry. Fold in sugar, a little at a time, then add egg yolks. Using a wire whip, fold in flour, sifting in about 4 or 5 tablespoons at a time. Bake in ungreased angel food tube pan (about 10" pan) at 350 F. about 1 hour. As soon as cake is done, invert pan 1 hour before removing cake.

NOTE   This cake can be baked in 2 layers and used for whipped-cream cake. When cool, spread layers with whipped cream.

* There are 1375 milligrams of cholesterol in 50 grams of whole egg as calculated from U.S.D.A. Handbook No. 8, pg. 146, item 12. Total 1375 milligrams divided by yield of 12 pieces of cake equals 115 average milligrams of cholesterol in each piece.

. . . .

RAW CARROT CAKE

F=Fair; G=Good; H=High; L=Low; t or T = trace; n/a = no information available; dashes = zero or unmeasurable

GRAM WT.	FOOD	VITAMINS	CAL	(mg) SOD	PRO	FAT	CARB	CHOL	FATTY ACIDS SAT	UNSAT	CALC	IRON	(mg) POTSM
100	AVERAGE EACH PIECE		388	188				(mg) 46					130
	Ingredients:												
330	1-1/2 cp cooking oil	---	2918	---	---	H	---	---	T	H	---	---	---
400	2 cp granulated sugar	---	1540	4	---	---	H	---	---	---	---	L	12
150	3 eggs	A B1 B2	225	183	G	G	L	H*	H	L	F	F	194
260	1 cp crushed undrained pineapple	A B1 B2 C	195	3	L	T	F	---	---	---	F	L	252
108	1 cp pecans, chopped	A B1 B2 C	740	T	L	H	F	---	---	---	F	F	651
220	2 cp carrots, shredded	A B1 B2 C	90	104	L	T	L	---	---	---	F	L	750
76	1 cp coconut,shredded	B1 B2	421	----	L	H	H	--------n/a------			L	L	266
230	2 cp presifted, all-purpose flour	B1 B2	840	4	F	L	G	---	---	---	L	F	219
n/a	2 tsp cinnamon	--------											---
8	2 tsp baking soda	---	6	878	L	T	G	---	---	---	H	---	.---
6	2 tsp baking powder	---	6	630	L	T	H	---	---	---	H	---	---
4	1 tsp salt	---	---	1569	---	---	---	---	---	---	G	---	T
n/a	2 tsp vanilla	--------						--------n/a-------					
1792	Recipe totals (gms; cal; sod. & potsm.)		6981	3375									2344

METHOD

Cream oil and sugar together thoroughly; add eggs and beat well; add pineapple, carrots, nuts and coconut and continue to mix well. Sift dry ingredients together and beat into the creamed mixture until smooth. Add vanilla, mix well and pour batter into greased 9" x 13" baking dish or in a greased and floured tubular pan and bake at 350 F. 55 to 60 minutes until done. This is a very rich cake and doesn't require frosting. Yield 18 pieces, 2" x 3".

*   There are 825 milligrams of cholesterol in 150 grams of whole egg as calculated from U.S.D.A. Handbook No. 8, pg. 146, item 12. Total 825 milligrams divided by yield of 18 pieces of cake equals 46 average milligrams of cholesterol per serving.

. . . .

172

WHITE TUBE CAKE

F=Fair; G=Good; H=High; L=Low; t or T = trace; n/a = no information available; dashes = zero or unmeasurable

GRAM WT.	FOOD	VITAMINS	CAL	(mg) SOD	PRO	FAT	CARB	CHOL	FATTY ACIDS SAT	UNSAT	CALC	IRON	(mg) POTSM
87	**AVERAGE EACH PIECE**		255	234									73
	Ingredients:												
113	1/2 cp margarine (1 stick)	A D	815	1115	L	H	L	---	L	H	L	---	26
300	1-1/2 cp granulated sugar	---	1155	3	---	---	H	---	---	---	---	L	9
240	2-1/2 cp sifted cake flour	B1 B2	875	5	F	L	G	---	---	---	L	F	228
9	3 tsp baking powder	---	9	945	L	T	H	---	---	---	H	---	---
1	1/4 tsp salt	---	---	393	---	---	---	---	---	---	G	---	---
246	1 cp 2% low-fat milk	A B1 B2 C	145	150	H	L	H	L *	L	L	H	L	431
n/a	1 tsp vanilla							--n/a--					
132	4 egg whites, stiffly beaten	B1 B2	60	192	L	T	T	---	---	---	L	T	183
1041	Recipe totals (gms; cal; sod. & potsm.)		3059	2803									877

METHOD

Line bottom and sides of lightly greased tube pan with waxed paper. Cut the paper for the bottom first, cut a hole in the middle for the tube, then cut a strip wide enough to circle the sides.

Cream margarine, add sugar a little at a time until fluffy. Sift flour, baking powder and salt together 3 times and add alternately with the milk and vanilla, beating until smooth after each addition. Fold in the stiffly beaten egg whites, then pour the batter in the tube pan and bake at 350 F. for 45 to 60 minutes. When cake is cold, ice with boiled frosting, or any confectioners' icing desired.

*   There are 3 milligrams of cholesterol in 100 grams of skim milk; in 246 grams, there are only 7 milligrams, a minimal amount in this recipe, as calculated from U.S.D.A. Handbook No. 8, pg. 146, item 29.

. . . .

CHOCOLATE CUPCAKES

F=Fair; G=Good; H=High; L=Low; t or T = trace; n/a = no information available; dashes = zero or unmeasurable

GRAM WT.	FOOD	VITAMINS	CAL	(mg) SOD	PRO	FAT	CARB	CHOL	FATTY ACIDS SAT	UNSAT	CALC	IRON	(mg) POTSM
42	AVERAGE PER CUPCAKE		140	139				(mg) 28					66
	Ingredients:												
84	3 squares bitter chocolate	A B1 B2	435	3	F	G	F	n/a	F	F	F	G	697
113	1/2 cp margarine (1 stick)	A D	815	1115	L	H	L	---	L	H	L	---	26
200	1 cp granulated sugar	---	770	2	---	---	H	---	---	---	---	L	6
100	2 eggs, well beaten	A B1 B2	150	122	G	G	L	H*	H	L	F	F	129
144	1-1/2 cp sifted cake flour	B1 B2	525	3	F	L	G	---	---	---	L	F	137
6	2 tsp baking powder	---	6	630	L	T	H	---	---	---	H	---	---
2	1/2 tsp salt	---	---	785	---	---	---	---	---	---	---	G	---
185	3/4 cp 2% low-fat milk	A B1 B2 C	107	113	H	L	H	L	L	L	H	L	324
n/a	1 tsp vanilla	---n/a---											
834	Recipe totals (gms; cal; sod. & potsm.)		2808	2773									1319

METHOD

Melt the chocolate in a small pan or double boiler over boiling water, then set aside. Cream margarine and sugar together until light and fluffy. Add eggs, one at a time, beating until batter is smooth. Add melted chocolate and beat again. Add sifted dry ingredients alternately with the milk and vanilla (mixed together). Fill greased cupcake pans 2/3 full of batter and bake at 350 F. about 20 minutes. Test with toothpick for doneness. When toothpick inserted in center comes out clean, cupcakes are ready. Frost when cool. Yield approximately 20 cupcakes.

* There are 550 milligrams of cholesterol in 100 grams of whole egg, and 6 milligrams of cholesterol in 185 grams of low-fat (considered skim) milk, as calculated from U.S.D.A. Handbook No. 8, pg. 146, items 12 and 29 respectively. Total 556 milligrams divided by 20 cup cakes equals 28 average milligrams of cholesterol per serving.

. . . .

F=Fair; G=Good; H=High; L=Low; t or T = trace; n/a = no information available;   dashes = zero or unmeasurable

GRAM WT.	FOOD	VITAMINS	CAL	(mg) SOD	PRO	FAT	CARB	CHOL	FATTY ACIDS SAT	UNSAT	CALC	IRON	(mg) POTSM
30	AVERAGE PER CUPCAKE		89	76				(mg) 23					25
	Ingredients:												
75	5-1/3 tblspn margarine	A D	534	741	L	H	L	---	L	H	L	---	17
200	1 cp granulated sugar	---	770	2	---	---	H	---	---	---	---	L	6
100	2 eggs	A B1 B2	150	122	G	G	L	H*	H	L	F	F	129
168	1-2/3 cp cake flourr	B1 B2	583	3	F	L	G	---	---	---	L	F	160
5	1-1/2 tsp baking powder	---	5	473	L	T	H	---	---	---	H	---	---
1	1/4 tsp salt	---	---	393	---	---	---	---	---	---	G	---	---
164	2/3 cp 2% low-fat milk	A B1 B2 C	96	100	H	L	H	L*	L	L	H	L	287
n/a	1 tsp vanilla or almond extract	---	---	---	---	---	---	-n/a-	---	---	---	---	---
713	Recipe totals (gms; cal; sod. & potsm.)		2138	1834									599

METHOD

Cream margarine and sugar together until light and fluffly. Add eggs one at a time, beating well after each addition. Sift the dry ingredients together; add the flavoring to the milk. Starting with the dry ingredients, add alternately with the milk to the first mixture, ending with the dry ingredients. Fill cupcakes pans (which have been greased generously) 2/3 full and bake at 400 F. 15 — 18 minutes or until done. Frost when cool with several flavors, such as chocolate, white, orange, etc.   Yield about 24 cupcakes.

VARIATIONS   For spice cup cakes, sift 1 teaspoon cinnamon, 1/4 teaspoon cloves, and 1/4 teaspoon nutmeg with the flour. If raisins are desired, add 1/2 cup to the flour before mixing with the milk.

*   There are 550 milligrams of cholesterol in 100 grams of whole egg and 5 milligrams of cholesterol in 164 grams of low-fat milk, as calculated from U.S.D.A. Handbook No. 8, pg. 146, items 12 and 29 respectively. Total 555 milligrams divided by yield of 24 cupcakes equals 23 average milligrams of cholesterol per serving.

. . . .

CREAM PUFFS

F=Fair; G=Good; H=High; L=Low; t or T = trace; n/a = no information available; dashes = zero or unmeasurable

GRAM WT.	FOOD	VITAMINS	CAL	(mg) SOD	PRO	FAT	CARB	CHOL	FATTY ACIDS SAT	UNSAT	CALC	IRON	(mg) POTSM
54	AVERAGE EACH PUFF		122	130				(mg) 92					31
113	Ingredients: 1/2 cp margarine (1 stick)	A D	815	1115	L	H	L	---	L	H	L	---	26
---	1/8 tsp salt	---	---	196	---	---	---	---	---	---	G	---	---
236	1 cup boiling water							---O---					
96	1 cp sifted cake flour	B1 B2	350	2	F	L	G	---	---	---	L	F	91
200	4 eggs	A B1 B2	300	244	G	G	L	H*	H	L	F	F	258
645	Recipe totals (gms; cal; sod. & potsm.)		1465	1557									375

METHOD

Add margarine and salt to 1 cup boiling water and heat to boiling. Reduce heat, add flour all at once and stir vigorously until mixture forms a ball around spoon, leaving pan clean. Remove from heat; add eggs, one at a time, beating thoroughly after each addition. Continue beating until mixture is thick and shiny and breaks off the spoon. Shape on ungreased cookie sheet with a teaspoon (if small puffs are desired) or a tablespoon (if large puffs are desired). Bake at 450 F. for 20 minutes, then reduce heat to 350 F. and bake about 20 minutes longer. Cool. Cut puffs about 1/3 from top, lift off and fill with sweetened whipped cream, flavored with vanilla, or dairy topping, or custard. Replace top, sieve a little powdered sugar over puffs and serve.

VARIATIONS

Eclairs: Shape cream puff dough into strips 1" wide by 4" long. Bake as for cream puffs. When cool, split lengthwise and fill with custard or sweetened whipped cream, flavored with vanilla, or dairy topping, and frost tops with uncooked chocolate icing. Yield approximately 12.

Cream puff cases are also good filled with chicken a la king, or creamed crab or tuna, or as cups for sliced peaches and ice cream, or any fruit and filled with custard (cold) sauce, or instant puddings and topped with dairy-type toppings and maraschino cherry or a dab of jam or jelly. They have many uses and are easy to make.

* There are 1100 milligrams of cholesterol in 20 grams of whole egg as calculated from U.S.D.A. Handbook No. 8, pg 146, item 12. Total 1100 milligrams divided by yield of 12 cream puffs equals 92 average milligrams of cholesterol per serving. (NOTE If smaller puffs are made, cholesterol will be decreased. For example, instead of 12 large puffs, make 24 small ones; cholesterol will average about 46 milligrams of cholesterol per puff.

. . . .

LITTLE GINGER CAKES

F=Fair; G=Good; H=High; L=Low; t or T = trace; n/a = no information available; dashes = zero or unmeasurable

GRAM WT.	FOOD	VITAMINS	CAL	(mg) SOD	PRO	FAT	CARB	CHOL	FATTY ACIDS SAT	UNSAT	CALC	IRON	(mg) POTSM
61	AVERAGE EACH CAKE		172	117				(mg) 34					175
	Ingredients:												
220	2/3 cp molasses	B1 B2	550	33	---	---	H	---	---	---	H	G	2024
100	1/2 cp granulated sugar	---	385	1	---	---	H	---	---	---	---	L	3
113	1/2 cp margarine (1 stick)	A D	815	1115	L	H	L	---	L	H	L	---	26
n/a	1 tsp ground ginger							-n/a-					
n/a	1 tsp cinnamon							-n/a-					
4	1 tsp baking soda	---	3	439	L	T	G	---	---	---	H	---	---
192	2 cp sifted cake flour	B1 B2	700	4	F	L	G	---	---	---	L	F	182
246	1 cp sour 2% low-fat milk	A B1 B2 C	145	150	H	L	H	L*	L	L	H	L	431
100	2 eggs, well beaten	A B1 B2	150	122	G	G	L	H*	H	L	F	F	129
975	Recipe totals (gms; cal; sod. & potsm.)		2748	1864									2795

METHOD

Heat the molasses, sugar, margarine, ginger and cinnamon to boiling, stirring continuously, then cool to lukewarm. Sift soda and flour together and add alternately with the milk and beaten eggs, blending thoroughly after each addition. Pour batter into well-greased muffin pans. Bake at 350 F. for 15 minutes. Frost when cold.   Yield 16 cakes.

*   There are 550 milligrams of cholesterol in 100 grams of whole egg and 7 milligrams of cholesterol in 2% low-fat milk, as calculated from U.S.D.A. Handbook No. 8, pg. 146, items 12 and 29 respectively. Total 557 milligrams divided by yield of 16 cakes equal 34 average milligrams of cholesterol per serving.

. . . .

LADYFINGERS

F=Fair; G=Good; H=High; L=Low; t or T = trace; n/a = no information available; dashes = zero or unmeasurable

GRAM WT.	FOOD	VITAMINS	CAL	(mg) SOD	PRO	FAT	CARB	CHOL	FATTY ACIDS SAT	UNSAT	CALC	IRON	(mg) POTSM
22	AVERAGE PER LADYFINGER		53	32				(mg) 69					20
	Ingredients:												
150	3 eggs, separated	A B1 B2	225	183	G	G	L	H*	H	L	F	F	194
60	1/2 cp sifted confectioners' sugar	---	230	1	---	---	H	---	---	---	--	L	2
n/a	1/2 tsp vanilla	----------------------						--n/a--					
48	1/2 cp sifted cake flour	B1 B2	175	1	F	L	G	---	---	---	L	F	46
---	1/8 tsp salt	---	---	196	---	---	---	---	---	---	G	---	---
258	Recipe totals (gms; cal; sod. & potsm.)		630	381									242

METHOD

Beat egg whites until stiff but not dry; add sugar gradually, beating after each addition. Beat egg yolks until thick, fold in egg whites, then fold in vanilla, flour and salt. Shape into 4-1/2" fingers on baking sheet that has been covered with heavy brown paper. Sprinkle with confectioners' sugar and bake at 350 F. for 10 to 12 minutes. Press together in pairs. Yield   12 Ladyfingers.

*   There are 825 milligrams of cholesterol in 150 grams of whole egg as calculated from U.S.D.A. Handbook No. 8, pg. 146, item 12. Total 825 milligrams divided by yield of 12 fingers equals 69 average milligrams of cholesterol per serving.

. . . .

BOILED FROSTING

F=Fair; G=Good; H=High; L=Low; t or T = trace; n/a = no information available; dashes = zero or unmeasurable

GRAM WT.	FOOD	VITAMINS	CAL	(mg) SOD	PRO	FAT	CARB	CHOL	FATTY ACIDS SAT	UNSAT	CALC	IRON	(mg) POTSM
28	AVERAGE PER OUNCE		70	6									6
	Ingredients:												
300	1-1/2 cp granulated sugar	---	1155	3	---	---	H	---	---	---	---	L	9
118	1/2 cp water	-----------	-----------	-----------	-----------	-----------	---------O--------	-----------	-----------	-----------	-----------
66	2 egg whites	B1 B2	30	96	F	T	L	---	---	---	L	L	92
n/a	1 tsp vanilla	-----------	-----------	-----------	-----------	-----------	--------n/a-------	-----------	-----------	-----------	-----------
484	Recipe totals (gms; cal; sod. & potsm.)		1185	99									101

METHOD

Cook the sugar and water together slowly, stirring until sugar is dissolved. Then continue to cook slowly, without stirring, until candy thermometer reaches 244 degrees. Remove from heat and set aside to cool. Beat egg whites until stiff then pour the sirup in a thin stream over them, beating the mixture constantly until it is thick enough to spread. Add vanilla and stir in thoroughly.

. . . .

F=Fair; G=Good; H=High; L=Low; t or T = trace; n/a = no information available; dashes = zero or unmeasurable

GRAM WT.	FOOD	VITAMINS	CAL	(mg) SOD	PRO	FAT	CARB	CHOL	FATTY ACIDS SAT	UNSAT	CALC	IRON	(mg) POTSM
28	AVERAGE PER OUNCE		110	57									9
	Ingredients:												
113	1/2 cp margarine softened (1 stick)	A D	815	1115	L	H	L	---	L	H	L	--	26
360	1 pkg powdered sugar	---	1380	3	---	---	H	---	---	---	---	L	11
30	5 tblspn cocoa	B1 B2	110	84	L	L	H	n/a	L	L	L	F	150
89	6 tblspn hot coffee							----O----					
n/a	1 tsp vanilla							----n/a----					
592	Recipe totals (gms; cal; sod & potsm.)		2305	1202									187

METHOD

Cream softened margarine with powdered sugar gradually, mashing any lumpy sugar. Stir in cocoa and hot coffee, add vanilla and stir until smooth, then beat until fluffy. If too stiff to spread, add a little more hot coffee (a few drops at a time). If too much coffee is added and frosting is too runny to spread, add more powdered sugar. This recipe will generously cover the inside layer, top layer and sides of a 9" cake.

VARIATIONS

1. For white icing, omit cocoa and use hot milk instead of coffee. Try almond flavoring for a delicious change.
2. For a different taste treat, use 3 tablespoons of instant coffee instead of cocoa, plus 4 tablespoons of coffee instead of six and add more if needed.
3. For pink icing,   delete the cocoa and coffee, add about 5 tablespoons of maraschino cherry juice, plus 1/4 teaspoon red coloring, chop some maraschino cherries (well-drained) and add to the icing if desired. Start with 1/4 cup and add more if necessary. Chopped walnuts or pecans may also be used with the cherries or other variations. If shredded coconut is sprinkled over the top, it should be added while frosting is still moist.

. . . .

CONFECTIONERS' FROSTING

F=Fair; G=Good; H=High; L=Low; t or T = trace; n/a = no information available; dashes = zero or unmeasurable

GRAM WT.	FOOD	VITAMINS	CAL	(mg) SOD	PRO	FAT	CARB	CHOL	FATTY ACIDS SAT	UNSAT	CALC	IRON	(mg) POTSM
28	AVERAGE PER OUNCE		74	15									15
33	Ingredients: 1 egg white	B1 B2	15	48	F	T	L	---	---	---	L	L	46
60	1/2 cp confectioners' sugar	---	230	T	---	---	H	---	---	---	---	L	2
n/a	1/2 tsp vanilla							n/a					
93	Recipe totals (gms; cal; sod. & potsm.)		245	48									48

METHOD

Beat egg white stiff then add sugar gradually and continue beating until the mixture is smooth and light. Add vanilla and blend well.

. . . .

F=Fair; G=Good; H=High; L=Low; t, or T = trace; n/a = no information available; dashes = zero or unmeasurable

GRAM WT.	. FOOD	VITAMINS	CAL	(mg) SOD	PRO	FAT	CARB	CHOL	FATTY ACIDS SAT	UNSAT	CALC	IRON	(mg) POTSM
28	AVERAGE PER OUNCE		73	7									6
	Ingredients:												
66	2 egg whites	B1 B2	30	96	F	T	L	---	---	---	L	L	92
300	1-1/2 cp granulated sugar	---	1155	3	---	---	H	---	---	---	---	L	9
21	1 tblspn light corn sirup	---	60	14	---	---	H	---	---	---	F	G	1
78	5 tblspn water							----O----					
n/a	1 tsp vanilla							----n/a----					
465	Recipe totals (gms; cal; sod. & potsm.)		1245	113									102

METHOD

Put all of the ingredients, except vanilla, in top of a double boiler and stir together until well blended, then place over boiling water and beat with a rotary (or electric mixer) until frosting holds in soft peaks -- test by lifting the beater – icing will hold on the beater blades. Remove from heat, add vanilla and beat until right consistency to spread. This will make enough frosting to ice an 8" or 9" layer cake.

VARIATIONS

1.	Maple frosting	use brown sugar instead of granulated and 1/2 teaspoon maple flavoring instead of vanilla.
2.	Chocolate frosting	let frosting cool, then fold in 2 squares of melted, cooled, unsweetened chocolate.
3.	Marshmallow frosting	as soon as the frosting is finished, add 2 tablespoons marshmallow cream, or 6 marshmallows cut in quarters (or smaller pieces) and beat until well blended.
4.	George Washington frosting	use maraschino cherry juice instead of the water in the recipe, also add 1/4 teaspoon red food coloring, 1/2 teaspoon almond extract and 1/ teaspoon of vanilla instead of 1 teaspoon of vanilla as called for in the recipe.

. . . .

LEMON FILLING

F=Fair; G=Good; H=High; L=Low; t or T = trace; n/a = no information available;   dashes = zero or unmeasurable

GRAM WT.	FOOD	VITAMINS	CAL	(mg) SOD	PRO	FAT	CARB	CHOL	FATTY ACIDS SAT	UNSAT	CALC	IRON	(mg) POTSM
28	AVERAGE PER OUNCE		45	8				(mg) 19					15
	Ingredients:												
14	2 tblspn flour	B1 B2	58	T	F	L	G	---	---	---	L	F	13
177	3/4 cp cold water	----------						----O----					-----
17	1 egg yolk	A B1 B2	60	9	F	G	T	H*	H	L	G	H	17
100	1/2 cp granulated sugar	---	385	1	---	---	H	---	---	---	---	L	3
54	1 lemon, juice and rind/grated	A B1 B2 C	12	1	L	T	F	---	---	---	F	L	162
10	2 tsp margarine	A D	68	92	L	H	T	---	L	H	L	---	2
372	Recipe totals (gms; cal; sod. & potsm.)		583	103									197

METHOD

Make a smooth paste of the flour and 2 tablespoons of the water. Cook the rest of the water, sugar, grated lemon rind and margarine together and when the sugar dissolves and mixture boils, stir in the flour and water mixture very slowly to avoid lumping. Cook until filling is clear and smooth, about 15 minutes. (Heat should be low enough to prevent filling from scorching or burning.) Add lemon juice and beaten egg yolk and cook 2 minutes longer. Cool before spreading on cake.   Yield about 13 ounces.

* There are 1500 milligrams of cholesterol in 100 grams of egg yolk, according to U.S.D.A. Handbook No. 8, pg 146, item 14; in 17 grams, there are 255 milligrams of cholesterol (1 egg yolk). Divide 255 by recipe yield of 13 ounces equals 19 average milligrams of cholesterol per ounce of filling.

. . . .

BROWN SUGAR COOKIES

F=Fair; G=Good; H=High; L=Low; t or T = trace; n/a = no information available; dashes = zero or unmeasurable

GRAM WT.	FOOD	VITAMINS	CAL	(mg) SOD	PRO	FAT	CARB	CHOL	FATTY ACIDS SAT	UNSAT	CALC	IRON	(mg) POTSM
15	AVERAGE		63	48				(mg) 5					26
	Ingredients:												
345	3 cp presifted, all-purpose flour	B1 B2	1260	6	F	L	G	---	---	---	L	F	328
6	2 tsp baking powder	---	6	630	L	T	H	---	---	---	H	---	---
1	1/4 tsp salt	---	---	393	---	---	---	---	---	---	G	---	---
170	3/4 cp margarine (1—1/2 sticks)	A D	1224	1680	L	H	L	---	L	G	L	---	39
330	1—1/2 cp brown sugar	B1 B2	1230	99	---	---	H	---	---	---	G	G	1135
50	1 egg, beaten	A B1 B2	75	61	G	G	G	H*	H	L	F	F	65
n/a	1 tsp vanilla	--						-O-					---------
902	Recipe totals (gms; cal; sod. & potsm.)		3795	2869									1567

1/3 cup finely chopped nuts may be added to the batter if desired.

METHOD

Sift flour, baking powder and salt together, then set aside. Cream softened margarine with the brown sugar until light and fluffy, making certain to press out any lumps of sugar. Add beaten egg and vanilla and mix thoroughly. Add flour mixture and blend well. Divide dough into 3 equal portions, shape into rolls and chill until firm. Slice thin and bake at 375 F. for 10 — 12 minutes. Yield about 60 (5 dozen).

*   There are 275 milligrams of cholesterol in 50 grams of whole egg as calculated from U.S.D.A. Handbook No. 8, pg. 146, item 12. Total 275 milligrams divided by yield of 60 equals 5 average milligrams of cholesterol per cookie.

. . . .

F=Fair; G=Good; H=High; L=Low; t or T = trace; n/a = no information available;   dashes = zero or unmeasurable

GRAM WT.	FOOD	VITAMINS	CAL	(mg) SOD	PRO	FAT	CARB	CHOL	FATTY ACIDS SAT	UNSAT	CALC	IRON	(mg) POTSM
12	AVERAGE EACH		47	22				(mg) 8					20
	Ingredients:												
48	1/2 cp cake flour	B1 B2	175	1	F	L	G	---	---	---	L	F	46
1	1/8 tsp salt	---	---	196	---	---	---	---	---	---	G	---	---
1	1/4 tsp baking powder	---	1	79	L	T	H	---	---	---	H	---	---
42	3 tblspn margarine	A D	300	418	L	H	L	---	L	H	L	---	10
100	1/2 cp granulated sugar	---	385	1	---	---	H	---	---	---	---	L	3
42	2 tblspns strained honey	B1 B2 C^t	130	2	L	---	H	---	---	---	L	L	21
42	2 tblspns light corn sirup	---	120	28	---	---	H	---	---	---	F	G	2
50	1 egg, beaten	A B1 B2	75	61	G	G	L	H*	H	L	F	F	65
28	1 square chocolate, melted	A B1 B2	145	1	F	G	F	n/a	F	F	F	G	232
15	1 tblspn hot water							O					
n/a	1 tsp vanilla							n/a					
54	1/2 cp pecans, chopped	A B1 B2 C	370	T	L	H	F	---	---	---	F	F	326
423	Recipe totals (gms; cal; sod. & potsm.)		1701	787									705

METHOD

Sift flour, salt and baking powder together. Cream margarine with sugar until light and fluffy. Add honey and corn sirup and continue to cream, then add egg and mix thoroughly. Melt chocolate over boiling water and add to the creamed mixture. Add dry ingredients, hot water and vanilla, a little at a time, and mix well. Blend in chopped nuts. Spread mixture in a greased 8'' x 8'' x 2 '' pan and bake at 350 F. for 20 minutes. If desired, sieve a little powdered sugar over brownies before cutting into squares. Yield   3 dozen.

* There are 275 milligrams of cholesterol in 50 grams of whole egg, as calculated from U.S.D.A. Handbook No. 8, pg. 146, item 12.   Total 275 milligrams divided by yield of 36 brownies equals 8 average milligrams of cholesterol per serving.

. . . .

SHORTBREAD

F=Fair; G=Good; H=High; L=Low; t or T = trace; n/a = no information available; dashes = zero or unmeasurable

GRAM WT.	FOOD	VITAMINS	CAL	(mg) SOD	PRO	FAT	CARB	CHOL	FATTY ACIDS SAT	FATTY ACIDS UNSAT	CALC	IRON	(mg) POTSM
8	AVERAGE PER COOKIE		42	43									11
	Ingredients:												
227	1 cp margarine (2 sticks)	A D	1633	2239	L	H	L	---	L	H	L	---	52
165	3/4 cp brown sugar, packed down	B1 B2	615	50	---	---	H	---	---	---	G	G	568
216	2-1/4 cp sifted cake flour	B1 B2	788	5	L	L	G	---	---	---	L	L	205
608	Recipe totals (gms; cal; sod. & potsm.)		3036	2294									825

METHOD

Cream softened margarine with sugar and work the flour in, then chill the dough. On a lightly-floured board, roll out the dough about 1/4" thick.   Cut out cookies with floured cutters (rectangles, squares, etc.) and bake at 325 F. (slow oven) from 15 — 20 minutes. Yield approximately 6 dozen.

. . . .

BUTTERSCOTCH COOKIES

F=Fair; G=Good; H=High; L=Low; t or T = trace; n/a = no information available; dashes = zero or unmeasurable

GRAM WT.	FOOD	VITAMINS	CAL	(mg) SOD	PRO	FAT	CARB	(mg) CHOL	FATTY ACIDS SAT	UNSAT	CALC	IRON	(mg) POTSM
13	AVERAGE PER COOKIE		59	41				6					27
	Ingredients:												
403	3-1/2 cp presifted,all-purpose flour	B1 B2	1470	7	F	L	G	---	---	---	L	F	383
6	2 tsp baking powder	---	6	630	L	T	H	---	---	---	H	---	---
2	1/2 tsp salt	---	---	785	---	---	---	---	---	---	G	---	---
227	1 cp margarine (2 sticks)	A D	1633	2239	L	H	L	---	L	H	L	---	52
440	2 cp brown sugar	B1 B2	1640	132	---	---	H	---	---	---	G	G	1514
100	2 eggs	A B1 B2	150	122	G	G	L	H*	H	L	F	G	129
n/a	1 tsp vanilla							n/a					
113	1 cp walnuts, chopped	A B1 B2 C	738	2	G	G	G	---	---	H	G	G	509
1291	Recipe totals (gms; cal; sod. & potsm.)		5637	3917									2587

METHOD

Sift flour, baking powder and salt together and set aside. Cream softened margarine and sugar together until fluffy; add eggs, one at a time, beating after each addition until batter is smooth. Add vanilla and nuts, then flour mixture, mixing thoroughly. Shape into rolls about 1-1/2" in diameter. Wrap in plastic wrap or heavy waxed paper and chill until firm. Then remove wrap or waxed paper and slice 1/4" thick, placing cookies about 1/2" apart on ungreased cookie sheets and bake at 400 F. for 8–10 nimutes or until done. Yield approximately 90 - 96 cookies.

* There are 550 milligrams of cholesterol in 100 grams of whole egg, per U.S.D.A. Handbook No. 8, pg 146, item 12. Total 550 milligrams divided by yield of 96 cookies equals approximately 6 average milligrams of cholesterol in each cookie.

. . . .

CHOCOLATE CHIP COOKIES

F=Fair; G=Good; H=High; L=Low; t or T = trace; n/a = no information available; dashes = zero or unmeasurable

GRAM WT.	FOOD	VITAMINS	CAL	(mg) SOD	PRO	FAT	CARB	CHOL	FATTY ACIDS SAT	UNSAT	CALC	IRON	(mg) POTSM
14	AVERAGE PER COOKIE		67	44				(mg) 6					26
	Ingredients:												
143	1-1/4 cp presifted, all-purpose flour	B1 B2	525	3	F	L	G	---	---	---	L	F	136
1	1/4 tsp baking soda	---	1	110	L	T	G	---	---	---	H	---	---
2	1/2 tsp salt	---	---	785	---	---	---	---	---	---	G	---	---
113	1/2 cp margarine (1 stick)	A D	815	1115	L	H	L	---	L	G	L	---	26
55	1/4 cp brown sugar, packed down	B1 B2	205	17	---	---	H	---	---	---	G	G	189
100	1/2 cp granulated sugar	---	385	1	---	---	H	---	---	---	---	L	3
50	1 egg, beaten	A B1 B2	75	61	G	G	L	H*	H	L	F	F	65
n/a	1 tsp vanilla							n/a					
170	6 oz. semi-sweet chocolate pieces	A B1 B2	860	3	L	G	G	n/a	G	F	L	F	553
58	1/2 cp walnuts, chopped	A B1 B2 C	369	1	G	G	G	---	---	H	G	G	255
692	Recipe totals (gms; cal; sod. & potsm.)		3235	2096									1227

METHOD

Sift the flour, soda and salt together and set aside. Cream softened margarine and sugars together until light and fluffy; add egg and vanilla and beat until batter is smooth. Add flour mixture in small amounts. Fold in chocolate pieces and walnuts. Drop dough from a teaspoon onto greased cookie sheets and bake at 350 F. about 10 minutes, or until done.   Yield about 4 dozen.

*   There are 275 milligrams of cholesterol in 50 grams of whole egg as calculated from U.S.D.A. Handbook No. 8, pg. 146, item 12. Total 275 milligrams divided by yield of 48 cookies equals 6 average milligrams of cholesterol per cookie.

;. . . .

NO BAKE CHOCOLATE COOKIES

F=Fair; G=Good; H=High; L=Low; t or T = trace; n/a = no information available; dashes = zero or unmeasurable

GRAM WT.	FOOD	VITAMINS	CAL	(mg) SOD	PRO	FAT	CARB	CHOL	FATTY ACIDS SAT	UNSAT	CALC	IRON	(mg) POTSM
18	AVERAGE PER COOKIE		71	27									43
	Ingredients:												
400	2 cp granulated sugar	---	1540	4	---	---	H	---	---	---	---	L	12
123	1/2 cp 2% low-fat milk	A B1 B2 C	73	75	H	L	H	L	L	L	H	L	215
113	1/2 cp margarine (1 stick)	A D	815	1115	L	H	L	---	L	H	L	---	26
252	3 cp uncooked oatmeal	B1 B2	984	5	L	L	G	---	---	---	L	L	887
48	1/2 cp cocoa	B1 B2	176	136	n/a	L	H	n/a	L	L	L	F	731
65	1/2 cp shredded coconut	B1 B2 C	225	---	L	F	G	---	---	---	L	F	229
72	1/2 cp salted peanuts	B1 B2	420	301	G	H	F	---	---	H	F	F	485
n/a	1 tsp vanilla							-n/a-					
1073	Recipe totals (gms; cal; sod. & potsm.)		4233	1636									2585

METHOD

Bring the sugar, milk and margarine to a boil over medium heat, then pour the mixture over the rest of the ingredients and beat until well blended. Drop by spoonsful on waxed paper until cool. (Yield will depend on size of spoon used. For example: if a teaspoon is used, yield will be more, but smaller cookies; a tablespoon will yield less, but larger cookies). NOTE to compute the average per cookie above, we used 5 dozen (60) cookies.

. . . .

CHOCOLATE DROPS

F=Fair; G=Good; H=High; L=Low; t or T = trace; n/a = no information available; dashes = zero or unmeasurable

GRAM WT.	FOOD	VITAMINS	CAL	(mg) SOD	PRO	FAT	CARB	CHOL	FATTY ACIDS SAT	UNSAT	CALC	IRON	(mg) POTSM
21	AVERAGE PER COOKIE		80	53				(mg) 9					38
	Ingredients:												
56	4 tblspn margarine	A D	400	558	L	H	L	---	L	H	L	---	13
110	1/2 cp brown sugar, packed down	B1 B2	410	33	---	---	H	---	---	---	G	G	378
50	1/4 cp granulated sugar	---	193	T	---	---	H	---	---	---	---	L	2
50	1 egg, beaten	A B1 B2	75	61	G	G	L	H*	H	L	F	F	65
28	1 square unsweetened chocolate	A B1 B2	145	1	F	G	F	n/a	F	F	F	G	232
115	1/2 cp sour cream	A B1 B2 C	242	53	L	G	L	n/a	H	L	G	L	n/a
n/a	1/2 tsp vanilla	-----------------						-----n/a-----					-------
157	1-1/4 cp +2 tblspn presifted flour	B1 B2	578	3	F	L	G	---	---	---	L	F	136
11	1/4 tsp baking soda	---	1	110	L	T	G	---	---	---	H	---	---
2	1/2 tsp salt	---	---	785	---	---	---	---	---	---	H	---	---
54	1/2 cp pecans, chopped	A B1 B2 C	370	T	L	H	F	---	---	---	F	F	326
633	Recipe totals (gms; cal; sod. & potsm.)		2414	1604									1152

METHOD

Cream margarine and sugars together then stir in beaten egg until well blended. Melt chocolate over boiling water and stir into creamed mixture along with sour cream and vanilla. Sift flour with soda and salt and add gradually to the creamed mixture. Beat until batter is smooth. Fold in pecans and blend well. Chill dough 1 hour. Drop rounded tablespoonsful of dough about 2" apart on greased cookie sheets. Bake at 375 F. about 10 minutes or until almost no fingerprint remains when cookies are touched lightly. When cool, cookies may be frosted with chocolate or any desired icing. Yield about 30.

* There are 275 milligrams of cholesterol in 50 grams of whole egg per U.S.D.A. Handbook No. 8, pg. 146, item 12. Total 275 milligrams divided by yield of approximately 30 cookies equals 9 average milligrams of cholesterol per serving.

. . . .

DATE BARS

F=Fair; G=Good; H=High; L=Low; t or T = trace; n/a = no information available; dashes = zero or unmeasurable

GRAM WT.	FOOD	VITAMINS	CAL	SOD (mg)	PRO	FAT	CARB	CHOL	FATTY ACIDS SAT	UNSAT	CALC	IRON	POTSM (mg)
28	AVERAGE PER BAR		99	48				(mg) 28					99
	Ingredients:												
178	1 cp dates, chopped	A B1 B2	490	2	L	L	H	---	---	---	G	H	1153
108	1 cp pecans, chopped	A B1 B2 C	740	T	L	H	F	---	---	---	F	F	651
120	1 cp confectioners' sugar, sifted	---	460	1	---	---	H	---	---	---	---	L	4
100	2 eggs, beaten	A B1 B2	150	122	G	G	L	H*	H	L	F	F	129
5	1 tsp margarine, melted	A D	34	47	L	H	T	---	L	H	L	---	1
	(to make 1 tablespoon)												
15	1 tblspn lemon juice	A B1 B2 C	4	T	L	T	F	---	---	---	F	L	21
29	1/4 cp presifted, all-purpose flour	B1 B2	105	T	F	L	G	---	---	---	L	F	28
2	1/2 tsp salt	---	---	785	---	---	---	---	---	---	G	---	---
557	Recipe totals (gms; cal; sod. & potsm.)		1983	957									1987

METHOD

Chop dates and nuts fine then blend with powdered sugar and beaten egg. Add 1 tablespoon melted margarine, lemon juice, flour and salt. Mix thoroughly. Spread batter evenly in a greased 10" x 6" x 2" pan. Bake at 375 F. for 30 – 35 minutes. While still warm place 2 tablespoons powdered sugar in a sieve and shake gently over the bars. Also while still warm, cut into 1" x 3" bars.   Yield   about 20 bars.

*   There are 550 milligrams of cholesterol in 100 grams of whole egg, per U.S.D.A. Handbook No. 8, pg. 146, item 12, Total 550 milligrams divided by yield of 20 date bars equals 28 average milligrams of cholesterol per serving.

. . . .

GINGERSNAPS

F=Fair; G=Good; H=High; L=Low; t or T = trace; n/a = no information available;   dashes = zero or unmeasurable

GRAM WT.	FOOD	VITAMINS	CAL	(mg) SOD	PRO	FAT	CARB	CHOL	FATTY ACIDS SAT	UNSAT	CALC	IRON	(mg) POTSM
24	AVERAGE PER COOKIE		100	73				(mg) 9					35
	Ingredients:												
340	1-1/2 cp margarine, soft (3 sticks)	A D	2248	3354	L	H	L	---	L	H	L	---	78
400	2 cp granulated sugar	---	1540	4	---	---	H	---	---	---	---	L	12
100	2 eggs	A B1 B2	150	122	G	G	L	H*	H	L	F	F	129
160	1/2 cp molasses	B1 B2	400	24	---	---	H	---	---	---	H	G	1472
460	4 cp presifted, all-purpose flour	B1 B2	1680	8	F	L	G	---	---	---	L	F	437
8	2 tsp baking soda	---	6	878	L	T	G	---	---	---	H	---	---
n/a	2 tsp cinnamon							---n/a---					
n/a	2 tsp cloves							---n/a---					
n/a	2 tsp ginger							---n/a---					
1468	Recipe totals (gms; cal; sod. & potsm.)		6024	4390									2128

METHOD

Cream margarine and sugar together. Beat in the eggs; add molasses and sifted dry ingredients and mix thoroughly. Roll dough into 1" balls then dip in sugar. Place on lightly greased cookie sheets about 2" apart. Bake at 375 F. for 15 — 18 minutes. Yield approximately 5 dozen.

*   There are 550 milligrams of cholesterol in 100 grams of whole egg, as calculated from U.S.D.A. Handbook no. 8, pg. 146, item 12. Total 550 milligrams divided by yield of 60 cookies equals 9 average·milligrams of cholesterol per cookie.

. . . .

YUMMY LEMON BARS

F=Fair; G=Good; H=High; L=Low; t or T = trace; n/a = no information available;   dashes = zero or unmeasurable

GRAM WT.	FOOD	VITAMINS	CAL	(mg) SOD	PRO	FAT	CARB	CHOL	FATTY ACIDS SAT	UNSAT	CALC	IRON	(mg) POTSM
38	AVERAGE PER COOKIE		144	112				(mg) 34					20
	Ingredients:												
113	1/2 cp margarine (1 stick)	A D	815	1115	L	H	L	---	L	H	L	---	26
30	1/4 cp powdered sugar	---	115	T	---	---	H	---	---	---	---	L	1
115	1 cp presifted, all-purpose flour	B1 B2	420	2	F	L	G	---	---	---	L	F	109
100	2 eggs	A B1 B2	150	122	G	G	L	H*	H	L	F	F	129
200	1 cp granulated sugar	---	770	1	---	---	H	---	---	---	---	L	6
2	1/2 tsp baking powder	---	2	158	L	T	H	---	---	---	H	---	---
1	1/4 tsp salt	---	---	393	---	---	---	---	---	---	G	---	---
30	2 tblspn lemon juice, fresh or reconstituted	A B1 B2 C	8	T	L	T	F	---	---	---	F	L	42
7	1-1/2 tsp lemon rind, grated	A B1 B2 C	n/a	2	L	L	F	---	---	---	F	L	11
8	1 tblspn powdered sugar	---	31	T	---	---	H	---	---	---	---	L	T
606	Recipe totals (gms; cal; sod. & potsm.)		2311	1793									324

METHOD

Lightly grease 8" x 8" x 2" baking dish, and preheat oven to 350 F.

FIRST STEP   Cream the softened margarine and powdered sugar together then work in the flour, blending it thoroughly. Press the mixture evenly into the dish or pan with the fingers until the entire surface is covered. Bake crust 20 minutes.   Do not overcook or crust will be hard and unpalatable.

SECOND STEP   Beat the rest of the ingredients together (except the tablespoon of powdered sugar which will be sprinkled over the top later). Pour the mixture over the cooked crust, covering it completely, then bake 25 minutes longer. Do not over bake. Cool on rack. Place the tablespoon of powdered sugar in a small sieve and shake sugar over entire surface. Allow cookies to cool a little, then cut in 16 squares. Lift out of dish carefully with spatula or pancake turner.

* There are 550 milligrams of cholesterol in 100 grams of whole, per U.S.D.A. Handbook No. 8, pg. 146, item 12. Total 550 milligrams divided by yield of 16 bars equals 34 average milligrams of cholesterol per serving.

. . . .

MOLASSES SPICE COOKIES

F=Fair; G=Good; H=High; L=Low; t or T = trace; n/a = no information available; dashes = zero or unmeasurable

GRAM WT.	FOOD	VITAMINS	CAL	(mg) SOD	PRO	FAT	CARB	CHOL	FATTY ACIDS SAT	UNSAT	CALC	IRON	(mg) POTSM
18	AVERAGE PER COOKIE		62	49				(mg) 8					71
	Ingredients:												
518	4-1/2 cp presifted, all-purpose flour	B1 B2	1890	9	F	L	G	---	---	---	L	F	492
7	2-1/4 tsp baking powder	---	7	709	L	T	H	---	---	---	H	---	---
2	3/8 tsp salt	---	---	588	---	---	---	---	---	---	G	---	---
3	3/4 tsp baking soda	---	3	330	L	T	G	---	---	---	H	---	---
n/a	3/4 tsp ground ginger	--n/a--											
n/a	2-1/4 tsp cinnamon	--n/a--											
170	3/4 cp margarine, melted (1-1/2 sticks)	A D	1224	1680	L	H	L	---	L	H	L	---	39
480	1-1/2 cp molasses	B1 B2	1200	72	---	---	H	---	---	---	H	G	4416
100	2 eggs, beaten	A B1 B2	150	122	G	G	L	H*	H	L	F	F	129
1280	Recipe totals (gms; cal; sod. & potsm.)		4474	3510									5076

METHOD

Sift the dry ingredients together. Combine margarine, molasses, 3 tablespoons warm water and beaten eggs then add to the dry ingredients. Mix thoroughly. Set aside about 10 — 12 minutes then roll out quite thinly on a floured board, cut with floured cookie cutters and place on ungreased cookie sheets. Bake at 400 F. about 12 — 15 minutes.

*   There are 550 milligrams of cholesterol in 100 grams of whole egg, as calculated from U.S.D.A. Handbook No. 8, pg. 146, item 12. Total 550 milligrams divided by yield of 6 dozen cookies equals 8 average milligrams of cholesterol per serving.

. . . .

PEANUT BUTTER COOKIES

F=Fair; G=Good; H=High; L=Low; t or T = trace; n/a = no information available; dashes = zero or unmeasurable

GRAM WT.	FOOD	VITAMINS	CAL	(mg) SOD	PRO	FAT	CARB	CHOL	FATTY ACIDS SAT	UNSAT	CALC	IRON	(mg) POTSM
21	AVERAGE PER COOKIE		97	82				(mg) 9					246
	Ingredients:												
259	2-1/4 cp presifted all-purpose flour	B1 B2	945	5	F	L	G	---	---	---	L	F	246
2	1/2 tsp baking soda	---	2	220	L	T	G	---	---	---	H	---	---
3	1 tsp baking powder	---	3	315	L	T	H	---	---	---	H	---	---
1	1/4 tsp salt	---	---	393	---	---	---	---	---	---	G	---	---
227	1 cp margarine (2 sticks)	A D	1633	2239	L	H	L	---	L	H	L	---	52
200	1 cp granulated sugar	---	770	2	---	---	H	---	---	---	---	L	6
220	1 cp brown sugar	B1 B2	820	66	---	---	H	---	---	---	G	G	757
100	2 eggs, beaten	A B1 B2	150	122	G	G	L	H*	H	L	F	F	129
256	1 cp creamy peanut butter	B1 B2	1520	1552	G	H	F	---	L	H	F	F	1715
n/a	1/4 tsp ground nutmeg	-----------						---n/a---					
n/a	1 tsp vanilla	-----------						---n/a---					
1268	Recipe total (gms; cal; sod. & potsm.)		5843	4914									2905

METHOD

Sift the flour, baking soda, baking powder and salt together and set aside. Cream the softened margarine and sugars together until light and fluffy; add the beaten eggs, peanut butter, nutmeg and vanilla and beat until well blended. Add the flour mixture a little at a time, stirring well after each addition. Drop dough from a teaspoon onto greased cookie sheets about 1" apart. Press cookies with tines of a fork twice, making crisscross design. Bake at 375 F. for 10 – 12 minutes. (Note: Before baking, cookies may be sprinkled with colored sugar or chocolate bits, or decorated with nuts or raisins). Yield   approximately 5 dozen cookies.

*   There are 550 milligrams of cholesterol in 100 grams of whole egg as calculated from U.S.D.A. Handbook No. 8, pg. 146, item 12. Total 550 milligrams divided by yield of 60 cookies equals 9 average milligrams of cholesterol per serving.

. . . .

SNICKERDODDLES

F=Fair; G=Good; H=High; L=Low; t or T = trace; n/a = no information available; dashes = zero or unmeasurable

GRAM WT.	FOOD	VITAMINS	CAL	(mg) SOD	PRO	FAT	CARB	CHOL	FATTY ACIDS SAT	UNSAT	CALC	IRON	(mg) POTSM
15	AVERAGE PER COOKIES		66	67				(mg) 9					7
	Ingredients:												
227	1 cp margarine (2 sticks)	A D	1633	2239	L	H	L	---	L	H	L	---	52
300	1-1/2 cp granulated sugar	---	1155	3	---	---	H	---	---	---	---	L	9
100	2 eggs	A B1 B2	150	122	G	G	L	H*	H	L	F	F	129
259	2-1/4 cp presifted,all-purpose flour	B1 B2	945	5	F	L	G	---	---	---	L	F	246
6	2 tsp cream of tartar	---	4	438	L	T	F	---	---	---	---	---	---
4	1 tsp baking soda	---	3	439	L	T	G	---	---	---	H	---	---
2	1/2 tsp salt	---	---	785	---	---	---	---	---	---	G	---	---
	Coating:												
12	2 tblspn sugar	---	48	T	---	---	H	---	---	---	---	L	---
n/a	2 tblspn cinnamon							-n/a-					
410	Recipe totals (gms; cal; sod. & potsm.)		3938	4031									436

METHOD

Cream the margarine, add sugar gradually, add the eggs and mix thoroughly. Sift the flour, salt, cream of tartar and soda together and stir in small amounts in the first mixture, beating until batter is smooth.

Chill dough about 1 hour then roll into balls about the size of small walnuts and roll in the coating mixture. Place cookies 2" apart on lightly greased cookie sheets and bake at 400 F. for 8 to 10 minutes until lightly browned. Yield approximately 5 dozen.

*   There are 550 milligrams of cholesterol in 100 grams of whole egg as calculated from U.S.D.A. Handbook No. 8, pg. 146, item 12. Total 550 milligrams of cholesterol divided by yield of 60 cookies equals 9 average milligrams of cholesterol per cookie.

. . . .

SPICY OATMEAL COOKIES

F=Fair; G=Good; H=High; L=Low; t or T = trace; n/a = no information available; dashes = zero or unmeasurable

GRAM WT.	FOOD	VITAMINS	CAL	(mg) SOD	PRO	FAT	CARB	CHOL	FATTY ACIDS SAT	UNSAT	CALC	IRON	(mg) POTSM
30	AVERAGE PER COOKIE		118	88				(mg) 11					87
	Ingredients:												
345	3 cp sifted all-purpose flour	B1 B2	1260	6	F	L	G	---	---	---	L	F	328
3	3/4 tsp salt	---	---	1178	---	---	---	---	---	---	G	---	---
3	3/4 tsp baking soda	---	3	330	L	T	G	---	---	---	H	---	---
9	3 tsp baking powder	---	9	945	L	T	H	---	---	---	H	---	---
n/a	3/4 tsp cloves							----n/a----					
n/a	1-1/2 tsp cinnamon							----n/a----					
n/a	1/2 tsp nutmeg							----n/a----					
340	1-1/2 cp margarine (3 sticks)	A D	2448	3354	L	H	L	---	L	H	L	---	78
495	2-1/4 cp brown sugar	B1 B2	1845	149	--	---	H	--	---	---	G	G	1703
150	3 eggs, beaten	A B1 B2	225	183	G	G	L	H*	H	L	F	F	194
246	1 cp sour milk (2% low-fat milk)	A B1 B2 C	145	150	H	L	H	L	L	L	H	L	431
189	2-1/4 cp rolled oats	B1 B2	738	4	L	L	G	---	---	---	L	L	665
248	1-1/2 cp raisins	A B1 B2 C	720	68	L	T	H	---	---	---	G	H	1892
162	1-1/2 cp pecans, chopped	A B1 B2 C	1110	T	L	H	F	---	---	---	F	F	977
2190	Recipe totals (gms; cal; sod. & potsm.)		8503	6367									6268

METHOD

Sift the flour with salt, soda, baking powder, cinnamon, cloves and nutmeg. Cream softened margarine with brown sugar until light and fluffy then add the beaten egg and mix well. Add flour mixture in small amounts alternately with the sour milk. Add rolled oats, raisins and nuts, and beat until smooth. Drop by teaspoons onto greased cookie sheets and bake at 350 F. until brown. Yield approximately 6 dozen cookies.

* There are 825 milligrams of cholesterol in 150 grams of whole egg as calculated from U.S.D.A. Handbook No. 8, pg. 146, item 12. Total 825 milligrams divided by yield of 72 cookies equals 11 average milligrams of cholesterol per serving.

. . . .

SPRITZ COOKIES

F=Fair; G=Good; H=High; L=Low; t or T = trace; n/a = no information available; dashes = zero or unmeasurable

GRAM WT.	FOOD	VITAMINS	CAL	(mg) SOD	PRO	FAT	CARB	CHOL	FATTY ACIDS SAT	UNSAT	CALC	IRON	(mg) POTSM
13	AVERAGE PER COOKIE		58	43				(mg) 13					7
	Ingredients:												
227	1 cp margarine (2 sticks)	A D	1633	2239	L	H	L	---	L	H	L	---	52
150	3/4 cp granulated sugar	---	578	2	---	---	H	---	---	---	---	L	5
50	1 egg	A B1 B2	75	61	G	G	L	H	H	L	F	F	65
34	2 egg yolks	A B1 B2	120	18	F	G	T	H	H	L	G	H	33
n/a	1-1/2 tsp vanilla	-----------						-----n/a-----					-----------
1	1/4 tsp baking powder	---	1	79	L	T	H	---	---	---	H	---	---
1	Dash salt	---	---	196	---	---	---	---	---	---	G	---	---
287	2-1/2 cp presifted, all-purpose flour	B1 B2	1050	5	F	L	G	---	---	---	L	F	273
750	Recipe total (gms; cal; sod. & potsm.)		3457	2600									428

METHOD

Preheat oven to 375 F. Do not grease cookie sheets.   Cream the softened margarine, and add sugar gradually, add beaten eggs and flavoring. Beat until smooth. Sift baking powder and salt with the flour and add to the creamed mixture in small amounts. Fill a cookie press or pastry tube, packing the dough firmly to   avoid leaving airspaces, and mold into desired shapes on ungreased cookie sheets. If desired, decorate with colored sugar, chocolate bits, or other decorating material, and bake at 375 F. for 12 – 15 minutes.   After cookies have cooled, additional trimming may be added, such as icing roses, stars, etc., made of confectioners' frosting, or commercial-types. These cookies make excellent Christmas gifts, especially when additional time is taken to decorate them as suggested. Attractive containers may be purchased during the holidays. If cookies are kept in plastic wrap or waxed paper in the containers and sealed, they will keep as fresh as the day they were made for about a week.   Yield   about 5 dozen cookies.

*   There are 785 milligrams of cholesterol in 50 grams of whole egg and 34 grams of egg yolk (fresh), as calculated from U.S.D.A. Handbook No. 8, pg. 146, items 12 and 14 respectively. Total 785 milligrams of cholesterol divided by yield of 60 cookies equals 13 average milligrams of cholesterol per cookie.

. . . .

SUGAR COOKIES

F=Fair; G=Good; H=High; L=Low; t or T = trace; n/a = no information available; dashes = zero or unmeasurable

GRAM WT.	FOOD	VITAMINS	CAL	(mg) SOD	PRO	FAT	CARB	CHOL	FATTY ACIDS		CALC	IRON	(mg) POTSM
									SAT	UNSAT			
12	AVERAGE PER COOKIE		52	44				(mg) 4					6
	Ingredients:												
227	1 cp margarine (2 sticks)	A D	1633	2239	L	H	L	---	L	G	L	---	52
200	1 cp granulated sugar	---	770	2	---	---	H	---	---	---	---	L	6
n/a	1 tsp vanilla	--n/a--											
50	1 egg, beaten	A B1 B2	75	61	G	G	L	H*	H	L	F	F	65
5	1 tsp water	--.0--											
345	3 cp presifted, all-purpose flour	B1 B2	1260	6	F	L	G	---	---	---	L	F	328
5	1-1/2 tsp baking powder	---	5	473	L	T	H	---	---	---	H	---	---
1	1/4 tsp salt	---	---	393	---	---	---	---	---	---	G	---	---
833	Recipe totals (gms; cal; sod. & potsm.)		3743	3174									451

METHOD

Cream the softened margarine and sugar together, add the egg beaten with the water and blend until batter is smooth. Stir in the flavoring. Sift the flour with the baking powder and salt and mix into the first mixture. Chill dough at least 1 hour. To hurry the chilling, dough can be divided into half or thirds. Roll dough to 1/8'' thickness or lightly-floured board. Cut into shapes with cookie cutters, or dip the edge of a medium size drinking glass in flour and cut plain, round cookies. Decorate with plain or colored sugar, nuts or seedless raisins, or candied cherries or pineapple. Bake at 375 F. 6 – 8 minutes on greased cookie sheets. Cool a few minutes, then remove from sheets with pancake turner. Yield approximately 6 dozen cookies.

*   There are 275 milligrams of cholesterol in 50 grams of whole egg as calculated from U.S.D.A. Handbook No. 8, pg. 146, item 12. Total 275 milligrams divided by yield of 72 cookies equals 4 average milligrams of cholesterol per serving.

. . . .

A LITTLE SOMETHING ABOUT PIES

Someone once said that a pie is only as good as its crust, but I believe that the filling is equally important. After all, if the crust is tough and the filling is delicious, one can always leave the crust, but if the filling is unpalatable, who will eat only the crust, no matter how flaky it is?

In making pie crust, quick handling is important. Shortening should never be mashed into the flower because this results in tough pastry. Ingredients should be cold; for beginners, even the flour should be chilled. Ice water is a must. Shortening should be cold and hard. Flour and salt should be sifted together first, in a cold mixing bowl, then the cold, hard shortening cut in with a pastry blender or two dinner knives as quickly as possible. Some cooks use their fingers to work the flour and shortening together, but the success of the pastry demands they work fast before the shortening softens. This takes experience and knowing by the feel of the mixture if it is ready for the ice water. When done this way, the mixture will feel like fine meal, the largest pieces of shortening will be about the size of small peas. DON'T add the water all at once. Sprinkle it, about a tablespoon at a time, over the dough, distributing it by tossing with a fork. Use about 2 to 4 tablespoons of ice water per cup of flour. When formed into a ball (by pressing the mixture together with the hands), the dough should hold its shape. If it feels a little crumbly, add a few more drops of water. Be sure to distribute the water evenly over the flour, pushing the moistened portions to one side before adding more water, so dry areas can be dampened each time. Too much water makes the crust hard; too little causes the crust to crack when being rolled out.

If a double crust is being made, divide the dough evenly into two mounds, chill the dough while you grease the pie pan and set the oven temperature called for in the recipe.

When dough is chilled, roll out one of the mounds on a lightly floured board with a floured rolling pin. (Don't use too much flour as this will make the pastry tough; just use enough flour to prevent dough from sticking to the board, and the rolling pin.) Roll from the center out, turning the circle of dough as it's rolled. If it sticks, add a little flour to the board and rolling pin. Properly rolled-out circle of pastry will be as thick at the center as it is at the edge. Circle of pastry should be rolled out large enough to fit the pie pan. Continue to roll out with quick, deft strokes, until pastry for the lower crust is 1" thick and a little thinner for the upper crust. Pastry should be about 1" wider than the pan.

Perhaps the easiest way for a beginner to get the circle of pastry into the pie pan is to roll the circle up on a floured rolling pin, then unroll into the pie pan, being careful not to stretch or break the dough while fitting it into the pan. If this happens, and the breaks are not long, press together with the fingers, first wetting the finger tips with a little water to seal the break.

Trim the edges with a sharp knife leaving about 1" of pastry overlapping the edge of the pan. If a single crust is to be used, turn this edge under, then flute all around the edge with the fingers, using the index finger of the right hand to push the dough into scallops and the index finger and thumb of the left hand to press the scallops into shape. Or, press the crust gently with the tines of a fork, around the entire edge.

BAKING THE SINGLE CRUST

If the recipe calls for a baked pie shell, roll out the dough 1" wider than the pan's diameter, as previously stated. Prick the bottom and sides gently with a fork in one or two places, after the dough has been placed in the pie pan. Flute the edge all around. Then grease the bottom of a second pie pan, the same size as the first, and press it carefully on top of the crust so that the fluted edge of the pastry shows a little beyond the rim of the second pan. Place in a preheated, 450 F. oven and bake 7 minutes. Then remove the empty pan and continue baking the crust about 7 — 8 minutes longer. Using this method, the pie crust will not shrink.

200

UNBAKED SINGLE CRUST

If recipe calls for an unbaked single crust, as used for custard or pumpkin pies, prepare the dough and fit crust into pan, flute the edge all around, then pour the uncooked filling carefully into the unbaked crust. Bake according to recipe instructions.

BAKING DOUBLE CRUST PIES

As in apple, berry, mince, and other fruit pies, double crusts are used. The bottom of a double crust pie is not fluted. It is rolled about 1/8"thick, while the top crust is rolled a little thinner. The top crust is trimmed about 2" wider than the pan so dough can be tucked under the lower crust and then fluted to create a seal. However, before adding the second crust, wet the edge of the bottom crust, all around the surface where the two crusts meet, with a little water to help seal the top crust. Press the top crust all the way around the edge, gently to avoid tearing, and to seal. Then trim and flute. Double crust pies will not overflow if the top crust is slashed in 1/2" cuts in two or three places and a chimney is placed in a small hole in the center of the pie. This is made by rolling a 2" piece of brown paper (such as that in market bags), by 4". This will allow steam to escape. However, if fruits are very juicy, it might be wise to put a cookie sheet on the rack below the pie. Sometimes, cornstarch or tapioca is used to thicken the fruit juice before adding to the pie crust.

Commercial pie crust mixes are economical for a small family and, except for the water, contain all the necessary ingredients.

Ready-made graham cracker crusts, and regular crusts are usually available in the market. These, along with instant pudding mixes and easy-to-prepare topping, can solve the dessert problem when your husband gives you an hour's warning that "the boss is coming to dinner."

SOME FACTS ABOUT SHORTENING

Shortening used for pie crusts by our grandmothers was always lard. Vegetable shortenings were unheard of and when they finally made their appearance, old-fashioned cooks wouldn't use them. Now the situation is reversed, possibly because of the increasing concern over cholesterol intake or possibly because they have found that vegetable shortenings make good pie crusts and are better for your health.

Lard and other animal fat contains 95 milligrams of cholesterol in 100 grams of edible portion, or 430 milligrams edible portion of 1pound (454 grams) as purchased, whereas all vegetable fat contains no cholesterol.

Some margarines contain 2/3 animal fat and 1/3 vegetable fat, so it's advisable to read the labels if you want a margarine that is free of cholesterol. Those made of all vegetable fat, such as corn oil, contain no cholesterol.

Butter contains 250 milligrams of cholesterol in 100 grams edible portion of 1135 milligrams in 1 pound (454 grams).

454 grams (1 pound)	SODIUM CONTENT OF SHORTENINGS
Lard	0
Margarine	4,477 milligrams in 1 pound (280 per ounce)
Butter	4,477 milligrams in 1 pound (280 per ounce)
Salad or cooking oils, such as corn, olive, soybean, etc.	0

The above information was taken from U.S.D.A. Handbook No. 8, pg. 146, items 3, 22, 25 and 26; pg. 94, items 1241, 1317 and 1401.

. . . .

GRAHAM CRACKER CRUST

F=Fair; G=Good; H=High; L=Low; t or T = trace; n/a = no information available; dashes = zero or unmeasurable

GRAM WT.	FOOD	VITAMINS	CAL	(mg) SOD	PRO	FAT	CARB	CHOL	FATTY ACIDS SAT	UNSAT	CALC	IRON	(mg) POTSM
40	1/7th of a 9" Pie AVERAGE EACH PIECE		208	282									74
	Ingredients:												
128	1-1/2 cp graham cracker crumbs	B1 B2	495	848	F	F	H	---	---	---	F	L	492
113	1/2 cp margarine, melted (1 stick)	A D	815	1115	L	H	L	---	L	H	L	---	26
36	3 tblspn granulated sugar	---	144	T	---	---	H	---	---	---	---	L	1
277	Recipe totals (gms; cal; sod. & potsm.)		1454	1973									519

METHOD

Combine cracker crumbs with melted margarine and sugar. Mix thoroughly. Turn mixture into a 9" pie pan and press firmly against the sides and bottom of the pan until crust is about 1/8" thick and there are no holes or spaces showing through to the pan. Chill about 20 minutes, or bake at 350 F. for 10 minutes before filling.

This crust is particularly good with lemon filling, or banana cream pie made with fresh sliced bananas and instant vanilla pudding mix. Topping can be either prepared dairy topping or meringue.

. . . .

BUTTERSCOTCH PIE FILLING

F=Fair; G=Good; H=High; L=Low; t or T = trace; n/a = no information available; dashes = zero or unmeasurable

GRAM WT.	FOOD	VITAMINS	CAL	(mg) SOD	PRO	FAT	CARB	CHOL	FATTY ACIDS SAT	UNSAT	CALC	IRON	(mg) POTSM
118	1/7th of a 9" Pie AVERAGE PER PIECE FILLING ONLY		261	86				(mg) 109					174
	Ingredients:												
330	1-1/2 cp brown sugar	B1 B2	1230	99	---	---	H	---	---	---	G	G	1135
354	1-1/2 cp water	---------	---	---	---	---	---	-O-	---	---	---	---	---
28	4 tblspn flour	B1 B2	105	1	F	L	G	---	---	---	L	F	27
36	4 tblspn cornstarch	---	136	T	L	T	H	---	---	---	---	---	T
---	1/8 tsp salt	---	---	196	---	---	---	---	---	---	G	---	---
51	3 egg yolks, beaten	A B1 B2	180	27	F	G	T	H*	H	L	G	H	50
28	2 tblspn margarine	A D	200	279	L	H	L	---	L	H	L	---	6
n/a	1 tsp vanilla	---------						-n/a-					---
827	Recipe totals (gms; cal; sod. & potsm.)		1851	602									1218

METHOD

Heat the brown sugar and 1-1/4 cups water to the boiling point, stirring to mix. Blend the flour, cornstarch and salt with the 1/4 remaining cup of water then pour the brown sugar sirup over the flour mixture, slowly, stirring constantly, cooking over low heat until thick. Add the beaten egg yolks, margarine and vanilla and cook 2 minutes longer. Set aside to cool. Stir before pouring into baked pie shell. Top with meringue, or non-dairy topping, or whipped cream. For meringue recipe, see the following page and total values of completed pie.

*   There are 765 milligrams of cholesterol in 3 egg yolks (51 grams), as calculated from U.S.D.A. Handbook No. 8. pg. 146, item 14. Total 765 milligrams divided by yield of 1/7th of a 9" pie equals 109 average milligrams of cholesterol per serving.

. . . .

MERINGUE FOR A 9" PIE

F=Fair; G=Good; H=High; L=Low; t or T = trace; n/a = no information available; dashes = zero or unmeasurable

GRAM WT.	FOOD	VITAMINS	CAL	(mg) SOD	PRO	FAT	CARB	CHOL	FATTY ACIDS SAT	UNSAT	CALC	IRON	(mg) POTSM
24	AVERAGE PER SERVING		48	20									20
	Ingredients:												
99	3 egg whites	B1 B2	45	144	G	T	T	---	---	---	L	–	138
72	6 tblspn granulated sugar	---	288	T	---	---	H	---	---	---	---	L	2
171	Recipe totals (gms; cal; sod. & potsm.)		333	144									140

METHOD

Beat the egg whites until stiff and dry; gradually add the sugar until well mixed. Spoon onto pie, spreading to edge of crust so that no filling is exposed to prevent meringue from shrinking. Bake at 425 F. until golden brown. Meringue should be watched closely so the meringue doesn't get too brown.

NOTE   There is no cholesterol in egg white.

TOTAL VALUES FOR FINISHED BUTTERSCOTCH PIE:

GRAM WT.	FOOD	VITAMINS	CAL	(mg) SOD	PRO	FAT	CARB	CHOL	FATTY ACIDS SAT	UNSAT	CALC	IRON	(mg) POTSM
309	1 baked single crust shell	B1 B2	1405	788				---					137
827	Butterscotch filling	A B1 B2 D	1851	602				765					1218
171	meringue	B1 B2	333	144				---					140
1307	Recipe total (gms; cal; sod. & potsm.)		3589	1534				765 (mg)					1495
187	AVERAGE EACH PIECE (1/7th)		513	219			109						214

. . . .

F=Fair; G=Good; H=High; L=Low; t or T = trace; n/a = no information available;   dashes = zero or unmeasurable

GRAM WT.	FOOD	VITAMINS	CAL	(mg) SOD	PRO	FAT	CARB	CHOL	FATTY ACIDS SAT	UNSAT	CALC	IRON	(mg) POTSM
76	1/6th of an 8" Pie AVERAGE FILLING ONLY		92	105				(mg) 43					114
	Ingredients:												
369	1-1/2 cp 2% low-fat milk, scalded	A B1 B2 C	218	225	H	H	L	L	L	L	H	L	646
50	1/4 cp granulated sugar	---	193	T	---	---	---	---	---	---	---	L	2
1	1/4 tsp salt	---	---	393	---	---	---	---	---	---	G	---	---
21	3 tblspn flour	B1 B2	78	T	F	L	G	---	---	---	L	F	20
17	1 egg yolk, beaten	A B1 B2	60	9	F	G	T	H*	H	L	G	H	17
n/a	1 tsp vanilla							---n/a---					
458	Recipe totals (gms; cal; sod. & potsm.)		549	627									685

METHOD

Scald only 1 cup of milk over boiling water. Mix sugar, salt, flour and remaining 1/2 cup of milk together; stir into hot milk and cook until thickened, stirring constantly, then cover and cook over hot water 5 minutes. Add mixture slowly to beaten egg yolk and cook 1 minute more; then add margarine and vanilla. Cool. Pour into baked pastry shell. Yield   enough filling for an 8" pie.

*   There are 255 milligrams of cholesterol in 17 grams of egg yolk as calculated in U.S.D.A. Handbook No. 8, pg. 146, item 12. Total 255 milligrams divided by yield of 6 pieces of pie equals 43 average milligrams of cholesterol per serving.

VARIATIONS

For a 9" pie, use 2 cups milk and 3 egg yolks. Values will change as follows:

INCREASE

+ 123	+ 1/2 cp milk	s a m e	+ 73	+ 75				same					+ 215
+ 34	+ 2 egg yolks	s a m e	+120	+ 18		same		+510		same			+ 34
+157	Total increase		+193	+ 93				+510					+249

FOR BANANA CREAM PIE

+700	Add 4 sliced bananas to cream filling in alternate layers	A B1 B2 C	+400	+ 8	L	L	G	---	---	---	F	F	+2590

FOR FRESH FRUIT CREAM PIES   Put sliced, sugared strawberries (about 4 cups) into baked or graham cracker crust. Pour creamed filling over them. Top with non-dairy topping or whipped cream. Other fruits, such as fresh peaches, huckleberries, loganberries, pineapple, raspberries and cut up oranges may be used. See food lists for values.

FOR CHOCOLATE CREAM PIE   Add 1 square melted chocolate and 2 tablespoons sugar to the hot milk, 2 minutes before adding to the eggs.

COCONUT CREAM PIE   Add 1-1/2 cups shredded coconut -- mix 1 cup in the filling and sprinkle 1/2 cup over the top of the meringue and brown slightly in the oven.

. . . .

CUSTARD PIE

F=Fair; G=Good; H=High; L=Low; t or T = trace; n/a = no information available; dashes = zero or unmeasurable

GRAM WT.	FOOD	VITAMINS	CAL	(mg) SOD	PRO	FAT	CARB	CHOL (mg)	FATTY ACIDS SAT	UNSAT	CALC	IRON	(mg) POTSM
193	1/7th of a 9" Pie AVERAGE EACH PIECE		361	268				160					242
200	Ingredients: (filling) 4 eggs, slightly beaten	A B1 B2	300	344	G	G	L	H*	H	L	F	F	260
1	1/4 tsp salt	---	---	393	---	---	---	---	---	---	G	---	---
100	1 cp granulated sugar	---	385	1	---	---	H	---	---	---	---	L	3
738	3 cp 2% low-fat milk	A B1 B2 C	435	450	H	L	H	L*	L	L	H	L	
n/a	1 tsp vanilla							--n/a--					
n/a	Nutmeg							--n/a--					
1039	Filling totals (gms; cal; sod. & potsm.)		1120	1088									1555
309	1 unbaked pie shell	B1 B2	1405	788		----------See recipe.----------							137

METHOD

Combine eggs, salt and sugar, then slowly add the scalded milk and vanilla. Mix thoroughly. Pour custard into unbaked pie shell slowly to avoid tearing or breaking the crust. Sprinkle nutmeg over the top and bake at 450 F. for 10 minutes, then reduce heat to 325 F. and bake 30 — 40 minutes longer, or until dinner knife blade inserted in center of custard comes out clean. Cool pie on rack.

* There are 1100 milligrams of cholesterol in 200 grams of whole egg and 22 milligrams of cholesterol in 738 grams of 2% low-fat milk, as calculated in U.S.D.A. Handbook No. 8, pg. 146, items 12 and 29 respectively. Total 1122 milligrams divided by yield of 1/7th of a 9" pie equals 160 average milligrams of cholesterol per serving.

. . . .

F=Fair; G=Good; H=High; L=Low; t or T = trace; n/a = no information available; dashes = zero or unmeasurable

GRAM WT.	FOOD	VITAMINS	CAL	SOD (mg)	PRO	FAT	CARB	CHOL	FATTY ACIDS SAT	UNSAT	CALC	IRON	POTSM (mg)
165	1/7th of a 9" Pie AVERAGE EACH PIECE		425	394				(mg) 73					115
	Ingredients: (Filling)												
200	1 cp granulated sugar	---	770	2	---	---	H	---	---	---	---	L	6
1	1/4 tsp salt	---	---	393	---	---	---	---	---	---	G	---	---
36	1/4 cp cornstarch	---	136	T	L	T	H	---	---	---	---	---	T
14	2 tblspn all-purpose flour	B1 B2	53	T	F	L	G	---	---	---	L	F	13
354	1-1/2 cp boiling water							-----O-----					
34	2 egg yolks, beaten	A B1 B2	120	18	F	G	T	H*	H	L	G	H	33
28	2 tblspn margarine	A D	200	279	L	H	L	---	L	H	L	---	6
14	Grated lemon rind (1)	A B1 B2 C	n/a	T	L	L	F	---	---	---	F	L	22
80	1/3 cp lemon juice	A B1 B2 C	21	T	L	T	F	---	---	---	F	L	113
761	Filling totals (gms; cal; sod. & potsm.)		1300	692									193
277	1 graham cracker crust	B1 B2	1454	1973	---------See recipe for these values---------								519
114	Meringue (see recipe below)	B1 B2	222	96									93
1152	Totals, complete pie (gms; cal; sod. & potsm.)		2976	2761									805

METHOD

FOR LEMON FILLING   In a saucepan, mix the sugar, salt, cornstarch and flour together, then add boiling water slowly, stirring into the mixture until smooth. Cook over low heat, stirring constantly until thick. Stir a little of the hot mixture into the beaten egg yolks, then add the yolks to the hot mixture gradually, beating hard. Cook about 2 minutes longer on low heat. Remove from heat and stir in margarine, lemon rind and juice. Cool about 15 minutes then pour into baked pie shell or graham cracker crust pie shell. Cover top with meringue, spreading it to the edge of the shell all around to prevent filling from "weeping" and shrinking. Bake in a preheated oven at 425 F. about 7 minutes until meringue is lightly browned. Watch carefully, so meringue doesn't brown too much. Cool pie on rack.

FOR MERINGUE   Beat 2 egg whites until stiff, add sugar gradually (about 4 tablespoons granulated). For a more generous meringue, use 3 egg whites and 6 tablespoons sugar.

*   There are 510 milligrams of cholesterol in 34 grams of fresh egg yolk, as calculated in U.S.D.A. Handbook No. 8, pg. 146, item 12. Total 510 milligrams divided by yield of one 9" pie equals 73 milligrams of cholesterol per 1/7 serving.

F=Fair; G=Good; H=High; L=Low; t or T = trace; n/a = no information available;   dashes = zero or unmeasurable

GRAM WT.	FOOD	VITAMINS	CAL	(mg) SOD	PRO	FAT	CARB	CHOL	FATTY ACIDS SAT	UNSAT	CALC	IRON	(mg) POTSM
165	1/7th of a 9" Pie AVERAGE EACH PIECE		471	216				(mg) 157					101
309	Ingredients: One Single crust, baked pie shell 9"		1405	788	----------see recipe----------								137
	FILLING & MERINGUE												
200	1 cp granulated sugar	---	770	2	---	---	H	---	---	---	---	L	6
7	1 envelope unflavored gelatin	---	25	---	H	L	---	---	---	---	---	---	---
1	1/4 tsp salt	---	---	393	---	---	---	---	---	---	G	---	---
n/a	1 tsp vanilla		----------n/a----------										
200	4 eggs, separated	A B1 B2	300	244	G	G	L	H*	H	L	F	F	258
118	1/2 cp water		----------0----------										
62	1/4 cp lime juice	A B1 B2 C	17	T	L	T	F	---	---	---	F	L	64
239	1 cp light whipping cream	A B1 B2 C	715	86	L	G	L	n/a	H	T	F	T	244
16	2 tblspn powdered sugar	---	62	T	---	---	H	---	---	---	---	L	---
n/a	Green food coloring		----------n/a----------										
5	1 tsp grated lime rind	A B1 B2 C	1	---	L	L	F	---	---	---	F	F	---
1157	Recipe total (gms; cal; sod. & potsm.)		3295	1513									709

METHOD

Combine half the sugar (1/2 cp), gelatin, salt, vanilla, egg yolks (slightly beaten), water and lime juice in a saucepan. Blend thoroughly and cook over low heat, stirring constantly, for about 10 minutes until gelatin dissolves and mixture will coat a metal spoon. Remove from heat. Chill, stirring several times for about 1 hour until mixture is as thick as an unbeaten egg white. Then beat the egg whites until foamy, add the remaining sugar, a tablespoon at a time, beating continuously until sugar is dissolved and meringue stands in firm peaks. To the gelatine mixture, carefully add a few drops of green food coloring until it is lime green. Then fold gelatine into meringue gently until well blended. Pour into pie shell and chill 3 – 4 hours. Prior to serving, beat whipping cream, add powdered sugar after cream is stiff enough to form peaks. Drop by teaspoons onto filling in pie to form a crown. Sprinkle with grated lime rind.

* There are 1100 milligrams of cholesterol in 200 grams of whole egg, as calculated from U.S.D.A. Handbook No. 8, pg. 146, item 12. Total 1100 milligrams divided by yield of one 9" pie equals 157 milligrams of cholesterol per 1/7th piece serving.

. . . .

ELAINE'S MYSTERY PIE

F=Fair; G=Good; H=High; L=Low; t or T = trace; n/a = no information available; dashes = zero or unmeasurable

GRAM WT.	FOOD	VITAMINS	CAL	(mg) SOD	PRO	FAT	CARB	CHOL	FATTY ACIDS SAT	UNSAT	CALC	IRON	(mg) POTSM
184	1/6th of a 9" Pie AVERAGE EACH PIECE		646	322				(mg) 138					251
	Ingredients:												
56	4 tblspn margarine (1 stick)	A D	400	558	L	H	L	---	L	H	L	---	13
100	1/2 cp granulated sugar	---	385	1	---	---	H	---	---	---	---	L	3
1	1/4 tsp salt	---	---	393	---	---	---	---	---	---	G	---	---
n/a	1/2 tsp cinnamon	--------------------------------------n/a-------------------------------------											
n/a	1/2 tsp cloves	--------------------------------------n/a-------------------------------------											
320	1 cp maple sirup	---	800	6	---	---	H	---	---	---	F	F	563
150	3 eggs	A B1 B2	225	183	G	G	L	H*	H	L	F	F	194
170	1 cp uncooked,quick-cooking oatmeal	B1 B2	663	3	L	L	H	---	---	---	F	G	598
309	1 unbaked 9" pie shell	B1 B2	1405	788	----------------See recipe for values-----------------								137
1106	Recipe totals (gms; cal; sod. & potsm.)		3878	1932									1508

METHOD

Cream margarine and sugar together; blend in salt, cinnamon and cloves, stir in maple sirup, then add eggs, one at a time, beating well after each addition. Stir in uncooked oatmeal until mixture is smooth. Pour into unbaked pie shell and bake at 350 F. for 1 hour. Serves 6. Add whipped cream or non-dairy topping if desired.

*   There are 825 milligrams of cholesterol in 150 grams of whole egg, as calculated in U.S.D.A. Handbook No. 8, pg. 146, item 12. Total 825 milligrams divided by yield of one pie equals 138 average milligrams of cholesterol per serving.

. . . .

ALABAMA PECAN PIE

F=Fair; G=Good; H=High; L=Low; t or T = trace; n/a = no information available; dashes = zero or unmeasurable

GRAM WT.	FOOD	VITAMINS	CAL	(mg) SOD	PRO	FAT	CARB	CHOL	FATTY ACIDS SAT	UNSAT	CALC	IRON	(mg) POTSM
159	1/7th of a 9" Pie AVERAGE EACH PIECE		594	178				(mg) 118					144
	Ingredients:												
309	One 9" pie shell, unbaked	B1 B2	1405	788	-------------See recipe for values-------------								137
	FILLING												
108	1 cp pecan halves	A B1 B2 C	740	T	L	H	F	---	---	---	F	F	651
150	3 eggs, beaten	A B1 B2	225	183	G	G	L	H*	H	L	F	F	194
5	1 tsp margarine, melt to 1 tblspn	A D	33	46	L	H	T	---	L	H	L	---	1
168	1/2 cp dark corn sirup	---	480	112	---	---	H	---	---	---	F	G	7
168	1/2 cp light corn sirup	---	480	112	---	---	H	---	---	---	F	G	7
n/a	1 tsp vanilla	--------------------------------------n/a-------------------------------------											
200	1 cp granulated sugar	---	770	2	---	---	H	---	---	---	---	L	6
7	1 tblspn flour	B1 B2	26	T	F	L	G	---	---	---	L	F	7
1115	Recipe totals (gms; cal; sod. & potsm.)		4159	1243									1010

METHOD

Line a greased 9" pie pan with pastry. Flute or crimp the edges. Arrange pecans on bottom of pie shell evenly. Beat the eggs; add melted margarine, corn sirups and vanilla. Combine the sugar and flour, then add egg mixture and blend well. Pour over pecans in pie shell. Wait until nuts rise to the surface, then bake at 350 F. for 45 minutes or until knife blade inserted in the center of the pie comes out clean.

* There are 825 milligrams of cholesterol in 150 grams of whole egg, as calculated in U.S.D.A. Handbook No. 8, pg. 146, item 12. Total 825 milligrams divided by yield of 7 pieces equals 118 average milligrams of cholesterol per serving.

. . . .

PUMPKIN PIE

F=Fair; G=Good; H=High; L=Low; t or T = trace; n/a = no information available;   dashes = zero or unmeasurable

GRAM WT.	FOOD	VITAMINS	CAL	(mg) SOD	PRO	FAT	CARB	CHOL	FATTY ACIDS SAT	UNSAT	CALC	IRON	(mg) POTSM
206	1/7th of a 9" Pie AVERAGE EACH PIECE		410	317				(mg) 79					404
309	Ingredients: One 9" pie shell, unbaked	B1 B2	1405	788	--------------See recipe for values------------							-----	137
	FILLING												
100	2 eggs, slightly beaten	A B1 B2	150	122	G	G	L	H*	H	L	F	F	129
456	2 cp canned pumpkin	A B1 B2 C	150	8	L	L	L	---	---	---	L	L	1094
55	1/4 cp brown sugar	B1 B2	205	17	---	---	H	---	---	---	G	G	189
100	1/2 cp granulated sugar	---	385	1	---	---	H	---	---	---	---	L	3
2	1/2 tsp salt	---	- ---	785	---	---	---	---	---	---	G	---	---
n/a	2 tsp cinnamon	--n/a--											
n/a	3/4 tsp ginger	--n/a--											
n/a	1/4 tsp cloves	--n/a--											
420	1-2/3 cp evaporated milk	A B1 B2 C	575	495	H	H	H	--------n/a--------			G	L	1273
1442	Recipe totals (complete) gms; cal; sod. & potsm.)		2870	2216									2825

METHOD

Beat eggs slightly, add pumpkin, sugars, salt and spices and mix thoroughly. Add milk, a little at a time, blending well after each addition. Pour mixture into unbaked pie shell and bake 15 minutes at 425 F., then reduce heat to 350 F. and continue to bake 35 — 45 minutes or until the blade of a silver knife, inserted in the center of the pie, comes out clean. Cool on rack. Serve with dairy topping, or whipped cream, or wedges of cheddar cheese.

* There are 550 milligrams of cholesterol in 100 grams of whole egg, per U.S.D.A. Handbook No. 8, pg. 146, item 12. Total 550 milligrams divided by yield of seven portions equals 79 average milligrams of cholesterol per serving.

. . . .

DOUBLE CRUST PIES
FLO'S DOUBLE CRUST PASTRY

F=Fair; G=Good; H=High; L=Low; t or T = trace; n/a = no information available; dashes = zero or unmeasurable

GRAM WT.	FOOD	VITAMINS	CAL	(mg) SOD	PRO	FAT	CARB	CHOL	FATTY ACIDS SAT	UNSAT	CALC	IRON	(mg) POTSM
67	1/7th of a 9" Pie AVERAGE EACH PIECE		310	169									31
	Ingredients:												
230	2 cp presifted, all-purpose flour	B1 B2	840	4	F	L	G	---	---	---	L	F	219
3	3/4 tsp salt	---	---	1178	---	---	---	---	---	---	G	---	---
150	12 tblspn vegetable shortening	---	1327	---	---	---	H	---	---	G	H	---	---	---
89	6 tblspn ice water							0					
472	Recipe totals (gms; cal; sod. & potsm.)		2167	1182									219

METHOD

Sift flour and salt together then cut in shortening until it is about the size of peas. Add water, a little at a time, until mixture holds together without feeling crumbly. Divide dough into two equal portions. On a floured board, roll out one portion with a floured rolling pin, stroking the dough from the center out, until circle is 1/8" thick. If dough sticks to the board, add a little flour, also to the rolling pin from time to time. Place circle of dough in a greased pie pan, very carefully to avoid breaking or cracking it. Do not stretch dough. With the back of the hands, gently press out any air bubbles (or bulges) in the dough. Trim excess dough with the blade of a knife, all around the edge. Should any breaks or holes in the pastry occur, use some of the trimmed dough to patch it, using a little water to make a seal. Add filling. Roll out top crust the same as the bottom, and carefully lift over the filling. (Before doing this, however, brush the edge of the bottom crust with a little water. This will make a seal when the top crust is added). Trim the top crust about 1/2" longer than the bottom crust so that it can be tucked under the bottom crust. Press the two edges of pastry together, tucking the top crust under the bottom crust, then flute all the way around, or press edges together with the tines of a fork to create a seal. Follow recipe for baking the pie. Also see "Baking Double Crust Pies" previously discussed in this chapter.

* There is no cholesterol in pie crust when vegetable shortening is used.

. . . .

FLO'S APPLE PIE

F=Fair; G=Good; H=High; L=Low; t or T = trace; n/a = no information available; dashes = zero or unmeasurable

GRAM WT.	FOOD	VITAMINS	CAL	(mg) SOD	PRO	FAT	CARB	CHOL	FATTY ACIDS SAT	UNSAT	CALC	IRON	(mg) POTSM
253	1/7th of a 9" Pie AVERAGE EACH PIECE		522	191									218
	Ingredients:												
472	1 recipe double crust pastry	B1 B2	2167	1182	------See recipe for values and how to make it--								219
1050	7 medium size cooking apples	A B1 B2 C	567	11	T	T	F	---	---	---	L	L	1155
150	3/4 cp granulated sugar	---	578	2	---	---	H	---	---	---	---	L	5
84	1/4 cp maple sirup	---	240	8	---	---	H	---	---	---	L	T	141
14	1 tblspn margarine	A D	100	139	L	H	T	---	L	H	L	---	3
n/a	1 tsp cinnamon	------------------------------n/a-------------------------											
n/a	1/2 tsp nutmeg	------------------------------n/a-------------------------											
1770	Recipe totals (gms; cal; sod. & potsm.)		3652	1342									1523

METHOD

Follow recipe for double crust pastry; grease pie pan generously and after bottom crust has been placed in the pan, slice peeled and cored apples quite thin into it, distributing them as evenly as possible. When half the apples have been used, sprinkle them with half the sugar and spices, then continue slicing the apples into the pie until all are used. Pie will seem quite full, but they will cook down when baked. Sprinkle remaining sugar over the apples, them pour maple sirup over them evenly all around the pie. Dot with margarine. Sprinkle remaining spices over all. Cover with top crust, flute, slash 3 or 4 slits in the top crust, about 1/2" in diameter to allow steam to escape. Make brown paper "chimney" about 2" long and insert in center of the pie. Bake at 400 F. for 30 minutes, reduce heat to 375 F. and continue baking about 30 minutes longer, or until crust is golden brown and apples are cooked. To test apples for doneness, insert a long-pronged fork into the pie near the center. The fork will pierce the pie crust and fruit easily. (Uncooked apples cannot be pierced easily.)

To prevent juice from boiling over onto the oven, bake pie on a cookie sheet. Sometimes, if the apples or other fruits are very juicy, even the insertion of a chimney will not prevent a boil-over, but it helps.

Cool pie on a rack. A little granulated sugar can be sprinkled over the top crust as the pie cools. For festive occasions, use colored sugar.

Serve wedges of cheddar cheese or non-dairy topping with pie.

. . . .

FRESH APRICOT PIE

F=Fair; G=Good; H=High; L=Low; t or T = trace; n/a = no information available; dashes = zero or unmeasurable

GRAM WT.	FOOD	VITAMINS	CAL	(mg) SOD	PRO	FAT	CARB	CHOL	FATTY ACIDS SAT	UNSAT	CALC	IRON	(mg) POTSM
227	1/7th of a 9" Pie AVERAGE EACH PIECE		483	170									400
	Ingredients:												
472	1 recipe double-crust pie (pastry)	B1 B2	2167	1182	------See recipe for values and method-----------								219
912	24 (approx.) fresh, pitted, halved apricots	A B1 B2 C	440	9	L	L	F	---	---	---	L	L	2563
200	1 cp granulated sugar	---	770	2	---	---	H	---	---	---	---	L	6
8	1-1/2 tsp lemon juice	A B1 B2 C	2	---	L	T	F	---	---	---	F	L	11
1592	Recipe totals (gms; cal; sod. & potsm.)		3379	1193									2799

METHOD

Preheat oven to 450 F. Grease 9" pie pan then line bottom with pastry. Blanch apricots in boiling water 1 minute, run cold water over them and slip off skins. Cut in half and remove pits. Fill pan with apricot halves, sprinkle with sugar and lemon juice and cover with top crust. Flute the edges of press edges with tines of a fork all around to seal top and bottom crusts. Cut 3 or 4 slits in top crust, insert a roll of brown paper 2 to 3" long and 2 to 3" wide, as a "chimney" in the center to allow steam to escape. Set pie on cookie sheet to catch any boil-over, and bake at 450 F. for 15 minutes, then reduce heat to 350 F. for 35 minutes longer. Cool on rack. Sprinkle a little sugar on the top crust.

. . . .

BLUEBERRY PIE

F=Fair; G=Good; H=High; L=Low; t or T = trace; n/a = no information available; dashes = zero or unmeasurable

GRAM WT.	FOOD	VITAMINS	CAL	(mg) SOD	PRO	FAT	CARB	CHOL	FATTY ACIDS SAT	UNSAT	CALC	IRON	(mg) POTSM
182	1/7th of a 9" Pie **AVERAGE EACH PIECE**		479	198									101
	Ingredients:												
472	1 recipe double-crust pie (pastry)	B1 B2	2167	1182	----------See recipe for values and method----------								219
560	4 cp blueberries	A B1 B2 C	340	6	L	L	F	---	---	---	F	F	454
200	1 cp granulated sugar	---	770	2	---	---	H	---	---	---	---	L	6
18	2 tblspn cornstarch	---	68	---	L	T	H	---	---	---	---	---	T
1	Dash salt	---	---	196	---	---	---	---	---	---	G	---	---
23	1-1/2 tblspn lemon juice	A B1 B2 C	6	---	L	T	F	---	---	---	F	L	32
1274	Recipe totals (gms; cal; sod. & potsm.)		3351	1386									711

METHOD

Preheat oven to 450 F. Grease 9" pie pan and line bottom with pastry. Wash and stem blueberries. Mix sugar, cornstarch and salt together and add to the berries, then add lemon juice and blend ingredients together. Fill pan with mixture, then cover with top crust. Flute the edges, or seal by pressing the tines of a fork all around the edge. Insert 3" roll of brown paper for chimny. Bake on cookie sheet at 450 F. for 10 minutes, then reduce heat to 350 F. for 20 — 30 minutes longer. Cool on rack. Sprinkle top with a little sugar.

. . . .

CHERRY PIE

F=Fair; G=Good; H=High; L=Low; t or T = trace; n/a = no information available; dashes = zero or unmeasurable

GRAM WT.	FOOD	VITAMINS	CAL	(mg) SOD	PRO	FAT	CARB	CHOL	FATTY ACIDS SAT	UNSAT	CALC	IRON	(mg) POTSM
180	1/7th of a 9" Pie AVERAGE EACH PIECE		529	227									156
	Ingredients:												
472	1 recipe for double-crust pie (pastry) unbaked	B1 B2	2167	1182	--------See recipe for values and method----------								219
300	1-1/2 cp granulated sugar	---	1156	4	---	---	H	---	---	---	---	L	9
36	4 tblspn cornstarch	---	136	T	L	T	H	---	---	---	---	---	---
1	1/4 tsp salt	---	---	393	---	---	---	---	---	---	G	---	---
**454	4 cp sour, red cherries	A B1 B2 C	242	8	L	L	F	---	---	---	L	L	867
1263	Recipe totals (gms; cal; sod. & potsm.)		3701	1587									1095

METHOD

Combine sugar, cornstarch and salt. Wash and pit cherries then mix with sugar mixture. Line bottom of a greased pie pan with pastry, add cherries and cover with top crust. Slash crust in two or three places, insert brown paper chimney to allow steam to escape, and bake pie at 450 F. for 10 minutes, then reduce heat to 350 F. and continue to bake 25 minutes longer. To avoid boil-over, if cherries are juicy, bake on cookie sheet.

** Estimated weight, since no fruit or figures were available.

. . . .

F=Fair; G=Good; H=High; L=Low; t or T = trace; n/a = no information available; dashes = zero or unmeasurable

GRAM WT.	FOOD	VITAMINS	CAL	(mg) SOD	PRO	FAT	CARB	CHOL	FATTY ACIDS SAT	UNSAT	CALC	IRON	(mg) POTSM
256	1/7th of a 9'' Pie AVERAGE EACH PIECE		675	282				(mg) 14					666
	Ingredients:												
472	1 recipe double-crust pastry	B1 B2	2167	1182	--------See recipe for values and method)--------								219
140	5 oz lean ground beef	A B1 B2	310	70	G	F	---	H*	H	L	L	F	---
28	2 tblspn beef suet	A B1 B2	239	---	L	H	---	------n/a------			L	L	--
450	3 tart apples	A B1 B2 C	210	4	L	L	F	---	---	---	L	L	495
330	2 cups seedless raisins	A B1 B2 C	960	90	L	T	H	---	---	---	G	H	2518
28	1 oz citron, chopped	n/a	89	82	L	L	H	---	---	---	F	L	34
n/a	1 tsp nutmeg		--------n/a--------										
100	1/2 cup granulated sugar	---	385	1	---	---	H	---	---	---	---	L	3
105	7 tblspn cider vinegar	---	14	1	---	L	---	---	---	---	L	L	105
140	7 tblspn molasses	B1 B2	350	21	---	---	H	---	---	---	H	G	1288
n/a	1/3 tsp cloves		--------n/a--------										
n/a	1/2 tsp cinnamon		--------n/a--------										
n/a	1/2 tsp mace		--------n/a--------										
1	1/3 tsp salt	---	---	523	---	---	---	---	---	G	---	---	
1794	Recipe totals (gms; cal; sod. & potsm.)		4724	1974									4662

METHOD

Cook ground beef in just enough water to cover then separate meat with a fork until it's the consistency of meal. (Do not throw away water in which meat is cooked.) Cool meat and stock. Cut suet into tiny pieces. Pare, core and cut apples fine or put suet and apples through a food chopper. Add remaining ingredients and the meat stock and simmer about an hour, stirring often. Add a little water if needed, but mixture should be thick.

Line a greased pie pan with pastry, pour in cooled filling and cover with top crust. Flute and trim edges, then slash 2 or 3 short cuts in top crust to allow steam to escape; also insert "chimney" of brown paper (the market bag type), about 2 to 3'' long by 3'' wide, in center of top crust. Bake on a cookie sheet at 450 F. for 10 minutes, reduce heat to 350 F. 30 minutes longer or until crust is golden brown. Cool on rack. Sprinkle a little granulated sugar over top crust.

*   In 140 grams of beef, there are 98 milligrams of cholesterol, as calculated from U.S.D.A. Handbook No. 8, pg. 146, item 1b. Divide 98 by 1/7th of a 9'' pie equals 14 average milligrams of cholesterol in each piece.

. . . .

PEACH PIE

F=Fair; G=Good; H=High; L=Low; t or T = trace; n/a = no information available; dashes = zero or unmeasurable

GRAM WT.	FOOD	VITAMINS	CAL	(mg) SOD	PRO	FAT	CARB	CHOL	FATTY ACIDS SAT	FATTY ACIDS UNSAT	CALC	IRON	(mg) POTSM
244	1/7th of a 9" Pie AVERAGE EACH PIECE		472	171									328
	Ingredients:												
472	1 recipe double-crust pastry	B1 B2	2167	1182	--------See recipe for values and method)--------								219
1026	9 medium size peaches	A B1 B2 C	315	10	L	T	L	---	---	---	L	L	2073
200	1 cup granulated sugar	---	770	2	---	---	H	---	---	---	---	L	6
14	1-1/2 tblspn cornstarch	---	51	---	L	T	H	---	---	---	---	---	---
n/a	1/2 tsp cinnamon	---n/a---											
1712	Recipe totals (gms; cal; sod. & potsm.		3303	1194									2298

METHOD

Set oven temperature at 450 F. Roll out lower crust and line greased pie pan with the pastry. Trim the edges.

Blanch peaches in boiling water about 1 minute, then immerse them in cold water and slip skins off. Remove pits, slice into a mixing bowl. Mix sugar and cornstarch together and blend into peaches. Pour into pie pan, sprinkle with cinnamon and cover with top crust. Trim pastry about 1/4 or 1/2" longer than the bottom crust, then tuck under the bottom crust and flute all the way around, or press to seal with the tines of a fork. Cut 2 or 3 one half inch slits in top crust; insert a 3" long brown paper chimney in the center of the top crust. Place pie on cookie sheet and bake at 450 F. for 15 minutes, then reduce heat to 350 F. and bake 35 minutes longer. Cool on rack. Sprinkle top crust with a little granulated sugar while still warm. Serve plain or with non-dairy topping or whipped cream.

. . . .

PINEAPPLE PIE

F=Fair; G=Good; H=High; L=Low; t or T = trace; n/a = no information available;   dashes = zero or unmeasurable

GRAM WT.	FOOD	VITAMINS	CAL	(mg) SOD	PRO	FAT	CARB	CHOL	FATTY ACIDS SAT	UNSAT	CALC	IRON	(mg) POTSM
174	1/7th of a 9" Pie AVERAGE EACH PIE		457	207				(mg) 79					125
	Ingredients:												
472	1 recipe double-crust pastry	B1 B2	2167	1182	--------See recipe for values and method)---------								219
100	2 eggs, beaten slightly	A B1 B2	150	122	G	G	L	H*	H	L	F	F	129
100	1/2 cup granulated sugar	---	385	1	---	---	H	---	---	---	---	L	3
15	1 tblspn lemon juice	A B1 B2 C	4	---	L	T	F	---	---	---	F	L	21
520	2 cp canned, shredded pineapple	A B1 B2 C	390	6	L	T	F	---	---	---	F	L	504
14	1 tblspn margarine	A D	100	139	L	H	L	---	L	H	L	---	3
1221	Recipe totals (gms; cal; sod. & potsm.)		3196	1450									879

METHOD

Beat eggs slightly, add sugar, lemon juice and pineapple. Line greased pie pan with pastry, pour in filling, dot with pieces of margarine, then cover with top crust. Insert 3" x 3" roll of brown paper to allow steam to escape, also cut 2 or 3 one-half inch slits in pastry near the center. Bake pie on cookie sheet at 450 F. about 10 minutes. Reduce heat to 350 F. and bake 35 minutes longer. Cool on rack. Sprinkle top with sugar.

*   There are 550 milligrams of cholesterol in 100 grams of whole egg, as calculated in U.S.D.A. Handbook No. 8, pg. 146, item 12.   Total 550 milligrams divided by 1/7th of a 9" pie equals 79 average milligrams of cholesterol per serving.

. . . .

RAISIN PIE

F=Fair; G=Good; H=High; L=Low; t or T = trace; n/a = no information available; dashes = zero or unmeasurable

GRAM WT.	FOOD	VITAMINS	CAL	(mg) SOD	PRO	FAT	CARB	CHOL	FATTY ACIDS SAT	UNSAT	CALC	IRON	(mg) POTSM
252	1/7th of a 9" Pie AVERAGE EACH PIECE		623	195									645
	Ingredients:												
472	1 recipe double-crust pastry	B1 B2	2167	1182	--------See recipe for values and method)---------								219
80	1/3 cp lemon juice	A B1 B2 C	21	T	L	T	F	---	---	---	F	L	113
7	1 tsp grated lemon rind	A B1 B2 C	n/a	2	L	L	F	---	---	---	F	L	11
124	1/2 cp orange juice	A B1 B2 C	55	1	L	L	F	---	---	---	F	L	248
10	2 tsp grated orange rind	A B1 B2 C	n/a	1	L	L	F	---	---	---	G	L	21
220	1 cp brown sugar	B1 B2	820	66	---	---	H	---	---	---	G	G	757
413	2-1/2 cp seedless raisins	A B1 B2 C	1200	113	L	T	H	---	---	---	G	H	3144
413	1-3/4 cp water	---n/a-----------------------											
27	3 tblspn cornstarch	---	102	T	L	T	H	---	---	---	---	---	---
1766	Recipe totals (gms; cal; sod. & potsm.)		4365	1365									4513

METHOD

Combine lemon rind and juice, orange rind and juice, sugar, raisins and only 1-1/4 cups of water, then heat to boiling. Mix cornstarch with remaining 1/2 cup water and stir until smooth. Add to hot mixture gradually, stirring constantly until thickened. Cook 5 – 6 minutes. Set aside. Line greased pie pan with pastry, pour in raisin mixture and cover with top crust. Trim and flute edges. Insert brown paper chimney, 3" x 3" into center of pie to allow steam to escape. Cut 2 or 3 one-half inch slits in pastry, also, near center. Bake on cookie sheet in 400 F. oven about 40 minutes until crust is golden brown. Cool on rack. Sprinkle top crust with a little granulated sugar.

. . . .

STRAWBERRY PIE

F=Fair; G=Good; H=High; L=Low; t or T = trace; n/a = no information available; dashes = zero or unmeasurable

GRAM WT.	FOOD	VITAMINS	CAL	(mg) SOD	PRO	FAT	CARB	CHOL	FATTY ACIDS SAT	UNSAT	CALC	IRON	(mg) POTSM
163	1/7th of a 9" Pie AVERAGE EACH PIECE		462	189									137
	Ingredients:												
472	1 recipe double-crust pastry	B1 B2	2167	1182	-------See recipe for values and method---------								219
447	3 cp fresh strawberries	A B1 B2 C	165	3	L	L	F	---	---	---	G	F	733
200	1 cp sugar	---	770	2	---	---	H	---	---	---	---	L	6
9	1 tblspn cornstarch	---	34	---	L	T	H	---	---	---	---	---	---
1	dash salt	---	---	----	---	---	---	---	---	---	G	---	---
14	1 tblspn margarine	A D	100	139	L	H	L	---	L	H	L	---	3
1143	Recipe totals (gms; cal; sod. & potsm.)		3236	1326									961

METHOD

Wash berries and remove caps. Mix sugar, cornstarch and salt together and add to berries. Line greased pie pan with pastry, add berry mixture, dot with pieces of margarine then cover with top crust. Trim and flute edges of pastry or seal edges by pressing with the tines of a fork all the way around. Insert a 3" x 3" roll of brown paper in the center of the crust to allow the steam to escape; also cut 2 or 3 one half inch slits in the pastry near the center. Bake 10 minutes at 450 F. on a cookie sheet. Reduce heat to 350 F. 30 minutes longer. Cool on a rack. Sprinkle top of crust with a little granulated sugar.

. . . .

CHEESE DISHES, EGGS, ICE CREAM and OTHER DAIRY PRODUCTS

DAIRY PRODUCTS, CHEESE DISHES, EGGS, ICE CREAM, CHEESE VARIETIES, DESCRIPTIONS AND ORIGINS
were carried on and improved by the monks in the monasteries of Europe. The origin of Gorgonzola cheese in the Po Valley in Italy dates back to 879 A.D., and Italy was the most advanced cheese-making center of Europe as early as the 10th Century. Roquefort cheese was first mentioned in the ancient records of the monastery at Conques, France, in 1070.

Cheese was included in the ship's supplies when the Mayflower made its famous voyage to America in 1620, but it wasn't until 1851 that the first cheese factory was started near Rome in Oneida County, New York. Herkimer County, adjoining Oneida County, was a center of the cheese industry from 1851 to about 1900. The market in the world for 30 years. As population increased, the industry gradually moved westward, settling in the rich lands of Wisconsin.

AMERICAN VARIETIES

AMERICAN CHEESE This is a pressed cheese, smooth-textured with a pleasant nutty flavor; a mild cheddar that originated in Cheddar, England. Its color is white to yellow.

BLUE OR BLEU Similar to Roquefort, but made in the United States from cows' milk, instead of goats' or ewes' milk as in France and Denmark. It is made in various sections of the country where limestone caves are available, which are necessary for proper ripening of the cheese. It is a semi-soft cheese, marbled with greenish-blue mold. It is used for dessert or in salads and salad dressings.

BRICK An American cheddar with a mild, sweetish taste, a rather elastic, smooth-textured, and many round, small holes or eyes. It is a rennet cheese made from whole milk and molded into brick shape.

BRIE A whole milk cheese with a soft center. It is ripened by bacteria in the United States; in Brie, France where it originated, it is ripened by mold. (See French cheeses).

CAMEMBERT A soft, creamy rennet cheese in the United States, but ripened by mold in Camembert, France where it originated. Serve as Brie. It is a dessert cheese. (See French cheeses).

CHEDDAR Several types of smooth, melt-in-the-mouth hard cheese, varying in flavor from mild to extra sharp, depending upon the time allowed for ripening. It may be made from whole milk, part skim or skim. This variety is sold in many shapes, such as daisies, longhorn, and young Americas. In recipes which do not specify a certain kind of cheese, this is the variety usually meant to use. (also see Herkimer and Pineapple cheeses). This cheese originated in Cheddar, England.

COTTAGE A soft curd cheese, also known as "Dutch" or "pot" cheese, made commercially from pasteurized sour milk, with or without rennet. It can be made in your own kitchen from sour skim or whole milk. One quart makes 1 cup of cheese. If sweet milk is used, it will be necessary to use 1 rennet tablet per quart. (See recipes for sweet cottage cheese, and sour cottage cheese following these varieties).

CREAM A soft, rich cheese with mild flavor. Genuine cream cheese is made from pasteurized rich cream thickened by souring, or from sweet cream thickened with rennet and whole milk. When fresh, it has a mild, delicate flavor. It must be kept under refrigeration. It is used as bases for mixtures with pimiento, crushed pineapple, etc. It is an unripened cheese, similar to the French cheese, Neufchatel.

EDAM (See Holland cheeses for description.)

GOUDA (See Holland cheeses for description.)

224

GRUYERE   In the United States, the name is generally applied to packaged, processed Swiss cheese. (See Swiss cheeses for description).

HERKIMER   An aged cheese with a sharp flavor. It is used in rarebits, cheese sauces and as a dessert.

LIEDERKRANTZ   Originated in Ohio, this cheese has a strong odor and flavor. It is a soft cheese of spreading consistency with a thin crust that should be eaten for fullest flavor. Similar to Camembert, or Limberger, but milder and softer. It should be kept refrigerated and warmed to room temperature before using

LIMBURGER   (See Belgium for description).

PINEAPPLE   A hard, highly colored cheddar made in pineapple shape, then hung and dried in a net, making diamond-shape corrugations on the surface. The outer coat is rubbed with oil, making it very hard and smooth. It is made from whole milk. It is grated and used like other cheddars.

NOTE   Of the grated, hard cheeses made in Switzerland and Italy, a considerable quantity of the Italian type is made in the United States and also imported from South America.

SAGE   A cheddar cheese, formerly made by adding sage leaves to the curd; now sage extract is generally used.

SWISS   Similar to Swiss-made Emmenthaler, but when processed, the characteristic holes are lost.

LIMBURGER   This cheese originated in Limburg in the eastern part of Belgium. It is famous for its very strong and disagreeable odor, but its texture is creamy and delicate, a semi-soft cheese made from whole milk, or partly or entirely skimmed milk.

ENGLISH VARIETIES

CHEDDAR   This cheese was first made in Cheddar, a village in Somerset, England. English Cheddar is hard, sharp, and white or yellow in color. It is made from sweet milk and sold as "full cream" (when whole milk is used), "part skim" or "skim," depending on the type of milk used.

CHESHIRE   A hard, rennet, yellow cheese, somewhat like English Cheddar but with a sharper flavor. It is made from whole milk and colored with annatto which is a yellowish-red dyestuff obtained from the pulp of annatto seeds (a tropical tree).

STILTON   A rich, unpressed, hard rennet cheese of waxy texture that is permeated with blue-green mold. It has a wrinkled, or ridged, rind or skin. Originally made at Stilton, a parish in Huntingdonshire, England, it is made from cows' milk with cream added, and usually allowed to ripen at least two years before being marketed. It is one of the principle English cheeses.

FRENCH VARIETIES

BRIE (Bre)   A mold-ripened, whole milk cheese with a soft center. It was first made in Brie, France. It is a dessert cheese. (Also see American-made Brie.)

CAMEMBERT (kam'em bar')   This is a creamy cheese that is ripened by mold. The inside softens as it ripens. It was first made at Camembert, a village in Normandy. It is a dessert cheese, excellent with fresh fruit.

LIVEROT   A strong rennet cheese, similar to Brie. It is made from skimmed milk and has a strong, pungent flavor.

MUENSTER   A semi-soft, creamy, yellow, fermented Alsatian cheese of milk flavor, originally made at Munster in northeastern France.

NEUFCHATEL (noo she tel)   A very soft, white rennet cheese made from skimmed or whole milk or cream, it was originally made at Neufchatel, a town in Bray, northern France.

PONT L'EVEQUE (pont levek)   A milk, soft-centered cheese made from whole milk, named after a town in northern France.

PORT du SALUT   (seloot)   A semi-hard, fermented cheese made originally by Trappist monks of LaTrappe, Normandy. Similar to brick but a little softer in texture and with a stronger flavor. The Canadian version is called OKRA or Trappist.

ROQUEFORT (rok'fert)   A marbled cheese made from goats' and ewes' milk. It contains a blue mold, Penicillium roqueforti. Made in Roquefort, a village in southern France, it is a semi-hard rennet cheese with streaks of blue and green mold. The mold is produced by adding a special wheat and barley bread which has been allowed to mold before grinding and combining with the curd. It is ripened in limestone caves. Holes are punched in the cheese during the curing process to allow air, essential to the growth of the mold, to enter.

EDAM   This is a hard, rennet cheese, small and round with a red paraffin rind; a pressed cheese, yellow in color, made from skimmed milk (or partly skimmed). It has a solid, dry, rather crumbly texture and a milk, slightly salty flavor. It is excellent served with fruit pies, salads, in rarebits, or as a dessert cheese. To serve, cut off the top and scoop out the inside as needed.

GOUDA   A mild, close-textured, pale yellow, hard rennet cheese, made from whole or partly skimmed milk and covered with a protective coating and red wax, similar to Edam cheese. Originally made in Gouda, a city in the western Netherlands, famous for its cheese markets.

ITALIAN VARIETIES

CACIOCAVALLO   A hard, beet-shaped rennet cheese made from whole or partly skimmed milk. It is slightly smoked.

GORGONZOLA   A pungent, blue-veined, cream-colored cheese made of pressed cows' milk. It was first made at Gorgonzola, a village near Milan, Italy.

MOZZARELLA This is a popular white curd cheese, soft, easily melted.

PARMEZAN (par'me zan)   Another popular cheese-hard, a rennet cheese made from partly skimmed milk. Usually served as a grated garnish (as on spaghetti), it has a sharp flavor, and a green or black rind. It will keep indefinitely. It originated in Parma, a city in northern Italy.

PROVOLE OR PROVOLONE   A hard round cheese held by a net. Made of cows' milk, it is similar to caciocavallo.

ROMANO A hard, dry cheese with a salty taste and a black coating.

SCANDINAVIAN VARIETIES

APPETITOST A semi-hard cheese made from buttermilk.

226

GJEDOST A hard cheese made from goats' milk. It is chocolate-colored and has a sweet taste.

MYSOST Semi-soft, whey cheese of light brown color. It has milk-sweetish flavor and is used as a snack or for a dessert.

NOKKELOST A hard cheese made from skimmed milk, with spices added.

SWISS VARIETIES

EMMENTHALER A hard, pale yellow rennet cheese with large holes and a mild somewhat sweetish flavor. Holes should be uniform, very shiny and about the same size as a quarter. It is made from whole milk and used for cooking, or salads and desserts.

GRUYERE A pale yellow, firm-textured cheese, with or without holes, made from whole milk. It has a nutty flavor. Originally made in Gruyere, a district in Switzerland.

SAPSAGO A hard cheese made from skim milk curd. It is green in color and mixed with blue meliot (a kind of clover honey).

. . . .

CHEESE DISHES, EGGS, ICE CREAM AND OTHER DAIRY PRODUCTS

F=Fair; G=Good; H=High; L=Low; t or T = trace; n/a = no information available; dashes = zero or unmeasurable

GRAM WT.	FOOD	VITAMINS	CAL	(mg) SOD	PRO	FAT	CARB	CHOL	FATTY ACIDS SAT	UNSAT	CALC	IRON	(mg) POTSM
	BUTTERMILK												
245	Fluid, cultured, made from skim milk, 1 cup	A B1 B2 C	90	319	H	L	H	---	---	---	F	L	319
120	Dried, packaged, 1 cup	A B1 B2	465	608	H	F	H	n/a	L	L	H	L	168
	CHEESE												
	Blue or Roquefort type												
28	1 ounce	A B1 B2	105	---	H	H	L	H	G	L	H	L	---
17	1 cubic inch	A B1 B2	65	---	H	H	L	H	G	L	H	L	---
100	Brick	A B1 ^{N} B2	370	---	F	F	L	H	H	T	H	L	---
	("N" means Niacin only)												
38	Camembert, 4 oz. package with 3 wedges per package, 1 wedge	A B1 B2	115	---	F	F	L	H	G	T	G	L	42
28	Cheddar, 1 ounce	A B1 B2	115	196	G	H	L	H	H	L	H	F	23
	Cottage cheese (large or small curd creamed)												
340	12 oz package (net weight)	A B1 B2	360	779	G	L	L	L	L	L	H	F	289
245	1 cup (curd pressed down)	A B1 B2	260	561	H	L	L	L	L	L	H	L	170
	uncreamed												
340	12 oz package (net weight)	A B1 B2	290	986	H	L	L	L	L	T	H	F	245
200	1 cup (curd pressed down)	A B1 B2	170	580	F	L	L	L	L	T	G	L	144
	cream												
227	1 package (8 ounces)	A B1 B2	850	568	L	H	L	H	H	L	F	L	168
85	1 package (3 ounces)	A B1 B2	320	193	L	H	L	H	H	L	F	L	63
	Parmesan, grated												
140	1 cup, pressed down	A B1 B2	655	1028	G	G	L	H	G	L	H	L	209
28	1 ounce	A B1 B2	130	206	G	G	L	H	G	L	H	L	42
5	1 tablespoon	A B1^t B2	25	37	G	G	L	H	G	T	H	L	7
	Swiss												
28	1 ounce	A B1^t B2	105	199	H	H	L	F	F	L	H	L	29
15	1 cubic inch	A B1^t B2	55	107	H	H	L	F	F	L	H	L	16
	Pasteurized, Process Cheese												
	American												
28	1 ounce	A B1 B2	105	318	H	H	L	H	H	L	H	L	22
18	1 cubic inch	A B1^t B2	65	204	H	H	L	H	H	L	H	L	14

CHEESE DISHES, EGGS, ICE CREAM AND OTHER DAIRY PRODUCTS

F=Fair; G=Good; H=High; L=Low; t or T = trace; n/a = no information available; dashes = zero or unmeasurable

GRAM WT.	FOOD	VITAMINS	CAL	(mg) SOD	PRO	FAT	CARB	CHOL	FATTY ACIDS SAT	UNSAT	CALC	IRON	(mg) POTSM
	Pasteurized Swiss												
28	1 ounce	A B1^t B2	100	327	H	H	L	F	F	L	H	L	28
18	1 cubic inch	A B1^t B2	65	210	H	H	L	F	F	L	H	L	18
	Pasteurized Process Cheese Food, American												
14	1 tablespoon	A B1^t B2	45	---	G	H	L	H	H	L	G	L	---
18	1 cubic inch	A B1^t B2	60	---	G	H	L	H	H	L	G	L	---
28	1 ounce, spread	A B1^t B2	80	455	G	H	L	--------n/a-------			G	L	67
	CREAM												
242	Half n' Half (cream and milk)												
	1 cup	A B1 B2 C	325	111	F	H	F	n/a	H	L	H	L	312
15	1 tablespoon	A B1^t B2 C^t	20	7	F	H	F	n/a	H	L	H	T	19
240	Light, coffee or table, 1 cup	A B1 B2 C	505	103	F	H	F	n/a	H	L	H	L	293
15	1 tablespoon	A B1^t B2 C^t	30	6	F	H	F	n/a	H	L	G	T	18
60	Whipped topping (pressurized)												
	1 cup	A B2	155	n/a	L	F	L	n/a	H	L	F	---	n/a
3	1 tablespoon	A B2^t	10	n/a	T	L	T	n/a	T	T	F	---	n/a
	Whipping cream, unwhipped (volume about double when whipped)												
239	Light, 1 cup	A B1 B2 C	715	86	L	G	L	n/a	H	L	H	L	244
15	1 tablespoon	A B1^t B2 C^t	45	5	T	G	L	n/a	H	L	H	T	15
238	Heavy, 1 cup	A B1 B2 C	840	86	L	H	L	n/a	H	L	F	L	212
15	1 tablespoon	A B1^t B2 C^t	55	5	T	H	L	n/a	H	L	F	T	13
	CREAM PRODUCTS (imitation) made with vegetable fat												
	Creamers												
94	powdered, 1 cup	A B1$^{(t-N)}$	505	541	L	F	G	n/a	F	L	F	L	n/a
	1 teaspoon	A^t	10	12	T	L	L	n/a	T	T	L	T	n/a
245	liquid (frozen) 1 cup	A	345	---	L	F	G	n/a	F	L	F	---	n/a
15	1 tablespoon	A	20	---	T	F	G	n/a	L	T	L	---	n/a

CHEESE DISHES, EGGS, ICE CREAM AND OTHER DAIRY PRODUCTS

F=Fair; G=Good; H=High; L=Low; t or T = trace; n/a = no information available; dashes = zero or unmeasurable

GRAM WT.	FOOD	VITAMINS	CAL	(mg) SOD	PRO	FAT	CARB	CHOL	FATTY ACIDS SAT	UNSAT	CALC	IRON	(mg) POTSM
235	Sour dressing (imitation sour cream) made with non-fat dry milk, 1 cup	A B1 B2 C	440	n/a	L	F	F	n/a	F	L	H	L	n/a
12	1 tablespoon	A^t B1^t B2^t C^t	20	n/a	T	L	L	n/a	T	T	H	T	n/a
	EGGS (Large, 24 oz per dozen) Raw or cooked in shell with nothing added (Chicken)												
50	whole, without shell, 1 egg	A B1 B2	75	61	G	G	L	H	H	L	F	F	65
33	white of 1 egg	B1^t B2	15	48	G	T	T	---	---	---	L	T	46
17	yolk, 1	A B1 B2	60	9	F	G	T	H	H	L	G	H	17
	cooked												
100	fried	A B1 B2	216	338	G	G	L	H	H	L	F	F	140
100	hard-cooked	A B1 B2	163	122	G	F	L	H	H	L	F	F	129
100	omelet	A B1 B2	173	257	G	F	L	H	H	L	F	F	146
100	poached	A B1 B2	163	271	G	F	L	H	H	L	F	F	128
64	scrambled with milk and fat, 1	A B1 B2	110	164	G	G	L	H	H	L	G	F	146
	Dried												
100	1 whole egg	A B1 B2	592	427	G	G	L	H	G	L	H	H	463
100	whole stabilized (glucose reduced)	A B1 B2	609	444	G	G	L	--------n/a-------			H	H	482
100	white, flakes	B1 B2	349	1033	G	L	L	---	---	---	F	F	937
100	yolk	A B1 B2	664	100	F	G	L	H	G	T	H	H	186
100	Duck, whole, fresh, raw	A B1 B2	191	122	F	F	L	--------n/a-------			F	F	(129)
100	Goose, whole, fresh, raw	---	185	---	F	F	L	--------n/a-------			---	---	---
100	Turkey, whole, fresh, raw	B1 $^{t(N)}$	170	---	F	F	L	--------n/a-------			---	---	---
	ICE CREAM												
1064	Regular (approx. 10% fat) 1/2 gallon	A B1 B2 C	2055	670	L	F	H	F	F	L	H	L	1926
133	1 cup	A B1 B2 C	255	82	L	F	H	F	F	L	H	L	241
50	3 fluid ounce cup	A B1 B2 C	95	32	L	F	H	F	F	L	H	T	91
	Rich (approx. 16% fat)												
1188	1/2 gallon	A B1 B2 C	2635	392	L	F	H	F	F	L	G	L	1129
148	1 cup	A B1 B2 C	330	49	L	F	H	F	F	L	G	T	141

CHEESE DISHES, EGGS, ICE CREAM AND OTHER DAIRY PRODUCTS

F=Fair; G=Good; H=High; L=Low; t or T = trace; n/a = no information available; dashes = zero or unmeasurable

GRAM WT.	FOOD	VITAMINS	CAL	(mg) SOD	PRO	FAT	CARB	CHOL	FATTY ACIDS SAT	UNSAT	CALC	IRON	(mg) POTSM
100	ICE CREAM CONES	A^t B1 B2 C^t	377	232	F	F	H	--------n/a--------		H	L	244
100	ICE MILK	A B1 B2 C	152	68	F	F	G	--------n/a--------		H	L	195
	MILK Cow												
	Regular type, fluid (pasteurized and raw)												
244	whole 3.5% fat, 1 cup	A B1 B2 C	160	122	H	H	H	H	H	L	H	L	251
245	nonfat (skim), 1 cup	A B1 B2 C	90	127	H	T	H	---	---	---	H	L	355
246	partly skimmed, 2%, 1 cup (non-fat milk solids added)	A B1 B2 C	145	150	H	L	H	L	L	L	H	L	431
	Regular type, canned, concentrated undiluted												
252	evaporated, unsweetened, 1 cup	A B1 B2 C	345	297	H	H	H	--------n/a-------		H	L	764
306	condensed, sweetened, 1 cup	A B1 B2 C	980	343	H	H	H	--------n/a-------		H	L	961
	(Note Most fluid, comercially-bought milk is fortified with vitamin D.)												
	dry non-fat; instant												
100	whole	A B1 B2 C	502	405	H	H	H	H	H	L	G	L	1330
100	skim (non-fat solids) regular	A B1 B2 C	363	532	H	L	H	L	L	L	H	L	1745
100	skim (non-fat solids) instant	A B1 B2 C	359	526	H	L	H	L	L	L	H	L	1725
	Miscellaneous												
100	goat milk	A B1 B2 C	67	34	L	L	L	n/a	L	L	G	L	180
100	human, U.S. samples	A B1 B2 C	77	16	L	L	L	n/a	L	L	F	L	51
100	reindeer	---	234	157	F	F	L	--------n/a-------		L	H	159
	Yoghurt												
245	from partially skimmed milk 1 cup	A B1 B2 C	125	125	L	L	L	L	L	L	G	T	350
	MILK, SOYBEAN See legumes, nuts vegetables & soups under beans												
	MILK BEVERAGES												
250	cocoa, homemade, 1 cup	A B1 B2 C	245	128	L	L	F	G	G	L	G	L	363
250	chocolate milk (made with skim milk & 2% butterfat added) 1 cp	A B1 B2 C	190	115	L	L	F	L	L	L	G	L	355

CHEESE DISHES, EGGS, ICE CREAM AND OTHER DAIRY PRODUCTS

F=Fair; G=Good; H=High; L=Low; t or T = trace; n/a = no information available;   dashes = zero or unmeasurable

GRAM WT.	FOOD	VITAMINS	CAL	(mg) SOD	PRO	FAT	CARB	CHOL	FATTY ACIDS SAT	UNSAT	CALC	IRON	(mg) POTSM
28	malted milk dry powder, approx. 1 ounce, 3 heaping teaspoons per ounce	A B1 B2 C	115	387	F	L	G	---	---	---	H	F	202
235	beverage, made with non-fat milk, 1 cup	A B1 B2 C	245	214	L	L	F	---	---	---	G	L	470
	MILK DESSERTS												
265	custard, baked, 1 cup	A B1 B2 C	305	209	L	L	F	F*	F*	F*	H	F	387
	(Note* Made with non-fat milk and one egg - if made with whole milk, values will read High (H) Chol; High (H) Sat. & Good (G) Unsat.)												

HOW TO MAKE COTTAGE CHEESE

SOUR MILK COTTAGE CHEESE

1 quart sour or clabbered milk
cream

METHOD

Heat milk over hot water until lukewarm (95 F.) and mixture appears to thicken and curdle. Remove from heat and let stand in a warm place a few minutes for curd to collect. Turn into a cheesecloth-lined strainer and let whey drain off thoroughly. If milk is very sour, rinse curd with cold water and drain again. Tie ends of cloth together and let curd hang until all whey has drained off. Moisten curd with a little cream. Do not salt -- allow each individual to season as he or she chooses. This will avoid overseasoning. (Use skim, whole, or buttermilk). For added flavor use a little grated onion; minced green onion tops; minced chives or a bit of fresh garlic, mashed; or caraway seeds. Yield: 1 cup. (See the food list heading this chapter for values, under CHEESE, Cottage.) Chill cottage cheese in covered container.

SWEET MILK COTTAGE CHEESE

1 rennet tablet
1 quart of milk
cream

METHOD

Crush rennet tablet to a powder and dissolve in a few tablespoons of the milk. Heat remaining milk to lukewarm (95 F.) stir in rennet, remove from heat and let stand in a warm place until mixture thickens. Break curd, pour into cheesecloth-lined strainer and let drain very thoroughly. Moisten with a little cream. Chill in covered container. Season individually. Yield 1 cup. Additional flavorings, as shown in Sour Milk Cottage Cheese, may be added, also fruits, such as canned pineapple (crushed or chunks), cherries, etc., or fresh fruits.

. . . .

F=Fair; G=Good; H=High; L=Low; t or T = trace; n/a = no information available; dashes = zero or unmeasurable

GRAM WT.	FOOD	VITAMINS	CAL	(mg) SOD	PRO	FAT	CARB	CHOL	FATTY ACIDS SAT	UNSAT	CALC	IRON	(mg) POTSM
137	AVERAGE PER ENCHALADA with sauce		358	326				(mg) 76					342
	Ingredients:												
222	12 corn tortillas	B1 B2	834	T	L	L	G	--------n/a--------			G	H	---
908	2 pounds ground beef	A B1 B2	1624	590	G	F	---	H	H	L	L	F	3223
110	1 onion, medium, chopped	A B1 B2 C	40	11	L	L	L	---	---	---	L	L	173
15	1 tblspn chili powder	A B1 B2 C	50	236	F	F	G	---	---	---	H	H	150
272	3 cp grated or shredded cheese (cheddar) 9-1/2 ozs.	A B1 B2	1083	1905	G	G	L	H**	H	L	H	F	223
	SAUCE												
70	5 tblspn margarine	A D	500	697	L	H	L	---	L	G	L	---	16
18	2-1/2 tblspn flour	B1 B2	66	T	F	L	G	---	---	---	L	F	17
30	2 tblspn chili powder	A B1 B2 C	100	472	F	F	G	---	---	---	H	H	300
1645	Recipe totals (gms; cal; sod. & potsm.)		4297	3911									4102

METHOD

Preparing the enchiladas -- Brown the beef in a little oil, breaking it up with a fork until free of lumps. Add chopped onion and chili powder and stir until well mixed. Set aside. Heat a little oil in a frying pan or round layer-cake pan. Using tongs, dip tortillas, one at a time, into the medium hot oil (so the tortilla doesn't burn). Leave tortilla in oil until it begins to puff slightly (this takes only a few seconds). Then lift it carefully with tongs and drain over pan a moment. Place tortilla, opened flat (like a pancake), in a lightly greased baking dish that is large enough to hold 12 folded tortillas. Divide meat into 12 equal portions. Fill tortilla with one of these portions, then add a generous amount of grated cheese (or cheese that has been shredded or cut into small pieces) then fold tortilla by placing the left side over the right, or vice versa, and holding it firmly to prevent contents from spilling, turn it over so that the folded side is on the bottom. Continue this process until all of the tortillas have been filled. Then prepare the sauce.

METHOD FOR SAUCE

In a frying pan, heat the margarine until slightly browned. Stir flour in gradually, add chili powder, then pour the hot water in a little at a time to avoid bubbling up and boiling over the pan. Stir quickly to prevent lumps from forming and continue to add water and stir until the sauce is consistency of medium-thick gravy. Add more water if sauce is too thick to pour. If a hotter sauce is desired, add another tablespoon of chili powder. Either reserve some of the sauce to use at the table, or pour all of it over the enchiladas. Sprinkle any remaining cheese over all and bake at 350 F. until sauce bubbles (about 30 minutes). NOTE Sometimes the sauce is prepared in a round cake pan and, after the tortillas are dipped in the oil, they are dipped into the sauce before filling. When doing it this way, I found the sauce spattered all over and added nothing to the taste, also tortillas were harder to handle because they broke easily, making them difficult to fill). For garnish, add chopped or whole ripe olives, additional grated cheese and shredded lettuce. Serves 6.

There are commercially prepared enchilada sauces on the market which may be used instead of the one above. Some are hot; some are mild.

* Corn tortillas nutritive information was calculated from Quaker-Oaks Instant Masa-Harina, 5—pound package, except sodium, which was estimated from item 860, corn flour, U. S. D. A. Handbook No. 8, "Composition of Foods."

** There are 640 milligrams of cholesterol in 2 pounds of lean, boneless beef and 270 milligrams of cholesterol in 270 grams of cheddar cheese, per U.S.D.A. Handbook No. 8, pg. 146, items 1b and 5 respectively. Total milligrams of cholesterol: 910 divided by 12 enchiladas equals 76 average milligrams of cholesterol per enchilada.

. . . .

CHEESE AND GREEN CHILI ENCHILADAS

F=Fair; G=Good; H=High; L=Low; t or T = trace; n/a = no information available; dashes = zero or unmeasurable

GRAM WT.	FOOD	VITAMINS	CAL	(mg) SOD	PRO	FAT	CARB	CHOL (mg)	FATTY ACIDS SAT	UNSAT	CALC	IRON	(mg) POTSM
106	AVERAGE EACH with sauce		269	262				23					57
	Ingredients:												
185	10 corn tortillas*	B1 B2	695	T	L	L	G	--------n/a--------			G	H	---
56	4 tblspn cooking oil	---	500	---	---	H	---	---	T	H	---	---	---
113	1 four oz can green chilies chopped (seeds removed)	A B1 B2 C	28	---	L	L	L	---	---	---	L	L	---
25	3 green onions w/tops, chopped	A^t B1 B2 C	11	1	L	L	F	---	---	---	F	L	58
227	1/2 lb cheddar cheese, grated or shredded. medium or sharp. (2-1/2cp) (No salt, season at the table)	A B1 B2	902	1588	G	G	L	H**	H	L	H	F	186
	SAUCE												
56	4 tblspn margarine	A D	400	558	L	H	L	---	L	G	L	---	13
14	2 tblspn flour	B1 B2	53	T	F	L	G	---	---	---	L	F	13
30	2 tblspn chili powder	A B1 B2 C	100	472	F	F	G	---	---	---	H	H	300
354	1-1/2 cp hot water		----------------------------0----------------------------										
1060	Recipe totals (gms; cal; sod. & potsm.)		2689	2619									570

METHOD

Lightly grease a baking dish that is large enough to hold 10 folded tortillas (a 13" dish should do). Set aside.

In a round layer-cake pan, heat the cooking oil until hot but not burning. Using tongs, dip the corn tortillas, one at a time, a few seconds in the hot oil until the tortilla begins to puff up a little, but not long enough to get crisp. Drain the tortilla over the pan then lift carefully to the baking dish and spread flat. Fill tortilla with a little green onion, 1/4 cup grated or shredded cheese, and about 3/4 to 1 teaspoon green chili (distributed over cheese), then roll or fold tortilla and place fold-side-down. Continue with each tortilla until all have been filled, folded and placed fold-side-down in the dish. Prepare sauce, pour over enchiladas and bake at 350 F. until sauce bubbles (about 30 minutes). These enchiladas may be frozen, but do not bake first, and leave the sauce off until ready to bake. Place enchiladas in foil, close tightly and freeze. An hour before baking, remove foil, place enchiladas in lightly greased baking dish. Prepare sauce and proceed as above, baking about 45 minutes or until sauce bubbles. Serves 5.

* Values for corn tortillas were calculated from Quaker Oats Instant Masa-Harina, 5-pound package, except sodium, which was estimated from item 860, corn flour, U.S.D.A. Handbook No. 8, "Composition of Foods."

**   There are 227 milligrams of cholesterol in 227 grams of cheddar cheese, per U.S.D.A. Handbook No. 8, pg. 146, item 5, or 23 milligrams of cholesterol average in each enchilada.

. . . .

GREEN CHILIES, CHEESE AND RICE CASSEROLE

F=Fair; G=Good; H=High; L=Low; t or T = trace; n/a = no information available; dashes = zero or unmeasurable

GRAM WT.	FOOD	VITAMINS	CAL	(mg) SOD	PRO	FAT	CARB	CHOL	FATTY ACIDS SAT	UNSAT	CALC	IRON	(mg) POTSM
179	AVERAGE PER SERVING		337	529				(mg) 31					48
	Ingredients:												
113	1 4-oz. can green chilies, chopped	A B1 B2 C	28	---	L	L	L	---	---	---	L	L	---
460	1 pint sour cream	A B1 B2 C	990	195	L	G	L	n/a	H	T	F	L	n/a
615	3 cp cooked rice	B1 B2	675	2300	L	L	F	---	---	---	L	L	172
227	1/2 lb cheddar cheese, cut in strips	A B1 B2	902	1588	G	H	L	H*	H	L	H	F	186
20	4 tblspn Parmesan grated cheese	A B1^t B2	100	148	G	G	L	G*	G	L	H	L	30
1435	Recipe totals (gms; cal; sod. & potsm.)		2695	4231									388

METHOD

Combine chilies with the sour cream, then starting with the cooked rice, layer a greased baking dish with all ingredients except the Parmesan cheese. (The second layer should be made up of the chilies and sour cream; the third cheddar cheese, etc., ending with the rice). Sprinkle the top with grated Parmesan cheese. Bake about 350 F. about 25 minutes or until the Parmesan cheese is melted. Yield   8 servings.

*There are 100 milligrams of cholesterol in 100 grams of cheddar cheese, and 85 milligrams of cholesterol in 100 grams of "Other" cheese (we have used this figure for the Parmesan cheese), as calculated in U.S.D.A. Handbook No. 8, pg 146, items 5 and 8 respectively. Total 244 milligrams divided by yield of 8 equals 31 average milligrams of cholesterol per serving.

. . . .

DIXIELAND HOMINY AND CHEESE

F=Fair; G=Good; H=High; L=Low; t or T = trace; n/a = no information available; dashes = zero or unmeasurable

GRAM WT.	FOOD	VITAMINS	CAL	(mg) SOD	PRO	FAT	CARB	CHOL	FATTY ACIDS SAT	UNSAT	CALC	IRON	(mg) POTSM
160	AVERAGE PER SERVING		131	297				(mg) 102					133
	Ingredients:												
490	2 cp cooked hominy	A B1 B2	250	1104	L	L	F	---	---	---	L	L	54
56	2/3 cp grated cheddar cheese	A B1 B2	226	397	G	H	L	H*	H	L	H	F	46
100	2 eggs, slightly beaten	A B1 B2	150	122	F	F	L	H*	H	L	F	F	129
** 20	2 tsp pimiento, chopped	A B1 B2 C	*5	---	L	L	L	---	---	---	L	F	---
8	2 tblspn parsley, chopped	A B1t B2 C	T	2	T	T	T	---	---	---	H	H	58
37	1/2 green pepper, med-size, cut in pieces	A B1 B2 C	8	5	L	L	L	---	---	---	L	L	79
246	1 cup 2% low-fat milk	A B1 B2 C	145	150	H	L	H	L*	L	L	H	L	431
957	Recipe total (gms; cal; sod. & potsm.)		784	1780									797

No salt was added to the ingredients; season at the table individually.

METHOD

Grease individual baking dishes. Set oven at 325 F. Combine ingredients and pour into baking dishes then place them in a pan of hot water and bake in a slow oven for about 30 minutes or until firm. Serves 6.

* There are 56 milligrams of cholesterol in 56 grams of cheddar cheese and 550 milligrams of cholesterol in 100 grams of whole egg and 7 milligrams of cholesterol in 246 grams of low-fat milk, according to U.S.D.A. Handbook No. 8, pg 146, items 5, 12, 18 and 29 respectively (fluid skim milk is 3 milligrams per 100 grams). Total 613 milligrams divided by yield of 6 equals 102 average milligrams of cholesterol per serving.

** Estimated.

. . . .

MACARONI AND CHEESE

F=Fair; G=Good; H=High; L=Low; t or T = trace; n/a = no information available; dashes = zero or unmeasurable

GRAM WT.	FOOD	VITAMINS	CAL	(mg) SOD	PRO	FAT	CARB	CHOL	FATTY ACIDS SAT	UNSAT	CALC	IRON	(mg) POTSM
104	AVERAGE PER SERVING		278	344				(mg) 39					147
	Ingredients:												
114	1 cp uncooked macaroni	B1 B2	420	2	L	L	G	---	---	---	L	L	225
246	1 cp 2% low-fat milk	A B1 B2 C	145	150	H	L	H	L*	L	L	H	L	431
227	1/2 lb cheddar, sharp or medium, cut up	A B1 B2	902	1588	G	H	L	H*	H	L	H	F	186
25	1/4 cp bread crumbs	A^t B1 B2 C^t	98	184	F	L	G	---	---	---	G	F	38
14	1 tblspn margarine	A D	100	139	L	H	T	---	L	H	L	---	3
	No Salt - - season at the table individually												
626	Recipe totals (gms; cal; sod. & potsm.)		1665	2063									883

NOTE   Because dry macaroni doubles in bulk when cooked, enough water must be used during the cooking process to prevent it from burning and to compensate for the expansion. One cup of dry macaroni will become about two cups when cooked.

METHOD

Cook the macaroni in at least 3 cups of boiling UNSALTED water until tender. Drain in a colander, then rinse slightly with warm water (this prevents the macaroni from sticking together). Place macaroni in a greased, medium size casserole. Heat milk, add the cut up cheese and stir until melted then pour over the macaroni and mix with a fork. Some of the cheese may be reserved and sprinkled over the top, if desired. Distribute bread crumbs over top evenly, then dot over all with margarine. Bake at 350 F. about 20 – 25 minutes. Yield   6 servings.

Another method for macaroni and cheese is to layer it with macaroni, cheese and a thin white sauce (made by heating the milk and thickening it with a little cornstarch and water, stirring continuously), and adding a few pieces of margarine between each layer, ending with macaroni and topping with breadcrumbs, then dotting with more margarine. However, this method increases the caloric content and sodium. (see the food list "Nutrition at your Fingertips," Chapter I, under Corn Products for cornstarch values, and this recipe for margarine values (1 tablespoon), and double the values if 2 tablespoons are used, triple them for 3 tablespoons, etc.). Bake the same as above.

*   There are 227 milligrams of cholesterol in 227 grams of cheddar cheese, and 7 milligrams of cholesterol in 246 grams of fluid skim milk, calculated from U.S.D.A. Handbook No. 8, pg. 146, items 5 and 29 respectively. Total 234 milligrams divided by yield of 6 equals 39 average milligrams of cholesterol per serving.

. . . .

CHEESE SOUFFLE

F=Fair; G=Good; H=High; L=Low; t or T = trace; n/a = no information available; dashes = zero or unmeasurable

GRAM WT.	FOOD	VITAMINS	CAL	(mg) SOD	PRO	FAT	CARB	CHOL	FATTY ACIDS SAT	UNSAT	CALC	IRON	(mg) POTSM
155	AVERAGE PER SERVING		333	446				(mg) 269					199
	Ingredients:												
57	4 tblspn margarine	A D	400	558	L	H	L	---	L	H	L	---	13
28	4 tblspn flour	B1 B2	105	1	F	L	G	---	---	---	L	F	27
369	1—1/2 cp 2% low-fat milk (hot)	A B1 B2 C	218	225	H	L	H	L*	L	L	H	L	646
n/a	dash cayenne pepper							-n/a-					
227	2-1/2 cp cheddar cheese, grated	A B1 B2	902	1588	G	H	L	H*	H	L	H	F	186
250	5 eggs, separated	A B1 B2	375	306	F	F	L	H*	H	L	F	F	323
	No salt, season at the table individually												
931	Recipe totals (gms; cal; sod. & potsm.)		2000	2678									1195

METHOD

In a medium-size sauce pan, melt the margarine slowly to prevent burning, then stir in the flour a little at a time and blend until smooth. Add the hot milk gradually, stirring constantly, cooking until thickened. Add the cayenne pepper and cheese. Continue heating until the cheese melts, then add the beaten egg yolks and mix well. Cool the mixture. While cooling, beat the egg whites until stiff then pour the cheese mixture into the egg whites, folding carefully until well blended. Bake in an ungreased, 2-quart baking dish (set pan in hot water while baking) at 300 — 325 F. for about 1 hour. When knife, inserted in the center, comes out clean, souffle is done. Serve at once. Yield approximately 6 servings.

*   There are 1375 milligrams of cholesterol in 250 grams of whole egg and 227 milligrams of cholesterol in 227 grams of cheddar cheese, and 11 milligrams of cholesterol in 369 grams of fluid skim milk, as calculated in U.S.D.A. Handbook No. 8, pg. 146, items 5, 12 and 29 respectively. Total 1613 milligrams divided by yield of 6 equals 269 average milligrams of cholesterol per serving.

. . . .

CHEESE—SPINACH SOUFFLE

F=Fair; G=Good; H=High; L=Low; t or T = trace; n/a = no information available; dashes = zero or unmeasurable

GRAM WT.	FOOD	VITAMINS	CAL	(mg) SOD	PRO	FAT	CARB	CHOL	FATTY ACIDS SAT	UNSAT	CALC	IRON	(mg) POTSM
125	AVERAGE PER SERVING		207	269				(mg) 154					219
	Ingredients:												
56	4 tblspn margarine	A D	400	558	L	H	L	---	L	H	L	---	13
18	2 tblspn cornstarch	---	68	---	L	T	H	---	---	---	---	---	---
246	1 cp 2% low-fat milk	A B1 B2 C	145	150	H	L	H	L*	L	L	H	L	431
n/a	dash pepper							n/a					
8	1 green onion and a little of the top	A^t B1 B2 C	3	T	L	L	F	---	---	---	F	L	18
91	1 cp grated cheddar cheese	A B1 B2	361	635	G	H	L	H*	H	L	H	F	75
180	1 cp spinach, chopped, cooked	A B1 B2 C	40	90	L	L	L	---	---	---	G	F	583
150	3 eggs, separated	A B1 B2	225	183	F	F	L	H*	H	L	F	F	194
	No Salt - - season at table individually												
749	Recipe total (gms; cal; sod. & potsm.)		1242	1616									1314

METHOD

While margarine is melting slowly in a sauce pan, mix the cornstarch with a little water (about 1/3 cup) and stir until smooth. Set aside. Add milk to the melted margarine and continue heating until milk is hot. Stir the cornstarch and water mixture then add slowly to the hot milk, sitrring constantly until sauce is very thick.   Blend in pepper. Add chopped onion and grated cheddar cheese, heating and stirring until cheese is melted. Add drained spinach and well-beaten egg yolks and mix thoroughly.   Fold in stiffly beaten egg whites. Pour into greased loaf pan, place pan in another pan of hot water and bake at 350 F. 45 minutes or until firm. Yield   approximately 6 servings.

*   There are 91 milligrams of cholesterol in 91 grams of cheddar cheese, 825 milligrams of cholesterol in 150 grams of whole egg and 7 milligrams of cholesterol in 246 grams of fluid skim milk, as calculated in U.S.D.A. Handbook No. 8, pg. 146, items 5, 12 and 29 respectively. Total 923 milligrams divided by yield of 6 equals 154 average milligrams of cholesterol per serving.

. . . .

CHEESE WAFFLES

F=Fair; G=Good; H=High; L=Low; t or T = trace; n/a = no information available; dashes = zero or unmeasurable

GRAM WT.	FOOD	VITAMINS	CAL	(mg) SOD	PRO	FAT	CARB	CHOL	FATTY ACIDS SAT	UNSAT	CALC	IRON	(mg) POTSM
164	(Four to a section) (2 section) AVERAGE PER WAFFLE		428	613				(mg) 151					195
	Ingredients:												
173	1-1/2 cp presifted,all-purpose flour	B1 B2	630	3	F	L	G	---	---	---	L	F	164
6	2 tsp baking powder	---	6	630	L	T	H	---	---	---	H	---	---
1	1/4 tsp salt	---	---	393	---	---	---	---	---	---	G	---	---
85	6 tblspn margarine	A D	600	837	L	H	L	---	L	H	L	---	20
100	2 eggs, separated	A B1 B2	150	122	F	F	L	H*	H	L	F	F	129
246	1 cp 2% low-fat milk	A B1 B2 C	145	150	H	L	H	L*	L	L	H	L	431
45	1/2 cp grated cheddar cheese	A B1 B2	181	318	G	H	L	H*	H	L	H	F	37
656	Recipe totals (gms; cal; sod. & potsm.)		1712	2453									781

METHOD

Sift flour with baking powder and salt into a medium-size mixing bowl. Cut in margarine with a table knife or mix with the finger tips until mixture resembles fine meal. Beat the egg yolks before adding them to the milk then blend well. Add to the flour mixture. Stir only until well moistened. Beat egg whites until stiff and fold them into the mixture gently, then add the cheddar cheese. Bake in a preheated waffle iron until steam ceases to escape from the grids. Yield about 4 waffles or 16 sections.

* There are 45 milligrams of cholesterol in 45 grams of cheddar cheese, 7 milligrams of cholesterol in 246 grams of low-fat milk and 550 milligrams of cholesterol in 100 grams of whole egg, as calculated from U.S.D.A. Handbook No. 8, pg 146, items 5, 12 and 29 respectively. Total 602 milligrams divided by yield of 4 equals 151 average milligrams of cholesterol per serving.

. . . .

MEXICAN FIESTA CASSEROLE

F=Fair; G=Good; H=High; L=Low; t or T = trace; n/a = no information available; dashes = zero or unmeasurable

GRAM WT.	FOOD	VITAMINS	CAL	(mg) SOD	PRO	FAT	CARB	CHOL	FATTY ACIDS SAT	UNSAT	CALC	IRON	(mg) POTSM
379	AVERAGE PER SERVING		593	1026				(mg) 114					769
	Ingredients:												
454	1 lb lean ground beef	A B1 B2	812	295	G	F	---	H*	H	L	L	F	1612
110	1 onion, medium-size	A B1 B2 C	40	11	L	L	L	---	---	---	L	L	173
227	1 8-oz can tomato sauce	A B1 B2 C	89	905	L	L	L	---	---	---	L	L	967
15	1 tblspn chili powder	A B1 B2 C	50	236	F	F	G	---	---	---	H	H	150
n/a	1/4 tsp black pepper							--n/a--					
136	1-1/2 cp grated cheddar cheese	A B1 B2 1	542	953	G	H	L	H*	H	L	H	F	112
111	6 corn tortillas**	B1 B2	417	T	L	L	G	--n/a--			G	H	---
227	1 cp pitted ripe chopped olives	A B1t B2t	420	1703	L	F	L	---	T	F	G	F	61
236	1 cp hot water							--0--					
	No Salt - - season at the table individually												
1516	Recipe totals (gms; cal; sod. & potsm.)		2370	4103									3075

METHOD

Brown meat with onions, breaking meat up with a fork; add tomato sauce, chili powder and pepper. Stir and blend thoroughly. Remove from heat. Set oven at 400 F. Spread a little soft margarine on one side of each tortilla. Place tortillas in lightly greased casserole dish, layering first tortillas then meat mixture, cheese and olives. Pour hot water over all and bake 20 – 25 minutes. Yield approximately 4 servings.

** Values for corn tortillas were calculated from Quaker Oaks Instant Masa-Harina, 5-pound package, except sodium which was estimated from item 860, corn flour, U.S.D.A. Handbook No. 8, "Composition of Foods."

* There are 320 milligrams of cholesterol in 454 grams of uncooked, boneless beef and 136 milligrams of cholesterol in 136 grams of cheddar cheese, as calculated from U.S.D.A. Handbook No. 8, pg. 146, items 1b and 5 respectively. Total 456 milligrams divided by yield of 4 equals 114 average milligrams of cholesterol per serving.

. . . .

NEBRASKA RED SNACK RAREBIT

F=Fair; G=Good; H=High; L=Low; t or T = trace; n/a = no information available; dashes = zero or unmeasurable

GRAM WT.	FOOD	VITAMINS	CAL	(mg) SOD	PRO	FAT	CARB	CHOL (mg)	FATTY ACIDS SAT	UNSAT	CALC	IRON	(mg) POTSM
128	AVERAGE PER SERVING		278	631				100					119
	Ingredients:												
227	1/2 lb sharp cheddar cheese	A B1 B2	902	1588	G	H	L	H*	H	L	H	F	186
---	1/4 tsp dry mustard	-------						--n/a--					-------
n/a	1/2 tsp garlic salt	-------						--n/a--					-------
n/a	1/2 tsp onion seasoning	-------						--n/a--					-------
245	1 cp tomato soup (1 can)	A B1 B2 C	90	970	L	L	F	---	---	---	F	L	230
50	1 egg, slightly beaten	A B1 B2	75	61	F	F	L	H*	H	L	F	F	65
115	5 slices toast	A^t B1 B2 C^t	325	535	F	L	G	---	---	---	F	F	114
637	Recipe totals (gms; cal; sod. & potsm.)		1392	3154									595

NOTE Inasmuch as there are 631 milligrams of sodium per serving, no salt has been included in the ingredients, also, there is sodium in garlic salt but no information was available on the amount.

METHOD

Shred or cut cheese in small pieces and melt in double boiler over hot water. Heat soup, as seasonings then the melted cheese gradually, stirring constantly. Add the beaten egg slowly and continue to heat and stir for 3 or 4 minutes. Serve hot on toast (or crisp crackers). Yield approximately 5 servings.

*   There are 227 milligrams of cholesterol in 227 grams of cheddar cheese and 275 milligrams of cholesterol in 50 grams of whole egg as calculated from U.S.D.A. Handbook No. 8, pg. 146, items 5 and 12 respectively. Total 502 milligrams divided by yield of 5 equals 100 average milligrams of cholesterol per serving.

. . . .

TACO—CHEESE CASSEROLE

F=Fair; G=Good; H=High; L=Low; t or T = trace; n/a = no information available; dashes = zero or unmeasurable

GRAM WT.	FOOD	VITAMINS	CAL	(mg) SOD	PRO	FAT	CARB	CHOL	FATTY ACIDS SAT	FATTY ACIDS UNSAT	CALC	IRON	(mg) POTSM
241	AVERAGE PER SERVING		467	656				(mg) 91					667
	Ingredients:												
454	1 lb lean ground beef	A B1 B2	812	295	G	F	---	H*	H	L	L	F	1612
75	1/2 cp chopped onion	A B1 B2 C	25	7	L	L	L	---	---	---	L	L	118
454	2 (8 oz.) cans tomato sauce	A B1 B2 C	177	1810	L	L	L	---	---	---	L	L	1934
15	1 tblspn chili powder	A B1 B2 C	50	236	F	F	G	---	---	---	H	H	150
222	12 corn tortillas**	B1 B2	834	T	L	L	G	--------n/a--------			G	H	---
227	2-1/2 cp grated or shredded ched-dar or jack cheese (8 ozs.)	A B1 B2	902	1588	G	H	L	H*	H	L	H	F	186
1447	Recipe totals (gms; cal; sod. & potsm.)		2800	3936									4000

METHOD

Brown the meat in a frying pan, breaking it up with a fork as it cooks. Add chopped onion, stir in tomato sauce and chili powder. Cut tortillas in halves. Alternate layers of sauce, tortillas and cheese in a 1-1/2 quart casserole. Bake at 325 F. about 30 minutes. Season at the table. Yield approximately 6 servings.

* There are 320 milligrams of cholesterol in 454 grams of boneless beef, and 277 milligrams of cholesterol in 227 grams of cheddar cheese, as calculated from U.S.D.A. Handbook No. 8, pg. 146 items 1b and 5 respectively. Total 547 milligrams divided by yield of 6 equals 91 average milligrams of cholesterol per serving.

** Corn tortillas   nutritive information was calculated from Quaker Oats Instant Masa-Harina, 5-pound package, except sodium which was estimated from item 860, corn flour, U.S.D.A. Handbook No. 8, "Composition of Foods."

. . . .

WELSH RAREBIT

F=Fair; G=Good; H=High; L=Low; t or T = trace; n/a = no information available; dashes = zero or unmeasurable

GRAM WT.	FOOD	VITAMINS	CAL	(mg) SOD	PRO	FAT	CARB	CHOL	FATTY ACIDS SAT	UNSAT	CALC	IRON	(mg) POTSM
178	AVERAGE PER SERVING		526	888				(mg) 184					193
	Ingredients:												
454	1 lb cheddar cheese, sharp, grated, about 5 cp	A B1 B2	1805	3175	G	H	L	H*	H	L	H	F	372
14	1 tblspn margarine	A D	100	139	L	H	T	---	L	H	L	---	3
5	1 tsp prepared mustard	---	4	63	L	L	L	---	---	---	F	F	7
3	1 tsp cornstarch	---	11	---	L	T	H	---	---	---	---	---	---
185	3/4 cp 2% low-fat milk	A B1 B2 C	110	113	H	L	H	L*	L	L	H	L	324
50	1 egg, slightly beaten	A B1 B2	75	61	F	F	L	H*	H	L	F	F	65
n/a	1 tblspn Worchestershire sauce	--n/a--											
711	Recipe totals (gms; cal; sod. & potsm.)		2105	3551									771

METHOD

In the top of a double boiler, over boiling water, melt the cheese and margarine. Mix the cornstarch and mustard together with a little milk and add with the remaining ingredients. Blend well. Cook until thickened. Serve on toast or crisp crackers. Yield   about 4 servings.

*   There are 455 milligrams of cholesterol in 455 grams of cheddar cheese, 275 milligrams of cholesterol in 50 grams of whole egg, and 6 milligrams of cholesterol in 185 grams of fluid skim milk, as calculated from U.S.D.A. Handbook No. 8, pg. 146, items 5, 12 and 29 respectively. Total 736 milligrams divided by yield of 4 equals 184 average milligrams of cholesterol per serving.

. . . .

A LITTLE SOMETHING ABOUT EGGS

Long before supermarkets, with their extensive system of mechanically refrigerated cases, came into existence, food supplies in communities were purchased from "corner grocery" stores which were usually located within walking distance of the surrounding neighborhoods.

In these stores, fresh meats, stone crocks of fresh-churned country butter and glass bottles of milk and cream were kept cool in huge wooden ice boxes which were stocked with hundreds of pounds of ice daily, but eggs were sold from baskets, or small wicker tubs that stood on counters, and were carried home in paper sacks. There were no fancy styrofoam cartons in those days; no stringent regulations imposed on egg producers; and no guarantee that the eggs were fresh.

Consequently, housewives often found one or two out of a dozen that were either rotten, or already occupied by an unborn chick. To prevent this rather abruptly revolting experience, housewives began testing eggs for freshness, setting the bad ones aside for refunds from the grocer. Some of these tests are as follows:

1.   Place an egg in a full glass of water; if it falls to the bottom and lays on it's side, it's fresh.

    a.   If the egg rises slightly at the large end, it is somewhat stale.

    b.   If it stands on end and floats, it is very stale.

2.   If it rattles when it is shaken, it is stale.

3.   Freshness was also determined by the appearance of the shell: if fresh, the shell was thought to have a "bloom;" if stale, a shiny shell.

Today, freshness of eggs is more or less taken for granted. Over the last few decades, housewives have only to bring them home from the store and put them in the refrigerator. However, eggs should still be checked -- at the store. The carton should be opened and if any are cracked, these should be given to the clerk for replacement. Cracked eggs can become lethal with salmonella bacteria. If an egg is cracked at home, it should be used as soon as possible.

DO NOT WASH EGGS   Although nature provides a protective coating which washing destroys, conscientious egg producers now make the egg safer than the hen is capable of doing. Eggs are washed, rinsed and sprayed with mineral oil which seals egg pores. Bacteria cannot penetrate this seal and eggs stay fresh. The membrane inside the shell also helps to protect the egg from bacteria.

Neither the taste nor the nutritional value of eggs is affected by the color of their shells. This indicates the breed of chickens that laid them, such as: white eggs come from White Leghorns; brown eggs from Rhode Island Red Chickens, etc.

The average chicken egg white measures about 2 tablespoons (or 1 ounce). A cup of whites usually requires from 8 to 11 eggs while a cup of egg yolks requires from 12 to 14 eggs.

The white of an egg (called albumin) contains a small amount of sodium, but it is a poor source of fat and carbohydrate, has no cholesterol and contains no saturated or unsaturated fatty acids. However, it is a good source of protein, and has only 15 calories.

The yellow part of the egg (or yolk) is low in sodium content, but is high in cholesterol, saturated fatty acids and contains a trace of unsaturated fatty acids. It is good in fat and poor in carbohydrate and fair in protein. The average yolk contains about 60 calories.

HOW TO SEPARATE EGGS

In many recipes, it is necessary to separate the whites of eggs from the yolks (as in fluffy omelets, white cakes, boiled icing, meringues, etc.). This can be done in several ways.

1. To separate eggs easier, use them direct from the refrigerator. If you're doing this for the first time, it's a good idea to work over two dishes in the sink -- a sauce dish for the yolks, a bowl for the whites in which they will be whipped.

    Hold an egg firmly in the right hand, small top up, and crack it near the middle by rapping it sharply against the inside surface of the sink hard enough to break the shell cleanly. Then, still holding it upright to prevent the contents from spilling, transfer it quickly to the bowl for the whites and lift off the top part of the shell carefully. After the white has drained off, empty the contents of the bottom into the top part of the shell, carefully to avoid breaking the yolk. Continue to juggle the contents of both shell halves until all of the white is in the bowl, then empty the yolk into the sauce dish. Should some of the yolk get into the whites, remove it with a paper towel, or a cloth wrung out in warm water, or use a piece of egg shell, because the whites will not whip to stiff peaks if they contain yolk.

2. Our grandmothers separated eggs by cracking them into a dish and very carefully lifting the yolk out with the fingers.

3. Another way is to place a slotted spoon into a bowl, breaking an egg over it, then lifting the spoon carefully, keeping it level. The whites drop through the slots in the spoon, leaving the yolk intact.

    Make a hole in the small end of the egg, let the white run out and leave the yolk in the shell until needed. However, such yolks should either be used at once, because of the danger of salmonella, by gently heating them in water until set then refrigerated and used as garnishes for salads, or mixed with mayonnaise and used for egg sandwiches. Raw yolks can be used in custards with one whole egg and one yolk to 1 cup of milk and also in sauces and soups. Unused whites can be used for thickening sauces.

HOW TO COOK EGGS

The term HARD-BOILED eggs, or SOFT-BOILED eggs are misnomers because eggs should never be boiled. This toughens their texture and some of their food value can be lost. Eggs should be coddled, which means cooking them at temperatures less than boiling. Therefore, SOFT-COOKED or HARD-COOKED means they are heated until the whites are set (and yolks). Soft-cooked eggs are heated in hot water just long enough to coagulate (or set) the whites and yolks to the desired consistency.

To cook eggs hard -- Place them in a small, deep saucepan, cover them with cold water and a tight lid. Heat slowly to the boiling point then reduce heat and simmer from 8 to 10 minutes. Remove pan from the fire, drain hot water off, run cold water over the eggs and peal at once, cracking the ends first which makes them easier to peel, or store eggs a short time in the refrigerator unshelled.

To cook eggs soft -- Place them in a small, deep saucepan, cover with cold water and a tight lid. Heat slowly to the boiling point, then reduce heat and simmer 1 minute or 2 to 3 minutes, depending upon the degree of softness desired. Remove pan from the fire, drain, run cold water over eggs to stop the cooking process and serve at once.

Poached eggs -- Although regular poaching pans are available on the market for this purpose, a frying pan or shallow utensil can be used. Fill the pan with water to a depth of at least 1" (enough water to completely cover the eggs). Bring to the boiling point, but do not boil. Carefully slip eggs, one at a time, into the simmering water, cover and cook until whites are firm and yolks are set, out not hard (unless desired), or with a long-handled spoon, baste water over the egg yolks until a white film appears. Turn off the heat. Remove eggs with a slotted spoon or pancake turner, being careful that they do not slip off, and place on a slice of dry, or buttered toast (on a warm plate). For decoration, sprinkle with a few dried parsley flakes or a dash of paprika.

Poached eggs may be served with bacon, ham or sausage, or on corned-beef hash rounds, also in clear soups, or Welsh Rarebit, or spinach, or on toasted English muffin rounds.

Another method of poaching eggs is to separate the whites from the yolks. Beat the whites until stiff then spoon them into custard cups that have been greased with a little margarine. Drop a yolk in the center of the whites. Set the dishes in hot water until the eggs are set. Garnish with a little margarine, parsley flakes or paprika or grated cheese and serve in the ramekins.

Fried eggs -- In a frying pan, melt about 2 tablespoons of margarine (slowly so it doesn't burn). Break the eggs in a sauce dish (one at a time) and gently slip each one into the pan. If cooked uncovered, baste the eggs by spooning some of the melted shortening over them. If covered, cook until the whites are set and the yolks have a white film over them. Cook slowly. Use a pancake turner to remove the eggs to a warm plate or platter. Garnish if desired.

Baked eggs -- Preheat the oven to 300 F. Melt 1 teaspoon margarine into individual baking dishes (Pyrex custard cups or other individual ramekins are ideal for this purpose.) Break 1 or 2 eggs in each dish. Bake in slow oven until eggs are set but not hard. Serve in the same dishes.

Shirred -- Use small ramekins, such as custard cups or egg-shirrers. Grease each dish, put in a layer of buttered crumbs, break an egg over them and cover with crumbs. Bake in slow oven until eggs are set and crumbs are browned. Season at the table.

Other variations of baked eggs

1.   Partially cook strips of bacon, drain on paper towels. Arrange 1 or 2 strips around the inside of individual baking dishes. Break an egg into each bacon ring. Bake at 350 F. until set but not hard. Serve in the same dishes and season at the table.

2.   Grease small baking dishes and measure about 2 tablespoons of margarine in each one. Add a poached egg. Cover with 1 tablespoon of grated cheddar cheese and bake at 450 — 500 F. until cheese is browned.

3.   Poach yolks at slow simmer until cooked. Beat the whites very stiff. Moisten the edges of unbuttered toast and lift the egg yolks carefully, using a slotted spoon or pancake turner, and place them on the slices of toast. Spread the egg whites around each yolk and brown in at 350 F. oven.

Deviled eggs -- Hard-cook eggs, allowing at least 1 per person. Cool eggs in cold water, drain, then peel off shells. Cut the eggs either crosswise of lengthwise, carefully to avoid tearing the whites. Remove yolks to a bowl. Mash them with a fork, then mix with enough prepared mustard (about 1 teaspoonful to 3 egg yolks) and enough mayonnaise to moisten -- start with a teaspoonful and increase. Add a little vinegar and mix well. Yolks should be fluffy, not runny. Stuff the whites with the yolk mixture, garnish each with paprika and parsley flakes. (See recipe in this chapter).

If using the deviled eggs as garnish in a salad plate, they will " stay put" easier if a very thin slice is carefully pared off the bottom of the whites. If eggs are to be taken on a picnic, put two halves together and wrap in airtight plastic, twist each end securely and refrigerate until the last moment. If using for a salad or meal extender, refrigerate eggs, cooked but not shelled, and prepare at the last possible moment, or prepare 30 minutes before serving and store in an airtight container.

. . . .

F=Fair; G=Good; H=High; L=Low; t or T = trace; n/a = no information available; dashes = zero or unmeasurable

GRAM WT.	FOOD	VITAMINS	CAL	(mg) SOD	PRO	FAT	CARB	CHOL	FATTY ACIDS SAT	FATTY ACIDS UNSAT	CALC	IRON	(mg) POTSM
166	AVERAGE PER SERVING		206	337				(mg) 275					276
	Ingredients:												
28	2 tblspn margarine	A D	200	279	L	H	F	---	L	G	L	---	6
15	1/4 medium green pepper, chopped	A B1 B2 C	5	2	L	L	L	---	---	---	L	L	32
18	2 tblspn cornstarch	---	68	---	L	T	H	---	---	---	---	---	---
482	2 cp tomatoes, canned	A B1 B2 C	100	626	L	L	L	---	---	---	L	L	1046
3	1/2 tsp chili powder	A B1 B2 C	8	39	F	F	G	---	---	---	H	H	30
2	1/2 tsp granulated sugar	---	8	T	---	---	H	---	---	---	---	L	---
8	1 tblspn minced green onion	A B1 B2 C	3	T	L	L	F	---	---	---	F	L	18
---	dash red pepper	A B1 B2 C	2	9	F	F	G	---	---	---	H	H	---
300	6 poached eggs	A B1 B2	450	366	F	F	L	H*	H	L	F	F	387
138	6 slices toast	A^t B1 B2 C^t	390	702	F	L	G	---	---	---	F	F	138
994	Recipe totals (gms; cal; sod. & potsm.)		1234	2023									1657

METHOD

Melt margarine slowly in a saucepan. Add chopped green pepper and cook and stir until soft. Combine cornstarch with about 1/2 cup of tomatoes, stir until smooth then add to the remaining tomatoes and stir in chili powder, sugar, green onion and red pepper. Add to green pepper and cook and stir until sauce is clear and thick. Poach eggs, arrange on toast then pour sauce over all. Yield 6 servings.

NOTE   This sauce is also good over poached eggs on thin pancakes.

* There are 1650 milligrams of cholesterol in 300 grams of whole egg as calculated from U.S.D.A. Handbook No. 8, pg. 146, item 12.   Total 1650 milligrams divided by yield of 6 equals 275 average milligrams of cholesterol per serving.

. . . .

DEVILED EGGS

F=Fair; G=Good; H=High; L=Low; t or T = trace; n/a = no information available;   dashes = zero or unmeasurable

GRAM WT.	FOOD	VITAMINS	CAL	(mg) SOD	PRO	FAT	CARB	CHOL	FATTY ACIDS SAT	UNSAT	CALC	IRON	(mg) POTSM
56	AVERAGE PER EGG		101	98				(mg) 275					69
	Ingredients:												
200	4 hard-cooked eggs	A B1 B2	300	244	F	F	L	H*	H	L	F	F	260
5	1 tsp vinegar	---	T	T	---	L	---	---	---	---	L	L	5
5	1 tsp prepared mustard	---	4	63	L	L	L	---	---	---	F	F	7
14	1 tblspn mayonnaise	A B1^t B2	100	84	T	H	T	n/a	G	G	F	L	5
	No salt -- season at the table												
224	Recipe totals (gms; cal; sod. & potsm.)		404	391									277

METHOD

Hard cook the eggs, immerse in cold water, crack each end then peel, washing off any bits of shell. Cut the eggs in half, either lengthwise or crosswise and scoop out the yolks carefully to avoid breaking the whites. (Sometimes, by gently squeezing the whites, the yolks will pop out by themselves). If yolks are stubborn, dislodge with the tip of a paring knife. Set the whites aside, mash the yolks with a fork, add the vinegar, mustard and mayonnaise. A little green onion, minced very fine, may also be added, if desired. Fill the whites with the yolk mixture, top with a bit of dried parsley flakes and a sprinkle of paprika, or a few strips of pimiento. To prevent eggs from slipping around on the place, pare a thin slice off the bottom.

*   There are 1100 milligrams of cholesterol in 200 grams of whole egg, as calculated from U.S D.A. Handbook No. 8, pg. 146, item 12. Total 1100 milligrams divided by yield of 4 equals 275 average milligrams of cholesterol per serving.

. . . .

EGG FOO YUNG

F=Fair; G=Good; H=High; L=Low; t or T = trace; n/a = no information available; dashes = zero or unmeasurable

GRAM WT.	FOOD	VITAMINS	CAL	(mg) SOD	PRO	FAT	CARB	CHOL	FATTY ACIDS SAT	UNSAT	CALC	IRON	(mg) POTSM
180	AVERAGE PER SERVING with sauce		281	556				(mg) 252					250
	Ingredients:												
56	4 tblspn corn or peanut oil	---	500	---	---	H	---	---	T	H	---	---	---
28	2 tblspn margarine	A D	200	279	L	H	L	---	L	H	L	---	6
38	4 tblspn minced onion	A B1 B2 C	13	4	L	L	L	---	---	---	L	L	60
21	1-1/2 tblspn soy sauce	B1 B2	14	1557	L	L	L	---	---	---	F	F	77
161	1-1/2 cp bean sprouts, drained	A B1 B2 C	74	---	L	L	L	---	---	---	F	L	---
250	5 eggs, well beaten	A B1 B2	375	305	F	F	L	H*	H	L	F	F	323
227	1 cp white meat of chicken, cooked, diced	A B1 B2	447	154	H	L	O	L*	L	G	L	F	985
	SAUCE Chinese												
14	1-1/2 tblspn cornstarch	---	51	---	L	T	H	---	---	---	---	---	---
30	2 tblspn cold water	--O--											
240	1 cp chicken broth	--n/a--											
1	1/4 tsp sugar	---	4	---	---	---	H	---	---	---	---	L	---
14	1 tblspn soy sauce	B1 B2	10	1038	L	L	L	---	---	---	F	F	51
1080	Recipe totals (gms; cal; sod. & potsm.)		1688	3337									1502

METHOD

Melt margarine in a frying pan, add oil and heat slowly to prevent burning. Combine onion, soy sauce, bean sprouts, well beaten eggs and white meat of chicken in a medium-size mixing bowl and stir gently until well blended. Drop from large spoon into the hot fat. Brown on one side, turn and brown on the other. Serve hot with Chinese Sauce. Yield 6 servings.

SAUCE

Blend the cornstarch and water until smooth. Stir mixture slowly into boiling chicken broth and continue to cook and stir 5 minutes then add the sugar and soy sauce.

* There are 1375 milligrams of cholesterol in 250 grams of whole egg and 136 milligrams of cholesterol in 227 grams of raw chicken meat (no figure for cooked meat was available). Total milligrams of cholesterol are 1511, divided by 6 servings equals 252 average milligrams of cholesterol in each serving, as calculated from U.S.D.A. Handbook No. 8, pg. 146, items 10 and 12 respectively.

. . . .

SCRAMBLED EGGS

F=Fair; G=Good; H=High; L=Low; t or T = trace; n/a = no information available; dashes = zero or unmeasurable

GRAM WT.	FOOD	VITAMINS	CAL	(mg) SOD	PRO	FAT	CARB	CHOL	FATTY ACIDS SAT	UNSAT	CALC	IRON	(mg) POTSM
118	AVERAGE PER SERVING		207	210				(mg) 459					153
	Ingredients:												
250	5 eggs, beaten	A B1 B2	375	305	F	F	L	H*	H	L	F	F	323
75	5 tblspn 2% low-fat milk	A B1 B2 C	46	47	H	L	H	L*	L	L	H	L	131
28	2 tblspn margarine	A D	200	279	L	H	L	---	L	H	L	---	6
	No salt -- season at the table individually												
353	Recipe totals (gms; cal; sod. & potsm.)		621	631									460

METHOD

Beat eggs slightly, add milk and blend. Melt the margarine in a frying pan slowly to avoid burning, and tip the pan until shortening covers the entire bottom surface. Add the eggs and cook slowly a few minutes without stirring, or until eggs begin to set underneath. With a pancake turner, lift the edges of the egg mixture all around the pan, then turn the pancake turner over and run the blade in a scraping motion from one side of the pan to the other. This will fluff the eggs. Continue scraping and fluffing until eggs are almost set (moist, not dry). Serve at once. Yield 3 generous servings.

Variate scrambled eggs with crisp bacon crumbled into eggs just before serving, or chopped ham or sausage; or cook chopped green pepper and 1 or 2 chopped green onions together a few minutes before adding the eggs and sprinkle some grated cheese over the eggs a few minutes before serving.

* There are 1375 milligrams of cholesterol in 250 grams of whole egg and 2 milligrams of cholesterol in 75 grams of low-fat milk, as calculated from U.S.D.A. Handbook No. 8, pg. 146, items 12 and 29 respectively. Total 1377 milligrams divided by yield of 3 equals 459 milligrams of cholesterol per serving.

. . . .

F=Fair; G=Good; H=High; L=Low; t or T = trace; n/a = no information available; dashes = zero or unmeasurable

GRAM WT.	FOOD	VITAMINS	CAL	(mg) SOD	PRO	FAT	CARB	CHOL	FATTY ACIDS SAT	UNSAT	CALC	IRON	(mg) POTSM
163	AVERAGE PER 5 OZ. SERVING		154	106				(mg) 141					248
	Ingredients:												
100	2 eggs, separated	A B1 B2	150	122	F	F	L	H*	H	L	F	F	129
492	2 cp 2% low-fat milk	A B1 B2 C	290	300	H	L	H	L*	L	L	H	L	861
18	1-1/2 tblspn sugar	---	72	T	---	---	H	---	---	---	---	L	1
42	3 tblspn blended whiskey	---	105	1	---	---	T	---	---	---	---	---	1
---	dash nutmeg in each serving							--n/a--					
652	Recipe totals (gms; cal; sod. & potsm.)		617	423									992

METHOD

Beat the egg whites until stiff; beat the egg yolks until lemon-colored, add the sugar and stir, then add the milk slowly, stirring until well blended. Add whiskey, mix well. Fold yolk mixture into stiffly beaten egg whites. Fill cups or glasses, sprinkle tops with nutmeg and serve. Yield 4 five ounce servings.

* There are 550 milligrams of cholesterol in 100 grams of whole egg and 15 milligrams of cholesterol in 492 grams of low-fat milk, as calculated in U.S.D.A. Handbook No. 8, pg. 146, items 12 and 29 respectively. Total 565 milligrams divided by yield of 4 equals 141 average milligrams of cholesterol per serving.

. . . .

FLUFFY OMELET

F=Fair; G=Good; H=High; L=Low; t or T = trace; n/a = no information available; dashes = zero or unmeasurable

GRAM WT.	FOOD	VITAMINS	CAL	(mg) SOD	PRO	FAT	CARB	CHOL	FATTY ACIDS SAT	UNSAT	CALC	IRON	(mg) POTSM
118	AVERAGE PER SERVING		207	210				(mg) 459					153
250	Ingredients: 5 eggs, separated	A B1 B2	375	305	F	F	L	H*	H	L	F	F	323
75	5 tblspn 2% low-fat milk	A B1 B2 C	46	47	H	F	G	L*	L	L	H	L	131
28	2 tblspn margarine	A D	200	279	L	H	L	---	L	G	L	---	6
	No salt -- season at the table individually												
353	Recipe totals (gms; cal; sod. & potsm.)		621	631									460

METHOD

Beat the egg whites until stiff but not dry. Set aside. Beat the egg yolks until light yellow then add the milk and mix well. Fold the yolks gently into the whites until well blended. Melt margarine in a heavy, 10" skillet with a lid. Tip the pan until the melted shortening covers the bottom. Do not let the margarine burn. Reduce heat, then pour egg mixture into the pan, tipping it a little to distribute the mixture to all edges, or spread with a spoon. Cover tightly and cook slowly about 5 minutes then lift the lid and check the mixture. If eggs are still wet, cover again and cook a little longer. Remove lid and insert a spatula all around the edge to loosen the mixture, lifting it away from the pan a little. If the omelet comes away from the pan clean, and the bottom of the mixture is firm, but the top still appears uncooked, leave the cover off and continue to cook a few minutes longer. Remove from heat and cut almost through the center. Loosen the edges again and with two pancake turners, or two spatulas, fold the omelet in half and slip onto a warm platter, or cut in thirds and serve on warm, individual plates. Yield 3 servings.

Before folding the omelet in half, variate by sprinkling crumbled, crisp bacon over the top, or chopped ham (cooked leftover ham is very tasty) or spread grated cheese over the top, or pimiento strips; or dabs of jam or jelly. Chopped green onion is also good with this omelet.

* There are 1375 milligrams of cholesterol in 250 grams of whole egg and 2 milligrams of cholesterol in 75 grams of fluid skim milk, as calculated in U.S.D.A. Handbook No. 8, pg. 146, items 5 and 29 respectively. Total 1377 milligrams divided by yield of 3 equals 459 average milligrams of cholesterol per serving.

. . . .

FRENCH OMELET

F=Fair; G=Good; H=High; L=Low; t or T = trace; n/a = no information available;   dashes = zero or unmeasurable

GRAM WT.	FOOD	VITAMINS	CAL	(mg) SOD	PRO	FAT	CARB	CHOL	FATTY ACIDS SAT	UNSAT	CALC	IRON	(mg) POTSM
118	AVERAGE PER SERVING, plain		207	210				(mg) 459					153
	Ingredients:												
250	5 eggs, beaten	A B1 B2	375	305	F	F	L	H*	H	L	F	F	323
75	5 tblspn 2% low-fat milk	A B1 B2 C	46	47	H	L	H	L*	L	L	H	L	131
28	2 tblspn margarine	A D	200	279	T	H	T	---	L	H	F	---	6
	No salt - - season at the table individually												
353	Recipe totals (gms; cal; sod. & potsm.)		621	631									460

METHOD

Beat the eggs, add the milk and stir until well blended but not foamy. Set aside. Melt margarine in a heavy frying pan slowly to prevent burning. Pour in egg mixture and cook at low heat until it begins to thicken around the edges. With a spatula, lift the edges all around the pan which will allow any uncooked mixture to run underneath. Tip the pan to hurry the cooking, then let the mixture cook until set. Cut the omelet at the center, but not all the way through then lift one side and flip it over on the other half. Divide in thirds and serve on heated plates.

Variations   After the egg mixture has been poured into the pan, sprinkle some chopped green onion over it, distributing it evenly, then add some strips of green pepper and some grated cheese. The cheese will melt and look like part of the runny eggs, but when folded over will blend into the omelet and make it moist. Omelet is also good with crumbled, crisp bacon or chopped ham. Or spread omelet with 1/2 cup creole sauce (see recipe below), roll the omelet, arrange on a warm platter or individual serving plate and pour additional sauce over the top; or spread omelet with creamed chicken, fish or other seafood, thin slices of roast beef, mushrooms or vegetables and then roll. A thin white sauce or any left over gravy is also good over the French omelet.

*   There are 1375 milligrams of cholesterol in 250 grams of whole egg and 2 milligrams of cholesterol in 75 grams of fluid skim milk, as calculated in U.S.D.A. Handbook No. 8, pg. 146, items 5 and 29 respectively. Total 1377 milligrams divided by yield of 3 equals 459 average milligrams of cholesterol per serving.

. . . .

CREOLE SAUCE

F=Fair; G=Good; H=High; L=Low; t or T = trace; n/a = no information available; dashes = zero or unmeasurable

GRAM WT.	FOOD	VITAMINS	CAL	(mg) SOD	PRO	FAT	CARB	CHOL	FATTY ACIDS SAT	UNSAT	CALC	IRON	(mg) POTSM
140	**AVERAGE PER SERVING**		125	537									389
	Ingredients:												
28	2 tblspn margarine	A D	200	278	L	H	L	---	L	H	L	---	6
8	1 tblspn fine chopped green onion	A^t B1 B2 C	4	T	L	L	F	---	---	---	F	L	18
20	2 tblspn fine chopped green pepper	A B1 B2 C	4	2	L	L	L	---	---	---	L	L	49
14	1-1/2 tblspn cornstarch	---	51	---	L	T	H	---	---	---	---	---	---
227	1 can tomato sauce (8 oz.)	A B1 B2 C	89	905	L	L	L	---	---	---	L	L	967
100	1/2 cup beef bouillon	---	13	382	L	---	L	------- n/a --------			T	L	32
20	1/2 stalk celery, chopped fine	A B1 B2 C	3	25	L	L	L	---	---	---	F	L	68
1	1/4 tsp chili powder	A B1 B2 C	4	18	F	F	G	---	---	---	H	H	15
2	1 small clove fresh garlic	A^t B1 B2 C	7	T	L	L	F	---	---	---	L	F	11
420	Recipe totals (gms; cal; sod. & potsm.)		375	1610									1166

METHOD

Melt margarine in a saucepan, then saute onion and green pepper about 5 minutes. Blend cornstarch with a little tomato sauce, add to the rest of the tomato sauce and beef bouillon, then add the celery, garlic and chili powder. Heat to boiling, stirring constantly until sauce is slightly thickened. This will make about 1-1/2 cups of sauce. Serve over omelets, spaghetti, rice or fish. Yield about 3 servings.

. . . .

F=Fair; G=Good; H=High; L=Low; t or T = trace; n/a = no information available; dashes = zero or unmeasurable

GRAM WT.	FOOD	VITAMINS	CAL	(mg) SOD	PRO	FAT	CARB	CHOL	FATTY ACIDS SAT	UNSAT	CALC	IRON	(mg) POTSM
115	AVERAGE PER SERVING		118	81				(mg) 140					176
	Ingredients:												
492	2 cp 2% low-fat milk	A B1 B2 C	290	300	H	L	H	L*	L	L	H	L	861
150	3 eggs	A B1 B2	225	183	F	F	L	H*	H	L	F	F	194
48	4 tblspn granulated sugar	---	192	T	---	---	H	---	---	---	---	L	1
n/a	1 tsp vanilla							---n/a---					
n/a	1/2 tsp nutmeg							---n/a---					
690	Recipe totals (gms; cal; sod. & potsm.)		707	483									1056

METHOD

Scald the milk. Mix eggs, sugar and flavoring together until thoroughly blended then pour milk slowly in the mixture, stirring until combined. Pour into custard cups or a baking dish. Sprinkle with nutmeg. Set dish in a pan of hot water and bake at 300 F. until a dinner knife blade inserted in the center comes out clean. Yield 6 servings. (For soft custard, see soft custard sauce in this chapter).

* There are 825 milligrams of cholesterol in 150 grams of whole egg and 15 milligrams of cholesterol in 492 grams of fluid skim milk, as calculated in U.S.D.A. Handbook No. 8, pg. 146, items 12 and 29 respectively. Total 840 milligrams divided by yield of 6 servings equals 140 average milligrams of cholesterol per serving.

. . . .

SOFT CUSTARD SAUCE (OR PUDDING)

F=Fair; G=Good; H=High; L=Low; t or T = trace; n/a = no information available; dashes = zero or unmeasurable

GRAM WT.	FOOD	VITAMINS	CAL	(mg) SOD	PRO	FAT	CARB	CHOL	FATTY ACIDS SAT	UNSAT	CALC	IRON	(mg) POTSM
119	AVERAGE PER SERVING		116	111				(mg) 58					185
	Ingredients:												
492	2 cp 2% low-fat milk	A B1 B2 C	290	300	H	L	H	L*	L	L	H	L	861
50	1 egg, slightly beaten	A B1 B2	75	61	F	F	L	H*	H	L	F	F	65
6	2 tsp cornstarch	---	22	---	L	T	H	---	---	---	---	---	---
48	4 tblspn granulated sugar	---	192	----	---	---	H	H	---	---	---	---	L	1
1	dash salt (1/8 tsp)	---	---	193	---	---	---	---	---	---	G	---	---
n/a	1 tsp vanilla							-n/a-					
n/a	nutmeg							-n/a-					
597	Recipe totals (gms; cal; sod. & potsm.)		579	554									927

METHOD

Scald milk in top of double boiler over boiling water. Beat egg slightly, add cornstarch mixed with sugar and salt; add hot milk to sugar and egg mixture, slowly, stirring until well blended. Return to top of double boiler and cook and stir until custard coats the spoon. Remove from heat, add vanilla and mix until thoroughly combined. Pour into individual serving dishes, or a small casserole-type dish. If desired, sprinkle with nutmeg. Chill in the refrigerator, covered. Serve plain, or over fresh or canned fruit. Add a dab of jam or jelly on top. Yield about 4 or 5 servings.

*   There are 275 milligrams of cholesterol in 50 grams of whole egg and 3 milligrams of cholesterol in 100 grams of skim milk, as calculated in U.S.D.A. Handbook No. 8, pg. 146, items 12 and 29 respectively. Total 290 milligrams divided by yield of 5 equals 58 average milligrams of cholesterol per serving.

. . . .

FLOATING ISLAND

F=Fair; G=Good; H=High; L=Low; t or T = trace; n/a = no information available; dashes = zero or unmeasurable

GRAM WT.	FOOD	VITAMINS	CAL	(mg) SOD	PRO	FAT	CARB	CHOL (mg)	FATTY ACIDS SAT	UNSAT	CALC	IRON	(mg) POTSM
143	AVERAGE PER SERVING		161	97				168					211
	Ingredients:												
492	2 cp 2% low-fat milk	A B1 B2 C	290	300	H	L	H	L*	L	L	H	L	861
150	3 eggs	A B1 B2	225	183	F	F	L	H*	H	L	F	F	194
72	6 tblspn granulated sugar	---	288	T	---	---	H	---	---	---	---	L	2
n/a	1 tsp vanilla	------------						-n/a-					------
714	Recipe totals (gms; cal; sod. & potsm.)		803	483									1057

METHOD

Scald milk in top of a double boiler over boiling water. Beat 1 whole egg with 2 egg yolks and the sugar together. Set the 2 egg whites aside. Add hot milk to the egg and sugar mixture, slowly, blending well. Return mixture to double boiler and cook over hot water, stirring constantly until it coats the spoon. Add vanilla, blend in thoroughly. Remove from heat. Beat the 2 egg whites until stiff. Add a little powdered sugar if desired. Divide in half and set one half aside. Fold the other half of the meringue gently into custard. It will look lumpy. Spoon into custard cups or sauce dishes, spoon remaining meringue on top and decorate with a bit of jelly, jam, or candied pineapple or cherries. Chill until served. Yield about 5 servings.

*   There are 825 milligrams of cholesterol in 150 grams of whole egg and 15 milligrams in 492 grams of fluid milk, as calculated in U.S.D.A. Handbook No. 8, pg. 146, items 12 and 29 respectively. Total 840 milligrams divided by yield of 5 equals 168 average milligrams of cholesterol per serving.

. . . .

No. 1 (Thin, used in cream soups, light sauces)	No. 2 (Medium, gravies, sauces, scalloped dishes)	No. 3 (Thick, for croquetts, souffles, cutlets)
1 tblspn of either oil or margarine, or butter or other fat.	2 tblspn oil, or margarine, or butter or other fat.	3 tblspn oil or margarine, or butter or other fat.
1 tblspn flour or 1/2 tblspn cornstarch	2 tblspn flour, or 1 tblspn cornstarch	3 tblspns flour, or 1-1/2 tblspn cornstarch
1 cp 2% low-fat milk	1 cp 2% low-fat milk	1 cp 2% low-fat milk
Season at the table	Season at the table	Season at the table

METHOD

Blend flour (or cornstarch) with the shortening until smooth. Add milk slowly, stirring constantly until it reaches the boiling point. Reduce heat, cook 3 minutes longer. Keep hot over hot water, and cover tightly to prevent formation of film.

NOTE   Another method is to beat the milk slowly so it doesn't scorch, and in the meantime, blend the flour, or cornstarch together with the oil, margarine of other fat. Add a little hot milk to this mixture, slowly, so it doesn't lump, add a little more milk, stir in well, then add this mixture to the heated milk and stir constantly until sauce thickens.

For twice as much sauce, double the recipes.

. . . .

BAKED ALASKA

F=Fair; G=Good; H=High; L=Low; t or T = trace; n/a = no information available; dashes = zero or unmeasurable

GRAM WT.	FOOD	VITAMINS	CAL	(mg) SOD	PRO	FAT	CARB	CHOL	FATTY ACIDS SAT	UNSAT	CALC	IRON	(mg) POTSM
131	AVERAGE PER SERVING		292	142				(mg) 30					181
	Ingredients:												
198	6 egg whites	B1ᵗ B2	90	288	G	T	T	---	---	---	L	T	276
48	6 tblspn powdered sugar	---	188	T	---	---	H	---	---	---	---	L	1
1064	2 quart brick of ice cream	A B1 B2 C	2055	670	L	F	G	F*	G	L	G	L	1926
790	1 rectangular sponge cake	A B1 B2 Cᵗ	2345	1319	L	L	H	---	---	---	G	L	687
2100	Recipe totals (gms; cal; sod. & potsm.)		4678	2277									2890

METHOD

Preheat oven to 450 F. Place a thick layer of the sponge cake on a board, then beat the egg whites until light, add confectioners' sugar and beat until stiff and dry. Turn the brick of ice cream onto the sponge cake on the board. (Cake should extend 1/2" beyond the ice cream). Cover it completely with the meringue, spreading it smoothly. Sprinkle confectioners' sugar over all. The easy way to do this is to take a fine sieve that has a handle, place some powdered sugar in it and shake over the meringue. Place dessert in a very hot oven to brown. Watch carefully as this takes only a few minutes. Remove from oven, slip onto a platter and serve immediately. Yield will be 12 to 16 servings.

*   There are 479 milligrams of cholesterol in 1064 grams of icecream, as calculated in U.S.D.A. Handbook No. 8, pg. 146, item 19. Total 479 milligrams divided by yield of 16 servings equals 30 average milligrams of cholesterol per serving.

. . . .

VANILLA ICE CREAM

GRAM WT.	FOOD	VITAMINS	CAL	(mg) SOD	PRO	FAT	CARB	CHOL	FATTY ACIDS SAT	UNSAT	CALC	IRON	(mg) POTSM
139	AVERAGE PER (1/8) SERVING		325	52									147
960	Ingredients: (Recipe No. 1) 1 quart thin cream	A B1 B2 C	2020	412	L	F	L	n/a	H	L	H	L	1172
150	3/4 cp granulated sugar	---	578	2	---	---	H	---	---	---	---	L	5
n/a	1-1/2 tblspn vanilla							----n/a----					
1110	Recipe totals (gms; cal; sod. & potsm.)		2598	414									1177

METHOD

Mix ingredients and freeze.   Yield approximately 8 servings

. . . .

GRAM WT.	FOOD	VITAMINS	CAL	(mg) SOD	PRO	FAT	CARB	CHOL	FATTY ACIDS SAT	UNSAT	CALC	IRON	(mg) POTSM
145	AVERAGE PER SERVING		265	130				(mg) 24					176
492	Ingredients: (Recipe No. 2) 2 cp 2% low-fat milk, scalded	A B1 B2 C	290	300	H	L	H	L*	L	L	H	L	861
7	1 tblspn flour	B1 B2	26	---	F	L	G	---	---	---	L	F	7
200	1 cp granulated sugar	---	770	2	---	---	H	---	---	---	---	L	6
50	1 egg, slightly beaten	A B1 B2	75	61	G	G	L	H*	H	L	L	F	65
2	1/2 tsp salt	---	---	785	---	---	---	---	---	---	---	G	---
960	1 quart thin cream	A B1 B2 C	2020	412	L	F	L	n/a	H	L	H	L	1172
28	2 tblspn vanilla							----n/a----					
1739	Recipe totals (gms; cal; sod. & potsm.)		3181	1560									2111

METHOD

Scald the milk; mix flour and sugar together, add slightly beaten egg and salt, then add scalded milk gradually, blending thoroughly. Cook over hot water 20 minutes, stirring constantly at first. When cool, add cream and flavoring then strain and freeze   Yield approximately 12 servings.

* There are 275 milligrams of cholesterol in 50 grams of whole egg and 15 milligrams in 492 grams of 2% low-fat milk, as calculated in U.S.A.D. Handbook No. 8, pg. 146, items 5 and 29 respectively. Total 290 milligrams divided by yield of 12 equals 24 average milligrams of cholesterol per serving. . . . No figures for cholesterol in cream.

. . . .

CHOCOLATE ICE CREAM

F=Fair; G=Good; H=High; L=Low; t or T = trace; n/a = no information available; dashes = zero or unmeasurable

GRAM WT.	FOOD	VITAMINS	CAL	(mg) SOD	PRO	FAT	CARB	CHOL	FATTY ACIDS SAT	UNSAT	CALC	IRON	(mg) POTSM
160	AVERAGE PER SERVING		371	93									177
	Ingredients:												
48	1/2 cp cocoa	B1 B2	176	137	L	L	H	--------n/a-------		L	F	240
59	1/4 cp hot water	---n/a-------------------------------										
960	1 quart thin cream	A B1 B2 C	2020	412	L	F	L	n/a	H	L	H	L	1172
200	1 cp granulated sugar	---	770	2	---	---	H	---	---	---	---	L	6
---	dash salt	---	---	193	---	---	---	---	---	---	G	---	---
14	1 tblspn vanilla	---n/a-------------------------------										
1281	Recipe totals (gms; cal; sod. & potsm.)		2966	744									1418

METHOD

Mix cocoa with hot water gradually, stirring until smooth. Add enough additional water so that mixture pours easily. Add to cream, then add sugar, salt and flavoring. Blend thoroughly. Freeze. Yield about 8 servings.

. . . .

264

ORANGE ICE CREAM

F=Fair; G=Good; H=High; L=Low; t or T = trace; n/a = no information available; dashes = zero or unmeasurable

GRAM WT.	FOOD	VITAMINS	CAL	(mg) SOD	PRO	FAT	CARB	CHOL	FATTY ACIDS SAT	UNSAT	CALC	IRON	(mg) POTSM
134	AVERAGE PER SERVING		244	24									188
	Ingredients:												
238	1 cp heavy cream	A B1 B2 C	840	86	L	G	L	n/a	H	L	F	L	212
240	1 cp light cream	A B1 B2 C	505	103	L	F	L	n/a	H	L	H	L	293
496	2 cp orange juice*	A B1 B2 C	220	4	L	L	F	---	---	---	F	L	992
100	1/2 cp granulated sugar	---	385	1	---	---	H	---	---	---	---	L	3
1074	Recipe totals (gms; cal; sod. & potsm.)		1950	194									1500

METHOD

Combine creams and add slowly to orange juice. Add sugar (add a little more if necessary -- this will depend upon the sweetness or tartness of the orange juice). Stir mixture until well blended, then freeze. Yield about 8 servings.

* Pineapple juice may be substituted for orange juice.

. . . .

STRAWBERRY ICE CREAM

F=Fair; G=Good; H=High; L=Low; t or T = trace; n/a = no information available; dashes = zero or unmeasurable

GRAM WT.	FOOD	VITAMINS	CAL	(mg) SOD	PRO	FAT	CARB	CHOL	FATTY ACIDS SAT	UNSAT	CALC	IRON	(mg) POTSM
203	AVERAGE PER SERVING		399	52									229
	Ingredients:												
596	4 cp fresh strawberries	A B1 B2 C	220	4	L	L	F	---	---	---	G	F	976
400	2 cp granulated sugar	---	1540	4	---	---	H	---	---	---	---	L	12
1440	1-1/2 quarts thin cream	A B1 B2 C	3030	618	L	F	L	n/a	H	L	H	L	1758
2436	Recipe totals (gms; cal; sod. &potsm.)		4790	626									2746

METHOD

Wash and hull berries, sprinkle with sugar and let stand about 2 hours, then mash some of the berries and strain the rest through a sieve, or ricer. Freeze cream to the consistency of mush, gradually add the strained strawberry juice and mashed berries and finish freezing. Yield about 12 servings.

. . . .

FATS, OILS and DRESSINGS

FATS, OILS AND SALAD DRESSINGS

F=Fair; G=Good; H=High; L=Low; t or T = trace; n/a = no information available; dashes = zero or unmeasurable

GRAM WT.	FOOD	VITAMINS	CAL	(mg) SOD	PRO	FAT	CARB	CHOL	FATTY ACIDS SAT	UNSAT	CALC	IRON	(mg) POTSM
	BUTTER -- See Dairy Products												
	FATS, COOKING												
205	Lard, 1 cp	---	1850	---	---	H	---	H	H	L	---	---	---
13	1 tblspn	---	115	---	---	H	---	H	H	L	---	---	---
200	Vegetable fats, 1 cp	---	1770	---	---	H	---	---	G	H	---	---	---
13	1 tblspn	---	110	---	---	H	---	---	F	H	---	---	---
	MARGARINE												
	Regular, 4 sticks per pound												
113	Stick, 1/2 cp	A*	815	1115	L	H	L	---	L	H	L	---	26
14	1 tblspn approximately 1/8 stick	A*	100	138	L	H	T	---	L	H	L	---	3
5	1 Pat 1" square x 1/3" high	A*	35	49	T	H	T	---	L	H	L	---	1
	Whipped, 6 sticks per pound												
76	stick, 1/2 cp	A*	545	750	L	H	L	---	L	H	L	---	17
	soft, 2 tubs per lb. (8 oz. each)												
227	1 tub	A*	1635	2240	L	H	L	---	L	H	L	---	52
	1 tblspn, same as regular above												

(A* Values of Vitamin "A" are based on the average Vitamin "A" content of fortified margarines. Federal specifications for fortified margarine require a minimum of 15,000 International Units of Vitamin "A" per pound, according to U.S.D.A. Handbook No. 8.)

GRAM WT.	FOOD	VITAMINS	CAL	(mg) SOD	PRO	FAT	CARB	CHOL	SAT	UNSAT	CALC	IRON	(mg) POTSM
	OILS, SALAD OR COOKING												
220	corn oil, 1 cp	---	1945	---	---	H	---	---	L	H	---	---	---
14	1 tblspn	---	125	---	---	H	---	---	L	H	---	---	---
	cottonseed, olive oil, peanut oil,												
	safflower oil, the same as corn oil.												
	SALAD DRESSINGS												
15	blue cheese, 1 tblspn	A B1t B2 Ct	75	164	L	G	L	G	H	L	F	L	6
	(also Roquefort dressing)												
	commercial, mayonnaise-types												
15	regular, 1 tblspn	A B1t B2t	65	88	L	F	L	G	H	G	L	T	1
16	special dietary, low calorie,												
	1 tblspn	A B1t B2t	20	19	T	L	L	--------n/a---------			L	T	1

FATS, OILS AND SALAD DRESSINGS

F=Fair; G=Good; H=High; L=Low; t or T = trace; n/a = no information available; dashes = zero or unmeasurable

GRAM WT.	FOOD	VITAMINS	CAL	(mg) SOD	PRO	FAT	CARB	CHOL	FATTY ACIDS SAT	UNSAT	CALC	IRON	(mg) POTSM
	French												
16	regular, 1 tblspn	---	65	219	T	G	L	L	T	H	L	L	13
15	special dietary, low-fat with artificial sweeteners, 1 tblspn	---	T	118	T	T	T	L	T	H	L	L	13
16	home-cooked, boiled, 1 tblspn	A B1 B2 C^t	25	116	L	L	L	---	T	H	H	L	19
14	mayonnaise, 1 tblspn	A B1^t B2	100	84	T	H	T	H	G	G	F	L	5
16	Thousand Island, 1 tblspn	A B1^t B2^t	80	112	T	G	L	H	G	L	L	L	18

. . . .

269

BOILED SALAD DRESSING

F=Fair; G=Good; H=High; L=Low; t or T = trace; n/a = no information available; dashes = zero or unmeasurable

GRAM WT.	FOOD	VITAMINS	CAL	(mg) SOD	PRO	FAT	CARB	CHOL	FATTY ACIDS SAT	UNSAT	CALC	IRON	(mg) POTSM
21	AVERAGE PER TABLESPOON		29	19				(mg) 48					7
	Ingredients:												
18	1-1/2 tblspn granulated sugar	---	72	T	---	---	H	---	---	---	---	L	1
5	1/2 tblspn cornstarch	---	17	---	L	T	H	---	---	---	---	---	---
---	1 tsp dry mustard	-------	-------	-------	-------	-------	-------	--n/a--	-------	-------	-------	-------	-------
51	3 egg yolks, beaten	A B1 B2	180	27	F	G	L	H*	G	T	H	G	50
177	3/4 cp cold water	-------	-------	-------	-------	-------	-------	--0--	-------	-------	-------	-------	-------
60	1/4 cp vinegar	---	2	T	---	L	---	---	---	---	L	L	60
28	2 tblspn margarine	A D	200	279	L	H	L	---	L	H	L	---	6
339	Recipe totals (gms; cal; sod. & potsm.)		471	306									117

METHOD

Combine sugar, cornstarch and mustard together. Beat egg yolks slightly, add dry ingredients, water and vinegar and mix until smooth. Cook over low heat, stirring constantly until mixture thickens, then remove from heat and stir in margarine. If dressing is too thick when ready to serve, thin with a little milk. Yield approximately 1 cup.

* There are 765 milligrams of cholesterol in 51 grams of egg yolk, as calculated from U.S.D.A. Handbook No. 8, pg. 146, item 14. Total 765 milligrams divided by yield of 16 tablespoons equals 48 average milligrams of cholesterol per tablespoon.

. . . .

FRENCH DRESSING

F=Fair; G=Good; H=High; L=Low; t or T = trace; n/a = no information available; dashes = zero or unmeasurable

GRAM WT.	FOOD	VITAMINS	CAL	(mg) SOD	PRO	FAT	CARB	CHOL	FATTY ACIDS SAT	UNSAT	CALC	IRON	(mg) POTSM
14	AVERAGE PER TABLESPOON		83	T									5
2	Ingredients: 1 large clove garlic (for plain French, omit garlic)	A^t B1 B2 C	2	T	L	L	F	---	---	---	L	F	11
75	1/3 cp vinegar	---	11	T	---	L	---	---	---	---	L	L	75
n/a	2/3 tsp dry mustard							-n/a-					
4	1 tsp granulated sugar	---	16	T	---	---	H	---	---	---	---	L	T
n/a	1/3 tsp paprika							-n/a-					
146	2/3 cp salad oil	---	1291	T	---	H	---	---	L	H	---	---	---
2771	Recipe totals (gms; cal; sod. & potsm.)		1320	T									86

METHOD

Peel garlic clove and soak it in 1/3 cup vinegar about half an hour before making dressing. In a covered shaker bottle or jar, mix the dry ingredients. Remove garlic from vinegar and add vinegar to dry ingredients. Shake to blend. Pour oil in slowly. Shake each time before using. Store in refrigerator. Yield 1 cup (No salt -- season at the table).

. . . .

FRUIT DRESSING

F=Fair; G=Good; H=High; L=Low; t or T = trace; n/a = no information available; dashes = zero or unmeasurable

GRAM WT.	FOOD	VITAMINS	CAL	(mg) SOD	PRO	FAT	CARB	CHOL	FATTY ACIDS SAT	UNSAT	CALC	IRON	(mg) POTSM
25	AVERAGE PER TABLESPOON		54	6				(mg) 17					26
	Ingredients:												
67	1/3 cp granulated sugar	---	257	T	---	---	H	---	---	---	---	L	2
9	1 tblspn cornstarch	---	34	---	L	T	H	---	---	---	---	---	---
50	1 egg, beaten	A B1 B2	75	61	F	F	L	H*	H	L	F	F	65
14	1 tblspn salad oil	---	125	---	---	H	---	---	L	H	---	---	---
23	1-1/2 tblspn lemon juice	A B1 B2 C	6	---	L	T	F	---	---	---	F	L	32
32	2 tblspn orange juice	A B1 B2 C	14	---	L	L	F	---	---	---	F	L	64
125	1/2 cp pineapple juice	A B1 B2 C	68	T	L	T	F	---	---	---	F	L	186
79	1/3 cp heavy cream, whipped	A B1 B2 C	280	29	L	G	L	---	n/a	---	F	T	70
478	Recipe totals (gms; cal; sod. & potsm.)		1139	119									489

METHOD

Combine sugar with the cornstarch then add remaining ingredients (except cream). Cook on low heat, stirring constantly until thickened. When cool, fold in whipped cream. Yield 1 cup.

* There are 275 milligrams of cholesterol in 50 grams of whole egg as calculated from U.S.D.A. Handbook No. 8, pg. 146, item 12. Total 275 milligrams divided by yield of 16 tablespoons equals 17 average milligrams of cholesterol per tablespoon.

. . . .

MAYONNAISE

F=Fair; G=Good; H=High; L=Low; t or T = trace; n/a = no information available;   dashes = zero or unmeasurable

GRAM WT.	FOOD	VITAMINS	CAL	(mg) SOD	PRO	FAT	CARB	CHOL	FATTY ACIDS SAT	UNSAT	CALC	IRON	(mg) POTSM
16	AVERAGE PER TABLESPOON		125	1				(mg) 16					2
	Ingredients:												
34	2 egg yolks	A B1 B2	120	18	F	G	L	H*	G	T	H	G	33
n/a	1/4 tsp black pepper	--------						--n/a--					--------
n/a	1/4 tsp paprika	--------						--n/a--					--------
n/a	1/8 tsp dry mustard	--------						--n/a--					--------
45	3 tblspn vinegar	---	6	T	---	L	---	---	---	---	L	L	45
440	2 cp salad oil	---	3890	---	---	H	---	---	L	H	---	---	---
519	Recipe totals (gms; cal; sod. & potsm.)		4016	18									78

METHOD

Beat egg yolks, add seasonings and beat together until well blended. Add vinegar and beat again. Add the oil a teaspoon at a time and beat hard after each addition. Continue to add the oil in very small amounts, beating hard after each addition until nearly half the oil has been used, then add oil at a slightly faster rate until mixture is smooth and thick. If mayonnaise curdles, beat another egg yolk with a small quantity of oil and add in very small quantities to the curdled dressing, beating well after each addition. Yield 1 pint.

*   There are 510 milligrams of cholesterol in 34 grams of egg yolk as calculated from U.S.D.A. Handbook No. 8, pg. 146, item 14. Total 510 milligrams divided by yield of 32 tablespoons equals 16 average milligrams of cholesterol per tablespoon.

. . . .

ROQUEFORT DRESSING

F=Fair; G=Good; H=High; L=Low; t or T = trace; n/a = no information available; dashes = zero or unmeasurable

GRAM WT.	FOOD	VITAMINS	CAL	SOD (mg)	PRO	FAT	CARB	CHOL (mg)	FATTY ACIDS SAT	UNSAT	CALC	IRON	POTSM (mg)
18	MAYONNAISE VARIATION No. 1 AVERAGE PER TABLESPOON		132	1				17					3
	Ingredients:												
260	1 cup mayonnaise	A B1 B2	2008	9	F	H	T	H*	G	G	F	L	39
28	1 oz Roquefort cheese, mashed	A B1 B2	105	---	F	F	L	H*	G	L	H	L	---
5	1 tsp lemon juice	A B1 B2 C	1	---	L	T	F	---	---	---	F	L	7
293	Recipe totals (gms; cal; sod. & potsm.)		2114	9									46

METHOD

Combine mashed roquefort cheese and lemon juice with mayonnaise until well blended. Yield   about 1 cup.

*   As calculated from U.S.D.A. Handbook No. 8, pg. 146, items 8 and 14.

. . . .

RUSSIAN DRESSING

F=Fair; G=Good; H=High; L=Low; t or T = trace; n/a = no information available;   dashes = zero or unmeasurable

GRAM WT.	FOOD	VITAMINS	CAL	(mg) SOD	PRO	FAT	CARB	CHOL	FATTY ACIDS SAT	UNSAT	CALC	IRON	(mg) POTSM
23	MAYONNAISE VARIATION No. 2 AVERAGE PER TABLESPOON		131	58				(mg) 9					23
	Ingredients:												
260	1 cp mayonnaise	A B1 B2	2008	9	F	H	T	H*	G	G	F	L	39
68	4 tblspn tomato chili sauce	A B1 B2 C	72	912	L	L	F	---	---	---	F	F	252
25	3 green onions, chopped fine	A^t B1 B2 C	11	1	L	L	F	---	---	---	F	L	58
15	1 tblspn lemon juice	A B1 B2 C	4	---	L	T	F	---	---	---	F	L	21
368	Recipe totals (gms; cal; sod. & potsm.)		2095	922									370

METHOD

Combine ingredients and mix thoroughly.

* See recipe for mayonnaise for details.

. . . .

QUICK THOUSAND ISLAND DRESSING

F=Fair; G=Good; H=High; L=Low; t or T = trace; n/a = no information available; dashes = zero or unmeasurable

GRAM WT.	FOOD	VITAMINS	CAL	(mg) SOD	PRO	FAT	CARB	CHOL	FATTY ACIDS SAT	UNSAT	CALC	IRON	(mg) POTSM
22	MAYONNAISE VARIATION No. 3 AVERAGE PER TABLESPOON		131	76				(mg) 8					23
	Ingredients:												
260	1 cp mayonnaise	A B1 B2	2008	9	F	H	T	H*	G	G	F	L	39
90	1/3 cp tomato chili sauce	A B1 B2 C	95	1208	L	L	F	---	---	---	F	F	333
350	Recipe totals (gms; cal; sod. & potsm.)		2103	1217									372

METHOD

Mix mayonnaise and tomato chili sauce until well blended. If desired, more chili sauce may be added and some minced green onion, or a tablespoon of chopped green olives, or hard-cooked egg.

*   See recipe for mayonnaise for details.

. . . .

276

EGGLESS MAYONNAISE

F=Fair; G=Good; H=High; L=Low; t or T = trace; n/a = no information available; dashes = zero or unmeasurable

GRAM WT.	FOOD	VITAMINS	CAL	(mg) SOD	PRO	FAT	CARB	CHOL	FATTY ACIDS SAT	UNSAT	CALC	IRON	(mg) POTSM
16	AVERAGE PER TABLESPOON		98	5									13
	Ingredients:												
6	1-1/2 tsp granulated sugar	---	24	---	---	---	H	---	---	---	---	L	T
n/a	1/4 tsp paprika	--------						--n/a--					
n/a	1/4 tsp dry mustard	--------						--n/a--					
63	1/4 cp evaporated milk, undiluted	A B1 B2 C	86	74	L	L	L	n/a	L	L	H	L	191
19	1-1/4 tblspn vinegar	---	---	---	---	L	---	---	---	---	L	L	19
165	3/4 cp salad oil	---	1459	---	---	H	---	---	L	H	---	---	---
253	Recipe totals (gms; cal; sod. & potsm.)		1569	74									210

METHOD

Mix dry ingredients with milk, beat in vinegar, add oil slowly, and beat thoroughly. Yield 1 cup.

. . . .

OIL SPREAD
(As a substitute for butter or margarine)

F=Fair; G=Good; H=High; L=Low; t or T = trace; n/a = no information available; dashes = zero or unmeasurable

GRAM WT.	FOOD	VITAMINS	CAL	(mg) SOD	PRO	FAT	CARB	CHOL	FATTY ACIDS SAT	UNSAT	CALC	IRON	(mg) POTSM
31	AVERAGE PER TABLESPOON		194	86									4
	Ingredients:												
9	1 tblspn cornstarch	---	34	---	L	T	H	---	---	---	---	---	---
45	2/3 cp 2% low-fat dry milk	A B1 B2 C	163	239	G	T	G	---	---	---	H	L	79
4	1 tsp salt	---	---	1569	---	---	---	---	---	---	G	---	---
5	1 tsp lemon juice	A B1 B2 C	1	---	L	T	F	---	---	---	F	L	7
157	2/3 cp water							---0---					
440	2 cp oil (corn, safflower, peanut, olive, etc.)	---	3890	---	---	H	---	---	---	H	---	---	
---	Few drops yellow food coloring							---n/a---					
660	Recipe totals (gms; cal; sod. & potsm.)		4088	1808									86

METHOD

Sift the cornstarch, dry milk and salt together into the top of a double boiler. Combine lemon juice and water and gradually add to the starch mixture, blending until smooth. Cook over boiling water, stirring constantly until mixture thickens (about 4 minutes). Remove from heat then add 1/4 cup of oil at a time beating with rotary after each addition. After last addition, add food coloring. Yield 1 pound, 5 ounces. This mixture will spread, but will not melt. Store in refrigerator.

. . . .

WHITE SAUCE

(made with oil instead of butter or margarine)

F=Fair; G=Good; H=High; L=Low; t or T = trace; n/a = no information available; dashes = zero or unmeasurable

GRAM WT.	FOOD	VITAMINS	CAL	(mg) SOD	PRO	FAT	CARB	CHOL	FATTY ACIDS SAT	UNSAT	CALC	IRON	(mg) POTSM
18	AVERAGE PER TABLESPOON		29	9									28
	Ingredients:												
21	3 tblspn flour	B1 B2	78	T	F	L	G	---	---	---	L	F	20
28	2 tblspn oil	---	250	---	---	H	---	---	L	H	---	---	---
246	1 cp 2% low-fat milk	A B1 B2 C	145	150	H	L	H	L*	L	L	L	---	431
295	Recipe totals (gms; cal; sod. & potsm.)		473	150									451

METHOD

Combine flour and oil, add milk slowly, mixing until smooth. Cook over low heat, stirring until thickened. Use for cream dishes, such as fish, vegetables and soups.

* There are only 7 milligrams of cholesterol in the entire recipe, therefore the average per tablespoon would be just a trace at most.

. . . .

SOUR CREAM DRESSING

F=Fair; G=Good; H=High; L=Low; t or T = trace; n/a = no information available;   dashes = zero or unmeasurable

GRAM WT.	FOOD	VITAMINS	CAL	(mg) SOD	PRO	FAT	CARB	CHOL	FATTY ACIDS SAT	UNSAT	CALC	IRON	(mg) POTSM
18	AVERAGE PER TABLESPOON		34	5									3
	Ingredients:												
30	2 tblspn vinegar	---	T	T	---	L	---	---	---	---	L	L	30
12	1 tblspn granulated sugar	---	48	T	---	---	H	---	---	---	---	L	T
230	1 cp sour cream	A B1 B2 C	485	98	L	G	F	---------	-n/a-	-------	G	L	n/a
15	1 tblspn fresh lemon juice	A B1 B2 C	4	---	L	T	F	---	---	---	F	L	21
n/a	1 tsp dried parsley flakes	A B1 B2 C	*	---------------				--------	n/a-				-------
287	Recipe totals (gms; cal; sod. & potsm.)		537	98									51

METHOD

Combine ingredients in order given and blend thoroughly. This dressing is excellent on sliced cucumbers and onions, also on vegetable and seafood salads. Yield approximately 1 cup.

*   Fresh parsley contains 727 milligrams of potassium per 100 grams. No figures were available for dry parsley flakes. Vitamins are those contained in fresh parsley.

. . . .

FISH, SEAFOOD and SHELL FISH

FISH, SEAFOOD AND SHELLFISH

F=Fair; G=Good; H=High; L=Low; t or T = trace; n/a = no information available; dashes = zero or unmeasurable

GRAM WT.	FOOD	VITAMINS	CAL	(mg) SOD	PRO	FAT	CARB	CHOL	FATTY ACIDS SAT	UNSAT	CALC	IRON	(mg) POTSM
	ABALONE												
100	raw	B1th B2	98	---	G	L	L	--------n/a---------			F	F	---
100	canned	B1th	80	---	G	L	L	--------n/a---------			F	---	---
	(Note B1th means thiamine only)												
100	ALBACORE, raw (almost all of the catch is canned as tuna)	*about 5 mg/100 gms	177	40	G	F	---	n/a	L	H	F	---	29
	ALEWIFE												
100	raw	---	127	---	G	F	---	--------n/a---------			---	---	---
100	canned, liquids and solids	---	141	---	G	F	---	--------n/a---------			---	---	---
	ANCHOVY, pickled, with or without added oil, not heavily salted	---	176	---	G	F	L	--------n/a---------			H	---	---
100	BARRACUDA, Pacific, raw	---	113	---	G	F	---	--------n/a---------			H	---	---
	BASS, BLACK SEA												
100	raw	---	93	68	G	F	---	--------n/a---------			---	---	---
100	cooked (baked, stuffed, prepared with bacon, margarine, onion, celery and bread cubes)	---	259	--	G	G	F	--------n/a---------			---	---	---
	BASS, SMALLMOUTH & LARGE-MOUTH, raw	B1 B2 C	104	---	G	F	---	--------n/a---------			---	---	---
	BASS, STRIPED												
100	raw	---	105	---	G	F	---	--------n/a---------			---	---	---
100	cooked, oven-fried, prepared with milk, breadcrumbs, margarine, and salt	---	196	---	G	F	F	--------n/a---------			---	---	---
100	BASS, WHITE, raw	---	98	--	G	F	---	--------n/a---------			---	---	---
	BLACKFISH, see Tautog												
	BLUEFISH												
100	raw	B1 B2 C	117	74	H	F	---	--------n/a---------			G	L	---
85	cooked, baked with table fat, 3oz	A B1 B2	135	88	H	F	---	--------n/a---------			G	L	---
100	fried	B1 B2	205	146	H1	G	L	--------n/a---------			G	L	---

FISH, SEAFOOD AND SHELLFISH

F=Fair; G=Good; H=High; L=Low; t or T = trace; n/a = no information available; dashes = zero or unmeasurable

GRAM WT.	FOOD	VITAMINS	CAL	(mg) SOD	PRO	FAT	CARB	CHOL	FATTY ACIDS SAT	UNSAT	CALC	IRON	(mg) POTSM
100	BONITO, including Atlantic, Pacific and striped, raw	---	168	n/a	H	G	---	--------n/a--------			---	---	---
100	BUFFALOFISH, raw	---	113	52	H	L	L	--------n/a--------			---	---	293
100	BULLHEADS, BLACK, raw	---	84	---		G	L	--------n/a--------			---	---	---
	BUTTERFISH												
100	raw, from northern waters	n/a	169	n/a	H	F	---	--------n/a--------			---	---	---
100	raw, from gulf waters	n/a	95	n/a	H	L	---	--------n/a--------			---	---	---
100	CARP, raw	A B1 B2 C	115	50	H	L	---	--------n/a--------			F	L	286
100	CATFISH, freshwater, raw	B1 B2	103	60	H	L	---	--------n/a--------			---	L	330
	CAVIAR, sturgeon												
100	granular	---	262	2200	H	G	L	H**	n/a	n/a	H	H	180
100	pressed	---	316	---	H	G	L	--------n/a--------			---	---	---
100													
100	CHUB, raw	---	145	---		G	F	---	--------n/a--------			---	---	---
	CISCO see Lake Herring												
	CLAMS, raw, soft												
100	meat and liquid	---	54	---	F	L	L	n/a	---	---	---	---	---
100	meat only	---	82	36	G	L	L	n/a	---	---	---	G	235
	CLAMS, hard or round												
100	meat and liquid	B2	49	---	L	L	L	n/a	---	---	---	---	---
100	meat only	---	80	205	F	L	L	n/a	---	---	L	H	311
	hard, soft and unspecified												
100	meat and liquid	---	53	---	L	L	L	n/a	---	---	---	---	---
100	meat only	A B1 B2 C	76	120	F	L	L	n/a	---	---	L	H	181

* In U.S.D.A. Handbook No. 8, pg. 146, fish steaks and fillets (items 17 a&b) are listed in general as having 70 milligrams of cholesterol in 100 grams edible portion. Fish, per se (or by name is not listed)

** Caviar and roe cholesterol content shown in U.S.D.A. Handbook No. 8, pg. 146 item 4, is 300 milligrams per 100 grams of edible portion, no information available on fatty acids.

FISH, SEAFOOD AND SHELLFISH

F=Fair; G=Good; H=High; L=Low; t or T = trace; n/a = no information available; dashes = zero or unmeasurable

GRAM WT.	FOOD	VITAMINS	CAL	(mg) SOD	PRO	FAT	CARB	CHOL	FATTY ACIDS SAT	UNSAT	CALC	IRON	(mg) POTSM
	CLAMS, canned, including hard, soft, razor and unspecified												
100	solids and liquids	B1 B2	52	---	L	L	L	n/a	---	---	L	G	140
100	drained solids	---	98	---	G	L	n/a	n/a	---	---	---	---	---
100	liquor, bouillon, or nectar	---	19	---	L	L	l	n/a	---	---	---	---	---
100	chowder, Manhattan type, tomatoes, no milk, prepared with an equal amount of water	A B1 B2	33	383	L	L	L	n/a	---	---	L	L	75
245	chowder, New England type with milk, no tomatoes, prepared with equal volume of milk (frozen concentrate)	A B1 B2 C^t	210	1066	F	F	F		--------n/a---------		H	L	225
100	fritters, prepared with flour, baking powder, margarine and egg	B1 B2	311	---	G	G	H		--------n/a---------		L	G	147
	CODFISH												
100	raw	B1 B2 C	78	70*	G	L	---		--------n/a---------		L	L	382
	Sodium value is about 255 milligrams per 100 grams -- if cod has been dipped or rinsed in brine												
100	cooked, broiled	A B1 B2	170	110	H	L	---		--------n/a---------		L	L	407
100	canned	B2	85	---	G	L	---		--------n/a---------		---	---	---
100	dehydrated, salted lightly	B1 B2	375	8100	H	L	---		--------n/a---------		---	F	160
100	dried, salted	---	130	---	G	L	---		--------n/a---------		---	---	---
100	cakes, fried, prepared with potato and egg	---	172	---	F	F	F		--------n/a---------		---	---	---
	CRAB, including blue, Dungeness, rock and king												
100	cooked, steamed	A B1 B2 C	93	---	G	L	L	H*	n/a	n/a	F	L	---
	Cholesterol content (in shell-- or meat only) is 125 milligrams per 100 grams edible portion which is 55 milligrams more than in beef or lamb or pork. No figures for fatty acids are available in U.S.D.A. Handbook No. 8.												
85	canned, 3 oz.	B1 B2	85	850	F	L	L	H	n/a	n/a	F	L	94
100	deviled, prepared with bread cubes butter, parsley, eggs, lemon juice and catsup	B1 B2 C	188	867	F	F	F	H	n/a	n/a	F	F	166
100	imperial, prepared with butter, flour, milk, onion, green pepper, eggs and lemon juice	B1 B2 C	147	728	F	F	L	H	n/a	n/a	F	L	131
	(Note High (H) cholesterol is reflected in the crabmeat butter and eggs in the above 2 recipes)												
	CRAPPIE, WHITE												
100	raw	B1 B2	79	---	H	L	---		---------n/a---------		---	---	----

FISH, SEAFOOD AND SHELLFISH

F=Fair; G=Good; H=High; L=Low; t or T = trace; n/a = no information available; dashes = zero or unmeasurable

GRAM WT.	FOOD	VITAMINS	CAL	(mg) SOD	PRO	FAT	CARB	CHOL	FATTY ACIDS SAT	UNSAT	CALC	IRON	(mg) POTSM
100	CRAYFISH, freshwater and spiny lobster, raw	B1 B2	72	---	F	L	L	--------n/a--------		---	---	---
	CROAKER											
100	Atlantic, raw	A B1 B2	96	87	G	L	---	--------n/a--------		---	---	234
100	baked	A B1 B2	133	120	G	L	---	--------n/a--------		---	---	323
100	white, raw	---	84	---	G	L	---	--------n/a--------		---	---	---
100	yellowfin, raw	---	89	---	G	L	---	--------n/a--------		---	---	---
	CUSK											
100	raw	B1 B2	75	---	G	L	---	--------n/a--------		---	---	---
100	steamed	B1 B2	106	74	G	L	---	--------n/a--------		L	F	---
100	DOGFISH, spiny (grayfish) raw	B1	156	---	G	F		--------n/a--------		---	---	---
100	DRUM, freshwater, raw	---	121	70	G	F		--------n/a--------		---	---	286
100	red, (redfish) raw	B1 B2	80	55	G	L		--------n/a--------		---	---	273
	EEL											
100	American, raw	A B1 B2	233	---	G	G	---	--------n/a--------		L	L	---
100	smoked	---	330	---	G	H	---	--------n/a--------		---	----	---
100	EULACHON (smelt) raw	B1 B2	118	----	F	L	---	--------n/a--------		---	---	---
100	FILET OF SOLE, broiled also see Flatfishes	B1 B2	79	78	G	L	---	--------n/a--------		L	L	342
100	FINNAN HADDIE (smoked Haddock)	B1 B2	103	---	F	L	---	--------n/a--------		---	---	---
100	FISH LOAF, prepared with canned, flaked fish, bread cubes, egg, tomatoes, onions and fat	A B1 B2 C	124	---	F	F	F	--------n/a--------		---	---	---
100	FISH STICKS, frozen, cooked	B1 B2	176	---	G	F	F	--------n/a--------		L	L	---
100	FLATFISHES (flounders, soles and sanddabs, raw)	B1 B2	79	78	G	L	---	--------n/a--------		L	L	342
100	FLOUNDER see Flatfishes, raw baked	B1 B2 C	202	237	G	F	---	--------n/a--------		L	L	587

FISH, SEAFOOD AND SHELLFISH

F=Fair; G=Good; H=High; L=Low;   t or T = trace; n/a = no information available;   dashes = zero or unmeasurable

GRAM WT.	FOOD	VITAMINS	CAL	(mg) SOD	PRO	FAT	CARB	CHOL	FATTY ACIDS SAT	UNSAT	CALC	IRON	(mg) POTSM
100	FROG LEGS, raw	B1 B2	73	---	G	L	---	--------n/a--------			L	F	---
100	GROUPER, including red, black, and speckled hind, raw	B1[th]	87	---	G	L	---	--------n/a--------			---	---	---
	HADDOCK												
100	raw	B1 B2	79	61	G	L	---	--------n/a--------			L	L	304
85	fried, dipped in egg, milk and breadcrumbs, 3 oz. Reflected in the egg dip	B1 B2 C	140	150	G	F	F	F*	F*	G*	G	F	296
100	smoked, canned or not canned	B1 B2	103	---	H	L	---	--------n/a--------			---	---	---
100	HAKE, including Pacific, squirrel hake and silver or whiting, raw	B1 B2	74	74	G	L	---	--------n/a--------			L	---	363
	HALIBUT, Atlantic & Pacific												
100	raw	A B1 B2	100	54*	G	F	---	n/a	L	H	L	L	449
100	broiled	A B1 B2	171	134	G	F	---	n/a	L	H	L	L	252
100	smoked	---	224	---	H	G	---	n/a	L	H	---	---	---
	Two frozen, raw samples dipped in brine contained 360 milligrams of sodium per 100 grams, per U.S.D.A. Handbook No. 8, pg. 32, item 1103.												
100	California, raw	---	97	---	G	L	---	--------n/a--------			---	---	---
100	Greenland, raw	B1[th]	146	---	G	F	---	--------n/a--------			---	---	---
	HERRING (also see Lake Herring) raw												
100	Atlantic	A B1 B2	176	---	G	F	---	n/a	L	L	---	L	---
100	Pacific	A B1 B2 C	98	74	G	L	---	n/a	T	T	---	L	420
	canned, solids and liquid												
100	plain	B2	208	---	G	F	---	--------n/a--------			G	L	---
100	in tomato sauce	B1 B2	176	---	G	F	F	--------n/a--------			---	---	---
100	pickled, Bismarck type	---	223	---	G	g	---	--------n/a--------			---	---	---
100	salted or brined	B2	218	---	G	G	---	--------n/a--------			---	---	---
	smoked												
100	bloaters	---	196	---	G	F	---	--------n/a--------			---	---	---
100	hard	---	300	6231	H	G	---	--------n/a--------			---	---	157
100	kippered	B1 B2	211	---	G	F	---	--------n/a--------			G	F	---
100	INCONNU raw	---	146	---	G	F	---	--------n/a--------			G	F	---
100	JACK MACKEREL, raw	---	143	---	G	F	---	--------n/a--------			---	---	---

FISH, SEAFOOD AND SHELLFISH

F=Fair; G=Good; H=High; L=Low; t or T = trace; n/a = no information available; dashes = zero or unmeasurable

GRAM WT.	FOOD	VITAMINS	CAL	(mg) SOD	PRO	FAT	CARB	CHOL	FATTY ACIDS SAT	UNSAT	CALC	IRON	(mg) POTSM
100	KINGFISH, southern, gulf, and northern (whiting) raw	---	105	83	G	L	---	-------n/a-------			---	---	250
100	LAKE HERRING (cisco) raw	B1 B2	96	47	G	L	---	-------n/a-------			L	L	319
100	LAKE TROUT, raw	B1 B2	168	---	G	G	---	-------n/a-------			---	L	---
	siscowet, raw												
100	less than 6.5 lbs. round weight	---	241	---	G	G	---	-------n/a-------			---	---	---
100	over 6.5 lbs. round weight	---	524	---	L	H	---	-------n/a-------			---	---	---
100	LINGCOD, raw	B1 B2	84	59	G	L	---	-------n/a-------			---	---	433
	LOBSTER, Northern												
100	raw, whole	B1 B2	91	---	G	L	L	H	L	G	F	L	---
100	canned or cooked	B1 B2	95	210	G	L	L	H	L	G	G	L	180
100	Newburg, prepared with butter, egg yolks, sherry and cream	B1 B2	194	229	G	G	F	H*	H	L	G	L	171
100	paste, canned	B2	180	---	G	F	L	-------n/a-------			---	---	---
100	salad, prepared with onion, sweet pickle, celery, eggs, mayonnaise and tomatoes	B1 B2 C	110	124	F	F	L	H*	H	L	F	L	264

High cholesterol and saturated fatty acids is reflected in the eggs and mayonnaise In Newburg, the egg yolks raise the level of cholesterol and saturated fatty acids. Lobster meat is high in cholesterol having 200 milligrams per 100 grams edible portion.
spiny (see Crayfish)

GRAM WT.	FOOD	VITAMINS	CAL	(mg) SOD	PRO	FAT	CARB	CHOL	FATTY ACIDS SAT	UNSAT	CALC	IRON	(mg) POTSM
	MACKEREL												
100	Atlantic, raw	A B1 B2	191	---	G	F	---	-------n/a-------			L	F	---
100	canned solids and liquids	A B1 B2 *	183	---	G	F	---	-------n/a-------			H	F	---

Vitamins based on drained solids according to U.S.D.A. Handbook No. 8, pg. 38, item 1307, sub figure 98.

GRAM WT.	FOOD	VITAMINS	CAL	(mg) SOD	PRO	FAT	CARB	CHOL	FATTY ACIDS SAT	UNSAT	CALC	IRON	(mg) POTSM
100	broiled with butter or margarine	A B1 B2	236	---	G	F	---	-------n/a-------			G	F	---
100	Pacific, raw		159	---	G	L	---	-------n/a-------			L	F	---
100	canned, solids and liquids	A B1 B2 *	180	---	G	F	---	-------n/a-------			H	F	---

vitamins based on drained solids, per U.S.D.A. Handbook No. 8, pg. 38, item 1310, footnote no. 98

GRAM WT.	FOOD	VITAMINS	CAL	(mg) SOD	PRO	FAT	CARB	CHOL	FATTY ACIDS SAT	UNSAT	CALC	IRON	(mg) POTSM
100	salted	---	305	---	G	H	---	-------n/a-------			---	---	---
100	smoked	---	219	---	G	F	---	-------n/a-------			---	---	---
100	MENHADEN, Atlantic, canned, solids and liquids	---	172	---	F	F	---	-------n/a-------			---	---	---

FISH, SEAFOOD AND SHELLFISH

F=Fair; G=Good; H=High; L=Low; t or T = trace; n/a = no information available; dashes = zero or unmeasurable

GRAM WT.	FOOD	VITAMINS	CAL	(mg) SOD	PRO	FAT	CARB	CHOL	FATTY ACIDS SAT	FATTY ACIDS UNSAT	CALC	IRON	(mg) POTSM
100	MULLET, striped, raw	B1 B2	146	81	G	F	---		---------n/a-------		G	F	292
100	MUSKELLUNGE, raw	---	109	---	G	F	---		---------n/a-------		---	L	---
	MUSSELS, Atlantic and Pacific, raw												
100	meat and liquid	---	66	---	F	L	L		---------n/a-------		---	---	315
100	meat only	B1 B2	95	289	F	L	L		---------n/a-------		G	G	---
100	Pacific, canned, drained solids	B2	114	---	G	L	L		---------n/a-------		---	---	---
	OCEAN PERCH, Atlantic (redfish)												
100	raw	B1 B2	88	79	G	L	---	---	---	---	L	F	269
85	fried, dipped in egg, milk and bread crumbs, 3 oz.	B1 B2	195	130	G	F	G	---	---	---	F	L	241
100	frozen, breaded, fried, reheated	---	319	---	G	G	G		---------n/a-------		---	---	---
100	Pacific, raw	---	95	63	G	L	---		---------n/a-------		---	---	390
100	OCTOPUS, raw	B1 B2	73	---	G	L	---		---------n/a-------		F	---	---
	OYSTERS, raw, meat only												
100	Eastern	A B1 B2	66	73	L	L	L	H*	H	G	H	H	121
100	Pacific and Western (Olympia)	B1 C	91	---	L	L	L	H*	H	G	H	H	---
100	fried, dipped in egg, milk and breadcrumbs	A B1 B2	239	206	L	F	F	H*	H	G	H	H	440

Note   There are more than 200 milligrams of cholesterol in 100 grams of oysters. In fried oysters, the egg and milk dip increases the amount of cholesterol.

GRAM WT.	FOOD	VITAMINS	CAL	(mg) SOD	PRO	FAT	CARB	CHOL	SAT	UNSAT	CALC	IRON	(mg) POTSM
100	stew, commercial, frozen												
100	prepared with milk	A B1 B2	84	366	L	L	L	H	H	L	H	L	205

Note   If skim milk is used, cholesterol and saturated fatty acids will still be high, because oysters are high in these categories.

GRAM WT.	FOOD	VITAMINS	CAL	(mg) SOD	PRO	FAT	CARB	CHOL	SAT	UNSAT	CALC	IRON	(mg) POTSM
100	prepared with water	A B1 B2	51	340	L	L	L	H	H	L	H	L	102
	prepared for home recipe--per U.S.D.A. Handbook No. 8												
100	2 parts milk to 1 part oysters	A B1 B2	97	339	L	L	L	H	H	L	H	F	133
100	3 parts milk to 1 part oysters contains added salt and butter	A B1 B2	86	203	L	L	L	H	H	L	H	F	138
	PERCH												
100	white, raw	---	118	---	G	F	---		---------n/a-------		---	---	---
100	yellow, raw	---	91	68	G	L	---		---------n/a-------		---	L	230

FISH, SEAFOOD AND SHELLFISH

F=Fair; G=Good; H=High; L=Low; t or T = trace; n/a = no information available; dashes = zero or unmeasurable

GRAM WT.	FOOD	VITAMINS	CAL	(mg) SOD	PRO	FAT	CARB	CHOL	FATTY ACIDS SAT	UNSAT	CALC	IRON	(mg) POTSM
	PICKEREL												
100	chain, raw	---	84	---	G	L	---		--------n/a-------		---	L	---
113	cooked, 4 ozs.	---	95	---	F	L	---		--------n/a-------		---	---	n/a
	PIKE												
100	blue, raw	---	90	---	G	L	---		--------n/a-------		---	---	---
100	Northern, raw	---	88	--	G	L	---		--------n/a-------		---	---	---
100	walleye, raw	---	93	---	G	L	---		--------n/a-------		---	---	319
	POLLOCK												
100	raw	B1 B2	95	48	F	L	L		--------n/a-------		---	---	350
100	creamed, cooked prepared with flour, butter and milk, per U.S.D.A. Handbook No. 8.	B1 B2 C^t	128	111	L	L	L		--------n/a-------		---	---	238
100	**POMPANO**, raw	B1 B2	166	47	G	F	---		--------n/a-------		---	----	259
100	**PORGY AND SCUP**, raw	---	112	63	G	L	---		--------n/a-------		---	---	287
	RAJA FISH, see skate												
100	**RED AND GRAY SNAPPER**, raw	B1 B2	98	67	G	L	---		--------n/a-------		F	L	323
	REDFISH, see Drum, red and ocean perch, and Atlantic												
	ROCKFISH, including black, canary, yellowtail, rasphead and bocaccio												
100	raw	B1 B2	97	60	G	L	---		--------n/a-------		---	---	388
100	cooked, oven-steamed	B1 B2	107	68	G	L	L		--------n/a-------		---	---	446
	ROE, raw												
100	including carp, cod, haddock, herring, pike and shad	B1 B2 C	130	---	G	L	L		--------n/a-------		---	L	---
100	including salmon, sturgeon and turbot	B1 B2 C	**207**	---	G	F	L		--------n/a-------		---	---	---
100	cooked, baked or broiled, cod and chad, prepared with butter or margarine and lemon juice or												

NUTRITION AT YOUR FINGERTIPS

FISH, SEAFOOD AND SHELLFISH

F=Fair; G=Good; H=High; L=Low; t or T = trace; n/a = no information available; dashes = zero or unmeasurable

GRAM WT.	FOOD	VITAMINS	CAL	(mg) SOD	PRO	FAT	CARB	CHOL	FATTY ACIDS SAT	UNSAT	CALC	IRON	(mg) POTSM
	ROE (continued)												
	vinegar per U.S.D.A. Handbook No. 8	---	126	73	G	L	L	--------n/a-------			L	L	132
100	canned, including cod, haddock, and herring, solids and liquids	C	118	---	H	L	L	--------n/a-------			L	F	---
100	SABLEFISH, raw	B1 B2	190	56	F	F	---	--------n/a-------			---	---	358
100	SALMON, Atlantic, raw	B1 B2 C	217	---	G	F	---	n/a	L	H	F	L	---
100	canned, liquids and solids	---	203	---	G	F	---	n/a	L	H	---	---	---
100	Chinook (king) raw	A B1 B2	222	45	G	F	---	n/a	L	H	---	---	399
100	canned, solids and liquids	A B1 B2	210	*	G	F	---	n/a	L	H	H**	L	366
*	Sodium for product canned without added salt, value is approximately the same as for raw salmon. Calcium is based on total contents of can. If bones are discarded, value will be greatly reduced... per U.S.D.A. Handbook No. 8, pg. 54, footnotes 138 and 139 respectively.												
100	Chum, raw	B1 B2	---	53	---	---	---	--------n/a-------			---	---	429
100	canned, liquids and solids	A B1 B2	139	*See Above	G	L	---	--------n/a-------			**See Above	L	336
100	Coho (silver), raw	B1 B2	---	48***	---	---	---	--------n/a-------			H	---	421
***	Note Sample dipped in brine contained 215 milligrams of sodium per 100 grams												
100	canned, solids and liquids	A B1 B2	153	351* see above	G	L	---	--------n/a-------			H** see above	L	339
100	pink (humpback), raw	B1 B2	119	64****	G	L	---	n/a	L	H	---	---	306 ****
100	canned, solids and liquids	A B1 B2	141	387* see above	G	L	---	n/a	L	H	H** see above	L	361 ****
****	Note Values for pink humpback salmon, raw, dipped in brine averaged 473 mg. of sodium and 126 mg of potassium per 100 grams, per U.S.D.A. Handbook No. 8, pg. 54, item No. 1954, footnote 141.												
100	Sockeye (red), raw	A B1 B2	---	48	---	---	---	--------n/a-------			---	---	391
100	canned, solids and liquids	A B1 B2	171	522*	G	L	---	--------n/a-------			H**	F	344
100	Salmon, baked or broiled	A B1 B2	182	116	F	L	L	L	T	H	---	F	443
100	rice loaf	---	122	---	F	L	L	--------n/a-------			---	---	---
100	smoked (Lox)	---	176	---	G	L	---	--------n/a-------			L	---	---
	SANDDAB (see flatfishes)												
	SARDINES, Atlantic, canned in oil												
100	solids and liquids	A B1 B2	175	434	H	H	L	--------n/a-------			H	G	560
100	drained solids	A B1 B2	203	823	H	F	---	--------n/a-------			H	F	590

290

FISH, SEAFOOD AND SHELLFISH

F=Fair; G=Good; H=High; L=Low; t or T = trace; n/a = no information available;   dashes = zero or unmeasurable

GRAM WT.	FOOD	VITAMINS	CAL	(mg) SOD	PRO	FAT	CARB	CHOL	FATTY ACIDS SAT	UNSAT	CALC	IRON	(mg) POTSM
100	SARDINES, Pacific, raw	---	160	---	G	L	---		----n/a----		L	F	---
100	canned in brine or mustard, solids and liquids	A	196	760	G	F	L		----n/a----		H	G	260
100	in oil, drained solids	B1 B2	---	---	---	---	---	---	---	---	---	---	---
100	in tomato sauce, solids and liquid	A B1 B2	197	400	G	F	L		----n/a----		H	G	320
100	SAUGER, raw	---	84	---	G	L	---		----n/a----		---	---	---
100	SCALLOPS, Bay and Sea, raw	B1 B2	81	255*	G	L	F		----n/a----		L	F	396 *
*	Note Based on frozen scallops, possibly brined...per U.S.D.A. Handbook No. 8, pg. 56 item 2023 footnote 145.												
100	cooked, steamed	---	112	265	H	L	---		----n/a----		H	G	476
100	frozen, breaded, fried, reheated	---	194	---	G	F	F		----n/a----		---	---	---
	SCUP (see Porgy)												
100	SEABASS, white, raw	---	96	---	G	L	---		----n/a----		---	---	---
	SHAD or AMERICAN SHAD												
100	raw	B1 B2	170	54	G	F	---		----n/a----		L	L	330
100	cooked baked with butter or margarine and bacon slices	A B1 B2	201	79	G	F	---		----n/a----		L	L	377
100	Creole, prepared with tomatoes onion, green pepper, butter or margarine and flour	A B1 B2 C	152	73	F	L	L	n/a	---	---	L	L	280
100	canned, solids and liquid	B2	152	---	F	L	---		----n/a----		---	---	---
100	gizzard (gizzard shad), raw	---	200	---	F	F	---		----n/a----		---	---	---
	SHEEFISH (see Inconnu)												
100	SHEEPSHEAD, Atlantic, raw	---	113	101	G	L	---		----n/a----		---	---	234
	SHEEPSHEAD, freshwater. (see Drum)												
100	SHRIMP, raw	B1 B2	91	140	G	L	F		----n/a----		G	F	220
100	cooked, french-fried (dipped in egg, breadcrumbs and flour or in batter)	B1 B2	225	186	G	F	F	H*	n/a	n/a	G	F	229
*	Note There are 125 milligrams of cholesterol in 100 grams of shrimp, per U.S.D.A. Handbook No. 8, pg. 146 item 33b.												

FISH, SEAFOOD AND SHELLFISH

F=Fair; G=Good; H=High; L=Low; t or T = trace; n/a = no information available; dashes = zero or unmeasurable

GRAM WT.	FOOD	VITAMINS	CAL	(mg) SOD	PRO	FAT	CARB	CHOL	FATTY ACIDS SAT	UNSAT	CALC	IRON	(mg) POTSM
	SHRIMP (continued), canned												
100	wet pack, solids and liquid	A B1 B2	80	---	G	L	L	H	n/a	n/a	F	F	---
85	dry pack, or drained solids of wet pack, 3 ozs.	A B1 B2	100	---	H	L	L	H	n/a	n/a	H	G	104
100	frozen, breaded, raw, not more than 50% breading	B1 B2	139	---	F	L	G		--------n/a--------		L	F	---
100	shrimp or canned lobster paste	B2	180	---	G	F	L		--------n/a--------		---	---	---
	SISCOWET (see Lake Trout)												
100	SKATE (Raja Fish), raw	B1th	98	---	G	L	---		--------n/a--------		---	---	---
100	SMELT, Atlantic, jack and bay, raw	B1 B2	98	---	G	L	---		--------n/a--------		---	L	---
100	canned	---	200	---	G	F	---		--------n/a--------		H	L	---
100	SNAIL, raw	---	90	---	F	L	L		--------n/a--------		---	F	---
100	giant African, raw	---	73	---	L	L	L		--------n/a--------		---	---	---
	SNAPPER, RED (see Red and Gray snapper.												
	SOLE (see Flatfishes)												
	SPINY LOBSTER (see Crayfish)												
100	SPOT, raw *	B1 B2	219	61	G	G	---		--------n/a--------		---	---	---
*	Note Values are based on samples caught in October. Content of fat may vary greatly from this average at other seasons of the year, U.S.D.A. Handbook No. 8, pg. 59 item 2184, footnote No. 149.												
100	cooked, baked	---	295	312**	H	H	---		--------n/a--------		---	---	---
**	Note Based on fish with salt added in cooking, per U.S.D.A. Handbook No. 8, pg. 59, item 2185, footnote 150.												
100	SQUID, raw	B1 B2	84	---	G	L	L		--------n/a--------		F	---	---
100	STURGEON, raw	---	94	---	G	L	---		--------n/a--------		---	---	---
100	cooked, steamed	---	160	108	G	F	---		--------n/a--------		H	G	235
100	smoked	---	149	---	G	L	---		--------n/a--------		---	---	---
100	SUCKERS, including white and mullets, raw	B1	104	56	G	F	---		--------n/a--------		---	---	336
100	carp, raw	---	111	---	G	F	---		--------n/a--------		---	---	---

FISH, SEAFOOD AND SHELLFISH

F=Fair; G=Good; H=High; L=Low; t or T = trace; n/a = no information available; dashes = zero or unmeasurable

GRAM WT.	FOOD	VITAMINS	CAL	(mg) SOD	PRO	FAT	CARB	CHOL	FATTY ACIDS SAT	UNSAT	CALC	IRON	(mg) POTSM
100	SWORDFISH, raw	A B1 B2	118	---	G	F	L	--------n/a-------		G	L	---
100	broiled with butter or margarine	A B1 B2	174	---	H	F	---	--------n/a-------		G	L	---
100	canned, solids and liquid	A B1 B2	102	---	G	F	L	--------n/a-------		---	---	---
100	TAUTOG (Blackfish), raw	---	89	---	G	L	---	--------n/a-------		---	---	---
100	TERRAPIN (Diamond back), raw	---	111	---	G	F	---	--------n/a-------		---	---	---
100	TILEFISH, raw	---	79	---	G	L	---	--------n/a-------		---	---	---
100	baked	---	138	---	G	F	---	--------n/a-------		---	---	---
100	TOMCOD, Atlantic, raw	---	78	---	G	L	---	--------n/a-------		---	---	---
	TROUT (see Lake Trout)											
100	TROUT, Brook, raw	B2	101	---	G	L	---	--------n/a-------		---	---	---
100	Rainbow or Steelhead, raw	B1 B2	195	---	G	F	---	n/a	L	L	---	---	---
100	canned	---	209	---	G	F	---	--------n/a-------		---	---	---
100	TUNA , Bluefin, raw	---	145	---	H	F	---	n/a	L	L	---	L	---
100	Yellowfin, raw	---	133	37*	H	F	---	n/a	L	L	---	---	---
*	Note Brined sample of yellowfin contained 439 mg. of sodium per 100 grams, per U.S.D.A. Handbook No. 8, pg. 63, item 2322, footnote 162.												
	canned												
100	in oil, solids and liquids	A B1 B2	288	800	H	H	---	n/a	L	L	L	L	301
100	drained solids	A B1 B2	197	---	H	F	---	n/a	L	L	L	F	---
100	in water, solids and liquids	B1 B2	127	41**	H	L	---	--------n/a-------		L	F	279
**	Note One sample with salt added contained 875 mg. of sodium per 100 grams, and 275 mg. of potassium, per U.S.D.A. Handbook No. 8, pg. 63, item 2325, footnote 163.												
100	TUNA SALAD, prepared with tuna celery, mayonnaise, pickle, onion and egg	A B1 B2 C	170	---	F	F	F	n/a	L	L	L	F	---
	TURBOT, A European flatfish, similar to other flatfishes (no other information available)..except Turbot roe...see Roe.												
100	TURTLE, green, raw	---	89	---	G	L	---	--------n/a-------		---	---	---
100	canned	---	106	---	H	L	---	--------n/a-------		---	---	---
100	WEAKFISH, raw	B1 B2	121	75	F	L	---	--------n/a-------		---	---	317
100	cooked, broiled	B1 B2	208	560*	H	F	---	--------n/a-------		---	---	465
*	Note Based on fish with salt added in cooking. U.S.D.A. Handbook No. 8, pg. 65, item 2427, footnote 150.												

FISH, SEAFOOD AND SHELLFISH

F=Fair; G=Good; H=High; L=Low; t or T = trace; n/a = no information available; dashes = zero or unmeasurable

GRAM WT.	FOOD	VITAMINS	CAL	(mg) SOD	PRO	FAT	CARB	CHOL	FATTY ACIDS SAT	UNSAT	CALC	IRON	(mg) POTSM
100	WHALE MEAT, raw	A B1[th] C	156	78	H	L	---	-----	-n/a-	-----	L	---	22
100	WHITEFISH, lake, raw	A B1 B2	155	52	G	G	---	-----	-n/a-	-----	---	L	299
100	cooked, baked, stuffed (prepared with bacon, butter, onion, celery and breadcrumbs-- U.S.D.A. Handbook No. 8, pg. 66, footnote 172)	A B1 B2 C[t]	215	195	G	G	F	-----	-n/a-	-----	---	L	291
100	smoked	---	155	---	G	H	---	-----	-n/a-	-----	F	---	---
	WHITING (see Kingfish and Hake)												
100	WRECKFISH, raw	---	114	---	G	L	---	-----	-n/a-	-----	F	F	282
100	YELLOWTAIL (Pacific Coast), raw	---	138	---	G	L	---	-----	-n/a-	-----	---	---	---

A LITTLE SOMETHING ABOUT COOKING FISH

There are some excellent coating mixes on the market which can be used not only for baking fish, which is their primary purpose, but for frying and broiling fish. To improve the flavor further, try mixing together 1/2 package each of fish coating mix with 1/2 package of chicken coating mix and 1/2 package of pork coating mix and add about 1 teaspoon of oregano. Shake to blend. Then wash the fish in cold water, shake off the excess and either sprinkle both sides with the coating mixture by hand, or place mixture in a plastic or paper bag and drop a few pieces of fish in at a time, twist the top to prevent coating mix from spilling, and shake until well coated.

TO BAKE   Place fish in a greased, shallow pan. The coating mix prevents the fish from becoming dry (small fish can also be baked this way). However, if fish is lean, such as: cod, smelt, whiting, flounder, pike, yellow perch, pickerel, sea bass, red snapper and haddock, drizzle a little melted margarine or oil over it before baking to prevent fish from becoming too dry. Then follow directions on the box for baking time. Large, whole fish (3 to 5 pounds or more) can be baked this way, although it takes a longer time to cook.

NOTE   In the following recipes, no salt has been included in the ingredients. Season individually at the table. (For specific information on sodium content, refer to the food lists at the beginning of each chapter, or the recipes.) Controlling salt intake helps to control body weight because salt helps to retain body fluids.

TO FRY   (With coating mix)   In a frying pan, melt about 1/2 stick of margarine and allow to brown but not burn. Prepare fish the same as for baking (above), then place in the frying pan and brown both sides. Cooking time will depend on thickness of the fish, but fish does not take long to cook. When meat of the fish flakes with a fork, it is done. Remove to a warm plate or platter.

Another method is to dredge fish in flour, cornmeal, or fine cracker crumbs; or dip fish in crumbs then in beaten egg which has been diluted with 1 tablespoon of water for each egg, dip in crumbs again. Fry fish in a medium amount of oil or margarine and deep fry until brown. When done, the fish should flake easily when tested with a fork. If fried in deep fat, drain on paper towels.

TO BROIL FISH   Fat fish, such as eels, herring, lake trout, mackerel, mullet, bluefish, butterfish, white perch, pompano, salmon, shad, swordfish, tuna (albacore), and whitefish should be brushed generously with oil or melted margarine then dusted lightly with flour. Place in a greased broiler-pan, skin side down 6 to 12 minutes, depending on thickness of the fish, about 2" from heat. When done, fish should flake easily with a fork.

Fat fish need no basting during the broiling period, but lean fish should be basted often with margarine or oil.

Large fish should be split, opened and broiled flat. Lemon juice may be sprinkled over fish before broiling.

When serving fish, provide lemon wedges or slices for individual use.

TO POACH OR STEAM FISH   A French-fryer basked makes an excellent holder for poaching or steaming (if no regular steamer is available) because whole fish can be placed in it and lowered into water or Court Bouillon (for poaching) or steamed over rapidly boiling water.

Poaching fish is done by lowering the basket into simmering (never boiling) water or Court Bouillon. Add 1 tablespoon vinegar or lemon juice for every 2 quarts of water or bouillon. This keeps the flesh white and firm. Cook until flesh may be easily separated into flakes. Cook approximately 8 minutes for the first 4 pounds and 5 minutes for each additional pound. Remove to a warm plate or platter and garnish with fresh lemon slices and parsley.

To steam fish, oil upper part of steamer, place fish in it and lower over rapidly boiling water. Sprinkle lemon juice and a little salt over fish. Cook 10 to 15 minutes per pound. Do not reduce heat. Water should boil vigorously.

To make court Bouillon, simmer the following ingredients together about 30 to 40 minutes and then strain. This may be used as a base for fish sauce and any scraps of fish, fish heads, shrimp shells, fish tails, etc., and can be cooked with this basic sauce which will make the flavor richer and the sauce thicker after straining.

Mash 2 small cloves fresh garlic, slice 2 small onions, add 1 bayleaf, 1/4 teaspoon thyme, slice 1/2 carrot, add 1 teaspoon dried parsley flakes, 1-1/2 cups boiling water, 1/2 stalk diced celery and 1/2 cup dry white wine. Add any fish scraps as mentioned above. Strain after cooking about 30 to 40 minutes through a medium to fine sieve.

HOW MUCH FISH TO BUY

If fish is not dressed out (head, tail and bones left in), allow 1/2 pound per person; if fish is solid flesh, allow 1/3 pound per person, or about 5 ounces each.

. . . .

Have you ever pitched camp along a grassy bank of a crystal-clear mountain stream that was so full of trout you could almost reach down with a long-handled net and dip 'em out? And have you ever let your feelings of frustration get the best of you when all of the fancy-tied flies in the fish-box wouldn't tempt them to take the bait no matter what method of casting you tried? In your anger, did you then try throwing a few rocks at them while you lay in the grass glowering? Perhaps then you picked up your bait-box, skipped a few pebbles across that clear water, overcame your temptation to net enough for supper by remembering the Game Warden and chided yourself for being chicken. After all, you and your wife and sons had driven many miles to catch fresh trout and it made you drool to think about it. That night you settled for bacon and eggs which tasted almost as good as trout cooked over an open fire -- but not quite. During the meal, did your oldest son look up into your face, all innocent-eyed, and ask why you like to fish, while your dearest wife snickered behind her napkin as you replied, "Because it's fun!" And when your son answered, "Why is it fun when you don't catch anything?" you mumbled something in reply but secretly vowed to catch some trout that day -- and you did, was that the day you caught your limit in half an hour, or was that another time?

Or have you ever rowed an old flat bottom boat miles up a stump-filled stream to a place one of your buddies told you had "lots of pickerel" and you spent most of the day casting, with only a small hammerhead or two to show for your efforts, while your son sat quietly "still" fishing, using worms for bait, and was so busy bringing in pan fish, he had only to throw his long bamboo pole out when he'd have another bite?

To those of you who have never fished, congratulations! You've avoided frustraion, but you've also missed some of the most wonderfully exciting moments you could have experienced. There's something about the feel of the tug on your line as the fish take your bait that's inexplicable. To bring that fish in is a challenge and when you do it, you beam with pride, especially if it happens to be a big one.

And even if you don't catch a thing, and you camp where the trees are tall, and the moon is the only light, there's something awe-inspiring about the silence as you look up through the trees into the sky and see the stars as you've never seen them before.

. . . .

FISH SAUCES AND GARNISHES

Name	Broiled, steamed Poached — Sauces	Garnish	Baker - Whole (W) Stufffings	Steaks, Cutlets Fillets — Sauce	Garnish	Broiled Suggested Sauces	Garnishes
Black Bass						Melted Margarine	Lemon Parsley
Sea Bass			(W)Bread	Tomato	Tomato		
Bluefish			(W)Bread	Catsup	Parsley	Melted Margarine	Chopped Almonds
Butterfish						Lemon	Watercress
Cod			(W)Oyster	Egg	Lemon	Melted Margarine	Lemon
Codfish	Shrimp Melted Margarine Caper Oyster	Parsley Cress					
Cusk				Creole	Lemon		
Flounder (Sole)	Bechamel	Chopped Parsley		Egg Parsley Butter	Egg	Tomato	Parsley Lemon
Halibut	Bechamel Cream Egg	Parsley Cress		Brown Hollandaise	Tomato Parsley	Margarine Hollandaise	Parsley Lemon
Mackerel	Caper Parsley	Cucumber Lemon	Pickle Caper		Lemon	Maitre d'hotel	Lemon Cucumber
Mackerer (horse)					Lemon Margarine	Melted	Parsley
Perch						Capers Anchovy	Parsley Lemon
Pickerel			(W)Bread	Tomato	Lemon Parsley	Tomato	Parsley
Pompano						Maitre d'hotel Lemon Butter	Cucumber Cress Cucumbers
Red Snapper	Mushroom Creole	Parsley					
Salmon	Egg Hollandaise Tarter	Cress Lemon		Drawn Butter Lemon	Parsley & Lemon	Anchovy, Caper	Chopped Parsley

Name	Broiled, steamed Poached — Sauces	Garnish	Baker - Whole (W) Steaks, Cutlets Fillets — Stuffings	Sauce	Garnish	Broiled — Suggested Sauces	Garnishes
Shad			(W)Bread		Tomato	Maitre d'hotel Melted Margarine	Parsley Radishes
Sheepshead	Drawn Butter	Parsley Lemon					
Smelt						Remoulade Bechamel	Parsley
Tilefish			(W)Bread	Maitre d'hotel Tomato	Parsley		
Trout	Horseradish	Lemon				Melted Margarine	Lemon
Weakfish			Bread	Lemon	Cress		
Whitefish			Bread	Egg	Egg	Mushroom	Watercress
Haddock	Egg	Parsley, Cress	Pickle Caper	Drawn Butter	Lemon	Oyster	Lemon

FRIED BULLHEADS

F=Fair; G=Good; H=High; L=Low; t or T = trace; n/a = no information available; dashes = zero or unmeasurable

GRAM WT.	FOOD	VITAMINS	CAL	(mg) SOD	PRO	FAT	CARB	CHOL	FATTY ACIDS SAT	UNSAT	CALC	IRON	(mg) POTSM
142	AVERAGE PER SERVING		248	140				(mg) 80					17
	Ingredients:												
454	1 lb bullhead fillets	---	381	---	G	L	---	*	n/a	n/a	---	---	---
56	1/2 cup flour	B1 B2	210	1	F	L	G	---	---	---	L	F	53
56	4 tblspn margarine	A D	400	558	L	H	L	---	L	H	L	---	13
566	Recipe totals (gms; cal; sod. & potsm.)		991	559									66

METHOD

Wash skinned fillets; dry gently with paper towels. Place bullhead fillets in a plastic or paper bag with the flour, twist bag closed and shake to distribute flour evenly. Brown margarine in a heavy frying pan. Reduce heat to medium and fry fish quickly until brown on both sides. Yield 4 servings.

NOTE   Another method is to dip fish in beaten egg, roll in cornmeal or cracker crumbs, then in egg again and fry as above. However, this method will increase the cholesterol content of the recipe because of the egg.

*   There are 320 milligrams of cholesterol in 1 pound of fish fillets (unidentified as to type in U.S.D.A.Handbook No. 8, item 17b, page 146). Total 320 milligrams divided by yield of 4 equals 80 average milligrams of cholesterol per serving.

. . . .

F=Fair; G=Good; H=High; L=Low; t or T = trace; n/a = no information available;   dashes = zero or unmeasurable

GRAM WT.	FOOD	VITAMINS	CAL	(mg) SOD	PRO	FAT	CARB	CHOL	FATTY ACIDS SAT	UNSAT	CALC	IRON	(mg) POTSM
244	AVERAGE PER SERVING		222	369				(mg) 135					665
	Ingredients:												
1135	2-1/2 lbs flounder fillets	B1 B2	895	885	G	L	---	*	n/a	n/a	L	L	3878
28	2 tblspn margarine	A D	200	279	L	H	L	---	L	H	L	---	6
5	1/2 tblspn cornstarch	---	17	---	L	T	L	---	---	---	---	---	---
8	1 tblspn chopped green onion	A^t B1 B2 C	4	T	L	L	F	---	---	---	F	L	18
n/a	1/2 bayleaf		-------					-----n/a-----					-------
227	1 cp chicken broth	---	20	683	L	T	L	---	---	---	L	L	---
10	2 tsp lemon juice	A B1 B2 C	2	---	L	T	F	---	---	---	F	L	14
50	1/2 cp bread crumbs	A^t B1 B2 C^t	195	368	F	L	G	---	---	---	G	F	76
n/a	Dried parsley flakes		-------					-----n/a-----					-------
1463	Recipe totals (gms; cal; sod. & potsm.)		1333	2215									3992

METHOD

Cut flounder into serving pieces and place in well-greased baking dish. Melt margarine, add cornstarch and onion and blend well.   Add bayleaf to the chicken stock and simmer 15 minutes. Remove bayleaf and discard. Add lemon juice. Pour over fish and sprinkle crumbs and parsley flakes over the top. Bake at 425 F. about 20 minutes.
Yield 6 servings.

*   There are 70 milligrams of cholesterol in 100 grams of fish fillets. In 1135 grams, there are 795; divided by 6 servings equals 133 average milligrams of cholesterol in each. (U.S.D.A. Handbook No. 8, item 17b, pg. 146, states that fish fillets contain 320 milligrams of cholesterol in 454 grams of fish fillets. However, type of fish is not identified. Calculations were made from this general figure).

. . . .

BROILED FINNAN HADDIE

F=Fair; G=Good; H=High; L=Low; t or T = trace; n/a = no information available; dashes = zero or unmeasurable

GRAM WT.	FOOD	VITAMINS	CAL	(mg) SOD	PRO	FAT	CARB	CHOL	FATTY ACIDS SAT	UNSAT	CALC	IRON	(mg) POTSM
157	AVERAGE PER SERVING		189	47				(mg) 106					2
	Ingredients:												
908	2 lb finnan haddie	B1 B2	934	---	F	L	*	--------n/a--------		---	---	---	---
5	1 tsp lemon juice	A B1 B2 C	1	----	F	T	F	---	---	--	F	L	7
28	2 tblspn soft margarine	A D	200	279	L	H	L	---	L	H	L	---	6
n/a	pepper	-------------------------------------						-n/a-				------------	
941	Recipe totals (gms; cal; sod. & potsm.)		1135	279									13

METHOD

Cover finnan haddie with boiling water and let stand 10 minutes. Drain, then place on greased broiler rack. Sprinkle with lemon juice and brush with soft margarine. Brown under moderate heat, turn and brush the other side with lemon juice and margarine. Brown. Sprinkle lightly with pepper and serve with egg sauce. (See recipe for egg sauce in this chapter). Yield about 6 servings.

* According to U.S.D.A. Handbook No. 8, pg. 146, items 17a and 17b, there are 70 milligrams of cholesterol in 100 grams of fish steaks and fillets. In 908 grams, there are 636 milligrams of cholesterol divided by 6 servings equals 106 average milligrams of cholesterol per serving.

. . . .

POACHED FISH

F=Fair; G=Good; H=High; L=Low; t or T = trace; n/a = no information available;   dashes = zero or unmeasurable

GRAM WT.	FOOD	VITAMINS	CAL	(mg) SOD	PRO	FAT	CARB	CHOL	FATTY ACIDS SAT	UNSAT	CALC	IRON	(mg) POTSM
159	AVERAGE PER SERVING		121	118				(mg) 106					528
	Ingredients:												
22	1 thick slice of onion	A B1 B2 C	8	2	L	L	L	---	---	---	L	L	35
22	1/5 whole lemon	A B1 B2 C	4	T	L	T	L	---	---	---	F	L	30
n/a	1/2 tsp peppercorns	-------						--n/a--					---
n/a	1 bay leaf	-------						--n/a--					---
908	2 lbs fish fillets*	B1 B2	716	708	G	L	---	*	n/a	n/a	L	L	3102
952	Recipe totals (gms; cal; sod. & potsm.)		728	710									3167

METHOD

This is another way to poach fish besides that mentioned in the first part of this chapter under Poaching or Steaming which is done in a shallow pan. Poaching is done by simmering the fish in a small amount of seasoned water or other liquid which can be strained afterward and used for sauce if desired.

*Fill a skillet half full of water. Heat to boiling then add onion, lemon, peppercorns and bayleaf. Add the fillets. Reduce heat to simmer.   Cooking time will depend on thickness of the fish (from 5 to 15 minutes). Remove fish with a slotted spoon or pancake turner, carefully, to a hot platter or plate. Strain stock before preparing sauce (see next page). Yield 6 servings. Flatfish, flounder, sole and sanddab fillets are very good poached.

. . . .

SAUCE FROM POACHED FISH STOCK

F=Fair; G=Good; H=High; L=Low; t or T = trace; n/a = no information available; dashes = zero or unmeasurable

GRAM WT.	FOOD	VITAMINS	CAL	(mg) SOD	PRO	FAT	CARB	CHOL	FATTY ACIDS SAT	UNSAT	CALC	IRON	(mg) POTSM
78	AVERAGE PER SERVING		30	302									325
	Ingredients:												
454	2 cans tomato sauce (8-oz each)	A B1 B2 C	177	1810	L	L	L	---	---	---	L	L	1934
8	1 tblspn green onion, finely chopped	A B1 B2 C	4	T	L	L	F	---	---	---	F	L	18
462	Recipe totals (gms; cal; sod. & potsm.)		181	1810									1952

METHOD

Strain the fish stock used in poaching (be sure bayleaf is out), then add tomato sauce and green onions and bring to a boil. Cook 2 minutes, then pour over fish.

Add values for sauce to values for recipe under AVERAGE PER SERVING for individual portions.

*   There are 636 milligrams of cholesterol in 908 grams of fresh fish fillets, as calculated from U.S.D.A. Handbook No. 8, pg 146, item 17b. Total 636 milligrams divided by yield of 6 equals 106 average milligrams of cholesterol per serving.

. . . .

304

OVEN—CRISP TROUT

F=Fair; G=Good; H=High; L=Low; t or T = trace; n/a = no information available; dashes = zero or unmeasurable

GRAM WT.	FOOD	VITAMINS	CAL	(mg) SOD	PRO	FAT	CARB	CHOL (mg)*	FATTY ACIDS SAT	UNSAT	CALC	IRON	(mg) POTSM
290	AVERAGE PER SERVING		426	336				211					136
	Ingredients:												
1362	6 Trout (Approx. 3 lbs.)	---	1374	---	G	L	---	n/a*	L	L	---	---	---
56	4 tblspn soft margarine	A D	400	558	L	H	L	---	L	H	L	---	13
64	1/2 cp chopped fresh parsley	A B1t B2 C	28	29	L	L	L	---	---	---	H	H	465
50	1 egg	A B1 B2	75	61	F	F	L	H*	H	L	F	F	65
62	1/4 cp 2% low-fat milk	A B1 B2 C	37	38	H	L	H	L*	L	L	H	L	109
75	3/4 cp fine, dry breadcrumbs	At B1 B2 Ct	293	552	F	L	G	---	---	---	G	F	114
42	1/2 cp shredded Swiss cheese	A B1 B2	151	497	G	G	L	H	G	L	H	L	44
28	2 tblspn margarine	A D	200	279	L	H	T	---	L	H	L	---	6
1739	Recipe totals (gms; cal; sod. & potsm.)		2558	2014									816

METHOD

Wash trout and pat dry with paper towels. If desired, sprinkle the inside of each fish with a little lemon juice. (Since this is optional, lemon juice was not listed in the ingredients). Combine soft margarine and parsley (chopped fine) then spread the mixture inside the cavity of each trout. Beat the egg and milk together. Mix the breadcrumbs and cheese together. Dip each fish first in the egg and milk mixture then roll in the breadcrumb mixture, coating each side well. Generously grease a shallow baking dish or pan; arrange fish on it. If any of the crumb mixture is left, sprinkle it over the fish. Dot with pieces of the 2 tablespoons of margarine. Bake in a very hot oven (500 F.) for 15 – 20 minutes, or until fish are tender and browned. Yield 6 servings.

* There are 275 milligrams of cholesterol in 50 grams of whole egg; 2 milligrams in 62 grams of 2% low-fat milk; 953 milligrams in fish fillets or steaks; and 36 milligrams in Swiss cheese; a total measureable cholesterol in this recipe of 1267 milligrams as calculated in U.S.D.A. Handbook No. 8, pg. 146, item 8, "Other Cheeses," item 12, "Whole Eggs," items 17a and 17b, "fish fillets and steaks," and item 29, "fluid skim" milk. Total 1267 milligrams divided by yield of 6 equals 211 average milligrams of cholesterol per serving.

Since there is no specific category for Swiss cheese and trout, we used the figures in the general category as listed above. Therefore, averages shown for the cholesterol figure may or may not be accurate.

. . . .

SALMON CROQUETTES

F=Fair; G=Good; H=High; L=Low; t or T = trace; n/a = no information available; dashes = zero or unmeasurable

GRAM WT.	FOOD	VITAMINS	CAL	(mg) SOD	PRO	FAT	CARB	CHOL (mg)	FATTY ACIDS SAT	UNSAT	CALC	IRON	(mg) POTSM
150	AVERAGE PER CROQUETTE		190	328				69					505
	Ingredients:												
244	2 medium-size potatoes, mashed without salt	A^t B1 B2 C	160	4	L	T	F	---	---	---	L	L	993
227	1 can salmon (8 ozs.), flaked	A B1 B2	320	876*	G	L	---	--------n/a--------			H	L	819
25	3 green onions, chopped fine	A^t B1 B2 C	10	2	L	L	F	---	---	---	F	L	58
5	1 tspn lemon juice	A B1 B2 C	1	---	L	T	F	---	---	---	F	L	7
50	1/2 cp bread crumbs	A^t B1 B2 C^t	194	368	F	L	G	---	---	---	G	F	76
50	1 egg, beaten	A B1 B2	75	61	F	F	L	H**	H	L	F	F	65
601	Recipe totals (gms; cal; sod. & potsm.)		760	1311									2018

Note   If salt is added to the mashed potatoes, sodium content will increase extensively; for example -- 1/2 teaspoon of salt contains 785 milligrams of sodium.

METHOD

Combine mashed potatoes, salmon (flaked well), onions and lemon juice. Shape into croquettes, roll in crumbs then add in beaten egg and again in crumbs. Fry in hot, deep fat (380 F.) 3 to 5 minutes until golden brown. Drain on paper towels. Yield   4 generous croquettes. (Other flaked fish may be used instead of salmon).

*   High sodium is reflected in the salt used in the canning process.
**   There are 275 milligrams of cholesterol in 50 grams of whole egg, as calculated in U.S.D.A. Handbook No. 8, pg 146, item 12. Total 275 milligrams divided by yield of 4 croquettes equals 69 average milligrams of cholesterol per serving.

Croquettes may be served plain or with a thin white sauce to which a few minced raw onions have been added.

. . . .

SALMON LOAF

F=Fair; G=Good; H=High; L=Low; t or T = trace; n/a = no information available; dashes = zero or unmeasurable

GRAM WT.	FOOD	VITAMINS	CAL	(mg) SOD	PRO	FAT	CARB	CHOL **(mg)	FATTY ACIDS SAT	UNSAT	CALC	IRON	(mg) POTSM
122	AVERAGE PER SERVING		175	387				**（mg) 85					339
	Ingredients:												
454	1 can (16 oz) pink salmon	A B1 B2	640	1755*	G	L	---	---------n/a-------			H	L	1637
30	2 tblspn lemon juice	A B1 B2 C	8	T	L	L	T	F	---	---	---	F	L	42
34	2 egg yolks	A B1 B2	120	18	F	G	L	H**	H	T	H	G	33
n/a	1/4 tspn paprika							---------n/a-------					
50	1/2 cp soft bread crumbs	A^t B1 B2 C^t	195	368	F	L	G	---	---	---	G	F	76
62	1/4 cp hot milk (2% low-fat)	A B1 B2 C	37	38	H	F	G	L**	L	L	H	L	109
99	3 egg whites	B1 B2	50	145	F	T	L	---	---	---	L	L	138
729	Recipe totals (gms; cal; sod. & potsm.)		1050	2324									2035

METHOD

Flake salmon with a fork; remove any hard, round bones or tough skin. Combine salmon with lemon juice, beaten egg yolks, bread crumbs and hot milk. Fold in stiffly beaten egg whites (3). Pour into well greased loaf pan and bake at 400 F. from 1 to 1-1/4 hours. Yield 6 servings. May be eaten plain, or with Hollandaise, or drawn butter, or lemon sauce. See FISH SAUCES AND GARNISHES for other salmon accompaniments, or the end of this chapter for sauce recipes.

*   High sodium content is reflected in the salt used in the canning process.
**   There are 1500 milligrams of cholesterol in 100 grams of egg yolk; in 34, there are 510 (2 egg yolks); and 2 milligrams of cholesterol in 62 grams of low-fat milk, as calculated in U.S.D.A. Handbook No. 8, pg. 146, items 12 and 14 respectively. Total 512 milligrams divided by yield of 6 servings equals 85 average milligrams of cholesterol per serving.

. . . .

SAVORY SALMON MOLD WITH CUCUMBER CREAM DRESSING

F=Fair; G=Good; H=High; L=Low; t or T = trace; n/a = no information available; dashes = zero or unmeasurable

GRAM WT.	FOOD	VITAMINS	CAL	(mg) SOD	PRO	FAT	CARB	CHOL	FATTY ACIDS SAT	UNSAT	CALC	IRON	(mg) POTSM
146	AVERAGE PER SERVING		164	275				(mg)* 129					316
	Ingredients:												
7	1 tblspn gelatin	---	25	---	H	L	---	---	---	---	---	---	---
59	1/4 cp cold water	--0-----------------------											
n/a	1-1/2 tspn dry mustard	--n/a-------------------											
n/a	1/4 tspn cayenne pepper	--n/a-------------------											
34	2 egg yolks, slightly beaten	A B1 B2	120	18	F	G	L	H*	H	T	H	G	33
185	3/4 cp 2% low-fat milk	A B1 B2 C	110	113	H	F	G	L*	L	L	H	L	324
10	2 tspn margarine, melted	A D	67	92	T	H	T	---	L	H	F	---	2
61	4 tblspn lemon juice	A B1 B2 C	15	T	L	T	F	---	---	---	F	L	86
227	1 cp pink salmon, flaked	A B1 B2	320	878	G	L	---	---	---	---	H	L	819
583	Recipe totals (gms; cal; sod. & potsm.)		657	1101									1264

METHOD

Soften gelatin in cold water for about 5 to 6 minutes. Combine mustard and cayenne pepper then stir in slightly beaten egg yolks and milk. Cook in top of double boiler over hot water 5 to 10 minutes, stirring continuously until thickened. Add margarine, lemon juice and gelatin, stirring until gelatin is dissolved. Remove from heat. Fold in salmon. Turn into fish mold and chill until firm. Unmold on crisp lettuce leaves and serve with cucumber dressing. (Other flaked fish may be substituted for salmon). Yield   about 4 servings.

*   There are 510 milligrams of cholesterol in 34 grams of egg yolk and 6 milligrams of cholesterol in 185 grams of low-fat milk, as calculated from U.S.D.A. Handbook No. 8, pg. 146, items 14 and 29 respectively. Total 516 milligrams divided by yield of 4 servings equals 129 average milligrams of cholesterol in each serving.

(See next page for cucumber cream dressing).

. . . .

CUCUMBER CREAM DRESSING

F=Fair; G=Good; H=High; L=Low; t or T = trace; n/a = no information available; dashes = zero or unmeasurable

GRAM WT.	FOOD	VITAMINS	CAL	(mg) SOD	PRO	FAT	CARB	CHOL	FATTY ACIDS SAT	UNSAT	CALC	IRON	(mg) POTSM
28	AVERAGE PER OUNCE		54	5				---					32
	Ingredients:												
30	2 tblspn vinegar	---	T	T	---	L	---	---	---	---	L	L	30
24	2 tblspn granulated sugar	---	96	T	---	---	H	---	---	---	---	L	1
207	1 cp diced cucumber	A^t B1 B2 C	30	12	L	L	L	---	---	---	F	L	331
238	1 cp heavy cream, whipped	A B1 B2 C	840	86	L	G	L	n/a	H	T	F	T	212
499	Recipe totals (gms; cal; sod. & potsm.)		966	98									574

METHOD

Add vinegar and sugar to cucumber; fold in whipped cream. Yield 18 ounces.

. . . .

309

SALMON SOUFFLE

F=Fair; G=Good; H=High; L=Low; t or T = trace; n/a = no information available; dashes = zero or unmeasurable

GRAM WT.	FOOD	VITAMINS	CAL	(mg) SOD	PRO	FAT	CARB	CHOL	FATTY ACIDS SAT	UNSAT	CALC	IRON	(mg) POTSM
181	AVERAGE PER SERVING		219	409				(mg)* 94					439
	Ingredients:												
28	2 tblspn soft margarine	A D	200	279	L	H	L	---	L	H	L	---	6
9	1 tblspn cornstarch	---	34	---	L	T	H	---	---	---	---	---	---
492	2 cp 2% low-fat milk	A B1 B2 C	290	300	H	F	G	L*	L	L	H	L	861
100	2 eggs, separated	A B1 B2	150	122	F	F	L	H*	H	L	F	F	129
454	1 can pink salmon (16 ozs.)	A B1 B2	640	1755	G	L	---	----------n/a--------			H	L	1637
n/a	Parsley flakes	--------------------					-n/a-						--------
1083	Recipe totals (gms; cal; sod. & potsm.)		1314	2456									2633

METHOD

Make a white sauce of the margarine, cornstarch and milk. Add a small amount of the white sauce to the beaten egg yolks, then stir into the remaining sauce. Add flaked salmon. Fold in stiffly beaten egg whites. Bake at 325 F. for 45 minutes. Garnish with parsley flakes or lemon wedges. Serve at once. Yield 6 servings.

*   There are 550 milligrams of cholesterol in 100 grams of whole egg. There are 15 milligrams of cholesterol in 492 grams of low-fat milk, as calculated from U.S.D.A. Handbook No. 8, pg. 146, items 12 and 29 respectively. Total 565 milligrams divided by yield of 6 servings equals 94 average milligrams of cholesterol per serving.

. . . .

SALMON SALAD SANDWICHES

F=Fair; G=Good; H=High; L=Low; t or T = trace; n/a = no information available; dashes = zero or unmeasurable

GRAM WT.	FOOD	VITAMINS	CAL	(mg) SOD	PRO	FAT	CARB	CHOL	FATTY ACIDS SAT	FATTY ACIDS UNSAT	CALC	IRON	(mg) POTSM
141	AVERAGE PER SANDWICH		374	708				(mg)* 12					368
	Ingredients:												
210	1 (7½ ozs.) can pink salmon	A B1 B2	296	813	G	L	---	-------n/a--------			H	L	758
10	2 tspn prepared mustard	---	8	125	L	L	L	---	---	---	F	F	13
42	3 tblspn mayonnaise	A B1t B2	300	252	T	H	T	H*	H	H	F	L	14
25	3 green onions, chopped	A B1 B2 C	10	1	L	L	F	---	---	---	F	L	58
20	1/2 large stalk of celery	A B1 B2 C	3	25	T	T	T	---	---	---	F	L	68
200	8 slices whole wheat bread	At B1 B2 Ct	480	1056	F	L	G	---	---	---	F	F	546
56	4 tblspn margarine	A D	400	558	L	H	L	---	L	H	L	---	13
563	Recipe totals (gms; cal; sod. & potsm.)		1497	2830									1470

METHOD

Flake salmon with a fork until fine; add mustard, mayonnaise, onions and finely chopped celery. Mix well. Spread bread with margarine, add filling, distributing amounts evenly on 4 slices. If desired, add some crisp lettuce. Cut sandwiches in halves or quarters. Yield   4 sandwiches. (Sardines may be substituted for salmon, or tuna fish. If tuna is used, add about 1/4 chopped green pepper). This recipe may also be used for salad. For salmon salad, omit the prepared mustard and do not flake fish too fine; add hard-cooked, sliced egg. For tuna salad, add green pepper, chopped fine, and hard cooked egg. Omit mustard, add a little chopped dill pickle.

*   There are 16 milligrams of cholesterol in 14 grams of mayonnaise as calculated from mayonnaise recipe in this book (see chapter on Fats and Oils). In 42 grams, there are 48 milligrams of cholesterol, divided by 4 servings equals 12 average milligrams of cholesterol per sandwich.

. . . .

BROILED SMELT

F=Fair; G=Good; H=High; L=Low; t or T = trace; n/a = no information available;   dashes = zero or unmeasurable

GRAM WT.	FOOD	VITAMINS	CAL	(mg) SOD	PRO	FAT	CARB	CHOL	FATTY ACIDS SAT	UNSAT	CALC	IRON	(mg) POTSM
145	AVERAGE PER SERVING		265,	140									33
	Ingredients:												
56	4 tblspn margarine	A D	400	558	L	H	L	---	L	H	L	---	56
15	1 tblspn lemon juice	A B1 B2 C	4	T	L	L	F	---	---	---	F	L	21
454	1 pound smelt, dressed	B1 B2	445	---	G	F	---	------n/a--------			---	L	---
56	1/2 cp flour	B1 B2	210	1	F	L	G	---	---	---	L	F	53
581	Recipe totals (gms; cal; sod. & potsm.)		1059	559									130

METHOD

Melt margarine and blend in lemon juice. Clean smelt and split open (if they are large, or leave whole and do not split open if small). Dip fish in margarine and lemon juice mixture, then roll in flour (or shake in a paper bag). Place on double broiler rack and broil for 6 minutes, turning once. Season at the table. Yield about 4 servings.

. . . .

CREAMED TUNA AND PEAS

F=Fair; G=Good; H=High; L=Low; t or T = trace; n/a = no information available;   dashes = zero or unmeasurable

GRAM WT.	FOOD	VITAMINS	CAL	(mg) SOD	PRO	FAT	CARB	CHOL (mg)	FATTY ACIDS SAT	FATTY ACIDS UNSAT	CALC	IRON	(mg) POTSM
176	AVERAGE PER SERVING		221	101				2					189
	Ingredients:												
140	5 oz frozen peas	A B1 B2 C	95	162	L	L	F	---	---	---	L	F	210
492	2 cp 2% low-fat milk	A B1 B2 C	290	300	H	F	G	L*	L	L	H	L	861
25	3 green onions, chopped	A^t B1 B2 C	10	1	L	L	F	---	---	---	F	L	58
364	2 (6½ oz) cans tuna	A B1 B2	760	---	H	F	---	------n/a--------			L	F	---
n/a	Dash pepper, no salt	--------------------					n/a	---------					
14	1 tblspn margarine	A D	100	139	L	H	T	---	L	H	L	---	3
18	2 tblspn cornstarch	---	68	---	L	T	H	---	---	---	---	---	---
1053	Recipe totals (gms; cal; sod. & potsm.)		1323	602									1132

METHOD

Cook frozen peas in unsalted, boiling water about 5 minutes. Set aside. Combine cornstarch with a little water (about 1/4 cup) and stir until smooth. Scald the milk, add drained peas, onions, flaked tuna (drain oil off first), pepper and margarine, then stir in the cornstarch mixture slowly. Keep stirring until sauce thickens. Serve over toast, or saltine crackers, or cooked egg noodles or rice; or prepared patty shells. Yield · 6 servings.

*   There are only 2 average milligrams of cholesterol per serving, as calculated from U.S.D.A. Handbook No. 8, pg. item 29.

. . . .

SCALLOPED TUNA AND PEAS

F=Fair; G=Good; H=High; L=Low; t or T = trace; n/a = no information available; dashes = zero or unmeasurable

GRAM WT.	FOOD	VITAMINS	CAL	(mg) SOD	PRO	FAT	CARB	CHOL	FATTY ACIDS SAT	UNSAT	CALC	IRON	(mg) POTSM
160	AVERAGE PER SERVING		226	98				(mg) T*					153
	Ingredients:												
320	2 cp cooked peas	A B1 B2 C	230	3	L	L	F	---	---	---	L	F	627
454	2-1/2 cp cooked tuna	A B1 B2	760	---	H	F	---	------n/a-------			L	F	---
123	1/2 cp 2% low-fat milk	A B1 B2 C	73	75	H	F	G	L*	L	L	H	L	215
50	1/2 cp dry bread crumbs	A^t B1 B2 C	195	368	F	L	G	---	---	---	G	F	76
14	1 tblspn soft margarine	A D	100	139	L	H	L	---	L	H	L	---	3
961	Recipe totals (gms; cal; sod. & potsm.)		1358	585									921

METHOD

Place peas and tuna (flaked with a fork) in a greased baking dish in layers, ending with the fish. Pour milk over fish, cover with bread crumbs, dot with margarine and bake at 350 F. about 20 to 30 minutes until crumbs are golden brown. Yield   6 servings.

*   There are only 4 milligrams of cholesterol in 123 grams of low-fat milk, as calculated from U.S.D.A. Handbook No. 8, pg. 146, item 29 (fluid skim milk), total 4 milligrams divided by yield of 6 servings equals only a trace of cholesterol per serving.

. . . .

TUNA FISH SANDWICHES (Mock Chicken)

F=Fair; G=Good; H=High; L=Low; t or T = trace; n/a = no information available;   dashes = zero or unmeasurable

GRAM WT.	FOOD	VITAMINS	CAL	(mg) SOD	PRO	FAT	CARB	CHOL	FATTY ACIDS SAT	UNSAT	CALC	IRON	(mg) POTSM
150	**AVERAGE PER SANDWICH**		396	475				(mg) 12					209
	Ingredients:												
182	1 (6½ oz.) can tuna fish	A B1 B2	380	---	H	F	---	------n/a-------			L	F	---
25	3 green onions, minced	A B1 B2 C	10	1	L	L	F	---	---	---	F	L	58
20	1/2 large stalk celery, chopped	A B1 B2 C	3	25	T	T	T	---	---	---	F	L	68
18	1/4 green pepper, chopped	A B1 B2 C	4	3	L	L	L	---	---	---	L	L	38
42	3 tblspn mayonnaise.	A B1^t B2	300	252	T	H	T	H*	H	H	F	L	14
57	1/8 head lettuce shredded	A B1 B2 C	8	5	L	L	L	---	---	---	L	L	100
200	8 slices whole wheat bread	A^t B1 B2 C^t	480	1056	F	L	G	---	---	---	F	F	546
56	4 tblspn margarine	A D	400	558	L	H	L	---	L	H	L	---	13
600	Recipe totals (gms; cal; sod. & potsm.)		1585	1900									837

METHOD

Drain oil from tuna fish then flake fish with a fork; add onion, celery and green pepper and mix well. Stir in the mayonnaise until well blended. Add shredded lettuce, or add to filling separately. Spread 8 slices of bread with margarine. Distribute tuna mixture evenly on 4 slices, cover with other 4 slices of bread; cut in halves or quarters. If mixture is a little dry, add a little mayonnaise. Yield 4 sandwiches.

* Cholesterol in mayonnaise was calculated from recipe in this book under Fats and Oils Chapter. There are 16 milligrams of cholesterol in 14 grams of mayonnaise; 3 tablespoons equals 48 milligrams of cholesterol, divided by 4 sandwiches equals 12 average milligrams of cholesterol per sandwich.

. . . .

A LITTLE SOMETHING ABOUT CLAMS

There are many varieties of clams, which are called bivalve mollusks because their shells are of two separate parts that open and shut.

Soft, or long-necked clams, are sometimes referred to as the "true" clam, or "mya" (Mya Arenaria). Found along the eastern coast from Cape Hatteras to Greenland, and around the British Isles, they can survive in the iciest waters. A favorite food of the walrus, soft-shelled clams have also been used as bait by cod fishermen. Their delicate, tasty meat is enjoyed steamed, fried, in chowders, and at clambakes.

Truly an American custom, the seacoast clambake was taught to settlers in the early 1600's by the Indians, along with other edible foods and how to cook them. Although cooking of other foods has changed considerably over the years, the clambake method remains relatively the same.

The Indians dug pits in the sandy beach and lined them with flat stones. Over the stones they built a fire of driftwood which was kept burning by tossing on more and more wood until the flat stones were white hot. This took quite a while (from 2 to 3 hours) which allowed time to gather clams and seaweed and to pull the silk from the ears of corn which would be baked with the clams.

As soon as the stones were hot enough, the fire was brushed off with branches from nearby trees or long sticks (now we use rakes). Then the hot stones were covered with a layer of seaweed. On this the fresh, unshelled clams were laid, and unhusked corn topped by quantities of seaweed. When the pit was full of alternating layers of clams, corn and seaweed, it was finally covered with wet hide, or sometimes wet cloth, and the edges were held down securely with many stones. The clams and corn cooked about an hour or two. A delicious moist feast resulted when the hide or cloth and layers of seaweed were removed. Present day clambakes include potatoes in jackets, unshelled oysters, and other steamable foods.

Hard-shell, or littleneck clams (Venus Mercenaria) were called quahogs by the early Indians who not only enjoyed them as food, but they cut out the purple patches on the mature shells, strung them and used the shells as wampum (currency).

Hard-shell clams are strongly hinged and connected by two very powerful adductor muscles. Smaller and more difficult to open than soft-shelled clams, they are classified in three sizes: littleneck (small), cherrystone (medium or half grown) and the large chowder clams.

Littlenecks (or young specimens) are served raw on the half shell, while the flesh of large hard clams are used in stews, chowders, pies and even in griddle cakes.

On the central coast of California, Pismo clams (hard-shell) are highly esteemed, not only for their delicious meat but in the sport of digging for them with long-handled, long-pronged, steel forks (similar to pitch forks), as the clams bury themselves rather deep in the sand. There are many other species of clams found along the Pacific coast, but the Pismo seems to be the most popular.

Weights of clams vary greatly from a few ounces per specimen to as much as 600 pounds which may be attained by a giant clam found in the Far East.

When purchasing clams, be sure the shells are tightly closed or that they close to the touch, as this indicates they're alive. Open shells that do not close when touched mean the clams are dead and unfit for use.

OPENING AND CLEANING CLAMS

Before opening clams, scrub and rinse them thoroughly.

To clean the sand from clams, the modern way is to cover them with salt water (2/3 cup of salt to 2 gallons of water) for 20 minutes at a time. Water should be changed about 3 times. During this salting period, clams should expel the sand from their stomachs. Thirty or forty years ago, the method was quite different. Clams were covered with cold water and cornmeal was sprinkled over the top -- 1 cup cornmeal for each peck of clams. Then they were allowed to stand 3 hours or overnight to allow clams to take in the meal and work out any sand in them.

TO OPEN CLAMS (steaming or cutting)

1. Larger clams were usually steamed open, either by pouring a little boiling water over them, and letting them stand a few minutes until shells open, or steaming them for 10 minutes in a steamer until shells open.

2. By cutting --   Hold the clam over a bowl to catch any liquor, then grasp clam in one hand with shell hinge outward. Insert a strong, slim, sharp knife between the shells about 1/4 inch deep near the thickest end, cut around clam through muscles, pry open by twisting knife slightly, carefully, to avoid breaking off any pieces of shell which are difficult to see and remove, and which may get into the meat. After opening, wash meat to remove any additional sand. Meat may be minced or ground. Tender parts may be fried.

A WORD OF CAUTION

When the early settlers were enjoying clam delicacies, pollution was unknown. But nowadays clams can be poisonous if taken from areas contaminated by sewage disposal. They can also be poisonous if taken during the summer months when there is an increase of tiny organisms in the water that suffocate the clams and consequently poision those who eat them. However, not all clams may carry this poison, but if eaten during the months from May to November, it is wise to remove the clams' stomach contents. In California, certain beaches are quarantined during these months and are posted accordingly

. . . .

CLAM CAKES

F=Fair; G=Good; H=High; L=Low; t or T = trace; n/a = no information available; dashes = zero or unmeasurable

GRAM WT.	FOOD	VITAMINS	CAL	(mg) SOD	PRO	FAT	CARB	(mg) CHOL	FATTY ACIDS SAT	UNSAT	CALC	IRON	(mg) POTSM
110	AVERAGE PER SERVING		192	341				138*					145
	Ingredients:												
226	1 cp canned clam meat and liquor	B1 B2	120	---	L	L	L	---	---	---	G	G	316
113	1 cp soda cracker crumbs	A B1 B2	496	1243	F	F	H	---	---	---	L	F	136
100	2 eggs, beaten	A B1 B2	150	122	F	F	L	H*	H	L	F	F	129
439	Recipe totals (gms; cal; sod. & potsm.)		766	**1365									581

METHOD

Do not drain clams. Chop clams in medium-size pieces, mix with clam juice and crumbs and let stand 5 minutes. Add beaten eggs. Shape into cakes and fry in deep, hot fat (375 F.) until golden brown. Drain on paper towels. Yield   4 servings.

*   There are 550 milligrams of cholesterol in 100 grams of whole egg. Total 550, divided by 5 cakes equals 138 average milligrams of cholesterol per cake according to U.S.D.A. Handbook No. 8, pg. 146, item 12.

**High sodium is reflected in the preserving and canning process.

. . . .

NEW ENGLAND CLAM CHOWDER

F=Fair; G=Good; H=High; L=Low; t or T = trace; n/a = no information available; dashes = zero or unmeasurable

GRAM WT.	FOOD	VITAMINS	CAL	(mg) SOD	PRO	FAT	CARB	CHOL (mg)	FATTY ACIDS SAT	UNSAT	CALC	IRON	(mg) POTSM
353	AVERAGE PER SERVING		350	311				18*					789
	Ingredients:												
114	1/4 lb. salt pork (diced)	B1 B2	893	1312	L	H	---	H*	H	L	T	T	48
110	1 medium onion, chopped fine	A B1 B2 C	40	11	L	L	L	---	---	---	L	L	173
294	1 (10½ oz.)can minced clams	B1 B2	158	---	L	L	L	---	---	---	G	G	---
732	6 potatoes, medium size	A^t B1 B2 C	480	12	L	T	F	---	---	---	L	L	2979
1	1/2 tsp black pepper						---n/a---						
861	3-1/2 cp 2% low-fat milk	A B1 B2 C	508	525	H	F	G	L*	L	L	H	L	1507
4	1 tblspn parsley, chopped	A B1^t B2 C	20	3	L	L	F	---	---	---	F	L	29
2116	Recipe totals (gms; cal; sod. & potsm.)		2099	1863									4736

METHOD

In a deep kettle, brown the salt pork, add the chopped onion and cook 2 or 3 minutes. Arrange clams and diced potatoes in layers over the onions, add pepper and cover with cold water. Heat to boiling and simmer until potatoes are tender. Add scalded milk and heat to serving temperature. Serve in bowls that have been warmed, or cups, and garnish with finely chopped parsley. If desired, chowder may be thickened by adding 1 tablespoon of cornstarch mixed until smooth with 3 tablespoons of water, stirring it into the chowder about 10 minutes before serving. Yield 6 servings.

* There are 70 milligrams of cholesterol in 100 grams of pork (without bone) per U.S.D.A. Handbook No. 8, pg. 146, item 32b. In 114 grams, there are 80 milligrams. There are 26 milligrams of cholesterol in 861 grams of 2% low-fat (fluid skim) milk as calculated, item 29. Total 106 milligrams divided by 6 servings equals 18 average milligrams of cholesterol per serving.

. . . .

MANHATTAN CLAM CHOWDER

F=Fair; G=Good; H=High; L=Low; t or T = trace; n/a = no information available; dashes = zero or unmeasurable

GRAM WT.	FOOD	VITAMINS	CAL	(mg) SOD	PRO	FAT	CARB	CHOL	FATTY ACIDS SAT	UNSAT	CALC	IRON	(mg) POTSM
385	AVERAGE PER SERVING		291	517				(mg) 13*					900
	Ingredients:												
114	1/4 lb. salt pork (diced)	B1 B2	893	1312	L	H	---	H*	H	L	T	T	48
110	1 medium onion, chopped fine	A B1 B2 C	40	11	L	L	L	---	---	---	L	L	173
294	1 (10½ oz.) can minced clams	B1 B2	158	---	L	L	L	---	---	---	G	G	---
37	1/2 green pepper, chopped	A B1 B2 C	8	5	L	L	L	---	---	---	L	L	79
50	1/2 cp celery, chopped	A B1 B2 C	8	62	L	T	L	---	---	---	F	L	171
732	6 potatoes medium, diced	A^t B1 B2 C	480	12	L	T	F	---	---	---	L	L	2979
851	3-1/2 cp tomato juice	A B1 B2 C	158	1701	L	L	L	---	---	---	L	L	1954
n/a	dash cayenne, sage, thyme	---------					----n/a----						----
2188	Recipe totals (gms; cal; sod. & potsm.)		1745	** 3103									5404

METHOD

In a deep, heavy kettle, brown salt pork, add chopped onion and cook 2 or 3 minutes until onion looks clear; arrange clams and diced pepper, and celery over the clams then the diced potatoes. Cover with cold water and heat to boiling, then simmer until potatoes are tender. Add tomato juice, spices and herbs and heat only to boiling. Serve in warm bowls. Yield approximately 6 servings.

*   There are 70 milligrams of cholesterol in 100 grams of boneless pork; in 114 grams, there are 80, according to U.S.D.A. Handbook No. 8, pg. 146, item 32b. Total 114 milligrams of cholesterol divided by 6 servings equals 13 average milligrams of cholesterol per serving.

** High sodium is reflected in the preserving and canning process.

. . . .

CLAM GRIDDLE CAKES

F=Fair; G=Good; H=High; L=Low; t or T = trace; n/a = no information available;   dashes = zero or unmeasurable

GRAM WT.	FOOD	VITAMINS	CAL	(mg) SOD	PRO	FAT	CARB	CHOL	FATTY ACIDS SAT	UNSAT	CALC	IRON	(mg) POTSM
55	AVERAGE PER SERVING		83	157				(mg)* 28					51
	Ingredients:												
115	1 cp all-purpose flour	B1 B2	420	2	F	L	G	---	---	---	L	F	109
2	1/2 tsp salt	---	---	785	---	---	---	---	---	---	L G	---	---
5	1-1/2 tsp baking powder	---	2	473	L	T	H	---	---	---	H	---	---
5	1-1/2 tsp cornmeal	A B1 B2	10	T	L	L	G	---	---	---	L	F	6
6	1-1/2 tsp granulated sugar	---	24	T	---	---	H	---	---	---	---	L	T
50	1 egg	A B1 B2	75	61	F	F	L	H*	H	L	F	F	65
185	3/4 cp 2% low-fat milk	A B1 B2 C	110	113	H	F	G	L*	L	L	H	L	324
14	1 tblspn margarine	A D	100	139	L	H	T	---	L	H	L	---	3
170	1 (6 oz.) can minced clams	B1 B2	90	---	L	L	L	---	---	---	G	G	---
552	Recipe totals (gms; cal; sod. & potsm.)		831	1573									507

METHOD

Sift flour with salt, baking powder, cornmeal and sugar. Beat eggs, add milk and melted margarine. Add sifted ingredients and beat until smooth. Fold in undrained minced clams and blend well. Drop by spoonful on greased, hot griddle. When bubbles appear, turn with pancake turner to brown other side. Serve with crisp bacon and tomato chili sauce. Yield   10 servings.

*   There are 275 milligrams of cholesterol in 50 grams of whole egg and 6 milligrams of cholesterol in 185 grams of fluid skim milk, for a total of 281 milligrams, divided by 10 servings equals 28 average milligrams of cholesterol per serving as calculated from U.S.D.A. Handbook No. 8, pg. 146, items 12 and 29 respectively.

. . . .

STEAMED CLAMS

F=Fair; G=Good; H=High; L=Low; t or T = trace; n/a = no information available;   dashes = zero or unmeasurable

GRAM WT.	FOOD	VITAMINS	CAL	(mg) SOD	PRO	FAT	CARB	CHOL	FATTY ACIDS SAT	UNSAT	CALC	IRON	(mg) POTSM
135	AVERAGE PER SERVING		186	174									215
454	Ingredients: 2-1/2 dozen hard-shelled, medium clams, unshelled	B2	240	---	G	L	L	---	---	---	---	---	822
70	5 tblspn margarine	A D	500	696*	L	H	T	---	L	H	L	---	16
15	juice of 1/2 lemon	A B1 B2 C	4	---	L	T	F	---	---	---	F	L	21
	No salt, season at the table												
539	Recipe totals (gms; cal; sod. & potsm.)		744	696									859

METHOD

Scrub shells; wash to free sand in several waters. Steam clams for 10 minutes, or until they open, in a steamer. Melt margarine, blend in lemon juice. Serve margarine and lemon sauce in individual dishes. Dip clam meat in sauce. (The neck [or syphon] which is the thin, tough part of the clam, is not eaten.) Yield   4 servings.

*   Sodium content may be lowered to zero if oil is substituted for margarine (see Chapter IV, Fats, Oils and Salad Dressings under Oils: salad or cooking). However, calories will be increased to 625 instead of 500.

. . . .

322

OYSTER COCKTAIL

F=Fair; G=Good; H=High; L=Low; t or T = trace; n/a = no information available;   dashes = zero or unmeasurable

GRAM WT.	FOOD	VITAMINS	CAL	(mg) SOD	PRO	FAT	CARB	CHOL	FATTY ACIDS SAT	UNSAT	CALC	IRON	(mg) POTSM
151	AVERAGE PER SERVING		115	648				(mg) 150					326
	Ingredients:												
454	30 large eastern oysters, chilled	A B1 B2 C	300	330	L	L	L	H*	n/a	n/a	H	H	549
20													
20	Cocktail Sauce 2 tspn hot prepared horseradish	---	8	18	L	L	L	---	---	---	F	L	58
340	10 oz tomato catsup	A B1 B2 C	360	3540	L	L	F	---	---	---	L	L	1234
30	2 tblspn cider vinegar	---	4	---	T	---	L	---	---	---	L	L	30
61	4 tblspn lemon juice	A B1 B2 C	15	T	L	T	F	---	---	---	F	L	86
n/a	few drops tobasco sauce							----n/a----					
905	Recipe totals (gms; cal; sod. & potsm.)		687	3888									1957

METHOD

Chill oysters. Mix the sauce ingredients and store in refrigerator until ready to serve. Place oysters in chilled, individual serving dishes and pour sauce over them. Yield   6 servings.

*   There are more than 200 milligrams of cholesterol in 100 grams of oysters. In 450 grams, there are more than 900 milligrams of cholesterol, as calculated from U.S.D.A. Handbook No. 8, pg. 146, item 31b. Divide total of 900 milligrams by 6 servings equals more than 150 average milligrams of cholesterol per serving.

OYSTERS ON THE HALF SHELL

Open oysters and serve in the deepest part of the shell (the deepest half) over cracked ice. A soup plate is ideal for this. Place individual dishes of cocktail sauce (the same sauce used in the above recipe) in the center of the plate; garnish with a lemon wedge.

. . . .

FRIED OYSTERS

F=Fair; G=Good; H=High; L=Low; t or T = trace; n/a = no information available; dashes = zero or unmeasurable

GRAM WT.	FOOD	VITAMINS	CAL	(mg) SOD	PRO	FAT	CARB	CHOL	FATTY ACIDS SAT	UNSAT	CALC	IRON	(mg) POTSM
108	AVERAGE PER SERVING		188	149				(mg) 150*					122
	Ingredients:												
454	30 large, eastern oysters	A B1 B2	300	330	L	L	L	H*	n/a	n/a	H	H	549
115	1 cp flour	B1 B2	420	2	F	L	G	---	---	---	L	F	109
n/a	1 tblspn oregano		---------					---n/a---					
n/a	1/2 tsp thyme		---------					---n/a---					
n/a	1 tsp dried parsley flakes		---------					---n/a---					
56	4 tblspn corn oil margarine	A D	400	558	L	H	L	---	L	H	L	---	13
25	3 green onions, chopped fine	A^t B1 B2 C	10	1	L	L	F	---	---	---	F	L	58
650	Recipe totals (gms; cal; sod. & potsm.)		1130	891									729

METHOD

Drain and wash oysters, then set aside. Put flour, oregano, thyme and parsley flakes into a medium-size plastic bag and shake to mix. Then put in 5 or 6 oysters at a time, twist top of bag to prevent mixture from spilling and shake to coat. Melt margarine in a frying pan at medium heat. Drop minced onions in the fat, spreading evenly. Fry oysters 5 or 6 minutes or less until browned on both sides. Drain on paper towels. Serve with lemon wedges or cocktail sauce (see oyster cocktail recipe for sauce). Yield 6 servings.

* See recipe for Oyster Cocktail for cholesterol calculations.

. . . .

OYSTERS ROCKEFELLER

F=Fair; G=Good; H=High; L=Low; t or T = trace; n/a = no information available; dashes = zero or unmeasurable

GRAM WT.	FOOD	VITAMINS	CAL	(mg) SOD	PRO	FAT	CARB	CHOL	FATTY ACIDS SAT	UNSAT	CALC	IRON	(mg) POTSM
147	AVERAGE PER SERVING		241	344				(mg) 180*					201
	Ingredients:												
30	4 strips bacon	B1 B2	180	340	H	H	L	n/a	L	H	L	L	39
56	4 tblspn margarine	A D	400	558	L	H	L	---	L	H	L	---	13
3	4 tblspn fresh spinach	A B1 B2 C	12	2	L	L	L	---	---	---	G	F	14
8	2 tblspn fresh parsley	A B1^t B2 C	4	4	T	T	T	---	---	---	H	H	58
20	2 tblspn celery, chopped	A B1 B2 C	3	25	L	L	L	---	---	---	F	L	68
16	2 green onions, chopped fine	A^t B1 B2 C	6	T	L	L	F	---	---	---	F	L	46
61	4 tblspn fresh lemon juice	A B1 B2 C	15	T	L	T	F	---	---	---	F	L	86
n/a	2 drops anisette	---------						-n/a-					-----
7	1/2 tblspn white wine	---	6	T	T	---	L	---	---	---	L	L	6
25	4 tblspn dry bread crumbs	A^t B1 B2 C^t	98	184	F	L	G	---	---	---	G	F	38
360	24 oysters in half shells	A B1 B2	240	263	L	L	L	H*	n/a	n/a	H	H	436
	Rock salt												
586	Recipe totals (gms; cal; sod. & potsm.)		964	1376									804

METHOD

Fry bacon until crisp; drain on paper towels and set aside. Melt margarine in a saucepan, slowly to prevent burning.
Chop the spinach, parsley, celery and green onions fine, measure and add to melted margarine along with the fresh
lemon juice, anisette and white wine. Cook slowly about 10 to 15 minutes, stirring continuously, then set aside. Make
a layer of rock salt about 1" deep in pie pans. Place oysters on top. Put about a teaspoon of cooked mixture on each
oyster. Crumble bacon, sprinkle a little on each oyster then add bread crumbs on top of all. Broil at 400 F. from 3 to 5
minutes until crumbs are brown. Serve in pie tins. Yield 4 servings.

*   There are more than 720 milligrams of cholesterol in 360 grams of oysters, as calculated from U.S.D.A. Handbook No. 8, pg. 146, item 31b. Divide total of 720 milligrams of cholesterol by 4 servings equals more than 180
average milligrams of cholesterol per serving.

. . . .

F=Fair; G=Good; H=High; L=Low; t or T = trace; n/a = no information available; dashes = zero or unmeasurable

GRAM WT.	FOOD	VITAMINS	CAL	(mg) SOD	PRO	FAT	CARB	CHOL	FATTY ACIDS SAT	UNSAT	CALC	IRON	(mg) POTSM
373	AVERAGE PER SERVING		275	307				(mg)* 248					577
	Ingredients:												
984	4 cp 2% low-fat milk	A B1 B2 C	580	600	H	F	G	L*	L	L	H	L	1722
480	2 cp oysters	A B1 B2	320	350	L	L	L	H*	n/a	n/a	H	H	581
28	2 tblspn margarine	A D	200	279	L	H	L	---	L	H	L	---	6
n/a	paprika	-- n/a -------------------------------											
1492	Recipe totals (gms; cal; sod. & potsm.)		1100	1229									2309

METHOD

Scald milk. While milk is heating slowly, put cleaned oysters, strained oyster liquor, and margarine into a saucepan. Simmer until oysters begin to curl at the edges. Then add scalded milk to the oysters and paprika. Yield 4 servings.

NOTE   If a thickened sauce is desired, mix about 4 tablespoons of cornstarch with 1/4 to 1/3 cup of water until smooth. Add slowly to the scalded milk, a little at a time until desired thickness is reached. Then add to the oysters. A chopped green onion may also be added.

*   There are 960 milligrams of cholesterol in 480 grams of oysters and 30 milligrams of cholesterol in 984 grams of fluid skim milk for a total of 990 milligrams, as calculated from U.S.D.A. Handbook No. 8, pg. 146, items 29 and 31b respectively.

. . . .

DELUXE POORBOY SANDWICHES

F=Fair; G=Good; H=High; L=Low; t or T = trace; n/a = no information available; dashes = zero or unmeasurable

GRAM WT.	FOOD	VITAMINS	CAL	(mg) SOD	PRO	FAT	CARB	CHOL	FATTY ACIDS SAT	UNSAT	CALC	IRON	(mg) POTSM
451	AVERAGE PER SERVING		721	1680				(mg)* 421					610
	Ingredients:												
454	1 one pound loaf French bread	A^t B1 B2 C^t	1315	2631	L	L	G	n/a	L	T	L	L	408
567	2 (10 oz) jars Pacific oysters	A B1 B2	431	---	L	L	L	H	n/a	n/a	H	H	397
113	1/4 head iceberg lettuce, shredded	A B1 B2 C	15	10	L	L	L	---	---	---	L	L	198
100	2 eggs, plus 2 tblspn water	A B1 B2	150	122	F	F	L	H*	H	L	F	F	129
100	1 cp dry bread crumbs	A^t B1 B2 C^t	390	736	F	L	G	---	---	---	G	F	152
56	4 tblspn margarine	A D	400	558	L	H	L	---	L	H	L	---	13
65	1 dill pickle, sliced thin	A B1^t B2 C	10	928	L	L	L	---	---	---	L	F	130
200	1 medium tomato, sliced thin	A B1 B2 C	40	6	L	L	L	---	---	---	L	L	488
113	1/2 cp tomato chili sauce	A B1 B2 C	118	1517	L	L	F	---	---	---	L	L	418
37	4 tspn prepared horseradish	---	14	36	L	L	L	---	---	---	F	L	107
1805	Recipe totals (gms; cal; sod. & potsm.)		2883	6544									2440

METHOD

Split bread lengthwise (or cut loaf in quarters and split lengthwise). Allow oysters to drain 15 minutes. Wash lettuce, pat dry with a paper towel; cut 1/4 head remove hard heart and shred fine. Set aside. Mix 2 eggs with 2 tablespoons water and beat until light. Put breadcrumbs in a soup dish; melt margarine in a frying pan. Dip oysters in egg, then in breadcrumbs, then in egg again. Fry until both sides are brown. Drain on paper towels, then divide equally on four quarters of bread, or, if bread is left whole, spread oysters evenly on bottom of the loaf. Cover with thinly sliced dill pickles, tomatoes and shredded lettuce, then cover with top of loaf. Cut in fourths if loaf is whole. Mix tomato chili sauce and horseradish together and serve in a separate dish.

*   There are 1134 milligrams of cholesterol in 567 grams of oysters and 550 milligrams in 100 grams of whole egg, for a total of 1684 milligrams of cholesterol; divided by 4 servings equals 421 average milligrams of cholesterol in each sandwich, as calculated from U.S.D.A. Handbook No. 8, pg. 146, items 31b and 29 respectively.

. . . .

F=Fair; G=Good; H=High; L=Low; t or T = trace; n/a = no information available; dashes = zero or unmeasurable

GRAM WT.	FOOD	VITAMINS	CAL	(mg) SOD	PRO	FAT	CARB	CHOL	FATTY ACIDS SAT	UNSAT	CALC	IRON	(mg) POTSM
163	AVERAGE PER SERVING		191	706				(mg)* 85					268
	Ingredients:			**									
227	8 oz crabmeat, canned	B1 B2	229	2268	F	L	L	---	---	---	F	L	250
120	1 cp celery, chopped	A B1 B2 C	15	150	T	T	T	---	---	---	F	L	409
25	3 green onions, chopped	A B1 B2 C	20	3	L	L	F	---	---	---	F	L	58
30	2 tblspn lemon juice	A B1 B2 C	8	---	L	T	F	---	---	---	F	L	42
142	1/2 medium cucumber, diced	A^t B1 B2 C	15	6	L	L	L	---	---	---	F	L	227
56	4 tblspn mayonnaise	A B1^t B2^t	400	336	T	H	T	H*	H	H	F	L	19
50	1 hard-cooked egg	A B1 B2	75	61	F	F	L	H*	H	L	F	F	65
650	Recipe totals (gms; cal; sod. & potsm.)		762	2824									1070

METHOD

Drain crabmeat, remove cartilege and shred meat. Mix with remaining ingredients (except egg). Serve over salad greens, slice hard-cooked egg on top of each serving. For additional color, use strips of canned pimiento and Kosher dill pickles. Serves four.

VARIATIONS   Shrimp, lobster, salmon, tuna, sardines (drain oil), or other cooked fish or seafood may be used.

*   There are 275 milligrams of cholesterol in 50 grams of whole egg, and 64 milligrams of cholesterol in mayonnaise (see recipe in chapter on Fats and Oils). Total milligrams of cholesterol in this recipe equal 399, divided by 4 servings equals 85 average milligrams of cholesterol per serving, as calculated from U.S.D.A. Handbook No. 8, pg. 146, item 12.

**   Fresh cooked crabmeat has no measurable sodium. Salt is added in canning.

. . . .

SCALLOPS

If cooked properly, the scallop becomes a sweet, tender delicacy that is worth every effort, but if it is overcooked, it becomes tough and unpalatable. This bivalve has an attractive fluted shell that can be used as its own serving dish. The firm white cube of meat, which is the adductor muscle, is the only part used. Bay scallops are about 3/4" in diameter and the most tender and flavorful. Sea scallops, which are about 2" in diameter, are tastier if cut across the grain before cooking.

Recent experiments with shark meat resulted in the discovery, when substituted for scallop meat, the difference in taste is hardly detectable.

FRIED SCALLOPS are prepared the same as sauteed (see recipe), but are cooked in hot deep fat (380 F.) not over 5 minutes.

BROILED SCALLOPS are dipped in melted margarine or French dressing then rolled in cracker crumbs and placed on a greased baking sheet or broiler pan and browned quickly on all sides -- no longer than 5 minutes.

. . . .

SAUTEED SCALLOPS

F=Fair; G=Good; H=High; L=Low; t or T = trace; n/a = no information available; dashes = zero or unmeasurable

GRAM WT.	FOOD	VITAMINS	CAL	(mg) SOD	PRO	FAT	CARB	CHOL ** (mg)	FATTY ACIDS SAT	FATTY ACIDS UNSAT	CALC	IRON	(mg) POTSM
151	AVERAGE PER SERVING		208	489				69					504
	Ingredients:												
454	16 oz scallops	B1 B2	367	1157*	G	L	F	---	n/a	n/a	L	F	1798
100	1 cp dry bread crumbs	A^t B1 B2 C^t	390	736	F	L	G	---	---	---	G	F	152
50	1 egg, beaten	A B1 B2	75	61	F	F	L	H**	H	L	F	F	65
604	Recipe totals (gms; cal; sod. & potsm.)		832	1954									2015

METHOD

Drain scallops. Check carefully and remove any pieces of shell. Dip in bread crumbs, then in beaten egg and again in fine crumbs. Saute quickly in a small amount of hot oil or other fat. Brown both sides but DO NOT COOK LONGER THAN 5 MINUTES; overcooking toughens scallops. Drain on paper towels. Yield 4 servings.

*   Based on frozen scallops, possibly brined, per U.S.D.A. Handbook No. 8, pg 111, footnote 123, re item 2023.

** There are 275 milligrams of cholesterol in 50 grams of whole egg as calculated from U.S.D.A. Handbook No. 8, pg 146, item 12. Divide 275 total milligrams by 4 servings equals 69 average milligrams of cholesterol per serving.

NOTE   4 ounces scallops equals 1/2 cup; 8 ounces equals 1 cup.

. . . .

F=Fair; G=Good; H=High; L=Low; t or T = trace; n/a = no information available; dashes = zero or unmeasurable

GRAM WT.	FOOD	VITAMINS	CAL	(mg) SOD	PRO	FAT	CARB	CHOL (**mg)	FATTY ACIDS SAT	UNSAT	CALC	IRON	(mg) POTSM
154	AVERAGE PER SERVING		192	353				45					355
	Ingredients:												
454	2 cp scallops	B1 B2	367	1157*	G	L	F	---	n/a	n/a	L	F	1798
177	3/4 cp water							---0---					---
117	1/2 cp white wine	B1 B2	97	6	T	---	L	---	---	---	L	L	108
n/a	dash cayenne							n/a					---
25	3 green onions, chopped	A^t B1 B2 C	10	2	L	L	F	---	---	---	F	L	58
28	2 tblspn margarine	A D	200	279	L	H	L	---	L	H	L	---	6
9	1 tblspn cornstarch	---	34	---	L	T	H	---	---	---	---	---	---
1	1/2 clove garlic, pressed	A^t B1 B2 C	2	T	L	L	F	---	---	---	L	F	5
3	2 tspn parsley flakes	A B1^t B2 C	14	2	L	L	F	---	---	---	F	L	---
17	1 egg yolk	A B1 B2	60	9	F	G	L	H**	H	T	H	G	17
75	3/4 cp dry bread crumbs	A^t B1 B2 C^t	292	552	F	L	G	---	---	---	G	F	114
15	3 tblspn Parmesan cheese, grated	A B1 B2 C	75	111	G	G	L	H**	H	L	H	L	22
921	Recipe totals (gms; cal; sod. & potsm.)		1151	2118									2128

METHOD

Simmer scallops 5 minutes in water, wine and cayenne. Reserve liquid, after draining. Cook onions in 1-1/2 table-spoons margarine until tender; add cornstarch to drained liquid, blending until smooth then add to onions and cook until thickened, stirring constantly. Add garlic and parsley and cook 5 minutes longer then add gradually to beaten egg yolk. Mix well. Chop scallops and add to mixture. Place in greased scallop shells, top with bread crumbs, dot with remaining margarine and sprinkle with Parmesan cheese. Brown in hot oven (400 F.). Yield 6 servings.

*   Sodium is based on frozen scallops, possibly brined, per U.S.D.A. Hanbook No. 8, pg. 111, footnote 123, re item 2023.

**   There are 255 milligrams of cholesterol in 1 fresh egg yolk, and 13 milligrams of cholesterol in 15 grams of cheese, as calculated from U.S.D.A. Handbook No. 8, pg. 146, items 14 and 8 (Other Cheeses) respectively, for a total of 268 milligrams, divided by 6 servings equals 45 average milligrams of cholesterol per serving.

. . . .

SHRIMP CANTONESE

F=Fair; G=Good; H=High; L=Low; t or T = trace; n/a = no information available; dashes = zero or unmeasurable

GRAM WT.	FOOD	VITAMINS	CAL	(mg) SOD	PRO	FAT	CARB	CHOL	FATTY ACIDS SAT	UNSAT	CALC	IRON	(mg) POTSM
400	AVERAGE PER SERVING with sauce		376	405				(mg)* 222					558
	Ingredients:												
100	2 eggs, slightly beaten	A B1 B2	150	122	F	F	L	H*	H	L	F	F	129
236	1 cp water							0					
115	1 cp flour	B1 B2	420	2	F	L	G	---	---	---	L	F	109
908	2 pounds fresh shrimp	B1 B2	826	1270	G	L	F	F*	n/a	n/a	F	F	1996
1359	Recipe totals (gms; cal; sod. & potsm.)		1396	1394									2234

METHOD

PREPARING THE SHRIMP, blend eggs and water, add flour and mix lightly. Shell and devein shrimp, wash, then dip in flour and egg batter. Fry in deep hot fat until golden brown. Drain on paper towels. Yield about 6 servings.

*   There are 550 milligrams of cholesterol in 100 grams of whole egg, and 780 milligrams of cholesterol in 908 grams of fresh shrimp, for a total of 1330; divided by 6 servings equals 222 average milligrams of cholesterol per serving, as calculated from U.S.D.A. Handbook No. 8, pg. 146, items 12 and 33a respectively.

. . . .

(Note: See next page for sauce).

F=Fair; G=Good; H=High; L=Low; t or T = trace; n/a = no information available;   dashes = zero or unmeasurable

GRAM WT.	FOOD	VITAMINS	CAL	(mg) SOD	PRO	FAT	CARB	CHOL	FATTY ACIDS SAT	UNSAT	CALC	IRON	(mg) POTSM
	See previous page, SHRIMP CANTONESE, for figures.							(mg)*					
	Ingredients:												
762	2 (13-1/2 oz.) cans pineapple tidbits	A B1 B2 C	297	8	L	L	F	---	---	---	L	L	760
60	1/4 cp vinegar	---	8	1	---	L	---	---	---	---	L	L	60
100	1/2 cp sugar (granulated)	---	385	1	---	---	H	---	---	---	---	L	3
5	1 tsp soy sauce	B1 B2	3	346	L	L	L	---	---	---	F	F	----17
65	1/4 cp catsup	A B1 B2 C	69	677	L	T	L	---	---	---	L	L	236
n/a	dash tabasco (optional)							--n/a--					
18	2 tblspn cornstarch	---	68	---	L	T	H	---	---	---	--	---	---
28	2 tblspn water							--0--					
5	1 tsp toasted sesame seeds	A B1 B2 C	27	3	F	G	F	------n/a------			H	H	36
1043	Recipe totals (gms; cal; sod. & potsm.)		857	1036									1112

METHOD

TO PREPARE THE SAUCE, drain pineapple and set aside. Save the juice. Add enough water to juice to make 1 cup. Add vinegar, sugar, soy sauce, catsup and tobasco. Bring to a boil. Mix cornstarch and water until smooth then add slowly to hot mixture, stirring constantly. Cook 2 to 3 minutes longer then add pineapple. Pour over shrimp. Bake at 325 F. for 20 minutes. Garnish with sesame seeds. Yield   6 servings.

. . . .

F=Fair; G=Good; H=High; L=Low; t or T = trace; n/a = no information available; dashes = zero or unmeasurable

GRAM WT.	FOOD	VITAMINS	CAL	(mg) SOD	PRO	FAT	CARB	CHOL	FATTY ACIDS SAT	UNSAT	CALC	IRON	(mg) POTSM
161	AVERAGE PER SERVING with sauce		146	552				(mg)* 98					404
	Ingredients:												
454	1 pound fresh, unshelled, medium shrimp	B1 B2	413	635	G	L	F	F*	n/a	n/a	F	F	999
n/a	1 bayleaf							----n/a----					
n/a	1/4 tsp paprika							----n/a----					
	2 pans ice cubes												
454	Total for shrimp (gms; cal; sod. & potsm.)		413	635									999
	SAUCE (Dip)												
150	5 oz catsup	A B1 B2 C	159	1563	L	L	F	---	---	---	L	L	545
n/a	Worcester sauce							----n/a----					
30	2 tblspn lemon juice	A B1 B2 C	8	T	L	T	F	---	---	---	F	L	42
10	1 tsp hot horseradish	---	4	9	L	L	L	---	---	----	F	L	29
190	Total for sauce (gms; cal; sod. & potsm.)		171	1572									616
644	GRAND TOTAL FOR RECIPE (gms; cal; sod. & potsm.)		584	2207									1615

METHOD

Fill a 1-1/2 or 2-quart saucepan half full of water and bring to a rolling boil. Add shrimp, bayleaf and paprika. When water comes to a boil again, cover with a tight lid and simmer 3 to 5 minutes (until shrimp is pink and white). DO NOT OVERCOOK or shrimp will be mushy.

While shrimp is cooking, empty 1 pan of ice cubes into a medium-size bowl. Drain shrimp, discard bayleaf, and turn hot shrimp over the ice. Remove ice from second pan and pour on top of shrimp. Let stand until shrimp is cold, then shell and devein shrimp, rinse in cold water and store in a covered bowl in the refrigerator until ready to serve. Yield   about 4 servings.

SERVING SUGGESTION to keep shrimp crisp, serve in bowls over crushed ice, or in one large shallow dish over ice. French fries, vegetable salad and a fruit dessert make a good accompaniment to this dish.

For the busy hostess, Crispy Shrimp N' Dip can be prepared the day before, along with salad greens, for those special luncheons. Cheese sticks, or saltines, or hot rolls, and fresh fruit and cheddar cheese compliment the menu.

*   There are 390 milligrams of cholesterol in 1 pound of fresh, unshelled shrimp, per U.S.D.A. Handbook No. 8, pg. 146, item 33a. Divide 390 by 4 servings equals 98 average milligrams of cholesterol per serving.

A LITTLE SOMETHING ABOUT LOBSTERS

Would you believe that, at one time, lobsters were found that weighed from 16 to 25 pounds? This fact was mentioned on page 156 of the 1918 revised edition of Fanny Merritt Farmer's "Boston Cooking School Cookbook," published by Little, Brown and Company. It seems that most of those big fellows had been eliminated long before Fanny Farmer's famous cookbooks were written, however, but think about all of the Lobster Newburgh that could have been made from just one of them!

Lobsters are the highest form of Crustaceans. When fresh, their shells are mottled and a dark green color when taken from the water, except those found on sandy bottoms; their shells are quite red. Boiling also causes shells to turn bright red.

A lobster consists of a body, tail, two claws, and four pairs of small claws. On the lower side of the body, in front of the large claws, are various small organs which surround the mouth, and a long and short pair of feelers. Under the tail, there are several pairs of appendages. In the female lobster, also called hen lobster, the spawn is found. This is also known as coral and considered a delicacy.

To open cooked lobsters, take off the large claws, small claws, and separate the tail from the body. By using a fork to pry it out, tail meat may sometimes be withdrawn whole, but more often it is necessary to cut the thin shell portion underneath the tail, using scissors or even a can opener. Separate tail meat through the center and remove the small intestinal vein which runs the entire length; generally darker than the meat, it is sometimes the same color.

Hold the body shell firmly in the left hand, then, with the first two fingers and thumb of the right hand, draw out the body, leaving in the shell the stomach (known as the lady) which is not edible, and also some of the green part of the liver. The liver may be removed by shaking the shell. The sides of the body are covered with the lungs which are also discarded. Break the body through the middle and separate body bones, picking out meat that lies between them, which is tender and sweet. Separate large claws at the joints. If shells are thin, cut off a strip down the edge with a sharp knife so that shell can be broken apart and meat removed whole. If shell is thick, crack with a nut-cracker and use a nut pick to remove the meat, or break the shell with a hammer.

TO COOK LIVE LOBSTERS

1.   BOILING -- In a large, deep kettle bring enough water to a rolling boil that will more than cover the lobsters. Add about 2 teaspoons of salt for each quart of water. Keep water boiling. Grasp lobsters by their backs and plunge head first into the rapidly boiling water. Allow water to come to a boil again, then cover. Reduce heat and simmer no more than 7 minutes (for a one-pound lobster) and about 10 minutes for a two-pound lobster. Overcooking toughens and dries the meat. Remove lobsters immediately from the boiling water and plunge them into cold water, then rinse and drain.

When cool enough to handle, lay them on their backs on a cutting board and, using a heavy, sharp knife, cut them through the shell from end to end lengthwise. Remove and discard the stomach (also known as the "lady," this is a small sac behind the head on a spiny lobster), and the intestinal vein which runs from stomach to tail and must be entirely taken out, and the lungs which are spongy particles between the meat and the shell. Save the pink roe (or coral, found in female lobsters) and the liver, considered delicacies. The roe is usually served beaten into soft margarine or butter and may also be used to color mayonaise red, then placed on broiled lobster.

2.   BROILING -- Northern lobster may be killed by holding it on its back and inserting the point of a sharp knife between the body and tail shells, severing the spinal cord. Split lengthwise, remove the stomach and intestinal vein completely — to the end of the tail. Save the coral-colored roe, and the liver. Crack the large claws and lay the lobster flat. Brush the meat with margarine or oil, place under broiler, shell side down, about 4" from heat for 10 to

12 minutes, depending on size, until golden brown. Larger lobsters may take 15 to 20 minutes. Do not turn, as juices may be lost. Serve a small dish of brown butter or melted margarine with each lobster. A nutcracker is a useful tool for cracking claws.

. . . .

LOBSTER WITH CORAL SAUCE

F=Fair; G=Good; H=High; L=Low; t or T = trace; n/a = no information available; dashes = zero or unmeasurable

GRAM WT.	FOOD	VITAMINS	CAL	(mg) SOD	PRO	FAT	CARB	CHOL	FATTY ACIDS SAT	UNSAT	CALC	IRON	(mg) POTSM
309	AVERAGE PER SERVING		126	104				(mg)* 341					13
	Ingredients:												
681	1 boiled lobster	B1 B2	160	---	G	L	L	L*	n/a	n/a	F	L	---
42	3 tblspn margarine	A D	300	417	L	H	L	---	L	H	L	---	10
9	1 tblspn cornstarch	---	34	---	L	T	H	---	---	---	---	---	---
472	2 cp boiling water							---0---					
30	2 tblspn lemon juice	A B1 B2 C	8	---	L	T	F	---	---	---	F	L	42
1234	Recipe totals (gms; cal; sod. & potsm.)		502	417									52

METHOD

Dice lobster meat. Mash coral with 1 tablespoon margarine. Set aside. Blend cornstarch with a little cold water until smooth; add boiling water slowly, stirring quickly. Cook until thickened, stirring constantly. Add coral and additional margarine. Cook 4 minutes longer. Strain, add lobster meat and lemon juice and heat to boiling. Yield 4 servings.

*   There are 200 milligrams of cholesterol in 100 grams of lobster meat. In 681 grams, there are 1362 milligrams as calculated from U.S.D.A. Handbook No. 8, pg. 146, item 24a. Divide 1362 milligrams of cholesterol by 4 servings equals 341 average milligrams of cholesterol per serving.

. . . .

F=Fair; G=Good; H=High; L=Low; t or T = trace; n/a = no information available; dashes = zero or unmeasurable

GRAM WT.	FOOD	VITAMINS	CAL	(mg) SOD	PRO	FAT	CARB	CHOL	FATTY ACIDS SAT	UNSAT	CALC	IRON	(mg) POTSM
659	AVERAGE PER SERVING		499	437				(mg)* 691					528
	Ingredients:												
681	1 boiled lobster (approx. 1-1/2 lb)	B1 B2	160	---	G	L	L	L*	n/a	n/a	F	L	---
50	1/2 cp mushrooms, sliced	A^t B1 B2 C	15	8	L	T	L	---	---	---	L	L	207
56	4 tblspn margarine	A D	400	558	L	H	L	---	L	G	L	---	13
16	2 green onions, chopped fine	A^t B1 B2 C	6	T	L	L	F	---	---	---	F	L	37
n/a	dash paprika	------------						----n/a----					
n/a	1/8 tsp dry mustard	------------						----n/a----					
4	1 tblspn parsley, chopped	A B1^t B2 C	T	2	T	T	T	---	---	---	H	H	29
117	1/2 cp dry sherry wine	B1 B2	97	6	T	---	L	---	---	---	L	L	108
14	1-1/2 tblspn cornstarch	---	51	---	L	T	H	---	---	---	---	---	---
369	1-1/2 cp 2% low-fat milk	A B1 B2 C	218	225	H	F	G	L*	L	L	H	L	646
10	2 tblspn Parmesan cheese, grated	A B1^t B2 D	50	74	G	G	L	H*	G	L	H	L	15
1317	Recipe totals (gms; cal; sod. & potsm.)		997	873									1055

METHOD

Cut lobster in half. Remove meat and cut it in small pieces. Cook sliced mushrooms in margarine, add chopped green onions, paprika, mustard, parsley and sherry. Heat to boiling. Stir enough water in the cornstarch to make it smooth (scant 1/4 cup), add to milk and cook on medium to low heat until thickened, stirring constantly. Add mushroom mixture and lobster. Fill shell halves. Sprinkle with grated cheese and bake at 450 F. about 10 minutes. Serve with crisp green salad. Yield 2 servings.

*   In 681 grams of lobster meat there are 1362 milligrams of cholesterol; in 369 grams of 2% low-fat milk there are 11 milligrams and in 10 grams of Parmesan grated cheese there are 9 milligrams, for a total of 1382, which, when divided by 2 servings equals 691 average milligrams of cholesterol per servings, as calculated from U.S.D.A. Handbook No. 8, pg. 146, items 24a, 29, and 8 respectively.

. . . .

FRIED FROGS' LEGS

F=Fair; G=Good; H=High; L=Low; t or T = trace; n/a = no information available;   dashes = zero or unmeasurable

GRAM WT.	FOOD	VITAMINS	CAL	(mg) SOD	PRO	FAT	CARB	CHOL	FATTY ACIDS SAT	UNSAT	CALC	IRON	(mg) POTSM
244	AVERAGE PER SERVING		297	400				(mg)* 138					186
	Ingredients:												
227	6 pair frogs' legs	B1 B2	108	---	G	L	---	--------n/a--------		---	---	---	
110	Juice of 1 lemon	A B1 B2 C	20	3	L	T	L	---	---	---	F	L	155
50	1 egg	A B1 B2	75	61	F	F	L	H*	H	L	F	F	65
100	1 cp bread crumbs	A^t B1 B2 C^t	390	736	F	L	G	---	---	---	G	F	152
487	Recipe total (gms; cal; sod. & potsm.)		593	800									372

METHOD

If legs are not skinned, turn the skin over and slip off the legs (like taking off a glove inside-out). However, frogs' legs may be purchased in most supermarkets, in the frozen-food section, ready to cook.

After legs are thawed, wash in cold water and dry with a paper towel. Put legs in a dish or bowl and sprinkle with lemon juice. Let stand while beating the egg, then dip the legs in the beaten egg, then in the fine bread crumbs. (Cracker crumbs may also be used if preferred).   Fry in deep, hot fat (390 F.) 2 to 3 minutes until lightly browned. A French fryer basket is an ideal way to cook the legs. Drain on paper towels. Keep hot in oven (150 F.) until ready to serve. Cover lightly with foil to keep moist. Serve with tartar sauce. Yield   2 servings.

*   There are 275 milligrams of cholesterol in 50 grams of whole egg, according to U.S.D.A. Handbook No. 8, pg. 146, item 12.   Divide by 2 servings equals 138 average milligrams of cholesterol per serving.

. . . .

FISH SAUCES

Many sauces for fish have a white sauce base. Listed below is the recipe for medium-thick white sauce and variations.

WHITE SAUCE

F=Fair; G=Good; H=High; L=Low; t or T = trace; n/a = no information available;   dashes = zero or unmeasurable

GRAM WT.	FOOD	VITAMINS	CAL	(mg) SOD	PRO	FAT	CARB	CHOL	FATTY ACIDS SAT	UNSAT	CALC	IRON	(mg) POTSM
28	AVERAGE PER OUNCE		28	29				(mg)* 1					43
	Ingredients:												
246	1 cp 2% low-fat milk	A B1 B2 C	145	150	H	F	G	L*	L	L	H	L	431
14	1 tblspn margarine	A D	100	139	L	H	T	---	L	H	L	---	3
9	1 tblspn cornstarch	---	34	---	L	T	H	---	---	---	---	---	---
269	Recipe totals (gms; cal; sod. & potsm.)		279	289									434

METHOD

Heat milk and margarine together. Mix cornstarch with 1/4 cup water until smooth then stir into hot milk slowly and continue stirring until sauce thickens. Reduce heat to low and cook about 3 minutes longer. Watch carefully, stirring several times, to prevent scorching. Sauce may be thinned by adding more milk or thickened by adding more cornstarch mixture. Yield   10 ounces.   *Cholesterol content is minimal in basic recipe.

VARIATIONS

1.   Caper Sauce -- To 1 cup white sauce, add 2 to 4 tablespoons chopped capers (about 9 calories per tablespoon. Other nutrient information not available). Use this sauce with boiled, steamed or poached codfish and mackerel; broiled perch and salmon.

2.   Cream Sauce -- use half & half cream instead of milk in white sauce. Values will change accordingly.

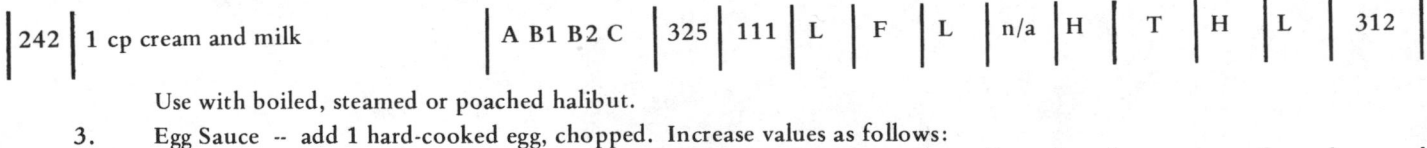

| 242 | 1 cp cream and milk | A B1 B2 C | 325 | 111 | L | F | L | n/a | H | T | H | L | 312 |

Use with boiled, steamed or poached halibut.

3.   Egg Sauce -- add 1 hard-cooked egg, chopped. Increase values as follows:

| 50 | 1 egg | A B1 B2 | 75 | 61 | F | F | L | H* | H | L | F | F | 65 |

*Although cholesterol values will change, 45 milligrams average per ounce, total per cup of egg sauce is only 275 milligrams plus 7 milligrams for the low-fat milk. By itself, an egg is high in cholesterol, but when it is mixed with other ingredients and divided into 3 or 4 servings, the cholesterol intake is reduced.

4.   Lobster Sauce -- Add 1/2 cp finely flaked, cooked lobster. Used creamed lobster on toast or crackers or in deviled lobster.

5.   Mushroom Sauce -- add 1/2 to 1/3 cup chopped or sliced, cooked mushrooms to white sauce. Values are as follows:

| 57 | 1/2 cp mushrooms | A^t B1 B2 C | 15 | 8 | L | T | L | --- | --- | -- | L | L | 236 |

Use boiled, steamed, poached red snapper and broiled white fish.

6.   Oyster Sauce -- heat 1 pint small oysters in their own liquor to boiling. Cook 1/2 minute, then remove from heat and combine with white sauce.

| 454 | 1 pint Eastern oysters | A B1 B2 | 299 | 331 | L | L | L | H* | n/a | n/a | H | H | 549 |

Use boiled, steamed, poached codfish or broiled haddock.

*   There are 908 milligrams of cholesterol in 454 grams of oysters.

7.   Parsley Sauce -- Add 2 to 4 tablespoons chopped, fresh parsley.

| 16 | 4 tblspn fresh parsley | A B1 B2 C | 7 | 8 | L | L | L | --- | --- | -- | H | H | 116 |

Use boiled, steamed, poached mackerel.

8.   Shrimp Sauce -- Add 1/2 cup cooked, chopped shrimp.

| 114 | 1/2 cp chopped shrimp | B1 B2 | 104 | 159 | G | L | F | F* | n/a | n/a | F | F | 261 |

Use boiled, steamed, poached codfish.

*   There are 98 milligrams of cholesterol in 114 grams of shrimp.

. . . .

ANCHOVY SAUCE

F=Fair; G=Good; H=High; L=Low; t or T = trace; n/a = no information available; dashes = zero or unmeasurable

GRAM WT.	FOOD	VITAMINS	CAL	(mg) SOD	PRO	FAT	CARB	CHOL	FATTY ACIDS SAT	UNSAT	CALC	IRON	(mg) POTSM
28	AVERAGE PER OUNCE		189	254									6
	Ingredients:												
56	4 tblspn (1/2 stick) corn oil margarine	A D	400	558	L	H	L	---	L	H	L	---	13
6	1 tsp anchovy paste	---	15	---	G	F	L		--n/a--		H	--	---
n/a	Cayenne pepper							-n/a-					
62	Recipe total (gms; cal; sod. & potsm.)		415	558									13

METHOD

Melt margarine slowly then stir in the anchovy paste and cayenne pepper (dash), blending well. Serve with either boiled or fried perch, or broiled salmon. Yield   2.2 ounces.

. . . .

BECHAMEL SAUCE

F=Fair; G=Good; H=High; L=Low; t or T = trace; n/a = no information available; dashes = zero or unmeasurable

GRAM WT.	FOOD	VITAMINS	CAL	(mg) SOD	PRO	FAT	CARB	CHOL	FATTY ACIDS SAT	UNSAT	CALC	IRON	(mg) POTSM
28	AVERAGE PER OUNCE		31	24				(mg)* 2					41
	Ingredients:												
110	1 small onion	A B1 B2 C	40	11	L	L	L	---	---	---	L	L	173
28	2 tblspn margarine	A D	200	279	L	H	L	---	L	H	L	---	6
56	1/4 cp ham, uncooked, lean, chopped	---	176	---	H	G	---	F*	H	L	---	---	---
18	2 tblspn cornstarch	---	68	---	L	T	H	---	---	---	---	---	---
492	2 cp 2% low-fat milk	A B1 B2 C	290	300	H	F	G	L*	L	L	H	L	861
	add salt at the table												
704	Recipe totals (gms; cal; sod. & potsm.)		774	590									1040

METHOD

Slice onion, melt margarine in a medium-size saucepan, add onion and ham and brown lightly. Add cornstarch, mix well, then add the milk. Stir constantly until it reaches the boiling point then cook over hot water for 10 minutes or longer. Strain before using. Yield about 25 ounces.

NOTE   Bechamel sauce is a white sauce for the most part. Sometimes a little nutmeg is added to the finished sauce; another Bechamel is a medium or thin white sauce using 1/2 cup of meat stock instead of half the milk. If an acid flavor is desired, add 1 teaspoon lemon juice to each cup of sauce. Still a third Bechamel is given above.

Bechamel is used on boiled, steamed, or poached flounder or halibut, or on baked, whole smelt.

*   There are 70 milligrams of cholesterol per 100 grams of boneless pork. In 56 grams, there are 39 milligrams. In skim milk, there are 3 milligrams per 100 grams. In 492 grams, there are 15 milligrams; total milligrams 54 divided by 25 ounces equals 2 average milligrams of cholesterol per ounce, as calculated from U.S.D.A. Handbook No.8, pg, 146, items 32b and 29 respectively.

. . . .

EASY CREOLE SAUCE

F=Fair; G=Good; H=High; L=Low; t or T = trace; n/a = no information available; dashes = zero or unmeasurable

GRAM WT.	FOOD	VITAMINS	CAL	(mg) SOD	PRO	FAT	CARB	CHOL	FATTY ACIDS SAT	FATTY ACIDS UNSAT	CALC	IRON	(mg) POTSM
28	**AVERAGE PER OUNCE**		6	46									64
	Ingredients:												
243	1 (8 oz.) can tomato sauce	A B1 B2 C	45	486	L	T	L	---	---	---	L	L	552
25	3 green onions, chopped	A^t B1 B2 C	10	2	L	L	F	---	---	---	F	L	58
10	1/4 stalk celery, chopped fine	A B1 B2 C	1	13	T	T	T	---	---	---	F	L	34
18	1/4 medium green pepper, chopped	A B1 B2 C	4	3	L	L	L	---	---	---	L	L	38
n/a	1/2 tsp oregano							-----n/a-----					
15	1 tblspn lemon juice	A B1 B2 C	4	---	L	T	F	---	---	---	F	L	21
311	Recipe totals (gms; cal; sod & potsm.)		64	504									703

METHOD

Mix all ingredients together, except lemon juice; simmer for 10 minutes, then stir in lemon juice and pour sauce over fish to be baked. Excellent with sea bass, halibut, pickerel and shad. Also may be used over baked pork chops and meat loaf. Yield about 11 ounces.

. . . .

DRAWN BUTTER SAUCE

F=Fair; G=Good; H=High; L=Low; t or T = trace; n/a = no information available; dashes = zero or unmeasurable

GRAM WT.	FOOD	VITAMINS	CAL	(mg) SOD	PRO	FAT	CARB	CHOL	FATTY ACIDS SAT	UNSAT	CALC	IRON	(mg) POTSM
28	AVERAGE PER OUNCE		30	37									1
	Ingredients:												
75	1/3 cp soft corn oil margarine	A D	534	740	L	H	L	---	L	H	L	---	17
18	2 tblspn cornstarch	---	68	---	L	T	H	---	---	---	---	---	---
472	2 cp boiling water	-------							------				------
565	Recipe totals (gms; cal; sod. & potsm.)		602	740									17

METHOD

Mix 4 level tablespoons margarine and all of the cornstarch together until well blended. Place mixture in a pan over hot water, then, very slowly and stirring constantly, add the 2 cups of boiling water until the sauce reaches the boiling point. Simmer until thick and smooth, stirring often. Just before serving, add the remaining margarine in small pieces, beating constantly. Yield   about 2 cups (20 ounces which is a little over 2 cups).

This sauce is excellent with boiled, poached or steamed sheepshead, or baked haddock or salmon, also with broiled roe. To serve with roe, add lemon juice and chopped parsley to the drawn butter sauce; let it cool slightly then add 2 beaten egg yolks. To 2 cups of sauce, add about 1 tablespoon lemon juice and 1 tablespoon chopped parsley.

. . . .

ESCARGOT (SNAIL) SAUCE

F=Fair; G=Good; H=High; L=Low; t or T = trace; n/a = no information available; dashes = zero or unmeasurable

GRAM WT.	FOOD	VITAMINS	CAL	(mg) SOD	PRO	FAT	CARB	CHOL	FATTY ACIDS SAT	UNSAT	CALC	IRON	(mg) POTSM
6	AVERAGE PER SNAIL		22	95									7
	Ingredients:												
35	2-1/2 tblspn margarine	A D	250	348	L	H	L	---	L	H	L	---	8
6	1-1/2 tblspn parsley flakes	A B1^t B2 C	T	3	L	T	T	---	---	---	H	H	---
4	1 medium clove fresh garlic	A^t B1 B2 C	3	T	L	L	F	---	---	---	L	F	21
25	2 green onions	A^t B1 B2 C	10	2	L	L	F	---	---	---	F	L	58
n/a	1/8 tblspn black pepper	---------						n/a					
2	1/2 tsp salt	---	---	785	---	---	---	---	---	---	G	---	---
n/a	dash nutmeg	---------						n/a					
72	Recipe totals (gms; cal; sod. & potsm)		263	1138									87

METHOD

Wash shells thoroughly inside and out, rinse and drain. Drain liquid from snails and rinse snails in cold water, then stuff each shell with 1 snail. Melt margarine, add chopped parsley, mashed garlic, chopped green onions. Stir once then remove from heat and spoon sauce over each snail, keeping snails upright in a flat baking dish to prevent the sauce from spilling out. Bake at 400 F. 15 to 20 minutes until sauce bubbles. Serve at once. Yield enough for 12 snails.

. . . .

HOLLANDAISE SAUCE

F=Fair; G=Good; H=High; L=Low; t or T = trace; n/a = no information available; dashes = zero or unmeasurable

GRAM WT.	FOOD	VITAMINS	CAL	(mg) SOD	PRO	FAT	CARB	CHOL	FATTY ACIDS SAT	UNSAT	CALC	IRON	(mg) POTSM
28	AVERAGE PER OUNCE		157	189				(mg)* 85					13
	Ingredients:												
34	2 egg yolks	A B1 B2	120	18	F	G	L	H*	H	T	G	H	33
113	1/2 cp (1 stick) margarine	A D	815	1115	L	H	L	---	L	H	L	---	26
n/a	dash cayenne pepper							---n/a---					
15	1 tblspn lemon juice	A B1 B2 C	4	---	L	T	F	---	---	---	F	L	21
162	Recipe total (gms; cal; sod. & potsm.)		939	1133									80

METHOD

Place egg yolks with 1/3 of the margarine, and the lemon juice in top of a double boiler. Do not let the water boil in the bottom of the boiler at any time, but keep it hot. Stir eggs, margarine and lemon juice constantly. When margarine melts, add another 1/3 of the margarine, stirring all of the time. As soon as mixture is thick, remove from heat and add cayenne pepper. Should sauce separate, beat in 2 tablespoons boiling water, drop by drop. Yield   about 3/4 cup. This sauce is delicious on vegetables, such as fresh asparagus, also on poached, steamed, or boiled halibut, or baked or broiled halibut, and in Eggs Benedict.

* There are 1500 milligrams of cholesterol in 100 grams of egg yolk, per U.S.D.A. Handbook No. 8, pg. 146, item 14. In 34 grams, there are 510 milligrams of cholesterol. Divide 510 milligrams of cholesterol by 6 ounces, equals 85 average milligrams of cholesterol per serving.

. . . .

HORSERADISH SAUCE

F=Fair; G=Good; H=High; L=Low; t or T = trace; n/a = no information available;   dashes = zero or unmeasurable

GRAM WT.	FOOD	VITAMINS	CAL	(mg) SOD	PRO	FAT	CARB	CHOL	FATTY ACIDS SAT	UNSAT	CALC	IRON	(mg) POTSM
28	AVERAGE PER OUNCE		59	15									44
	Ingredients:												
n/a	1 tspn dry mustard	--------						--n/a--					--
42	3 tblspn horseradish	---	15	41	L	L	L	---	---	---	F	L	122
n/a	dash cayenne pepper	--------						--n/a--					--
60	4 tblspn heavy cream	A B1^t B2 C^t	220	20	T	G	L	-------n/a-------			F	T	53
102	Recipe totals (gms; cal; sod. & potsm.)		235	61									175

METHOD

Mix dry mustard with a little water to make a smooth paste then combine with horseradish and cayenne. Whip the cream until stiff then fold the mustard and horseradish mixture into it. Salt may be added at the table individually. This sauce is excellent with ham or other meats, either hot or cold, such as cold roast beef, pork or tongue. It is especially good with poached or steamed trout. Yield   about 4 ounces.

. . . .

MAITRE d' HOTEL SAUCE

GRAM WT.	FOOD	VITAMINS	CAL	(mg) SOD	PRO	FAT	CARB	CHOL	FATTY ACIDS SAT	UNSAT	CALC	IRON	(mg) POTSM
28	AVERAGE PER OUNCE		33	36				(mg)* 23					5
	Ingredients:												
565	2 cp drawn butter sauce (see this chapter for recipe)	A D	602	740	L	H	H	---	L	H	L	---	17
15	1 tblspn lemon juice	A B1 B2 C	4	---	L	T	F	---	---	---	F	L	21
4	1 tblspn fresh parsley, chopped	A B1^t B2 C	T	2	T	T	T	---	---	---	H	H	29
34	2 egg yolks	A B1 B2	120	18	F	G	L	H*	H	T	G	H	33
	no salt - Season at the table												
618	Recipe totals (gms; cal; sod. & potsm.)		726	760									100

METHOD

Add lemon juice and fresh, chopped, parsley to the drawn butter sauce (see recipe this chapter). Cool slightly, then add beaten egg yolks. Do not boil sauce after egg yolks are added. This sauce is used on baked tilefish, shad, pompano, and mackerel. Yield about 22 ounces.

* There are 510 milligrams of cholesterol in 34 ounces of egg yolk as calculated from U.S.D.A. Handbook No. 8, pg. 146, item 14; divided by 22 ounces equals 23 average milligrams of cholesterol per ounce.

. . . .

F=Fair; G=Good; H=High; L=Low; t or T = trace; n/a = no information available; dashes = zero or unmeasurable

GRAM WT.	FOOD	VITAMINS	CAL	(mg) SOD	PRO	FAT	CARB	CHOL	FATTY ACIDS SAT	FATTY ACIDS UNSAT	CALC	IRON	(mg) POTSM
28	AVERAGE PER OUNCE		194	1				(mg)* 26					7
	Ingredients:												
34	2 hard-cooked egg yolks	A B1 B2	120	18	F	G	L	H*	H	T	G	H	33
n/a	1 tsp dry mustard							--n/a--					
17	1 raw egg yolk	A B1 B2	60	9	F	G	L	H*	H	T	G	H	17
45	3 tblspn tarragon vinegar	---	6	---	---	T	---	L	---	---	L	L	45
45	3 tblspn cider vinegar	---	6	---	---	T	---	L	---	---	L	L	45
440	2 cp oil	---	3890	---	---	---	H	---	---	L	H	---	---	---
1	1 tsp fresh parsley, chopped fine	A B1^{t} B2 C	---	1	T	T	T	---	---	---	H	H	10
582	Recipe totals (gms; cal; sod. & potsm.)		4082	28									150

METHOD

Work the hard-cooked yolks through a coarse wire sieve, then put them in a bowl with the egg yolk and dry mustard. Add 2 tablespoons of the vinegar and beat thoroughly five minutes. Next, add the oil 1 teaspoon at a time, beating 2 or 3 minutes after each addition. When 5 teaspoons of oil have been added, the remainder of the oil may be added in larger quantities (3 or 4 teaspoons at a time). If the sauce becomes so thick that the beater turns hard, add 1/2 tablespoon vinegar. Stir in parsley. Similar to mayonnaise, remoulade sauce may be used for meat, salads, asparagus, artichokes, and broccoli. It is also good with broiled smelt. Yield   about 21 ounces.

*   There are 765 milligrams of cholesterol in 51 grams of egg yolk, as calculated from U.S.D.A. Handbook No. 8, pg. 146, item 14; divided by 21 ounces equals 26 average milligrams of cholesterol per ounce.

. . . .

TARTAR SAUCE

F=Fair; G=Good; H=High; L=Low; t or T = trace; n/a = no information available; dashes = zero or unmeasurable

GRAM WT.	FOOD	VITAMINS	CAL	(mg) SOD	PRO	FAT	CARB	CHOL	FATTY ACIDS SAT	UNSAT	CALC	IRON	(mg) POTSM
28	AVERAGE PER OUNCE		179	175				(mg)* 57					16
	Ingredients:												
224	1 cp thick mayonnaise	A B1ᵗ B2	1600	1344	L	H	L	H*	H	H	F	L	76
17	2 green onions, chopped fine	Aᵗ B1 B2 C	6	T	L	L	F	---	---	---	F	L	39
16	1 tblspn finely chopped dill pickle	A B1ᵗ B2 C	3	232	L	L	L	---	---	---	L	F	32
n/a	1 tblspn capers (optional)	--------	----	----	----	----	----	--n/a--	----	----	----	----	----
257	Recipe totals (gms; cal; sod. & potsm.)		1609	1576									147

METHOD

Into the mayonnaise, mix the onions, dill pickle and capers until well blended. Cover tightly and refrigerate until needed. Tartar sauce should be thick. Serve with poached salmon or with other hot fish or seafood, also with meat or fish salads. Yield about 9 ounces.

* There are 510 milligrams of cholesterol in 1 cup mayonnaise (see recipe in chapter on Fats and Oils); divided by 9 ounces of tartar sauce equals 57 average milligrams of cholesterol per ounce.

. . . .

FRUITS and FRUIT PRODUCTS

FRUIT AND FRUIT PRODUCTS

F=Fair; G=Good; H=High; L=Low; t or T = trace; n/a = no information available; dashes = zero or unmeasurable

GRAM WT.	FOOD	VITAMINS	CAL	(mg) SOD	PRO	FAT	CARB	CHOL	FATTY ACIDS SAT	UNSAT	CALC	IRON	(mg) POTSM
150	APPLE, fresh, unpared, 1 medium	A B1 B2 C	70	2	L	L	F	---	---	---	L	L	165
100	APPLE BUTTER	B1 B2 C	181	2	L	L	G	---	---	---	L	L	252
100	APPLE CIDER, fresh, or APPLE JUICE, canned or bottled	B1 B2 C	47	1	L	T	F	---	---	---	L	L	101
	APPLE JELLY, see Fruit Jams, Jellies and Preserves												
255	APPLESAUCE, canned, sweetened, 1 cup	A B1 B2 C	230	2	L	T	F	---	---	---	L	F	199
251	APRICOT NECTAR, canned, 8 ozs.	A B1 B2 C	140	T	L	T	F	---	---	---	L	L	399
100	APRICOTS, canned, light sirup	A B1 B2 C	66	1	L	L	G	---	---	---	L	L	239
190	APRICOTS, fresh, 5 medium	A B1 B2 C	90	2	L	L	F	---	---	---	L	L	534
284	AVOCADO, fresh, whole fruit, mainly Fuerte (California, mid and late winter) 3-1/8" diameter	A B1 B2 C	370	11	L	G	F	n/a	L	H	F	L	1715
175	BANANA, fresh, common variety, 1 medium	A B1 B2 C	100	2	L	T	G	---	---	---	L	L	648
100	BANANA FLAKES, or powder, 1 cup	A B1 B2 C	340	4	L	L	G	---			F	F	1477
100	BLACKBERRIES, canned in light sirup	A B1 B2 C	72	1	L	L	G	---	---	---	F	L	111
144	BLACKBERRIES, fresh, 1 cup	A B1 B2 C	85	1	L	L	F	---	---	---	F	L	245
100	BLUEBERRIES, canned, extra heavy sirup	A B1 B2 C	101	1	L	L	H	---	---	---	F	L	55
113	BLUEBERRIES, canned, water pack 1/2 cup	A B1 B2 C	50	1	L	L	F	---	---	---	F	L	68
100	BLUEBERRIES, fresh	A B1 B2 C	62	1	L	L	F	---	---	---	F	F	81
100	BOYSENBERRIES, frozen, sweetened	A B1 B2 C	96	1	L	L	F	---	---	---	F	L	105
	CANTALOUPE, see Muskmelon												
100	CASABA MELON, fresh	A B1 B2 C	27	12	L	T	L	---	---	---	L	L	251
153	CATAWBA GRAPES, (American type, slip skin) 1 cup	A B1 B2 C	95	3	L	L	F	---	---	---	F	L	242

FRUIT AND FRUIT PRODUCTS

F=Fair; G=Good; H=High; L=Low; t or T = trace; n/a = no information available; dashes = zero or unmeasurable

GRAM WT.	FOOD	VITAMINS	CAL	(mg) SOD	PRO	FAT	CARB	CHOL	FATTY ACIDS SAT	UNSAT	CALC	IRON	(mg) POTSM
	CHERRIES												
	Fresh												
100	Sour, red	A B1 B2 C	58	2	L	L	F	---	---	---	L	L	191
100	Sweet	A B1 B2 C	70	2	L	L	F	---	---	---	L	L	191
	Canned, red, solids and liquid												
100	heavy sirup pack	A B1 B2 C	89	1	L	L	G	---	---	---	L	L	124
100	water pack	A B1 B2 C	43	2	L	L	F	---	---	---	L	L	130
	Sweet, solids and liquid												
100	heavy sirup pack	A B1 B2 C	81	1	L	L	G	---	---	---	L	L	126
100	water pack, with or without artificial sweetner	A B1 B2 C	48	1	L	L	F	---	---	---	L	L	130
100	Maraschino, bottled, liquid and solids	---	116	---	L	L	G	---	---	---	---	---	---
227	CRANBERRIES, fresh, approimately 2 cups	A B1 B2 C	104	5	L	L	F	---	---	---	L	L	186
250	CRANBERRY JUICE COCKTAIL 1 cup	A^t B1 B2 C^F	162	3	L	L	H	---	---	---	L	L	25

Note   C^F means that about 2 milligrams (mg) of Vitamin C per 100 grams is from cranberries. Ascorbic Acid (Vitamin C) is usually added to approximately 40 milligrams per 100 grams.

GRAM WT.	FOOD	VITAMINS	CAL	(mg) SOD	PRO	FAT	CARB	CHOL	SAT	UNSAT	CALC	IRON	(mg) POTSM
277	CRANBERRY SAUCE, 1 cp, sweet-ened, canned, strained	A B1 B2 C	405	3	L	L	H	---	---	---	F	L	83
	CURRANTS, fresh												

Production of the European black currant in particular, and, to less extent, of other currants and of gooseberries, is restricted by Federal and State regulations that prohibit shipment of the plants to certain designated states and areas within some states. The regulations have been enacted to prevent further spread of the white pine blister rust inasmuch as these plants are alternate hosts of this disease.

GRAM WT.	FOOD	VITAMINS	CAL	SOD	PRO	FAT	CARB	CHOL	SAT	UNSAT	CALC	IRON	POTSM
100	black, European	A B1 B2 C	54	3	L	L	F	---	---	---	F	F	372
100	red, and white *	A$^+$ B1 B2 C	50	2	L	L	F	---	---	---	F	F	257
60	DAMSON PLUMS, 1 fresh, 2" dia.	A B1 B2 C	25	1	T	T	F	---	---	---	F	L	179
89	DATES, domestic, natural, pitted, cut, 1/2 cup	A B1 B2	245	1	L	L	H	---	---	---	G	H	577
	FIGS												
100	canned, in light sirup	A B1 B2 C	65	2	L	L	H	---	---	---	G	L	152
	* Based on red currants only												

FRUIT AND FRUIT PRODUCTS

F=Fair; G=Good; H=High; L=Low; t or T = trace; n/a = no information available; dashes = zero or unmeasurable

GRAM WT.	FOOD	VITAMINS	CAL	(mg) SOD	PRO	FAT	CARB	CHOL	FATTY ACIDS SAT	UNSAT	CALC	IRON	(mg) POTSM
	FIGS (continued)												
21	dried, one, 2" x 1"	A B1 B2	60	7	L	L	H	---	---	---	H	L	134
100	fresh	A B1 B2 C	50	2	L	L	G	---	---	---	G	L	194
256	FRUIT COCKTAIL, canned, heavy sirup, 1 cup	A B1 B2 C	195	13	L	T	G	---	---	---	F	F	412
20	FRUIT JAMS AND PRESERVES (all) 1 tablespoon	A^t B1^t B2 C^t	55	---	T	T	H	---	---	---	F	L	15
18	FRUIT JELLIES (all) 1 tblspn.	A^t B1^t B2 C^t	50	3	T	T	H	---	---	---	F	L	14
193	FRUIT SHERBETS, 1 cup (orange)	A B1 B2 C	260	19	L	L	G	---	---	---	L	T	42
100	GOOSEBERRIES, fresh	A C	39	1	L	L	L	---	---	---	L	L	155
241	GRAPEFRUIT, white, 1/2 small	A B1 B2 C	45	1	L	L	F	---	---	---	F	L	325
241	pink or red, 1/2 small	A B1 B2 C	50	1	L	L	F	---	---	---	F	L	325
246	juice, fresh, 1 cup	A B1 B2 C	95	1	L	L	F	---	---	---	F	l	399
250	juice, canned, sweetened, 1 cup	A B1 B2 C	130	1	L	L	T	---	---	---	F	L	405
100	GRAPE JUICE, canned or bottled	B1 B2 C	66	2	L	T	G	---	---	---	F	L	116
153	GRAPES, American type (slip skins, such as: Concord, Delaware, Catawba Niagara and Scuppermong) 1 cup	A B1 B2 C	65	5	L	L	F	---	---	---	F	L	242
160	European type (adherent skins such as: Emperor, Flame Tokay Malaga,Muscat and Thompson Seedless),1 cup	A B1 B2 C	95	5	L	L	F	---	---	---	F	L	277
100	GREENGAGE PLUMS, water pack, with or without artificial sweetener	A B1 B2 C	33	1	L	L	F	---	---	---	L	L	82
	GUAVA, fresh												
100	common variety	A B1 B2 C	62	4	L	L	F	---	---	---	G	L	289
100	strawberry variety	A B1 B2 C	65	4	L	L	F	---	---	---	G	L	(289)
100	HONEYDEW MELON	A B1 B2 C	33	12	L	L	L	---	---	---	L	L	251
	HUCKELBERRIES (see blueberries)												
100	ICES, fruit, such as lime, etc.	A B1^t B2^t C	78	T	L	T	G	---	---	---	T	T	3
	JAMS, JELLIES AND PRESERVES see Fruit Jams & Preserves, also Fruit Jellies.												

FRUIT AND FRUIT PRODUCTS

F=Fair; G=Good; H=High; L=Low; t or T = trace; n/a = no information available; dashes = zero or unmeasurable

GRAM WT.	FOOD	VITAMINS	CAL	(mg) SOD	PRO	FAT	CARB	CHOL	FATTY ACIDS SAT	UNSAT	CALC	IRON	(mg) POTSM
100	KUMQUATS, fresh	A B1 B2 C	65	7	L	L	F	---	---	---	F	L	236
110	LEMON, 1 fresh, unpeeled	A B1 B2 C	20	3	L	T	L	---	---	---	F	L	160
248	LEMONADE, frozen concentrate, diluted with 4-1/3 parts water, by volume	A^t B1 B2 C	110	5	T	T	F	---	---	---	L	T	40
122	LEMON JUICE, fresh, 1/2 cup	A B1 B2 C	30	1	L	T	F	---	---	---	F	L	172
15	1 tablespoon	A B1 B2 C	4	T	L	T	F	---	---	---	F	L	21
247	LIMEADE, frozen concentrate, diluted with 4-1/3 parts water by volume	A^t B1^t B2^t C	100	T	T	T	F	---	---	---	L	T	32
123	LIME JUICE, fresh, 1/2 cup	A B1 B2 C	33	1	L	T	F	---	---	---	F	L	128
100	LIMES, acid type, fresh	A B1 B2 C	28	2	L	L	F	---	---	---	F	L	102
100	LOGANBERRIES, fresh	(A B1 B2 C)	62	(1)	L	L	F	---	---	---	F	F	170

NOTE Values in parentheses imputed from another form of the food or from a similar food - per U.S.D.A. Handbook No.8

GRAM WT.	FOOD	VITAMINS	CAL	(mg) SOD	PRO	FAT	CARB	CHOL	FATTY ACIDS SAT	UNSAT	CALC	IRON	(mg) POTSM
100	MANGO, fresh	A B1 B2 C	66	7	L	L	F	---	---	---	L	L	189
	MARASCHINO CHERRIES (see Cherries)												
100	MARMALADE, citrus	B1 B2 C	257	14	L	L	H	---	---	---	G	L	33
	MARMALADE, plums, (see Sapotes)												
385	MUSKMELON (cantaloupe)1/2 med.	A B1 B2 C	60	46	L	L	L	---	---	---	F	L	966
100	NECTARINE, fresh	A C	64	6	L	T	F	---	---	---	F	L	294
180	ORANGE, fresh, 1 medium.	A B1 B2 C	65	2	L	L	F	---	---	---	F	L	360
	ORANGE JUICE												
248	fresh, all varieties, 1 cup	A B1 B2 C	110	2	L	L	F	---	---	---	F	L	496
249	canned, unsweetened, 1 cup	A B1 B2 C	120	2	L	L	F	---	---	---	F	F	496
249	frozen concentrate, diluted with 3 parts water, by volume,1cup	A B1 B2 C	120	2	L	L	F	---	---	---	F	L	463
113	dehydrated crystals, 4 ozs.	A B1 B2 C	430	9	L	L	H	---	---	---	G	F	1953
249	ORANGE-APRICOT JUICE DRINK 1 cup	A B1 B2 C	125	T	L	T	F	---	---	---	L	L	122
182	PAPAYA, fresh, 1 cup of 1" cubes	A B1 B2 C	70	5	L	L	F	---	---	---	F	L	426

FRUIT AND FRUIT PRODUCTS

F=Fair; G=Good; H=High; L=Low; t or T = trace; n/a = no information available; dashes = zero or unmeasurable

GRAM WT.	FOOD	VITAMINS	CAL	(mg) SOD	PRO	FAT	CARB	CHOL	FATTY ACIDS SAT	UNSAT	CALC	IRON	(mg) POTSM
	PEACHES												
257	canned in heavy sirup, 1 cup	A B1 B2 C	200	5	L	T	G	---	---	---	L	L	334
245	canned, water pack, 1 cup	A B1 B2 C	75	5	L	T	F	---	---	---	L	L	336
114	fresh, 1 med., 2" diameter	A B1 B2 C	35	---	L	T	L	---	---	---	L	L	230
	PEARS												
182	fresh, 1 medium	A B1 B2 C	100	4	L	L	F	---	---	---	L	L	237
100	canned in heavy sirup	A^t B1 B2 C	76	1	L	L	F	---	---	---	L	L	84
100	canned, water pack with or without artificial sweetener	A^t B1 B2 C	32	1	L	L	L	---	---	---	L	L	88
100	nectar, approx. 40% fruit	A^t B1^t B2 C^t	52	1	L	L	L	---	---	---	L	L	39
	PERSIAN MELON												
	(no information available)												
	PERSIMMONS, raw												
100	Japanese or kaki	A B1 B2 C	77	6	L	L	F	---	---	---	L	L	174
100	Native	C	127	1	L	L	G	---	---	---	L	G	310
	PINEAPPLE												
140	fresh, diced, 1 cup	A B1 B2 C	75	1	L	T	F	---	---	---	L	L	204
	Canned in heavy sirup, solids and liquids												
260	crushed, 1 cup	A B1 B2 C	195	3	L	T	F	---	---	---	F	L	250
122	sliced, slices and juice, 2 small or 1 large	A B1 B2 C	90	1	T	T	F	---	---	---	L	L	179
100	water pk, all styles except crushed	A B1 B2 C	39	1	L	L	F	---	---	---	L	L	99
259	juice, 1 cup unsweetened	A B1 B2 C**	135	1	L	T	F	---	---	---	F	L	371

** This is the amount from the fruit. Additional acorbic acid may be added by the manufacturer. Refer to the label for this information, per U.S.D.A. Home & Garden Bulletin No. 72.

GRAM WT.	FOOD	VITAMINS	CAL	(mg) SOD	PRO	FAT	CARB	CHOL	SAT	UNSAT	CALC	IRON	(mg) POTSM
	RASPBERRIES												
100	black, fresh	A^t B1 B2 C	73	1	L	L	F	---	---	---	F	L	199
123	red, fresh, 1 cup	A B1 B2 C	70	1	L	L	F	---	---	---	F	G	207
100	black, canned	A^t B1 B2 C	51	1	L	L	F	---	---	---	F	L	135
100	red, canned	A B1 B2 C	35	1	L	L	F	---	---	---	F	L	114
100	red, frozen, not thawed	A B1 B2 C	98	1	L	L	F	---	---	---	F	L	100

FRUIT AND FRUIT PRODUCTS

F=Fair; G=Good; H=High; L=Low; t or T = trace; n/a = no information available; dashes = zero or unmeasurable

GRAM WT.	FOOD	VITAMINS	CAL	(mg) SOD	PRO	FAT	CARB	CHOL	FATTY ACIDS SAT	UNSAT	CALC	IRON	(mg) POTSM
272	RHUBARB, cooked with sugar,1cp	A B1 B2 C	385	2	L	L	G	---	---	---	G	L	552
100	SAPOTES, marmalade plums, fresh	A B1 B2 C	125	---	L	L	F	---	---	---	F	F	---
	STRAWBERRIES												
149	fresh, 1 cup	A B1 B2 C	55	1	L	L	F	---	---	---	G	F	244
100	canned, solids and liquid, with or without artificial sweeteners, water pack	A B1 B2 C	22	1	L	L	F	---	---	---	L	L	111
284	frozen, 10 ozs, not thawed,1crtn	A B1 B2 C	310	3	L	L	G	---	---	---	L	L	295
	PLUMS (all except prunes) also see Damson and Greengage												
60	fresh, 2" diameter, 2 ozs. 1 plum	A B1 B2 C	25	1	T	T	L	---	---	---	L	L	179
256	canned, heavy sirup, purple Italian prunes, 1 cup	A B1 B2 C	205	3	L	L	G	---	---	---	L	L	364
100	POMEGRANATE, pulp, fresh	A^t B1 B2 C	63	3	L	L	F	---	---	---	L	L	259
256	PRUNE JUICE, canned or bottled 1 cup	B1 B2	200	8	L	L	G	---	---	---	F	G	602
270	PRUNES, cooked, unsweetened 1 cup	A B1 B2 C	295	8	L	L	G	---	---	---	F	F	883
	RAISINS, seedless												
14	packaged, 1/2 oz or 1-1/2 tblspn per package, 1 package	A^t B1 B2 C^t	40	4	L	L	H	---	---	---	F	G	107
165	1 cup pressed down	A B1 B2 C	480	45	L	T	H	---	---	---	G	H	1259
116	TANGERINES, fresh, 2-3/8", 1	A B1 B2 C	40	2	L	L	F	---	---	---	F	L	146
249	TANGERINE JUICE, fresh, 1 cp.	A B1 B2 C	125	2	L	L	F	---	---	---	L	L	443
925	WATERMELON, 4" x 8" slice	A B1 B2 C	115	9	L	L	L	---	---	---	L	L	925

. . . .

A LITTLE SOMETHING ABOUT FRUIT

The importance of fruit goes back to the Garden of Eden. Not only has it been mentioned in the Bible, but it has been painted on canvas, done in charcoal, sketched in crayon, and consumed by man.

Besides the nutritional factor, fruit is a source of enjoyment in our diet. Without it, there would be no sparkling Burgundies and champagnes, no delicious fruit pies, no jams or jellies, no fruit cobblers, fruit cakes, fruit cookies, canned fruit, no fruit juices for breakfast, and no oranges to stuff in the traditional Christmas stockings!

The abundance of fruit in American markets is taken for granted today, thanks to the advent of refrigerated railroad cars and trucks, but many people will remember when citrus fruits were only available during the Thanksgiving and Christmas holidays. This was particularly true of the northcentral and northeastern states. Large navel oranges were considered a luxury. Poor families couldn't afford them at all, and middle class families bought them as special treats to stuff into the toes of our white-lisle stockings along with pink-fleshed snow apples, nuts, and decorated hard candies as a gift from Santa Claus.

Today's children are more blase about their Christmas stockings. They can have oranges every day, and apples and candy. (Thank heavens they'll never know about rickets and beri-beri). They grow tall and healthy. They take their vitamins. Their life span will be longer than ours. A little over half a century ago the average life span was 40; today it's in the 70's -- will theirs be 80? I hope so.

. . . .

VITAMINS IN FRUIT

It makes sense to start the day with some form of fruit rich in Vitamin C, such as citrus, strawberries or cantaloupe, otherwise you could fall short of your daily quota of this important vitamin. Fruits highest in Vitamin C, and their juices, are those of the citrus family such as oranges, grapefruit, kumquats, lemons, limes and tangerines. (At this writing, no information was available on tangelos). Guavas are also rich in Vitamin C. Fresh or canned tomatoes are also a good source of Vitamin C, but it takes three times as much as orange juice to give you an equal amount. In frozen fruits, there is little loss of Vitamin C. To get more vitamins and minerals from the pulp of citrus fruits, do not strain it.

In canned fruits, vitamins are retained best when stored in a cool place. Only about 10% of Vitamin C is lost when fruits (and vegetables) are stored for a year at 65 F. When the temperature is 80 F. losses may reach 25% in a year.

Carotene, a precursor of Vitamin A, is well retained in canned fruits. Losses average only about 10% in a year when stored at 80 F.

A few fruits are good sources of Vitamin A, some are mainstay sources of Vitamin C, and their juices supply other vitamins in small amounts, also some calcium and iron. Fruits high in Vitamin A are yellow-fleshed, such as apricots, yellow peaches, cantaloupe (the deep colored varieties) and mangoes and papayas.

The values of fruit in our diet can be seen in a study of the following pages titled "Nutrition at Your Fingertips." A glance down the "Vitamins" column will show that most fruits contain Vitamins A B1 B2 & C.

. . . .

BAKED APPLES

F=Fair; G=Good; H=High; L=Low; t or T = trace; n/a = no information available; dashes = zero or unmeasurable

GRAM WT.	FOOD	VITAMINS	CAL	(mg) SOD	PRO	FAT	CARB	CHOL	FATTY ACIDS SAT	UNSAT	CALC	IRON	(mg) POTSM
201	AVERAGE PER SERVING		248	54									249
	Ingredients:												
600	4 tart cooking apples	A B1 B2 C	280	8	L	L	F	---	---	---	L	L	660
50	4 tblspn granulated sugar	---	193	T	---	---	H	---	---	---	---	L	2
55	4 tblspn brown sugar	---	205	17	---	---	H	---	---	---	G	G	189
n/a	1/2 tspn cinnamon							---n/a---					
n/a	1/2 tspn nutmeg							---n/a---					
19	4 tsp margarine	A D	134	185	L	H	T	---	L	H	L	---	4
80	4 tblspn maple sirup	---	180	8	---	---	H	---	---	---	L	T	141
804	Recipe totals (gms; cal; sod. & potsm.)		992	218									996

METHOD

Wash and thoroughly core apples so that no seeds nor part of the core remains. Stand apples upright on lightly greased foil squares. Be sure foil is large enough to completely cover apples. Press foil against apples and leave tops uncovered. Place in a glass baking dish about an inch apart. Carefully fill the core of apples with 1 tablespoon granulated sugar each. Mix the brown sugar and spices together and spoon equally into each apple until all is used. Place 1 teaspoon margarine on top of each, pressing it down a little. Bring foil up over tops of apples, sealing it by pinching together. This prevents juices from cooking out. Bake at 350 F. for 1 hour, or until apples are tender (test by inserting prongs of a cooking fork through top of foil which will prevent loss of juices). If apples are cooked, remove from oven, untwist top and spread foil open a little, leaving the foil cupped until juices can be poured over apple. Lift apples out with tongs and place in sauce dishes. Pour any sirup over them from foil cups. When lifting apples out of foil, be careful not to squeeze them or they will lose their shape. If desired, top with cream of dairy topping or whipped cream. Yield 4 servings.

. . . .

APPLE BROWN BETTY

F=Fair; G=Good; H=High; L=Low; t or T = trace; n/a = no information available;   dashes = zero or unmeasurable

GRAM WT.	FOOD	VITAMINS	CAL	(mg) SOD	PRO	FAT	CARB	CHOL	FATTY ACIDS SAT	UNSAT	CALC	IRON	(mg) POTSM
208	AVERAGE PER SERVING		304	317									199
	Ingredients:												
42	3 tblspn melted margarine	A D	300	417	L	H	T	---	L	H	L	---	10
200	2 cp bread crumbs	A^t B1 B2 C	780	1472	F	L	G	---	---	---	G	F	304
750	5 cooking apples	A B1 B2 C	350	10	L	L	F	---	---	---	L	L	825
n/a	1/ tsp cinnamon							---n/a---					
n/a	1/2 tsp nutmeg							---n/a---					
100	1/2 cp granulated sugar	---	385	1	---	---	H	---	---	---	---	L	3
37	juice and grated rind of 1 lemon	A B1 B2 C	8	2	L	L	F	---	---	---	F	L	52
118	1/2 cp water						-0-						
1247	Recipe totals (gms; cal; sod. & potsm.)		1823	1902									1194

METHOD

Mix well margarine with bread crumbs. Wash, peel and core apples and slice thin. Arrange layers of apples and crumbs in a greased baking dish. (Reserve some of the crumbs for the top). Mix spices and sugar together and sprinkle each layer with a little. Mix lemon rind and water together. Add to apple and crumbs, distributing evenly. Sprinkle top with crumbs. Bake in a covered baking dish at 350 F. 45 minutes until apples are tender, then remove cover and bake 15 to 20 minutes longer. Serve hot or cold with nutmeg sauce, or with cream. Yield 6 servings.
(See next page for nutmeg sauce).

. . . .

F=Fair; G=Good; H=High; L=Low; t or T = trace; n/a = no information available; dashes = zero or unmeasurable

GRAM WT.	FOOD	VITAMINS	CAL	(mg) SOD	PRO	FAT	CARB	CHOL	FATTY ACIDS SAT	UNSAT	CALC	IRON	(mg) POTSM
118	AVERAGE PER SERVING		150	56									5
	Ingredients:												
200	1 cp granulated sugar	---	770	2	---	---	H	---	---	---	---	L	6
7	1 tblspn flour	B1 B2	26	T	F	L	G	---	---	---	L	F	7
1	dash salt (1/8 tsp)	---	---	196	---	---	---	---	---	---	G	---	---
472	2 cp boiling water							-0-					
14	1 tblspn margarine	A D	100	139	L	H	T	---	L	H	L	---	3
15	1 tblspn vinegar	---	2	T	T	---	L	---	---	---	L	L	15
n/a	1 tsp grated nutmeg							-n/a-					
709	Recipe totals (gms; cal; sod. & potsm.)		898	337									31

METHOD

Mix the sugar, flour and salt together until well blended. Add water gradually, stirring constantly. Add margarine and cook 5 minutes on medium heat. Remove from fire and stir in vinegar and nutmeg. Serve hot on Brown Betty Pudding. This sauce is also good on cottage pudding, plum pudding, any apple puddings and dumplings.

. . . .

APPLE COBBLER

F=Fair; G=Good; H=High; L=Low; t or T = trace; n/a = no information available; dashes = zero or unmeasurable

GRAM WT.	FOOD	VITAMINS	CAL	(mg) SOD	PRO	FAT	CARB	CHOL	FATTY ACIDS SAT	UNSAT	CALC	IRON	(mg) POTSM
297	AVERAGE PER SERVING		437	176				(mg) 1 *					339
	FILLING												
1200	8 medium-size tart apples	A B1 B2 C	560	16	L	L	F	---	---	---	L	L	1320
150	3/4 cp granulated sugar	---	578	2	---	---	H	---	---	---	---	L	5
110	1/2 cp brown sugar	---	410	33	---	---	H	---	---	---	G	G	378
n/a	1 tsp cinnamon	-----------						-n/a-					
n/a	1/2 tsp nutmeg	-----------						-n/a-					
28	2 tblspn margarine	A D	200	279	L	H	L	---	L	H	L	---	6
	CRUST												
5	1-1/2 tspn baking powder	---	5	450	---	---	---	---	---	---	H	---	---
115	1 cp presifted flour	B1 B2	420	2	F	L	G	---	---	---	L	F	109
1	dash salt (1/8 tsp)	---	---	196	---	---	---	---	---	---	G	---	T
12	1 tblspn granulated sugar	---	48	T	---	---	H	---	---	---	---	L	T
39	3 tblspn vegetable shortening	---	330	---	---	H	---	---	F	H	---	---	---
123	1/2 cp 2% low-fat milk	A B1 B2 C	73	75	H	F	G	L	L	L	H	L	215
1763	Total for filling & Crust (gms; cal; sod. & potsm.)		2624	1053									2033

METHOD FOR FILLING

Wash, peel, core and slice apples quite thin then combine them with sugars and spices. Place in a greased baking dish, and distribute them evenly. (A 1-1/2 lb. bread-loaf pan will do). Dot apples with margarine.

METHOD FOR CRUST

Measure baking powder into the flour, add salt, sugar, and sift once. Cut in shortening until mixture looks like coarse meal. Add milk and stir in with a fork until flour is moistened. Knead lightly on a floured board for a few seconds, then roll, or pat, to 1/2" thickness, into the size of the baking dish. Fit over apples, seal edges of dough to the pan all around. Cut 2 or 3 slits in center of dough to allow steam to escape. Bake at 400 F. approximately 25 to 30 minutes, or until crust is light brown. Test apples for doneness by inserting a fork into center of crust. Serve with warm milk to which 1 tablespoon on granulated sugar has been added; or serve with cream or hard sauce. Yield 6 servings.

* Cholesterol in this recipe is minimal.

VARIATION—Peach Cobbler — METHOD

Use 3 cups fresh, sliced peaches. Combine 2/3 Cp. sugar and 1 tblspn flour, stir into peaches and cook and stir constantly over low heat until peaches are tender. Then combine with spices. Delete brown sugar. Bake at 425 F. 25 to 30 minutes until crust is golden brown. Serve with warm, sweetened milk.

APPLE COBBLER (continued)

VARIATION – Peach Cobbler (continued)

Average grams per serving – 172 (with crust)

Average calories per serving – 301 (with crust)

Average milligrams of sodium per serving – 168 (with crust)

Average milligrams of potassium per serving – 248 (with crust)

Cholesterol content – minimal

APPLE DUMPLINGS

F=Fair; G=Good; H=High; L=Low; t or T = trace; n/a = no information available; dashes = zero or unmeasurable

GRAM WT.	FOOD	VITAMINS	CAL	(mg) SOD	PRO	FAT	CARB	CHOL	FATTY ACIDS SAT	UNSAT	CALC	IRON	(mg) POTSM
265	AVERAGE PER SERVING		584	311									299
	FILLING												
900	6 large cooking apples	A B1 B2 C	420	12	L	L	F	---	---	---	L	L	990
165	3/4 cp brown sugar	---	615	54	---	---	H	---	---	---	G	G	568
1	dash salt (1/8 tsp)	---	---	196	---	---	---	---	---	---	G	---	T
n/a	1 tsp cinnamon							-n/a-					
n/a	1/2 tsp nutmeg							-n/a-					
7	1 tsp grated lemon rind	A B1 B2 C	---	2	L	L	F	---	L	---	F	L	11
42	3 tblspn margarine	A D	300	417	L	H	L	---	L	H	L	---	9
	PASTRY												
230	2 cp presifted all-purpose flour	B1 B2	840	4	F	L	G	---	---	---	L	F	219
3	3/4 tsp salt	---	---	1178	---	---	---	---	---	---	G	---	T
150	12 tblspn vegetable shortening	---	1327	---	---	---	H	---	H	H	---	---	---
89	6 tblspns ice water							-0-					
1587	Recipe total, filling & crust (gms; cal; sod. & potsm.)		3502	1863									1797

METHOD FOR FILLING

Wash, peel and core apples. Set whole apples aside. Combine brown sugar, salt, spices and lemon rind, pressing out any lumps in the brown sugar.

METHOD FOR PASTRY

Sift the flour and salt once. Work in the shortening with a pastry blender, or with the fingers until mixture is the consistency of coarse meal. With a fork, stir in lightly 2 tablespoons of ice water, then 2 more. Flour the hands. Gather dough into a ball (as you would a snowball). If it sticks together, do not add more water, but if the dough crumbles under the hand pressure, add 1 more tablespoon of water, sprinkling it over the dough, and working in quickly. If needed to hold the dough together, the 6th tablespoon may be added. Again gather the dough into the hands, squeezing it into a ball. Work it a little to make it smooth, but work quickly and deftly. Too much handling toughens pastry. Place ball of dough on a lightly floured board, sprinkle it with a little flour to prevent sticking, also flour the rolling pin, then roll out by pressing from center of the dough outward, forming a long rectangle (or a large square of dough) 1/8" thick. Cut in squares, each one large enough to cover an apple. Place apples on squares and fill each core cavity with the sugar-spice mixture. Add 1-1/2 teaspoons margarine on top of each apple. Carefully bring corners of dough squares together at top of apples, and pinch together to form a seal to keep the juices in. If a hole appears in the pastry, dampen edges with a little water, and seal. Grease a shallow baking dish or pan; set apples in the dish about an inch apart and bake at 400 F. for 40 to 45 minutes until apples are tender. Test for tenderness by inserting a long-pronged fork into top of the dumpling, piercing the apple. If apples are not done, reduce heat to 350 F. and cook until tender. Dough should be golden brown. Serve with cream, or hot, sweetened milk, or any dairy topping desired. Serves 6. Pitted apricots or peaches may be substituted for apples. Omit the spices.

Note   Jam or jelly tarts can be made out of any left over dough.

. . . .

APPLE PANDOWDY

F=Fair; G=Good; H=High; L=Low; t or T = trace; n/a = no information available; dashes = zero or unmeasurable

GRAM WT.	FOOD	VITAMINS	CAL	SOD (mg)	PRO	FAT	CARB	CHOL	FATTY ACIDS SAT	UNSAT	CALC	IRON	POTSM (mg)
358	AVERAGE PER SERVING		562	119									347
	PASTRY												
144	1-1/4 cp pre-sifted all-purpose flour	B1 B2	525	3	F	L	G	---	---	---	L	F	137
1	dash salt (1/8 tsp)	---	---	196	---	---	---	---	---	---	G	---	T
104	8 tblspn vegetable shortening	---	880	---	---	H	---	---	F	H	---	---	---
59	4 tblspn ice water							----------0----------					
28	2 tblspn melted margarine	A D	200	279	L	H	L	---	L	H	L	---	6
	FILLING												
1500	10 tart cooking apples	A B1 B2 C	700	20	L	L	F	---	---	---	L	L	1650
133	2/3 cp granulated su gar	---	513	1	---	---	H	---	---	---	---	L	4
n/a	1/2 tsp cinnamon							----------n/a----------					
n/a	1/2 tsp nutmeg							----------n/a----------					
160	1/2 cp maple sirup	---	403	3	---	---	H	---	---	---	L	T	282
21	1-1/2 tblspn melted margarine	A D	150	209	L	H	L	---	L	H	L	---	5
---	water, about 1/4 cp							----------0----------					
2150	Recipe totals (gms; cal; sod. & potsm.)		3371	711									2084

METHOD FOR PASTRY

In a medium size mixing bowl, measure flour, add salt, and cut in the shortening with a knife or pastry blender. Add water, 1 tablespoon at a time, mixing lightly and quickly with a fork until pastry holds together. (If mixture crumbles, add more water, a little at a time, until pastry holds together. Too much water will make pastry tough). Roll pastry out onto a lightly floured board, brush with melted margarine, fold over and roll again. Divide in half, wrap in a plastic bag, and chill while preparing the filling.

METHOD FOR FILLING

Wash, peel, core and slice apples very thin. Mix with sugar and spices and set aside.

PUTTING IT ALL TOGETHER

Roll out one-half of the pastry on a lightly floured board until thicker than pie crust. Line the bottom of a greased baking dish with the pastry. Distribute sliced apples evenly on top. Mix maple sirup (molasses may be used instead) with the melted margarine and water and pour over apples carefully distributing it all around the dish. Roll out second half of pastry, cover the apples with it and seal the edges by crimping or pressing top and bottom of pastry together with tines of a dinner fork. Place dish in an oven preheated to 400 F. at least 10 minutes. Remove from oven and cut (or dowdy) the crust into the apples, using a sharp knife. Bake 1 hour longer. Remove from oven and cool a few minutes before serving. Sprinkle crust with a little granulated sugar. Serve with cream, ice cream or daily topping. Yield 6 servings.

. . . .

F=Fair; G=Good; H=High; L=Low; t or T = trace; n/a = no information available; dashes = zero or unmeasurable

GRAM WT.	FOOD	VITAMINS	CAL	(mg) SOD	PRO	FAT	CARB	CHOL	FATTY ACIDS SAT	UNSAT	CALC	IRON	(mg) POTSM
201	AVERAGE PER SERVING		243	54									385
	Ingredients:												
510	1 can apricots (2-1/2 size)	A B1 B2 C	337	5	L	L	G	---	---	---	L	L	1219
179	3/4 cp light whipping cream	A B1 B2 C	536	65	L	G	L	n/a	H	L	F	T	183
14	1 tblspn rum	---	55	T	---	---	L	---	---	---	---	---	---
99	3 egg whites	B1 B2	45	144	F	T	L	---	---	---	L	L	138
802	Recipe totals (gms; cal; sod. & potsm.)		973	214									1540

METHOD

Drain apricots and save juice for other beverages. Either mash fruit through a sieve or put in a blender to make pulp. Combine with stiffly beaten egg whites and whipped cream. Fold in rum and serve cold. Yield   4 servings.

. . . .

PINEAPPLE AMBROSIA

F=Fair; G=Good; H=High; L=Low; t or T = trace; n/a = no information available; dashes = zero or unmeasurable

GRAM WT.	FOOD	VITAMINS	CAL	(mg) SOD	PRO	FAT	CARB	CHOL	FATTY ACIDS SAT	UNSAT	CALC	IRON	(mg) POTSM
132	AVERAGE PER SERVING		303	30									89
	Ingredients:												
280	2 cp fresh pineapple	A B1 B2 C	150	2	L	T	F	---	---	---	F	L	272
227	8 oz marshmallows	B1^{tN}* B2^{t}	724	89	L	T	H	---	---	---	L	F	14
	* Trace niacin only												
238	1 cp heavy whipping cream	A B1 B2 C	840	86	L	G	L	n/a	H	L	F	T	212
24	2 tblspn granulated sugar	---	96	T	---	---	H	---	---	---	---	L	1
n/a	1/2 tsp vanilla							------n/a------					
23	1-1/2 tblspn lemon juice	A B1 B2 C	6	---	L	T	F	---	---	---	F	L	32
792	Recipe totals (gms; cal; sod. & potsm.)		1816	177									531

METHOD

Peel pineapple, cut out the eyes and core, then shred meat fine with a fork or cut fine. Cut the marshmallows in small pieces with scissors, or use minature marshmallows. Mix pineapple with marshmallows, cover and let stand in bottom of refrigerator (the coldest part) until thoroughly chilled. Just before serving, whip cream until it stands in peaks, add sugar and vanilla and blend to mix. Add lemon juice to pineapple, fold in whipped cream and serve. Yield   6 servings.

Note   No figures for cholesterol in heavy whipping cream were available at time of this writing).

. . . .

PRUNE WHIP

F=Fair; G=Good; H=High; L=Low; t or T = trace; n/a = no information available; dashes = zero or unmeasurable

GRAM WT.	FOOD	VITAMINS	CAL	(mg) SOD	PRO	FAT	CARB	CHOL	FATTY ACIDS SAT	UNSAT	CALC	IRON	(mg) POTSM
99	AVERAGE PER SERVING		132	27									251
	Ingredients:												
405	1-1/2 cp· pitted, unsweet. prunes	A B1 B2 C	482	17	L	L	G	---	---	---	F	F	1332
22	1-1/2 tblsp lemon juice	A B1 B2 C	6	---	L	T	F	---	---	---	F	L	31
99	3 egg whites	B1 B2	45	144	F	T	L	---	---	---	L	L	138
67	1/3 cp granulated sugar	---	257	T	---	--	H	---	---	---	---	L	2
n/a	1 tsp vanilla	--- n/a ---											
593	Recipe Totals (gms; cal; sod. & potsm.)		790	161									1503

METHOD

Chop, mash or blend cooked prunes. Mix lemon juice and prune pulp together. Beat egg whites until stiff, add sugar and vanilla and fold into prune mixture until well blended. Serve in individual sauce dishes. If desired, chopped nuts may be sprinkled on top. Yield 6 servings.

. . . .

FRUIT SHERBETS MADE WITH GELATIN
BASIC RECIPE
F=Fair; G=Good; H=High; L=Low; t or T = trace; n/a = no information available;   dashes = zero or unmeasurable

GRAM WT.	FOOD	VITAMINS	CAL	(mg) SOD	PRO	FAT	CARB	CHOL	FATTY ACIDS SAT	UNSAT	CALC	IRON	(mg) POTSM
	AVERAGE (see below)												
7	1 tblspn gelatin	---	25	---	H	L	----	---	---	---	---	---	---
354	1-1/2 cp cold water	---0---											
118	1/2 cp boiling water	---0---											
200	1 cp sugar	---	770	2	---	---	H	---	---	---	---	L	6
	Fruit juice-see below												
679	(add to variations below)		795	2									6
	Variation No. 1 — Use the strained juice of 6 lemons* to make lemon sherbet.												
180	Values for lemon juice*	A B1 B2 C	48	T	L	T	F	---	---	---	F	L	254
859	Lemon sherbet total (gms; cal; sod.& potsm.)		843	2									260
107	Average 8 1/2 cp servings each		105	T									33
	Variation No. 2 — For orange sherbet, use strained juice of 6 oranges and 2 lemons												
60	Lemon Juice	A B1 B2 C	16	T	L	T	F	---	---	---	F	L	85
650	Orange Juice	A B1 B2 C	286	6									1300
1389	Orange Sherbert total (gms; cal; sod. & potsm.)		1097	8									1391
174	Average per serving		137	1									174

METHOD

Soak gelatin in 1/2 cup cold water, add the boiling water and stir until dissolved. Then add the sugar, remainder of the cold water and juices, stirring until well blended. Freeze.

. . . .

CRANBERRY SHERBET

F=Fair; G=Good; H=High; L=Low; t or T = trace; n/a = no information available; dashes = zero or unmeasurable

GRAM WT.	FOOD	VITAMINS	CAL	(mg) SOD	PRO	FAT	CARB	CHOL	FATTY ACIDS SAT	UNSAT	CALC	IRON	(mg) POTSM
239	AVERAGE PER SERVING		238	1									18
	Ingredients:												
7	1 tblspn gelatin	---	25	---	H	L	---	---	---	---	---	---	---
944	1 quart water							---0---					
400	2 cp granulated sugar	---	1540	4	---	---	H	---	---	---	---	L	12
60	juice of 2 lemons	A B1 B2 C	16	T	L	T	F	---	---	---	F	L	85
500	1 pint cranberry juice	A^t B1 B2 C	324	6	L	L	H	---	---	---	L	L	50
1911	Recipe totals (gms; cal; sod. & potsm.)		1905	10									147

METHOD

Soften gelatin in a little cold water and dissolve over heat in a small saucepan, stirring constantly. Remove from heat and set aside. Boil water and sugar together 5 minutes, stirring until sugar is dissolved. Cool sirup a little then add gelatin, lemon juice and cranberry juice. Strain, cool and freeze, Yield   about 8 servings.

. . . .

RASPBERRY SHERBET

F=Fair; G=Good; H=High; L=Low; t or T = trace; n/a = no information available; dashes = zero or unmeasurable

GRAM WT.	FOOD	VITAMINS	CAL	(mg) SOD	PRO	FAT	CARB	CHOL	FATTY ACIDS SAT	UNSAT	CALC	IRON	(mg) POTSM
102	AVERAGE PER SERVING		109	T									5
	Ingredients:												
14	2 tblspn gelatin	---	50	---	H	L	---	---	---	---	---	---	---
708	3 cp cold water						--0--						
236	1 cp boiling water						--0--						
400	2 cp granulated sugar	---	1540	4	---	---	H	---	---	---	---	L	12
227	1 cp strained raspberry juice*	A B1 B2 C	136	1	L	L	H	F	---	---	F	L	n/a
45	3 tblspn lemon juice	A B1 B2 C	12	T	L	T	F	---	---	---	F	L	63
1630	Recipe totals (gms; cal; sod. & potsm.)		1738	5									75

METHOD

Soften gelatin in 1/2 cup cold water, then dissolve in 1 cup boiling water. Add sugar, fruit juice and remaining cold water. Stir to dissolve sugar. Freeze. Yield 2 quarts sherbet.

* 1 cup strained strawberry juice may be used instead.

. . . .

373

FRUIT DESSERTS MADE WITHOUT GELATIN

LEMON SHERBET (with water)

F=Fair; G=Good; H=High; L=Low; t or T = trace; n/a = no information available; dashes = zero or unmeasurable

GRAM WT.	FOOD	VITAMINS	CAL	(mg) SOD	PRO	FAT	CARB	CHOL	FATTY ACIDS SAT	UNSAT	CALC	IRON	(mg) POTSM
224	AVERAGE PER SERVING (8)		298	13									46
	Ingredients:												
944	1 quart water	----------						---0---					----
600	3 cp granulated sugar	---	2310	6	---	---	H	---	---	---	---	L	18
183	3/4 cp lemon juice	A B1 B2 C	45	2	L	T	H F	---	---	---	F	L	258
66	2 egg whites	B1 B2	30	96	F	T	L	---	---	---	L	L	92
1793	Recipe totals (gms; cal; sod. & potsm.)		2385	104									368

METHOD

Boil water and sugar together about 5 minutes, stirring until sugar is dissolved. Stir in lemon juice. Cool and freeze until mushy. Add stiffly beaten egg whites then continue freezing.

. . . .

LEMON SHERBET (with milk)

F=Fair; G=Good; H=High; L=Low; t or T = trace; n/a = no information available;   dashes = zero or unmeasurable

GRAM WT.	FOOD	VITAMINS	CAL	(mg) SOD	PRO	FAT	CARB	CHOL	FATTY ACIDS SAT	UNSAT	CALC	IRON	(mg) POTSM
176	AVERAGE PER SERVING		221	75				(mg) 4 *					239
	Ingredients:												
122	1/2 cp lemon juice	A B1 B2 C	30	1	L	T	F	---	---	---	F	L	172
300	1-1/2 cp granulated sugar	---	1155	3	---	---	H	---	---	---	---	L	9
984	4 cp low-fat 2% milk	A B1 B2 C	580	600	H	F	G	L*	L	L	H	L	1722
1406	Recipe totals (gms; cal. sod. & potsm.)		1765	604									1903

METHOD

Mix the strained lemon juice and sugar together and add to the milk slowly, stirring constantly. (By adding the lemon juice and sugar mixture to the milk there is less chance of curdling). Freeze.   Yield 8 servings.

*   There are 29.52 milligrams of cholesterol in 984 grams of fluid skim milk, as calculated from U.S.D.A. Handbook No. 8, pg. 146, item 29. Divided by 8 servings equals 3.69 milligrams of cholesterol per serving (rounded out to 4 milligrams).

. . . .

PINEAPPLE SHERBET

F=Fair; G=Good; H=High; L=Low; t or T = trace; n/a = no information available; dashes = zero or unmeasurable

GRAM WT.	FOOD	VITAMINS	CAL	(mg) SOD	PRO	FAT	CARB	CHOL	FATTY ACIDS SAT	UNSAT	CALC	IRON	(mg) POTSM
245	AVERAGE PER SERVING		246	13									81
	Ingredients:												
944	4 cp water	---------------						---0---					------
400	2 cp granulated sugar	---	1527	4	---	---	H	---	---	---	---	L	12
520	2 cp crushed pineapple, fresh or canned	A B1 B2 C	390	6	L	T	F	---	---	---	F	L	504
30	juice of 1 lemon	A B1 B2 C	8	T	L	T	F	---	---	---	F	L	42
66	2 egg whites	B1 B2	30	96	F	T	L	---	---	---	L	L	92
1960	Recipe totals (gms; cal; sod. & potsm.)		1968	106									650

METHOD

Boil water and sugar together about 5 minutes, stirring to dissolve sugar. Scald pineapple in the boiling sirup then rub through a sieve. Cool, add lemon juice, and freeze to a mush. Add stiffly beaten egg whites and continue freezing. Yield 8 servings.

. . . .

RASPBERRY SHERBET

F=Fair; G=Good; H=High; L=Low; t or T = trace; n/a = no information available; dashes = zero or unmeasurable

GRAM WT.	FOOD	VITAMINS	CAL	(mg) SOD	PRO	FAT	CARB	CHOL	FATTY ACIDS SAT	UNSAT	CALC	IRON	(mg) POTSM
93	AVERAGE PER SERVING		134	7									113
	Ingredients:												
200	1 cp granulated sugar	---	770	2	---	---	H	---	---	---	---	L	6
492	1 qt. fresh red raspberries	A B1 B2 C	280	4	L	L	F	---	---	---	F	G	827
15	2 tblspn lemon juice	A B1 B2 C	4	---	L	T	F	---	---	---	F	L	21
33	1 egg white	B1 B2	15	48	F	T	L	---	---	---	L	L	46
740	Recipe totals (gms; cal; sod. & potsm.)		1069	54									900

METHOD

Add sugar to the washed berries, and let stand in refrigerator for 2 hours. If not sweet enough, add more sugar. Add lemon juice and freeze until mushy. Then add the stiffly beaten egg whites and continue freezing. Yield 8 servings.

. . . .

CRANBERRY ICE

F=Fair; G=Good; H=High; L=Low; t or T = trace; n/a = no information available; dashes = zero or unmeasurable

GRAM WT.	FOOD	VITAMINS	CAL	(mg) SOD	PRO	FAT	CARB	CHOL	FATTY ACIDS SAT	UNSAT	CALC	IRON	(mg) POTSM
250	AVERAGE PER SERVING		314	2									49
	Ingredients:												
454	1 qt fresh cranberries	A B1 B2 C	200	9	L	L	F	---	---	---	L	F	372
944	1 qt boiling water	-------						---0---					
600	3 cp granulated sugar	---	2310	6	---	---	H	---	---	---	---	L	18
1998	Recipe total (gms; cal; sod. & potsm.)		2510	15									390

METHOD

Wash cranberries. Remove any stems and bad berries and discard. Cook cranberries in a small amount of water until soft, or until they begin to pop. Press berries through a sieve. Make a sirup by boiling the water and sugar together for 5 minutes. Add berries, cool and freeze. Yield   8 servings.

. . . .

LEMON ICE

F=Fair; G=Good; H=High; L=Low; t or T = trace; n/a = no information available; dashes = zero or unmeasurable

GRAM WT.	FOOD	VITAMINS	CAL	(mg) SOD	PRO	FAT	CARB	CHOL	FATTY ACIDS SAT	UNSAT	CALC	IRON	(mg) POTSM
191	AVERAGE PER SERVING		198	1									34
	Ingredients:												
944	1 qt water	-----------------------------n/a-----------------------------											
400	2 cp granulated sugar	---	1540	4	---	---	H	---	---	---	---	L	12
183	3/4 cp lemon juice, strained	A B1 B2 C	45	2	L	T	F	---	---	---	F	L	258
1527	Recipe totals (gms; cal; sod. & potsm.)		1585	6									270

METHOD

Make a sirup by adding sugar to the boiling water, cooking and stirring about 5 minutes until dissolved. Stir in strained lemon juice, cool and freeze. Yield   8 servings.

. . . .

ORANGE ICE

F=Fair; G=Good; H=High; L=Low; t or T = trace; n/a = no information available; dashes = zero or unmeasurable

GRAM WT.	FOOD	VITAMINS	CAL	(mg) SOD	PRO	FAT	CARB	CHOL	FATTY ACIDS SAT	UNSAT	CALC	IRON	(mg) POTSM
241	AVERAGE PER SERVING		222	1									136
	Ingredients:												
944	1 quart water	--0---------------------------											
400	2 cp granulated sugar	---	1540	4	---	---	H	---	---	---	---	L	12
496	2 cp orange juice	A B1 B2 C	220	5	L	L	F	---	---	---	F	L	992
61	1/4 cp lemon juice	A B1 B2 C	15	T	L	T	F	---	---	---	F	L	86
28	grated rinds of 2 oranges	A B1 B2 C	n/a*	1	L	L	F	---	---	---	F	L	---
1929	Recipe totals (gms; cal; sod. & potsm.)		1775	10									1090

METHOD

Bring water to boiling, add sugar and cook and stir about 5 minutes until sugar is dissolved. Add fruit juices and grated orange peel. Stir until blended. Strain, cool and freeze. Yield   8 servings.

*Value cannot be calculated - inasmuch as digestibility is unknown, per U.S.D.A. Handbook No. 8, pg. 43, Footnote No. 93.

. . . .

LOGANBERRY PUDDING

F=Fair; G=Good; H=High; L=Low; t or T = trace; n/a = no information available; dashes = zero or unmeasurable

GRAM WT.	FOOD	VITAMINS	CAL	(mg) SOD	PRO	FAT	CARB	CHOL	FATTY ACIDS SAT	UNSAT	CALC	IRON	(mg) POTSM
93	AVERAGE PER SERVING		210	249				(mg) 92 *					107
	Ingredients:												
173	1-1/2 cp presifted flour	B1 B2	630	3	F	L	G	---	---	---	L	F	164
6	2 tspn baking powder	---	6	630	L	T	H	---	---	---	H	---	---
1	1/3 tsp salt	---	---	523	---	---	---	---	---	---	G	---	T
67	1/3 cp sugar	---	257	T	---	---	H	---	---	---	---	L	2
123	1/2 cp 2% low-fat milk	A B1 B2 C	73	75	H	F	G	L*	L	L	H	L	215
100	2 eggs, beaten	A B1 B2	150	122	F	F	L	H*	H	L	F	F	129
14	1 tblspn margarine, melted	A D	100	139	L	H	L	---	L	H	L	---	3
75	1 cp fresh loganberries	A B1 B2 C	45	1	L	L	F	---	---	---	F	F	128
559	Recipe totals (gms; cal; sod. & potsm.)		1261	1493									641

METHOD

Sift first four ingredients together. Combine milk, beaten eggs and melted margarine together and add to the sifted dry ingredients, stirring only until smooth. Fold loganberries into batter carefully, then pour into well greased molds. (Bottoms of molds should be lined with waxed paper). Cover and steam 45 minutes. Serve warm with Hard Sauce or Berry Sauce (see recipes in this chapter). Yield 6 servings. Other berries or chopped fruit may be substituted for loganberries.

*   There are 550 milligrams of cholesterol in 100 grams of whole egg and 4 milligrams of cholesterol in 123 grams of 2% milk, for a total of 554 milligrams, as calculated from U.S.D.A. Handbook No. 8, pg. 146, items 12 and 29 respectivly. Divide 554 milligrams of cholesterol by 6 servings equals 92 average milligrams per serving.

. . . .

FRUIT MERINGUES

F=Fair; G=Good; H=High; L=Low; t or T = trace; n/a = no information available; dashes = zero or unmeasurable

GRAM WT.	FOOD	VITAMINS	CAL	(mg) SOD	PRO	FAT	CARB	CHOL	FATTY ACIDS SAT	UNSAT	CALC	IRON	(mg) POTSM
9	**AVERAGE PER MERINGUE**		23	18									5
	Ingredients:												
66	2 egg whites	B1 B2	30	96	F	T	L	---	---	---	L	L	92
---	1/8 tsp cream of tartar	---	T	27	L	T	F	-------	-n/a-	-----	---	---	---
---	dash salt (1/8 tsp)	---	---	196	---	---	---	---	---	---	G	---	---
100	1/2 cp granulated sugar	---	385	1	---	---	H	---	---	--	---	L	3
n/a	1/2 tsp vanilla	----------						-n/a-					
166	Recipe totals (gms; cal; sod. & potsm.)		415	320									95

METHOD

Beat egg whites with cream of tartar and salt until stiff but not dry (soft peaks). Add 1 tablespoon of sugar at a time, beating until stiff after each addition. Fold in vanilla. Heap in rounds or press through a pastry bag onto lightly greased baking sheet or onto baking sheet covered with heavy, ungreased paper. Make a shallow indentation in top of each. (Note: If paper is used, after baking, remove meringues at once). Bake in very slow over (275 F.) 40 to 60 minutes or until lightly browned. Yield 18 large meringues. Serve with sliced strawberries, peaches or other fruit, or ice cream and sauce.

. . . .

STRAWBERRY SHORTCAKE

F=Fair; G=Good; H=High; L=Low; t or T = trace; n/a = no information available; dashes = zero or unmeasurable

GRAM WT.	FOOD	VITAMINS	CAL	SOD (mg)	PRO	FAT	CARB	CHOL	FATTY ACIDS SAT	UNSAT	CALC	IRON	POTSM (mg)
212	AVERAGE PER SERVING		393	485									266
	Ingredients:												
288	2-1/2 cp presifted flour	B1 B2	1050	4	F	L	G	---	---	---	L	F	274
12	4 tspn baking powder	---	12	1260	L	T	H	---	---	---	H	---	---
2	1/2 tsp salt	---	---	785	---	---	---	---	---	---	G	---	T
12	1 tblspn sugar	---	48	T	---	---	H	---	---	---	---	L	T
75	5-1/3 tblspn margarine	A D	534	740	L	H	L	---	L	H	L	---	17
185	3/4 cp 2% low-fat milk	A B1 B2 C	110	113	H	F	G	L*	L	L	H	L	324
596	4 cp strawberries	A B1 B2 C	220	4	L	L	F	---	---	---	L	L	977
100	1/2 cp sugar	---	385	1	---	---	H	---	---	---	---	L	3
1270	Recipe totals (gms; cal; sod. & potsm.)		2359	2907									1595

METHOD

Mix and sift dry ingredients; cut in margarine with a knife or pastry blender. Add milk gradually to make a soft dough. Turn out on a lightly floured board and knead a few minutes. Form into a smooth ball then roll lightly to 1/2" thickness. Cut biscuits a little larger than regular type...(flour the rim of a drinking glass and use instead of traditional biscuit cutter) or bake biscuit dough in flat, greased pan. Cake can be cut in squares instead of traditional biscuit shapes. Brush tops with melted margarine and bake in 450 F. oven 15 minutes. Split biscuits and spread with margarine. Crush washed and hulled strawberries, reserving a few whole berries for garnish. Add sugar and mix well. Place bottom half of biscuits in individual dishes and spoon some of the crushed berries over them. Cover with tops of biscuits and spoon remaining berries over each, distributing evenly. Add whole berries and serve. If desired, serve with non-dairy topping, sweetened whipped cream or plain cream.

*   There are only 6 milligrams of cholesterol in 185 grams of 2% low-fat milk, as calculated from U.S.D.A. Handbook No. 8, pg. 146, item 29, an average of 1 milligram of cholesterol per serving.

. . . .

NOTE   other fruit may be substituted for strawberries such as peaches, respberries, sliced bananas, diced pineapple, blackberries, blueberries, apricots and applesauce.

LEMONADE

F=Fair; G=Good; H=High; L=Low; t or T = trace; n/a = no information available; dashes = zero or unmeasurable

GRAM WT.	FOOD	VITAMINS	CAL	(mg) SOD	PRO	FAT	CARB	CHOL	FATTY ACIDS SAT	UNSAT	CALC	IRON	(mg) POTSM
210	AVERAGE PER CUP		94	T									43
	Ingredients:												
180	juice of 6 lemons	A B1 B2 C	48	1	L	T	F	---	---	---	F	L	254
944	4 cp water							0					
133	2/3 cp sugar	---	513	1	---	---	H	---	---	---	---	L	4
1257	Recipe totals (gms; cal; sod. & potsm.)		561	2									258

METHOD

Mix fruit juice with water and sugar and stir until sugar is dissolved. Store in covered container in refrigerator. Serve over ice cubes. Yield about 6 cups.

. . . .

384

LIMEADE

F=Fair; G=Good; H=High; L=Low; t or T = trace; n/a = no information available; dashes = zero or unmeasurable

GRAM WT.	FOOD	VITAMINS	CAL	(mg) SOD	PRO	FAT	CARB	CHOL	FATTY ACIDS SAT	UNSAT	CALC	IRON	(mg) POTSM
221	AVERAGE PER CUP		136	T									32
	Ingredients:												
180	juice of 6 limes	A B1 B2 C	48	1	L	T	F	---	---	---	F	L	187
944	4 cp water	---------------------------------------0--------------------------------------											
200	1 cp sugar	---	770	2	---	---	H	---	---	--	---	L	6
1324	Recipe totals (gms; cal; sod. & potsm.)		818	3									193

METHOD

Mix fruit juice with water and sugar and stir until sugar is dissolved. Store in covered container in refrigerator. Serve over ice cubes. Yield   about 6 cups.

. . . .

ORANGEADE

F=Fair; G=Good; H=High; L=Low; t or T = trace; n/a = no information available; dashes = zero or unmeasurable

GRAM WT.	FOOD	VITAMINS	CAL	(mg) SOD	PRO	FAT	CARB	CHOL	FATTY ACIDS SAT	UNSAT	CALC	IRON	(mg) POTSM
212	AVERAGE PER CUP		57	1									153
	Ingredients:												
435	4 oranges (juice only)	A B1 B2 C	191	3	L	L	F	---	---	---	F	L	870
30	1 lemon (juice only)	A B1 B2 C	8	T	L	T	F	---	---	---	F	L	42
100	1/2 cp granulated sugar	---	385	1	---	---	H	---	---	---	---	L	3
708	3 cp water	----------						----0----					----------
1273	Recipe totals (gms; cal; sod. & potsm.)		584	4									915

METHOD

Mix orange and lemon juice with sugar and water, then stir until sugar is dissolved. Store in covered container in refrigerator. Serve over ice cubes. Yield   about 6 cups.

. . . .

HOLIDAY PUNCH

F=Fair; G=Good; H=High; L=Low; t or T = trace; n/a = no information available; dashes = zero or unmeasurable

GRAM WT.	FOOD	VITAMINS	CAL	(mg) SOD	PRO	FAT	CARB	CHOL	FATTY ACIDS SAT	UNSAT	CALC	IRON	(mg) POTSM
195	AVERAGE PER CUP		107	2									206
	Ingredients:												
1012	4 cp Concord grape juice	B1 B2 C	668	18	L	T	G	---	---	---	F	L	1174
506	2 cp white grapejuice	B1 B2	334	9	L	T	G	---	---	---	F	L	587
1305	juice of 12 oranges	A B1 B2 C	573	9	L	L	F	---	---	---	F	L	2610
360	juice of 12 lemons	A B1 B2 C	96	2	L	T	F	---	---	---	F	L	508
500	2 cp cranberry juice	A^t B1 B2 C^F	324	6	L	L	H	---	---	---	L	L	50
	F – fortified, if cranberry juice cocktail, commercial-type.												
672	2 (12 oz each) bottles ginger-ale	---	208	---	---	---	F	---	---	---	---	---	---
236	1 cp water						---0---						
100	1 cp sugar (granulated)	---	385	1	---	---	H	---	---	---	---	L	3
4691	Recipe totals (gms; cal; sod. & potsm.(		2588	45									4932

METHOD

Mix all ingredients together, except sugar and water. Make a sirup of the sugar and water by boiling together about 10 minutes, stirring until sugar is dissolved. Cool, then mix into the fruit mixture, a little at a time until desired sweetness is reached. Chill and serve over crushed ice. Yield about 24 (7 ounce) servings.

Note   If you do not have a regular punch bowl, use a large mixing bowl. Wrap the outside in either foil or festive holiday paper and tie with a 2" sash and bow. Use Scotch tape to hold the sash and bow in place.

. . . .

F=Fair; G=Good; H=High; L=Low; t or T = trace; n/a = no information available;   dashes = zero or unmeasurable

GRAM WT.	FOOD	VITAMINS	CAL	(mg) SOD	PRO	FAT	CARB	CHOL	FATTY ACIDS SAT	UNSAT	CALC	IRON	(mg) POTSM
210	AVERAGE PER SERVING		211	138				(mg)* 21					272
	Ingredients:												
900	2 cp diced apples	A B1 B2 C	420	12	L	L	F	---	---	---	L	L	990
100	1 cp diced celery	A B1 B2 C	15	126	L	T	L	---	---	---	F	L	341
112	1/2 cp mayonnaise	A B1ᵗ B2	800	672	T	H	T	H*	¡H¡	H	F	L	38
150	6 iceberg lettuce leaves	A B1 B2 C	30	15	L	L	L	---	---	---	F	F	263
1262	Recipe totals (gms; cal; sod. & potsm.)		1265	825									1632

METHOD

Red-skinned apples, such as red delicious, left unpeeled, add color to this salad. However, apples should be washed and cored then diced. To prevent apples from turning brown, mix diced pieces with 1/2 teaspoon of ascorbic acid. Wash celery stalks separately and peel off the outside tough fibers. Dice a little smaller than the apples. Fold mayonnaise in gently until well blended.   Serve on lettuce leaves that have been washed and blotted with paper towels. To make this a Waldorf Salad, add walnut pieces.   Yield   6 servings.

*   There are 128 milligrams of cholesterol in 1/2 cup mayonnaise, as calculated from U.S.D.A. Handbook No. 8, pg. 146, item 12. Divided by 6 servings equals 21 average milligrams of cholesterol in each .

. . . .

FESTIVE LIME AND PEAR SALAD

F=Fair; G=Good; H=High; L=Low; t or T = trace; n/a = no information available; dashes = zero or unmeasurable

GRAM WT.	FOOD	VITAMINS	CAL	(mg) SOD	PRO	FAT	CARB	CHOL	FATTY ACIDS SAT	UNSAT	CALC	IRON	(mg) POTSM
104	AVERAGE PER SERVING		75	99				(mg) 10					35
	Ingredients:												
155	1 large package lime gelatin	---	575	493	L	---	G	---	---	---	---	---	---
345	6 canned pear halves	A^t B1 B2 C	225	3	L	L	F	---	---	---	---	L	293
48	1/2 small package cream cheese	A B1 B2	160	97	L	H	L	H*	H	T	F	F	36
76	12 maraschino cherries **	---	90	---	L	L	G	---	---	---	---	---	---
	** Other small fruits or berries may be used instead, such as raspberries, huckleberries, etc.												
624	Recipe totals (gms; cal; sod. & potsm.)		1050	593									329

METHOD

Prepare lime gelatin according to package directions. Pour into square glass dish and set in refrigerator. Drain pear halves. Divide half package of cream cheese into 6 equal parts. Roll each part between the palms of the hands until a ball is formed. Press 1 ball into each pear cavity. When lime gelatin is cold and slightly thick, invert pear halves into it allowing space between each. To prevent cheese from floating to the top while inverting pear halves, hold pears with two fingers placed over cheese. Place a cherry at top and bottom of pear halves. Refrigerate until gelatin is set. To serve, cut into squares, lift out with a pancake turner and place cheese-side-up on crisp lettuce. Mayonnaise or other desired dressing may be provided in a separate bowl.

*   There are 120 milligrams of cholesterol in 100 grams of cream cheese, per U.S.D.A. Handbook No. 8, pg 146, item 7. In 48 grams, there are 58 milligrams, divided by 6 servings equals 10 average milligrams of cholesterol per serving of salad.

. . . .

CANDLE SALAD

F=Fair; G=Good; H=High; L=Low; t or T = trace; n/a = no information available; dashes = zero or unmeasurable

GRAM WT.	FOOD	VITAMINS	CAL	(mg) SOD	PRO	FAT	CARB	CHOL (mg)	FATTY ACIDS SAT	UNSAT	CALC	IRON	(mg) POTSM
149	AVERAGE PER SERVING		258	184				* 24					188
	Ingredients:												
350	2 medium-size bananas	A B1 B2 C	200	4	L	T	G	---	---	---	L	L	130
100	4 lettuce leaves	A B2 B2 C	20	9	L	L	L	---	---	---	F	F	175
64	4 tblspn peanut butter	B1 B2	380	388	G	H	F	---	L	H	F	F	429
56	6 tblspn mayonnaise	A B1^t B2	400	336	T	H	T	H*	H	H	F	L	19
25	4 maraschino cherries**	---	30	---	L	L	G	---	---	---	---	---	---
	** Other fruits, such as strawberries, etc., may be used for garnish instead of cherries.												
595	Recipe totals (gms; cal; sod. & potsm.)		1030	737									753

METHOD

Peel bananas and cut in half crosswise. Place on lettuce leaves cut side down. Mix peanut butter and mayonnaise together until well blended, then drizzle it from top of bananas. Place a maraschino cherry on top.

*   Cholesterol rating is reflected in the egg yolk in the mayonnaise. There are approximately 16 milligrams of cholesterol per tablespoon in a home recipe (see under Fats and Oils chapter). In this recipe, 6 tablespoons of mayonnaise times 16 milligrams of cholesterol per tablespoon totals 96 milligrams of cholesterol. Divide by 4 servings will equal 24 average milligrams of cholesterol per serving.

. . . .

CITRUS – AVOCADO SALAD

F=Fair; G=Good; H=High; L=Low; t or T = trace; n/a = no information available; dashes = zero or unmeasurable

GRAM WT.	FOOD	VITAMINS	CAL	(mg) SOD	PRO	FAT	CARB	CHOL	FATTY ACIDS SAT	UNSAT	CALC	IRON	(mg) POTSM
340	AVERAGE PER SERVING		212	8									975
	Ingredients:												
482	1 medium-size white grapefruit	A B1 B2 C	188	5	L	T	F	---	---	---	F	L	651
180	1 medium-size orange	A B1 B2 C	65	2	L	L	F	---	---	---	G	L	360
284	1 avocado, peeled	A B1 B2 C	370	11	L	G	F	n/a	L	H	F	L	1715
75	3 lettuce leaves	A B1 B2 C	14	7	L	L	L	---	---	---	F	F	198
1021	Recipe totals (gms; cal; sod. & potsm.)		637	25									2924

METHOD

Peel and remove Membranes from grapefruit and orange sections. Pull sections apart carefully. Peel and remove seed from avocado and slice to conform to grapefruit and orange sections. Beginning with grapefruit, arrange sections alternately, overlapping on lettuce leaves, and ending with grapefruit. Serve with tart French dressing recipe on next page. Also note dressings No. 1 and No. 2.

. . . .

TART FRENCH DRESSING

F=Fair; G=Good; H=High; L=Low; t or T = trace; n/a = no information available;   dashes = zero or unmeasurable

GRAM WT.	FOOD	VITAMINS	CAL	(mg) SOD	PRO	FAT	CARB	CHOL	FATTY ACIDS SAT	UNSAT	CALC	IRON	(mg) POTSM
231	AVERAGE PER CUP		1324	1									84
	Ingredients:												
2	1 clove garlic (optional)	A^t B1 B2 C	3	T	L	L	F	---	---	---	L	F	11
240	1 cp vinegar	---	32	3	T	---	L	---	---	---	L	L	240
n/a	2 tsp dry mustard							-------n/a-------					
12	1 tblspn granulated sugar	---	48	T	---	---	H	---	---	---	---	T	T
n/a	1 tsp paprika							-------n/a-------					
n/a	1 tsp black pepper							-------n/a-------					
440	2 cp salad oil	---	3890	---	---	H	---	---	L	H	---	---	---
	no salt—season at the table												
694	Recipe totals (gms; cal; sod. & potsm.)		3973	3									251

METHOD

Soak garlic in vinegar 30 minutes. Mix dry ingredients together and place in a covered bottle or jar. Remove garlic from vinegar and add vinegar to dry ingredients. Add oil slowly. Store in covered jar in refrigerator. Shake well before using. Yield   3 cups.

No. 1   If making tarragon dressing, mustard, sugar and paprika may be omitted.

No. 2   For fruit salads, use 1/4 cup each of lemon, lime or orange juice instead of half the vinegar.

Reduce mustard to 1/2 teaspoon; paprika to 1/2 teaspoon. (Do not use any salt — season at the table).
Increase sugar to 3/4 cup; add 7-1/2 teaspoons Worcester Sauce and omit pepper and garlic.

. . . .

HEAVENLY SALAD

F=Fair; G=Good; H=High; L=Low; t or T = trace; n/a = no information available;   dashes = zero or unmeasurable

GRAM WT.	FOOD	VITAMINS	CAL	(mg) SOD	PRO	FAT	CARB	CHOL	FATTY ACIDS SAT	UNSAT	CALC	IRON	(mg) POTSM
225	AVERAGE PER SERVING	A B1 B2 C	274	18									242
	Ingredients:												
240	8 canned, peeled apricots	A B1 B2 C	200	2	L	L	G	---	---	---	L	L	574
113	18 maraschino cherries*	---	135	---	L	L	G	---	---	---	---	---	---
	*or other small fruits, such as raspberries, strawberries, etc.												
488	8 medium slices canned pineapple	A B1 B2 C	360	4	T	T	F	---	---	---	L	L	473
257	7 canned peach halves	A B1 B2 C	200	5	L	T	G	---	---	---	L	L	342
114	1/4 pound marshmallows	B1^t B2^t	360	4	L	T	H	---	---	---	L	F	7
345	6 canned pear halves	A^t B1 B2 C	225	3	L	L	F	---	---	---	L	L	293
239	1 cp whipping cream	A B1 B2 C	715	86	L	G	L	n/a	H	L	F	T	244
1796	Recipe totals (gms; cal; sod. & potsm.)		2195	144									1933

METHOD

Remove any pits from fruit, then cut apricots and cherries in half; cut pineapple in pieces; peaches in half; marshmallows in pieces (or use miniature marshmallows). Cut pears in 4 pieces each. Mix all together and store in a covered container in the refrigerator. A few minutes before serving, whip cream and fold into the fruit. Serve on lettuce leaves. Garnish with a cherry on top. Yield   8 servings.

Note   Date-nut bread or thin slices of brown bread spread with cream cheese makes a tasty accompaniment for this salad.

. . . .

GINGERALE SALAD

F=Fair; G=Good; H=High; L=Low; t or T = trace; n/a = no information available; dashes = zero or unmeasurable

GRAM WT.	FOOD	VITAMINS	CAL	(mg) SOD	PRO	FAT	CARB	CHOL	FATTY ACIDS SAT	UNSAT	CALC	IRON	(mg) POTSM
99	AVERAGE PER SERVING		110	49									112
	Ingredients:												
85	1 package lime gelatin	---	315	270	L	---	H	---	---	---	---	---	---
244	8 ounce ginger ale	---	77	---	---	---	F	---	---	---	---	---	---
210	1-1/4 cp fresh peaches, diced	A B1 B2 C	81	2	---	L	T	---	---	---	L	L	424
27	1/4 cp chopped pecans	A B1 B2 C	185	---	L	H	F	---	---	---	F	F	163
25	1/4 cp chopped celery	A B1 B2 C	4	22	L	L	L	---	---	---	G	L	85
608	Recipe totals (gms; cal; sod. & potsm.)		662	294									672

METHOD

Dissolve lime gelatin in 1 cup boiling water. Add ginger ale and chill until slightly thickened. Fold in drained, diced peaches, also nutmeats and celery. Turn into 1 quart mold or 6 individual molds and chill until firm. Dip individual molds in hot water a few seconds and unmold on lettuce leaves. Serve with any desired dressing. Yield   6 servings.

. . . .

FRUIT SALAD COMBINATIONS

1. Melon balls (cantaloupe) and cherry tomatoes and lettuce.

2. Pitted prunes (cooked), stuffed with cottage cheese or cream cheese, on pineapple slices or chicory.

3. Peach halves on cottage cheese and lettuce.

4. Pineapple slices and cottage cheese or cream cheese balls on lettuce.

5. Fresh or canned pears and cottage cheese or cream cheese balls on lettuce.

6. Grapefruit wedges and avocado slices on romaine.

7. Avocado and orange wedges on watercress.

8. Avocado, tangerine wedges and pecans on lettuce.

9. Sliced oranges, French dressing on lettuce.

10. Pear halves, canned or fresh, canned white pitted cherries on lettuce with either French dressing or mayonnaise.

11. Pineapple chunks, seedless grapes on cottage cheese, lettuce and 1 teaspoon mayonnaise.

12. Fruit jello molded in muffin cups, unmolded and served on lettuce leaves, garnished with cottage cheese.

. . . .

APPLE SAUCE

F=Fair; G=Good; H=High; L=Low; t or T = trace; n/a = no information available; dashes = zero or unmeasurable

GRAM WT.	FOOD	VITAMINS	CAL	(mg) SOD	PRO	FAT	CARB	CHOL	FATTY ACIDS SAT	UNSAT	CALC	IRON	(mg) POTSM
140	AVERAGE PER 1/2 CUP		133	2									133
	Ingredients:												
600	4 large tart apples	A B1 B2 C	280	8	L	L	F	---	---	---	L	L	660
100	1/2 c p granulated sugar	---	385	1	---	---	H	---	---	---	---	L	3
n/a	1/2 tsp cinnamon	----------						0					
n/a	1/4 tsp nutmeg	----------						0					
700	Recipe totals (gms; cal; sod. & potsm.)		665	9									663

METHOD

Wash, peel and core apples. Cut in quarters then cut quarters in half. Place fruit in enamel sauce pan with just enough water to prevent apples from burning. Boil until tender on medium to low heat. Cool then put apples in blender with sugar and spices. Mix until nearly liquified.   Yield   5 (1/2 cup) servings.

. . . .

RHUBARB SAUCE

F=Fair; G=Good; H=High; L=Low; t or T = trace; n/a = no information available; dashes = zero or unmeasurable

GRAM WT.	FOOD	VITAMINS	CAL	(mg) SOD	PRO	FAT	CARB	CHOL	FATTY ACIDS SAT	UNSAT	CALC	IRON	(mg) POTSM
151	AVERAGE PER 1/2 CUP		160	3									246
	Ingredients:												
454	1 lb fresh rhubarb	A B1 B2 C	62	8	L	L	L	---	---	---	F	L	979
150	3/4 cp granulated sugar	---	578	2	---	---	H	---	---	---	---	L	5
604	Recipe totals (gms; cal; sod. & potsm.)		640	10									984

METHOD

If there are any leaves on the rhubarb, cut off every bit as they are deadly poisonous. Wash the stalks but don't peel them. Cut in 1" pieces. Place rhubarb in sauce pan with enough water to prevent burning and cook until tender. Add sugar while rhubarb is still hot and blend well. Yield   4 (1/2 cup) servings.

. . . .

BERRY SAUCE

F=Fair; G=Good; H=High; L=Low; t or T = trace; n/a = no information available; dashes = zero or unmeasurable

GRAM WT.	FOOD	VITAMINS	CAL	(mg) SOD	PRO	FAT	CARB	CHOL	FATTY ACIDS SAT	UNSAT	CALC	IRON	(mg) POTSM
28	AVERAGE PER OUNCE		67	14									22
	Ingredients:												
150	2 cp berries	A B1 B2 C	90	2	L	L	F	---	---	---	F	F	255
12	1 tblspn granulated sugar	---	48	T	---	---	H	---	---	---	---	L	T
14	1 tblspn soft margarine	A D	100	139	T	H	T	---	L	H	F	---	3
180	1-1/2 cp powdered sugar	---	690	2	---	---	H	---	---	---	---	L	5
33	1 egg white	B1^t B2	15	48	F	T	L	---	---	---	L	L	46
389	Recipe totals (gms; cal; sod. & potsm.)		943	191									309

METHOD

Place the washed berries in a bowl, mash slightly, then add the granulated sugar and blend by folding into the berries carefully. Cover bowl and refrigerate until time to serve. Then beat margarine to a cream, add the powdered sugar a little at a time, blending well. Then add the stiffly beaten egg white. Just before serving, combine with the mashed berries. Yield   about 14 ounces.

Small fruits, such as strawberries, raspberries and blackberries make excellent sauces for custards, steamed puddings and ice cream.

. . . .

HARD SAUCE

F=Fair; G=Good; H=High; L=Low; t or T = trace; n/a = no information available;   dashes = zero or unmeasurable

GRAM WT.	FOOD	VITAMINS	CAL	(mg) SOD	PRO	FAT	CARB	CHOL	FATTY ACIDS SAT	UNSAT	CALC	IRON	(mg) POTSM
28	AVERAGE PER OUNCE		144	107									3
	Ingredients:												
75	1/3 cp soft margarine	A D	534	740	L	H	T	---	L	H	L	---	17
120	1 cp powdered sugar*	---	460	1	---	---	H	---	---	---	---	L	4
n/a	1 tsp vanilla							--------n/a--------					
195	Recipe totals (gms; cal; sod. & potsm.)		994	741									21

METHOD

Cream the margarine until very soft then blend in sugar and vanilla until smooth. Keep in a cool place, covered, until ready to use. A little grated lemon peel, or nutmeg or cinnamon may be substituted for vanilla. Also, to make more sauce, a little cream or milk may be added with more sugar. Yield 6.9 ounces.

*Granulated, brown or maple sugar may be used instead of powdered sugar.
This sauce is delicious with hot puddings, such as plum pudding, loganberry pudding, or steamed puddings, or on apple pie.

. . . .

PICKLED PEACHES

F=Fair; G=Good; H=High; L=Low; t or T = trace; n/a = no information available; dashes = zero or unmeasurable

GRAM WT.	FOOD	VITAMINS	CAL	(mg) SOD	PRO	FAT	CARB	CHOL	FATTY ACIDS SAT	UNSAT	CALC	IRON	(mg) POTSM
977	AVERAGE PER PINT		1240	9									1055
	Ingredients:												
2724	6 lb peaches	A B1 B2 C	900	24	L	L	L	---	---	---	L	L	4782
56	2 oz stick cinnamon	-------	-----	-----	-----	-----	------	-n/a-	------	------	-----	-----	-----
28	1 oz whole cloves	-------	-----	-----	-----	-----	------	-n/a-	------	------	-----	-----	-----
1362	3 lb granulated sugar	---	5238	15	---	---	H	---	---	---	---	L	41
480	2 cp vinegar	---	64	5	T	---	L	---	---	---	L	L	454
236	1 cp water	-------	-----	-----	-----	-----	------	-0-	------	------	-----	-----	-----
4886	Recipe totals (gms; cal; sod. & potsm.)		6202	44									5277

METHOD

Dip peaches into boiling water about 10 seconds, then plunge into cold water and slip off the skins. Break cinnamon stick into pieces. Tie spices in a bag. Combine sugar, vinegar, water and bag of spices and boil together stirring until sugar dissolves and sirup is clear (about 15 minutes). Add enough peaches to fill only one jar at a time and cook until tender. Pack into hot, sterilized jar. Cover to keep hot. Repeat until all are cooked. Fill each jar with hot sirup to overflowing. Insert a silver dinner knife into jar to allow air bubbles to escape. Seal. Yield   about 5 pints.

Note   Instead of breaking cinnamon, add it whole to the sirup and stick several cloves into each peach. Pears may be pickled as above. If desired, add 1 ounce ginger to above spices. Stick cloves into pears instead of a bag.

. . . .

LITTLE PICKLED PEARS

F=Fair; G=Good; H=High; L=Low; t or T = trace; n/a = no information available;   dashes = zero or unmeasurable

GRAM WT.	FOOD	VITAMINS	CAL	(mg) SOD	PRO	FAT	CARB	CHOL	FATTY ACIDS SAT	UNSAT	CALC	IRON	(mg) POTSM
958	AVERAGE PER PINT		1325	14									723
	Ingredients:												
3178	7 lb small pears	A B1 B2 C	1764	56	L	L	F	---	---	---	L	L	3759
n/a	1 tblspn cinnamon							---n/a---					
n/a	1 tblspn allspice							---n/a---					
n/a	1 tblspn cloves							---n/a---					
28	1 oz fresh ginger root	A B1 B2 C	13	2	L	L	L	---	---	---	L	F	74
480	1 pint vinegar	---	64	5	T	---	L	---	---	---	L	L	454
472	2 cp water							---0---					
1589	3-1/2 lb sugar (7 cups)	---	6111	18	---	---	H	---	---	---	---	L	48
5747	Recipe totals (gms; cal; sod. & potsm)		7952	81									4335

METHOD

Peel pears, leaving stems on. Tie spices in a bag and add to vinegar, water and sugar. Stir. Boil mixture 5 minutes. Add pears a few at a time and cook until tender and clear. Spoon pears into hot, sterilized jars, pour hot liquid over them until jar is overflowing. Insert dinner knife to allow air bubbles to escape. Seal. Yield   about 6 pints.

. . . .

PICKLED PLUMS

F=Fair; G=Good; H=High; L=Low; t or T = trace; n/a = no information available; dashes = zero or unmeasurable

GRAM WT.	FOOD	VITAMINS	CAL	(mg) SOD	PRO	FAT	CARB	CHOL	FATTY ACIDS SAT	UNSAT	CALC	IRON	(mg) POTSM
822	AVERAGE PER PINT		1332	10									1333
	Ingredients:												
2270	5 lb Damson plums	A B1 B2 C	1360	40	L	T	L	---	---	---	L	L	6170
1362	3 lb granulated sugar	---	5238	5	---	---	H	---	---	---	---	L	41
n/a	1 tblspn cinnamon	---------------------						-n/a-					------
480	2 cp vinegar	---	64	5	T	---	L	---	---	---	L	L	454
n/a	1/2 tblspn whole cloves	---------------------						-n/a-					------
n/a	1/2 tblspn whole allspice	---------------------						-n/a-					------
4112	Recipe totlas (gms; cal; sod. & potsm.)		6662	50									6665

METHOD

Wash plums, remove stems, then prick with a fork. Boil remaining ingredients together about 5 minutes, stirring until sugar is dissolved. Pour boiling sirup over plums. Let stand 3 days, then scoop plums out, boil sirup down until quite thick, add plums and heat to boiling point. Pour into hot, sterilized jars and seal. Yield   about 5 pints.

. . . .

402

WATERMELON PICKLES

F=Fair; G=Good; H=High; L=Low; t or T = trace; n/a = no information available;   dashes = zero or unmeasurable

GRAM WT.	FOOD	VITAMINS	CAL	(mg) SOD	PRO	FAT	CARB	CHOL	FATTY ACIDS SAT	UNSAT	CALC	IRON	(mg) POTSM
1385	AVERAGE PER PINT		*1582	*10									317
	Ingredients:												
908	2 lb watermelon rind	A B1 B2 C	n/a	---	---	---	---	---	---	---	---	---	---
480	2 cp vinegar	---	64	8	T	---	L	---	---	---	L	L	454
472	2 cp water		---	---	---	---	---	0	---	---	---	---	---
800	4 cp sugar	---	3080	8	---	---	H	---	---	---	---	L	24
n/a	1 stick cinnamon		---	---	---	---	---	n/a	---	---	---	---	---
n/a	1 tsp whole cloves		---	---	---	---	---	n/a	---	---	---	---	---
n/a	1 tsp whole allspice		---	---	---	---	---	n/a	---	---	---	---	---
110	1 lemon, sliced thin	A B1 B2 C	20	3	L	T	L	---	---	---	L	L	155
2770	Recipe totals (gms; cal; sod. & potsm.)		*3164	19*									633

*Without rind — no information was available.

METHOD

Pare the green outside skin from watermelon rind and remove any pink portions. Cut rind into 2" x 1" pieces, 1/2" thick or into 3/4" to 1" cubes. Weigh. Soak rind overnight in brine made by dissolving 1/4 cup of salt in each cup of water. Drain rind, wash in fresh water and drain. Cook rind in fresh water until tender. Combine remaining ingredients and boil 5 minutes. Add rind, a few pieces at a time, and cook until rind is clear. Pack rind in hot sterilized jars, cover with boiling sirup and seal. Yield   2 pints.

. . . .

LEGUMES, NUTS and VEGETABLES

LEGUMES, NUTS AND VEGETABLES

F=Fair; G=Good; H=High; L=Low; t or T = trace; n/a = no information available; dashes = zero or unmeasurable

GRAM WT.	FOOD	VITAMINS	CAL	(mg) SOD	PRO	FAT	CARB	CHOL	FATTY ACIDS SAT	UNSAT	CALC	IRON	(mg) POTSM
	ASPARAGUS												
100	raw spears	A B1 B2 C	26	2	L	L	L	---	---	---	L	F	278
	cooked, drained												
60	spears 1/2" at base, 4	A B1 B2 C	10	1	L	L	L	---	---	---	L	L	110
145	pieces, 1 cp, 1-1/2 to 2" lengths	A B1 B2 C	30	1	L	L	L	---	---	---	L	L	265
244	canned, solids and liquid, 1 cp	A B1 B2 C	45	576*	L	L	L	---	---	---	L	F	447
	(* High sodium due to salt used in the canning process.)												
	Soups, commercially canned (creamed)												
100	condensed	A B1 B2	54	820*	L	L	L	** ---	** ---	** ---	L	L	100
	(* Values depend on type of milk, whether whole, or skim.)												
100	prepared with equal volume of water	A B1 B2	27	410*	L	L	L	** ---	** ---	** ---	L	L	50
100	prepared with equal volume of whole milk	A B1 B2 C^t	60	436*	L	L	L	H	H	L	F	L	123
	ALMONDS												
100	dried	B1 B2 C^t	598	4	F	G	F	---	L	H	H	G	773
100	roasted and salted	B1 B2	627	198	F	G	F	---	L	H	H	G	773
142	shelled, whole kernels, 1 cp	B1 B2 C^t	850	6	F	G	F	---	L	H	H	G	1097
100	sugar-coated	B1 B2	456	20	F	G	H	---	L	H	G	F	255
100	meal, partially defatted	B1 B2 C^t	408	7	G	F	F	---	L	H	H	H	1400
	ARTICHOKES												
100	Globe or French, raw	A B1 B2 C	**	43	L	L	F	---	---	---	F	F	430
100	cooked, boiled, drained	A B1 B2 C	**	30	L	L	F	---	---	---	F	F	301
	(** Values range from 9 calories per 100 grams for freshly harvested, raw artichokes, to as many as 47 for stored product, the corresponding range for boiled artichokes is 8 to 44 calories.)												
100	Jerusalem, raw	A B1 B2 C	***	---	L	L	F	---	---	---	L	F	---
	(*** Values range from 7 calories per 100 grams, for freshly harvested Jerusalem artichokes, to 75 calories for those stored for a long period.) Note The Jerusalem artichoke is not really an artichoke, but a member of the sunflower family, the edible portion being the potato-like tubers which grow underground.												

LEGUMES, NUTS AND VEGETABLES

F=Fair; G=Good; H=High; L=Low; t or T = trace; n/a = no information available; dashes = zero or unmeasurable

GRAM WT.	FOOD	VITAMINS	CAL	(mg) SOD	PRO	FAT	CARB	CHOL	FATTY ACIDS SAT	UNSAT	CALC	IRON	(mg) POTSM
	ASPARAGUS (continued)												
	Special dietary pack (low-sodium)												
100	canned, solids and liquid	A B1 B2 C	16	4	L	L	L	---	---	---	L	L	166
100	drained solids	A B1 B2 C	19	4	L	L	L	---	---	---	L	L	166
100	drained liquid	A^t B1 B2 C	8	4	L	T	L	---	---	---	L	L	166
	Frozen												
100	cut and tips, not thawed	A B1 B2 C	23	2	L	L	L	---	---	---	L	F	239
100	cooked, boiled, drained	A B1 B2 C	22	1	L	L	L	---	---	---	L	F	220
100	spears, not thawed	A B1 B2 C	24	2	L	L	L	---	---	---	L	F	259
100	cooked, boiled, drained	A B1 B2 C	23	1	L	L	L	---	---	---	L	F	238
100	BAMBOO SHOOTS, raw	A B1 B2 C	27	---	L	L	L	---	---	---	L	L	533
	BEANS, Dry, Common varieties as												
	Great Northern, navy and others												
	cooked												
180	Great northern, 1 cp	B1 B2	210	13	L	L	F	---	---	---	F	F	749
190	Navy (pea), 1 cp	B1 B2	225	13	L	L	F	---	---	---	F	F	790
	Canned, solids and liquid, white with Frankfurters,												
255	sliced, 1 cp	A B1 B2 C^t	365	18	L	L	F	H	H	L	F	F	n/a
255	Pork and tomato sauce, 1 cp	A B1 B2 C	310	1181	L	L	F	L	L	T	F	F	536
255	Pork and sweet sauce, 1 cp	A B1 B2 C	385	969	L	L	F	------n/a------			F	F	---
100	without pork	A B1 B2 C	120	338	L	L	F	------n/a------			F	F	268
255	Red Kidney, 1 cp	A B1 B2	230	8	L	L	F	---	---	---	L	F	867
100	Pinto, calico and red Mexican, raw	B1 B2	349	10	F	L	G	---	---	---	G	G	984
100	Other, including black, brown and												
	Bayo, raw	A B1 B2	330	25	F	L	G	---	---	---	G	G	1038
250	Soup, Navy bean with pork prepared with an equal volume of												
	water 1 c p.	A B1 B2 C	170	1008	L	L	L	T	T	T	L	L	395
190	Lima beans, cooked, boiled,												
	drained, 1 cp	A B1 B2 C	260	2	L	L	F	---	---	---	F	F	802
100	canned, drained solids	A B1 B2 C	96	236	L	L	F	---	---	---	L	F	222
100	special dietary pack (low-sodium) drained solids	A B1 B2 C	95	4	L	L	F	---	---	---	L	F	222

LEGUMES, NUTS AND VEGETABLES

F=Fair; G=Good; H=High; L=Low; t or T = trace; n/a = no information available; dashes = zero or unmeasurable

GRAM WT.	FOOD	VITAMINS	CAL	(mg) SOD	PRO	FAT	CARB	CHOL	FATTY ACIDS SAT	UNSAT	CALC	IRON	(mg) POTSM
	BEANS (continued)												
100	frozen Fordhooks, cooked and drained	A B1 B2 C	99	101	L	L	F	---	---	---	L	F	426
100	frozen, Baby limas, cooked and drained	A B1 B2 C	118	129	L	L	F	---	---	---	L	F	394
100	mature seeds, cooked	B1 B2	138	2	L	L	F	---	---	---	L	F	612
100	Bean flour, lima	---	343	---	F	L	G	---	---	---	---	---	---
125	Snap, green, cooked, drained 1 cp	A B1 B2 C	30	5	L	L	L	---	---	---	F	L	189
239	canned, liquids & solids 1 cp	A B1 B2 C	45	564	L	L	L	---	---	---	L	F	227
125	Yellow ,fresh, cooked, drained,1cp	A B1 B2 C	30	4	L	L	L	---	---	---	F	L	189
239	canned, solids & liquids, 1 cp	A B1 B2 C	45	564	L	L	L	---	---	---	L	F	227
100	special dietary pack, solids and liquids, green beans	A B1 B2 C	16	2	L	L	L	---	---	---	L	F	95
100	Yellow wax, solids/liquids	A B1 B2 C	15	2	L	L	L	---	---	---	L	F	95
100	Frozen, cut, green, cooked and drained	A B1 B2 C	25	1	L	L	L	---	---	---	F	L	152
100	Yellow wax, cooked/drained	A B1 B2 C	27	1	L	L	L	---	---	---	L	L	164
100	French style green, cooked and drained	A B1 B2 C	26	2	L	L	L	---	---	---	L	L	136
125	Mung (sprouted) cooked and drained, 1 cp	A B1 B2 C	35	5	L	L	L	---	---	---	L	L	195
100	Soybeans, immature seeds cooked, boiled and drained	A B1 B2 C	118	---	L	L	F	---	---	---	F	F	---
100	canned, solids and liquid	B1 Th B2	75	236	L	L	L	---	---	---	F	F	---
100	mature seeds, cooked	A B1 B2	130	2	H	F	F	---	---	---	H	L	540
100	Soybeans, fermented products Natto	B1 B2	167	---	F	L	F	---	---	---	G	F	249
100	Miso (cereal & Soybeans)	A B1 B2	171	2950	F	L	F	---	---	---	F	F	334
100	sprouted seeds, cooked, drained	A B1 B2 C	38	---	L	L	L	---	---	---	F	L	---
100	soybean curd (tofu)	B1 B2	72	7	L	L	L	---	---	---	G	F	42
100	Soybean flours full-fat	A B1 B2	421	1	G	G	G	---	---	---	H	H	1660
100	high-fat	B1 B2	380	1	G	F	G	---	---	---	H	H	1775

LEGUMES, NUTS AND VEGETABLES

F=Fair; G=Good; H=High; L=Low; t or T = trace; n/a = no information available; dashes = zero or unmeasurable

GRAM WT.	FOOD	VITAMINS	CAL	(mg) SOD	PRO	FAT	CARB	CHOL	FATTY ACIDS SAT	UNSAT	CALC	IRON	(mg) POTSM
	BEANS, soybean flours (cont'd)												
100	low-fat	A B1 B2	356	1	G	L	G	---	---	---	H	H	1859
100	defatted	A B1 B2	326	1	G	L	G	---	---	---	H	H	1820
	Soybean Milk												
100	fluid	A B1 B2	33	---	L	L	L	--------n/a-------			L	L	---
100	powder	---	429	---	G	F	F	--------n/a-------			H	---	---
	(Values apply to products without added vitamins and minerals)												
100	liquid concentrate	A^t B1 B2	126	43	L	L	L	--------n/a-------			F	L	237
100	powder	A B1 B2	452	1	F	F	G	--------n/a-------			G	G	915
100	soybean protein	---	322	210	G	L	F	--------n/a-------			G	---	180
100	soybean proteinate	---	312	1200	G	L	L	--------n/a-------			---	---	---
100	Soy Sauce	B1 B2	68	7325	L	L	L	---	---	---	F	F	366
100	BEECHNUTS	---	568	---	F	G	F	---	L	H	---	---	---
	BEETS, cooked, drained, peeled												
100	whole 2", 2 each	A B1 B2 C	30	43	L	L	L	---	---	---	L	L	208
170	diced or sliced, 1 cup	A B1 B2 C	55	73	L	T	L	---	---	---	L	L	354
100	canned, liquids	A B1 B2 C	34	236	L	L	L	---	---	---	L	L	167
100	special dietaryppack (low sodium) liquids and solids	A B1 B2 C	32	46	L	T	L	---	---	---	L	L	167
145	Beet greens, leaves, stems, cooked and drained, 1 cp	A B1B2·C	25	110	L	L	L	---	---	---	L	L	332
	BLACKEYE PEAS -- See Cowpeas												
100	BRAZIL NUTS	A^t B1 B2	654	1	F	G	F	---	---	---	H	F	715
	BROCCOLI, cooked, drained												
155	Stalks cut in 1/2" pieces, 1 cp	A B1 B2 C	40	16	L	L	L	---	---	---	F	L	414
250	chopped, (10 oz. frozen pk) 1-3/8 cups	A B1 B2 C	65	25	L	L	L	---	---	---	F	L	530
180	whole stalks, med. size. 1 stalk	A B1 B2 C	45	18	L	L	L	---	---	---	F	F	481
	BRUSSELS SPROUTS												
100	raw	A B1 B2 C	45	14	L	L	L	---	---	---	L	F	390
155	cooked, 7 to 8 sprouts per cp	A B1 B2 C	55	22	L	L	L	---	---	---	L	F	423
100	frozen, cooked, drained	A B1 B2 C	33	14	L	L	L	---	---	---	L	L	295

NUTRITION AT YOUR FINGERTIPS

LEGUME, NUTS AND VEGETABLES

F=Fair; G=Good; H=High; L=Low; t or T = trace; n/a = no information available; dashes = zero or unmeasurable

GRAM WT.	FOOD	VITAMINS	CAL	(mg) SOD	PRO	FAT	CARB	CHOL	FATTY ACIDS SAT	UNSAT	CALC	IRON	(mg) POTSM
100	BUTTERNUTS	---	629	---	F	G	L	---	T	H	---	G	---
	CABBAGE, common varieties, raw												
70	coarse shredded or sliced, 1 cp	A B1 B2 C	15	14	L	L	L	---	---	---	L	L	163
90	finely shredded or chopped, 1	A B1 B2 C	20	18	L	L	L	---	---	---	L	L	210
145	cooked, 1 cp	A B1 B2 C	30	29	L	L	L	---	---	---	L	L	236
70	red, raw, coarse shred, 1 cp	A B1 B2 C	20	18	L	L	L	---	---	---	F	L	188
70	coarsely shredded or sliced, 1 cp	A B1 B2 C	15	15	L	L	L	---	---	---	F	L	188
75	celery or chinese, raw, cut in pieces, 1 cp	A B1 B2 C	10	17	L	L	L	---	---	---	L	L	190
170	spoon (or white mustard or Pakchoy) 1 cp	A B1 B2 C	25	44	L	L	L	---	---	---	H	L	520
100	cooked	A B1 B2 C	14	18	L	L	L	---	---	---	H	L	214
100	coleslaw, with French dressing homemade	A B1 B2 C	120	131	L	F	L	L	T	H	F	L	197
100	French dressing, commercial	A B1 B2 C	95	268	L	L	L	L	L	H	F	L	205
100	mayonnaise	A B1 B2 C	144	120	L	F	L	H	H	H	F	L	199
100	salad dressing, mayonnaise type	A B1 B2 C	99	124	L	L	L	L	T	H	F	L	192
	CARROTS, raw												
50	whole, 5½ by 1" (25 ea.) 1 carrot	A B1 B2 C	20	24	L	T	L	---	---	---	F	L	171
110	grated, 1 cp	A B1 B2 C	45	52	L	L	L	---	---	---	F	L	375
145	cooked, diced, 1 cp	A B1 B2 C	45	48	L	T	L	---	---	---	F	L	322
28	canned, strained or chopped, (baby food) 1 oz.	A B1 B2 C	10	66	T	T	L	---	---	---	L	L	51
100	special dietary pack, drained solids, (low sodium)	A B1 B2 C	25	39	L	L	L	---	---	---	L	L	120
100	Dehydrated	A B1 B2 C	341	268	L	L	H	---	---	---	H	H	1944
140	CASHEW NUTS, roasted, 1 cp	A B1 B2	785	21	F	G	F	---	L	H	F	F	650
100	CAULIFLOWER, RAW	A B1 B2 C	27	13	L	L	L	---	---	---	F	F	295
120	cooked (flower buds), 1 cp	A B1 B2 C	25	11	L	T	L	---	---	---	F	L	247
100	frozen, cooked, drained	A B1 B2 C	18	10	L	L	L	---	---	---	L	L	207
100	CELERIAC, root, raw	B1 B2 C	40	100	L	L	L	---	---	---	F	L	300
40	CELERY, all, including green and yellow varieties, 1 stalk, raw	A B1 B2 C	5	50	T	T	T	---	---	---	F	L	136

LEGUME, NUTS AND VEGETABLES

F=Fair; G=Good; H=High; L=Low; t or T = trace; n/a = no information available; dashes = zero or unmeasurable

GRAM WT.	FOOD	VITAMINS	CAL	(mg) SOD	PRO	FAT	CARB	CHOL	FATTY ACIDS SAT	UNSAT	CALC	IRON	(mg) POTSM
	CELERY, continued												
100	pieces, diced, 1 cp	A B1 B2 C	15	126	L	T	L	---	---	---	F	L	341
100	cooked, boiled, drained	A B1 B2 C	14	88	L	L	L	---	---	---	F	L	239
100	soup, cream, with equal												
	parts water (canned)	A B1 B2 C^t	36	398	L	L	L	F	F	L	L	L	45
100	with equal parts milk	A B1 B2 C	69	424	L	L	L	F	F	L	F	L	118
100	CHARD, SWISS, cooked, drained	A B1 B2 C	18	86	L	L	L	---	---	---	F	F	321
100	CHAYOTE, raw	A B1 B2 C	28	5	L	L	L	---	---	---	L	L	102
	CHESTNUTS												
100	fresh	B1 B2	194	6	L	L	G	-------n/a-------			L	F	454
100	dried	B1 B2	377	12	L	L	H	-------n/a-------			F	F	875
100	chestnut flour	B1 B2	362	11	L	L	H	-------n/a-------			F	F	847
	CHICKPEAS, see Garbanzos												
100	CHICORY GREENS, raw	A B1 B2 C	20	---	L	L	L	---	---	---	F	L	420
100	CHILI CON CARNE, canned, beans	A B1 B2	133	531	L	L	F	F	F	L	F	F	233
100	CHILI POWDER	A B1 B2 C	340	1574	F	F	G	---	---	---	H	H	1000
	CHILI SAUCES, see Peppers, hot, and Tomato Chili Sauce under Tomatoes												
100	CHIVES, raw	A B1 B2 C	28	---	L	L	L	---	---	---	F	F	250
	COCONUT, fresh, meat only												
45	2" x 2" x ½" piece (approx)	B1 B2 C	155	10	L	H	L	n/a	H	T	L	L	115
130	shredded, grated, 1 cp packed firm	B1 B2 C	450	30	L	H	F	n/a	H	T	L	L	333
113	dried, sweetened, shredded, 1 cp	B1 B2 C	622	---	L	H	H	n/a	F	T	L	L	339
	COLESLAW, see cabbage												
190	COLLARDS, cooked, boiled, drained, 1 cup	A B1 B2 C	55	48	L	L	L	---	---	---	H	L	498
100	frozen, cooked, drained	A B1 B2 C	30	16	L	L	L	---	---	---	H	F	236
	CORN												
100	field, whole-grain, raw	A B1 B2	348	1	L	L	G	---	---	---	L	F	284
140	sweet, cooked, 1 ear 5" x 1¾",	A B1 B2 C	70	1	L	L	F	---	---	---	L	L	274
	creamed style, canned, white												
100	and yellow, solids & liquid	A B1 B2 C	82	236	L	L	F	---	---	---	L	L	(97)

LEGUME, NUTS AND VEGETABLES

F=Fair; G=Good; H=High; L=Low; t or T = trace; n/a = no information available; dashes = zero or unmeasurable

GRAM WT.	FOOD	VITAMINS	CAL	(mg) SOD	PRO	FAT	CARB	CHOL	FATTY ACIDS SAT	UNSAT	CALC	IRON	(mg) POTSM
	CORN, continued												
100	whole kernel, wet pack, solids & liquid	A B1 B2 C	66	236	L	L	F	---	---	---	L	L	(97)
	special dietary pack (low sodium)												
100	white/yellow, cream style	A B1 B2 C	82	2	L	L	F	---	---	---	L	L	(97)
	whole kernel, special dietary pack												
100	(low sodium) wet, solids & liquid	A B1 B2 C	57	2	L	L	F		---	---	L	L	97
100	frozen cut kernels, cooked	A B1 B2 C	79	1	L	L	F	---	---	---	L	L	184
336	2 cp, uncooked	A B1 B2 C	275	4	L	L	F	---	---	---	L	L	477
100	Cob, cooked, drained	A B1 B2 C	94	L	L	L	F	---	---	---	L	L	231
	COWPEAS (blackeye peas), cooked,												
160	immature seeds, 1 cp	A B1 B2 C	175	2	l	L	F	---	---	---	L	F	606
100	CRESS, garden or field, raw	A B1 B2 C	32	14	L	L	L	---	---	---	F	F	606
	CUCUMBERS												
207	7½" X 2", raw, pared, 1	A^t B1 B2 C	29	12	L	L	L	---	---	---	F	L	331
	CUCUMBER PICKLES, see Pickles												
	DAIKON, see radishes, oriental												
180	DANDELION GREENS, cooked,1cp	A B1Th B2 C	60	79	L	L	L	---	---	---	G	F	418
	DASHEENS, see Taros												
100	DOCK, (curly or narrowleaf dock,												
	broadleaf dock and sheep sorrel)												
	cooked	A B1 B2 C	19	3	L	L	L	---	---	---	F	L	198
100	EGGPLANT, cooked, drained	A B1 B2 C	19	1	L	L	L	---	---	---	L	L	150
57	ENDIVE curly, including												
	escarole, 2 ozs.	A B1 B2 C	10	8	L	L	L	---	---	---	F	F	168
	ESCAROLE, see Endive												
100	FENNEL	A C	28	---	L	L	L	---	---	---	F	F	397
100	FILBERTS, (hazelnuts)	B1 C	634	2	F	G	F	---	---	---	H	G	704
100	GARBANZOS, chickpeas,												
	uncooked, dry	A B1 B2	360	26	F	L	G	---	---	---	H	H	797
2	GARLIC, raw, 1 small clove	A^t B1 B2 C	3	T	L	L	F	---	---	---	L	F	11
	GINGER ROOT												
100	Crystallized (candied)	---	340	---	L	L	H	---	---	---	---	---	---

LEGUME, NUTS AND VEGETABLES

F=Fair; G=Good; H=High; L=Low; t or T = trace; n/a = no information available; dashes = zero or unmeasurable

GRAM WT.	FOOD	VITAMINS	CAL	(mg) SOD	PRO	FAT	CARB	CHOL	FATTY ACIDS SAT	UNSAT	CALC	IRON	(mg) POTSM
	GINGER ROOT continued												
100	fresh	A B1 B2 C	49	6	L	L	L	---	---	---	L	F	264
	GREEN BEANS, see Beans, Snap												
	GREEN ONIONS, see Onions												
	GREEN PEAS, see Peas												
	GREEN PEPPERS, see Peppers												
	HAZELNUTS, see Filberts												
100	HICKORY NUTS	A B1^N B2	673	---	F	H	F	---	---	---	T	F	---
100	HORSERADISH, prepared	---	38	96	L	L	L	---	---	---	F	L	290
100	raw	B1Th C	87	8	L	L	F	---	---	---	G	F	564
100	HYACINTH, beans, raw, young pods	A B1 B2 C	35	---	L	L	L	--------n/a-----			F	F	285
	JERUSALEM ARTICHOKES,												
	see Artichokes												
	JICAMA, No information available												
	See Recipe												
	KALE												
100	leaves only, raw	A B1 B2 C	53	75	L	L	L	---	---	---	H	F	(378)
110	cooked, leaves and stems, 1 cp	A C	30	47	L	L	L	---	---	---	G	G	243
100	frozen, cooked, drained	A B1 B2 C	31	21	L	L	L	---	---	---	G	F	193
100	KOHLRABI, (thickened, bulblike stems, cooked, drained)	A B1 B2 C	24	6	L	L	L	---	---	---	L	L	260
100	LEEKS, raw (bulb & lower leaf)	A B1 B2 C	52	5	L	L	L	---	---	---	F	F	347
100	LENTILS, mature seeds, cooked	A B1 B2	106	---	L	T	F	---	---	---	L	F	249
	LETTUCE, raw												
220	butterhead, as Boston types (and Romaine) 4" in diameter, 1 head	A B1 B2 C	30	20	L	L	L	---	---	---	L	F	581
454	crisphead, as Iceberg, 4¾" diameter, 1 head	A B1 B2 C	60	41	L	L	L	---	---	---	L	L	795
50	looseleaf, or bunching varieties, leaves, 2 large	A B1 B2 C	10	5	L	L	L	---	---	---	F	F	132
	LIMA BEANS, see Beans												
100	LITCHI NUTS, dried	A	277	3	L	L	G	---	---	H	F	F	1100
100	MACADAMIA NUTS	B1 B2	691	---	L	G	F	--------n/a--------			F	F	264

LEGUMES, NUTS AND VEGETABLES

F=Fair; G=Good; H=High; L=Low; t or T = trace; n/a = no information available; dashes = zero or unmeasurable

GRAM WT.	FOOD	VITAMINS	CAL	(mg) SOD	PRO	FAT	CARB	CHOL	FATTY ACIDS SAT	FATTY ACIDS UNSAT	CALC	IRON	(mg) POTSM
	MARGARINE See Chapter on												
	Fat & Oils												
	MATAI, see Waterchestnut, Chinese												
	MIXED VEGETABLES, see Vegetables, mixed												
244	MUSHROOMS, canned, solids & liquid , 1 cp	A^t B1 B2 C	40	976	L	T	L	---	---	---	L	L	481
140	MUSTARD GREENS, cooked, 1 cp	A B1 B2 C	35	25	L	L	L	---	---	---	G	F	308
100	MUSTARD SPINACH (tendergreen) cooked	A C	16	---	L	L	L	---	---	---	H	L	---
100	NEW ZEALAND SPINACH, cooked, drained	A B1 B2 C	13	92	L	L	L	---	---	---	F	F	463
85	OKRA, cooked, pod 3 X 3/8", 8pod	A B1 B2 C	25	2	L	L	L	---	---	---	F	L	148
	ONIONS												
110	mature, raw, 2½" diameter, 1	A B1 B2 C	40	11	L	L	L	---	---	---	L	L	173
210	cooked, 1 cp	A B1 B2 C	60	15	L	T	L	---	---	---	L	L	231
100	dehydrated, flaked	A B1 B2 C	350	88	L	L	H	---	---	---	G	F	1383
	Note Vitamin A value is based on yellow-fleshed varieties; white fleshed varieties contain only a trace.												
50	green young, without tops, 6	A^t B1 B2 C	20	3	L	L	F	---	---	---	F	L	116
	OYSTERPLANT, see Salsify												
4	PARSLEY, raw, chopped, 1 tblspn	A B1^t B2 C	T	2	T	T	T	---	---	---	H	H	29
155	PARSNIPS, cooked, 1 cp	A B1 B2 C	100	7	L	L	F	---	---	---	F	L	587
144	PEANUTS, roasted, salted, 1 cp	B1 B2	840	602	G	H	F	---	---	---	F	F	971
16	PEANUT BUTTER, 1 tblspn	B1 B2	95	97	G	H	F	---	L	H	F	F	107
100	PEANUT FLOUR, defatted	B1 B2	371	9	G	L	F	-------n/a--------			G	G	1186
	PEAS												
100	edible-podded, cooked, boiled, drained	A B1^{Th*} B2 C	43	---	L	L	L	---	---	---	F	L	119
	* Thiamine only.												
100	green, immature, cooked,drained	A B1 B2 C	71	1	L	L	F	---	---	---	L	F	196

LEGUMES, NUTS AND VEGETABLES

F=Fair; G=Good; H=High; L=Low; t or T = trace; n/a = no information available; dashes = zero or unmeasurable

GRAM WT.	FOOD	VITAMINS	CAL	(mg) SOD	PRO	FAT	CARB	CHOL	FATTY ACIDS SAT	UNSAT	CALC	IRON	(mg) POTSM
	PEAS: (Continued)												
100	canned (early/June) regular pack	A B1 B2 C	66	236	L	L	F	---	---	---	L	F	96
100	canned (low sod.) dietary pack	A B1 B2 C	55	3	L	L	L	---	---	---	L	F	96
100	frozen, cooked, drained	A B1 B2 C	68	115	L	L	F	---	---	---	L	F	135
250	split, dry, cooked, 1 cp	A B1 B2	290	33	L	L	F	---	---	---	L	F	296
28	canned, baby food, strained 1 oz.	A B1 B2 C	15	54	L	L	L	---	---	---	L	F	28
100	**PEAS AND CARROTS**												
	cooked, frozen and drained	A B1 B2 C	53	84	L	L	F	---	---	---	L	F	157
108	**PECANS**, halves, 1 cp	A B1 B2 C	740	T	L	H	F	---	---	---	F	F	651
	PEPPERS												
15	hot, red (ground chili powder, added seasonings), 1 tblspn	A B1 B2 C	50	236	F	F	G	---	---	---	H	H	1000
100	hot, green chili, deseeded, canned	A B1 B2 C	25	---	L	L	L	---	---	---	L	L	---
74	sweet, green, without stems, seeds, 1 pod	A B1 B2 C	15	---	L	L	L	---	---	---	L	L	158
73	cooked, boiled, drained 1 pod	A B1 B2 C	15	7	L	L	L	---	---	---	L	L	109
100	stuffed with beef and crumbs	A B1 B2 C	170	314	F	L	F	--------n/a--------			F	F	258
100	red, raw, mature, excluding seeds	A B1 B2 C	31	---	L	L	L	---	---	---	L	L	564
	PICKLES (cucumber)												
65	dill, medium, whole, 3-3/4" long, 1-1/4" diameter, 1 pickle	A B1[t] B2 C	10	928	L	L	L	---	---	---	L	F	130
15	fresh, sliced, as in bread-and-butter pickles, 2 slices, 1-1/2" and 1/4" thick	A B1[t] B2[t] C	10	101	T	T	L	---	---	---	L	F	---
100	sour	A B1 B2 C	10	1353	L	L	L	---	---	---	L	F	---
15	sweet gherkin, small, whole, 2-1/2 inches long, 3/4" diameter, 1	A B1[t] B2[t] C	20	---	T	T	F	---	---	---	L	F	---
15	sweet relish, 1 tblspn	---	20	79	T	T	F	---	---	---	L	F	---
100	**PIMIENTOS**, canned, solids and liquid	A B1 B2 C	27	---	L	L	L	---	---	---	L	L	---
	PINENUTS												
100	pignolias	B1[Th]	552	---	G	G	F	---	---	---	L	---	---
100	pinon	A B1 B2 C[t]	635	---	F	G	F	---	---	L	L	G	---

LEGUMES, NUTS AND VEGETABLES

F=Fair; G=Good; H=High; L=Low; t or T = trace; n/a = no information available; dashes = zero or unmeasurable

GRAM WT.	FOOD	VITAMINS	CAL	(mg) SOD	PRO	FAT	CARB	CHOL	FATTY ACIDS SAT	UNSAT	CALC	IRON	(mg) POTSM
100	PISTACHIO NUTS	A B1	594	---	F	G	F	---	L	H	G	H	972
	POTATOES												
	raw, med-size, 3 per pound, approx.												
99	baked, peeled after baking, 1	A^t B1 B2 C	90	4	L	T	F	---	---	---	L	L	498
136	boiled, peal after boiling, 1	A^t B1 B2 C	105	4	L	T	F	---	---	---	L	L	554
122	peal before boiling, 1	A^t B1 B2 C	80	2	L	T	F	---	---	---	L	L	348
57	french-fried, 2" x 1/2" x 1/2"												
	cooked in deep fat, 10 pieces	A^t B1 B2 C	155	3	L	F	G	---	---	---	F	F	486
57	frozen, heated, 10 pieces	A^t B1 B2 C	125	2	L	L	F	---	---	---	L	F	123
195	Mashed, milk added, 1 cp	A B1 B2 C	125	587	L	L	F	---	---	---	L	F	509
	Cholesterol values will depend on type of milk and fat used. If whole milk and butter are used, there will be cholesterol												
	readings; if skim milk and margarine are used, there will be none.												
20	potato chips, 2" diameter, 10	A^t B1 B2 C	115	---	L	F	G	--------n/a-------			F	F	226
	Note Sodium content is variable and may be as high as 1000 mg. per 100 grams. Also, see recipe for Mashed Potatoes,												
	using skim milk, margarine and no salt.												
100	potato flour	A^t B1 B2 C	351	34	L	L	H	--------n/a-------			F	H	1588
100	potato salad, from home recipe,												
	with mayonnaise and French												
	dressing, hard-cooked eggs, and												
	seasonings	A B1 B2 C	145	480	L	L	F	---	T	G	L	L	318
100	potato sticks	A^t B1 B2 C	544	*	L	F	G	--------n/a-------			F	F	1130
228	PUMPKIN, canned, 1 cp	A B1 B2 C	75	4	L	L	L	---	---	---	L	L	547
100	PURSLANE, leaves, including stems,												
	cooked, boiled, drained	A B1 B2 C	15	---	L	L	L	---	---	---	F	F	---
	RADISHES, raw												
40	common, without tops, 4	A B1 B2 C	5	7	T	T	L	---	---	---	L	F	129
100	oriental, including daikon												
	Japanese and Chinese	A B1 B2 C	19	---	L	L	L	---	---	---	L	L	180
100	RUTABAGAS, raw	A B1 B2 C	46	5	L	L	F	---	---	---	F	L	239
100	cooked, boiled, drained	A B1 B2 C	35	4	L	L	F	---	---	---	F	L	167
100	SAFFLOWER SEED MEAL,												
	partially defatted	B1 B2	355	---	F	L	F	---	---	---	F	---	---
	* variable												

LEGUMES, NUTS AND VEGETABLES

F=Fair; G=Good; H=High; L=Low; t or T = trace; n/a = no information available; dashes = zero or unmeasurable

GRAM WT.	FOOD	VITAMINS	CAL	(mg) SOD	PRO	FAT	CARB	CHOL	FATTY ACIDS SAT	UNSAT	CALC	IRON	(mg) POTSM
100	SALSIFY (Oysterplant), cooked, drained	A B1 B2 C	*	---	L	L	F**	---	---	---	F	F	266

Note *Caloric values for raw salsify range from 15 calories per 100 grams for freshly harvested vegetable to 82 calories for the product after storage; corresponding range for boiled salsify is 12 to 70 calories.

** A large portion of the carbohydrate in the unstored product may be inulin, which is of doubtful availability. During storage inulin is converted to sugars.

	SAUERKRAUT												
235	canned, solids and liquid, 1 cp	A B1 B2 C	45	1755*	L	L	L	---	---	---	L	L	329
100	juice, canned	B1 B2 C	10	787	L	T	L	---	---	---	L	F	---

Note *Sodium values for sauerkraut and sauerkraut juice are based on salt contents of 1.9 and 2.0 respectively in the finished product. The amounts in some samples may vary significantly from this estimate.

100	SESAME SEEDS, dry, whole	A B1 B2	563	60	F	G	F	--------n/a-------			H	H	725
100	SHALLOT BULBS, raw	A[t] B1 B2 C	72	12	L	L	F	---	---	---	F	F	334
	SPINACH												
180	canned, drained solids, 1 cp	A B1 B2 C	45	424*	L	L	L	---	---	---	G	F	450

Note *reflects salt used in canning.

180	fresh, cooked, 1 cp	A B1 B2 C	40	90	L	L	L	---	---	---	G	F	583
100	frozen, cooked, drained	A B1 B2 C	23	52	L	L	L	---	---	---	G	F	333
	MUSTARD SPINACH, see Mustard Spinach												
	NEW ZEALAND, see New Zealand Spinach												
	SQUASH												
210	cooked, summer, diced, 1 cp	A B1 B2 C	30	6	L	T	L	---	---	---	L	L	296
205	cooked, winter, baked, 1 cp	A B1 B2 C	130	2	L	L	F	---	---	---	L	L	945
100	SUCCOTASH, frozen, cooked	A B1 B2 C	93	38	L	L	F	---	---	---	L	F	246
100	SUNFLOWER SEED KERNELS, dry	A B1 B2	560	30	F	G	F	--------n/a-------			G	G	920
100	SUNFLOWER SEED FLOUR												
	partially defatted	B1 B2	339	56	G	L	G	--------n/a-------			H	H	1080
	SWEET POTATOES												
	cooked, med. 5" x 2" weight raw, about 6 ozs.												
110	baked, peeled after baking, 1	A B1 B2 C	155	13	L	L	F	---	---	---	L	L	330
147	boiled, peeled after boiling, 1	A B1 B2 C	170	17	L	L	F	---	---	---	L	L	357
175	candied, 3-1/2" x 2-1/2", 1	A B1 B2 C	295	74	L	L	F	---	---	---	L	L	333

LEGUMES, NUTS AND VEGETABLES

F=Fair; G=Good; H=High; L=Low; t or T = trace; n/a = no information available; dashes = zero or unmeasurable

GRAM WT.	FOOD	VITAMINS	CAL	(mg) SOD	PRO	FAT	CARB	CHOL	FATTY ACIDS SAT	FATTY ACIDS UNSAT	CALC	IRON	(mg) POTSM
	SWEET POTATOES, continued												
218	canned, vacuum or solid pack, 1 cp	A B1 B2 C	235	105*	L	L	F	---	---	---	L	L	436
	Note *reflects salt used in canning.												
	SWISS CHARD, see Chard, Swiss												
	TAROS												
100	corms and tubers	A B1 B2 C	98	7	L	L	F	----------n/a-----			L	F	514
100	leaves and stems	C	40	---	L	L	L	----------n/a-----			F	F	---
	TOMATOES												
100	green, raw	A B1 B2 C	24	3	L	L	L	---	---	---	L	L	244
200	red, raw, 3" dia. 2-1/8" high approx. 7 ozs. 1	A B1 B2 C	40	6	L	L	L	---	---	---	L	L	488
241	regular canned, solids and liquids, 1 cp	A B1 B2 C	50	313*	L	L	L	---	---	---	L	L	523
	Note *reflects salt used in canning												
100	dietary pack (low-sodium)	A B1 B2 C	20	3	L	L	L	---	---	---	L	L	217
273	catsup, 1 cp	A B1 B2 C	290	2845*	L	L	F	---	---	---	L	L	991
15	catsup, 1 tblspn	A B1 B2 C	15	156*	T	T	F	---	---	---	L	L	54
113	chili sauce, 1/2 cp	A B1 B2 C	118	1517*	L	L	F	---	---	---	L	L	418
243	juice, canned, 1 cp	A B1 B2 C	45	486*	L	T	L	---	---	---	L	L	552
182	juice, canned, 6 ozs.	A B1 B2 C	35	364*	L	T	L	---	---	---	L	L	413
168	paste, canned, 6 ozs.	A B1 B2 C	138	66*	L	L	L	---	---	---	L	F	1492
100	puree, canned regular pack	A B1 B2 C	39	399*	L	L	L	---	---	---	L	L	426
100	dietary pack, low-sodium	A B1 B2 C	39	6	L	L	L	---	---	---	L	L	426
245	soup, canned, prepared with equal volume of water, 1 cup	A B1 B2 C	90	970*	L	L	F	---	---	---	F	L	230
	Note * reflects salt used in canning.												
	TURNIPS												
155	cooked, diced, 1 cp	A[t] B1 B2 C	35	53	L	L	L	---	---	---	L	L	291
145	greens, cooked, 1 cp	A B1 B2 C	20	---	L	L	L	---	---	---	G	F	---
100	VEGETABLE JUICE COCKTAIL canned	A B1 B2 C	17	200	L	L	L	---	---	---	L	L	221
	VEGETABLE-OYSTER, see Salsify												
100	VINE SPINACH (basella), raw	A B1 C	19	---	L	L	L	---	---	---	G	F	---

LEGUMES, NUTS AND VEGETABLES

F=Fair; G=Good; H=High; L=Low; t or T = trace; n/a = no information available; dashes = zero or unmeasurable

GRAM WT.	FOOD	VITAMINS	CAL	(mg) SOD	PRO	FAT	CARB	CHOL	FATTY ACIDS SAT	UNSAT	CALC	IRON	(mg) POTSM
	WALNUTS												
126	black, or native, 1 cp chopped	A B1 B2	790	4	G	G	G	---	---	H	T	G	580
100	English or Persian	A B1 B2 C	651	2	G	G	G	---	---	H	G	G	450
100	WATER CHESTNUT, Chinese												
	(matai, waternut), raw	B1 B2 C	79	20	L	L	F	--------n/a-------			L	L	500
100	WATERCRESS, leaves, including												
	stems	A B1 B2 C	19	52	L	L	L	---	---	---	H	F	282
100	YAM, tuber, raw	A^t B1 B2 C	101	---	L	L	F	---	---	---	L	L	600
	YELLOW WAX BEANS, see beans, (snap)												

THE IMPORTANCE OF VEGETABLES IN THE DIET

Vegetables are one of three groups of foods that protect our growth and vitality; the others are milk and fruits. Vegetables provide starches and sugars for energy, plus several forms of protein, also large amount of vitamins, and mineral salts — especially calcium, phosphorous, iron, copper, manganese, potassium and sulphur, as well as iodine (in those grown near the seashore). For sound health and vitality, vegetables help to keep up the body's normal alkaline balance.

ACID-FORMING VEGETABLES AND NUTS

Corn
Lentils
Peanuts
Walnuts

ALKALINE-FORMING VEGETABLES AND NUTS

Almonds	Cauliflower	Lettuce
Asparagus	Celery	Parsnips
Beans: pods, snap, lima,	Chard	Peas
kidney, navy, and soy.	Chestnuts	Potatoes
Beets	Chickory	Radishes
Broccoli	Cucumbers	Rutabagas
Brussels Sprouts	Eggplant	Sweet potatoes
Cabbage	Endive	Tomatoes
Carrots	Kohlrabi	Turnips and tops

. . . .

A LITTLE SOMETHING ABOUT COOKING VEGETABLES

Certain vegetables may be eaten raw, while others must be cooked to make then palatable. Raw vegetables retain all of their values; when cooked, some of their values are lost. As an example: boiling, which does the most damage to fresh vegetables, yet it is the most frequently used method of cooking them. Most mineral salts in vegetables are easily dissolved in water. Loss of vitamins occurs by overheating; by prolonged exposure to air, and by dissolving in the cooking water. When cooking water is drained off, so are the vitamins. It is a wise housewife who uses this water to her family's health advantage. She uses it in gravies, soups, sauces and stews. To prevent waste of vitamins, use only the smallest amount of water necessary to keep vegetables from burning. Water should be boiling rapidly when vegetables are dropped in. They should be cooked only until tender for better flavor. By this time, the water will have evaporated.

Greens, such as spinach and chard, need to cook in only the water that is left on the leaves after washing them. Put them in a cold pot, then turn on the heat.

Baking is the best method to preserve vitamins and minerals in vegetables, especially baking with the skins on, such as: potatoes, sweet potatoes, squash, turnips, parsnips and carrots. Rolled in foil and sealed tightly against loss of juices, flavor is enhanced too. But there is one important rule to remember before sealing the foil: dab pieces of margarine over the vegetables and sprinkle with a little water. This keeps them moist.

Cooking time will depend upon the size of vegetables to be baked; the larger the vegetable, the longer the baking time. In a 325 F. oven, allow 1-1/2 to 2 hours for medium to large potatoes, halves of squash, plump yams and sweet potatoes, etc. If vegetables are cooked before the meat is ready, leave them sealed in foil; they'll stay plump and tasty.

Test for doneness by piercing foil with a long-pronged cooking fork.

When serving vegetables, open foil carefully, pour off juices into the gravy.

Another way to retain food values is cooking in deep fat. This prevents little loss because vegetables are cooked quickly.

All cooking methods for vegetables tend to reduce Vitamin C content with the exception of tomatoes and baked potatoes, which retain most of theirs.

For good nutrition, the family's daily diet should include fresh vegetables and fruit.

. . . .

ARTICHOKES

It has been said that one has to acquire the taste for artichokes, but there are some who'll disagree, claiming they were addicted at first bite! My first reaction to them was they they were a nothing vegetable — vegetable? Not so. They're from the thistle family — or are they? Webster's Dictionary states they're related to the daisy. Oh well—

If you don't have the courage, or curiosity, to try cooking one, don't be discouraged. They're easy to prepare. All it takes is a pair of sharp scissors with which to cut off the spiny part of the leaves; a very sharp knife, a lemon cut in half, a pan with a tight lid and some boiling water.

1. Select artichokes that show dark purple streaks near the base of the stems. These are fresh. Avoid artichokes with too many brown spots.
2. Wash under COLD water. Hot water causes discoloration.
3. Place artichokes on a cutting board to drain a minute while you fill a deep enough kettle to hold the chokes upright, and fill it about a quarter full of water. Add a sprinkle of salt, a tablespoon of cooking oil (for 3 or 4 artichokes: for 1 or 2, 1/2 teaspoon). The oil gives the leaves a glossy appearance. Cover and bring water to a boil while preparing the artichokes.
4. Grasp an artichoke firmly with the left hand, carefully to avoid spines. With your right hand, use the sharp knife to cut off about an inch or two of the top. This is the hardest part of the preparation because artichokes are stubborn about giving up their spines and have to be pressed hard against the board while cutting them off. Scissors won't work. Then cut the stem off level to the base of the choke. Rub cut places with fresh lemon to prevent discoloration.
5. Strip off about a layer of outer leaves and discard. Then take the scissors and cut off enough of each leaf left to remove the spines—(about 1/3 or less). Keep cutting around and around until all leaves have been de-spined. Rub entire surface with lemon generously.
6. Place artichokes in boiling water, upright. To keep them upright, place a china soup dish over them, or something similar, but nothing aluminum or metal, as this will cause discoloration.
7. Reduce heat to boil gently for about 50 minutes (if artichokes are large). less time if small. Continue to simmer until done. Test by piercing stem end with a long-pronged cooking fork for tenderness.
8. Drain artichokes. Place on cutting board to cool and drain.
9. Artichokes can be served either with or without the choke. Some people like to remove their own. This nest of fibers is situated in the center of the artichoke below the leaves. It can be scooped out with a spoon. Underneath it is the best part of the artichoke, a gray, unappetizing looking mass, but delicious. This is eaten with a fork; and usually dipped in a little mayonnaise. Mayonnaise should be served with each artichoke. The leaves are picked off, one by one and dipped into the dressing, then pulled through the teeth. The fibrous part of the leaf is discarded. (In very small artichokes, it is not necessary to remove the choke. However, I always do).

Cooked artichokes, if covered closely in plastic wrap, will keep several days in the refrigerator.

Just for the record: if you're not fond of mayonnaise, there are other dressing that can be used instead.

Unlike the French, or globe type artichokes described above, the Jerusalem artichokes are washed, peeled and boiled like potato, then either seasoned with margarine and chopped parsley or they can be creamed.

. . . .

To clean   Snap off tough ends of asparagus by bending the stalk until tender and tough parts separate. Discard tough ends then carefully wash tender tops well to remove any sand. Pay particular attention to the scales that run up and down the stalk as sand accumulates underneath them. Also, handle stalks carefully at the bud ends to prevent them from breaking off.

To cook   It is reasonable to assume that the lower part of the stalks will take longer to cook than the tender tips. That is probably why we were taught to tie stalks in bunches and stand them upright in a pan of boiling water that covers two-thirds of the stalks. This method is much more successful in keeping the buds from falling off. However, I have had as much success in cooking asparagus in a breadloaf pan, gently simmering the stalks until fork tender, then lifting them out with a slotted spoon under the tips. If spoon is large enough to take two-thirds of the stalk and tips at the same time, little damage occurs to the tips. Whichever method is used, cooking time is rarely longer than 10-12 minutes unless stalks are large.

It is not necessary to salt the boiling water — season at the table individually.

To serve   Asparagus can be eaten plain, or with a little margarine and grated cheese, or with traditional Hollandaise Sauce. However, food values will increase with the addition of margarine, cheese, or sauce. (See Nutrition at Your Fingertips at the beginning of this chapter in which values for 4 spears are given).

Note   Frozen asparagus takes about half the time to cook as fresh—follow directions on the package. Stalks are ready to cook—do not need preliminary preparation as do the fresh, but they should be treated as gently as fresh asparagus.

. . . .

There are so many recipes for baked beans, it would be impossible to include them in this book. Baked beans mean many things to many housewives: some follow the recipes for Boston Baked to the letter, others perk up the flavor by adding tomato sauce, or barbecue sauce — add bacon instead of salt pork or pieces of smoked ham; while other cooks add frankfurters during the last hour of baking, or smoked pork chops. Resourceful cooks use navy and pink beans, mixing them in a ratio of 1/2 cup of pink beans to 1-1/2 cups of navy with smoked ham hocks instead of salt pork. Hocks are cooked with the beans and a medium-size chopped onion. When beans are cooked, remove the hocks to a cutting board and lift out the small bones, then strip off the rind. Cut ham in bite-size pieces and return to the beans, then follow directions for Boston Baked Beans in this chapter.

Although many cooks believe beans should be soaked overnight, there is an effective shortcut: rinse and pick over beans as usual, then put them in a large kettle and pour enough boiling water over them to cover. Let stand 2 hours. Do not drain. Add more water, chopped onion and meat and cook until tender. Then proceed as for Boston Baked, or your regular method. The addition of one 8 oz. can of tomato sauce gives beans more flavor.

For the working housewife, beans could be the answer to the menu for her days off. Friday night, put beans to soak; Saturday morning cook them and have bean soup for lunch. Bake the remaining beans for supper and include an easy-to-make pineapple and cottage cheese salad, or sliced tomatoes on crisp head lettuce, and brown bread spread with cream cheese.

Soy beans could probably top the list for versatility, because they are not only an excellent food, but many, many products are made from them, such as: soybean oil, soy sauces, soy flour and meal. Their experimentation continues in Japan and the United States.

To cook miscellaneous frozen beans, such as baby limas, snap beans, etc., follow directions on the package then add some of your own ideas.

Try a sprinkle of celery salt, or minced green onion and a tablespoon of margarine after the beans are cooked and drained. Then stir in 1/2 teaspoon of dried parsley flakes and a dash of paprika. Or spice the beans with a tablespoon (or less) of chili powder.

Miscellaneous dried beans (pinto, kidney, etc.) may be soaked from a few hours to overnight before preparation.

Frozen beans take less time to cook because they have been blanched before freezing. It is not necessary to salt the cooking water. The only thing salt does is to make the water boil a little quicker, but it is also absorbed by the vegetables which increases the sodium content. It does little or nothing for the flavor. The most effective way to enhance the flavor is to season at the table. if added during the boiling process, seasoning goes down the drain with the rest of the liquid, except the amount absorbed. For people on low-sodium diets, even a small percentage of absorption could affect their daily allowance. If butter or margarine is added to the beans before serving, flavor may be increased, but so will calories and sodium content. (See Fats and Oils food list for margarine values and Dairy Products food list for those of butter).

. . . .

F=Fair; G=Good; H=High; L=Low; t or T = trace; n/a = no information available; dashes = zero or unmeasurable

GRAM WT.	FOOD	VITAMINS	CAL	(mg) SOD	PRO	FAT	CARB	CHOL	FATTY ACIDS SAT	UNSAT	CALC	IRON	(mg) POTSM
101	AVERAGE PER SERVING		162	3				(mg)* 24					426
	Ingredients:												
227	1-1/2 cp dried lima beans	A B1 B2 C	279	5	L	L	F	---	---	---	L	F	1476
168	1 ham hock, smoked, 6 oz	B1 B2	490	---	G	G	---	H	H	L	L	F	479
110	1 medium-size onion	A B1 B2 C	40	11	L	L	L	---	---	---	L	L	173
505	Recipe totals (gms; cal; sod. & potsm.)		809	16									2128

METHOD

Wash lima beans in colander; pick over and discard any that are discolored. Put beans in a large mixing bowl, cover with water and soak overnight (about twice as much water as beans). The next day, drain water from beans and pour beans into a large saucepan or kettle; a Dutch oven is ideal. Cover beans with cold water, add the ham hock and onion (which has been chopped fine), cover kettle and cook beans slowly until tender. Remove ham, skin off rind, take out small bones and discard. Cut meat into small pieces. If there is too much liquid, drain some off and save for soups or gravies. Yield 5 three quarter cup servings. Beans can be baked in a covered dish at 300F. 4 or 5 hours, adding bean liquid as needed. Beans should not be too dry. If desired, 1/4 cup of honey or brown sugar may be added just before baking and 1/4 teaspoon dry mustard.

LIMAS

    3 cups uncooked equals 7 cups cooked
    1 cup uncooked equals 1-1/3 cups cooked
    1-1/2 cups uncooked equals 3-1/2 cups cooked.

* There are 70 milligrams of cholesterol in 100 grams of pork, per U.S.D.A. Handbook No. 8, pg. 146, item 32a. In 168 grams, there are 118 milligrams of cholesterol; divided by 5 servings equals 24 average milligrams of cholesterol per serving.

. . . .

424

BAKED SOY BEANS

F=Fair; G=Good; H=High; L=Low; t or T = trace; n/a = no information available; dashes = zero or unmeasurable

GRAM WT.	FOOD	VITAMINS	CAL	(mg) SOD	PRO	FAT	CARB	CHOL	FATTY ACIDS SAT	UNSAT	CALC	IRON	(mg) POTSM
80	AVERAGE PER SERVING		139	124									675
	Ingredients:												
227	2 cp dry soy beans	A B1 B2 C	914	12	H	F	F	---	---	---	H	L	3806
110	1 medium-size onion	A B1 B2 C	40	11	L	L	L	---	---	---	L	L	173
2	1 clove garlic, mashed (or chopped fine)	A^t B1 B2 C	3	T	L	L	F	---	---	---	L	F	11
33	1/3 cp celery, chopped	A B1 B2 C	5	42	L	L	L	---	---	---	F	L	113
20	1/3 cp parsley, finely chopped	A B1 B2 C	9	9	L	L	L	---	---	---	H	H	145
20	1 tblspn molasses	B1 B2	50	3	---	---	H	---	---	---	H	H	184
227	1 (8 oz) can tomato sauce	A B1 B2 C	88	*905	L	L	L	---	---	---	L	L	967
639	Recipe totals (gms; cal; sod. & potsm.)		1109	982									5399

METHOD

Wash beans thoroughly then place in a deep bowl, cover with water and soak 12 hours. Drain. Put beans in a large kettle, cover with fresh water and simmer until beans are tender. Then drain, save the liquid for adding to the beans as they cook. Pour beans in a large bean pot or baking dish and stir in the rest of the ingredients. Container should be quite deep.   Add enough liquid to nearly cover. If bean pot has a lid, cover and bake 8 to 10 hours at 300 F., if not, make a cover out of foil. At the end of the baking period, beans should not be dry, nor should they be soupy. Add liquid from time to time during the baking process to control moisture content. Soy beans take a much longer time to cook than navy beans, but they make a delicious, high protein meal. Yield   approximately 8 servings.

*   High sodium is reflected in the canning process.

. . . .

BEETS AND BEET GREENS

Select small to medium-size beets which are more tender and flavorful. Sometimes, very large beets have a woody taste and take a long time to cook. Greens from small beets are more tender, too. Those from very large beets are often tough and undersirable.

To prepare beets for cooking, remove leaves by cutting them off about an inch from the beets. Scrub beets to remove any soil. They're a root vegetable (which means they grow underground) and when harvested, some of the dirt may cling to their outer surfaces. This must be washed off.

Do not remove rootlets from the beets as they contain flavor and juices. Unless beets are to be cooked in a pressure cooker, they should be cooked in plenty of water in a covered container. Length of cooking time will depend upon tenderness and age of beets. Young beets take from 1-1/2 to 2 hours; old beets from three to four hours or longer. Test for tenderness by piercing each beet with a fork because cooking time for each beet may vary as much as fifteen minutes. When all of the beets are tender, drain off liquid then run cold water over them and slip off the skins with the hands, also removing the rootlets. Rinse out the pot in which the beets were cooked, making certain no sand remains. Use this pot to cook the greens. Beets can be put in a bowl and set aside until greens are cooked.

To prepare beet greens for cooking: Cut off stems about an inch from base of the leaves and discard. Go over the leaves carefully, keeping only those that are unblemished. Wilted leaves may be all right when opened out — if they are not brown or tough or full of holes. Wash each leaf on both sides in running water because sand can cling to the veins of the leaves. Finger the leaves as they're washed; if they feel smooth, they should be clean. Drain on paper towels and set aside until beets are cooked. About 15 minutes before serving, put the greens in about an inch of boiling water in the kettle in which the beets were cooked. Cover and cook until greens are limp (about 8 minutes). Add skinned beets and continue cooking until beets are heated through (about 5 minutes).

NOTE Before adding the beets, it is easier to slice the cooled beets before adding them to the greens than it is to cut them while hot. If beets are small, they are good left whole; if larger, they can be sliced or cut in pieces if preferred. When beets are heated, drain off liquid and discard. Add about a tablespoon of margarine to the beets and greens, stir gently, cover about 1 minute until margarine melts. Serve hot. Season individually at the table.

. . . .

HARVARD BEETS

F=Fair; G=Good; H=High; L=Low; t or T = trace; n/a = no information available; dashes = zero or unmeasurable

GRAM WT.	FOOD	VITAMINS	CAL	(mg) SOD	PRO	FAT	CARB	CHOL	FATTY ACIDS SAT	UNSAT	CALC	IRON	(mg) POTSM
130	AVERAGE PER SERVING		132	106									194
	Ingredients:												
340	2 cp cooked beets	A B1 B2 C	110	146	L	T	L	---	---	---	L	L	707
28	2 tblspn margarine	A D	200	279	L	H	L	---	L	H	L	---	6
5	1-1/2 tspn cornstarch	---	17	---	L	T	H	---	---	---	---	---	T
50	1/4 cp sugar	---	193	T	T	---	---	H	---	---	---	---	L	2
60	1/4 cp vinegar	---	8	---	T	---	---	L	---	---	---	L	L	60
38	2-1/2 tblspns water								---0---				
---	1/8 tsp black pepper								n/a				
	No salt, season at the table												
521	Recipe totals (gms; cal; sod & potsm.)		528	425									775

METHOD

Skin freshly cooked beets, then slice or dice. (Canned beets may be used). Set aside. Melt margarine in a saucepan, remove from heat and blend in cornstarch. Add sugar, vinegar, water and pepper. Return to heat and cook, stirring constantly until mixture is clear and thick. Remove from heat, add beets carefully, folding in until all are coated. Allow flavors to blend about 5 minutes. Yield   4 servings.

. . . .

EASY BEET RELISH

F=Fair; G=Good; H=High; L=Low; t or T = trace; n/a = no information available;   dashes = zero or unmeasurable

GRAM WT.	FOOD	VITAMINS	CAL	(mg) SOD	PRO	FAT	CARB	CHOL	FATTY ACIDS SAT	UNSAT	CALC	IRON	(mg) POTSM
351	AVERAGE PER PINT		231	406									576
	Ingredients:												
680	4 cp diced, cooked beets	A B1 B2 C	220	292	L	T	L	---	---	---	L	L	1414
280	4 cp chopped cabbage	A B1 B2 C	60	56	L	L	L	---	---	---	L	L	652
113	1/2 cp grated horseradish	---	42	108	L	L	L	---	---	---	L	L	328
4	1 tspn salt	---		1569	---	---	---	---	---	---	G	---	T
---	1/4 tsp pepper							n/a					
480	2 cp vinegar	---	64	5	T	---	L	---	---	---	L	L	480
200	1 cp granulated sugar	---	770	2	---	---	H	---	---	---	---	L	6
1757	Recipe totals (gms; cal; sod. & potsm.)		1156	2032									2880

METHOD

Combine beets, cabbage, horseradish, and salt and pepper. Scald vinegar, dissolve sugar in it, add the vegetables and cook until tender. Seal in hot, sterilized jars. Yield 5 pints.

. . . .

BROCCOLI

A variety of cauliflower and broccoli is green instead of white. One pound of raw cauliflower has only 270 International Units of Vitamin A, and 354 milligrams of Vitamin C, while raw broccoli has 8,840 units of Vitamin A and 400 milligrams of Vitamin C. (See the list of foods at the beginning of this chapter for calorie and sodium comparisons).

Although broccoli was grown along the east coast, it wasn't until western growers promoted it that it became as popular as cauliflower. It is nearly always lower priced than cauliflower, perhaps because it is often more abundant.

Broccoli heads should be bright green and crisp; yellow flowers indicate age. Only that part of the stalk which is hard should be discarded. It will be difficult to insert a knife in the hard part, but by moving the knife up the stalk a little, it's easy to cut off. Wash under running water, store in a plastic bag in the refrigerator if it is not to be used immediately. This will insure freshness.

To cook: If stalks are large enough, split them in four pieces; if not, split them in two. Use a deep kettle large enough to hold the heads without crushing them. Bring water to a rapid boil then insert the heads carefully, stem end down to avoid breaking the flowers. Add soda the size of a small pea around the stems. Do not submerge heads. When water boils up again, cook from 15 to 25 minutes, depending on freshness. Test for tenderness by piercing stem with a fork. Flowers cook before the stems, and if they are submerged, they'll turn mushy before the stems are cooked. Serve plain with margarine, or Hollandaise Sauce, or sprinkle with grated cheese.

Another way to cook broccoli is to wash the stalks, being careful not to break the flowers. Cut flowers off stems and save. Peel stems, cut in pieces about an inch long and cook slowly in tomato juice until tender. Add a little fresh, mashed garlic (about 1/4 clove) or sprinkle a little garlic salt in the tomato juice. Cook the flowers in a small amount of boiling water about 5 minutes, drain and add to the cooked stems, stirring carefully to avoid mashing them.

. . . .

BAKED BROCCOLI

F=Fair; G=Good; H=High; L=Low; t or T = trace; n/a = no information available; dashes = zero or unmeasurable

GRAM WT.	FOOD	VITAMINS	CAL	(mg) SOD	PRO	FAT	CARB	CHOL (mg)*	FATTY ACIDS SAT	UNSAT	CALC	IRON	(mg) POTSM
	COMPLETE WITH SAUCE							(mg)*					
346	AVERAGE PER SERVING		205	220				8					868
	Ingredients:												
1135	2-1/2 lb fresh broccoli	A B1 B2 C	283	133	L	L	L	---	---	---	F	F	3380
510	2 cp medium white sauce (below)	A B1 B2 C	358	300	G	F	H	L	L	L	G	G	861
50	1/2 cp bread crumbs	A^t B1 B2 C^t	195	368	F	L	G	---	---	---	G	F	76
14	1 tblspn margarine	A D	100	139	T	H	T	---	L	H	F	---	3
23	1/4 cp grated cheese	A B1 B2	90	159	G	G	L	H	H	L	H	F	19
1732	Recipe totals (mgs; cal; sod. & potsm.)		1026	1099									4339

METHOD

Wash broccoli; cut off about 1/2" of thick stems and discard. Split stems up toward flowers in about 2 or 3 pieces. Cook in small amount of boiling water, flowers-up and not submerged, until stems are fork tender. Drain. Place in a greased baking dish and cover with white sauce. Sprinkle with bread crumbs, dot with margarine and sprinkle cheese over all, distributing it as evenly as possible. Bake at 350 F. 25 to 30 minutes. Yield 5 servings.

RECIPE FOR WHITE SAUCE

GRAM WT.	FOOD	VITAMINS	CAL	(mg) SOD	PRO	FAT	CARB	CHOL (mg)*	FATTY ACIDS SAT	UNSAT	CALC	IRON	(mg) POTSM
102	AVERAGE PER SERVING		72	60				(mg)* 3					172
	Ingredients:												
18	2 tblspn cornstarch	---	68	---	L	T	H	---	---	---	---	---	T
492	2 cp 2% low-fat milk	A B1 B2 C	290	300	H	F	G	L	L	L	H	L	861
n/a	Dash pepper							-----n/a-----					
	No salt, season individually at table.												
510	Recipe totals (gms; cal; sod. & potsm.)		358	300									861

METHOD

Mix cornstarch in about 1/4 cup of water, stirring until smooth. Heat milk slowly (DO NOT BOIL). Add cornstarch mixture, stirring constantly until sauce thickens. Add pepper and blend.

NOTE   When adding the cornstarch and water mixture, it's a good idea to add a little at a time instead of all at once to prevent sauce from thickening too fast.   Margarine has been omitted in order to reduce calories and sodium content.

*   There are 100 milligrams of cholesterol in 100 grams of cheddar cheese, per U.S.D.A. Handbook No. 8, pg. 146, item 5. In 23 grams, there are 23 milligrams of cholesterol. In non-fat skim milk, there are 3 milligrams of cholesterol, per U.S.D.A. Handbook No. 8, pg. 146, item 29 fluid skim. In 492 grams (2 cups) of milk, there are 15 milligrams of cholesterol for a total in this recipe of 38, divided by 5 servings equals 8 average milligrams per serving.

. . . .

BRUSSEL SPROUTS

This vegetable, which resembles little cabbages, should be soaked in cold, salted water for 30 minutes to dispel any insects or worms that burrow deep inside. Then drain, peel off any yellow outside leaves, cut off a little of the hard stems and boil in very small amount of water (or steam) until just tender. Drain in a colander over a bowl, saving the liquid which contains vitamins. Sprouts may be served plain, or with a dab or two of margarine, or may be creamed by adding milk to the liquid that was drained off. Heat milk and water mixture almost to the boiling point. Mix one tablespoon cornstarch with water until smooth then add slowly, stirring constantly, to the heated mixture until a medium-thick cream sauce. Add sprouts, folding in carefully, sprinkle with grated cheese (Cheddar or Parmesan) and serve. Yield   3 or 4 medium-size sprouts makes one serving. Salt may be added individually at the table.

* There are 390 milligrams of potassium in 100 grams of brussel sprouts, uncooked, and 273 milligrams cooked, per U.S.D.A. Handbook No. 8, pg. 18, items 489 and 490 respectively. (See Nutrition at Your Fingertips list of foods heading this chapter).

. . . .

CREAMED WHITE OR RED CABBAGE

F=Fair; G=Good; H=High; L=Low; t or T = trace; n/a = no information available; dashes = zero or unmeasurable

GRAM WT.	FOOD	VITAMINS	CAL	(mg) SOD	PRO	FAT	CARB	CHOL	FATTY ACIDS SAT	FATTY ACIDS UNSAT	CALC	IRON	(mg) POTSM
124	AVERAGE PER SERVING INCLUDING WHITE SAUCE		85	93				(mg)* 1					232
	Ingredients:												
454	1 small head cabbage	A B1 B2 C	98	82	L	L	L	---	---	---	L	L	951
283	1 recipe white sauce (below)		379	429									437
5	1 tsp margarine	A D	34	46	L	H	T	---	L	H	L	---	1
4	Paprika & dried parsley flakes	A B1t B2 C	T	2	T	T	T	---	---	---	H	H	---
746	Recipe totals (gms; cal; sod. & potsm.)		511	559									1389

METHOD

Wash cabbage under running water then remove any wilted or yellow outer leaves and discard. Cut in pieces, remove core, and place cabbage in a kettle that is 1/4 full of boiling water. Cover and cook until fork tender. Drain through a colander, and set aside. Make the following white sauce for this recipe.

WHITE SAUCE

GRAM WT.	FOOD	VITAMINS	CAL	(mg) SOD	PRO	FAT	CARB	CHOL	FATTY ACIDS SAT	FATTY ACIDS UNSAT	CALC	IRON	(mg) POTSM
47	FOR SAUCE ONLY PER SERVING		63	72				(mg)* 1					73
	Ingredients:												
246	1 cp 2% low-fat milk	A B1 B2 C	145	150	H	F	G	L	L	L	H	L	431
28	2 tblspn margarine	A D	200	279	L	H	L	---	L	G	L	---	6
9	2 tblspn cornstarch	---	34	---	L	T	H	---	---	---	---	---	---
n/a	Dash black pepper, no salt							n/a					
283	Recipe totals (gms; cal; sod. & potsm.)		379	429									437

METHOD

Heat milk, but do not boil. Mix cornstarch with a little water until smooth. Stir into milk a little at a time, continuing to stir until sauce thickens. Sprinkle pepper into sauce, add cooked cabbage. Just before serving, dot with margarine, shake paprika and parsley flakes lightly over the top. Yield 6 servings.

. . . .

STUFFED CABBAGE LEAVES

F=Fair; G=Good; H=High; L=Low; t or T = trace; n/a = no information available; dashes = zero or unmeasurable

GRAM WT.	FOOD	VITAMINS	CAL	(mg) SOD	PRO	FAT	CARB	CHOL	FATTY ACIDS SAT	UNSAT	CALC	IRON	(mg) POTSM
147	AVERAGE PER SERVING		304	342				(mg)* 53					325
	Ingredients:												
454	1 lb lean ground beef	A B1 B2	812	295	G	F	---	H	H	L	L	F	1612
100	1 cp bread crumbs	A^t B1 B2 C^t	390	736	F	L	G	---	---	---	G	F	152
56	4 tblspn margarine	A D	400	558	L	H	L	---	L	H	L	---	13
110	1 medium onion, minced	A B1 B2 C	40	11	L	L	L	---	---	---	L	L	173
n/a	1/2 tsp ground sage	--n/a--											
n/a	1/2 tsp pepper	--n/a--											
n/a	6 large cabbage leaves	A B1 B2 C	---	------------------no measurement available, including cal. & sod.)--									
165	1 cp cooked minute rice	B1	180	450	L	T	F	---	---	---	L	L	T
885	Total for recipe (gms; cal; sod. & potsm.)		1822	2050									1950

METHOD

Mix ground beef, crumbs, margarine, onion and seasonings together. Place cabbage leaves in boiling water; turn off heat and let them stand about 5 minutes, then drain. Divide meat mixture into 6 even amounts and place 1 portion in center of 1 cabbage leaf until all are filled. Make a depression in the center of each of the meat mixtures and fill with cooked rice. (To cook rice, follow directions on the package). Fold leaves over meat and fasten with string or toothpicks. Place in a frying pan, or baking dish, cover with boiling water, cover pan and either cook on top of the stove 30 minutes or in a 350 F. oven, 45 minutes. If desired, bake cabbage leaves in tomato juice instead of water — heat before pouring over leaves, then cover.

*   There are 70 milligrams of cholesterol in 100 grams of boneless beef, per U.S.D.A. Handbook No. 8, pg. 146, item 1b. In 1 pound of beef (454 grams) there are 318 milligrams of cholesterol divided by 6 servings equals 53 average milligrams of cholesterol per serving.

. . . .

CARROTS

To Boil: Wash fresh carrots, cut off the ends and scrape or pare as thinly as possible. If carrots are small, boil whole; if old or large, slice or cut in strips or pieces. Carrots absorb cooking water fast so they should be covered with water and watched closely, adding water as needed until tender. Test for tenderness by piercing with a fork. Drain, add a little margarine, cover and shake gently to distribute fat, then serve. Salt individually at the table.

To Bake: Prepare as for boiling. Line a baking dish with foil, place the whole or sliced carrots in it, dot them with butter, and drizzle a little water over them. (If desired, add some brown sugar). Close foil tightly and bake at 350 F. 1 hour or until carrots are tender. Or prepare carrots as for boiling and bake around a roast. Add just enough water to prevent them from burning, checking from time to time, turning or stirring them, adding more water as needed. In a 325 F. oven, carrots will take almost as long to cook as a roast of beef that weighs about 3 pounds.(2 To 2-1/2 hours medium rare).

To Steam: Prepare carrots as for boiling. Place on a rack in a steamer over boiling water and cook until tender, dot with margarine and serve.

To Cook in a Pressure-Cooker: Prepare carrots as for boiling, then following directions given for the cooker.

NOTE   Frozen, canned, or fresh peas may be combined with carrots a short time before serving.

Seasoning Cooked Carrots: Try celery salt after margarine has been added to the carrots, OR some minced onion, OR sprinkle some brown sugar over them and stir to blend.

. . . .

CARROT MOLDS

F=Fair; G=Good; H=High; L=Low; t or T = trace; n/a = no information available;   dashes = zero or unmeasurable

GRAM WT.	FOOD	VITAMINS	CAL	(mg) SOD	PRO	FAT	CARB	CHOL	FATTY ACIDS SAT	UNSAT	CALC	IRON	(mg) POTSM
87	AVERAGE PER SERVING		118	158				(mg)* 92					196
	Ingredients:												
220	2 cp raw carrots, grated	A B1 B2 C	90	104	L	T	L	---	---	---	F	L	750
50	1/2 cp bread crumbs	A^ت B1 B2 C^t	195	368	F	L	G	---	---	---	G	F	76
100	2 large eggs	A B1 B2	150	122	F	F	L	H	H	L	F	F	129
28	2 tblspn melted margarine	A D	200	279	L	H	T	---	L	H	L	---	6
123	1/2 cp 2% low-fat milk	A B1 B2 C	74	75	H	F	G	L	L	L	H	L	215
521	Recipe totals (gms; cal; sod. & potsm.)		709	948									1176

METHOD

Mix grated carrots with bread crumbs. Beat the eggs, add margarine and milk and add to carrots and crumb mixture. Fill a greased ring mold, or muffin pans, or other individual baking dishes and set in a pan of hot water. Bake in a slow oven 250 F. to 325 F. until firm. Yield   4 to 6 servings, depending upon size of serving dishes.

*   There are 550 milligrams of cholesterol in 100 grams of whole egg and 4 milligrams of cholesterol in 123 grams of fluid skim milk, for a total of 554, as calculated from U.S.D.A. Handbook No. 8, pg. 146, items 12 and 29 respectively. Divide 554 by 6 servings equals 92 average milligrams of cholesterol per serving.

. . . .

CAULIFLOWER

When buying cauliflower, select firm, white heads with crisp green leaves, and few brown blemishes. These indicate age and should be cut out when preparing to cook.

Cauliflower may be eaten raw (as in salads), boiled, steamed, creamed, or baked. To prepare: remove the green leaves and cut out any bruised or brown spots. Place head downward in a deep bowl of cold, salted water for about 30 minutes to draw out any dust or insects. Drain, rinse, then cook in enough boiling water to nearly cover, whole or broken into flowerlets, 12 to 15 minutes until just tender. To retain white color, add 1 or 2 tablespoons of lemon juice to 1 pint of water. In a salad, cauliflower is delicious raw. Cut flowerlets very thin and marinate in French dressing 30 minutes, then toss with other salad greens.

. . . .

CAULIFLOWER AU GRATIN

F=Fair; G=Good; H=High; L=Low; t or T = trace; n/a = no information available;   dashes = zero or unmeasurable

GRAM WT.	FOOD	VITAMINS	CAL	(mg) SOD	PRO	FAT	CARB	CHOL	FATTY ACIDS SAT	UNSAT	CALC	IRON	(mg) POTSM
151	AVERAGE PER SERVING		127	143				(mg)* 9					338
	Ingredients:												
454	1 lb head of cauliflower	A B1 B2 C	122	59	L	L	L	---	---	---	F	F	1339
369	1-1/2 cp 2% low-fat milk	A B1 B2 C	218	225	H	F	G	L	L	L	H	L	647
14	1-1/2 tblspn cornstarch	---	51	---	L	T	H	---	---	---	---	---	---
28	2 tblspn margarine	A D	200	279	L	H	L	---	L	H	L	---	6
42	1/2 cp grated cheddar cheese	A B1 B2	169	297	G	G	L	H	H	L	H	F	34
n/a	Dash black pepper						-----n/a-----						
1	1 tsp parsley flakes	A B1^t B2 C	T	T	T	T	T	---	---	---	H	H	---
908	Recipe totals (gms; cal; sod. & potsm.)		760	860									2026

METHOD

Trim off all green leaves, cut stem end from cauliflower, and soak upside down in cold, salted water for 30 minutes. Drain and rinse in fresh water. Cook cauliflower in enough boiling water to prevent burning, until fork tender. Drain. Heat milk in a saucepan slowly, mix cornstarch with water until smooth (about 1/4 cup water), add margarine, grated cheese and pepper. Stir until cheese is melted and sauce thickens. Place whole cauliflower head in a serving dish and pour cheese sauce over it. Sprinkle with parsley flakes. Serve hot. Yield   6 servings. This is delicious with fish, chicken and meat loaf.

*   There are 42 milligrams of cholesterol in 42 grams of cheddar cheese, and 11 milligrams of cholesterol in 369 grams of fluid skim milk, for a total of 53 milligrams of cholesterol as calculated from U.S.D.A. Handbook No. 8, pg. 146, items 5 and 29 respectively. Divide 53 by 6 servings equals 9 average milligrams of cholesterol per serving.

. . . .

CELERY

To Prepare: Cut off about 2" of the root end. Do not discard as this can be used in soups or other dishes. Wash each stalk carefully until all sand or other dirt has been removed. Cut off most of the leafy ends and save for soups, stews and gravies. With a potato peeler, or sharp paring knife, bend at the leaf-end of the stalk and peel off the tough, stringy fibers. Place cleaned celery in a plastic bag, twist closed and keep in refrigerator crisper until needed. Store leaves, root ends in a separate bag.

Stuffed Celery: Select firm, rather large stalks. The number of pieces will depend upon number of people to be served (about 3 per person). Cut stalks in 2" pieces. Wash and peel tough fibers off, place in a bowl of cold water while stuffing is prepared.

Moisten Philadelphia-type cream cheese with mayonnaise to the consistency desired, but mixture should not be runny. Amount of cheese to use will also depend upon number of people to be served. Add a few drops of onion juice or green onion minced very fine and blend until smooth. Stuff celery pieces with the mixture. Garnish with a sprinkle of paprika and parsley flakes or stuffed olives cut in rounds. Place celery on a serving dish, cover with a plastic bag, twist to close, and store in refrigerator until needed.

Creamed Celery: Wash and peel tough fibers from celery stalks; cut in 1" pieces, cook until tender in as little water as possible. Save 1/2 cup of the water, drain the remaining liquid in a bowl and store in the refrigerator to add to soups, gravies, etc. Make a medium white sauce (See Creamed Cabbage recipe) but using the 1/2 cup of celery water and 1/2 cup 2% low-fat milk instead of a whole cup of milk. Mix celery and cream sauce together, garnish with paprika or parsley flakes and a dab of margarine on top. If desired, garnish with minced green onion instead of parsley.

. . . .

CHAYOTE MEDLEY

Of the squash family, Chayotes are prepared in the same way.

F=Fair; G=Good; H=High; L=Low; t or T = trace; n/a = no information available; dashes = zero or unmeasurable

GRAM WT.	FOOD	VITAMINS	CAL	(mg) SOD	PRO	FAT	CARB	CHOL	FATTY ACIDS SAT	UNSAT	CALC	IRON	(mg) POTSM
213	**AVERAGE PER SERVING**		110	10									376
	Ingredients:												
454	1 lb chayote	A B1 B2 C	108	19	L	L	L	---	---	---	L	L	463
42	3 tblspn oil	---	375	---	---	H	---	---	L	H	---	---	---
110	1 medium onion	A B1 B2 C	40	11	L	L	L	---	---	---	L	L	173
74	1 green pepper	A B1 B2 C	15	10	L	L	L	---	---	---	L	L	158
600	3 fresh tomatoes approx. 7 oz each	A B1 B2 C	120	18	L	L	L	---	---	---	L	L	1464
n/a	Dash pepper						-n/a-						
1280	Recipe totals (gms; cal; sod. & potsm.)		658	58									2258

METHOD

Wash and cut chayote in 1/4" slices. Add oil to heavy skillet with a close-fitting cover. While oil is heating slowly, peel and slice onion thin, wash and cut green pepper in half, deseed, destem, cut out membranes inside, and cut in pieces. Wash and slice tomatoes then arrange vegetables in layers, starting with squash and ending with tomatoes on top. Sprinkle pepper over all. Salt at the table individually. Add 1/4 cup of hot water and cover and cook slowly about 45 minutes or until vegetables are tender. Yield 6 servings.

. . . .

CELERIAC

This vegetable is a variety of celery grown for its root instead of its stalks.

To Prepare: Trim tops off, wash and peel bulb and drop it in boiling water. Cook for 30 minutes, or until tender. It may be eaten plain, or creamed, scalloped, or used cold in salads. Flavor is similar to celery. It is not necessary to salt the water in which it is cooked. Season at the table. See the food list "Nutrition at Your Fingertips" at the beginning of this chapter for its food components.

CHARD

This green, leafy vegetable is a member of the beet family, but has no bulbous root. Its foliage is raised for greens, the stems for a vegetable.

To Prepare: It is cooked like fresh spinach and prepared in the same way. Wash the leaves thoroughly, both tops of the leaves and undersides. Cook in very little water until tender. It may be eaten plain, with a little margarine, or with lemon juice or vinegar added just before serving. See the food list "Nutrition at Your Fingertips" for its food components.

CHESTNUTS

To Boil: Chestnuts have a flat side which must be cut to allow steam to escape and to loosen skins that cover the meat inside. Make a gash in each chestnut with a sharp knife — be sure to penetrate the shell — then put chestnuts into a saucepan with enough water to cover — water must be boiling. Reduce heat and simmer chestnuts approximately 5 minutes. Drain. Dry nuts with paper towels. Remove shells and inner skins while still hot. Place chestnuts in a saucepan again, cover with boiling water and cook slowly 20 to 30 minutes until tender.

To Roast: Cut a gash in flat sides of chestnuts. Distribute nuts on cookie sheet and roast in a 350 F. preheated oven about 20 minutes. Test a chestnut with a fork — if tender remove from oven, if not, roast a little longer, then strip off shells and brown outer skins of nuts. Serve as is. (For chestnut stuffing, see Meats and Poultry Chapter).

. . . .

CHESTNUTS AND RED CABBAGE

F=Fair; G=Good; H=High; L=Low; t or T = trace; n/a = no information available;   dashes = zero or unmeasurable

GRAM WT.	FOOD	VITAMINS	CAL	(mg) SOD	PRO	FAT	CARB	CHOL	FATTY ACIDS SAT	UNSAT	CALC	IRON	(mg) POTSM
110	AVERAGE PER SERVING		160	48									276
	Ingredients:												
280	4 cp red cabbage, shredded	A B1 B2 C	80	72	L	L	L	---	---	---	F	L	753
14	1 tblspn margarine	A D	100	139	L	H	T	---	L	H	L	---	3
144	1/2 cp grape jelly, melted	A^t B1^t B2 C	400	24	L	L	H	---	---	---	L	F	108
n/a	Dash pepper						----n/a----						
114	4 oz French chestnuts, fresh	B1 B2	220	7	L	L	G		-----n/a-----		L	F	518
552	Recipe totals (gms ; cal; sod. & **potsm.**)		800	242									1382

METHOD

Select firm red cabbage, discard outer leaves and soak head in water 5 or 10 minutes. Drain and thinly shred 4 cups. At this point prepare chestnuts — see below. In a saucepan, melt margarine, add jelly, cabbage, chestnuts, 1/2 cup water and pepper. Cover and cook very slowly until tender (about 30 minutes). Yield   about 5 servings.

To Prepare Chestnuts: Slash flat sides of chestnuts, piercing the shells. Pour enough boiling water over them to cover and boil 5 minutes. Drain, dry thoroughly and remove shells and outer skins.

. . . .

COLLARD GREENS

Collards are a variety of kale and may be cooked the same way. They are often cooked with fat bacon and served with corn pones or egg bread.

CORN

Corn-on-the-cob is at its perfection when just picked, husked, dropped into boiling, unsalted water all within 30 minutes of serving time. As fresh picked as that, only 5 minutes cooking time is required. Unfortunately, the majority of corn-on-the-cob is shipped to market, resulting in a great amount of flavor loss. To prevent some loss, husks should not be removed until the last possible minute before boiling. In fact, water in a deep kettle should be at the boiling point before husking begins. Corn should be cooked in UNSALTED water because salting makes kernels tough, for no longer than 7 to 12 minutes. Time will depend on size of ears.

If corn is to be served without individual corn holders, run a little cold water over the ears just before serving to make handling easier.

BAKED CORN-ON-THE-COB IN HUSKS

Selected as freshly-picked corn as possible, with all of the husks. Use a very sharp knife to cut off about an inch or two of the stalk end. Peel each husk off until all of the corn is exposed and save the husks. Remove as much of the silk as possible. Tear squares of foil large enough to wrap each ear in a double thickness which will prevent scorching. Put an ear on a square of foil and spread it entirely with some soft margarine. DO NOT SALT. Then rewrap the ears with the husks lengthwise, as they were originally around the ear until completely covered. Holding the ear tightly with one hand to prevent husks from coming off, place it at the edge of the foil and roll up tight, crimping the ends to seal. Place ears on oven rack, foil edge up, and bake at 350 F. for 1 hour or 400 F. for 45 minutes. When ready to serve, unwrap foil carefully. Corn will be very hot. Discard foil and husks. Serve on a heated platter or on warm, individual plates. Each person may add additional margarine, if desired, and season to his own preference.

Prepared this way, corn is much more flavorful and kernels are juicy and tender.

. . . .

CORN RELISH

F=Fair; G=Good; H=High; L=Low; t or T = trace; n/a = no information available; dashes = zero or unmeasurable

GRAM WT.	FOOD	VITAMINS	CAL	(mg) SOD	PRO	FAT	CARB	CHOL	FATTY ACIDS SAT	UNSAT	CALC	IRON	(mg) POTSM
563	AVERAGE PER PINT		492	993									1045
	Ingredients:												
1134	2 (20 oz packages) frozen whole kernel corn	A B1 B2 C	930	13	L	L	F	---	---	---	L	F	2291
148	2 large green peppers	A B1 B2 C	30	20	L	L	L	---	---	---	L	L	315
100	2 sweet red peppers	A B1 B2 C	31	---	L	L	L	---	---	---	L	L	---
90	1 cp finely shredded cabbage	A B1 B2 C	20	18	L	L	L	---	---	---	L	L	210
440	4 medium onions	A B1 B2 C	160	44	L	L	L	---	---	---	L	L	691
100	1 cp chopped celery	A B1 B2 C	15	126	L	T	L	---	---	---	F	L	341
908	4 cp vinegar	---	128	10	T	---	L	---	---	---	L	L	908
440	2 cp brown sugar	B1 B2	1640	132	---	---	H	---	---	---	G	G	1514
15	1 tblspn salt	---	---	5592							G		
n/a	3 tblspn dry mustard							-------n/a-------					
3375	Recipe totals (gms; cal; sod. & potsm.)		2954	5955									6270

METHOD

Partly thaw corn in a large mixing bowl. While waiting, wash and seed peppers, chop; shred cabbage (remove outer leaves), peel onions and chop. Mix all vegetables together, add remaining ingredients, stir, and cook until tender, 20 to 30 minutes. Stir occasionally. Pack into hot, sterilized jars. Yield about 6 pints.

. . . .

CORN SOUFFLE

F=Fair; G=Good; H=High; L=Low; t or T = trace; n/a = no information available; dashes = zero or unmeasurable

GRAM WT.	FOOD	VITAMINS	CAL	(mg) SOD	PRO	FAT	CARB	CHOL	FATTY ACIDS SAT	UNSAT	CALC	IRON	(mg) POTSM
155	AVERAGE PER SERVING		159	85				(mg)* 139					258
	Ingredients:												
14	1 tblspn margarine	A D	100	139	L	H	T	---	L	H	L	---	3
7	1 tblspn flour	B1 B2	26	T	F	L	G	---	---	---	L	F	7
123	1/2 cp 2% low-fat milk	A B1 B2 C	73	75	H	F	G	L	L	L	H	L	215
n/a	1 tsp paprika	-----------					-n/a-						-----------
n/a	Dash black pepper	-----------					-n/a-						-----------
38	1 canned pimento	A B1 B2 C	10	---	L	L	L	---	---	---	L	---	---
336	2 cp frozen whole kernel corn	A B1 B2 C	275	4	L	L	F	---	---	---	L	L	679
100	2 eggs, separated	A B1 B2	150	122	F	F	L	H	H	L	F	F	129
618	Recipe totals (gms; cal; sod. & potsm.)		634	340									1033

METHOD

Preheat oven to 375 F. Grease a baking dish and set aside.

Make a thick white sauce of the margarine, flour and milk and add paprika and pepper. Rub the pimiento through a sieve and add to the sauce, then add the corn and blend well. Let the mixture become almost cold before adding the well-beaten egg yolks. Fold in about one third of the stiffly beaten egg whites at a time. Turn mixture into well greased casserole dish, set in a pan of hot water and bake until egg is set, about 30 minutes. Yield 4 servings.

* There are 554 milligrams of cholesterol in whole egg and 4 milligrams of 2% low-fat milk as calculated from U. S.D.A. Handbook No. 8, pg. 146, items 12 and 29 respectively. Divide 554 by the 4 servings equals 139 average milligrams of cholesterol in each serving.

. . . .

BAKED COW PEAS

(Blackeye Peas)

F=Fair; G=Good; H=High; L=Low; t or T = trace; n/a = no information available; dashes = zero or unmeasurable

GRAM WT.	FOOD	VITAMINS	CAL	(mg) SOD	PRO	FAT	CARB	CHOL	FATTY ACIDS SAT	UNSAT	CALC	IRON	(mg) POTSM
218	AVERAGE PER SERVING		191	342									434
	Ingredients:												
320	2 cps cooked cow peas	A B1 B2 C	350	4	L	L	F	---	---	---	L	F	1213
330	2 cps boiled rice	B1 B2	360	901	L	T	L	---	---	---	L	F	92
484	2 cp stewed tomatoes	A B1 B2 C	100	626	L	L	L	---	---	---	L	L	1046
110	1 medium onion, chopped	A B1 B2 C	40	11	L	L	L	---	---	---	L	L	173
50	1/2 cp dry bread crumbs	A^t B1 B2 C^t	195	368	F	L	G	---	---	---	G	F	76
n/a	Dash black pepper	--------------------					-n/a-						
14	1 tblspn margarine	A D	100	139	L	H	T	---	L	H	L	---	3
1308	Recipe totals (gms; cal; sod. & potsm.)		1145	2049									2603

METHOD

In a greased baking dish, arrange vegetables in layers: peas, rice, tomatoes and onion. Cover with breadcrumbs, sprinkle with black pepper and dot with margarine over all. Bake in a 400 F. oven until browned. Yield about 6 servings.

. . . .

CUCUMBERS

Although cucumbers are usually thought of as salad vegetables, there are many ways to serve them, a few of which are given in the following pages.

CUCUMBER LUNCHEON CUPS

Cut unpeeled cucumbers into pieces 2" long and cook until tender in boiling water. Allow to cool then scoop out the center of each, leaving 1/2" thickness all around the sides and bottoms, forming green cups. These may be filled with creamed dishes, such as: chicken, sweetbreads, shrimp, mushrooms, or any filling made with a white sauce.

. . . .

CREAMED CUCUMBERS

F=Fair; G=Good; H=High; L=Low; t or T = trace; n/a = no information available; dashes = zero or unmeasurable

GRAM WT.	FOOD	VITAMINS	CAL	(mg) SOD	PRO	FAT	CARB	CHOL (mg)*	FATTY ACIDS SAT	UNSAT	CALC	IRON	(mg) POTSM
166	AVERAGE PER SERVING		105	101				2					278
	Ingredients:												
246	1 cp 2% low-fat milk	A B1 B2 C	145	150	H	F	G	L	L	L	H	L	431
17	2 green onions, chopped	A B1 B2 C	7	T	L	L	F	---	---	---	F	L	39
9	1 tblspn cornstarch	---	34	---	L	T	H	---	---	---	---	---	---
14	1 tblspn margarine	A D	100	139	L	H	T	---	L	G	L	---	3
n/a	Dash black papper							-n/a-					
207	1 medium cucumber	A^t B1 B2 C	29	12	L	L	L	---	---	---	F	L	331
4	1 tblspn fresh parsley, chopped	A B1 B2 C	T	2	T	T	T	---	---	---	H	H	29
497	Recipe totals (gms; cal; sod. & potsm.)		315	303									833

METHOD

Pour milk into a saucepan, add finely chopped green onions and heat, but do not boil. Mix cornstarch and pepper with a little water until smooth. Stir into hot milk slowly and continue to stir until sauce thickens. Add margarine and blend. Keep sauce hot by placing pan over hot water. Peel cucumber. Cut in half lengthwise then cut halves lengthwise again. Cut the four strips into 1" size pieces, drop into boiling water and cook 15 minutes. Drain and add to white sauce. Sprinkle servings with chopped parsley. Yield   2 or 3 servings.

Variation: Fold in 8 ozs. tiny cocktail shrimp in the white sauce after it's thickened. Add cooked cucumbers. Serve on crisp toast. Yield   4 or 5 servings.

*   There are 125 milligrams of cholesterol in 100 grams of shrimp. In 227 grams in above variation, there are 284 milligrams as calculated from U.S.D.A. Handbook No. 8, pg. 146, item 33b. In 246 grams of non-fat milk, there are 7 milligrams of cholesterol, for a total of 291. Divide 291 by 4 servings equals 73 average milligrams of cholesterol in each serving with shrimp
In 227 grams of shrimp, there are 207 calories, 318 milligrams of sodium and 520 milligrams of potassium, and A, B1 and B2 Vitamins.

. . . .

CUCU SAUTE

F=Fair; G=Good; H=High; L=Low; t or T = trace; n/a = no information available; dashes = zero or unmeasurable

GRAM WT.	FOOD	VITAMINS	CAL	(mg) SOD	PRO	FAT	CARB	CHOL	FATTY ACIDS SAT	UNSAT	CALC	IRON	(mg) POTSM
128	AVERAGE PER SERVING		118	76									193
	Ingredients:												
414	2 (10 oz) cucumbers	A^t B1 B2 C	58	24	L	L	L	---	---	---	F	F	662
*28	2 tblspn margarine	A D	200	279	L	H	L	---	L	H	L	---	6
56	1/2 cp flour	B1 B2	210	1=	F	L	G	---	---	---	L	F	53
4	1 tblspn parsley	A B1^t B2 C	T	2	T	T	T	---	---	---	H	H	32
**8	1 tblspn chives	A^t B1 B2 C	4	T	L	L	L	---	---	---	F	F	20
510	Recipe totals (gms; cal; sod. & potsm.)		472	306									773

METHOD

Peel and cut cucumbers lengthwise, then cut in half. Boil without any water for 3 minutes. Drain. If desired, sprinkle a little pepper over them, roll in flour (or shake in a plastic bag of flour) and saute in margarine until tender. Just before cooking is completed, sprinkle with chives (or onions). Yield 4 servings. Garnish with parsley.

NOTE   *If oil is used instead of margarine, sodium will be reduced to O, and calories will increase to 250 as shown in the following: 28   2 tblspns oil   ---   250 --- --- H --- --- L H --- ---   ---

NOTE   **If chives are not available, mince 1 tablespoon green onion instead.

. . . .

448

DILL PICKLES

F=Fair; G=Good; H=High; L=Low; t or T = trace; n/a = no information available; dashes = zero or unmeasurable

GRAM WT.	FOOD	VITAMINS	CAL	(mg) SOD	PRO	FAT	CARB	CHOL	FATTY ACIDS SAT	UNSAT	CALC	IRON	(mg) POTSM
240	AVERAGE PER PICKLE		18	2643									183
2600	Ingredients: 25 cucumbers, 4", unpeeled	A[t] B1 B2 C	400	150	L	L	L	---	---	---	F	L	4160
	BRINE												
168	3/4 cp salt	-------------		65922	------	------------					G	---	7
2832	3 quarts water	-------------				---0---							
	VINEGAR SOLUTION												
n/a	1/4 small horseradish root, diced	-------------				--n/a--							
n/a	small bunch of dill	-------------				--n/a--							
398	1-3/4 cp vinegar	---	48	8	T	---	L	---	---	---	L	L	398
5998	Recipe totals (gms; cal; sod. & potsm.)		448	66080									4565

METHOD

Select cucumbers that are 3-1/2 to 4" long, and thin. Wash thoroughly, dry on paper towels. Dissolve 1/2 cup salt in 2 quarts water, add cucumbers and let stand 12 hours. Be sure cucumbers are under brine. If not, weigh down with a plate or something similar; add a little more brine if necessary to cover. After 12 hours drain cucumbers and wipe dry. Place in sterilized jars with layers of diced horseradish and dill, top and bottom of the jar. Combine remaining quart of water with 1/4 cup salt and 1-3/4 cup vinegar. Heat to boiling and pour over cucumbers. Partly seal. When fermentation stops, pour enough fresh, cooled brine, containing vinegar, to cover. Seal. Makes 3 quarts or 6 pints.

For Kosher dills, add 2 small peeled cloves garlic and 2 small hot peppers to each jar.

. . . .

14—DAY SWEET PICKLES

Into a clean stone crock, put 2 gallons of 2-1/2 to 3" cucumbers which have been washed thoroughly and sliced lengthwise. Slicing, regardless of size, prevents shriveling. Dissolve 2 cups salt in 1 gallon (4 quarts) of boiling water and pour, while hot, over the pickles. Cover pickles and weigh down. Let stand, undisturbed for 1 week. On the 8th day, drain, then pour 1 gallon of boiling water over them and let stand 24 hours. On the 9th day, drain and pour 1 gallon of boiling water, with 1 tablespoon powdered alum mixed into the water, over the pickles and let stand 24 hours. (Alum makes the pickles crisp). On the following day again drain, pour 1 gallon of boiling water over the pickles and let stand 24 hours then drain.

Pickling Mixture: Combine 5 pints boiling hot vinegar, 6 cups sugar dissolved in the vinegar, 1/2 oz. celery seed, 1 oz. cinnamon stick. Pour this mixture over the pickles. For 3 mornings, drain mixture off and reheat each morning, adding 1 cup granulated sugar each time. With third and last heating, pack pickles in sterilized jars, pour hot liquid over them, insert silver knife into jar before sealing to remove air bubbles, then seal at once.

. . . .

BREAD AND BUTTER PICKLES

F=Fair; G=Good; H=High; L=Low; t or T = trace; n/a = no information available; dashes = zero or unmeasurable

GRAM WT.	FOOD	VITAMINS	CAL	(mg) SOD	PRO	FAT	CARB	CHOL	FATTY ACIDS SAT	UNSAT	CALC	IRON	(mg) POTSM
796	AVERAGE PER PINT		279	5521									1129
	Ingredients:												
2352	12 cucumbers, 7 oz. ea. approx.	A[t] B1 B2 C	192	72	L	L	L	---	---	---	F	L	3763
330	3 onions (2-1/2" diameter)	A B1 B2 C	120	33	L	L	L	---	---	---	L	L	518
56	1/4 cp salt	---	---	21974	-------				-------		G	-------	-------
n/a	1-1/2 tspn mustard seed	-------					-n/a-						-------
n/a	1-1/2 tspn celery seed	-------					-n/a-						-------
n/a	1-1/2 tspn curry powder	-------					-n/a-						-------
227	1 cp vinegar	---	32	3	T	---	L	---	---	---	L	L	227
200	1 cp sugar	---	770	2	---	---	H	---	---	---	---	L	6
118	1/2 cp water	-------					-0-						-------
3183	Recipe totals (gms; cal; sod. & potsm.)		1114	22084									4514

METHOD

Wash and slice cucumbers fairly thin; wash, peel and slice onions thin. Arrange in layers and sprinkle salt on each layer.
Let stand 2 or 3 hours. Drain. Combine remaining ingredients and heat to boiling. Add cucumbers and onions and
simmer 10 minutes. Pack into hot, sterilized jars. Yield   4 pints.

. . . .

DANDELION GREENS

F=Fair; G=Good; H=High; L=Low; t or T = trace; n/a = no information available;   dashes = zero or unmeasurable

GRAM WT.	FOOD	VITAMINS	CAL	(mg) SOD	PRO	FAT	CARB	CHOL	FATTY ACIDS SAT	UNSAT	CALC	IRON	(mg) POTSM
188	AVERAGE PER SERVING		103	166									729
	Ingredients:												
908	2 lb dandelion greens	A B1^{*N} B2 C	408	690	L	L	L	---	---	---	G	F	3605
	*N = Niacin only												
17	2 green onions, chopped	A^t B1 B2 C	7	T	L	L	F	---	---	---	F	L	39
14	1 tblspn margarine	A D	100	139	L	H	T	---	L	H	L	---	3
939	Recipe totals (gms; cal; sod. & potsm.)		515	829									3647

METHOD

Pick greens before they blossom, otherwise they'll have a bitter taste. Cut off roots, pick over very carefully and wash greens in several waters to remove sand. Place in a large kettle with the chopped onions, add a small amount of boiling water and cook until tender. Drain through a colander and press down to eliminate as much water as possible. Chop greens and add margarine. Season at the table individually. Yield   5 servings.

. . . .

BROILED EGGPLANT

F=Fair; G=Good; H=High; L=Low; t or T = trace; n/a = no information available; dashes = zero or unmeasurable

GRAM WT.	FOOD	VITAMINS	CAL	(mg) SOD	PRO	FAT	CARB	CHOL	FATTY ACIDS SAT	UNSAT	CALC	IRON	(mg) POTSM
142	AVERAGE PER SERVING		188	1								7	207
	Ingredients:												
454	1 medium eggplant (1 lb)	A B1 B2 C	92	7	L	L	L	---	---	---	L	L	786
113	1/2 cp French dressing*	---	660	T	T	G	L	---	L	H	L	L	42
567	Recipe totals (gms; cal; sod. & potsm.)		752	7									828

METHOD

Wash and cut off stem end and about an inch off the bottom of the eggplant. Do not peel. Cut in 1/2" slices, marinate in French Dressing about 15 minutes. Broil until tender and light brown, turning once. (Test with fork for tenderness). Serve at once. Yield about 4 servings.

* For French Dressing recipe see page 271.

. . . .

FRIED EGGPLANT

F=Fair; G=Good; H=High; L=Low; t or T = trace; n/a = no information available; dashes = zero or unmeasurable

GRAM WT.	FOOD	VITAMINS	CAL	(mg) SOD	PRO	FAT	CARB	CHOL	FATTY ACIDS SAT	UNSAT	CALC	IRON	(mg) POTSM
166	AVERAGE PER SERVING		252	663				(mg)* 69					252
	Ingredients:												
454	1 medium eggplant (1 lb.)	A B1 B2 C	92	7	L	L	L	---	---	---	L	L	786
4	1 tsp salt	---	---	1569	---	---	---	---	---	---	G	---	T
100	1 cp breadcrumbs (dry)	A^t B1 B2 C^t	390	736	F	L	G	---	---	---	G	F	152
50	1 egg	A B1 B2	75	61	F	F	L	H	H	L	F	F	65
28	1 tblspn margarine	A D	200	279	L	H	L	---	L	H	L	---	6
28	2 tblspns oil	---	250	---	---	H	---	---	L	H	---	---	---
664	Recipe totals (gms; cal; sod. & potsm.)		1007	2652									1009

METHOD

Cut off top and bottom of eggplant, then cut eggplant into 1/2" slices, peel and sprinkle each with a little salt. Stack slices on top of each other on a soup plate. Let stand 1 hour to draw out the bitter flavor. Half an hour before serving, rinse slices in cold water, dry with a paper towel. Beat the egg until frothy. Place breadcrumbs in a flat dish large enough to dip the slices of eggplant. Heat margarine in a skillet until medium-hot. Dip eggplant in egg, then in breadcrumbs and saute in oil until golden brown on both sides and fork tender. (Flour may be substituted for crumbs, and milk for egg). Eggplant must be watched closely as it burns easily. Also, add more margarine or oil if needed. During the frying process, crumbs (or flour) absorb the fat. Yield 4 servings.

* There are 275 milligrams of cholesterol in 50 grams of whole egg, per U.S.D.A. Handbook No. 8, pg. 146, item 12. Divide 275 by 4 servings equals 69 average milligrams of cholesterol per serving.

. . . .

454

STUFFED EGGPLANT

F=Fair; G=Good; H=High; L=Low; t or T = trace; n/a = no information available;   dashes = zero or unmeasurable

GRAM WT.	FOOD	VITAMINS	CAL	(mg) SOD	PRO	FAT	CARB	CHOL	FATTY ACIDS SAT	UNSAT	CALC	IRON	(mg) POTSM
158	AVERAGE PER SERVING		138	356									394
	Ingredients:												
454	1 eggplant (1 lb.)	A B1 B2 C	92	7	L	L	L	---	---	---	L	L	786
23	3 slices crisp bacon	B1 B2	135	230	H	H	L	n/a	L	H	L	L	54
25	3 green onions	A^t B1 B2 C	10	2	L	L	F	---	---	---	F	L	58
8	2 tblspn parsley	A B1^t B2 C	T	4	T	T	T	---	---	---	H	H	58
50	1/2 cp chopped celery	A B1 B2 C	8	63	L	T	L	---	---	---	F	L	171
227	1 (8 oz) can tomato sauce	A B1 B2 C	89	906	L	L	L	---	---	---	L	L	967
37	1/2 green pepper, chopped	A B1 B2 C	8	5	L	L	L	---	---	---	L	L	79
125	1-1/4 cp breadcrumbs	A^t B1 B2 C^t	488	920	F	L	G	---	---	---	G	F	190
949	Recipe totals (gms; cal; sod. & potsm.)		830	2137									2363

METHOD

Wash eggplant, then cut in half lengthwise, scoop out the pulp in the center, leaving rind and meat 1/2" thick to keep shape firm. Cover shells with cold water. Chop center pulp fine, cook in a frying pan in a little bacon fat for 10 minutes, stirring well. Drain. Mix pulp with chopped bacon and vegetables, except 1/4 cup bread crumbs. Drain shells, fill with mixture, sprinkle remaining bread crumbs over the the top, dot with bacon fat. Bake at 375 F. for 30 minutes. Yield 6 servings. Season at the table individually.

. . . .

ENDIVE

Related to chickory, endive (escarole) makes an excellent salad green used either alone or in combination with other greens. It can also be cooked.

To Cream Endive: Wash carefully, remove outer leaves, using only the white part. Boil until tender. Drain thoroughly, return to the kettle and nearly cover with a medium white sauce seasoned with a little chopped green onion, and pimiento.

To Braise Endive: Wash carefully, remove outer leaves, bring to a boil in as little water as possible, add some margarine and chopped green onion, then simmer in a covered earthenware, or glass baking dish in a 325 F. oven 1-1/2 hours. Serve hot in its own liquid.

Cooked endive may also be served cold with vinaigrette sauce.

. . . .

BRAISED FENNEL

F=Fair; G=Good; H=High; L=Low; t or T = trace; n/a = no information available; dashes = zero or unmeasurable

GRAM WT.	FOOD	VITAMINS	CAL	(mg) SOD	PRO	FAT	CARB	CHOL	FATTY ACIDS SAT	UNSAT	CALC	IRON	(mg) POTSM
204	AVERAGE PER SERVING		133	254									583
	Ingredients:												
908	2 lb fennel	A C	236	---	L	L	L	---	---	---	F	F	3350
75	1/3 cp margarine	A D	534	740	L	H	L	---	L	H	L	---	17
240	1 cp meat stock (or beef broth)	A^t B1 B2	30	782	L	---	L		--n/a--		T	L	130
n/a	Dash black pepper (no salt)							--n/a--					
1223	Recipe totals (gms; cal; sod. & potsm.)		800	1522									3497

METHOD

Wash fennel thoroughly. Cut into 1" pieces. Simmer in margarine until lightly browned. Add meat stock or beef broth and pepper. Simmer 20 minutes, or until tender. Yield 6 servings.

. . . .

JICAMA
(Hickama)

Although jicama is familiar to Mexican markets, it is not as well known in the United States, but it is gaining in popularity in markets in the southwest. It should; it's delicious, a fact one wouldn't know by its appearance! It looks like a very fat, overgrown beet or turnip with an unappetizing gray brown exterior, but under its ugliness it has the whitest meat, something like a potato, but crisp as water chestnuts, and much less expensive. One medium jicama could substitute for many, many water chestnuts in Chinese recipes. A very versatile vegetable, it can be eaten raw or cooked.

Preparation is easy, jicama skin is quite thin. Peeling is no chore. It can be sliced thick or thin and mixed with salad combinations, or sliced very thin and dipped in French dressing or cheese dips. It perks up the conversation at any hostess' table. Or try it sliced thin and diced in your favorite beef stew!

A good source of ways to serve it can be found in Sunset Magazine's "Mexican Cook Book" published by Lane Books of Menlo Park, California.

Unfortunately, there was no information available on food components for jicama at this writing.

. . . .

KALE

()= values imputed from another, similar food, per U.S.D.A. Handbook No. 8.
F=Fair; G=Good; H=High; L=Low; t or T = trace; n/a = no information available; dashes = zero or unmeasurable

GRAM WT.	FOOD	VITAMINS	CAL	(mg) SOD	PRO	FAT	CARB	CHOL	FATTY ACIDS SAT	UNSAT	CALC	IRON	(mg) POTSM
55*	AVERAGE PER SERVING		63*	90*									108*
	Ingredients:												
385*	4 lb kale (cooked equals about 3-1/2 cp	A B1 B2 C	105*	(165)*	(L)	(L)	L	---	---	---	G	F	(851)*
56	4 tblspn margarine	A D	400	558	L	H	L	---	L	H	L	---	13
n/a	dash pepper	--------					----n/a----						
441	Recipe totals (gms; cal; sod. & potsm.)		505	723									864

METHOD

Wash kale with as much care as spinach. Remove all heavy stems. Chop and cook kale uncovered in small amount of water (boiling) 15 to 20 minutes or until tender. Drain. Season with margarine and pepper — sale at the table individually. Yield about 8 servings. Kale is delicious with sausage, ham or bacon. It may also be served creamed, or scalloped with grated cheese, cream sauce and chopped, hard-cooked eggs.

*Values are for cooked kale.

. . . .

459

F=Fair; G=Good; H=High; L=Low; t or T = trace; n/a = no information available; dashes = zero or unmeasurable

GRAM WT.	FOOD	VITAMINS	CAL	(mg) SOD	PRO	FAT	CARB	CHOL (mg)*	FATTY ACIDS SAT	UNSAT	CALC	IRON	(mg) POTSM
204	AVERAGE PER SERVING		84	57				2					444
	Ingredients:												
681**	6 Kohlrabi	A B1 B2 C	144	39	L	L	L	---	---	---	F	F	1771
	** Estimated weight — no firm data available.												
30	2 tblspn vinegar	---	4	---	T	---	L	---	---	---	L	L	30
18	2 tblspn cornstarch	---	68		---	L	T	H	---	---	---	---	---
492	2 cp 2% low-fat milk	A B1 B2 C	290	300	H	F	G	L	L	L	H	L	861
n/a	Paprika							-n/a-					
1221	Recipe totals (gms; cal; sod. & potsm.)		506	339									2662

METHOD

Remove any leaves. Wash and pare kohlrabi rather thickly and cut into cubes or slices. Mix vinegar with cold water and allow kohlrabi to soak in this mixture about 1 hour, then drain and rinse in cold water. Boil about 20 minutes in as little water as possible (to prevent burning) until fork tender. Drain. Keep hot. Mix the cornstarch with a small amount of water (about 1/4 cup) until smooth. Heat milk but do not let it boil. Add cornstarch mixture to milk slowly, stirring constantly until sauce thickens then stir and cook slowly about 5 minutes. Pour over kohlrabi, sprinkle paprika on top. Kohlrabi may also be steamed until tender and served plain with margarine, or with Hollandaise Sauce. Yield   about 6 servings, 3/4 cup each.

*   There are 15 milligrams of cholesterol in 492 grams of 2% low-fat milk, as calculated from U.S.D.A. Handbook No. 8, pg. 146, item 29. Divide 15 milligrams by 6 servings equals 2 average milligrams of cholesterol in each serving of creamed kohlrabi.

. . . .

LEAKS AU GRATIN

F=Fair; G=Good; H=High; L=Low; t or T = trace; n/a = no information available; dashes = zero or unmeasurable

GRAM WT.	FOOD	VITAMINS	CAL	(mg) SOD	PRO	FAT	CARB	CHOL (mg)*	FATTY ACIDS SAT	UNSAT	CALC	IRON	(mg) POTSM
119	AVERAGE PER SERVING		53	43				6					399
	Ingredients:												
908	2 bunches of leeks	A B1 B2 C	246	24	L	L	L	---	---	---	F	F	3151
n/a	Dash pepper						----n/a----						
45	1/2 cp grated cheddar cheese	A B1 B2	181	318	G	G	L	H	H	L	H	F	37
953	Recipe totals (gms; cal; sod. & potsm.)		427	342									3188

METHOD

Wash and trim leeks. Cook until tender (about 15 minutes), in enough boiling water to cover. Leeks may be cooked whole or cut into pieces. Drain. Arrange in greased baking dish and sprinkle with pepper and cheese. Heat under broiler until cheese is melted. Yield   8 servings.

NOTE   Leeks look like large green onions and have an asparagus-onion flavor. To clean, strip leaves down from the top to remove grit (similar to cleaning green onions). Cut off root ends.

*   There are 45 milligrams of cholesterol in 45 grams of cheddar cheese, as calculated from U.S.D.A. Handbook No. 8, pg. 146, item 5. Divide 45 milligrams by 8 servings equals 6 average milligrams of cholesterol per serving.

. . . .

SAUTEED LENTILS with SMOKED HAM

F=Fair; G=Good; H=High; L=Low; t or T = trace; n/a = no information available; dashes = zero or unmeasurable

GRAM WT.	FOOD	VITAMINS	CAL	(mg) SOD	PRO	FAT	CARB	CHOL	FATTY ACIDS SAT	UNSAT	CALC	IRON	(mg) POTSM
								(mg)*					
84	AVERAGE PER SERVING		280	52				15					454
	Ingredients:												
454	2-1/3 cp lentils	A B1 B2	1542	136	L	T	F	---	---	---	L	F	3587
28	2 tblspn margarine	A D	200	279	L	H	L	---	L	H	L	---	6
17	2 green onions, chopped	A B1 B2 C	6	T	L	L	F	---	---	---	F	L	39
170	6 ozs smoked ham, diced	B1 B2	490	---	G	G	---	H	H	L	F	F	---
---	1 clove minced garlic	A^t B1 B2 C	2	3	L	L	F	---	---	---	L	F	---
669	Recipe totals (gms; cal; sod. & potsm.)		2240	418									3632

METHOD

Wash lentils and soak in cold water overnight. Simmer in the same water until tender, adding water if needed. Test for doneness by mashing lentil with a fork. They should be soft with no hard centers. Melt margarine in frying pan, add lentils and remainder of ingredients. Cook and stir about 15 to 20 minutes. Yield   about 8 servings.

* At this writing, no information on cholesterol in smoked ham was available. Therefore, the figures for pork listed on page 146 of the U.S.D.A. Handbook No. 8 were used to calculate cholesterol in this recipe. In 170 grams, there are 119 milligrams of cholesterol. Divide 119 milligrams by 8 servings equals 15 average milligrams of cholesterol per serving.

. . . .

LETTUCE

The leaf variety contains more Vitamin A than head lettuce. In one pound of the loose leaf or bunching varieties (also COS or Romaine), there are 5520 International Units of Vitamin A in comparison to 1420 units in good quality crisphead varieties. Lettuce also contains low amounts of B1, B2, and C Vitamins.

A one pound head of lettuce will serve 4 people, 1/4 head each, or will provide garnish for 8 to 10 salad plates.

When cleaning, cut out core and run cold water into it to separate the leaves.

Good lettuce leaves that are not suitable for salads can be cooked like spinach, or cooked in soups, or used for wilted lettuce with sauce of bacon fat, cut up cooked bacon and a small amount of hot vinegar poured over them.

MUSHROOMS

To keep fresh mushrooms from turning black, drop them into a bowl of water that contains the juice of half a lemon, or 1 tablespoon of vinegar.

To prepare mushrooms for cooking, in any recipe, cut off the stalks, pare the caps (or brush well if fresh and tender). This should be done before putting them in lemon juice and water. If stalks are tender and solid, they may be pared, cooked and served with the caps.

Mushrooms enhance the flavor of many foods; in gravies, spaghetti, and other sauces; in soups; or sauteed in a little margarine 5 or 6 minutes, and served with broiled steak or chops, or roasts. They are especially good sliced raw in salads, or cooked; or uncooked, as stuffed canapes. Fresh mushrooms, cleaned of any specks of dirt by brushing carefully, are excellent sauteed in a little margarine, with a dash of garlic salt, and a little minced green onion, served with scrambled eggs.

For an entree, large mushrooms are delicious cleaned and dipped in melted margarine, stuffed with seafood, such as cooked lobster, crabmeat or shrimp, then sprinkled with grated cheese, dotted with margarine, and browned in a 400 F. oven until cheese melts.

One-half pound of good quality, fresh mushroons weight 227 grams, has 62 calories, 33 milligrams of sodium, no cholesterol, and 940 milligrams of potassium. They contain a trace of Vitamin A, B1, B2 and C. They are low in protein, fat and carbohydrates, have no fatty acids, are low in calcium and iron.

Mushrooms should be cooked gently and never too long as they are inclined to toughen with overcooking.

MUSTARD GREENS

Cook like spinach. Add a little diced bacon to the cooking water or season with dry mustard and vinegar. Wash greens thoroughly. For values, see "Nutrition at your Fingertips," the food list at the beginning of this chapter.

. . . .

OKRA

F=Fair; G=Good; H=High; L=Low; t or T = trace; n/a = no information available;   dashes = zero or unmeasurable

GRAM WT.	FOOD	VITAMINS	CAL	(mg) SOD	PRO	FAT	CARB	CHOL	FATTY ACIDS SAT	UNSAT	CALC	IRON	(mg) POTSM
179	AVERAGE PER SERVING		74	40									397
	Ingredients:												
450	2 cp okra	A B1 B2 C	140	12	L	L	L	---	---	---	F	L	971
227	3 tomatoes	A B1 B2 C	45	7	L	L	L	---	---	---	L	L	554
25	3 green onions, minced	A^t B1 B2 C	10	2	L	L	F	---	---	---	F	L	58
14	1 tblspn margarine	A D	100	139	L	H	T	---	L	H	L	---	3
716	Recipe totals (gms; cal; sod. & potsm.)		295	160									1586

METHOD

Wash pods well, remove stems and cut pods into crosswise slices. Place in a granite saucepan, cover with boiling water and simmer very gently until tender 15 to 35 minutes. Peel and cut up tomatoes, add to okra along with the minced onion and cook 10 minutes longer. Add margarine and serve. Yield   about 4 servings.

NOTE   To test okra for freshness, break off tip of pods. If there are tough strings that will not break easily, pods are too old to be served as a vegetable, but can be used for soups or sauce which is to be strained. Okra is valuable for its mucilagenous content, and needs special care in handling during cleaning to prevent breaking.

. . . .

ONIONS

A liliaceous Asiatic plant (Allium cepa); its bulb is edible and has a pungent taste and odor.

To cooks all over the world, the fact that onions belong to the lily family is probably immaterial; the only fact that matters to them is that this "vegetable" is a must in hundreds of dishes they prepare, with garlic, leeks and chives running a close second.

Peeling and cutting raw onions can stimulate the tear ducts to such an extent that people cry during their preparation. To prevent the irritation, onions should be held under cold running water during peeling. To remove onion odor from knives, run blades through a raw potato; to remove odor from hands, apply a little vanilla to them, or hold hands under cold water a few minutes, or rub with cut celery.

CREAMED ONIONS

Although pearl onions are probably the best size for creaming, their preparation is tedious because it takes so many of them and each must be skinned and tops and root ends cut off individually. To save time, use larger onions and cut in pieces. Boil in as little water as possible until tender, then drain. (Save the water for soups and gravies). Make a medium white sauce, combine with onions, and garnish with parsley flakes or paprika, or both.

TO BOIL ONIONS

Wash, skin and cut root ends and tops off, cut in pieces, or leave whole if onions are medium size. Pearl onions are cooked whole; they have a bland flavor in comparison to the flat, white onions, or yellow and red varieties. Cook in boiling water until tender, then drain, dot with margarine and season at the table. Plain, boiled onions are good with roast beef, roast pork, and poultry dishes.

. . . .

STUFFED ONIONS

F=Fair; G=Good; H=High; L=Low; t or T = trace; n/a = no information available;   dashes = zero or unmeasurable

GRAM WT.	FOOD	VITAMINS	CAL	(mg) SOD	PRO	FAT	CARB	CHOL (mg)*	FATTY ACIDS SAT	UNSAT	CALC	IRON	(mg) POTSM
173	AVERAGE PER SERVING		189	170				14					243
	Ingredients:												
660	6 onions, 2-1/2" diameter	A B1 B2 C	240	66	L	L	L	---	---	---	L	L	1036
114	1/2 cp smoked ham, chopped	B1 B2	326	---	G	G	---	H	H	L	L	F	---
25	1/3 of 1 medium green pepper	A B1 B2 C	5	3	L	L	L	---	---	---	L	L	53
50	1/2 cp breadcrumbs	A^t B1 B2 C^t	195	368	F	L	G	---	---	---	G	F	76
14	1 tblspn margarine	A D	100	139	L	H	T	---	L	G	L	---	3
50	1/2 cp breadcrumbs	A^t B1 B2 C^t	195	368	F	L	G	---	---	---	G	F	76
123	1/2 cp 2% low-fat milk	A B1 B2 C	73	75	H	F	G	L	L	L	H	L	215
1036	Recipe totals (gms; cal; sod. & potsm.)		1134	1019									1459

METHOD

Wash and peel onions. Slice off tops and cut out root end, being careful not to cut too far. Parboil (covered) until nearly tender. Drain, remove centers, making 6 little cups. Chop onion that was scooped out and combine with ham, green pepper and 1/2 cup of breadcrumbs. Stuff each onion cup with mixture, dot with margarine and place onions in a greased baking dish. Cover with remaining breadcrumbs, add milk, distributing it as evenly as possible, and bake at 400 to 450 F. until fork tender.

*   There are 70 milligrams of cholesterol in boneless pork, per U.S.D.A. Handbook No. 8, pg. 146, item 32b — no figures are given for smoked pork, therefore, we used the boneless pork values — in 114 grams of pork there are 80 milligrams of cholesterol. Divide by 6 servings equals 13 average milligrams per serving, plus 1 milligram per serving in skim milk equals 14 average milligrams of cholesterol per serving.

. . . .

SAUTEED PARSNIPS

F=Fair; G=Good; H=High; L=Low; t or T = trace; n/a = no information available; dashes = zero or unmeasurable

GRAM WT.	FOOD	VITAMINS	CAL	(mg) SOD	PRO	FAT	CARB	CHOL	FATTY ACIDS SAT	UNSAT	CALC	IRON	(mg) POTSM
96	AVERAGE PER SERVING		160	79	L	L	F	---	---	---	F	L	421
	Ingredients:												
300	6 medium young parsnips	A B1 B2 C	228	36	L	L	F	---	---	---	F	L	1623
56	1/2 cp flour	B1 B2	210	1	F	L	G	---	---	---	L	F	53
28	1 tblspn margarine	A D	200	279	L	H	L	---	L	H	L	---	6
384	Recipe totals (gms ; cal; sod. & potsm.)		638	316									1682

METHOD

Peel or scrape parsnips, rinse under cold water, then cover with boiling water and cook until tender. Drain. When cold, cut in long, then sections (about 1/3'' thick). If parsnips are not young, remove woody core. Coat pieces with flour and saute in margarine until each side is browned. Drain off any fat and serve hot. (Additional margarine may be needed to finish cooking the parsnips).

To Boil Parsnips or To Serve Plain: Wash and peel parsnips as for sauteeing and boil in enough water to prevent burning, until fork tender. Cut in half lengthwise, remove any woody core, and add a little margarine. Serve hot. Season individually at the table.

. . . .

PEAS

Whether they're frozen, canned, or fresh, out of the pod, the flavor of peas can be ruined if overcooked. Perhaps an exception would be canned peas because any canned vegetable should be cooked at the boiling point for at least 10 minutes to prevent botulism. (To be safe, I prefer 15 minutes).

Frozen vegetables should be cooked in as little water as possible. The moisture surrounding the vegetable from the freezing process provides additional moisture. Carefully read the package directions — after all, they've been written by experts who are continuing to test for ways to improve their product for best results.

Fresh, unshelled peas should not be prepared until needed, to retain more flavor. If curly-cues appear on peas, these are tendrils indicating peas are old, have started roots. Remove. Fresh, young peas will require very little boiling water and will cook in 5 to 8 minutes; mature peas will take longer.

Fresh, young peas, have green, supple pods; older peas feel hard through their pods and show brown spots on the pods.

One pound of unshelled peas will yield 2 to 3 servings. See equivalents, in the addendum.

To cream peas, prepare 1 cup medium white sauce, combine with 2 cups cooked, frozen or fresh, or drained canned peas and serve hot. Add some minced green onion, if desired.

. . . .

POTATOES — FIRST, THE BAD: THEN THE GOOD

As a result of an article in the Santa Barbara (California) Press, September 16, 1971 issue, titled, "Don't Eat or Chew Leaves — POISONOUS PLANTS" by Dorothea M. Brooks, dateline New York (UPI), I have been very concerned, especially where there are children in the family. The article was an eye-opener — I had no idea that so many common plants are deadly.

Children have a natural curiosity — a pretty flower — a bright green leaf — a tempting berry, even an old twig, if chewed, can be fatal, if they happen to belong to one of these poison-plants.

Vital facts about these plants and others have been published by Geigy Agriculture Chemicals, Ardsley, NY. Other lists are available by other companies. I don't know their names, or the titles of their articles. Perhaps the poison centers in your community can tell you where they may be acquired —or the library might know a source.

We have no small children, but many of our friends do who visit us. There was an oleander bush in our back yard. After reading the above article, we had it removed. The leaves of this lovely plant contain a deadly heart stimulant and some people have died merely from eating steaks that have been speared on oleander twigs and roasted over an open fire!

The POTATO plant is POISONOUS, too; the leaves, stems, EYES — only the tuber is edible. I read somewhere recently that it is believed that the green spots on the tuber are also poisonous — so please, don't buy potatoes that have green coloring, and DO CUT OUT THE EYES. Also be careful of potato sprouts — they can poison — they're part of the plant — cut them off.

For your sake, your family's sake and your pet's sake, don't take my word for it. Write the U. S. Department of Agriculture; check with your library, perhaps the school knows where these lists of poisonous plants can be obtained. But first: educate your children not to touch, or eat anything that grows in your back yard, or in the park, or on your vacation trips. If children are very small, they're more vulnerable. Your love and awareness of these dangers around them may save their lives.

To Bake Potatoes: Select smooth, plump potatoes of medium size. Scrub with a "chore girl" or scrape with the broad side of a paring knife. Dig out the eyes with the tip of a paring knife then wash in cold water to remove any skin scrapings. Remove dark blemish spots. Rub surface of potatoes with soft margarine, or oil. Cut off a small slice from each end then wrap potatoes in foil, either separately or in one group. Seal tightly, crimp the edges together and bake at 350 F. about 1 hour. Pierce through top of potatoes with a long-pronged fork. If fork penetrates potatoes easily, they're baked. (Piercing potatoes through the foil keeps them firm and unwrinkled). Also, if dinner is to be a bit late, reduce oven temperature to 160 F. and leave potatoes in the foil. They'll stay hot and plump until serving time. Just before bringing them to the table, cut a cross 2" long and wide in top center of potatoes. Pinch potatoes together with the fingers, forcing the white fleshy part up through the cuts. Sprinkle with paprika or parsley (dried flakes or fresh, chopped fine). If potatoes are individually wrapped in foil, cut cross through the foil, as above, and peel it back to expose entire top.

Top with sour cream or margarine, if desired.

To Boil Potatoes: Prepare the same as for baking. Cook in boiling water until fork tender. Remove skins, if desired. (Potatoes may be peeled before boiling, but valuable minerals under the skin will be lost).

To Cream Potatoes: Wash and scrub potatoes, remove eyes and blemishes. Cook in boiling water until fork tender (not quite as soft as boiled potatoes, to prevent mushiness). Drain. Cool slightly, then peel. Cut lengthwise, then crosswise into strips, then into 1/2" pieces. Make a medium white sauce, add 1 tablespoon minced green onion after sauce has thickened. Add potatoes carefully to avoid breaking the pieces into mush. Season at the table. Number of potatoes and amount of white sauce to make will depend upon number of people to be served. 2 Cups of diced cold or warm potatoes, and 1-1/2 cups of medium white sauce will serve 6.

American Fried Potatoes: Cut boiled potatoes into 1/2" pieces, add some minced or chopped onions and saute in a small amount of margarine, bacon fat, oil or other fat, stirring often until browned. Reduce heat, add a little fat, stir and cover. Cook slowly 5 to 8 minutes.

French Fried Potatoes: Select long, plump potatoes. Wash and peel. Cut in 1/2" wide lengths. Fry in deep oil at 395 F. until golden. Stir often to brown evenly. Drain on paper towels.

Frozen French Fries: Follow directions on the package.

To Bake French Cut Raw Potatoes: Prepare as for French frying. Dip in oil. Spread pieces on cookie sheet 1/4" apart. Bake in preheated oven 400 to 450 F. until brown on top. Turn carefully with metal pancake turner and continue baking until they look like French fries.

O'Brien Potatoes: Wash, peel and dice raw potatoes. Saute in just enough fat to prevent burning. When tender, add chopped pimientos and onion juice.

Lyonnaise Potatoes: Prepared from boiled, cold potatoes. Dice and saute some onion in fat until clear. Add diced potatoes and stir with a fork until all sides are brown. Sprinkle chopped parsley over top.

Potatoes Baked Around A Roast: Select medium potatoes. Wash, peel and place around roast beef, allowing 1 hour and 20 minutes to cook. Turn frequently, and baste with juice from the roast. To shorten the cooking time, parboil potatoes 15 minutes before placing them in the roaster. Allow 45 minutes additional time. As with raw potatoes, turn parboiled potatoes often to brown evenly.

Raw Fries, Small: (Allow 1 medium potato per person). Wash and peel potatoes, cut in half lengthwise, then in slices. Stack the slices and dice in 1/4" to 1/3" thick cubes. Add to hot fat in a heavy skillet. Stir until potatoes have a yellow cast and are cooking well then do not stir, allowing them to brown. Turn with a pancake turner. Brown, without stirring. If desired, add a tablespoon of chopped onion when potatoes are half cooked.

Raw Fries, Large: Prepare potatoes the same as for small raw fries. Cut in 1/4" slices and lay them side by side in melted margarine in a heavy frying pan. Allow potatoes to brown before turning each slice carefully to avoid breaking, and/or separate browned part. After turning, add a small amount of chopped green onions. While second side is browning, cover pan about 10   minutes (this cooks the potatoes through a little faster). Remove lid and test for doneness by piercing with a fork. If tender, remove potatoes with a pancake turner to double thickness of paper towels. Keep warm until serving time in 160 F. oven, but potatoes are tastier if served immediately while crisp. They're inclined to soften in the oven.

Sweet Potatoes and Yams: See following succotash.

. . . .

MASHED POTATOES

F=Fair; G=Good; H=High; L=Low; t or T = trace; n/a = no information available; dashes = zero or unmeasurable

GRAM WT.	FOOD	VITAMINS	CAL	(mg) SOD	PRO	FAT	CARB	CHOL	FATTY ACIDS SAT	UNSAT	CALC	IRON	(mg) POTSM
147	AVERAGE PER SERVING		128	63				(mg)* 1					488
	Ingredients:												
408	3 medium potatoes	A^t B1 B2 C	315	12	L	T	F	---	---	---	L	L	1661
164	2/3 cp 2% low-fat milk	A B1 B2 C	97	100	H	F	G	L	L	L	H	L	287
14	1 tblspn margarine	A D	100	139	L	H	T	---	L	H	L	---	3
	No salt												
586	Recipe totals (gms; cal; sod. & potsm)		512	251									1951

METHOD

Wash and peel potatoes, cut in thirds and boil until tender. Drain. Force through a ricer (use a potatoe masher if no ricer is available), add a little of the milk and the margarine and beat. Continue adding milk a little at a time until the desired consistency is reached. Potatoes should be fluffy and light. Spoon into a warm serving dish, add a dot of margarine in the center and a dash of paprika if desired.   Yield   about 4 servings.

*   There are 5 milligrams of cholesterol in 164 grams of 2% low-fat milk, as calculated from U.S.D.A. Handbook No. 8, pg. 146, item 29. Divide 5 milligrams by 4 servings equals 1 average milligram of cholesterol per serving.

. . . .

MASHED POTATO CAKES

F=Fair; G=Good; H=High; L=Low; t or T = trace; n/a = no information available; dashes = zero or unmeasurable

GRAM WT.	FOOD	VITAMINS	CAL	(mg) SOD	PRO	FAT	CARB	CHOL (mg)*	FATTY ACIDS SAT	UNSAT	CALC	IRON	(mg) POTSM
165	AVERAGE PER SERVING		149	79				70					519
	Ingredients:												
586	2 cp mashed potatoes	A B1 B2 C	512	251	L	T	F	---	---	---	L	L	1951
50	1 egg, beaten	A B1 B2	75	61	F	F	L	H	H	L	F	F	65
25	3 green onions, minced	A^t B1 B2 C	10	2	L	L	F	---	---	---	F	L	58
n/a	dash black pepper	----------					--n/a--						----------
661	Recipe totals (gms; cal; sod. & potsm.)		597	314									2074

METHOD

In a medium size bowl, mix potatoes with a fork until light. Add beaten egg, chopped onions and pepper, and blend in thoroughly. Make 4 even mounds of the mixture on a molding board, or wax paper, until they resemble hamburger patties. Saute in a small amount of margarine in a heavy frying pan. (Bacon fat or oil may be used instead of margarine). Serve plain, or with cream or brown gravy. (Brown both sides).

NOTE   Instant potatoes may be used instead of fresh. Values above are for fresh taken from mashed potato recipe in this chapter.

*   There are 275 milligrams of cholesterol in 50 grams of egg and 5 milligrams in 164 grams of milk used in the mashed potatoes for a total of 280, divided by 4 servings equals 70 average milligrams of cholesterol per serving, as calculated from U.S.D.A. Handbook No. 8, pg. 146, items 12 and 29 respectively.

. . . .

472

POTATOES AU GRATIN

F=Fair; G=Good; H=High; L=Low; t or T = trace; n/a = no information available; dashes = zero or unmeasurable

GRAM WT.	FOOD	VITAMINS	CAL	(mg) SOD	PRO	FAT	CARB	CHOL (mg)*	FATTY ACIDS SAT	UNSAT	CALC	IRON	(mg) POTSM
242	AVERAGE PER SERVING		245	204				6					730
	Ingredients:												
816	6 medium potatoes	A^t B1 B2 C	630	24	L	T	F	---	---	---	L	L	3321
492	2 cp 2% low-fat milk	A B1 B2 C	290	300	H	F	G	L	L	L	H	L	861
18	2 tblspn cornstarch	---	68	---	L	T	H	------	------	------	------	------	------
23	1/4 cp cheddar cheese, grated	A B1 B2	90	159	G	G	L	H	H	L	H	F	19
4	1 tblspn parsley	A^t B1^t B2 C	T	2	T	T	T	------	------	------	H	H	29
100	1 cp breadcrumbs	A^t B1 B2 C	390	736	F	L	G	------	------	------	G	F	152
1453	Recipe totals (gms; cal; sod. & potsm.)		1468	1221									4382

METHOD

Wash potatoes, remove eyes and boil until tender in a covered saucepan. Heat the milk, mix cornstarch with 1/4 cup water until smooth, add slowly to the hot milk, stirring constantly until sauce thickens. Fold in grated cheese and blend. Set aside. When potatoes are cooked, peel and slice into a greased casserole. Add the white sauce. Sprinkle parsley and breadcrumbs over top and bake at 400 F. until crumbs are brown. Season individually at the table. Yield 6 servings.

*   There are 23 milligrams of cholesterol in 23 grams of cheddar cheese and 15 milligrams of cholesterol in 492 grams of fluid skim milk, for a total of 38 milligrams of cholesterol, as calculated from U.S.D.A. Handbook No. 8, pg. 146, items 5 and 29 respectively. Divide38 milligrams by 6 servings equals 6 average milligrams of cholesterol per serving.

. . . .

SCALLOPED POTATOES

F=Fair; G=Good; H=High; L=Low; t or T = trace; n/a = no information available; dashes = zero or unmeasurable

GRAM WT.	FOOD	VITAMINS	CAL	(mg) SOD	PRO	FAT	CARB	CHOL	FATTY ACIDS SAT	UNSAT	CALC	IRON	(mg) POTSM
271	AVERAGE PER SERVING		213	94				(mg)* 3					849
	Ingredients:												
816	6 medium potatoes	A^t B1 B2 C	630	24	L	T	F	------	------	------	L	L	3321
25	3 chopped green onions	A^t B1 B2 C	10	2	L	L	F	------	------	------	F	L	58
515	2 cp thin white sauce	see below-------	424	439	------	------	see below	------	------	------	------		864
1356	Recipe totals (gms; cal; sod. & potsm.)		1064	465									4243
	Thin White Sauce - Ingredients:												
492	2 cp 2% low-fat milk	A B1 B2 C	290	300	H	F	G	L	L	L	H	L	861
9	1 tblspn cornstarch	---	34	---	L	T	H	------	------	------	------		
14	1 tblspn soft margarine	A D	100	139	L	H	T	---	L	H	L	---	3
n/a	dash black pepper	------	------	------	------	------	n/a	------	------	------	------		
515	Total for White Sauce (gms; cal; sod. & potsm.)		424	439									864

METHOD

Wash, peel, and slice potatoes into a greased casserole. Heat milk, mix cornstarch with a small amount of cold water, until smooth; add slowly to heated milk and stir constantly until sauce is thickened; add margarine and pepper and blend. Pour over sliced potatoes, distributing it evenly, add chopped onions, sprinkling them over the top. Cover casserole and bake at 350 F. until potatoes are tender. Remove cover and bake 15 minutes longer to allow top to brown. Yield   5 servings.

*   There are 15 milligrams of cholesterol in 492 grams of fluid skim milk, as calculated from U.S.D.A. Handbook No. 8, pg. 146, item 29. Divide by 5 servings equals 3 average milligrams of cholesterol per serving.

. . . .

474

POTATO PANCAKES

F=Fair; G=Good; H=High; L=Low; t or T = trace; n/a = no information available;   dashes = zero or unmeasurable

GRAM WT.	FOOD	VITAMINS	CAL	(mg) SOD	PRO	FAT	CARB	CHOL (mg)*	FATTY ACIDS SAT	UNSAT	CALC	IRON	(mg) POTSM
113	AVERAGE PER SERVING		90	29				92					408
	Ingredients:												
567	3 cp grated raw potatoes	A^t B1 B2 C	349	14	L	T	F	---	---	---	L	L	2308
100	2 eggs, well beaten	A B1 B2	150	122	F	F	L	H	H	L	F	F	129
11	1-1/2 tblspn flour	B1 B2	39	T	F	L	G	---	---	---	L	F	10
---	1/8 tsp baking powder	---	1	40	L	T	H	---	---	---	H	---	---
n/a	1/2 tsp onion juice	-------	---	----	----	----	---n/a---	---	---	---	---	---	----
678	Recipe totals (gms; cal; sod. & potsm.)		539	176									2447

METHOD

Wash and pare about 4 medium potatoes. Cover with cold water, add a little lemon juice and let stand a couple of hours. Drain. Grate potatoes. Drain well. Add beaten eggs, mix lightly then stir in remaining ingredients. Drop from tablespoon onto hot, well greased frying pan or griddle and brown both sides.   Yield   12 pancakes.

* There are 550 milligrams of cholesterol in 100 grams of whole egg, per U.S.D.A. Handbook No. 8, pg. 146, item 12. Divide 550 by 6 servings equals 92 average milligrams of cholesterol per serving (2 pancakes).

. . . .

RUTABAGAS

Perhaps the more common name for this vegetable is yellow turnip. It is an edible root that averages a pound each and it is a good source of Vitamin A. In one pound, there are 2,240 International Units, whereas in one pound of white turnip, there is only a trace, according to U.S.D.A. Handbook No. 8.

Turnips are related to the mustard family and have a distinct flavor enjoyed in food combinations, such as: soups, stews, and with mashed potatoes. They're also good served plain, with a small amount of margarine as seasoning.

To Boil Rutabagas: Wash and peel off the tough outer layer. Cut into pieces and boil until tender. Drain. Serve mashed or in pieces, as desired. Mashed rutabagas have the consistency of applesauce.

SALSIFY (OYSTERPLANT)

A root vegetable, salsify is also called oysterplant because of its taste, a distinct oyster flavor.

To Prepare: Peel under water to which a little milk has been added. This will prevent staining the hands. To prevent salsify from discoloring, place it at once into cold water to which lemon juice or vinegar has been added. Cut into one inch slices and cook in boiling water until tender. Drain and combine with medium white sauce.

For fried salsify, prepare as above then follow directions for sauteed parsnips.

SAUERKRAUT

To reduce the sour taste, add about a third of a medium potato, grated, while sauerkraut is cooking.

Sauerkraut makes an excellent accompaniment with spareribs; fresh ham hocks; frankfurters and sausage.

Although sauerkraut juice is refreshing, it is also high in sodium.

To Make Sauerkraut: 10 Pounds of cabbage, shredded about as thick as a nickel and 1/2 cup of salt should yeild 6 or 7 quarts. Do not shred cabbage any thinner or sauerkraut will turn mushy, and if too thick, it will be unattractive.

Fermentation should occur at 60 F. for 4 to 6 weeks in a covered stone crock; higher temperatures may cause spoilage. Stir the kraut occasionally during "working" period.

Cabbage should be placed in a stone crock in layers: start with shredded cabbage, then sprinkle salt over the first layer; add a second layer of shredded cabbage and sprinkle with salt, etc., until cabbage and salt is used. Cover and keep as near as 60 F. as possible. (See above).

SPINACH

This versatile vegetable is used in many ways. It's delicious in salads, or cooked in souffles, or boiled, or steamed and served with margarine or lemon juice or vinegar; or creamed.

Preparation of fresh spinach can be tedious because each leaf must be washed and washed again to get rid of the sand. This is probably one reason why frozen and canned spinach is used more frequently than fresh.

To Boil Fresh Spinach: Remove roots and wilted leaves. Wash in several waters to remove sand — both sides of leaves must be washed — then place in a large kettle without additional water. Cover and cook slowly until tender. Young spinach will cook in a shorter time then older. When spinach is tender, drain, chop, season with margarine and salt and pepper individually at the table. Serve a few slices of lemon with it, or vinegar, if desired. One pound of fresh spinach will yield 3 to 4 servings.

. . . .

SPINACH SOUFFLE

F=Fair; G=Good; H=High; L=Low; t or T = trace; n/a = no information available; dashes = zero or unmeasurable

GRAM WT.	FOOD	VITAMINS	CAL	(mg) SOD	PRO	FAT	CARB	CHOL (mg)*	FATTY ACIDS SAT	UNSAT	CALC	IRON	(mg) POTSM
115	AVERAGE PER SERVING		58	76				138					324
	Ingredients:												
360	2 cp cooked spinach	A B1 B2 C	80	180	L	L	L	---	---	---	G	F	1166
100	2 eggs, separated	A B1 B2	150	122	F	F	L	H	H	L	F	F	129
460	Recipe totals (gms; cal; sod. & potsm.)		230	302									1295

METHOD

Place spinach in a granite, glass, or china saucepan; add the beaten egg yolks, heat slowly and stir until egg sets. Remove from heat and set aside. When cold, fold in stiffly beaten egg whites. Fill greased baking cups half full of the mixture, set in a pan of hot water and bake in a moderate oven of 375 F. for 20 to 30 minutes. To prevent souffle from falling, serve at once. Yield 4 servings.

* There are 550 milligrams of cholesterol in 100 grams of whole egg, per U.S.D.A. Handbook No. 8, pg. 146, item 12. Divide 550 milligrams by 4 servings equals 138 average milligrams of cholesterol per serving.

. . . .

478

BAKED ACORN SQUASH (OR TABLE QUEEN)

F=Fair; G=Good; H=High; L=Low; t or T = trace; n/a = no information available; dashes = zero or unmeasurable

GRAM WT.	FOOD	VITAMINS	CAL	(mg) SOD	PRO	FAT	CARB	CHOL	FATTY ACIDS SAT	UNSAT	CALC	IRON	(mg) POTSM
232	AVERAGE PER SERVING		110	48									1091
	Ingredients:												
908	2 acorn squash (1 lb. each)	A B1 B2 C	304	6	L	L	F	---	---	---	L	L	4358
19	4 tspn margarine	A D	134	185	L	H	T	---	L	H	L	---	4
927	Recipe totals (gms; cal; sod. & potsm.)		438	191									4362

METHOD

Wash squash, dry with a paper towel, then cut in half lengthwise. (Squash are hard to cut — use a heavy bladed knife, very sharp, and pound blade through squash with a hammer). Scoop out seeds before. or after baking. It makes little difference. To make squash lie flat on baking dish, cut a thin slice off the bottom. Place the 4 halves in a foil-lined baking dish; use enough foil to cover squash. Add 2 tablespoons water to each half in the seed cavity and 1 teaspoon margarine. Cover squash with foil loosely. Bake at 350 F. 1 hour or until fork tender. Remove from oven, scoop out seeds and stringy fibers; serve in shells. Yield 4 servings.

. . . .

BAKED HUBBARD SQUASH

F=Fair; G=Good; H=High; L=Low; t or T = trace; n/a = no information available; dashes = zero or unmeasurable

GRAM WT.	FOOD	VITAMINS	CAL	(mg) SOD	PRO	FAT	CARB	CHOL	FATTY ACIDS SAT	UNSAT	CALC	IRON	(mg) POTSM
121	AVERAGE PER SERVING	·	79	71									248
	Ingredients:												
454	1 lb Hubbard Squash	A B1 B2 C	117	3	L	L	F	---	---	---	L	L	985
28	2 tblspn margarine	A D	200	279	L	H	L	---	L	H	L	---	6
482	Recipe totals (gms; cal; sod. & potsm.)		317	282									991

METHOD

Seal pieces of Hubbard squash in foil and place on a cookie sheet. (If desired, dot with margarine before sealing in foil). Bake at 350 F. for 1 hour or until fork tender. Spoon squash out of shell and mash with a potato masher. Add remaining margarine and serve at once. Yield   about 4 servings.

. . . .

SUMMER SQUASH
Yellow crookneck and pale green squash with scalloped edges.

Wash squash then cut in pieces and cook together. These two varieties of squash make a colorful dish that's a tasty accompaniment to nearly every kind of meat or fowl.

Cook squash in as little water as possible to prevent burning. When fork tender, drain, then add some chopped green onion and a dash of garlic salt or celery salt. For a new taste experience, sprinkle grated cheese over the squash just before serving.

NOTE   If squash is young, it is not necessary to remove the seeds, but cut off the stem ends.

BUTTERNUT SQUASH

Wash squash, then cut in half lengthwise. Since this is a hard squash, it may be necessary to use a sharp, heavy knife and a hammer (as in cutting through table queen squash). Sprinkle with celery salt and dot with margarine. Seeds may be scooped out before or after baking. Drizzle a little water over the tops then seal halves in heavy duty foil, and place on a shallow cooking sheet.   Bake at 350 F for 1 hour and 20 minutes, or longer if squash is not tender. Serve by scooping squash out of shell and mashing with a fork, or by cutting halves for individual servings.

Butternut squash tastes like sweet potatoes and is delicious with many dishes. It may also be peeled and steamed.

. . . .

ZUCCHINI SQUASH CASSEROLE

F=Fair; G=Good; H=High; L=Low; t or T = trace; n/a = no information available;   dashes = zero or unmeasurable

GRAM WT.	FOOD	VITAMINS	CAL	(mg) SOD	PRO	FAT	CARB	CHOL (mg)*	FATTY ACIDS SAT	UNSAT	CALC	IRON	(mg) POTSM
203	**AVERAGE PER SERVING**		308	452				107					333
	Ingredients:												
681	1-1/2 lb small zucchini	A B1 B2 C	110	6	L	L	L	---	---	---	F	F	1376
84	6 tblspn margarine	A D	600	834	L	H	L	---	L	H	L	---	19
110	1 medium onion, chopped	A B1 B2 C	40	11	L	L	L	---	---	---	L	L	173
91	1 cp grated cheddar cheese	A B1 B2	361	635	G	G	L	H	H	L	H	F	75
n/a	1 tsp accent (optional)	----------------					---n/a---						------
n/a	dash black pepper	----------------					---n/a---						------
100	2 eggs, beaten	A B1 B2	150	122	F	F	L	H	H	L	F	F	129
150	1-1/2 cp soft breadcrumbs	A^t B1 B2 C^t	585	1104	F	L	G	---	---	---	G	F	228
1216	Recipe totals (gms; cal; sod. & potsm.)		1846	2712									2000

METHOD

Wash zucchini and cut off stem ends. Do not peel. Cook whole in a small amount of water until slightly underdone. Drain and set aside to cool. Saute chopped onion in the margarine, saving 2 tablespoons for last. When onions are yellow, cut squash into cubes and add to them. Stir in cheese and pepper. Mix lightly with beaten eggs. Pour into one quart baking dish. Melt remaining margarine, add to breadcrumbs, toss with a fork, then sprinkle over zucchini. Bake at 350 F. for 30 to 45 minutes, or until knife inserted in center comes out clean. Yield   6 servings.

*   There are 550 milligrams of cholesterol in 100 grams of whole egg, and 91 milligrams of cholesterol in 91 grams of cheddar cheese, for a total of 641 milligrams, as calculated from U.S.D.A. Handbook No. 8, pg. 146, items 12 and 5 respectively. Divide 641 by 6 servings equals 107 average milligrams of cholesterol per serving.

. . . .

ZUCCHINI - TOMATO CASSEROLE

F=Fair; G=Good; H=High; L=Low; t or T = trace; n/a = no information available;   dashes = zero or unmeasurable

GRAM WT.	FOOD	VITAMINS	CAL	(mg) SOD	PRO	FAT	CARB	CHOL	FATTY ACIDS SAT	UNSAT	CALC	IRON	(mg) POTSM
180	AVERAGE PER SERVING		56	181				(mg)* 4					436
	Ingredients:												
681	1-1/2 lb small zucchini	A B1 B2 C	110	6	L	L	L	---	---	---	F	F	1376
110	1 medium onion, chopped	A B1 B2 C	40	11	L	L	L	---	---	---	L	L	173
37	1/2 sweet green pepper	A B1 B2 C	8	5	L	L	L	---	---	---	L	L	79
227	1 (8oz can tomato sauce	A B1 B2 C	88	906	L	L	L	---	---	---	L	L	967
	High sodium reflects salt used in the canning process.												
23	1/4 cp grated cheddar cheese	A B1 B2	90	159	G	G	L	H	H	L	H	F	19
1078	Recipe totals (gms; cal; sod. & potsm.)		336	1087									2614

METHOD

Wash and cut off stem ends from zucchini. Slice in half inch pieces and place in a greased baking dish with a cover. Add chopped onion, chopped green pepper (remove seeds and white membrane inside the pod). Pour tomatoe juice over all, sprinkle with grated cheese and bake at 350 F. for 1 hour or until zucchini is tender.   Yield   6 servings.

*   There are 23 milligrams of cholesterol in 23 grams of cheddar cheese, as calculated from U.S.D.A. Handbook No. 8, pg. 146, item 5. Divide 23 milligrams by 6 servings equals 4 average milligrams of cholesterol per serving.

. . . .

SUCCOTASH

F=Fair; G=Good; H=High; L=Low; t or T = trace; n/a = no information available; dashes = zero or unmeasurable

GRAM WT.	FOOD	VITAMINS	CAL	(mg) SOD	PRO	FAT	CARB	CHOL (mg)	FATTY ACIDS SAT	UNSAT	CALC	IRON	(mg) POTSM
124	AVERAGE PER SERVING		126	115				Less than 1					372
	Ingredients:												
336	2 cp frozen whole-kernel corn	A B1 B2 C	275	4	L	L	F	---	---	---	L	L	679
380	2 cp frozen lima beans	A B1 B2 C	388	490	L	L	F	---	---	---	F	F	1862
246	1 cp 2% low-fat milk	A B1 B2 C	145	150	H	F	G	L	L	L	H	L	431
28	2 tblspn margarine	A D	200	279	L	H	L	---	L	H	L	---	6
990	Recipe totals (gms; cal; sod. & potsm.)		1008	923									2978

METHOD

Combine vegetables and cook in as little water as possible to prevent burning. When limas are tender, drain and add milk and margarine and cook slowly about 5 minutes longer until milk is hot. Season individually at the table. Yield 8 servings.

NOTE   Canned whole kernel or cream-style corn and lima beans may be used instead, but sodium will increase due to salt added in the canning process. Use only 1/2 cup milk, and 1/2 cup of liquid drained from vegetables, adding more if necessary. Simmer vegetables about 10 minutes.

*   There is less than 1 average milligram of cholesterol per serving, as calculated from U.S.D.A. Handbook No. 8, pg. 146, item 29.

. . . .

SWEET POTATOES

To Boil: Wash and peel (unless potatoes are to be cooked in their jackets). Cut up or cook whole in a small amount of water in a covered pan. Potatoes should be watched closely to prevent scorching. Serve either plain or with margarine.

To Bake: Wash, but do not peel. Cut out any bad spots. Cut off a thin slice from each end of the potato, then roll up in heavy foil. Crimp edges to seal and place on a pie pan or similar baking dish and bake at 350 F. about 1 hour or until tender when pierced with a long pronged fork through the foil. Peel before serving.

. . . .

CANDIED SWEET POTATOES

F=Fair; G=Good; H=High; L=Low; t or T = trace; n/a = no information available;   dashes = zero or unmeasurable

GRAM WT.	FOOD	VITAMINS	CAL	(mg) SOD	PRO	FAT	CARB	CHOL	FATTY ACIDS SAT	UNSAT	CALC	IRON	(mg) POTSM
217	AVERAGE PER SERVING		323	51									533
	Ingredients:												
1008	6 medium sweet potatoes	A B1 B2 C	1020	102	L	L	F	---	---	---	L	L	2439
220	1 cp brown sugar	B1 B2	820	66	---	---	H	---	---	---	G	G	757
59	1/4 cp water		------------------------------------0------------------------------------										
14	1 tblspn margarine	A D	100	139	L	H	T	---	L	H	L	---	3
1301	Recipe totals (gms; cal; sod. & potsm.)		1940	307									3199

METHOD

Wash potatoes, boil with their skins on until tender, then drain. Strip off skins. Make a sirup of boiling water and sugar together and set aside. Cut potatoes in half lengthwise, or in thick slices. Dip each half, or slice, in sirup and lay flat on a greased baking dish. Dot with margarine. When all potatoes are in the dish, pour remaining sirup over them. Brown potatoes quickly, baking in a 400 to 450 F. oven. Yield   6 servings.

. . . .

486

TOMATOES

Perhaps the most common vegetable grown in the family garden today, yet, only a little over a hundred years ago, it was considered poisonous, and the tomato was cultivated as an ornamental curiosity. Perhaps fear of this nutritious food stemmed from the fact that it belongs to the dreaded Nightshade family which is known for their poisonous characteristics.

Tomatoes originated in western South America and, in their wild state, were perennials but when cultivated in botannical gardens and similar places, they are treated as annuals.

The red variety of tomatoes is more popularly grown; the yellow variety is gaining in popularity because it is a trifle milder in taste but just as delicious. There are also pink and white varieties, but there is little information on them at this writing.

For a long time, the tomato was called Love Apple and sometimes Gold Apple. It has been called a berry; a fruit; dictionaries refer to it as an herb. In America it is a vegetable, and tomato products are found in the vegetable section of supermarkets. Whatever its identity, the tomato is delicious raw or cooked and a source of vitamins in both pulp and juice.

Four small tomatoes will weigh about a pound; 14 pounds in a peck, and 56 pounds in a bushel. For canning purposes, 2-1/4 lbs. of tomatoes are needed to produce a pint; 1 peck will yield 8 pints and 1 bushel, 18 quarts of whole tomatoes. When tomatoes separate from the juice and rise to the top of the jar, they may have been processed too long, or were overripe, or preheated too much before packing.

To Use Green Tomatoes: Wash and slice them about 1/2" thick, dip in a thin batter, or coat with flour, and fry in hot oil — enough fat to cover bottom of the pan (about 1/4" to 1/2" deep) until brown on both sides. (Solid, red tomatoes are also delicious fried and served with toast for breakfast). Green tomatoes are also used in pickling, jams, preserves and conserves.

To ripen green tomatoes, put in a brown paper bag and keep in a dark place until red; or wrap in newspaper. Wrap separately.

Red Tomatoes: To peel quickly, spear stem end with a long-pronged fork, dip in boiling water, count ten seconds, run cold water over them immediately, then slip off the skins.

Tomatoes are more flavorful when used at room temperature, though some people prefer them chilled for salads.

Cherry tomatoes are very prolific and can be grown in deep flower pots. This variety of tomato is delicious in salads, or just eaten whole as a snack. They're a tasty and nutritious addition to lunch boxes, too, and much easier to handle.

To Stuff Tomatoes For Baking: Mix cooked rice with a little onion and green pepper (coarsely chopped). Cut out some tomato pulp around the stem end, large enough to make room for the stuffing. Save as much of the pulp as possible to add to the stuffing mixture. Discard the hard stem section. If desired, add a little fresh celery chopped fine. Place tomatoes in a greased casserole or baking dish and sprinkle with grated cheddar cheese. Bake at 350 to 400 F. until tender.   Tomatoes should be the large, slicing type with firm meat for best results.

To Make Tomato Paste: Follow the recipe for tomato sauce (puree) in this chapter; spread thick puree in flat, oiled pans. As soon as a film appears over the top, loosen paste with a spatula and turn it onto a screen covered with cheese-cloth, then dry in the sun or a very slow oven. When it is dry enough to handle without sticking, roll in waxed paper and store in a metal box or glass jar. This paste has many uses; in sauces, soups, scalloped dishes, etc. Soak in cold water until paste is soft before adding to any hot mixture. One teaspoon of paste makes 1 cup of soup.

. . . .

STEWED TOMATOES

F=Fair; G=Good; H=High; L=Low; t or T = trace; n/a = no information available;   dashes = zero or unmeasurable

GRAM WT.	FOOD	VITAMINS	CAL	(mg) SOD	PRO	FAT	CARB	CHOL	FATTY ACIDS SAT	UNSAT	CALC	IRON	(mg) POTSM
206	AVERAGE PER SERVING		41	7									500
	Ingredients:												
1200	6 medium tomatoes	A B1 B2 C	240	36	L	L	L	---	---	---	L	L	2928
25	1/3 pod green pepper, chopped	A B1 B2 C	5	3	L	L	L	---	---	---	L	L	53
8	1 chopped green onion	A B1 B2 C	3	T	L	L	F	---	---	---	F	L	18
1233	Recipe totals (gms; cal; sod. & potsm.)		248	39									2999

METHOD

Spear tomatoes with a long pronged cooking fork and dip them, one by one, into boiling water for about 10 seconds, then rinse under cold, running water. Slip off skins, cut out hard stem ends. Cut into pieces, add chopped onion and pepper and cook slowly without adding water until tender. (Do not cook tomatoes in pans made of aluminum; use granite, glass, or Corningware type utensils). Tomatoes may be cooked without onions and green pepper, if desired. Salt and pepper at the table individually. Yield   6 servings.

. . . .

TOMATO CHILI SAUCE

F=Fair; G=Good; H=High; L=Low; t or T = trace; n/a = no information available; dashes = zero or unmeasurable

GRAM WT.	FOOD	VITAMINS	CAL	(mg) SOD	PRO	FAT	CARB	CHOL	FATTY ACIDS SAT	UNSAT	CALC	IRON	(mg) POTSM
935	AVERAGE PER SERVING		281	1436									1902
	Ingredients:												
2400	12 large ripe tomatoes	A B1 B2 C	480	72	L	L	L	---	---	---	L	L	5856
330	3 onions (2-1/2" diameter)	A B1 B2 C	120	33	L	L	L	---	---	---	L	L	518
296	4 green peppers	A B1 B2 C	60	40	L	L	L	---	---	---	L	L	630
15	1 tblspn salt	---	---	5592					--------0--------				
100	1/2 cp granulated sugar	---	385	1	---	---	H		---	---	---	L	3
n/a	1-1/2 tspn cinnamon							-------n/a-------					
n/a	1 tsp ground cloves							-------n/a-------					
600	2-1/2 cps vinegar	---	80	6	T	---	L	---	---	---	L	L	600
3741	Recipe totals (gms; cal; sod. & potsm.)		1125	5744									7607

METHOD

To peel tomatoes — spear them, one at a time, through stem ends with a two pronged, long handle cooking fork, then dip into boiling water for 10 to 12 seconds, immersing completely. Remove tomato to rinse quickly in cold running water. Skins should slip off easily. Peel onions. Wash peppers, cut off tops, remove seeds and white inner membrane, then chop vegetables fine. Mix vegetables together, add salt, sugar, spices and vinegar. Cook slowly in a non-aluminum kettle 45 to 60 minutes, or until thick, stirring often. Pour into hot, sterilized jars and seal. Yield 4 pints.

For a zippier sauce, add 2 sweet red peppers, seeded and chopped and 2 hot red peppers, seeded and chopped, to the above recipe.

. . . .

490

TOMATO CATSUP

F=Fair; G=Good; H=High; L=Low; t or T = trace; n/a = no information available; dashes = zero or unmeasurable

GRAM WT.	FOOD	VITAMINS	CAL	(mg) SOD	PRO	FAT	CARB	CHOL	FATTY ACIDS SAT	UNSAT	CALC	IRON	(mg) POTSM
746	AVERAGE PER PINT		210	512									1662
	Ingredients:												
7264	16 lb ripe tomatoes	A B1 B2 C	1600	224	L	L	L	---	---	---	L	L	17724
660	6 medium onions	A B1 B2 C	240	66	L	L	L	---	---	---	L	L	1036
4	2 small cloves fresh garlic	A^t B1 B2 C	6	T	L	L	F	---	---	---	L	F	21
200	2 sweet red peppers	A B1 B2 C	62	---	L	L	L	---	---	---	L	L	---
n/a	2 whole bay leaves						--n/a--						
15	1 tblspn salt	---	---	5592	---	---	---	---	---	---	G	---	T
200	2 cp chopped celery	A B1 B2 C	30	252	L	T	L	---	---	---	F	L	682
n/a	1 tsp cayenne pepper												
n/a	1/2 tsp cinnamon						--n/a--						
133	2/3 cp sugar	---	513	4	---	---	H	---	---	---	---	L	4
480	2 cp vinegar	---	64	5	T	---	L	---	---	---	L	L	480
8956	Recipe totals (gms; cal; sod. & potsm.)		2515	6143									19947

METHOD

Wash and cut up tomatoes then put in a large enamel kettle; add peeled, chopped onions and garlic. Wash peppers, cut off tops and remove seeds, then cut in pieces and add to tomatoes. Add the whole bay leaves, salt and celery. Cook until vegetables are soft. Remove bay leaves. Strain mixture through a sieve or ricer. Tie spices in a small cheese-cloth bag, securely to prevent them from spilling into the mixture, add to strained tomatoes, stir in sugar until well mixed. Boil rapidly, stirring often to prevent burning. When catsup is thick or reduced to one-half the original amount, remove from heat, remove spices, add vinegar, stir, return to heat and bring to a boil and cook 10 minutes. Pour into hot, sterilized jars. Yield   about 6 quarts (12 pints).

. . . .

TOMATO SAUCE (PUREE)

Puree

F=Fair; G=Good; H=High; L=Low; t or T = trace; n/a = no information available;   dashes = zero or unmeasurable

GRAM WT.	FOOD	VITAMINS	CAL	(mg) SOD	PRO	FAT	CARB	CHOL	FATTY ACIDS SAT	UNSAT	CALC	IRON	(mg) POTSM
632	AVERAGE PER HALF PINT		141	553									1529
	Ingredients:												
3632	8 lb ripe tomatoes	A B1 B2 C	800	112	L	L	L	---	---	---	L	L	8862
110	1 onion	A B1 B2 C	40	11	L	L	L	---	---	---	L	L	173
40	1 stalk celery	A B1 B2 C	5	50	T	T	T	---	---	---	F	L	136
n/a	1 bay leaf							-------n/a-------					
8	2 tspn salt	---	---	3142	---	---	---	---	---	---	G	---	T
n/a	1/4 tsp paprika							-------n/a-------					
3790	Recipe totals (gms; cal; sod. & potsm.)		845	3315									9171

METHOD

Wash tomatoes and cut in pieces; wash, peel and dice onions. Wash celery and pare off the tough, outside fibers, then cut in pieces. Put tomatoes, onion, celery, bay leaf, salt and paprika in a large non-aluminum kettle and boil until vegetables are tender. Remove bay leaf. Rub vegetables through a sieve or ricer. Boil pulp slowly until volume is reduced half the original amount. Pour in hot, sterilized pints or half-pint jars and seal. Yield   3 pints (6 half-pints).

. . . .

TURNIPS

The white variety of turnips average about 4 to the pound, which, when cooked, yields about 2 cups diced which is approximately four 1/2 cup servings.

Rutabagas (the yellow turnips) are rich in Vitamin A, but in one pound of white turnips there was only a trace in samples tested by the Department of Agriculture for their Handbook No. 8. Vitamins B1 and B2 are comparable in the two varieties.

To Cook White Turnips: Wash well, then peel 'round and 'round. Dice or slice and boil in a small amount of water, but watch them because turnips absorb the water and additional must be added before they're cooked. They can be served plain or mashed with a little margarine. White turnips are good combined with mashed potatoes; and diced, they're good with a medium white sauce.

To Make Turnip Cups: Peel the whole turnip, remove the centers leaving 1/2" shells. Cook shells in boiling water until tender. Use as cases for creamed or buttered vegetables, such as peas, carrots or beets; or for creamed meats such as, chipped beef, chicken, turkey and tuna. For garnish, use parsley, hard-cooked eggs, or minced green onions.

. . . .

NUTS

To Toast Nutmeats: Place in a shallow pan, add 1/8" depth of salad oil or melted margarine, spread nuts evenly into the oil and coat each one well. Brown in a hot oven, stirring occasionally until desired browning is reached. Remove from oven. Drain on paper towels. Sprinkle lightly with salt, if desired.

Nuts with skins, such as almonds and large peanuts, should be blanched before roasting and their skins removed. (Small Spanish peanuts may be toasted, salted and eaten with their skins on).

Other miscellaneous nuts may be roasted in the oven, or in an iron frying pan using enough oil or melted margarine to coat them, and browning in hot fat. However, they must be watched closely to prevent overbrowning.

To Blanch Almonds: Shell the nuts and pour boiling water over them. Let stand from 2 to 5 minutes until the brown skins can be slipped off with the fingers. Pour off the water and remove the skins.

To Glaze Nuts: Make a sirup of 1 cup sugar, 1/2 cup water and 1/3 cup light corn sirup. Boil without stirring to the hard crack stage (300 F.). Remove pan from heat and put it into an outer pan of boiling water to keep sirup from hardening. Drop in well-drained nutmeats, a few at a time, skim out with slotted spoon and place on heavy waxed paper to dry. (Fruits may also be glazed this way).

To Bake Peanuts: Cover 4 cups shelled, raw peanuts with cold water and soak over night. In the morning, place them over a fire and boil ten minutes. Remove from fire and drain; dry on paper towels. Add 4 tablespoons salad oil and mix well. Place mixture in a greased baking dish and bake at 400 F. until peanuts are soft and well browned. Salt, if desired.

. . . .

ALMOND PASTE (MARZIPAN)

F=Fair; G=Good; H=High; L=Low; t or T = trace; n/a = no information available; dashes = zero or unmeasurable

GRAM WT.	FOOD	VITAMINS	CAL	(mg) SOD	PRO	FAT	CARB	CHOL	FATTY ACIDS SAT	UNSAT	CALC	IRON	(mg) POTSM
28	AVERAGE PER OUNCE		115	9									101
	Ingredients;												
142	1 cp whole almonds	B1 B2 C^t	850	6	F	G	F	---	L	H	H	G	1098
66	2 egg whites	B1 B2	30	96	F	T	L	---	---	---	L	L	92
120	1 cp powdered sugar	---	460	1	---	---	H	---	---	---	---	L	4
n/a	1 tsp almond flavoring						-n/a-						
328	Recipe totals (gms; cal; sod. & potsm.)		1340	103									1194

METHOD

Blanch almonds: cover with water and bring to the boiling point. Drain. Slip off skins and dry almonds on paper towels. Using the finest knife of the food chopper, grind almonds 3 or 4 times. Beat egg whites until foamy — mix with almonds and add sugar until mixture is stiff. Add almond flavoring a few drops at a time, blending well. If paste is too stiff, add a few drops of lemon juice, mixing with hands until paste is the right consistency. Let stand 24 hours before shaping into balls, fruits, vegetables, or other designs. To color, divide paste and add a few drops of yellow food coloring for carrots, red for cherries, etc. Balls may be rolled in grated chocolate, coconut (shredded), or finely chopped nuts.

. . . .

SOUPS

Canned, frozen, and dry package soups are much in demand. They're easy to make and tasty. Resourceful cooks also use them as a base for their own concoctions to spice up the taste of dishes such as meat loaf, stuffed green peppers, stews, etc., and in special sauces. But, for all of their goodness and convenience, there is something about the flavor of homemade vegetable, navy-bean, or split-pea soup that can't be found in a can.

VEGETABLE SALADS

There are so many vegetables that can go into the making of a salad, the combinations are almost limitless. All it takes to put a flavorful salad together is some fresh greens, vegetables, your favorite dressing or lemon juice, herbs such as: peppergrass, sorrel, celery, chervil, fresh or dried parsley, mint, nasturtium leaves, garlic, savory, tarragon, hyssop, fennel, costmary, chives, borage, anise, balm, basil leaves, marjoram, thyme, and a bit of imagination.

A few favorite salads are given in this chapter, but it's fun creating your own. All vegetables should be washed thoroughly. Greens should be crisp — to keep them crisp, soak in cold water after washing, then dry on paper towels. Store in plastic bags in the refrigerator until 30 minutes before they are to be used. Bowl for the salad should be cold to keep greens crisp and fresh. The salad should be one of the last dishes brought to the table. Supply salad bowls for individual servings, and two or three kinds of dressings — if salad in one with fresh greens and vegetables, serve vinegar and oil, thousand island, and mayonnaise or bleu cheese. It is the gracious hostess who allows guests to choose their own dressing preference. Perhaps an exception to this would be when potato salad is served — but mayonnaise should be folded into the salad at the last minute; and this goes for cold slaw, too, otherwise the salads become runny and distasteful in appearance.

Dressing for fruit salads should be served separately at the table, as with vegetable salads. See the chapter on fruits.

Garbanzo beans, mixed with a dab of mashed fresh garlic, fresh parsley and minced green onion, dressed with vinegar and oil, is an unusual but delicious combination salad that compliments a light meal. Garnishes of sliced tomatoes and strips of pimiento add color to this salad.

Canned kidney beans, drained, mixed with chopped celery and thin slices of yellow onions is another hearty salad combination. Dress with thin mayonnaise, lemon juice.

To dress up a vegetable salad, use flowers from broccoli and cauliflower; bits of red onion; crisp bacon pieces; finely shredded lettuce; sliced deviled eggs with pimiento strips; combine cottage cheese with strips of unpeeled cucumber sprinkled with vinegar or lemon juice. Use tiny bits of diced cheddar cheese for garnish; or slices of white radishes, or thin slices of jicama.

The list goes on and on, but the suggestions above may give you some creative ideas of your own. Making salads is fun — and sometimes, they're the best part of the meal, because vegetables have more vitamins than meat, and no cholesterol.

. . . .

NAVY AND PINTO BEAN SOUP WITH HAM

F=Fair; G=Good; H=High; L=Low; t or T = trace; n/a = no information available; dashes = zero or unmeasurable

GRAM WT.	FOOD	VITAMINS	CAL	(mg) SOD	PRO	FAT	CARB	CHOL	FATTY ACIDS SAT	UNSAT	CALC	IRON	(mg) POTSM
127	AVERAGE PER SERVING		346	14				(mg)* 30					839
	Ingredients:												
454	2 cp navy beans	B1 B2	1542	86	L	L	F	---	---	---	F	F	5425
113	1/2 cp pinto beans	B1 B2	394	11	F	L	G	---	---	---	G	G	1112
110	1 medium chopped onion	A B1 B2 C	40	11	L	L	L	---	---	---	L	L	173
342	2 smoked ham hocks	**B1 B2	795	---	G	G	---	H	H	L	L	F	---
1019	Recipe totals (gms; cal; sod. & potsm.)		2771	108									6710

** No information was available on ham hocks; these figures are from smoked picnics (3/4 pound).

METHOD

Wash beans thoroughly, pick them over and discard any that are wilted and discolored, then put them in a bowl large enough to allow for expansion of the beans, and cover with water. Soak overnight. Drain. Cover with fresh water, add chopped onion and smoked ham hocks. Cover with a tight lid and cook until beans are tender (about 1 hour) at medium to slow heat. Add more water as needed and stir occasionally. To test beans for tenderness, remove a few with a spoon and mash with a fork. Uncooked beans will be hard in the center.

At the end of an hour, remove ham hocks and, when cool enough to handle, remove rind and small bones. There will be three or four bones in each hock. Cut meat fairly small. Set aside and mash beans in pot until soup is thick (leave some whole beans), then add ham pieces, stir and reheat. Yield 8 servings.

* There are 239 milligrams of cholesterol in 342 grams of pork with bone, as calculated from U.S.D.A. Handbook No. 8, pg. 146, item 32a. Divide 239 by 8 servings equals 30 average milligrams of cholesterol per serving.

. . . .

SPLIT PEA SOUP

F=Fair; G=Good; H=High; L=Low; t or T = trace; n/a = no information available; dashes = zero or unmeasurable

GRAM WT.	FOOD	VITAMINS	CAL	(mg) SOD	PRO	FAT	CARB	CHOL (mg)*	FATTY ACIDS SAT	UNSAT	CALC	IRON	(mg) POTSM
102	AVERAGE PER SERVING		251	21				27					396
	Ingredients:												
227	1 cp split peas	A B1 B2	790	90	L	L	F	---	---	---	L	F	2032
50	1 carrot, raw, medium	A B1 B2 C	20	24	L	T	L	---	---	---	F	L	171
110	1 medium onion	A B1 B2 C	40	11	L	L	L	---	---	---	L	L	173
227	1 cp diced, smoked ham	B1 B2	656	---	G	G	---	H	H	L	L	F	---
614	Recipe totals (gms; cal; sod. & potsm.)		1506	125									2376

METHOD

Wash peas in a colander, cover with cold water and soak overnight. Grate carrot, chop onion, and set aside. Drain peas and cover with at least 3 quarts of water. Add carrots, onion and ham. Cook about 1 hour until peas are soft. Mash peas, or run through a blender. Reheat soup and serve hot. Yield 6 generous servings.   Instead of ham, cut frankfurters in slices and add to the soup when it is reheating. Cook about 20 minutes, covered.

*   In 227 grams of boneless pork, there are 159 milligrams of cholesterol as calculated from U.S.D.A. Handbook No. 8, pg. 146, item 32b. Divide 159 milligrams by 6 servings equals 27 average milligrams of cholesterol per serving.

. . . .

MAIN COURSE BEEF/VEGETABLE SOUP

F=Fair; G=Good; H=High; L=Low; t or T = trace; n/a = no information available; dashes = zero or unmeasurable

GRAM WT.	FOOD	VITAMINS	CAL	(mg) SOD	PRO	FAT	CARB	CHOL (mg)*	FATTY ACIDS SAT	UNSAT	CALC	IRON	(mg) POTSM
230	AVERAGE PER SERVING		261	204				40					713
	Ingredients:												
454	1 lb rump beef	A B1 B2	1374	295	H	F	---	H	H	L	L	G	1612
28	2 tblspn margarine	A D	200	279	L	H	L	---	L	H	L	---	6
110	1 medium onion, chopped	A B1 B2 C	40	11	L	L	L	---	---	---	L	L	173
2	1 clove fresh garlic, mashed	A^t B1 B2 C	3	T	L	L	F	---	---	---	L	F	11
227	1/2 lb cabbage, shredded	A B1 B2 C	49	41	L	L	L	---	---	---	L	L	529
50	1 carrot, sliced or diced	A B1 B2 C	20	24	L	T	L	---	---	---	F	L	171
40	1 large stalk celery and a few leaves, cut up	A B1 B2 C	5	50	T	T	T	---	---	---	F	L	136
76	1/2 cp lima beans	A B1 B2 C	93	2	L	L	F	---	---	---	F	F	494
57	1/2 cp green beans, cut up	A B1 B2 C	16	5	L	L	L	---	---	---	F	L	139
454	1 lb fresh tomatoes, cut	A B1 B2 C	100	14	L	L	L	---	---	---	L	L	1108
114	1/2 cp peas	A B1 B2 C	95	2	L	L	L	---	---	---	F	L	360
227	1 (8oz) can tomato sauce	A B1 B2 C	89	905	**L	L	L	---	---	---	L	L	967
	** High sodium is reflected in the salt used in the canning process.												
1839	Recipe totals (gms; cal; sod. & potsm.)		2084	1628									5706

METHOD

Cut up rump beef in pieces and brown on all sides in margarine, in a Dutch oven or deep kettle with a lid. Cover meat with water, add remaining ingredients, except peas and tomato sauce, which should be added about 30 minutes before serving time. Lima beans and green beans may be fresh, canned or frozen. This is a thick, rich soup. It may be necessary to add a little water from time to time. The longer this soup simmers, the tastier it is; in fact, it seems to be more flavorful the second day. Serve with crackers crisped in the oven, also serve wedges of jack or cheddar cheese and a green salad. Yield about 8 servings.

* In 454 grams of rump beef, there are 318 milligrams of cholesterol as calculated from U.S.D.A. Handbook No. 8, page 146, item 1b. Divide 318 milligrams by 8 servings equals 40 average millirgrams of cholesterol per serving.

. . . .

POTATO SALAD

F=Fair; G=Good; H=High; L=Low; t or T = trace; n/a = no information available; dashes = zero or unmeasurable

GRAM WT.	FOOD	VITAMINS	CAL	(mg) SOD	PRO	FAT	CARB	CHOL (mg)*	FATTY ACIDS SAT	UNSAT	CALC	IRON	(mg) POTSM
168	AVERAGE PER SERVING		149	91				102					422
	Ingredients:												
454	3 medium potatoes	A^t B1 B2 C	279	11	L	L	F	---	---	---	L	L	1495
25	3 green onions	A B1 B2 C	10	2	L	L	T	---	---	---	F	L	58
40	1 large stalk celery	A B1 B2 C	5	50	T	T	T	---	---	---	F	L	136
100	1 small cucumber	A^t B1 B2 C	15	6	L	L	L	---	---	---	F	L	160
100	2 eggs, hard-cooked	A B1 B2	150	122	F	F	L	H	H	L	F	F	139
50	2 small, fresh tomatoes	A B1 B2 C	10	1	L	L	L	---	---	---	L	L	122
114	1/4 head lettuce, shredded	A B1 B2 C	15	10	L	L	L	---	---	---	L	L	200
40	4 radishes	A B1 B2 C	5	7	T	T	L	---	---	---	L	F	129
n/a	1 tsp dried parsley flakes	---------					-n/a-						---------
56	4 tblspn mayonnaise	A B1^t B2 C	400	336	T	H	T	H	H	H	F	L	65
30	2 tblspn vinegar	---	2	T	T	---	L	---	---	---	L	L	30
n/a	1 tsp dry mustard	---------					-n/a-						---------
1009	Recipe totals (gms; cal; sod. & potsm.)		891	545									2534

METHOD

Wash potatoes. Do not peel. Boil potatoes until tender, then set aside to cool, after draining. Store in refrigerator until thoroughly chilled. Wash green onions, strip off outer skins and discard. Chop fine. Wash celery, pare off tough outer fibers, cut off root end and discard. Chop fine or in small pieces. Peel cucumber in small pieces. Cook eggs hard, peel off shells and place eggs in a plastic bag and chill in refrigerator. Wash tomatoes. Peel if skins are tough. Remove seeds then cut tomatoes in pieces. Wash lettuce and shred fine or cut small. Wash radishes and slice thin. Mix all of the above ingredients together except eggs and potatoes. Mix parsley flakes, mayonnaise, vinegar and mustard together. Slice eggs; remove skins from potatoes and dice or cut into bite-size pieces. Add potatoes to salad mixture then add the mayonnaise mixture, folding in carefully. Garnish top with sliced eggs. Cover bowl and refrigerate until needed. However, if salad is not to be used within 30 minutes, do not fold in mayonnaise until a few minutes before serving. Yield about 6 servings.

* There are 550 milligrams of cholesterol in 100 grams of whole egg, per U.S.D.A. Handbook No. 8, pg. 146, item 12. There are no figures on values for mayonnaise in the Handbook, so we used the average per tablespoon of cholesterol in the recipe in Chapter IV, Fats, Oils and Salad Dressings and arrived at a total of 614 milligrams of cholesterol in this recipe. Divide 614 by 6 servings equals 102 average milligrams of cholesterol per serving.

. . . .

MEATS and POULTRY

THE SANTA MARIA BARBECUE STORY

The Santa Maria Style Beef Barbecue is not only a tradition, but a way of life to the people of Santa Maria Valley — in the Central Coast area of California.

In the early days of the huge ranchos, the rancheros, along with their vaqueros, friends and neighbors, gathered frequently under the oaks of the serene little valley for Spanish-style barbecues. The present Santa Maria styled barbecue grew out of this tradition, and achieved its style when local residents began stringing their beef on skewers and cooking it over the hot oak coals of a red oak fire — some fifty years ago.

The only secret of the Santa Maria style barbecue is its simplicity. It consists of prime top sirloin, about three inches thick, aged for a minimum of 20 days, and cooked over a fire of coals from the Santa Maria Valley Red Oak wood. The sirloin usually comes in blocks weighing 10 to 12 pounds, sometimes slightly heavier; they are trimmed, cut in half, and strung on rods or skewers, whichever suits the individual doing the cooking, after they have been rolled thoroughly in a mixture of salt, pepper, and a little garlic salt, to give that superb flavor. The rods of meat are placed over the hot coals, where cooking time runs from 1-1/2 to 2-1/2 hours with frequent turning of the rods to insure evenness of cooking. Rotating the meat also allows the flavors of the seasoning to penetrate the meat during the cooking process. Length of time to cook the steaks depends upon personal preference as to degree of doneness.

When cooking is completed, steaks are removed from the rods and sliced into individual servings about 3/4" thick and placed into large meat pans for serving, with the juices of the meat adding that super delicious taste to the finished product.

The usual menu complimenting the Santa Maria Styled barbecues is made up of French bread toasted on a screen over the hot coals then dipped into melted butter which has been flavored with garlic salt, also Pinquinto beans, a special kind of bean raised only in the Santa Maria Valley and Lompoc Valley. They are cooked to perfection by members of every crew each of whom has a little different slant on what seasonings should be used, but the end result of every crew and its particular beans is the best eating ever. Also, most of our barbecues are served with a tossed green salad, and sometimes a macaroni or potato salad are added as well.

The barbecue tradition is closely associated with the Santa Maria Valley and on any given day one is apt to find a barbecue in progress. Nearly every backyard has a barbecue pit of some kind or another; some are stationary and others are portable. At large barbecue parties, it's not uncommon to see half a dozen "extra" portables lined up beside the host's.

A must to top of the Santa Maria Styled barbecues is our famous Salsa Sauce, which adds just that perfect touch to the meal fit for a king.

And for those who feel that no meal is really complete without dessert, we'd suggest something light such as an ice cream cup, a dish of sherbet, or a dish of jello.

At the present time, the Santa Maria Elks Lodge No. 1538 is doing its share to promote our famous Santa Maria Styled barbecuse for crowds of four to five thousand people. Large, portable pits, and the red oak wood have been hauled for hundreds of miles to insure their success by teams of excellent cooks who are members of the Elks' Lodge. And with that kind of dedication, the popularity and future of the Santa Maria Styled Barbecuse is assured.

The above information was provided by the Santa Maria Elks Lodge No. 1538, Benevolent and Protective Order of Elks, Santa Maria, California.   . . . .

THE BEANS

F=Fair; G=Good; H=High; L=Low; t or T = trace; n/a = no information available; dashes = zero or unmeasurable

GRAM WT.	FOOD	VITAMINS	CAL	(mg) SOD	PRO	FAT	CARB	CHOL (mg)*	FATTY ACIDS SAT	UNSAT	CALC	IRON	(mg) POTSM
153	AVERAGE PER SERVING		281	199				20					796
	Ingredients:												
681	3 cp Pinquito beans	B1 B2	2375	68	G	L	H	---	---	---	F	L	6695
	Note If Pinquito beans are not available, use other pink beans. Values for Pinquito beans were not available; we used those in U.S.D.A. Handbook No. 8, pg 71, item 162 "Pinto, calico and red Mexican beans, raw."												
6	3 cloves garlic, minced	A[t] B1 B2 C	9	T	L	L	F	---	---	---	L	F	33
220	2 medium chopped onions	A B1 B2 C	80	22	L	L	L	---	---	---	L	L	346
454	2 (8 oz cans tomato sauce	A B1 B2 C	177	1810**	L	L	L	---	---	---	L	L	1932
	** Sodium content in the tomato sauce is reflected in the salt used in the canning process.												
n/a	1/2 cp bacon drippings							-n/a-					
30	2 tblspn chili powder	A B1 B2 C	100	472	F	F	G	---	---	---	H	H	310
n/a	1/4 tsp powdered cumin seed or comin (optional)							-n/a-					
	Brown and add 1 of the following:												
339	3/4 lb ground beef, ham or sausage. We used lean beef	A B1 B2	608	---	G	F	---	H	H	L	H	F	---
111	1-1/2 green pepper—deseeded	A B1 B2 C	24	14	L	L	L	---	---	---	L	L	236
1841	Recipe totals (gms; cal; sod. & potsm.)		3373	2386									9552

METHOD

Wash and pick over beans, discarding any that are withered or bad. Beans should be covered with 1-1/2 times more water than beans to allow for absorption. For a quicker method, put washed beans in a large kettle and cover them with boiling water. Let stand until cool. Drain. Cover beans with boiling water again and add remaining ingredients. (Green peppers should be washed, deseeded and the white inside membrane removed, then cut into strips or pieces before adding to the beans). Cover kettle and bring water to a boil, then reduce heat and simmer gently 2 to 3 hours, or until beans are tender and sauce is thick and rich. Stir occasionally. As needed, add a little boiling water. When beans are done, they should be neither dry nor soupy. This recipe should serve 10 to 12 people.

* In 339 grams of boneless beef, there are 237 milligrams of cholesterol. Divide by 12 servings equals 20 average milligrams of cholesterol per serving, as calculated from U.S.D.A. Handbook No. 8, pg. 146, item 1a.

. . . .

F=Fair; G=Good; H=High; L=Low; t or T = trace; n/a = no information available; dashes = zero or unmeasurable

GRAM WT.	FOOD	VITAMINS	CAL	(mg) SOD	PRO	FAT	CARB	CHOL	FATTY ACIDS SAT	UNSAT	CALC	IRON	(mg) POTSM
217	AVERAGE PER CUP		48	389									439
	Ingredients:												
2382	3 Can (No. 1, 12 oz) peeled tomatoes, whole peeled tomatoes	A B1 B2 C	499	3098*	L	L	L	---	---	---	L	L	5067
	* Sodium content reflects the salt used in the canning process.												
99	1 can (3-1/2 oz) whole green chilies, chopped fine — deseeded	A B1 B2 C	25	---	L	L	L	---	---	---	L	L	---
6	3 cloves fresh garlic, mashed	A^t B1 B2 C	9	T	L	L	F	---	---	---	L	F	33
110	1 chopped onion (2-1/2" diameter)	A B1 B2 C	40	11	L	L	L	---	---	---	L	L	173
4	1 level tsp salt	---	---	1569	---	---	---	---	---	---	G	---	---
2	pinch black pepper	---											-------
n/a	dash Tobasco sauce	--n/a---------------------------------------											
2603	Recipe totals (gms; cal; sod. & potsm.)		573	4678									5273

METHOD

Pour tomatoes into a large mixing bowl and squeeze through the fingers, breaking them into pieces. DO NOT SIEVE — DO NOT USE A BLENDER — this makes the sauce too mushy. The secret of the sauce is the pieces of the tomatoes and the only way to obtain it is to use the fingers. Add chopped green chilies, mashed garlic and chopped onions. Add seasoning and stir to mix. Yield about 3 quarts (12 cups). Serve separately in small dishes or a large bowl.

Recipe courtesy of Far Western Tavern, Guadalupe, California.

. . . .

THE MEAT

A 10 to 12 pound "top block" of sirloin of beef will serve ten to twelve people. To season it, mix 8 tablespoons of black pepper and 2 tablespoons garlic salt. Pour this mixture into a shallow pan that is large enough to roll the meat. Spread the seasoning around until the pan is nearly covered then roll the meat into it on all sides. If the meat is cut in thirds, roll each piece into the seasoning.

If meat is to be barbecued whole, cook on the rack 3 to 4 hours, turning occasionally; if cut in thirds, barbecue on the rack 1-1/2 hours, turning as needed to cook evenly.

To serve, cut meat in 2 to 3" slices or hunks.

NOTE   Serve warm French bread, spread with garlic butter, which is an excellent accompaniment with the beans, meat and sauce.

. . . .

BOSTON BAKED BEANS

F=Fair; G=Good; H=High; L=Low; t or T = trace; n/a = no information available; dashes = zero or unmeasurable

GRAM WT.	FOOD	VITAMINS	CAL	(mg) SOD	PRO	FAT	CARB	CHOL (mg)*	FATTY ACIDS SAT	FATTY ACIDS UNSAT	CALC	IRON	(mg) POTSM
93	AVERAGE PER SERVING		330	179				20					763
	Ingredients:												
454	2 cp navy (pea) beans	B1 B2	1542	86	L	L	F	---	---	---	F	F	5425
110	1 medium-size onion	A B1 B2 C	40	11	L	L	L	---	---	---	L	L	173
114	1/4 lb salt pork	B1 B2	853	1320	L	H	---	H	H	L	T	T	48
n/a	1 tsp dry mustard		----------				-n/a-						----------
40	2 tblspn molasses	B1 B2	100	6	---	---	H	---	---	---	H	H	368
27	2 tblspn brown sugar	B1 B2	103	9	---	---	H	---	---	---	G	G	93
745	Recipe totals (gms; cal; sod. & postm.)		2638	1432									6107

METHOD

Wash beans in colander through several rinse waters then pick over and discard any that are discolored. Soak beans in water overnight. (About 4 cups of water to cover, because beans expand as they absorb the water). Drain. In a large kettle, cover beans with fresh water and add coarsely chopped onion. Bury the salt pork in the beans, rind-side-up. Cook slowly until beans mash under the tines of a fork—or until skins burst. DO NOT DRAIN.

In an 8 ounce cup, mix the dry mustard, molasses and brown sugar. Fill the cup with hot water, stirring until well mixed. Over a large mixing bowl, or over a pan large enough to catch the bean liquid, drain beans through a colander and set liquid aside.

Fill a bean pot or a deep casserole with the beans. Cut off a small strip from the salt pork, also cut off rind, then either cut in two or three pieces or leave whole, if desired, and bury in the beans. Set remainder of the pork aside. Pour the mustard mixture over beans and stir to blend. Pour enough of the drained liquid over beans to almost cover them. Save remainder of liquid to add to the beans during the long cooking process. Any liquid left over can be used to mix with any left-over beans with which to make soup. Cover beans and bake in a slow oven (300 F.) for 6 to 8 hours. Remove cover occasionally and add more liquid as needed. Beans should not be too dry. At the end of 4 hours, place the rest of the salt pork on a Pyrex pie plate, cut off the rind, score the top and put in the oven to brown until crisp to serve with the beans. During the last hour or hour and a half, remove cover from beans to brown the top. Yield 8 Servings.

BOSTON BAKED BEANS continued

*There are no figures for salt port in U.S.D.A. Handbook No. 8, giving cholesterol content. Therefore, we used the values for boneless pork (pg. 146, item 32b), 70 milligrams of cholesterol in 100 grams for our calculations. In 227 grams, there are 159 milligrams of cholesterol which, when divided by 8 servings, equals 20 average milligrams of cholesterol per serving. To reduce caloric and sodium content, omit pork, and use slab bacon, or pieces of smoked ham.

. . . .

Rich in protein, essential minerals and Vitamin B, meat is very important in the diet because it nourishes our bodies, repairing and regenerating them, keeping them fit. When meat is not included in the diet, protein-rich substitutes should be used, such as: beans, cheese, soybean flour, peanut butter, etc.

BEEF AND VEAL

Beef is identified as from the adult animal. Veal is from immature beef (usually calves less than a year old). Beef should be bright red in color, well marbled with creamy fat and the flesh should be firm and fine-grained. If bones are porous and red, beef is from a young animal; old beef bones are white and hard as flint. Veal has little surface fat and no marbling. The flesh is grayish-pink and fine-grained; the fat is white and firm, bones are porous and red.

LAMB

As the animal grows older, the meat darkens in color. In an old animal, the color is deep red. Young lamb fat is slightly pink, and quite soft; as it grows older, it becomes harder and whiter.

PORK

If good quality, pork is grayish-pink in young animals, and rose-pink in older. Flesh is marbled with firm-white fat.

Meat shrinks 1/3 to 1/2 in the cooking process. Allow 1/4 pound without bone and 1/2 pound of meat with bone and fat for each serving.

HOW TO COOK MEAT

To Broil: Cook by direct heat, such as under an electric unit or a gas flame, or on the barbecue over hot coals. On less expensive cuts of meat, use tenderizer — directions are on container.

To Braise: Brown meat in a small amount of fat in a heavy frying pan, or Dutch oven. (Pork chops are good this way because they should be cooked slowly for a long time, also pot roasts, Swiss steaks, brisket and less tender cuts.) After browning on both sides of meat, cover tightly and cook slowly in juices from meat, or add water (as in pork chops, pot roasts, etc.) or milk (as in country ribs of pork, smoked ham slices) or in vegetable juices (liquid saved from cooking vegetables).

Fricassee, and smothered steaks, are also cooked by braising.

To Pan Broil: Heavy iron frying pans make good utensils in which to pan broil. Allow pan to get very hot — test by dropping a bit of water on the pan — if it spatters and rolls around, disappearing at once, pan is hot enough. Use no fat. Steaks or meat should sizzle as soon as they're put in the pan. Before reducing heat, brown meat on both sides, then lower heat and pour off any accumulated fat. Cook until desired doneness is reached. To prevent meat from curling, slash through each side into the lean.

To Roast: A rack should be put into the roasting pan if meat is boneless, such as rolled beef, as an example. Prime rib of beef does not need a rack as it will stand on the ribs, fat side up.

Most meats should be roasted at 325 F., which prevents shrinking, and loss of juices. Hot temperatures dry the meat.

If gravy is to be made, add enough water to cover bottom of roaster when meat is half cooked; otherwise, do not use any water and do not baste the roast. If roast is very lean, put two strips of bacon over the top. Rib roasts usually have enough fat.

For roasting temperatures, see recipes for roast beef, pork, veal, and lamb in this chapter.

To Boil: Place meat in a Dutch oven, or similar utensil, cover with boiling water. Bring water to a boil, then reduce heat to simmer and cook until meat is tender.

To Stew: Cut meat into pieces, dredge in flour and brown on all sides in hot fat. Cover with boiling water and simmer, covered, until tender, adding additional water as necessary. Vegetables should be added about 30 minutes before serving time.

To Fry or Saute: Frying is usually done by using more fat than in sauteing. Breaded chops (such as: veal, smoked pork chops and chicken)   can be fried, also steaks (these are tastier barbecued or broiled, however), and lamb chops and hamburger.

Sauteing is done in less fat; meat is browned on both sides then liquid is added; meat is covered and simmered until tender. Pork chops are delicious this way. They can be floured or coated with dry bread or cracker crumbs then dipped in egg and milk which has been beaten together, then in the crumbs. Try a sprinkle of oregano over the chops 15 minutes prior to serving.

BACON

Broiled: Set oven indicator to "broil." Place bacon on the broiler rack 4" below the heat. Broil 2 minutes then turn. Cook 2 minutes longer or until desired crispness is reached.

Baked: Place strips of bacon on the wire rack over a shallow baking pan. (The broiler pan will do). Bake in a 400 F. oven about 12 minutes or to desired crispness. Do not turn.

Fried: Place strips of bacon in a cold frying pan over low heat. Cook slowly to desired crispness, turning frequently. Pour off fat as it accumulates. Drain bacon on 1 or 2 thicknesses of paper towels. Until serving time, keep bacon hot in a 160 F. oven.

Fried With Eggs: After bacon is cooked, break eggs separately in a sauce dish and, one by one, slip then gently into warm, NOT HOT, bacon grease in the pan and cook slowly until set. Or rinse frying pan under hot running water, after the bacon has been cooked. Dry with paper towels. Add two tablespoons margarine, melt at low heat, add eggs and proceed as above.

HAM

Broiled: Cut off rind from around the edges of sliced ham, and also trim the fat. To prevent meat from curling, slash through fat into lean about 1/4" on each side and the ends. Arrange ham on broiling rack and place 4" from the broiler (which should be preheated to 350 F.). Broil a 1/2" slice that weighs 3/4 to 1 pound, about 10 minutes on each side. Broil a 1" slice that weighs 1-1/2 to 2 pounds, about 15 minutes on each side.

Fried: Trim the rind and fat and slash each side and ends of the ham slice to prevent it from curling. Unless the meat is very lean, place it in a hot pan and cook without additional fat until browned on both sides. Reduce heat. Add a little water to prevent ham from cooking too hard. Pork should always be thoroughly cooked.

Fried With Cream Gravy: Remove ham to a warm platter and keep it warm in a preheated oven (150 to 170 F.). Add about 1-1/2 cups of milk to the ham fat left in the pan and heat to the boiling point, but do not boil. Reduce heat to low. Then stir in a mixture of cornstarch and water (1 tablespoon cornstarch to 1/4 cup water mixed until smooth), add slowly until gravy is the desired consistency. Cook about 5 minutes, pour over ham and serve.

510

SAUSAGE

Broiled: Arrange sausages on a cold broiler rack. Place 4 to 5" from broiler heat. Turn oven indicator to broil and cook 10 to 12 minutes, turning frequently, until all sides are browned. Pork should be cooked thoroughly.

Fried: Place sausages in a cold frying pan and cook slowly, turning frequently until browned. Fat should be poured off as it accumulates.

. . . .

MEATS AND POULTRY

F=Fair; G=Good; H=High; L=Low; t or T = trace; n/a = no information available; dashes = zero or unmeasurable

GRAM WT.	FOOD	VITAMINS	CAL	(mg) SOD	PRO	FAT	CARB	CHOL	FATTY ACIDS SAT	UNSAT	CALC	IRON	(mg) POTSM
15	Bacon, 2 strips (crisp)	B1 B2	90	153	H	H	L	n/a	F	F	L	L	35
100	Bacon, Canadian style	B1 B2	277	2555	H	H	L	n/a	F	F	L	L	432
100	Brains (all kinds: beef, calf, hog and sheep)	B1 B2 C	125	125	G	G	L	H	n/a	n/a	L	L	219
	BEEF												
4	Bouillon, 1 cube	---	5	960	L	T	T	---	---	---	---	---	4
	Canned:												
100	Beef-vegetable stew	A B1 B2 C	79	411	F	F	F	--------n/a-------			L	L	250
85	Corned beef, medium fat, 3 ozs.	A B1 B2	185	---	G	F	---	n/a	H	L	G	G	---
85	Corned beef hash, with potatoes 3 ozs.	B1 B2	155	459	F	F	F	n/a	H	L	L	F	170
	Dried or chipped beef:												
57	Cooked, creamed, 2 ozs.	B1 B2	115	408	G	L	F	n/a	H	T	G	L	87
100	Uncooked	(B1 B2)	203	4300	G	L	---	n/a	L	L	L	H	200
56	Frankfurters, all meat (8 per lb.)	B1 B2	170	---	F	G	L	--------n/a-------			L	L	---
	Hamburger:												
85	Lean, broiled, 3 ozs.	A B1 B2	185	41	G	F	---	H	H	L	L	F	474
85	Regular, broiled, 3 ozs.	A B1 B2	245	40	G	F	---	H	H	L	L	F	383
100	Heart, braised	A B1 B2 C	188	104	H	L	L	F	---	---	L	H	232
100	Kidney, braised	A B1 B2	252	253	H	F	L	H	n/a	n/a	L	H	324
128	Kidney (Berkshire) stew see recipe	A B1 B2 C	182	162	F	L	L	H	H	L	L	F	344
57	Liver, fried, 2 ozs.	A B1 B2 C	130	105	H	F	L	H	H	L	L	H	217
227	Potpie, commercial, 8 ozs.	A B1 B2	560	831	G	G	G	n/a	F	L	F	H	211
100	Potted beef	B1 B2	248	---	G	G	---	--------n/a-------			---	---	---
	Roasts:												
72	Pot roast, lean 2.5 ozs.	A B1 B2	140	43	G	L	---	H	H	L	L	F	266
85	Pot roast, lean/fat, 3 ozs.	A B1 B2	245	51	G	G	---	H	H	L	L	F	315
85	Rib roast, lean/fat, 3 ozs.	A B1 B2	375	51	G	G	---	H	H	L	F	F	315
78	Round, heel, lean, 2.7 ozs.	A[t] B1 B2	125	47	G	L	---	H	H	L	L	F	289
85	Round, heel, lean/fat, 3 ozs.	A B1 B2	165	51	G	L	---	H	H	L	L	F	315

MEATS AND POULTRY

F=Fair; G=Good; H=High; L=Low; t or T = trace; n/a = no information available; dashes = zero or unmeasurable

GRAM WT.	FOOD	VITAMINS	CAL	(mg) SOD	PRO	FAT	CARB	CHOL	FATTY ACIDS SAT	UNSAT	CALC	IRON	(mg) POTSM
	BEEF continued												
100	Rump roast, lean	A B1 B2	208	60	H	F	---	H	H	L	L	G	370
100	Chuck steak, rib, lean	A B1 B2	303	65	H	G	---	H	H	L	L	F	370
100	Flank steak	A B1 B2	196	60	H	L	---	H	H	L	L	F	370
100	Porterhouse, choice, broiled	A B1 B2	465	60	G	G	---	H	H	L	L	F	370
85	Rib steak, broiled	A B1 B2	386	51	H	H	---	H	H	L	L	F	315
68	Round steak, lean 2.4 ozs.	A B1 B2	130	41	H	L	---	H	H	L	L	F	252
	Salisbury steak, see Hamburger												
56	Sirloin, lean, broiled, 2 ozs.	A B1 B2	115	34	G	L	---	H	H	L	L	F	207
85	Spencer, lean/fat, broiled, 3 ozs.	A B1 B2	330	51	H	H	---	H	H	L	L	F	315
193	Swiss steak, see recipe	A B1 B2 C	341	452	G	F	---	H	H	L	L	L	669
85	T-bone, lean/fat, broiled, 3 ozs.	A B1 B2	330	51	G	G	---	H	H	L	L	F	315
100	Tenderloin (filet mignon) broiled	A B1 B2	207	60	G	L	---	H	H	L	L	F	370
273	Steak/Kidney Pie, see recipe	A B1 B2 C	378	279	G	L	L	H	H	L	L	F	740
100	Tongue, whole, canned or pickled	---	267	---	H	H	L	H	H	L	---	---	---
100	Tripe, commercial	B1 B2	100	72	H	L	---	H	H	L	F	F	9
	Cervelat. See Sausage, cold cuts and luncheon meats.												
	CHICKEN												
85	Broiled, 3 ozs.	A B1 B2	115	56	G	L	L	L	L	H	F	F	233
100	whole, fried (1-3/4 lbs.)	A B1 B2	250	---	H	F	L	L	L	H	L	F	381
100	breast, fried	A B1 B2	203	---	H	F	L	L	L	H	L	F	---
100	Drumstick, fried	A B1 B2	235	---	H	F	L	L	L	H	L	F	---
100	Thigh, fried	A B1 B2	237	---	H	F	L	L	L	H	L	F	---
100	Wing, fried	A B1 B2	268	---	H	F	L	L	L	H	L	F	---
100	Roasted	A B1 B2	290	---	H	H	---	L	L	H	L	F	---
100	Capons, uncooked	---	283	---	H	H	---	L	L	H	---	---	---
100	Chicken a la king, home recipe	A B1 B2 C	191	310	F	F	L	L	L	G	G	F	165
85	canned, boneless, 3 ozs.	A B1 B2 C	170	---	G	G	---	L	L	H	F	F	117
113	Chicken chop suey, 1/2 cp.	A B1 B2 C	136	467	F	L	L	L	L	H	L	F	192
100	Chicken chow mein, home recipe	A B1 B2 C	102	287	F	L	L	L	L	H	L	L	189

MEATS AND POULTRY

F=Fair; G=Good; H=High; L=Low; t or T = trace; n/a = no information available; dashes = zero or unmeasurable

GRAM WT.	FOOD	VITAMINS	CAL	(mg) SOD	PRO	FAT	CARB	CHOL	FATTY ACIDS SAT	UNSAT	CALC	IRON	(mg) POTSM
	CHICKEN, continued												
100	Liver, cooked, simmered	A B1 B2 C	115	61	H	L	L	H	H	L	L	G	151
227	Potpie, baked (4-1/4" dia.)	A B1 B2 C	535	581	F	F	G	F	F	F	L	F	336
100	DUCK, domesticated, flesh only, uncooked	B1 B2	165	74	G	F	---	L	L	H	L	F	285
100	GOOSE, roasted	B1 B2	233	134	G	L	---	L	L	H	L	L	---
100	GUINEA HEN, uncooked, total edible	---	156	---	F	L	---	L	L	H	---	---	---
	KIDNEY: See particular kind												
	Kidney and beefsteak pie-see												
	Beef, Steak and Kidney Pie.												
	LAMB												
137	Loin chop, thick, broiled 4.8ozs.	B1 B2	400	96	H	H	---	H	H	L	L	F	397
85	Leg roast, lean, 2.5 ozs.	B1 B2	130	60	G	L	---	L	L	L	L	F	247
64	Shoulder roast, lean only	B1 B2	130	45	G	L	---	L	L	L	L	F	186
100	Kidney, uncooked	A B1 B2 C	105	200	F	F	L	H	H	L	L	G	230
100	liver, broiled	A* B1 B2 C	261	85	H	F	L	H	H	T	L	H	331

* (Vitamin A values in all kinds of liver vary widely, ranging from 100 International Units (I.U.) to more than 100,000 I.U.'s per 100 grams. Per U.S.D.A. Handbook No. 8, pg. 37, item 1275).

GRAM WT.	FOOD	VITAMINS	CAL	(mg) SOD	PRO	FAT	CARB	CHOL	SAT	UNSAT	CALC	IRON	(mg) POTSM
43	MEAT BALLS												
	broiled 1-1/2 oz. lean/fat (1)	A B1 B2	123	21	G	G	L	H	H	L	G	F	n/a
100	in spaghetti with tomato sauce	A B1 B2 C	134	407	G	G	G	L	L	L	G	L	268
168	MEAT LOAF, no pork, see recipe	A B1 B2 C	177	219	F	F	L	F	F	L	L	F	549
252	Peppers, green, stuffed with hamburger - see recipe	A B1 B2 C	243	311	F	F	F	F	H	L	F	F	815
100	PHEASANT, uncooked, total edible	---	151	---	H	L	---	L	L	H	---	---	---
	PORK, cured												
15	Bacon, 2 strips, cooked crisp	B1 B2	90	153	H	H	L	L	L	H	L	L	35
100	Bacon, Canadian style	B1 B2	277	2555	H	H	L	L	L	H	L	L	432
57	Ham, boiled, 2 ozs. sliced	B1 B2	135	---	H	G	---	H	H	L	F	F	---
85	Ham, roasted, 3 ozs.	B1 B2	245	---	G	G	---	H	H	L	L	F	277
100	Ham croquettes	A B1 B2 C^t	251	342	G	G	F	H	H	L	F	F	83

MEATS AND POULTRY

F=Fair; G=Good; H=High; L=Low;   t or T = trace;   n/a = no information available;   dashes = zero or unmeasurable

GRAM WT.	FOOD	VITAMINS	CAL	(mg) SOD	PRO	FAT	CARB	CHOL	FATTY ACIDS SAT	UNSAT	CALC	IRON	(mg) POTSM
	PORK, fresh												
48	Chopped, lean, baked or broiled 1.7 ozs.	B1 B2	130	31	G	F	---	H	H	L	F	F	187
100	Kidney, raw	A B1 B2 C	106	115	F	F	L	H	H	L	L	G	230
100	Liver, fried	A B1 B2 C	241	111	H	F	L	H	H	L	L	H	395
100	Loin roast, medium fat	B1 B2	362	65	G	G	---	H	H	L	L	F	390
	Salt Cured												
100	Salt pork, uncooked	(B1 B2)	783	1212	L	H	---	H	H	L	T	L	42
	Miscellaneous												
454	Spareribs, uncooked	B1 B2	976	190	G	H	---	H	H	L	L	F	3519
100	QUAIL, uncooked, total edible	---	168	---	G	L	---	L	L	H	---	---	---
100	RABBIT, stewed (domesticated)	B1 B2	216	41	H	F	---	L	L	H	L	F	368
100	RACCOON, roasted	B1 B2	255	---	H	F	---	------n/a-------			---	---	---
100	REINDEER, lean only, uncooked	B1 B2	127	---	G	L	---	------n/a-------			---	H	---
	SAUSAGE and LUNCHEON MEAT												
13	Bologna, slice 3" x 1/8" dia.	B1 B2	40	169	F	G	T	H	H	L	L	L	30
10	Braunschweiger, slice 2" x 1/4"	A B1 B2 C	33	---	F	G	T	H	H	L	F	F	---
100	Brown n' serve Sausage, browned	---	422	---	G	H	L	H	H	L	---	---	---
100	Cervelat - dry	B1 B2	451	---	G	H	L	H	H	L	L	F	---
100	Cervelat - soft	B1 B2	307	---	G	G	L	H	H	L	L	F	---
100	Country style sausage	B1 B2	345	---	G	H	---	H	H	L	L	F	---
13	Deviled ham, canned, 1 tblspn	B1 B2	45	---	G	H	---	H	H	L	L	F	---
	Frankfurters (hot dogs), see frankfurters.												
100	Headcheese	B1 B2	268	---	F	G	L	H	H	L	L	F	---
100	Knockwurst	B1 B2	278	---	G	G	L	H	H	T	L	L	---
100	Liverwurst, smoked	A B1 B2	319	---	G	G	L	H	H	L	L	H	---
26	Pork sausage links, cooked, two 3" (16 links per lb. raw or bulk)	B1 B2	125	192	F	H	T	H	H	L	L	L	70
57	Pork, spiced or unspiced luncheon meat, canned, 2 ozs.	B1 B2	165	703	F	G	L	H	H	L	L	F	127
100	Meat loaf	B1 B2	200	---	F	F	L	H	H	L	L	F	---

MEATS AND POULTRY

F=Fair; G=Good; H=High; L=Low; t or T = trace; n/a = no information available; dashes = zero or unmeasurable

GRAM WT.	FOOD	VITAMINS	CAL	(mg) SOD	PRO	FAT	CARB	CHOL	FATTY ACIDS SAT	UNSAT	CALC	IRON	(mg) POTSM
	SAUSAGE and												
	LUNCHEON MEAT, continued												
100	potted (beef, chicken, turkey)												
	(also see Beef, potted)	B1 B2	248	---	G	G	---	L*	L*	H *	---	---	---
	* Chicken and turkey only												
100	Minced ham	B1 B2	228	---	F	F	F	H	H	L	L	F	---
100	Mortadella	B1 B2	315	---	F	G	L	H	H	L	L	F	---
100	Polish style sausage	B1 B2	304	---	F	G	L	H	H	L	L	F	---
28	Salami, dry type, 1 oz.	B1 B2	130	---	G	H	T	H	H	T	L	F	---
28	Salami, cooked, 1 oz.	B1 B2	90	---	G	G	T	H	H	T	L	L	---
100	Scrapple	B1 B2	215	---	L	F	F	------n/a------			L	F	---
100	Thuringer	B1 B2	307	---	G	G	L	------n/a------			L	F	---
16	Vienna, canned, 7 sausages per												
	5 oz. can, 1 sausage	B1 B2	40	---	F	F	L	---	---	---	L	F	---
100	Pigs feet, pickled	---	199	---	F	F	---	------n/a------			---	---	---
100	SQUAB (pigeon), raw, total edible	---	279	---	G	G	---	L	L	H	---	---	---
100	SUET(beef kidney fat), uncooked	---	854	---	L	H	---	H	H	L	---	---	---
	TURKEY (all classes)												
100	Total edible, cooked, roasted	A B1 B2	263	---	H	F	---	L	L	H	---	---	---
100	Light meat, roasted	A B1 B2	176	82	H	L	---	L	L	H	---	F	411
100	Dark meat, roasted	A B1 B2	203	99	H	L	---	L	L	H	---	F	398
100	Giblets, simmered (some fat)	B2	233	---	G	G	---	L	L	H	---	---	---
100	Canned, meat only	B1 B2	202	---	G	F	---	L	L	H	---	F	---
100	Potpie, commercial, frozen												
	unheated	A B1 B2 C	197	369	L	F	G	L	L	H	L	L	198
	VEAL												
85	Cutlet, medium-fat, cooked 3ozs.	B1 B2	185	68	G	L	L	L	L	H	L	G	425
85	Roast, 3 ozs.	B1 B2	230	68	G	L	---	H	H	L	L	F	425
100	VENISON, uncooked, lean	B1 B2	126	---	G	L	---	------n/a------			L	---	---
	VIENNA SAUSAGE, see Sausage												
	and Luncheon meat.												

FILET MIGNON

This cut of beef is the tenderloin from the underside of the loin which may be purchased ready to use at the market. Because it is very lean, it should be baked with strips of bacon or fat salt pork, or the entire surface should be brushed with soft margarine, salad oil or other fat, then dredged with flour and sprinkled lightly with garlic salt. Should any skin or ligament remain on the roast, this should be removed with a very sharp knife before roasting or broiling. Place meat in a small pan without water and bake slowly in at 300 F. oven. Or cut tenderloin into steaks about 1" each and broil. Brush generously with margarine and sprinkle lightly with garlic salt, if desired. Or 1" steaks can be placed on a rack in a shallow roasting pan, brushed with margarine or salad oil and baked at 450 F. for 20 minutes. Filets will be browned on the outside and rare on the inside. Serve with melted margarine, sauteed mushrooms, or any desired sauce. If mushrooms are served with the filet mignon, saute caps in margarine, cut stems in pieces and brown with the caps, stirring frequently. Add a small amount of water, then pour over filet mignon.

PRIME RIB ROAST OF BEEF

Season roast with a light sprinkle of garlic salt and place fat-side-up in an uncovered roasting pan. No rack is necessary because bones act as a rack. If a thermometer is used, insert in the meat at the fullest point making certain it doesn't touch the bone, or the fat. It is not necessary to add water but I found the roast stays juicier if water is added to cover the bottom of the pan; also, the gravy is better because the drippings from the roast don't dry out and brown on the bottom of the pan. As water evaporates, add more water. Roast at 325 F. until desired doneness is reached.

HAMBURGERS

Although ground meat originated in Hamburg, Germany, the idea of putting it on a bun and adding everything from sauerkraut to chopped onions was created in the United States of America.

To make hamburgers, select "extra lean" ground beef because it has less fat than regular and therefore less cholesterol and calories. "Super lean" ground beef is almost too dry and requires more fat in which to cook it. Be sure ground meat is fresh; meat will be bright red to pink, depending on how much fat has been added.

Divide a pound of hamburg into four, five or six mounds. If you want the large "quarter-pounder," divide meat in four mounds (113 grams each; 4 ozs.) or 5 (91 grams each; about 3-1/4 ozs. each) or 6 (76 grams each; about 2.7 ozs. each). With the hands, mold each mound into a ball, squeezing the meat together; this prevents the meat from separating into pieces and falling apart when it is cooking. After balls are formed, flatten them by pushing with the palm of the hand, or with a pancake turner. Heat a frying pan to the medium-hot stage; add about a tablespoon of margarine or oil and tip pan to distribute fat evenly. Then, with a pancake turner, lift flattened patties and place in the pan. Cooking time will depend on degree of doneness desired. Brown on both sides. Serve on warm, buttered buns, with "fixings" provided on the side, such as: chopped onions, sliced tomatoes, pickles, sauerkraut, etc.

To make cheeseburgers: prepare as above, add a slice of cheese to the meat when it has been turned over to brown the other side. The cheese will melt on top of the cooked side as the second side browns.

To make patty melts: Fry hamburgers (or broil) as usual. In another frying pan, or on a griddle, place two slices of bread for each hamburger. Butter only one side of the bread then flip over so that buttered side is next to pan (or griddle). Before turning on heat to brown the bread, place a slice of processed cheese on top of each slice of bread. Turn on the heat. Cheese will melt as the bread browns. Watch the bread closely, as it burns quickly. Turn off heat and lift bread out to warm plates. Place a patty of hamburg on one slice and cover it with another. If mustard is desired on patty melts, put it on unbuttered sides of bread before adding cheese.

SALISBURY STEAK

Mix hamburg with chopped onion and a sliver of mashed garlic. Press mixture flat to about 3/4". Cut in oblong pieces and either fry in a little browned margarine, or broil on a broiler pan about 4" from the heat until cooked to desired doneness. Turn once. Cook other side until steak is rare, medium or well-done.

HOT DOGS

Originally known as "red hots" in America at the Polo Grounds in New York, hot dogs (or frankfurters) have been in America since the 1880's or thereabouts.

Hot dogs are made in a "foot-long" size and a regular size; both are easy to prepare. They can be boiled in a covered saucepan; grilled in a frying pan in a small amount of fat; baked at 425 F. for 20 to 30 minutes, broiled, or barbecued. They're good with sauerkraut, macaroni and cheese, baked beans, cut up in split pea or cream of potato soup, and just as good wrapped in a piece of buttered bread and eaten plain. Perhaps they're best of all stuck on the end of a long stick or fork and held over an outdoor fire or barbecue, or eaten on a dry bun at a baseball game and swallowed down with a bottle of pop, or with popcorn at a circus or carnival. But they are particularly good in a warm hot dog bun, with mustard, onions, catsup or relish. As the hamburger is, they're as American as apple pie and one of our favorite foods in any age group.

. . . .

STUFFED BEEF HEART

F=Fair; G=Good; H=High; L=Low; t or T = trace; n/a = no information available; dashes = zero or unmeasurable

GRAM WT.	FOOD	VITAMINS	CAL	(mg) SOD	PRO	FAT	CARB	CHOL (mg)*	FATTY ACIDS SAT	UNSAT	CALC	IRON	(mg) POTSM
183	AVERAGE PER SERVING		266	305				227					341
	Ingredients;												
28	2 tblspn margarine	A D	200	279	L	H	L	---	L	H	L	---	6
17	2 green onions, chopped	A B1 B2 C	7	1	L	L	F	---	---	---	F	L	39
100	1 cp dry breadcrumbs	A^t B1 B2 C	390	736	F	L	G	---	---	---	G	F	152
n/a	dash pepper	---n/a---											
n/a	1/2 tsp oregano	---n/a---											
13	1/3 stalk celery, chopped	A B1 B2 C	2	17	T	T	T	---	---	---	F	L	44
30	2 tblspn 2% low-fat milk	A B1 B2 C	18	19	H	F	G	L	L	L	H	L	53
908	1 beef heart (2 lbs.)	A B1 B2 C	980	780	H	L	L	F	n/a	n/a	L	F	1752
1096	Recipe totals (gms; cal; sod. & potsm.)		1597	1832									2046

METHOD

Melt 2 tablespoons margarine in a frying pan; add chopped green onions and saute until tender. Cook slowly to prevent burning. Add breadcrumbs, pepper, oregano, celery and stir until well mixed. Add milk and blend into mixture. Remove from heat. Wash heart under cold water; trim muscle fibers, then fill with stuffing and tie heart firmly with string. Add 1-1/2 cups water to the frying pan, stir to take up any juices left, then put meat in a casserole, add the water, and bake, covered at 350 F. about 3-1/2 hours. Or simmer heart in a covered Dutch oven with the 1-1/2 cups water until tender (about 2 hours). Add water as needed. Thicken liquid left in the pan with the cornstarch mixed with a small amount of water until smooth. If there isn't enough liquid to make gravy, add some water. Bring to a boil, then add the cornstarch and water slowly until gravy is the desired consistency.

*   There are 150 milligrams of cholesterol in 100 grams of beef heart; in 908 grams, there are 1362; divided by 6 servings equals 227 average milligrams of cholesterol per serving. In 2 tablespoons (30 grams) of milk, there are only .9 or approximately 1 milligram of cholesterol. Calculations are based on U.S.D.A. Handbook No. 8, pg. 146, items 18 and 29 respectively.

. . . .

BRISKET OF BEEF

F=Fair; G=Good; H=High; L=Low; t or T = trace; n/a = no information available; dashes = zero or unmeasurable

GRAM WT.	FOOD	VITAMINS	CAL	(mg) SOD	PRO	FAT	CARB	CHOL (mg)*	FATTY ACIDS SAT	UNSAT	CALC	IRON	(mg) POTSM
363	AVERAGE PER SERVING		408	152				159					1360
	Ingredients:												
1362	3 lb beef brisket	A B1 B2	1812	885	G	G	---	H	H	L	L	F	4830
n/a	dash celery salt						---n/a---						---
2	1 clove fresh garlic	A^ت B1 B2 C	3	T	L	L	F	---	---	---	L	F	11
816	6 boiled potatoes	A^t B1 B2 C	630	24	L	T	F	---	---	---	L	L	3321
2180	Recipe totals (gms; cal; sod. & potsm.)		2445	909									8162

METHOD

In a deep kettle, cover meat with boiling water, add celery salt and slivered garlic and simmer 3 hours or until meat is tender. Turn brisket once during the cooking period. Remove meat from pot and place in a shallow pan for baking, skin-side-up. Score several times across the top. Peel skins from potatoes and place them in the kettle in which the brisket was cooked. Let stand a few minutes to soak up some of the meat juices, then place them around the meat. Brown meat and potatoes in a hot oven (450 F.) about 20 minutes. Make gravy with remaining liquid in the kettle by adding a thickening of cornstarch mixed with water to the boiling juices and stir it in gradually until gravy is desired consistency.

Egg noodles are also good with beef brisket, but do not brown with the roast. Boil until tender, then drain.

* There are 70 milligrams of cholesterol in 100 grams of boneless beef. In 1362 grams, there are 953 milligrams as calculated from U.S.D.A. Handbook No. 8, pg. 146, item 1b. Divide 953 milligrams by 6 servings equals 159 milligrams of cholesterol per serving.

. . . .

CORNED BEEF BOILED DINNER

F=Fair; G=Good; H=High; L=Low; t or T = trace; n/a = no information available; dashes = zero or unmeasurable

GRAM WT.	FOOD	VITAMINS	CAL	(mg) SOD	PRO	FAT	CARB	CHOL	FATTY ACIDS SAT	UNSAT	CALC	IRON	(mg) POTSM
580	AVERAGE PER SERVING		533	151				(mg)* 80					1716
	Ingredients:												
454	1 lb corned beef	A B1 B2	1329	295	G	G	---	H	H	L	L	F	1612
544	4 potatoes, raw, peeled	A^t B1 B2 C	420	16	L	T	F	---	---	---	L	L	2214
440	4 medium onions	A B1 B2 C	160	44	L	L	L	---	---	---	L	L	691
200	4 large carrots	A B1 B2 C	80	96	L	L	L	---	---	---	F	L	682
454	1 lb head cabbage (green)	A B1 B2 C	98	82	L	L	L	---	---	---	L	L	1058
227	2 white turnips, diced	A B1 B2 C	44	72	L	L	L	---	---	---	L	L	608
2319	Recipe totals (gms; cal; sod. & potsm.)		2131	605									6865

METHOD

With a pair of scissors, cut open the plastic case the corned beef was packed in and slide the meat out being careful not to spill the juices from the sack. Place meat and juices in a Dutch oven or deep kettle. Fill sack with water and pour over beef then cover corned beef with enough additional water to cover. Bring water to a boil, reduce heat to simmer and cook meat, covered, from 2 to 2-1/2 hours until fork tender. While meat is cooking, prepare vegetables; keep fresh in cold water until needed. Cabbage can be quartered just before cooking time, about 40 minutes before meat is done.

A Word Of Caution   Most corned-beef is now packed with spices, such as bayleaf and pickling spices. When bayleaf is whole, it can be removed easily, but when it is in pieces, such as in the plastic bags of corned-beef, it is almost impossible to discard.   And it MUST be discarded, because it can choke you.

At this point, you are probably wondering why bayleaf is used at all, but it does give a very pleasant and special flavor to meat, stews, soups, and other dishes which would otherwise be quite bland.

If you purchase corned beef that is packaged in plastic bags, with loose spices, cut open top of the bag and remove meat to the sink. Fill the plastic bag with water and strain into a bowl or into the kettle in which the corned beef will be cooked. Be sure all spices are out. Then rinse meat under cold water and pick out spices, running the fingers under loose flaps of meat and under the fat and sides. When spices have been removed, place meat in the cooking kettle and proceed as stated above. Add your own spices— 2 whole bayleaves, and 2 tablespoons of pickling spice tied securely in a small cheesecloth bag. Remove bag before adding the vegetables about 40 minutes before corned beef is done.

*   There are 70 milligrams of cholesterol in 100 grams of boneless beef; in 454 grams, there are 318 milligrams as calculated from U.S.D.A. Handbook No. 8, pg. 146, item 1b. Divide 318 by 4 servings equals 80 average milligrams of cholesterol per serving.

CANNED CORNED BEEF HASH

F=Fair; G=Good; H=High; L=Low; t or T = trace; n/a = no information available;   dashes = zero or unmeasurable

GRAM WT.	FOOD	VITAMINS	CAL	(mg) SOD	PRO	FAT	CARB	CHOL (mg)*	FATTY ACIDS SAT	FATTY ACIDS UNSAT	CALC	IRON	(mg) POTSM
123	AVERAGE PER SERVING		256	682				80					232
	Ingredients:												
454	1 lb can corned beef hash with potatoes	B1 B2	821	2449	L	L	L	H	H	L	L	F	908
28	2 tblspn margarine	A D	200	279	L	H	L	---	L	H	L	---	6
8	1 tblspn minced onion	A B1 B2 C	4	T	L	L	F	---	--	---	F	L	13
490	Recipe totals (gms; cal; sod. & potsm.)		1025	2728									927

METHOD

Open each end of can and push corned-beef through by pressing on lid, forcing lid through with the meat to the bottom. Meat stays in cylindrical shape and is easy to cut. Divide into 4 equal circles with a sharp knife. Melt margarine in a heavy frying pan and place the four circles of corned beef in it. Cook on medium heat until one side is browned. Turn carefully with a pancake turner then sprinkle minced onion over each. When brown on both sides, serve.

Poached eggs may be served on top, but cholesterol will increase to 355 milligrams per serving.

*   There are 70 milligrams of cholesterol in 100 grams of boneless beef. In 454 grams, there are 318 milligrams, divided by 4 servings equals 80 average milligrams of cholesterol per serving, as calculated from U.S.D.A. Handbook No. 8, pg. 146, item 1b.

. . . .

LIVER AND BACON

F=Fair; G=Good; H=High; L=Low; t or T = trace; n/a = no information available; dashes = zero or unmeasurable

GRAM WT.	FOOD	VITAMINS	CAL	(mg) SOD	PRO	FAT	CARB	CHOL	FATTY ACIDS SAT	UNSAT	CALC	IRON	(mg) POTSM
161	AVERAGE PER SERVING		448	413				(mg)* 341					377
	Ingredients:												
227	1/2 lb sliced bacon *	B1 B2	1508	1542	H	H	L	n/a	F	F	L	L	295
	* Instead of bacon, chop 2 medium onions. Brown in melted margarine until clear and starting to brown but not burned. Remove from pan and keep hot in 180 F. oven. Cook liver as below; smother with onions and serve.												
681	1-1/2 lb beef liver	A B1 B2 C	953	926	G	L	L	H	H	L	L	F	1914
58	1/2 cp flour	B1 B2	210	1	F	L	G	---	---	---	L	F	55
n/a	dash black pepper	---n/a---											
966	Recipe totals (gms; cal; sod. & potsm.)		2671	2469									2264

METHOD

Start bacon in a cool frying pan on low heat. Turn often. Pour off excess fat. When bacon is cooked to the desired consistency, drain on paper towels. Keep hot in a 180 F. oven. Dredge liver in flour and pepper and brown on both sides in bacon fat, at reduced heat, about 5 to 8 minutes. Do not overcook as this makes liver tough. Yield   6 serving.

*   There are 300 milligrams of cholesterol in 100 grams of liver; in 681 grams, there are 2043 as calculated from U.S.D.A. Handbook No. 8, pg. 146, item 23. Divide 2043 milligrams by 6 servings equals 341 milligrams of cholesterol per serving. (No information available on cholesterol in bacon at this writing).

. . . .

523

STEAK AND KIDNEY PIE

F=Fair; G=Good; H=High; L=Low; t or T = trace; n/a = no information available; dashes = zero or unmeasurable

GRAM WT.	FOOD	VITAMINS	CAL	(mg) SOD	PRO	FAT	CARB	CHOL (mg)*	FATTY ACIDS SAT	UNSAT	CALC	IRON	(mg) POTSM
273	AVERAGE PER SERVING		603	279				221					703
	Ingredients:												
681	1-1/2 lb top round steak	A B1 B2	1347	443	H	L	---	H	H	H	L	F	2415
227	1/2 lb beef kidney	A B1 B2 C	295	399	G	F	L	H	H	L	L	H	504
115	1 cp flour	B1 B2	420	2	F	L	G	---	---	---	L	F	109
n/a	1 tsp garlic salt	---------	---	---	---	---	---	n/a	---	---	---	---	---
n/a	dash pepper	---------	---	---	---	---	---	n/a	---	---	---	---	---
55	1 small onion, chopped	A B1 B2 C	20	6	L	L	L	---	---	---	L	L	86
4	1 tblspn minced parsley	A B1[t] B2 C	T	2	T	T	T	---	---	---	H	H	29
227	1/2 lb fresh mushrooms, sliced	A[t] B1 B2 C	62	33	L	T	L	---	---	---	L	L	940
309	1 recipe single crust pastry	B1 B2	1405	788	F	H	G	---	F	H	G	F	137
18	2 tblspn cornstarch	---		68	---	L	T	H	---	---	---	---	---	---
1636	Recipe totals (gms; cal; sod. & potsm.)		3617	1673									4220

METHOD

Trim fat from round steak. Separate fat from lean in kidney until only the lean remains. Discard fat. Cut steak and kidney into 1/2" cubes. Put flour, garlic salt, pepper and meat cubes into a plastic sack and shake until meat is well coated. Shake off excess. Brown meat in a heavy skillet in a small amount of margarine or other fat until all sides are browned. Add enough water to cover meat, then add onion, parsley and mushrooms. Cover and simmer about an hour until meat is fork tender. Add water as needed to keep meat covered. When meat is nearly tender, preheat oven to 450 F. Make a single crust of pastry (see recipe in pie section of Cakes, Cookies and Pies in Chapter 1). Mix cornstarch with 1/4 cup of water until smooth. Increase heat under meat until it bubbles a little then add cornstarch mixture slowly, stirring continuously until gravy thickens. Reduce heat to low. Roll out pastry crust. Pour meat and gravy into a greased casserole. Cover with single crust pastry. Flute the edges and prick the middle of the pastry with a fork to allow the steam to escape — two or three places will do — then bake at 450 F. about 15 minutes until crust is golden brown. Yield 6 servings.

To make plain meat pie: use 2 pounds rump beef cut up, instead of the steak and kidney. Add 2 carrots cut up instead of the mushrooms, and 1/2 cup frozen fresh peas. Do not add the peas to the meat until 10 minutes before making gravy.

*   There are 70 milligrams of cholesterol in 100 grams of boneless beef; in 681 grams, there are 477 milligrams. In 100 grams of raw kidney, there are 375 milligrams of cholesterol; in 227 grams, there are 851 milligrams as calculated from U.S.D.A. Handbook No. 8, pg. 146, items 1b and 20 respectively. Divide 1328 milligrams of cholesterol by 6 servings equals 221 average milligrams of cholesterol per serving.

. . . .

STUFFED GREEN PEPPERS

F=Fair; G=Good; H=High; L=Low; t or T = trace; n/a = no information available; dashes = zero or unmeasurable

GRAM WT.	FOOD	VITAMINS	CAL	(mg) SOD	PRO	FAT	CARB	CHOL (mg)*	FATTY ACIDS SAT	UNSAT	CALC	IRON	(mg) POTSM
252	AVERAGE PER SERVING		243	311				80					815
	Ingredients:												
454	1 lb lean ground beef	A B1 B2	812	295	G	F	---	H	H	L	L	F	1612
296	4 medium green peppers	A B1 B2 C	60	40	L	L	L	---	---	---	L	L	630
32	4 green onions	A^t B1 B2 C	12	2	L	L	F	---	---	---	F	L	50
227	1 (8 oz) can tomato sauce	A B1 B2 C	89	906	L	L	L	---	---	---	L	L	967
1009	Recipe totals (gms; cal; sod. & potsm.)		973	1243									3259

METHOD

Divide meat into four equal parts. Wash green peppers, cut off the tops, remove seeds and pithy membrane and discard. Clean green onions, cut off root ends and 1/3 of the tops. Slice one into each green pepper. Stuff mound of meat into peppers and smooth the top. Place peppers into a greased casserole standing up. Pour tomato sauce over the top, cover and bake at 325 F. 1 hour and 45 minutes. If baking dish has no lid, cover with foil. Yield 4 servings.

*   There are 70 milligrams of cholesterol in 100 grams of boneless beef; in 454 grams, there are 318 milligrams of cholesterol. Divide by 4 servings equals 80 average milligrams of cholesterol per serving.

. . . .

MEAT LOAF WITHOUT PORK

F=Fair; G=Good; H=High; L=Low; t or T = trace; n/a = no information available; dashes = zero or unmeasurable

GRAM WT.	FOOD	VITAMINS	CAL	(mg) SOD	PRO	FAT	CARB	CHOL (mg)*	FATTY ACIDS SAT	UNSAT	CALC	IRON	(mg) POTSM
168	AVERAGE PER SERVING		177	226				99					549
	Ingredients:												
454	1 lb lean ground beef	A B1 B2	812	295	G	F	---	H	H	L	L	F	1612
50	1 egg	A B1 B2	75	61	F	F	L	H	H	L	F	F	65
110	1 medium onion	A B1 B2 C	40	11	L	L	L	---	---	---	L	L	173
74	1 green pepper	A B1 B2 C	15	10	L	L	L	---	---	---	L	L	158
50	1 medium carrot, sliced thin	A B1 B2 C	20	24	L	T	L	---	---	---	F	L	171
40	1 stalk celery, diced	A B1 B2 C	5	50	T	T	T	---	---	---	F	L	136
2	1 clove garlic, crushed	A^t B1 B2 C	3	T	L	L	F	---	---	---	L	F	11
n/a	1/8 tsp thyme & savory	--------	-----	-----	-----	-----	--n/a--						-----
n/a	1/4 tsp oregano	--------	-----	-----	-----	-----	--n/a--						-----
227	1 (8 oz) can tomato sauce	A B1 B2 C	89	906	L	L	L	---	---	---	L	L	967
1007	Recipe totals (gms; cal; sod. & potsm.)		1059	1357									3293

METHOD

Mix ground beef and egg together. Add diced onion and green pepper, diced carrot and celery, mashed garlic, savory and thyme. Blend thoroughly, either with a fork or the hands. Mold into a bread loaf pan, greased, about a 1 pound size, then pour tomato sauce over all, distributing it evenly until no meat shows through the sauce. Set pan on a cookie sheet in a cold oven and bake at 325 F. for 1-1/2 hours.

*   There are 318 milligrams of cholesterol in 454 grams of boneless beef and 275 milligrams of cholesterol in 50 grams of whole egg, for a total of 593 milligrams as calculated from U.S.D.A. Handbook No. 8, pg. 146, items 1b and 12 respectively. Divide 593 milligrams by 6 servings equals 99 average milligrams of cholesterol per serving.

. . . .

PIZZABURGER LOAF

F=Fair; G=Good; H=High; L=Low; t or T = trace; n/a = no information available;   dashes = zero or unmeasurable

GRAM WT.	FOOD	VITAMINS	CAL	(mg) SOD	PRO	FAT	CARB	CHOL (mg)*	FATTY ACIDS SAT	UNSAT	CALC	IRON	(mg) POTSM
229	AVERAGE PER SERVING		337	186				148					709
	Ingredients:												
	SAUCE												
76	1/2 cp onion, chopped	A B1 B2 C	25	7	L	L	L	---	---	---	L	L	119
168	1 (6 oz) can tomato paste	A B1 B2 C	138	66	L	L	L	---	---	---	L	F	1492
236	1 cp water	---0--------------------------------------											
	LOAF												
681	1-1/2 lb ground beef	A B1 B2	1218	443	G	F	---	H	H	L	L	F	2418
50	1 egg	A B1 B2	75	61	F	F	L	H	H	L	F	F	65
50	1 cp soft breadcrumbs	A^t B1 B2 C^t	140	254	L	L	G	---	---	---	F	F	76
n/a	1 tsp oregano	---n/a-------------------------------------											
n/a	1/4 tsp basil	---n/a-------------------------------------											
114	1/4 lb mozzarella cheese	n/a	424	284	L	G	L	H	H	L	F	L	84
1375	Recipe totals (gms; cal; sod. & potsm.)		2020	1115									4254

METHOD

Combine ingredients for the sauce in a pan and stir to blend then simmer 20 minutes, stirring occasionally, Mix remaining ingredients together, except the cheese, and form into a loaf to fit a 10" x 6" x 2" pan. Bake at 375 F. about 50 minutes, then pour the sauce over the loaf and arrange slices of mozzarella cheese on top. Bake 15 minutes longer until cheese melts. Yield   6 servings.

*   In 681 grams of boneless beef, there are 477 milligrams of cholesterol. In 50 grams of whole egg, there are 275 milligrams of cholesterol. There were no figures available for mozzarella cheese, therefore, we used figures for cream cheese which is similar. In 114 grams, there are 136 milligrams of cholesterol as calculated from U.S.D.A. Handbook No. 8, pg. 146, items 1b, 12 and 7 respectively. Divide 888 milligrams by 6 servings equals 148 average milligrams of cholesterol per serving.

. . . .

POT ROAST OF BEEF

F=Fair; G=Good; H=High; L=Low; t or T = trace; n/a = no information available; dashes = zero or unmeasurable

GRAM WT.	FOOD	VITAMINS	CAL	(mg) SOD	PRO	FAT	CARB	CHOL (mg)*	FATTY ACIDS SAT	UNSAT	CALC	IRON	(mg) POTSM
238	AVERAGE PER SERVING		570	200				159					817
	Ingredients:												
1816	4 lb lean rump pot roast	A B1 B2	4148	1180	G	L	---	H	H	L	L	F	6447
28	1/4 cp flour	B1 B2	105	1	F	L	G	---	---	---	L	F	27
42	3 tblspn margarine	A D	300	417	L	H	L	---	L	H·	L	---	10
17	2 green onions, chopped	A^{t}B1 B2 C	7	1	L	L	F	---	---	---	F	L	39
2	1 small clove fresh garlic	A^t B1 B2 C	3	T	L	L	F	---	---	---	L	F	11
1905	Recipe totals (gms; cal; sod. & potsm.)		4563	1599									6534

METHOD

Dredge both sides of the meat with flour. Melt margarine in a Dutch oven or similar type of kettle, allowing fat to brown a little before placing the meat in it. Brown pot roast on both sides. Add water to half cover the meat, add chopped onions and mashed garlic, cover and simmer 3 to 4 hours or until tender. About 30 minutes before serving, add carrots, small whole potatoes and pearl onions, if desired. Cover again and cook until vegetables are tender. Remove vegetables with a slotted spoon to a hot platter; keep warm in a 180 F. oven. Bring liquid in kettle to a boil, reduce heat and thicken with a mixture of cornstarch and water, stirring until gravy is the right consistency. Yield about 8 servings.

*   There are 1271 milligrams of cholesterol in 1816 grams beef with bone, as calculated from U.S.D.A. Handbook No. 8, pg. 146, item 1a. Divide 1271 milligrams by 8 servings equals 159 average milligrams of cholesterol per serving.

. . . .

FLO'S AMERICAN SPAGHETTI SAUCE

F=Fair; G=Good; H=High; L=Low; t or T = trace; n/a = no information available; dashes = zero or unmeasurable

GRAM WT.	FOOD	VITAMINS	CAL	(mg) SOD	PRO	FAT	CARB	CHOL (mg)*	FATTY ACIDS SAT	UNSAT	CALC	IRON	(mg) POTSM
319	AVERAGE PER SERVING		570	448				72					783
	Ingredients:												
56	1/2 stick margarine	A D	400	558	L	H	L	---	L	H	L	---	13
56	1/2 cp flour	B1 B2	210	1	F	L	G	---	---	---	L	F	53
681	1-1/2 lb rump beef	A B1 B2	1416	409	H	F	---	H	H	L	L	G	2418
330	3 medium onions	A B1 B2 C	120	33	L	L	L	---	---	---	L	L	518
12	6 large cloves fresh garlic	A B1 B2 C	18	2	L	L	F	---	---	---	L	F	63
482	1 (16 oz) can whole tomatoes in puree sauce	A B1 B2 C	100	626	L	L	L	---	---	---	L	L	1046
61	2 (2 oz) can button mushrooms	A^t B1 B2 C	10	244	L	T	L	---	---	---	L	L	120
18	2 tblspn cornstarch	---	68	---	L	T	H				---	---	---
59	1/4 cp water	---------------------------------------0---------------------------------											
227	1 (8 oz) can tomato sauce	A B1 B2 C	89	905	L	L	L	---	---	---	L	L	967
454	16 oz uncooked spaghetti	B1 B2	1674	9	L	L	F	---	---	---	L	L	894
113	1-1/4 cp grated Parmesan cheese	A B1 B2	451	794	G	G	L	H	H	L	H	F	168
2549	Recipe totals (gms; cal; sod. & potsm.)		4556	3581									6260

METHOD

Melt margarine in a Dutch oven until lightly browned. Put flour in a plastic sack; cut the meat in pieces and add to the flour. Shake to dredge. Shake off excess, add meat to margarine to brown on all sides. Then carefully add enough hot water to nearly cover the meat. (It'll cook down). Chop onions and add to meat. Cover and simmer about 3 hours. Check often, stirring occasionally, adding water if needed. Strain tomatoes through a ricer or sieve and add with the garlic (mashed) to the sauce. Let cook about 30 minutes. Add mushrooms. Mix cornstarch and water together until smooth. Set aside. Put water for spaghetti on to boil in a deep kettle. Add tomato sauce to the meat sauce. Stir. Add spaghetti to boiling water, stir with a fork, reduce heat to medium to prevent water from boiling over, and cook spaghetti until it is tender. Reduce heat to keep spaghetti hot while sauce is thickened.

Stir cornstarch and water mixture, add to boiling spaghetti sauce and stir and cook until sauce is the right consistency (thick gravy). If more cornstarch is needed for desired consistency, mix another tablespoon or two with water and add slowly. Serve over drained spaghetti. Provide Parmesan cheese at the table for individual use.

Note   To drain spaghetti, use a colander, run a little hot water over it to prevent spaghetti from sticking together, then return colander to the kettle and let it drain. Serve with tongs.

* In 681 grams of boneless beef, there are 477 milligrams of cholesterol and in cheese 96 milligrams in 113 grams, as calculated from U.S.D.A. Handbook No. 8, pg. 146, items 1b and 8 respectively. Divide 573 milligrams by 8 servings equals 72 average milligrams of cholesterol per serving.

. . . .

DELUXE SPANISH RICE

F=Fair; G=Good; H=High; L=Low; t or T = trace; n/a = no information available; dashes = zero or unmeasurable

GRAM WT.	FOOD	VITAMINS	CAL	(mg) SOD	PRO	FAT	CARB	CHOL (mg)*	FATTY ACIDS SAT	FATTY ACIDS UNSAT	CALC	IRON	(mg) POTSM
226	AVERAGE PER SERVING		264	435				56					661
	Ingredients:												
28	1 tblspn margarine	A D	200	279	L	H	L	---	L	H	L	---	6
454	1 lb lean ground beef	A B1 B2	812	295	G	F	---	H	H	L	L	F	1612
33	4 green onions with some tops	A B1 B2 C	13	2	L	L	F	---	---	---	F	L	76
74	1 green pepper, deseeded	A B1 B2 C	15	10	L	L	L	---	---	---	L	L	158
2	1 clove garlic, mashed	A^t B1 B2 C	3	T	L	L	F	---	---	---	L	F	11
40	1 stalk celery, diced	A B1 B2 C	5	50	T	T	T	---	---	---	F	L	136
454	2 (8 oz) cans tomato sauce	A B1 B2 C	178	1812	L	L	L	---	---	---	L	L	1934
248	1-1/2 cp instant rice	B1 B2	270	3	L	T	F	---	---	---	L	F	---
23	1/4 cp grated Parmesan cheese	A B1 B2	90	159	G	G	L	H	H	L	H	F	34
1356	Recipe totals (gms; cal; sod. & potsm.)		1586	2610									3967

METHOD

In a large frying pan, melt the margarine, add the ground beef and brown lightly, breaking it up with a fork until it's crumbly. Reduce heat to low, add chopped onions, chopped green pepper, mashed garlic, diced celery and one of the cans of tomato sauce, plus 1/2 can water. Stir to blend, then cover. Simmer about 30 minutes, stirring occasionally.

Prepare rice according to box directions, or boil 1-1/2 cups water, add 1-1/2 cups instand rice, cover and let stand 5 minutes. (Rice can be prepared while sauce is cooking).

As soon as meat sauce is cooked, stir in the rice and the second can to tomato sauce, but no more water. Simmer 15 minutes longer, covered, or pour mixture into an uncovered, greased casserole and bake at 350 F. about 30 minutes. Just before serving, sprinkle grated Parmesan cheese over the top. Yield 6 servings.

*   There are 318 milligrams of cholesterol in 454 grams of boneless beef and 20 milligrams of cholesterol in 85 grams of cheese as calculated from U.S.D.A. Handbook No. 8, pg. 146, items 1b and 8 (other cheeses) respectively. Divide 338 milligrams by 6 servings equals 56 average milligrams of cholesterol per serving.

. . . .

BERKSHIRE KIDNEY STEW

F=Fair; G=Good; H=High; L=Low; t or T = trace; n/a = no information available; dashes = zero or unmeasurable

GRAM WT.	FOOD	VITAMINS	CAL	(mg) SOD	PRO	FAT	CARB	(mg)* CHOL	FATTY ACIDS SAT	UNSAT	CALC	IRON	(mg) POTSM
128	AVERAGE PER SERVING		182	162				340					250
	Ingredients:												
454	1 lb beef kidney	A B1 B2 C	590	798	G	F	L	H	H	L	L	H	1021
58	1/2 cp flour	B1 B2	210	1	F	L	G	---	---	---	L	F	55
n/a	1 bayleaf						-n/a-						
110	1 medium onion	A B1 B2 C	40	11	L	L	L	---	---	---	L	L	173
18	2 tblspn cornstarch	---	68	---	L	T	H	---	---	---	---	---	---
640	Recipe totals (gms; cal; sod. & potsm.)		908	810									1249

METHOD

Wash kidney under cold water. Remove any membrane. Separate lean meat from fat. Discard fat. Cut meat in pieces, dredge in flour, shake off excess, and brown in a little margarine in a heavy skillet. Cover with water, add bayleaf and chopped onion and bring to a boil. Reduce heat and simmer, covered, until meat is fork tender. As soon as meat is tender, remove bayleaf carefully, to avoid breaking any pieces off in the stew. (Hard pieces of bayleaf can get caught in the throat and cause choking). Mix cornstarch with 1/4 cup of water and stir until smooth. Add to simmering stew and stir until it thickens. Cook about 10 minutes longer. Serve over rice, noodles, or dry toast. Yield 5 servings.

* There are 375 milligrams of cholesterol in 100 grams of uncooked kidney; in 454 grams there are 1702 milligrams as calculated from U.S.D.A. Handbook No. 8, pg. 146, item 20. Divide 1702 milligrams by 5 servings equals 340 average milligrams of cholesterol per serving.

. . . .

LEFTOVER BEEF STEW

F=Fair; G=Good; H=High; L=Low; t or T = trace; n/a = no information available; dashes = zero or unmeasurable

GRAM WT.	FOOD	VITAMINS	CAL	(mg) SOD	PRO	FAT	CARB	CHOL	FATTY ACIDS SAT	FATTY ACIDS UNSAT	CALC	IRON	(mg) POTSM
								(mg)*					
174	AVERAGE PER SERVING		206	54				53					542
	Ingredients:												
454	1 lb leftover rump roast of beef	A B1 B2	944	272	H	F	---	H	H	L	L	G	1680
110	1 medium onion, diced	A B1 B2 C	40	11	L	L	L	---	---	---	L	L	173
50	1 large carrot, sliced thin	A B1 B2 C	20	24	L	L	L	---	---	---	F	L	171
136	1 medium potato, raw, diced	A^t B1 B2 C	105	4	L	T	F	---	---	---	L	L	554
76	1/2 cp green beans	A B1 B2 C	21	5	L	L	L	---	---	---	F	L	185
200	1 medium tomato, peeled	A B1 B2 C	40	6	L	L	L	---	---	---	L	L	488
18	2 tblspn cornstarch	---	68	T	L	T	H	---	---	---	---	---	---
1044	Recipe totals (gms;cal;sod. & potsm.)		1238	322									3251

METHOD

Cut meat into bite-size cubes, place in a Dutch oven or other pan with a tight lid, cover meat with water and add chopped onion. Bring to a boil then reduce heat and simmer for an hour. Add sliced carrot, diced potato, cut-up green beans and sliced tomato. Stir in any leftover gravy and cook about 30 minutes longer, until carrots are tender. Mix cornstarch with 1/4 cup water and blend until smooth. Add gradually to simmering stew, stirring until gravy is medium thick. Serve plain, or over egg noodles which have been cooked in boiling water until tender, then drained; or with dumplings. Bisquick dumplings are light, fluffy and easy to make. Follow directions on the box, or use the following recipe on the next page.

*   In 454 grams of boneless beef, there are 318 milligrams of cholesterol as calculated from U.S.D.A. Handbook No. 8, pg. 146, item 1b. Divide 318 by 6 servings equals 53 average milligrams of cholesterol per serving.

. . . .

DUMPLINGS

F=Fair; G=Good; H=High; L=Low; t or T = trace; n/a = no information available; dashes = zero or unmeasurable

GRAM WT.	FOOD	VITAMINS	CAL	(mg) SOD	PRO	FAT	CARB	CHOL	FATTY ACIDS SAT	UNSAT	CALC	IRON	(mg) POTSM
35	AVERAGE PER DUMPLING		87	118									42
	Ingredients:												
230	2 cp presifted flour	B1 B2	840	4	F	L	G	---	---	---	L	F	219
4	1-1/4 tsp baking powder	---		4	394	L	T	H	---	---	---	H	---	---
2	1/2 tsp salt	---	---	785	---	---	---	---	---	---	G	---	---
14	1 tblspn margarine	A D	100	139	L	H	T	---	L	H	L	---	3
164	2/3 cp 2% low-fat milk	A B1 B2 C	97	100	H	F	G	L	L	L	H	L	287
414	Recipe totals (gms; cal; sod. & potsm.)		1041	1422									509

METHOD

Sift flour, baking powder and salt together then cut in margarine with a pastry blender or knife, until mixture is like meal. Add enough milk to make a soft dough (not all of the milk may be needed). Drop dough by tablespoon into simmering stew. Cover pan with a tight lid and cook 20 to 25 minutes. Stew should just simmer because it has been thickened and could scorch. You may prefer to thicken stew after dumplings have been made. In this case, after dumplings have been cooked, remove them with a slotted spoon to a hot serving dish. Keep warm in a 180 F. oven until stew is thickened, then pour stew over the dumplings in the serving dish.   Yield 12 dumplings.

Note Cholesterol in the milk is minimal.

. . . .

BAKED BEEF STEW

F=Fair; G=Good; H=High; L=Low; t or T = trace; n/a = no information available;   dashes = zero or unmeasurable

GRAM WT.	FOOD	VITAMINS	CAL	(mg) SOD	PRO	FAT	CARB	CHOL (mg)*	FATTY ACIDS SAT	UNSAT	CALC	IRON	(mg) POTSM
348	AVERAGE PER SERVING		348	403				80					939
	Ingredients:												
454	1 lb round steak	B1 B2	894	295	G	F	---	H	H	L	L	F	1612
110	1 medium onion, chopped	A B1 B2 C	40	11	L	L	L	---	---	---	L	L	173
100	2 carrots, sliced	A B1 B2 C	40	48	L	T	L	---	---	---	F	L	341
40	1 large stalk celery	A B1 B2 C	5	50	T	T	T	---	---	---	F	L	136
114	1/2 cp sherry wine	B1 B2	96	**6	T	---	L	---	---	---	L	L	102
301	1 (10-3/4 oz) can tomato soup	A B1 B2 C	108	1192	L	L	F	---	---	---	F	L	283
272	2 raw potatoes, diced	A B1 B2 C	210	8	L	T	F	---	---	---	L	L	1107
1391	Recipe totals (gms; cal; sod. & potsm.)		1393	1610									3754

METHOD

Cut meat into bite-size pieces, add chopped onion, sliced carrots, celery (cut coarse), the wine, tomato soup, and peeled and diced raw potatoes and mix thoroughly, then pour into a greased casserole. Cover and bake at 250 F. for 5 hours. Yield 4 servings.

*   There are 70 milligrams of cholesterol in 100 grams of boneless beef, according to U.S.D.A. Handbook No. 8, pg. 146, item 1b; in 454 grams, there are 318 milligrams of cholesterol. Divide by 4 servings equals 80 average milligrams of cholesterol per serving.

NOTE   ** High sodium reflects salt used in the canning process. For those on low-sodium diets, substitute 1 pound of raw tomatoes, peeled, which equals 14 milligrams of sodium. Average per serving would equal 108 instead of 403 milligrams of sodium and recipe total for sodium would be 432 instead of 1610.

. . . .

F=Fair; G=Good; H=High; L=Low; t or T = trace; n/a = no information available; dashes = zero or unmeasurable

GRAM WT.	FOOD	VITAMINS	CAL	(mg) SOD	PRO	FAT	CARB	CHOL (mg)*	FATTY ACIDS SAT	UNSAT	CALC	IRON	(mg) POTSM
255	AVERAGE PER SERVING		310	507				55					678
	Ingredients:												
138	1 cp yellow cornmeal	A B1 B2 C	500	1	L	L	G	---	---	---	L	F	166
492	1 cp 2% low-fat milk	A B1 B2 C	290	300	H	F	G	L	L	L	H	L	861
567	1-1/4 lb ground beef	A B1 B2	1015	369	G	F	---	H	H	L	F	F	2013
110	1 medium onion, chopped	A B1 B2 C	40	11	L	L	L	---	---	---	L	L	173
2	1 clove garlic, mashed	A^t B1 B2 C	3	T	L	L	F	---	---	---	L	F	11
10	2 tsp chili powder	A B1 B2 C	34	158	F	F	G	---	---	---	H	H	100
454	2 (8 oz) cans tomato sauce	A B1 B2 C	178	1810 **	L	L	L	---	---	---	L	L	1934
113	1 cp whole kernel corn	A B1 B2 C	75	267	L	L	F	---	---	---	L	L	110
126	1 small can chopped ripe olives	A B1 B2	232	945	L	F	L	---	T	F	G	F	34
28	1 oz grated cheddar cheese	A B1 B2	113	198	G	G	L	H	H	L	H	F	23
	** High sodium is reflected in the salt used in the canning process.												
2040	Recipe totals (gms; cal; sod. & potsm.)		2480	4059									5425

METHOD

Soak cornmeal in the milk at least 4 hours. Brown the humburger with onion, add crushed garlic and chili powder, add tomato sauce, corn, and chopped olives. Add the cornmeal and milk mixture and mix all together thoroughly. Pour mixture into a greased casserole and sprinkle grated cheese on top. Cover and bake at 350 F. approximately 1 hour and 20 minutes. If a crusty brown top is desired, bake uncovered, otherwise cover casserole the entire baking period. Yield 6 to 8 servings.

*   In 492 grams of fluid skim milk, there are 15 milligrams of cholesterol; in 567 grams of boneless beef, there are 397 milligrams and in 28 grams of cheddar cheese there are 28 milligrams as calculated from U.S.D.A. Handbook No. 8. Divide 440 milligrams of cholesterol by 8 servings equals 55 average milligrams of cholesterol per serving.

. . . .

SWISS STEAK

F=Fair; G=Good; H=High; L=Low; t or T = trace; n/a = no information available; dashes = zero or unmeasurable

GRAM WT.	FOOD	VITAMINS	CAL	(mg) SOD	PRO	FAT	CARB	CHOL (mg)*	FATTY ACIDS SAT	FATTY ACIDS UNSAT	CALC	IRON	(mg) POTSM
193	AVERAGE PER SERVING		342	452				80					652
	Ingredients:												
681	1-1/2 lb round steak	A B1 B2	1347	443	G	F	---	H	H	H	L	F	2415
56	1/2 cp flour	B1 B2	210	1	F	L	G	---	---	---	L	F	53
42	3 tblspn margarine	A D	300	418	L	H	L	---	L	H	L	---	10
25	3 green onions, chopped	A^t B1 B2 C	10	2	L	L	F	---	---	---	F	L	58
37	1/2 green pepper, chopped	A B1 B2 C	8	**5	L	L	L	---	---	---	L	L	79
227	1 (8oz) can tomato sauce	A B1 B2 C	89	906	L	L	L	---	---	---	L	L	967
90	6 tblspn tomato catsup	A B1 B2 C	90	**936	T	T	F	---	---	---	L	L	327
	** High sodium is reflected in the salt used in the canning, preserving process.												
1158	Recipe totals (gms; cal; sod. & potsm.)		2054	2711									3909

METHOD

Trim off fat from meat then cut in 6 equal pieces. Pound flour into both sides of the meat with the edge of a heavy butterplate or saucer, as the sharp edge acts as a tenderizer, cutting the flour into the steak. Melt margarine in a large frying pan, add meat and brown on both sides; add onions, green pepper, tomato sauce and 1 cup hot water. On each piece of meat spread 1 tablespoon catsup (tomato chili sauce may be used instead). Cover tightly and simmer for 2 hours, checking often to add water as needed. Do not pour water on the meat or catsup will run off. When serving, spoon some of the unthickened sauce over the meat. Yield   6 servings.

*   In 681 grams of beef, there are 477 milligrams of cholesterol; divided by 6 servings equals 80 milligrams of cholesterol per average serving, as calcualted from U.S.D.A. Handbook No. 8, Pg. 146, item 1b.

. . . .

ROAST BEEF WITH YORKSHIRE PUDDING

F=Fair; G=Good; H=High; L=Low; t or T = trace; n/a = no information available;   dashes = zero or unmeasurable

GRAM WT.	FOOD	VITAMINS	CAL	(mg) SOD	PRO	FAT	CARB	CHOL (mg)*	FATTY ACIDS SAT	FATTY ACIDS UNSAT	CALC	IRON	(mg) POTSM
285	AVERAGE PER SERVING		776	280				229					890
	Ingredients:												
1816	4 lb rolled roast of beef	A B1 B2	5496	1180	H	F	---	H	H	L	L	G	6447
n/a	garlic salt	-------------------					-n/a-						
	YORKSHIRE PUDDING												
115	1 cp sifted flour	B1 B2	420	2	F	L	G	---	---	---	L	F	109
2	1/2 tspn salt	---	---	785	---	---	---	---	---	---	G	---	---
246	1 cp 2% low-fat milk	A B1 B2 C	145	150	H	F	G	L	L	L	H	L	431
100	2 eggs	A B1 B2	150	122	F	F	L	H	H	L	F	F	129
n/a	drippings from the roast	-------------------					-n/a-						
2279	Recipe totals (gms; cal; sod. & potsm.)		6211	2239									7116

METHOD FOR MEAT

Wipe roast with damp cloth. Sprinkle garlic salt lightly all over the meat. Place fat side up on roasting pan on a rack. If meat has little fat, place strips of bacon over the top. This will baste the meat and no other basting will be necessary. Insert meat thermometer into thickest part of the roast. Set oven at 325 F; for rare, cook 2-1/4 to 2-3/4 hours or 140 F; medium 2-3/4 to 3-1/4 hours or 160 F; well done 3-1/4 to 3-1/2 or 170 F. on the thermometer. When roast is removed from the oven, if not cut at once, it will continue to cook 30 to 45 minutes. Allow 1/2 pound per person.

METHOD FOR YORKSHIRE PUDDING

Set oven to 400 F. Mix presifted flour with salt. Combine milk and eggs, add to flour and salt and beat with a rotary egg beater until smooth. Pour hot meat drippings into a shallow pan (about 8" x 10") to a depth of 1". Pour in mixture quickly and bake at 400 F. 15 minutes. Cut in squares and put in pan around the roast. Make gravy with remaining beef drippings. Yield   about 8 servings.

*   In 1816 grams of boneless beef, there are 1271 milligrams of cholesterol; in 246 grams of fluid skim milk, there are 7 milligrams of cholesterol, and in 100 grams of whole egg, there are 550 milligrams of cholesterol for a total measureable in this recipe of 1828. Divide by 8 servings equals 229 average milligrams of cholesterol per serving.

. . . .

BEEF CHOP SUEY

F=Fair; G=Good; H=High; L=Low; t or T = trace; n/a = no information available; dashes = zero or unmeasurable

GRAM WT.	FOOD	VITAMINS	CAL	(mg) SOD	PRO	FAT	CARB	CHOL (mg)*	FATTY ACIDS SAT	FATTY ACIDS UNSAT	CALC	IRON	(mg) POTSM
492	AVERAGE PER SERVING		510	726				80					732
	Ingredients:												
681	1-1/2 lb lean rump beef, diced	A B1 B2	1076	443	H	F	---	H	H	L	L	G	2418
55	1/4 cp oil	---	486	---	---	H	---	---	L	H	---	---	---
28	2 tblspn soy sauce	B1 B2	19	2051	L	L	L	---	---	---	F	F	102
200	5 large stalks celery, diced	A B1 B2 C	25	250	L	L	L	---	---	---	F	L	682
220	2 medium onions, chopped	A B1 B2 C	80	22	L	L	L	---	---	---	L	L	345
21	1 tblspn molasses	---	60	14	---	---	H	---	---	---	F	G	193
480	2 cp beef bouillon	---	62	1565	L	T	T	---	---	---	---	---	259
250	2 cp canned bean sprouts	A B1 B2 C	70	10	L	L	L	---	---	---	L	L	390
27	3 tblspn cornstarch	--	102	T	L	T	H	---	---	---	---	---	---
n/a	dash black pepper	---------------					=n/a				---------------		
990	6 cp hot, cooked, instant rice	B1 B2	1080	---	L	L	F	---	---	---	L	F	---
2952	Recipe totals (gms; cal; sod. & potsm.)		3060	4355									4389

NOTE   Do not add salt to the rice in order to reduce sodium content per serving.

METHOD

Fry beef in oil over high heat for 3 minutes, stirring constantly. Stir in soy sauce. Remove meat and keep hot in 180 F. oven. To remaining oil in frying pan, add celery, onions, molasses and bouillon. Bring to a boil; cook 10 minutes, stirring frequently. Add canned, drained bean sprouts and cook 3 minutes. Add fried beef. Mix cornstarch and pepper with 1/4 cup water until smooth then add to chop suey, stirring while it thickens. Serve with hot rice. Yield 6 servings. Additional soy sauce may be served at the table.

*   There are 477 milligrams of cholesterol in 681 grams of boneless beef; divided by 6 servings equals 80 milligrams average per serving, as calculated from U.S.D.A. Handbook No. 8, pg. 146, item 1b.

. . . .

BEEF–TORTILLA CASSEROLE

F=Fair; G=Good; H=High; L=Low; t or T = trace; n/a = no information available; dashes = zero or unmeasurable

GRAM WT.	FOOD	VITAMINS	CAL	(mg) SOD	PRO	FAT	CARB	CHOL (mg)*	FATTY ACIDS SAT	UNSAT	CALC	IRON	(mg) POTSM
262	AVERAGE PER SERVING		442	483				57					402
	Ingredients:												
28	2 tblspn margarine	A D	200	279	L	H	L	---	L	H	L	---	6
151	1 cp chopped onion	A B1 B2 C	50	14	L	L	L	---	---	---	L	L	237
454	1 lb lean ground beef	A B1 B2	812	295	G	F	---	H	H	L	L	F	1612
14	2 tblspn flour	B1 B2	52	T	F	L	G	---	---	---	L	F	13
45	3 tblspn chili powder	A B1 B2 C	150	708	F	F	G	---	---	---	H	H	450
236	1 cp water	------------------------------- 0 -------------------------------											
368	1-1/2 cp tomato soup	A B1 B2 C	135	1455	L	L	F	---	---	---	F	L	346
360	1-1/2 cp light cream	A B1 B2 C	758	155	L	F	L	n/a	H	L	H	L	439
302	12 corn tortillas	B1 B2	834	2	L	L	F	---	---	---	F	F	n/a
136	1-1/2 cp grated cheddar cheese	A B1 B2	542	953	G	G	L	H	H	L	H	F	112
2094	Recipe totals (gms; cal; sod. & potsm.)		3533	3861									3215

METHOD

Melt the margarine in a frying pan, add half the onions and saute until soft. Add meat and cook until brown, breaking it up with a fork until crumbly. Add the flour and chili powder and cook 5 minutes, then add the water. Cover and simmer until thick, stirring frequently. Mix soup, cream, remaining onion. Cut tortillas in strips and place in greased, shallow casserole. Alternate with meat, soup mixture, some grated cheese, ending with grated cheese on top. Bake at 325 F. until bubbly and browned. Yield   about 8 servings.

*   In 454 grams of boneless beef, there are 318 milligrams of cholesterol; in 136 grams of cheddar cheese, there are 136 milligrams of cholesterol, for a total of 454 measureable milligrams of cholesterol in this recipe. Divide by 8 servings equals 57 average milligrams of cholesterol per serving.

. . . .

QUICK CHILI-CON-CARNE

F=Fair; G=Good; H=High; L=Low; t or T = trace; n/a = no information available; dashes = zero or unmeasurable

GRAM WT.	FOOD	VITAMINS	CAL	(mg) SOD	PRO	FAT	CARB	CHOL (mg)*	FATTY ACIDS SAT	UNSAT	CALC	IRON	(mg) POTSM
274	AVERAGE PER SERVING		366	364				80					946
	Ingredients:												
55	1/4 cp olive oil	---	486	---	---	H	---	---	L	L	---	---	---
908	2 lb lean ground beef	A B1 B2	1624	590	G	F	---	H	H	L	L	F	3223
227	1-1/2 cp chopped onions	A B1 B2 C	75	21	L	L	L	---	---	---	L	L	356
4	2 cloves fresh garlic, mashed	A^t B1 B2 C	6	T	L	L	F	---	---	---	L	F	21
30	2 tblspn chili powder	A B1 B2 C	100	472	F	F	G	---	---	---	H	H	300
n/a	1 tblspn paprika	-------------------------------n/a-------------------------------											
n/a	2 tsp oregano	-------------------------------n/a-------------------------------											
454	2 (8oz) cans tomato sauce	A B1 B2 C	177	1810	L	L	L	---	---	---	L	L	1934
510	2 cp red kidney beans	A B1 B2	460	16	L	L	F	---	---	---	L	F	1734
2188	Recipe totals (gms; cal; sod. & potsm.)		2928	2909									7568

METHOD

Heat the olive oil, add the meat, breaking it up with a fork until it's crumbly, and brown. Add onions and garlic and cook about 5 minutes, stirring continuously. Stir in chili powder, paprika, and oregano. Add tomato sauce; cover and cook about 45 minutes, then add the cooked kidney beans and cook 15 minutes longer. Yield about 8 servings.

*   In 908 grams of beef, there are 636 milligrams of cholesterol as calculated from U.S.D.A. Handbook No. 8, pg. 146, item 1b (boneless beef). Divide 636 by 8 servings equals 80 average milligrams of cholesterol per serving.

. . . .

ROAST VEAL

There is less fat on veal, so it is necessary to put strips of bacon or salt pork over the roast or to brush it with soft margarine. It is also a rather bland meat and a sprinkle of oregano, or curry powder, or garlic salt will enhance its flavor.

Bread stuffing is delicious with veal, one with sage or oregano, for the reason stated above. Have the butcher cut a pocket in the roast, and this may be stuffed with a good bread, celery, onion and either oregano or sage mixture like the recipe for turkey dressing. Day-old, firm crust bread makes better stuffing because it doesn't pack into a doughy mass, unless, of course, you've used too much moisture. Water or stock should always be added a little at at time. Feel the mixture with the hands— it shouldn't feel wet. Since you will not be making as much dressing as for turkey, less herbs will also be used. A good rule of thumb is to start with half a teaspoon, Mix them in, smell it —if the sage or oregano is not fairly strong, add a little more — but it's better to have a dressing that's under-seasoned than over-seasoned, and this takes experimentation. Keep a record of what you used and how much. It's so easy to forget; file this information with the recipe for roast veal—it'll come in handy next time.

Roast veal at 325 F. Allow about 1/3 pound per serving. Arrange roast on a rack. Sprinkle with oregano then add bacon strips or salt pork across the top. Do not baste or add water. If a thermometer is used, place it in the fleshiest part of the meat, not touching any bone. Roast until 180 F. is reached.

Number of Minutes Per Pound: A center cut leg roast should be cooked 25 minutes per pound; a loin roast — 30 to 35 minutes per pound; a rack of 4 to 6 ribs — 30 to 35 minutes per pound; shoulder with bone — 25 minutes per pound; boneless shoulder (rolled)— 25 to 40 minutes per pound.

MORE ON USE OF HERBS FOR VEAL

Herbs, such as marjoram, oregano, lovage, celery and thyme, give that extra flavor that perks up the blandness of veal. Start with a little. It's easier to correct the amount than starting with too much which can make the flavor bitter and ruin the meat. And, if you have never used herbs, please start with one or two until you know more about them. For instance; marjoram, in its wild stage, is oregano. But marjoram is known as a sweet herb and oregano as a bitter one. They are seldom used together in the same recipe. However, marjoram is usually teamed up with thyme. Onions and garlic are used together in many recipes. Though related, they compliment each other.

Herbs accent the flavor of foods. Once you've tried them, you'll probably never go back to cooking without them. But remember that too many herbs in the same recipe can kill the flavor of the food. Their use should be subtle, not overpowering. Used improperly, then can turn food into a bitter, unappetizing meal.

But don't let this discourage you — go in and try them! The difference in taste will be a pleasant surprise for you and your family.

. . . .

VEAL BIRDS

F=Fair; G=Good; H=High; L=Low; t or T = trace; n/a = no information available; dashes = zero or unmeasurable

GRAM WT.	FOOD	VITAMINS	CAL	(mg) SOD	PRO	FAT	CARB	CHOL (mg)*	FATTY ACIDS SAT	UNSAT	CALC	IRON	(mg) POTSM
181	AVERAGE PER SERVING		370	250				136					514
	Ingredients:												
908	2 lb veal steak cut 1/4" thick	B1 B2	1570	820	H	L	L	H	L	L	L	F	2906
75	1 cp bread stuffing	see below	138	258	--------------- see			below			----------------		114
58	1/2 cp flour	B1 B2	210	1	F	L	G	---	---	---	L	F	55
42	3 tblspn margarine	A D	300	418	L	H	L	---	L	G	L	---	10
	Water												
1083	Recipe totals (gms; cal; sod. & potsm.)		2218	1497									3085
	BREAD STUFFING												
48	2 slices firm white bread	A[t] B1 B2 C[t]	130	244	L	L	G	---	---	---	F	F	41
10	1/4 stalk celery, cut fine	A B1 B2 C	1	13	T	T	T	---	---	---	F	L	34
17	2 green onions, cut fine	A[t] B1 B2 C	7	1	L	L	F	---	---	---	F	L	39
n/a	1/2 tsp oregano	-------------------						-n/a-					-------------------
75	total for dressing recipe (gms; cal; sod. & potsm.)		138	258									114

METHOD

Make the dressing first. In a medium mixing bowl, pull the bread into very small pieces, add the finely chopped celery and onions, then stir in the oregano and mix ingredients thoroughly. Add about 2 tablespoons of water, one at a time, mixing with the hands — dressing should not feel wet, just moist enough to hold together lightly.

Trim any skin or fat from edge around the meat then cut in 6 pieces, about 3" x 4" in size. Place a mound of stuffing on each piece, fold or roll veal over the stuffing and tie across and lengthwise with double strands of white thread. (This keeps the stuffing in). Roll meat in flour and brown in margarine in a frying pan. Add enough water to cover the bottom of the pan, cover, and simmer until tender. Check occasionally to add more water as necessary. When meat is tender, remove to a hot platter and keep warm in a 180 F. oven. If gravy is desired, add milk to the pan juices, and thicken with a mixture of about 2 tablespoons cornstarch to 1/4 cup of water (stirred with a spoon until smooth before adding to the milk). Allow milk to heat to the boiling point, but do not boil. Stir in cornstarch mixture slowly, and continue to stir until gravy is the desired consistency. Season at the table individually.

*   In 908 grams of veal there are 817 milligrams of cholesterol as calculated from U.S.D.A. Handbook No. 8, pg. 146, item 35b. Divide 817 milligrams by 6 servings equals 136 average milligrams of cholesterol per serving.

. . . .

VEAL CUTLETS WITH CREAM GRAVY

F=Fair; G=Good; H=High; L=Low; t or T = trace; n/a = no information available; dashes = zero or unmeasurable

GRAM WT.	FOOD	VITAMINS	CAL	(mg) SOD	PRO	FAT	CARB	CHOL	FATTY ACIDS SAT	UNSAT	CALC	IRON	(mg) POTSM
								(mg)*					
234	AVERAGE PER SERVING		361	374				229					604
	Ingredients:												
908	2 lb veal cutlets	B1 B2	1146	820	G	L	---	H	L	L	L	F	2900
100	2 eggs, beaten	A B1 B2	150	122	F	F	L	H	H	L	F	F	129
100	1 cp dry bread crumbs	A^t B1 B2 C	390	736	F	L	G	---	---	---	G	F	152
42	3 tblspn margarine	A D	300	418	L	H	L	---	L	H	L	---	10
9	1 tblspn cornstarch	---	34	---	L	T	H	---	---	---	---	---	---
246	1 cp 2%, low-fat milk	A B1 B2 C	145	150	H	F	G	L	L	L	H	L	431
n/a	dash black pepper						--------n/a--------						
n/a	1/2 tsp marjoram or oregano						--------n/a--------						
1405	Recipe totals (gms; cal; sod. & potsm.)		2165	2246									3622

METHOD

Divide meat into 6 pieces. Trim edges of tough muscle, then dip cutlets into the beaten egg first, then into bread-crumbs. Brown both sides of the meat in margarine which has been melted in a heavy frying pan, add 1/2 cup of water and cover and cook slowly until meat is tender. Mix cornstarch with 2 or 3 tablespoons of water and set aside. When meat is tender, remove it to a hot platter and keep warm in a 180 F. oven. Add milk to pan drippings, bring almost to a boil, reduce heat, then stir in cornstarch and water mixture a little at a time until gravy thickens. Add pepper and marjoram and blend. Remove from heat, pour in a bowl and serve with the meat. Yield 6 servings.

* In 908 grams of veal, there are 817 milligrams of cholesterol, in 100 grams of whole egg, there are 550 milligrams of cholesterol; in 246 grams of fluid skim milk, there are 7 milligrams of cholesterol for a total of 1374 milligrams as calculated from U.S.D.A. Handbook No. 8, pg 146, item 35b. Divide 1374 milligrams by 6 servings equals 229 average milligrams of cholesterol per serving.

VEAL SCALLOPINI

F=Fair; G=Good; H=High; L=Low; t or T = trace; n/a = no information available; dashes = zero or unmeasurable

GRAM WT.	FOOD	VITAMINS	CAL	(mg) SOD	PRO	FAT	CARB	CHOL (mg)*	FATTY ACIDS SAT	FATTY ACIDS UNSAT	CALC	IRON	(mg) POTSM
216	AVERAGE PER SERVING		278	274				77					445
	Ingredients:												
681	1-1/2 lb thin veal round	B1 B2	947	615	G	L	---	H	L	L	L	F	2179
56	4 tblspn cooking oil	---	500	---	---	H	---	---	L	H	---	---	---
2	1 clove fresh garlic	A^t B1 B2 C	3	T	L	L	F	---	---	---	L	F	11
n/a	dash black pepper						-n/a-						
56	1/2 cp flour	B1B2	210	1	F	L	G	---		---	L	F	53
n/a	1 tsp rosemary						-n/a-						
117	1/2 cp sherry wine	B1 B2	97	6	T	---	L	---	---	---	L	---	88
117	1/2 cp chablis wine	B1 B2	97	6	T	---	L	---	---	---	L	---	88
244	1 cp mushrooms, canned, sliced	A^t B1 B2 C	40	976	L	T	L	---	---	---	L	L	481
454	2 cp frozen peas	A B1 B2 C	331	585	L	L	L	---	---	---	L	F	680
1727	Recipe totals (gms; cal; sod. & potsm.)		2225	2189									3580

METHOD

Have the butcher slice the veal thin (about 1/4" or thinner, if possible). Cut meat into 2" strips. Heat the oil, add mashed garlic and cook until clear but not brown. Remove with a slotted spoon and discard. In a plastic sack, mix pepper with the flour. Shake to blend. Put in the meat and shake until well coated with the flour mixture. Shake off excess. Brown in hot oil. Add 1 cup hot water (or meat or chicken stock if available). Cover pan tightly and simmer about 1-1/2 hours, adding more water as needed. When meat is fork tender, remove it to a hot platter and keep warm in a 180 F. oven.

To the simmering juices in the pan, add rosemary, wines and mushrooms. Mix well, Cook 5 minutes, then add the peas and cook 3 to 5 minutes longer or until peas are tender but not overcooked. Thicken sauce with your favorite thickening, or mix 1 or 2 tablespoons of cornstarch with 1/4 cup water until smooth, then add slowly to the sauce, stirring continuously until desired consistency. Pour over meat. Yield 6 to 8 servings. Scallopini may be served with rice or noodles or just plain, with a green salad.

*   There are 90 milligrams of cholesterol in 100 grams of veal according to U.S.D.A. Handbook No. 8, pg. 146, item 35b. In 681 grams, there are 613, divide by 8 servings equals 77 average milligrams of cholesterol per serving.

WIENER SCHNITZEL

F=Fair; G=Good; H=High; L=Low; t or T = trace; n/a = no information available; dashes = zero or unmeasurable

GRAM WT.	FOOD	VITAMINS	CAL	(mg) SOD	PRO	FAT	CARB	CHOL (mg)*	FATTY ACIDS SAT	UNSAT	CALC	IRON	(mg) POTSM
231	AVERAGE PER SERVING		388	245				285					577
	Ingredients:												
908	6 veal chops	B1 B2	1146	820	G	L	---	H	L	L	L	F	2906
100	2 eggs, slightly beaten	A B1 B2	150	122	F	F	L	H	H	L	F	F	129
56	1/2 cp flour	B1 B1	210	1	F	L	G	---	---	---	L	F	53
422	3 tblspn margarine	A D	300	418	L	H	L	---	L	H	L	---	10
45	3 tblspn lemon juice	A B1 B2 C	12	T	L	T	F	---	---	---	F	L	63
7	1 tblspn flour	B1 B2	26	T	F	L	G	---	---	---	L	F	1
230	1 cp thick sour cream	A B1 B2 C	485	106	L	G	L	H	H	L	G	L	297
1388	Recipe totals (gms; cal; sod. & potsm.)		2329	1467									3459

METHOD

Dip chops in slightly beaten eggs, then dip into flour and shake off excess. Melt margarine in a heavy frying pan and brown chops in it.   Cover and cook slowly about 1 hour. Remove chops to a hot platter and sprinkle them with lemon juice. Keep them warm in a 180 F. oven. Blend flour with fat in the frying pan, add sour cream and cook 3 minutes, stirring continuously. Serve with chops. Lemon slices may be used as a garnish if desired. Yield   6 servings.

*   In 908 grams of veal, there are 817 milligrams of cholesterol; in 100 grams of whole egg, there are 550 milligrams of cholesterol; in 230 grams of sour cream, there are 345 milligrams for a total of 1712 according to U.S.D.A. Handbook No. 8, pg. 146, items 35a and 12 respectively. Divide 1712 milligrams by 6 servings equals 285 average milligrams of cholesterol per serving.

. . . .

ROAST LEG OF LAMB

Lamb should be placed fat-side-up on a rack in an uncovered roasting pan and cooked in a moderately slow oven (300 to 325 F.) allowing 30 to 35 minutes per pound or until meat thermometer registers 180 F.

To prepare leg-of-lamb for roasting, do not cut off the fell (the thick skin covering the meat). Season with slivers of fresh garlic tucked into slits in the surface of the roast, or rub the meat with cut garlic; or sprinkle surface of the meat lightly with curry powder; or rub roast with cut mint leaves, basting the meat frequently the last hour with 3/4 cup grape jelly melted in hot water; or 1 hour before meat is done, cover roast with drained pineapple slices and brush with melted margarine to brown the fruit.

BROILED LAMB CHOPS

Select loin chops 1-1/2" thick. If desired, sprinkle just a hint of garlic salt over them, then arrange chops on broiler rack. Place them 3" below broiler heat and brown chops on both sides. Cook 15 minutes for rare; 18 minutes for medium. If chops have only a little fat, brush with margarine before broiling. Allow 2 chops per serving.

BRAISED SHOULDER CHOPS

Although shoulder lamb chops have more meat on them than loin chops, they are not as tender. It takes long, slow cooking to tenderize them.

Remove any tough skin around outside of the chops, sprinkle with a little garlic salt, if desired, or curry powder, and brown on both sides in a small amount of margarine. Reduce heat, add enough water to cover bottom of the frying pan, cover and simmer until fork tender. Check often and add water as needed. When chops are tender, remove them to a hot platter and keep warm in a 180 F. oven. To make gravy, add a little water to the frying pan and bring to a boil. Thicken with your favorite mixture or with 1 to 2 tablespoons cornstarch and water mixed until smooth. Add gradually to the boiling juices, stirring constantly until desired consistency.

. . . .

LEFTOVER LAMB CURRY WITH RICE

F=Fair; G=Good; H=High; L=Low; t or T = trace; n/a = no information available; dashes = zero or unmeasurable

GRAM WT.	FOOD	VITAMINS	CAL	(mg) SOD	PRO	FAT	CARB	CHOL	FATTY ACIDS SAT	UNSAT	CALC	IRON	(mg) POTSM
261	AVERAGE PER SERVING		392	352**				(mg)* 106					499
	Ingredients:												
908	4 cp leftover lamb roast	B1 B2	1664	560	G	L	---	H	H	L	L	F	2679
110	1 medium onion, diced	A B1 B2 C	40	11	L	L	L	---	---	---	L	L	173
14	1 tblspn margarine	A D	100	139	L	H	T	---	L	H	L	---	3
40	1 large stalk celery, diced	A B1 B2 C	5	50	T	T	T	---	---	---	F	L	136
n/a	1 tblspn curry powder						-n/a-						
495	3 cp instant-cooked rice	B1 B2	540	1351**	L	T	F	---	---	---	L	F	---
1567	Recipe totals (gms; cal; sod. & potsm.)		2349	2111**									2991

METHOD

Cut leftover lamb in bite-size pieces. Set aside. Cook onion in margarine only until clear, not brown. Add meat, chopped celery, 2 cups leftover gravy or hot water, and stir until well blended. Cover and simmer about 1 hour. Stir in curry powder. Add more water if needed and cook 30 minutes longer. Prepare instant rice according to instructions on the box. Thicken lamb gravy with cornstarch mixed with water until smooth, stirring constantly until thickened. Serve on hot plates over rice. Garnish with tomato wedges. Yield about 6 servings.

* There are 70 milligrams of cholesterol in 100 grams of boneless lamb; in 908 grams there are 636 milligrams, according to U.S.D.A. Handbook No. 8, pg. 146, item 21b. Divide 636 milligrams by 6 servings equals 106 average milligrams of cholesterol per serving.

** To reduce sodium content of this recipe, do not use salt when cooking the rice. Instead, season at the table individually. In 495 grams of cooked instant rice, without salt, there are only 5 milligrams of sodium, which would reduce total sodium in this recipe to 765, an average of 128 milligrams per servings instead of 352.

. . . .

PORK

All pork must be cooked thoroughly because of Trichinella, a parasitic nematode worm that causes trichinosis, a disease resulting from eating inadequately cooked trichinized pork.

ROAST LOIN OF PORK

A 5 to 6 pound roast will serve 6 people. If the bone along the loin is solid, have the butcher crack each chop through for easier cutting and serving.

Place a roast on a rack in a shallow roasting pan. If fat is thick, slice some of it off and discard. Score remaining fat lightly. Sprinkle entire surface with oregano and garlic salt — not heavy, but enough to flavor the meat. Roast in a preheated 325 F. oven, 35 to 40 minutes per pound. A 4 to 7 pound roast will take 3-1/2 to 4-1/4 hours, and if a thermometer is used, 170 F. internal temperature. At the end of 1 hour, add about 1 cup of water and baste roast frequently, adding water as needed. Before making gravy, skim off as much fat from the juices as possible.

To test for doneness, remove meat from the oven, and cut into the center section far enough to see if the meat is pink. If it is, the roast is not cooked and should be returned to the oven.

BRAISED PORK CHOPS

Allow 1 chop, with tenderloin, per person. Rinse chops with cold water to remove any fine bone left when they were cut. Wipe dry with a paper towel. Dredge with flour, shake off excess and place in a heavy frying pan in 2 tablespoons melted margarine. Sprinkle lightly with oregano. Brown chops on both sides at medium heat. Reduce heat, add 1/4 cup of water, cover and cook slowly until water evaporates, then add 1/2 cup of water and cook slowly about 1 hour or until very tender. Turn chops occasionally.

To Make Milk Gravy: Remove chops to a hot platter and keep hot in a 180 F. oven. Add milk to pan drippings and bring almost to the boiling point then thicken with cornstarch mixed with water until smooth, (about 1 tablespoon cornstarch to 1 cup of milk) depending on thickness of gravy desired. Serve with chops separately. Season at the table.   NOTE: Fresh pork steaks may be prepared the same way.

SPARERIBS

Allow 1 pound of spareribs per person. Spareribs should be cooked slowly and thoroughly, from 40 to 45 minutes per pound.

To Roast: Place ribs in a shallow baking dish and season with sage or oregano. Roast in a 325 F. oven, or   Cover spareribs with foil and roast half the time, then uncover for remaining time. Just before taking meat from oven, sprinkle with 1 cup breadcrumbs seasoned with 1/4 teaspoon sage and 1/4 teaspoon minced onion. Baste with drippings and roast 5 minutes longer.

BARBECUED RIBS

Place 2 pounds of spareribs on a broiler rack and brown both sides. Remove ribs to a roasting pan, cover with barbecue sauce, and bake in a covered pan at 325 F. for 1-1/2 hours. Yield   2 to 3 servings.

COUNTRY RIBS

These are the meaty ribs which take longer to cook. Place 2 or 3 ribs per serving in a roasting pan. Brown, uncovered in a 450 F. oven. Drain fat, add 1/2 cup water. Reduce heat to 325 F., cover pan and return to oven for about 30 minutes. Then pour barbecue sauce over the ribs, cover pan and continue baking about 45 minutes longer or until fork tender.

STUFFED SPARERIBS

Select 2 strips of spareribs, as nearly matched as possible. Place strips on a broiler rack and brown only one side. Remove ribs to a roasting pan and place one strip brown-side-down. Cover it with a bread, celery and sage stuffing (see recipe in poultry section for turkey and dressing). Place second strip over this, brown-side-up. Tie together with string or skewer edges together. Bake at 325 F. from 1-1/2 to 2 hours.

SPARERIBS WITH SAUERKRAUT

Brown spareribs under the broiler; place sauerkraut in a greased baking dish. Sprinkle with brown sugar; add 1/2 cup water and arrange spareribs on top. Cover dish and bake at 350 F. for 1 hour.

. . . .

BARBECUE SAUCE
(FOR PORK CHOPS, SPARERIBS & COUNTRY RIBS)

F=Fair; G=Good; H=High; L=Low; t or T = trace; n/a = no information available; dashes = zero or unmeasurable

GRAM WT.	FOOD	VITAMINS	CAL	(mg) SOD	PRO	FAT	CARB	CHOL	FATTY ACIDS SAT	UNSAT	CALC	IRON	(mg) POTSM
94	AVERAGE PER SERVING		25	166									206
	Ingredients:												
110	1 medium onion, minced	A B1 B2 C	40	11	L	L	L	---	---	---	L	L	173
227	1 (8oz) can tomato sauce	A B1 B2 C	88	905	L	L	L	---	---	---	L	L	967
177	3/4 cp water						---n/a---						
45	3 tblspn cider vinegar	---	6	T	T	---	L	---	---	---	L	L	45
n/a	2 tblspn Worcestershire sauce						---n/a---						
n/a	1 tsp paprika						---n/a---						
5	1 tsp chili powder	A B1 B2 C	17	79	F	F	G	---	---	---	H	H	50
n/a	1/2 tsp pepper						---n/a---						
n/a	1/4 tsp cinnamon						---n/a---						
n/a	1/8 tsp ground cloves						---n/a---						
564	Recipe totals (gms; cal; sod. & potsm.)		151	995									1235

METHOD

Combine ingredients in the order given and blend thoroughly.

. . . .

STUFFED PORK CHOPS

F=Fair; G=Good; H=High; L=Low; t or T = trace; n/a = no information available; dashes = zero or unmeasurable

GRAM WT.	FOOD	VITAMINS	CAL	(mg) SOD	PRO	FAT	CARB	CHOL (mg)*	FATTY ACIDS SAT	UNSAT	CALC	IRON	(mg) POTSM
175	AVERAGE PER SERVING		397	159				106					393
	Ingredients:												
908	6 medium thick pork chops	B1 B2	2130	520	G	F	---	H	H	L	F	F	2120
80	2 cp breadcrumbs	A^t B1 B2 C^t	220	404	L	L	G	---	---	---	F	F	122
17	2 green onions, minced	A^t B1 B2 C	6	1	L	L	F	---	---	---	F	L	39
n/a	2 tsp oregano							---n/a---					
45	3 tblspn 2% low-fat milk	A B1 B2 C	27	27	H	F	G	L	L	L	H	L	79
1050	Recipe totals (gms; cal; sod. & potsm.)		2383	952									2360

METHOD

Cut a pocket on the bone-side of each chop. Combine next 4 ingredients and mix well. Stuff each chop with this mixture. Brown chops in a small amount of oil or margarine then place them side-by-side in a large casserole or roasting pan. Add a little water. Cover and bake at 350 F. about 1 hour, or until tender. Yield 6 servings.

* There are 636 milligrams of cholesterol in 908 grams of pork with bone, as calculated from U.S.D.A. Handbook No. 8, pg. 146, item 32b. Divide 636 milligrams by 6 servings equals 106 average milligrams of cholesterol per serving. Milk has only 1 milligram of cholesterol for this entire recipe, which does not affect the average per serving.

. . . .

PORK CHOPS AND SCALLOPED POTATOES

F=Fair; G=Good; H=High; L=Low; t or T = trace; n/a = no information available; dashes = zero or unmeasurable

GRAM WT.	FOOD	VITAMINS	CAL	(mg) SOD	PRO	FAT	CARB	CHOL (mg)*	FATTY ACIDS SAT	UNSAT	CALC	IRON	(mg) POTSM
490	**AVERAGE PER SERVING**		532	181				72					1265
	Ingredients:												
454	3 medium potatoes	A^t B1 B2 C	279	11	L	L	F	---	---	---	L	L	1495
110	1 medium onion	A B1 B2 C	40	11	L	L	L	---	---	---	L	L	173
150	3 carrots	A B1 B2 C	60	84	L	L	L	---	---	---	L	L	512
37	1/2 green pepper	A B1 B2 C	8	5	L	L	L	---	---	---	F	L	79
56	1/2 cp flour	B1 B2	210	1	F	L	G	---	---	---	L	F	53
369	1-1/2 cp 2% low-fat milk	A B1 B2 C	218	225	H	F	G	L	L	L	H	L	646
294	3 lean pork chops with tenderloin 3.5 oz each	B1 B2	780	206	G	F	---	H	H	L	F	F	838
n/a	Pepper and oregano						-n/a-						
1470	Recipe totals (gms; cal; sod. & potsm.)		1595	543									3796

METHOD

Grease a medium size casserole. Wash vegetables; peel and slice potatoes, peel and dice onions, scrape carrots and cut in half; remove seeds and white membrane from inside green pepper, then cut in small pieces. Put flour in a plastic sack, add sliced potatoes, twist top closed, and shake to coat, then spread them in casserole, distributing as evenly as possible. Add onions, carrots and green peppers, then 1 cup of the milk. Trim fat from the chops and arrange them on top of the vegetables. Pour remaining milk over each; sprinkle pepper and oregano on top, and cover and bake in a 350 F. oven 45 minutes, then uncover and continue baking 45 minutes longer until chops are brown and carrots are tender.

* In 369 grams of fluid skim milk, there are 11 milligrams of cholesterol; in 294 grams of pork with bone, there are 206 milligrams of cholesterol, for a total measureable cholesterol in this recipe of 217, according to U.S.D.A. Handbook No. 8, pg. 146, items 29 and 32a respectively. Divide 217 by 3 servings equals 72 average milligrams of cholesterol per serving.

. . . .

FRESH PORK BUTT AND SAUERKRAUT

F=Fair; G=Good; H=High; L=Low; t or T = trace; n/a = no information available; dashes = zero or unmeasurable

GRAM WT.	FOOD	VITAMINS	CAL	(mg) SOD	PRO	FAT	CARB	CHOL (mg)*	FATTY ACIDS SAT	UNSAT	CALC	IRON	(mg) POTSM
246	AVERAGE PER SERVING		434	672				106					609
	Ingredients:												
908	2 lb fresh pork butt	B1 B2	2440	520	G	F	---	H	H	L	F	F	2588
470	2 cp canned sauerkraut	A B1 B2 C	90	3510	L	L	L	---	---	---	L	L	658
	NOTE Values for sauerkraut and sauerkraut juice are based on salt contents of 1.9 and 2.0 per cent respectively in the finished products. The amounts of some samples may vary significantly from this estimate. (U.S.D.A. Handbook No. 8, pg. 55, item 1977).												
100	1 small raw potato, grated	A B1 B2 C	76	3	L	L	F	---	---	---	L	L	407
1478	Recipe totals (gms; cal; sod. & potsm.)		2606	4033									3653

METHOD

Cut pork into chunks, and cook about 5 minutes in enough boiling water to cover. Reduce heat, cover, and simmer 2-1/2 to 3 hours until meat is fork tender. Twenty minutes before serving, pour off most of the water and add sauerkraut and grated potato. Heat thoroughly. Serve on a hot platter. Yield   6 servings.

*   In 908 grams of pork there are 636 milligrams of cholesterol according to U.S.D.A. Handbook No. 8, pg. 146, item 32 b. Divide 636 milligrams by 6 servings equals 106 average milligrams of cholesterol per serving.

. . . .

PORK TENDERLOIN WITH SOUR CREAM

F=Fair; G=Good; H=High; L=Low; t or T = trace; n/a = no information available; dashes = zero or unmeasurable

GRAM WT.	FOOD	VITAMINS	CAL	(mg) SOD	PRO	FAT	CARB	CHOL (mg)*	FATTY ACIDS SAT	UNSAT	CALC	IRON	(mg) POTSM
120	AVERAGE PER SERVING		348	137				96					263
	Ingredients:												
454	1 lb pork tenderloin	B1 B2	1216	320	G	G	---	H	H	L	L	F	1294
56	1/2 cp flour	B1 B2	210	1	F	L	G	---	---	---	L	F	53
42	3 tblspn margarine	A D	300	418	L	H	L	---	L	H	L	---	10
n/a	1/2 tsp oregano							-n/a-					
170	3/4 cp sour cream	A B1 B2 C	363	80	L	G	L	H	H	L	G	L	219
722	Recipe totals (gms; cal; sod. & potsm.)		2089	819									1576

METHOD

Cut tenderloin crosswise into 2" slices. Flatten with meat tenderizer tool or the flat side of a meat cleaver; dredge with flour, shake off excess and place meat in a hot frying pan with melted margarine, and brown on both sides. Reduce heat, add sour cream, cover and simmer 30 minutes. Yield   6 servings.

*   In 454 grams of boneless pork, there are 318 milligrams of cholesterol; in 170 grams of sour cream, there are 255 milligrams of cholesterol according to U.S.D.A. Handbook No. 8, pg. 146, item 32b.   Divide 573 milligrams by 6 servings equals 96 average milligrams of cholesterol per serving.

FRIED SALT PORK WITH CREAM GRAVY

F=Fair; G=Good; H=High; L=Low; t or T = trace; n/a = no information available; dashes = zero or unmeasurable

GRAM WT.	FOOD	VITAMINS	CAL	(mg) SOD	PRO	FAT	CARB	CHOL	FATTY ACIDS SAT	UNSAT	CALC	IRON	(mg) POTSM
								(mg)*					
334	AVERAGE PER SERVING		1303	1860				111					368
	Ingredients:												
454	1 lb salt pork	B1 B2	3410	5278	L	H	---	H	H	L	T	L	191
56	1/2 cp flour	B1 B2	210	1	F	L	G	---	---	---	L	F	53
492	2 cp 2% low-fat milk	A B1 B2 C	290	300	H	F	G	L	L	L	H	L	861
n/a	dash pepper						--n/a--						
1002	Recipe totals (gms; cal; sod. & potsm.)		3910	5579									1105

METHOD

Slice pork thin, place in cold water and let stand about an hour, then drain. Dry on paper towels. Dip each slice in flour, shake off excess and fry in hot skillet until crisp. Remove meat to a hot platter and keep warm in a 180 F. oven. Drain off all but 2 tablespoons fat; stir in 2 tablespoons flour, and cook and stir 2 minutes, then reduce heat and add milk very slowly. Stir until thickened. Blend in pepper. Serve over meat. Yield 3 servings.

* In 454 grams of pork there are 318 milligrams of cholesterol. In 492 grams of fluid skim milk, there are 15 milligrams according to U.S.D.A. Handbook No. 8, pg. 146, items 32b and 29 respectively. Divide 333 milligrams of cholesterol by 3 servings equals 11 average milligrams per serving.

. . . .

BAKED HAM

Most hams purchased today are precooked and need only to be heated through. Directions usually come with them. However, if the ham is not cooked or if directions are not included, it can be baked as follows:

NOTE Directions are for modern-cured hams only, not for old-method country cured).

Preheat oven to 325 F.

For a whole ham, weighing 9 to 12 pounds, allow 18 to 20 minutes per pound cooking time. (Internal temperature when cooked — 160F.).

A whole ham, weighing 12 to 16 pounds, allow 16 to 18 minutes per pound. Internal temperature 160 F.

Half a ham, weighing 6 to 8 pounds, allow 25 to 27 minutes per pound, internal temperature 160 F.

METHOD

Place ham in a shallow roasting pan, fat-side-up. Do not cover or add water. An hour before ham has finished cooking, take it from the oven, remove rind and slash a series of crisscross cuts across the fat; patterns may be in diamonds or squares. Spread with one of the following glazes, then insert a whole clove in each square or diamond shape. Return to the oven for 1 hour.

GLAZES FOR HAM

Pour about one pint of sweet gingerale over the ham, then sprinkle with cinnamon.

Mix 1 cup brown sugar, 2 teaspoons dry mustard and 1/4 teaspoon ground cloves. Use as a dry glaze or mix with a little melted fat and spread the paste over the ham.

Place pineapple slices over the ham, add a maraschino cherry in the center of each slice.

Pour 1 cup pineapple juice over the ham.

Pour 1 glass of melted currant jelly over the ham.

Pour canned apricot juice over the ham, or pureed apricots.

Peel and core a large apple, or 2 small ones, cut in thin rings, arrange over the ham and pour 1/2 cup maple sirup over them.

Pour 1/2 cup honey over the ham.

Pour fresh apple cider or apple juice over the ham.

Mix applesauce with cinnamon and nutmeg and spread evenly over the ham.

BROILING SMOKED HAM

A 1/2" slice of ham, 9 to 12 ounces in weight, broil 10 to 12 minutes. Trim any fat around the edge; slash sides, top and bottom about 1" into the meat to prevent curling. Broil plain, or with one of the glazes mentioned above, about 3" from the heat.

BOILED HAM

Wash ham in cold water — cover with boiling water, bring to the boiling point and simmer at 20 minutes to the pound, or until internal temperature reaches 160 F. For cold-boiled ham, allow it to cool down in the cooking water then remove rind and slice. To serve hot, remove rind and glaze as for Baked Ham, or follow packer's directions.

. . . .

FRIED HAM WITH CREAM GRAVY

F=Fair; G=Good; H=High; L=Low; t or T = trace; n/a = no information available; dashes = zero or unmeasurable

GRAM WT.	FOOD	VITAMINS	CAL	(mg) SOD	PRO	FAT	CARB	CHOL (mg)*	FATTY ACIDS SAT	UNSAT	CALC	IRON	(mg) POTSM
215	AVERAGE PER SERVING		412	38				108					108
	Ingredients:												
908	2 1/2" slice smoked ham	B1 B2	2200	n/a	G	G	---	H	H	L	L	F	---
369	1-1/2 cp 2% low-fat milk	A B1 B2 C	218	225	H	F	G	L	L	L	H	L	646
14	1-1/2 tblspn cornstarch	---	51	---	L	T	H	---	---	---	---	---	---
n/a	dash pepper						---n/a---						
1291	Recipe totals (gms; cal; sod. & potsm.)		2469	225									646

METHOD

Score meat around the edge to prevent curling. Cook in a large frying pan until browned on each side. Reduce heat, add 1/2 cup water, cover and cook about 15 minutes. Remove to a hot platter, keep warm in the oven at 180 F. Pour milk into frying pan; heat slowly. Mix cornstarch with 1/4 cup water and stir until smooth. When milk is hot (do not boil) stir in cornstarch mixture a little at a time, stirring constantly, until gravy is thickness desired. Serve over ham or in a separate bowl. Yield   6 servings.

*   There are 636 milligrams of cholesterol in 908 grams of pork and 11 milligrams of cholesterol in 369 grams of fluid skim milk, for a total of 647 milligrams as calculated from U.S.D.A. Handbook No. 8, pg. 146, items 32a and 29 respectively. Divide 647 milligrams by 6 servings equals 108 average milligrams of cholesterol per serving.

. . . .

WESTERN SANDWICH

F=Fair; G=Good; H=High; L=Low; t or T = trace; n/a = no information available; dashes = zero or unmeasurable

GRAM WT.	FOOD	VITAMINS	CAL	(mg) SOD	PRO	FAT	CARB	CHOL	FATTY ACIDS SAT	UNSAT	CALC	IRON	(mg) POTSM
								(mg)*					
186	AVERAGE PER SANDWICH		342	311				305					190
	Ingredients:												
84	3 oz chopped smoked ham	B1 B2	245	---	G	G	---	H	H	L	L	F	---
37	1/2 green pepper, chopped	A B1 B2 C	8	5	L	L	L	---	---	---	L	L	79
55	1/2 medium onion, chopped	A B1 B2 C	20	6	L	L	L	---	---	---	L	L	86
100	2 eggs, beaten	A B1 B2	150	122	F	F	L	H	H	L	F	F	129
n/a	dash pepper							-n/a-					
96	4 slices bread	A^t B1 B2 C^t	260	488	L	L	G	---	---	---	F	F	85
372	Recipe totals (gms; cal; sod. & potsm.)		683	621									379

METHOD

Fry ham about 10 minutes; add green pepper and onion and cook until nearly tender. Add beaten eggs and pepper and cook until eggs are set. Turn to brown the other side slightly. Divide in half and place on two pieces of bread; cover with the other two. Yield   2 sandwiches.

*   There are 550 milligrams of cholesterol in 100 grams of whole egg; in 84 grams of pork, there are 59 for a total of 609 milligrams of cholesterol according to U.S.D.A. Handbook No. 8, pg. 146, items 12 and 32b respectively. Divide 609 milligrams of cholesterol by 2 servings equals 305 average milligrams per serving.

. . . .

Poultry should be plump, have soft, smooth legs and feet and smooth, moist skin. If feet are scaly and skin is hard, the bird is old. Pinfeathers are a sign the bird is young; long hairs a sign the bird is old.

Birds with yellow skins are likely to be fat; those with white skins are likely to be tender.

The lower end of the breastbone should feel flexible and the skin should be easily broken when twisted between the thumb and finger; also joints of the wings should yield readily when turned backward.

Select dry-picked birds — flavor is impaired in birds which are scalded before plucking.

Poultry and game should not be kept long uncooked unless frozen.

Large tom turkeys are more satisfactory than large hens. However, small, plump, young hens are flavorful and satisfactory.

ROAST CHICKEN

Select a whole roaster-fryer weighing about 3 pounds. Prepare desired stuffing, and set aside. Rinse giblets in cold water, put in a saucepan, add about 2 cups of water and 2 minced green onions, a 2" piece of celery cut fine, and a sprinkle of oregano or sage. Cover and simmer until giblets are tender. Add water as needed.

While giblets are cooking, rinse chicken in cold water inside and out. Pat dry with a paper towel. Singe long hairs. Remove any pinfeathers. Fill neck (or crop area) with stuffing. Pull neck-skin over opening and either secure with a skewer or use white thread, double strand, to sew area closed. Stitch loosely. Fill body cavity next. Do not pack the dressing tightly — otherwise stuffing will become a doughy mass — loosely packed dressing allows flavors to mingle through the bread. However, some pressure must be used to get the stuffing inside the bird, but do this gently.

Sew outside skin over the cavity opening loosely, or secure with skewers. Fold the wings under the back. Bring legs close to the body and tie them, ending around and under the tail. Brush entire surface of bird either with soft margarine or oil. Sprinkle oregano or sage over the breast, legs and wings. Place chicken breast-up in a shallow roasting pan on a rack. Bake at 375 F. about 2 hours. Test for doneness by moving drumsticks up and down. If they move easily, chicken is ready to serve. Yield about 4 servings.

NOTE Some cooks cover chicken half time. They believe this cooks the chicken through. However, they add about 1 cup of water to the roaster pan. We've tried it both ways, and prefer the covered method because there are no pink, or raw areas when cooked this way, and by removing the cover at the end of an hour, chicken browns beautifully and seems juicier. When we used the uncovered method, we basted the chicken frequently to keep it moist and juicy.

GIBLET-MILK GRAVY

As soon as giblets are tender, remove from the heat and set aside to cool. About 40 minutes before serving time, cut meat off the gizzard and discard gristle. Cut up liver; strip neck of skin; pull neck meat and cut once or twice. Measure liquid from the giblets and add enough 2% low-fat milk to make 2 cups of liquid. Bring to a boil, but do not boil; add finely cut celery and one green onion, also cut fine. Celery adds to the flavor, but an inch or 1-1/2" piece, cut fine, should be sufficient in this amount of liquid. Simmer until celery is cooked. Add 1/2 teaspoon oregano. Thicken gravy with 2 tablespoons cornstarch mixed with 1/4 cup water until smooth, adding slowly to the right consistency, stirring constantly. Add giblets and cook until heated through (heart is left whole).

NOTE   Giblets can be prepared earlier, adding onions and celery and simmering until tender, then covered and set aside to cool. Add milk and oregano about 15 to 20 minutes before serving, bring to a boil, then thicken.

OREGANO DRESSING

In a large mixing bowl, pull 10 or 11 slices of day-old bread into pieces about the size of a dime. Add 1 tablespoon oregano and mix well. Add 1 medium onion, cut small, plus 1/2 stalk of celery, cut fine, and a dash of black pepper. Mix in 3 tablespoons water, one at a time, with the fingers, feeling the dressing after each addition. If dressing seems dry, add 1 more tablespoon, distributing it around the bowl. Press some of the bread between the fingers and add 1 more tablespoon if needed. Dressing should feel moist, but too much water will cause bread to pack into a doughy mass. The dressing will absorb juices from the chicken during the baking period, therefore, it is important not to add too much water. A good rule to remember is that dressing should be moist enough to stick together, but dry enough to crumble.

. . . .

CHICKEN FRICASSEE

Clean, singe, and cut up chicken. Dredge in flour, brown on both sides in melted margarine. Add water to half cover chicken then add 1 teaspoon of oregano, distributing it evenly, or 1 teaspoon of sage. Add 1 medium onion, cut small, 1/2 stalk celery, cut small, and a sprinkle of black pepper. Cover and simmer until chicken is tender (about 1 hour). Replenish water as needed. Remove chicken to a hot platter and keep warm in a 180 F. oven. If desired, strain broth, then thicken with cornstarch and water mixed together until smooth (1 tablespoon cornstarch to 1 cup liquid). Bring broth to the boiling point, add cornstarch and water slowly, stirring constantly until the desired thickness is reached. Pour over chicken or serve separately. To enrich gravy, add 1 cup milk or light cream before thickening.

. . . .

CHICKEN SOUP

Place the bones left from roast chicken, or fried chicken, and any skin into a kettle and cover with water. Simmer about 2 hours, adding water as needed. Strain through a colander into a large mixing bowl. Discard bones and return broth to the kettle. Add sliced carrots, diced celery, diced onion, and 1 teaspoon oregano. Cook until vegetables are tender. If desired, add 1/2 cup of long grain rice 30 minutes before serving. (Noodles may be used instead of rice.)

Turkey bones and skin may be used instead of the chicken, but use enough water to cover and double the amount of vegetables and oregano.

. . . .

FLO'S BATTER-FRIED CHICKEN

F=Fair; G=Good; H=High; L=Low; t or T = trace; n/a = no information available; dashes = zero or unmeasurable

GRAM WT.	FOOD	VITAMINS	CAL	(mg) SOD	PRO	FAT	CARB	CHOL (mg)*	FATTY ACIDS SAT	UNSAT	CALC	IRON	(mg) POTSM
287	AVERAGE PER SERVING		520	268				119					76
	Ingredients:												
794	1-3/4 lb frying chicken	A B1 B2	668	---	H	F	L	L	L	H	L	F	---
56	4 tblspn margarine	A D	400	558	L	H	L	---	L	H	L	---	13
n/a	Oregano						--------n/a--------						
	Batter Ingredients:												
258	2-1/4 cp sifted flour	B1 B2	945	5	F	L	G	---	---	---	L	F	246
1	1/4 tsp salt	---	---	393	---	---	---	---	---	---	G	---	---
7	1-1/2 tsp margarine, melted	A D	51	69	L	H	L	---	L	H	L	---	2
n/a	Lukewarm water						--------0--------						
33	1 egg white	B1 B2	15	48	F	T	L	---	---	---	L	L	46
1149	Recipe totals (gms; cal; sod. & potsm.)		2079	1073									307

METHOD

Cut up chicken. Melt margarine in a large skillet. Sprinkle oregano over melted fat then reduce heat. Dip chicken pieces in batter; let excess drip off. Place chicken in hot margarine. Cook until chicken is golden brown on both sides.

METHOD FOR BATTER

In a large mixing bowl, sift the flour and salt together. Add the melted margarine and enough lukewarm water to make a fairly thin batter. Stir until smooth. Just before dipping the chicken in it, add the white of egg whisked to a froth.

* There are 476 milligrams of cholesterol in 794 grams of Chicken as calculated from U.S.D.A. Handbook No. 8, pg 146, item 10. Divide 476 milligrams of cholesterol by 4 servings equals 119 average milligrams per serving. There is no cholesterol in egg white.

. . . .

563

CHICKEN A LA KING

F=Fair; G=Good; H=High; L=Low; t or T = trace; n/a = no information available; dashes = zero or unmeasurable

GRAM WT.	FOOD	VITAMINS	CAL	(mg) SOD	PRO	FAT	CARB	CHOL (mg)*	FATTY ACIDS SAT	UNSAT	CALC	IRON	(mg) POTSM
227	AVERAGE PER SERVING		262	232				90					240
	Ingredients:												
56	4 tblspn margarine	A D	400	558	L	H	L	---	L	H	L	---	13
28	4 tblspn flour	B1 B2	105	1	F	L	G	---	---	---	L	F	27
37	1/2 green pepper, chopped fine	A B1 B2 C	8	5	L	L	L	---	---	---	L	L	79
50	6 green onions, minced	A^t B1 B2 C	20	3	L	L	F	---	---	---	F	L	116
20	1/2 stalk celery, chopped fine	A B1 B2 C	3	25	T	T	T	---	---	---	F	L	68
492	2 cp 2% low-fat milk	A B1 B2 C	290	300	H	F	G	L	L	L	H	L	861
454	2 cp diced chicken meat	A B1 B2	613	---	H	F	L	L	L	H	L	F	---
122	1/2 cp mushrooms, canned, sliced	A^t B1 B2 C	20	488	L	T	L	---	---	---	L	L	240
17	1 egg yolk, slightly beaten	A B1 B2	60	9	F	G	L	H	H	T	H	G	17
28	2 tblspn sherry wine	---	38	3	T	---	L	---	---	---	L	L	21
56	2 oz canned pimiento, chopped	A B1 B2 C	15	---	L	L	L	---	---	---	L	L	---
n/a	1 tsp oregano						--0--						
1360	Recipe totals (gms; cal; sod. & potsm.)		1572	1392									1442

METHOD

Melt margarine in top of double boiler over direct heat; add flour gradually until mixture is smooth. Add green pepper, onions and celery then add milk slowly and stir until mixture is thickened. Add chicken and mushrooms, then place top of double boiler over boiling water to heat mixture thoroughly. Mix egg yolk and wine together and add to hot mixture. Heat two or three minutes then fold in chopped pimiento and oregano. Yield 6 small or 4 large servings. Spoon over toast, or into patty shells, or serve over noodles, rice or biscuits.

* There are 255 milligrams of cholesterol in 17 grams of egg yolk; there are 272 milligrams of cholesterol in 454 grams of chicken meat; there are 15 milligrams of cholesterol in 492 grams of fluid skim milk, as calculated from U.S.D.A. Handbook No. 8, pg. 146, items 14, 10 and 29 respectively. Divide 542 milligrams of cholesterol by 6 servings equals 90 average milligrams per serving.

. . . .

CHICKEN AND DUMPLINGS

F=Fair; G=Good; H=High; L=Low; t or T = trace; n/a = no information available; dashes = zero or unmeasurable

GRAM WT.	FOOD	VITAMINS	CAL	(mg) SOD	PRO	FAT	CARB	CHOL (mg)*	FATTY ACIDS SAT	FATTY ACIDS UNSAT	CALC	IRON	(mg) POTSM
394	AVERAGE PER SERVING		502	356				170					142
1135	Ingredients: 2-1/2 lb broiler-fryer, cut up	A B1 B2	955	---	H	F	L	L	L	H	L	F	---
n/a	oregano						n/a						---
25	3 green onions, cut fine	A^t B1 B2 C	10	2	L	L	F	---	---	---	F	L	58
414	Dumplings (see recipe)		1041	1422			see recipe						509
1574	Recipe totals (gms; cal; sod. & potsm.)		2006	1424									567

METHOD

Rinse chicken under cold water then dry with a paper towel. Remove any pinfeathers and singe hair from legs and wings. Place chicken in a kettle and nearly cover with water. Add oregano and onions. Cover kettle and simmer gently about 2 hours. Prepare dumplings about 20 minutes before serving time and add to the chicken (see dumpling recipe for leftover beef stew in this chapter). Before making gravy, remove chicken and dumplings to a hot platter or serving dish and keep warm in the oven at 180 F. Thicken gravy with a mixture of cornstarch and water stirred until smooth then add to the simmering broth, stirring constantly until desired consistency is reached. Pour over chicken and dumplings. Yield   about 4 servings.

*   There are 681 milligrams of cholesterol in 1135 grams of chicken, as calculated from U.S.D.A. Handbook No. 8, pg. 146, item 10. Divide 681 milligrams of cholesterol by 4 servings equals 170 average milligrams per serving.

. . . .

BREASTS OF CHICKEN WITH WHEAT GERM DRESSING

F=Fair; G=Good; H=High; L=Low; t or T = trace; n/a = no information available; dashes = zero or unmeasurable

GRAM WT.	FOOD	VITAMINS	CAL	(mg) SOD	PRO	FAT	CARB	CHOL (mg)*	FATTY ACIDS SAT	FATTY ACIDS UNSAT	CALC	IRON	(mg) POTSM
206	AVERAGE PER SERVING		412	191				46					338
	Ingredients:												
113	1/2 cp toasted wheat germ	A B1 B2	442	2	F	F	F	---	---	---	F	G	935
33	4 green onions, chopped	A^t B1 B2 C	12	2	L	L	F	---	---	---	F	L	76
n/a	1/2 tsp basil	---n/a---											
n/a	1/4 tsp garlic powder	---n/a---											
56	4 tblspn melted margarine	A D	400	558	L	H	L	---	L	H	L	---	13
n/a	2 tspn seasoned chicken stock base	---n/a---											
14	2 tblspn flour	B1 B2	52	T	F	L	G	---	---	---	L	F	13
168	3/4 cp chablis wine or white dinner wine	B1 B2	144	8	T	---	L	---	---	---	L	L	155
121	1/2 cp half and half	A B1 B2 C	163	56	L	F	L	n/a	H	T	H	L	156
304	2 whole chicken breasts, halved and boned	A B1 B2	334	---	H	F	L	L	L	H	L	F	---
14	1 tblspn margarine	A D	100	139	L	H	T	---	L	H	L	---	3
823	Recipe totals (gms; cal; sod. & potsm.)		1647	765									1351

METHOD

Mix wheat germ, onion, basil and garlic powder into melted margarine. Combine chicken stock base and flour, then gradually add wine and half and half. Stir until smooth. Add 1 tablespoon of sauce to wheat germ mixture. Set remainder aside. Place chicken breasts skin-side-down on cutting board. Remove skin, if desired. Cover with waxed paper and flatten chicken with a mallet. Place an equal amount of wheat germ dressing in center of each chicken breast. Roll breasts around stuffing. Fasten with toothpicks. Brown rolls in 1 tablespoon margarine over high heat. Transfer to a 1-1/2 quart baking dish. Pour wine sauce over chicken. Cover and bake in 400 F. oven 45 to 50 minutes, or until tender. Yield   4 servings.

* There are 182 milligrams of cholesterol in 304 grams of chicken, as calculated from U.S.D.A. Handbook No. 8, pg. 146, item 10. Divide 182 milligrams of cholesterol by 4 servings equals 46 average milligrams per serving.

. . . .

CHICKEN CACCIATORE

F=Fair; G=Good; H=High; L=Low; t or T = trace; n/a = no information available; dashes = zero or unmeasurable

GRAM WT.	FOOD	VITAMINS	CAL	(mg) SOD	PRO	FAT	CARB	CHOL	FATTY ACIDS SAT	UNSAT	CALC	IRON	(mg) POTSM
								(mg)*					
502	AVERAGE PER SERVING		528	726				163					800
	Ingredients:												
110	1/2 cp corn oil	---	973	---	---	H	---	---	L	H	---	---	---
1362	1 frying chicken, cut up (3 lbs)	A B1 B2	1146	---	H	F	L	L	L	H	L	F	---
908	4 (8 ozs) cans tomato sauce	A B1 B2 C	356	3624	L	L	L	---	---	---	L	L	3868
	Note High sodium is reflected in the salt used in the canning process.												
17	2 green onions, chopped	A^t B1 B2 C	7	1	L	L	F	---	---	---	F	L	39
2	1 clove garlic, mashed	A^t B1 B2 C	3	T	L	L	F	---	---	---	L	F	11
n/a	pepper	------						n/a					------
113	1/2 cp dry white wine	---	157	5	T	---	L	---	---	---	L	L	85
2512	Recipe totals (gms; cal; sod. & potsm.)		2642	3630									4003

METHOD

Heat the oil in a large frying pan or Dutch oven. Wash chicken, dry with a paper towel, singe off any hair, then brown in hot oil until golden brown. Pour tomato sauce over the chicken, add onions, garlic and a sprinkle of black pepper. Cover and simmer until meat is tender and sauce is thick. To hasten sauce thickening, remove cover during the last 15 minutes of the cooking period. Add wine, stirring to blend. Yield   5 servings.

*   There are 817 milligrams of cholesterol in 1362 grams of chicken, as calculated from U.S.D.A. Handbook No. 8, pg. 146, item 10. Divide 817 milligrams of cholesterol by 5 servings equals 163 average milligrams per serving.

. . . .

CHICKEN (or turkey) SALAD

F=Fair; G=Good; H=High; L=Low; t or T = trace; n/a = no information available; dashes = zero or unmeasurable

GRAM WT.	FOOD	VITAMINS	CAL	(mg) SOD	PRO	FAT	CARB	CHOL	FATTY ACIDS SAT	UNSAT	CALC	IRON	(mg) POTSM
138	AVERAGE PER SERVING		268	145				(mg)* 68					501
	Ingredients:												
570	2-1/2 cp chicken, cooked, diced	A B1 B2	1163	376	G	L	L	L	L	H	F	F	2405
120	3 large stalks celery	A B1 B2 C	15	150	T	T	T	---	---	---	F	L	409
50	6 green onions, diced	A^t B1 B2 C	20	3	L	L	F	---	---	---	F	L	116
15	1 tblspn fresh lemon juice	A B1 B2 C	4	---	L	T	F	---	---	---	F	L	21
15	1/4 green pepper, diced	A B1 B2 C	4	3	L	L	L	---	---	---	L	L	38
56	4 tblspn mayonnaise (see recipe)		400	336	T	T	T	H	H	H	F	L	19
826	Recipe totals (gms; cal; sod. & potsm.)		1606	868									3008

METHOD

Strip skin from chicken and discard. Cut meat into bite-size pieces. Wash and pare outside fibers from celery, then cut fine. Wash onions, cut off root ends, strip off tough outside leaves, cut off tough portion of tops, then cut in small pieces. Mix chicken, celery and onions together. Blend in lemon juice. Wash pepper, cut out a quarter section, remove seeds and tough white membranes on the inside, then cut in pieces. Pare vinyl-like outside skin off and chop pepper into small pieces. Stir into first mixture. Add mayonnaise, a tablespoon at a time, until desired consistency is reached. Serve on crisp iceberg lettuce. Garnish with stuffed olives, pimiento strips or hard-cooked eggs.

* In 570 grams of chicken there are 342 milligrams of cholesterol; divided by 6 servings equals 57 average milligrams of cholesterol per serving. In 4 tablespoons of mayonnaise, there are 64 milligrams of cholesterol (see recipe in chapter on fats and oils.), divided by 6 servings equals 11 average milligrams per serving, for a total of 68 milligrams per serving as calculated from U.S.D.A. Handbook No. 8, pg. 146, item 10 and the recipe.

. . . .

568

TURKEY

Since the first Thanksgiving in 1631, when Americans shared their first turkey dinner together, this truly American holiday has been traditionally observed. However, preparations for the feast have changed dramatically — what used to take nearly a week to prepare, can now be ready the same day. There are varieties of convenience foods that make this day a little easier on the cooks: frozen pumpkin pies, canned pumpkin (some canned pumpkin includes all ingredients necessary to make a pie); mince pies (ready for the oven); rolls, breads and stuffings; canned, frozen and fresh vegetables; canned, jellied or stuffed cranberries; even predressed fowls, frozen or fresh, ready for the dressing. It's true — it's no longer necessary to shoot your own bird!

A word of warning, though — if turkey is frozen — to avoid food poisoning, it is safer to thaw the bird in the refrigerator in its own wrapping, or, if time is short, start thawing at room temperature and finish in the refrigerator. And, DO NOT STUFF TURKEY until just before roasting. After dinner, immediately remove remaining dressing from the bird and store in a covered bowl in the refrigerator. Turkey should be cooled in the refrigerator as quickly as possible, then wrapped in foil to keep it moist. When stuffing is left in the bird, it remains hot longer than the turkey, which prevents the meat from cooling and which retards the growth of dangerous bacteria. Gravy should also be chilled at once.

Stuffing may be prepared a day ahead if stored in a sealed container or covered bowl in the refrigerator. Under no circumstances should the turkey be stuffed ahead of time.

. . . .

ROAST TURKEY

Preparation is similar to roast chicken, but on a larger scale. If turkey is frozen, wait until it is completely thawed then wash it inside and out. Remove giblets, rinse in cold water, put them in a saucepan with the neck and cover with water. Add some chopped onion, some celery cut up with a few leaves and a sprinkle of sage or oregano. Cover pan and bring water to a boil, then reduce heat and simmer until giblets are tender. Continue with the turkey: pull out any pinfeathers and singe off hairs (these are usually found on the wings and legs). Wash turkey inside and out again. If oil bag has not been cut out of the tail, do so. Unless you know how to remove leg tendons, forget it, as meat could be mangled in the process.

Wipe the outside of the turkey with a paper towel. Stand the bird upright in the sink. To keep it from slipping while it's being stuffed, put a couple of paper towels underneath it. Pull back the loose skin over the neck (this is the crop area). With the left hand, hold the skin open like a sack; with the right, stuff the neck cavity. Do not pack the dressing — leave it loose and fluffy to prevent compaction. Pull skin over dressing and secure with a skewer, or sew with double strands of white thread, pulling thread firmly through but not too tight to allow for expansion. Turn the bird over and stuff the body cavity. Close skin over the opening and skewer or sew, again not too tight, as stuffing will expand as it absorbs the juices from the turkey. Lift the bird into the roaster and place it on the rack, and rub it all over with softened margarine or oil. Sprinkle with oregano or sage then turn it breast-side-down. Twist wing tips until they lie flat against the back of the turkey. Pull legs close to the body, and sprinkle sage or oregano over the back. Place strips of bacon over the back and legs. Roast in an uncovered 325 F. oven 25 minutes to the pound. (Large birds take less time than smaller birds).

Roasting time for Stuffed birds

8 to 10 pounds — 4 to 4-1/2 hours
10 to 14 pounds — 5 to 5-1/4 hours
14 to 20 pounds — 6 to 6-1/2 hours

Baste turkey often during the roasting period. At half time, turn the turkey on its back and cover it loosely with a foil "tent," tucking the foil inside the roasting pan to keep moisture from dripping into the oven. An hour before end of the baking period, remove foil to allow turkey to brown.

To test for doneness: move a leg joint up and down — it should do so easily. The fleshy part of the leg should feel soft. The old-fashioned way to test for doneness was to prick turkey with a fork between leg and body or between wing and body and if the juice ran out, it wasn't cooked. But it is now thought that pricking the meat results in loss of juices, and makes the meat dry. Consequently the leg test is considered better.

(Note: I have used both methods for testing for doneness, and have found little, if any, difference in the meat's moistness.)

BREAD STUFFING

F=Fair; G=Good; H=High; L=Low; t or T = trace; n/a = no information available; dashes = zero or unmeasurable

GRAM WT.	FOOD	VITAMINS	CAL	(mg) SOD	PRO	FAT	CARB	CHOL	FATTY ACIDS SAT	UNSAT	CALC	IRON	(mg) POTSM
60	AVERAGE PER SERVING		127	236									70
	Ingredients:												
454	1 (1 lb) loaf day-old bread, firm, white	A^t B1 B2 C^t	1225	2300	L	L	G	---	---	---	F	L	386
110	1 medium onion, chopped	A B1 B2 C	40	1	L	L	L	---	---	---	L	L	173
40	1 medium stalk celery, chopped	A B1 B2 C	5	50	T	T	T	---	---	---	F	L	136
n/a	2 tblspn oregano or sage	-----------------					---n/a---						----
n/a	2 tblspn turkey broth from giblets	-----------------					---n/a---						----
604	Recipe totals (gms; cal; sod. & potsm.)		1270	2361									695

METHOD

Break bread lightly, into a large mixing bowl, in small pieces. Add onion and celery and mix well. Add oregano or sage. Drizzle hot broth over mixture and stir in lightly. If dressing is not to be used right away, cover bowl and store in refrigerator.

To make Giblet Stuffing   Follow directions for bread stuffing, add chopped giblets last. Mix well. Reduce turkey broth to 4 tablespoons instead of 6.

To make oyster stuffing   For a large turkey, add 2 jars of oysters and liquid, omitting turkey broth. Oysters may be used whole or cut up.

(Note: Stuff part of the bird with oyster dressing, and part with sage dressing)

. . . .

CORNBREAD STUFFING

F=Fair; G=Good; H=High; L=Low; t or T = trace; n/a = no information available; dashes = zero or unmeasurable

GRAM WT.	FOOD	VITAMINS	CAL	(mg) SOD	PRO	FAT	CARB	CHOL (mg)*	FATTY ACIDS SAT	UNSAT	CALC	IRON	(mg) POTSM
128	AVERAGE PER SERVING		308	411				73					134
	Ingredients:												
861	1 (1-1/2 lb) loaf firm white bread	A^t B1 B2 C^t	1838	3450	L	L	G	---	---	---	F	L	579
336 (est.)	3 cp cornbread, crumbled or about 4 muffins	A B1 B2 C	870	1254	L	L	G	F	F	L	G	F	454
227	1/2 lb ground sausage	B1 B2	783	---	L	F	---	H	H	L	L	L	---
100	2 eggs	A B1 B2	150	122	F	F	L	H	H	L	F	F	129
n/a	dash black pepper	---------						n/a					
n/a	2 tsp oregano	---------						n/a					
110	1 onion, minced	A B1 B2 C	40	11	L	L	L	---	---	---	L	L	173
80	2 stalks celery, cut up	A B1 B2 C	10	100	T	T	T	---	---	---	F	L	273
1534	Recipe totals (gms; cal; sod. & potsm.)		3691	4937									1608

METHOD

Brown sliced bread in slow oven, then shred fine and mix well with remaining ingredients. Moisten with just enough water to hold together. Yield Dressing for a 16-pound turkey (approximately 12 servings).

* There are a total of 870 measureable milligrams of cholesterol in this recipe, divide by 12 servings equals 73 average milligrams of cholesterol per serving.

. . . .

CHESTNUT STUFFING

F=Fair; G=Good; H=High; L=Low; t or T = trace; n/a = no information available;   dashes = zero or unmeasurable

GRAM WT.	FOOD	VITAMINS	CAL	(mg) SOD	PRO	FAT	CARB	CHOL	FATTY ACIDS SAT	UNSAT	CALC	IRON	(mg) POTSM
239	AVERAGE PER SERVING		709	946									538
	Ingredients:												
908	2 lb unshelled chestnuts	B1 B2	1426	44	L	L	G	-------	n/a	------	L	L	3336
340	3 sticks margarine	A D	2450	3359	L	H	L	---	L	H	L	---	78
220	2 onions, chopped fine	A B1 B2 C	80	22	L	L	L	---	---	---	L	L	345
120	3 stalks celery, chopped	A B1 B2 C	15	150	T	T	T	---	---	---	F	L	409
800	8 cp dry breadcrumbs	Aᵗ B1 B2 Cᵗ	3120	5888	F	L	G	---	---	---	G	F	1216
n/a	1 tsp powdered thyme	-----------					n/a						-------
n/a	2 tsp oregano	-----------					n/a						-------
2388	Recipe totals (gms; cal; sod. & potsm.)		7091	9463									5384

METHOD

With a sharp, pointed knife, make a slit on the flat side of each chestnut, then put chestnuts in a saucepan, pour enough boiling water over them to cover, and simmer about 5 to 7 minutes. While hot, remove shells and dark brown inner skins from chestnuts, then put them in the pan again, pour boiling water over them and cook about 30 minutes, or until tender. Drain. Chop coarsely. Melt margarine in a large saucepan, add chopped onion and celery and cook until onion is clear but not brown. Transfer to a large mixing bowl and add breadcrumbs, 2 cups at a time, and mix thoroughly. Add thyme and oregano and blend well. Add coarsely-chopped chestnuts. Yield enough dressing for a 12 to 14 pound turkey, approximately 9 to 10 servings.

. . . .

DUCKS

Removing feathers and down from ducks can be a frustrating experience. It can take hours to clean off all of the down — but there is an easier way to do it. First, pluck the large feathers, then line a large bowl or pan with heavy foil, set the duck on top of it and pour hot, melted parrafin over the entire bird. Wait until cool, peel off wax and feathers and cut the cleaning time in half. Then just throw foil and feathers away.

Of course there's an easier way — buy the duck already cleaned and dressed at the store!

ROAST DUCK

Allow 1 pound per serving. Roast uncovered in 350 F. oven 20 to 30 minutes to the pound for a well-cooked, fully grown, domestic bird. Baste every 30 minutes with pan drippings. For a young duck, if desired rare-cooked without stuffing, truss the bird, sprinkle with oregano, pepper and flour and roast in a very hot oven (500 F.) 15 to 30 minutes.

To absorb the strong flavor of ducks, place cored and quartered apples inside cavity of each bird, or celery or onions, and remove before serving, or combine 2 tablespoons chopped onion to each cup of chopped celery (tops and leaves may be used), mixing well before placing in the duck/ducks. This is very effective.

Hot potato stuffing may also be used. Oregano or sage dressing is also good, and cut up the giblets fine and include with this stuffing; use a full cup of chopped celery. Make gravy from the broth in which the giblets were cooked and pour over the duck. Serve with tart jelly and green peas.

. . . .

POTATO STUFFING

F=Fair; G=Good; H=High; L=Low; t or T = trace; n/a = no information available; dashes = zero or unmeasurable

GRAM WT.	FOOD	VITAMINS	CAL	(mg) SOD	PRO	FAT	CARB	CHOL	FATTY ACIDS SAT	UNSAT	CALC	IRON	(mg) POTSM
99	AVERAGE PER SERVING		177	412									217
	Ingredients:												
390	2 cp hot mashed potatoes	A B1 B2 C	250	1174	L	L	F	---	---	---	F	L	1018
100	1 cp dry breadcrumbs	A^t B1 B2 C^t	390	736	F	L	G	---	---	---	G	F	152
n/a	1/2 tsp pepper						--n/a--						
n/a	1 tsp sage or oregano						--n/a--						
56	4 tblspn margarine	A D	400	558	L	H	L	---	L	H	L	---	13
50	6 green onions, chopped fine	A^t B1 B2 C	20	3	L	L	F	---	---	---	F	L	116
596	Recipe totals (gms; cal; sod. & potsm.)		1060	2471									1299

METHOD

Mix ingredients together, starting with mashed potatoes and folding in thoroughly.   Yield   3 cups, enough for an 8 pound duck.

. . . .

ROAST GOOSE

A young goose about 4 to 5 months old is better roasted; an older one is tastier braised. If the bird is already dressed, singe the hairs off, wash carefully in warm to hot water and dry the outside with a paper towel. Remove giblets, rinse in cold water and put them on to cook in enough water to cover, adding a few sprigs of celery leaves and green onion tops. Stuff goose with mashed potato dressing (see Roast Duck). If goose is lean, lay strips of salt pork or bacon over the breast. Truss and bake in very hot oven (500 F.) 45 minutes then remove from the oven, pour off fat, sprinkle with pepper and a little salt, brush with flour and return it to a 350 F. oven. When flour is brown, pour 1 cup of hot water into the roasting pan and baste the goose often, dredging it each time with a light sifting of flour to absorb the fat.

For a young goose, allow 20 minutes to the pound; 25 minutes for an older bird.

When giblets are tender, skim out of the broth with a slotted spoon, cut fine and return to broth. (Celery and onions may be removed, if desired). Add 1/2 teaspoon sage or oregano to the broth then bring to a boil. Thicken with a mixture of cornstarch and water stirred until smooth. Garnish goose with fresh parsley. Serve with applesauce.

Instead of potato stuffing, a bread dressing may be used.

. . . .

GUINEA HEN FRICASSEE

Clean and cut up the fowl. Fry bacon to extract the fat, add guinea hen and cook until well browned. Remove pieces of fowl. Add 2 tablespoons flour to fat in the pan and stir until thoroughly mixed. Add 2 cups hot water gradually, stirring constantly until gravy boils. Add 1 small clove garlic. Put pieces of guinea hen back in the pan, cover and simmer 1-1/2 to 2 hours or until meat is tender. Add water as needed. Add a dash of pepper just before serving. Yield   about 4 servings.

. . . .

GAME BIRDS

The flesh of quail, partridges and pheasant is white meat and, like chicken, should be thoroughly cooked. The flesh of ducks, pigeons, squab (young pigeons), grouse (prairie chicken), snipe and woodcock is dark meat which some gourmets prefer cooked rare and served very hot.

But epicurean delight or bourgeois, however they're cooked is strictly a matter of palatable preference for each individual. For instance, I prefer fowl or birds browned on the outside, not dry on the inside, juicy and succulent, and cooked until the meat nearly falls from the bones, flavored with just a hint of delicate herbs.

Strips of bacon or salt pork wrapped around small birds, or laid over the breasts and legs of larger fowl, and frequent basting while roasting, helps to prevent the meat from drying. Foil tents used over the birds half time, then removed to brown the other half, have been very effective in keeping the birds moist. A covered baking dish serves the same purpose as foil tents, and the addition of a little water braises the birds until tender.

To repeat, the way birds are cooked is a matter of individual tastes; to attain yours, experiment. Write down what you do, step by step. Add dabs of this and that to the basic recipe until you're happy with the finished product. After all, a basic recipe is just that — basic. It's how you put it all together that makes the difference.

To Broil: Clean birds, remove any shot, split them down the back, dust with flour — this keeps the juices — place on the broiler rack with inside toward the heat. Allow about 10 minutes for quail; 25 to 40 minutes for pheasant and partridges. When done, brush generously all over with oil or margarine.

If breasts are quite thick, cover with foil for half the time, then remove to brown.

GROUSE

To be palatable, grouse should be larded because they're dry birds. To prepare — clean and wipe with a damp towel. On each bird lay thin slices of bacon over entire surface, holding bacon in place by tying it on with white string or thread. Place in a roasting pan and pour enough boiling water over them sufficient to baste birds while cooking. Roast at 500 F. 15 to 25 minutes, basting every 7 to 8 minutes. After 15 minutes, reduce heat to 350 F. When finished, remove bacon, brush birds all over with margarine or oil, dredge with flour and place in oven again until brown. Dilute gravy in the pan with a little water, add a sprinkle of marjoram or oregano, thicken with cornstarch and water mixed together until smooth. Garnish birds with rings of green pepper sauteed a little, and the strips of bacon roasted with the birds.

ROAST QUAIL

Dress, clean, remove any shot, then stuff each bird with 1 large oyster. Place bacon strips over breast and legs. Tie on with soft white twine, and complete trussing. Place birds in roasting pan, pour boiling water over them, enough to use for basting during the cooking period. Bake at 500 F. 15 to 20 minutes, basting 3 or 4 times. When done, reduce heat to 350 F. Remove bacon and save it to serve with birds. Brush quail with margarine or oil, sift flour over them and return to oven to brown. When a golden, rich brown, remove birds to a hot platter and keep warm in a 180 F. oven while making gravy from liquor in the roasting pan. Add a little water, if needed, to liquid in the roaster. Place roaster over a stove burner on medium heat, or pour liquid into saucepan, bring to a boil, and slowly add a mixture of cornstarch and water stirred until smooth (1 tablespoon cornstarch in 1/4 cup water for every cup of liquid to thickened). Sprinkle a little oregano into the gravy; blend well.

WILD MALLARD DUCK

These ducks are good if stuffed with bread dressing, but are inclined to be dry when roasted. To avoid this, they should be trussed and placed in a large kettle in a small quantity of water. Add a few slices of onion, a sprinkle of thyme then cover and cook slowly about 1 hour. Birds should be turned often during the cooking process and water replenished as needed, just enough to prevent burning. When cooked, remove from kettle, add a cup of water to juices in the kettle and thicken with a mixture of cornstarch and water, stirring until gravy is desired consistency. Pour over birds and serve.

. . . .

BREAD SAUCE

F=Fair; G=Good; H=High; L=Low; t or T = trace; n/a = no information available; dashes = zero or unmeasurable

GRAM WT.	FOOD	VITAMINS	CAL	(mg) SOD	PRO	FAT	CARB	CHOL (mg)*	FATTY ACIDS SAT	UNSAT	CALC	IRON	(mg) POTSM
204	AVERAGE PER SERVING		215	321				4					370
	Ingredients:												
100	1 cp dry breadcrumbs	A^t B1 B2 C^t	390	736	F	L	G	---	---	---	G	F	152
492	2 cp 2% low-fat milk	A B1 B2 C	290	300	H	F	G	L	L	L	H	L	861
110	1 onion, studded with cloves	A B1 B2 C	40	11	L	L	L	---	---	---	L	L	173
14	1 tblspn margarine	A D	100	139	L	H	L	---	L	H	L	---	3
100	1/3 cp prepared horseradish	---	38	96	L	L	L	---	---	---	F	L	290
816	Recipe totals (gms; cal; sod. & potsm.)		858	1282									1479

METHOD

Add crumbs to hot milk (do not boil); add onion and cook 12 minutes. Remove onion and add 1 tablespoon of margarine, then stir in horseradish.

This sauce may be served with roast chicken, duck, or other fowl or meats, also wild duck, guinea hen, pheasant, quail and squab.

* In 492 grams of fluid skim milk, there are 15 milligrams of cholesterol; divided by 4 servings equals 4 average milligrams of cholesterol per serving, as calculated from U.S.D.A. Handbook No. 8, pg. 146, item 29.

. . . .

VENISON

Although the word venison means to hunt game and the flesh of any game animal, such as deer, elk, moose and caribou, the word is more closely associated with the flesh of wild deer.

The meat of wild deer (venison) is short-fibered and dark-colored, with a high game flavor. Tastes differ in the way it is cooked. Some prefer it medium-rare, declaring it is best when cooked this way, while others prefer it well done — but isn't this the case with all meat cooking? People who like their beefsteak rare believe the flavor is ruined when well-cooked, and so it always goes — back to preference.

Many professional chefs marinate venison, believing it not only improves the flavor, but suppresses the gaminess.

Articles on venison suggest that it should be hung about two weeks in a cool, dry place to develop better flavor and to tenderize the meat, but this seems to be true of most meat. Hanging breaks down tough muscles and fibers.

VENISON MARINADE

Cut steaks or chops in individual portions. Sprinkle a little powdered clove over the meat, then salt and black pepper. Arrange venison in a china dish. Wash, pare and slice onions and carrots thin, depending on amount of meat to be used, plus fresh parsley, a sprinkle of thyme and whole bay leaves. Place over meat in layers. Add crushed garlic. Cover all with dry red wine distributed evenly over all. Cover dish and store in refrigerator 2 days.

This marinade may also be used for roasts or pot roasts but meat should be turned once a day and left in the refrigerator 2 more days.

STEAKS AND CHOPS

Drain meat as dry as possible. Brown steaks or chops on both sides in very hot, melted margarine to usual degree of doneness for beefsteak, then discard margarine. Add marinade to the pan, add stock or water with beef bouillon or extract; bring to a boil and thicken gravy with a mixture of cornstarch and water at reduced heat, stirring until desired consistency is reached, then add a few tablespoons of grape, currant, or other jelly. Cook slowly for 10 to 15 minutes longer, then strain and either pour over the meat or serve separately.

POT ROAST

Follow first of above directions, but after discarding margarine and adding marinade, add enough water to nearly cover meat (or beef stock made with extract or bouillon), reduce heat, cover pan, and simmer until tender. Remove meat to a hot platter; make gravy (as above); add jelly, if desired, and strain. Serve separately, or pour gravy over meat.

580

LEG OF VENISON

Wipe meat with a damp paper towel. Remove the dry skin. Lard with strips of bacon or salt pork. Rub soft margarine all over the leg (or bacon fat). Insert slivers of garlic into tiny cuts in the fleshy part of the leg. Dredge with flour. Place meat on a rack in a roasting pan, sprinkle bottom of the pan with a little flour. Preheat oven to 500 F. Place roaster in oven about 5 minutes and watch carefully until flour browns, then add enough boiling water to cover the bottom of the pan. Baste meat every 15 minutes, thoroughly. (This is very important because it makes the meat juicier). After the first 15 minutes, reduce heat to 325 F. Bake at 12 to 15 minutes to the pound for rare; 15 to 20 minutes for medium and 20 to 25 minutes for well done.

Meat can be covered during the roasting period, and less basting is necessary, but wait until after the first basting period before covering.

. . . .

Venison can be used in ground meat dishes, such as patties, sausage, and meat loaf; chops may be rolled in bread crumbs or fine potato chips; substitute venison for beef in meat pies and stews; liver, kidneys, tongue and heart may be used in other tasty dishes.

FREEZING GAME ANIMALS

Deer, elk, moose, bear, and other large game, should be handled in the same way as beef or veal. To prevent spoilage, which can occur quickly, prompt attention to bleeding and thorough chilling should be given even as in domestic animals.

. . . .

MISCELLANEOUS ITEMS

MISCELLANEOUS ITEMS

F=Fair; G=Good; H=High; L=Low; t or T = trace; n/a = no information available; dashes = zero or unmeasurable

GRAM WT.	FOOD	VITAMINS	CAL	(mg) SOD	PRO	FAT	CARB	CHOL	FATTY ACIDS SAT	UNSAT	CALC	IRON	(mg) POTSM
3	Baking Powder, 1 tsp.	---	4	345	T	---	G	---	---	---	H	---	---
250	Barbecue sauce, 1 cp	A B1 B2 C	230	2038	L	L	L	---	---	---	F	F	435
	Beverages, Alcoholic												
360	Beer, 12 fluid ozs.	B1 B2	150	25	L	---	L	---	---	---	L	T	90
	Gin, rum, vodka, whiskey												
42	80-proof, 1-1/2 fluid oz.	---	100	1	---	---	T	---	---	---	---	---	1
42	86-proof, 1-1/2 fluid oz.	---	105	1	---	---	T	---	---	---	---	---	1
42	90-proof, 1-1/2 fluid oz.	---	110	1	---	---	T	---	---	---	---	---	1
42	94-proof, 1-1/2 fluid oz.	---	115	1	---	---	T	---	---	---	---	---	1
42	100-proof, 1-1/2 fluid oz.	---	125	1	---	---	T	---	---	---	---	---	1
	Wines												
103	Dessert, 3-1/2 fluid oz. glass	B1 B2	140	4	T	---	L	---	---	---	L	---	77
102	Table, 3-1/2 fluid oz. glass	B1 B2	85	5	T	---	L	---	---	---	L	L	94
	Beverages, Non-alcoholic												
	(sweetened)												
366	Carbonated water, 12 fluid ozs.	---	115	---	---	---	F	---	---	---	---	---	---
369	Cola type, 12 fluid ozs.	---	145	---	---	---	F	---	---	---	---	---	---
372	Fruit-flavored soda, 12 fluid ozs.	---	170	---	---	---	F	---	---	---	---	---	---
	(Citrus, cherry, grape, strawberry,												
	Tom Collins mix, other)												
	(10% to 13% sugar)												
366	Ginger ale, 12 fluid ozs.	---	115	---	---	---	F	---	---	---	---	---	---
370	Root beer, 12 fluid ozs.	---	150	---	---	---	F	---	---	---	---	---	---
4	Bouillon Cubes, approximately												
	1/2" cube (or powder)	---	5	960	F	L	L	---	---	---	---	---	4
	Chocolate												
28	bitter or baking, 1 oz. square	A B1 B2	145	1	F	G	F	n/a	F	F	F	G	232
170	semi-sweet, small pieces, 1 cp	A B1 B2	860	3	L	G	G	n/a	H	F	L	F	553
	Gelatin												
7	Plain, dry powder in 1 envelope	---	25	---	H	L	---	---	---	---	---	---	---
85	Dessert powder, 3 oz. pkg.	---	315	270	L	---	H	---	---	---	---	---	---
240	Dessert, prepared with water, 1 cp	---	140	122	L	---	F	---	---	---	---	---	---

MISCELLANEOUS ITEMS

F=Fair; G=Good; H=High; L=Low; t or T = trace; n/a = no information available; dashes = zero or unmeasurable

GRAM WT.	FOOD	VITAMINS	CAL	(mg) SOD	PRO	FAT	CARB	CHOL	FATTY ACIDS SAT	UNSAT	CALC	IRON	(mg) POTSM
	Mustard												
n/a	dry	---------------------------------n/a-----------------------.											
100	prepared, brown	---	91	1307	L	L	L	---	---	---	G	F	130
100	prepared, yellow	---	78	1252	L	L	L	---	---	---	F	F	130
	Olives, Pickled (canned or bottled)												
16	Green, 4 medium or 3 extra large or 2 giant	A	15	384	L	F	L	---	T	F	F	F	9
10	Ripe, mission, 3 small or 2 large	A B1^t B2^t	15	75	L	F	L	---	T	F	G	F	3
	Pickles (See Chapter Two, Food List)												
	Popcorn (See Chapter One, Food List)												
95	Popsicle, 3 fluid ozs. size, 1	---	70	n/a	---	---	F	---	---	---	---	T	n/a
	Puddings Home recipe, starch base												
260	Chocolate, 1 cp.	A B1 B2 C	385	146	L	L	F	L*	L*	L*	F	L	445
	* If made with non-fat milk and cocoa, no eggs and cornstarch; but if made with melted chocolate, whole milk and eggs, cholesterol will be high (H), saturated fats high (H) and unsaturated low (L)												
255	Vanilla (blanc mange) 1 cp	A B1 B2 C	285	168	L	L	F	H*	H*	T*	G	T	352
	*(see note above)												
113	Pudding mix, dry form, 4-oz pk, 1	A^t B1 B2	410	457	L	L	H	-------n/a--------			L	F	96
193	Sherbet, 1 cp (for fruit sherbet see Chapter Six)	A B1 B2 C	260	19	L	L	F	---	---	---	L	T	42
4	Table salt, 1 tsp	---	---	1569	---	---	---	---	---	---	G	---	T
152	Tapioca, dry, quick-cooking, 1 cp	---	535	5	L	L	H	---	---	---	L	L	27
250	Tapioca desserts, apple, 1 cp	A B1^t B2^t C^t	295	128	L	L	F	---	---	---	L	L	65
165	cream pudding, 1 cp	A B1 B2 C	220	257	L	L	F	H	H	L	G	L	223
14	Tartar sauce, regular, 1 tblspn.	A B1^t B2^t C^t	75	99	L	G	L	L	L	H	L	L	11
15	Vinegar, 1 tblspn	---	T	T	---	L	---	---	---	---	L	L	15
250	White sauce, medium, 1 cp	A B1 B2 C	405	948	L	F	L	L*	L*	L*	G	L	348
	*. Cholesterol and saturated fatty acids will be low if non-fat skim or 2% low-fat milk is used instead of whole milk and corn oil margarine is used in place of butter. See recipes.												
	Yeast												
7	Baker's dry, active, 1 pkg.	A^t B1 B2 C^t	20	4	F	L	F	---	---	---	F	H	140
100	Compressed	A^t B1 B2 C^t	86	16	F	L	F	---	---	---	L	G	610

MISCELLANEOUS ITEMS

F=Fair; G=Good; H=High; L=Low; t or T = trace; n/a = no information available; dashes = zero or unmeasurable

GRAM WT.	FOOD	VITAMINS	CAL	(mg) SOD	PRO	FAT	CARB	CHOL	FATTY ACIDS SAT	UNSAT	CALC	IRON	(mg) POTSM
8	Yeast, continued Brewer's dry, 1 tblspn Yoghurt See Dairy Products Chapter Four	A^t B1 B2 C^t	25	10	F	L	F	---	---	---	H	H	152

F=Fair; G=Good; H=High; L=Low; t or T = trace; n/a = no information available;   dashes = zero or unmeasurable

GRAM WT.	FOOD	VITAMINS	CAL	(mg) SOD	PRO	FAT	CARB	CHOL	FATTY ACIDS SAT	UNSAT	CALC	IRON	(mg) POTSM
28	AVERAGE PER OUNCE		92	13				(mg)* 25					25
	Ingredients:												
50	1 egg, separated	A B1 B2	75	61	F	F	L	H	H	L	F	F	65
24	2 tblspn granulated sugar	---	96	T	---	F	H L	H	---	---	---	F L	1
238	1 cp heavy whipping cream	A B1 B2 C	840	86	L	G	L		--------n/a---------		F	T	212
n/a	1/3 cp brandy	----------------------						--n/a--					
312	Recipe totals (gms; cal; sod. & potsm.)		1011	147									278

METHOD

Separate egg, beat the white until soft peaks form. Add sugar gradually; beat in slightly-beaten egg yolk. Whip the cream and fold into the meringue then stir in brandy. Yield   about 11 ounces.

*   There are 275 milligrams of cholesterol in 50 grams of whole egg; divided by 11 ozs. equals 25 average milligrams of cholesterol per ounce.

NOTE   Brandy sauces are used with bread, plum or other types of puddings, also on ice creams or on leftover cakes and pies. No. 1 Brandy Sauce (above) is uncooked; No. 2 is cooked and usually served over hot plum pudding, or hot mince pie.

. . . .

BRANDY SAUCE NO. 2

F=Fair; G=Good; H=High; L=Low; t or T = trace; n/a = no information available; dashes = zero or unmeasurable

GRAM WT.	FOOD	VITAMINS	CAL	(mg) SOD	PRO	FAT	CARB	CHOL	FATTY ACIDS SAT	UNSAT	CALC	IRON	(mg) POTSM
28	AVERAGE PER OUNCE		79	87									1
	Ingredients:												
200	1 cp granulated sugar	---	770	2	---	---	H	---	---	---	---	L	6
14	1-1/2 tblspn cornstarch	---	51	---	L	T	H	---	---	---	---	---	---
2	1/2 tsp salt	---	---	785	---	---	---	---	---	---	H	---	---
118	1/2 cp water						----n/a----						
56	4 tblspn margarine	A D	400	556	L	H	L	---	L	G	L	---	13
42	3 tblspn brandy						----n/a----						
n/a	1 tsp vanilla						----n/a----						
432	Recipe totals (gms; cal; sod. & potsm.)		1221	1343									19

METHOD

Mix 1/2 cup sugar with cornstarch and salt in a small saucepan; add water and blend well. Cook and stir over medium heat until sauce is smooth and thick. Cream margarine and remaining sugar until light and fluffy. Add to first mixture and stir only until sugar is dissolved. Add brandy and vanilla and reheat only to serving temperature. Yield about 1-3/4 cups. To serve hot over plum pudding; add a sprinkle of nutmeg.

. . . .

587

HOT COCOA FUDGE SAUCE

F=Fair; G=Good; H=High; L=Low; t or T = trace; n/a = no information available;   dashes = zero or unmeasurable

GRAM WT.	FOOD	VITAMINS	CAL	(mg) SOD	PRO	FAT	CARB	CHOL	FATTY ACIDS SAT	UNSAT	CALC	IRON	(mg) POTSM
								(mg)*					
28	AVERAGE PER OUNCE		82	24				T					24
	Ingredients:												
300	1-1/2 cp granulated sugar	---	1155	3	---	---	H	---	---	---	---	L	9
24	4 tblspn cocoa	B1 B2	88	68	L	L	H	n/a	L	L	L	L	120
185	3/4 cp 2% low-fat milk	A B1 B2 C	110	113	H	F	G	L	L	L	H	L	324
28	2 tblspn margarine	A D	200	279	L	H	L	---	L	H	L	---	6
n/a	1 tsp vanilla						-n/a-						
537	Recipe totals (gms; cal; sod. & potsm.)		1553	463									459

METHOD

Mix sugar and cocoa together in a saucepan. Press out any lumps. Stir in milk. Heat slowly to boiling, stirring until sugar dissolves. Cook slowly until sirup reaches 238 F., or until soft ball forms when dropped in cold water in a sauce dish. Remove from heat, add margarine and vanilla. Allow to cool a few minutes, then beat 2 or 3 minutes. Serve over ice cream. Yield about 19 ounces.

* Cholesterol is minimal.

. . . .

PLAIN NUTMEG SAUCE

F=Fair; G=Good; H=High; L=Low; t or T = trace; n/a = no information available;   dashes = zero or unmeasurable

GRAM WT.	FOOD	VITAMINS	CAL	(mg) SOD	PRO	FAT	CARB	CHOL	FATTY ACIDS SAT	UNSAT	CALC	IRON	(mg) POTSM
28	AVERAGE PER OUNCE		36	13									1
	Ingredients:												
200	1 cp granulated sugar	---	770	2	---	---	H	---	---	---	---	L	6
7	1 tblspn flour	B1 B2	26	T	F	L	G	---	---	---	L	F	7
1	dash salt	---	---	196	---	---	---	---	---	---	G	---	---
472	2 cp boiling water	------					n/a						
14	1 tblspn margarine	A D	100	139	L	H	T	---	L	H	L	---	3
n/a	1 tsp nutmeg	------					n/a						
694	Recipe totals (gms; cal; sod. & potsm.)		896	337									16

METHOD

Mix sugar, flour and salt together, add boiling water, stirring constantly, then add margarine and cook 5 minutes. Remove from heat and stir in nutmeg. Serve hot on apple dumplings, berry puddings, or puddings made with biscuit dough. Yield   about 25 ounces.

. . . .

VINEGAR-NUTMEG SAUCE

F=Fair; G=Good; H=High; L=Low; t or T = trace; n/a = no information available; dashes = zero or unmeasurable

GRAM WT.	FOOD	VITAMINS	CAL	(mg) SOD	PRO	FAT	CARB	CHOL	FATTY ACIDS SAT	UNSAT	CALC	IRON	(mg) POTSM
28	AVERAGE PER OUNCE		45	34									3
	Ingredients:												
100	1/2 cp granulated sugar	---	385	1	---	---	H	---	---	---	---	L	3
9	1 tblspn cornstarch	---	34	---	L	T	H	---	---	---	---	---	---
236	1 cp boiling water						-----n/a-----						
1	dash salt	---	---	196	---	---	---	---	---	---	H	---	---
28	2 tblspn margarine	A D	200	279	L	H	L	---	L	G	L	---	6
30	2 tblspn vinegar	---	4	---	T	---	L	---	---	---	L	L	30
n/a	1 tblspn grated nutmeg						-----n/a-----						
404	Recipe totals (gms; cal; sod. & potsm.)		623	476									39

METHOD

Mix sugar and cornstarch together; add boiling water gradually and a dash of salt. Boil until clear and thick. Continue cooking over hot water (as in a double-boiler) for 20 minutes. Beat in margarine, vinegar and nutmeg. Yield about 14 ounces. Use this sauce on plum pudding, cottage pudding, and brown betty.

. . . .

QUICK CARAMEL SAUCE

F=Fair; G=Good; H=High; L=Low; t or T = trace; n/a = no information available; dashes = zero or unmeasurable

GRAM WT.	FOOD	VITAMINS	CAL	(mg) SOD	PRO	FAT	CARB	CHOL	FATTY ACIDS SAT	UNSAT	CALC	IRON	(mg) POTSM
								(mg)					
28	AVERAGE PER OUNCE		75	45				T					50
	Ingredients:												
227	20 vanilla caramels	A B1 B2 C^t	905	513	L	F	H	--------n/a--------			G	F	436
123	1/2 cp 2% low-fat milk	A B1 B2 C	73	75	H	F	G	L	L	L	H	L	215
350	Recipe totals (gms; cal; sod. & potsm.)		978	588									651

METHOD

Heat caramels in a double-boiler until melted. Add milk gradually and stir until thoroughly mixed. Yield   about 1 cup.

. . . .

CARAMEL SAUCE

F=Fair; G=Good; H=High; L=Low; t or T = trace; n/a = no information available; dashes = zero or unmeasurable

GRAM WT.	FOOD	VITAMINS	CAL	(mg) SOD	PRO	FAT	CARB	CHOL	FATTY ACIDS SAT	UNSAT	CALC	IRON	(mg) POTSM
28	AVERAGE PER OUNCE		45	7									T
	Ingredients:												
200	1 cp sugar	---	770	2	---	---	H	---	---	---	---	L	6
15	1 tblspn cold water						n/a						
315	1-1/3 cps hot water						n/a						
9	1 tblspn cornstarch	---	34	---	L	T	H	---	---	---	---	---	---
14	1 tblspn margarine	A D	100	139	L	H	T	---	L	H	L	---	3
n/a	1 tsp vanilla						n/a						
553	Recipe totals (gms; cal; sod. & potsm.)		904	141									9

METHOD

Mix sugar and 1 tablespoon cold water together in a pan. Cook and stir until sugar is a clear brown sirup, but not as dark as caramel, then add hot water slowly, stirring until thoroughly mixed. Blend cornstarch with a little cold water until smooth, then add to sirup, stirring until well mixed. Boil 5 minutes. Continue cooking over hot water 15 minutes. Remove from heat, beat in margarine and vanilla. Yield about 2-1/4 cups.

. . . .

HARD SAUCE

F=Fair; G=Good; H=High; L=Low; t or T = trace; n/a = no information available; dashes = zero or unmeasurable

GRAM WT.	FOOD	VITAMINS	CAL	(mg) SOD	PRO	FAT	CARB	CHOL	FATTY ACIDS SAT	UNSAT	CALC	IRON	(mg) POTSM
28	AVERAGE PER OUNCE		142	106									3
	Ingredients:												
75	1/3 cp soft margarine	A D	534	740	L	H	L	---	L	H	L	---	17
120	1 cp sifted powdered sugar	---	460	1	---	---	H	---	---	---	---	L	4
n/a	1 tsp vanilla, rum or almond flavoring	--n/a--											
195	Recipe totals (gms; cal; sod. & potsm.)		994	741									21

METHOD

Cream margarine, add sugar gradually, pressing out any lumps. Beat until fluffy. Add flavoring. Store in a covered jar or bowl in the refrigerator until needed. Yield about 3/4 cup.

Use hard sauce on puddings, gingerbread, and on mince pie (add 1/2 teaspoon maple flavoring).
NOTE See Fruit Desserts in Chapter Six, Loganberry Pudding.

. . . .

BREAD PUDDING

F=Fair; G=Good; H=High; L=Low; t or T = trace; n/a = no information available; dashes = zero or unmeasurable

GRAM WT.	FOOD	VITAMINS	CAL	(mg) SOD	PRO	FAT	CARB	CHOL	FATTY ACIDS SAT	UNSAT	CALC	IRON	(mg) POTSM
								(mg)*					
192	AVERAGE PER SERVING		307	363				73					389
	Ingredients:												
200	2 cp dry breadcrumbs	A^t B1 B2 C^t	780	1472	F	L	G	---	---	---	G	F	304
984	4 cp hot 2% low-fat milk	A B1 B2 C	580	600	H	F	G	L	L	L	H	L	1722
100	1/2 cp granulated sugar	---	385	1	---	---	H	---	---	---	---	L	3
1	1/4 tsp salt	---	---	393	---	---	---	---	---	---	G	---	---
100	2 eggs, beaten	A B1 B2	150	122	F	F	L	H	H	L	F	F	129
28	2 tblspn margarine, melted	A D	200	279	L	H	L	---	L	H	L	---	6
124	3/4 cp seedless raisins	A B1 B2 C	360	33	L	T	H	---	---	---	G	H	946
n/a	1 tsp vanilla	-----------						-n/a-					------
n/a	cinnamon and nutmeg	-----------						-n/a-					------
1537	Recipe totals (gms; cal; sod. & potsm.)		2455	2900									3110

METHOD

Add breadcrumbs to hot milk and set aside to cool slightly. Mix sugar, salt and beaten eggs together, add margarine, raisins and vanilla. Combine with bread and milk. Pour into lightly greased casserole dish. Sprinkle with cinnamon and nutmeg. Bake at 325 F. about 1 hour or until center is set and slightly brown. Serve with Brandy Sauce No. 1 (see recipe in this chapter), or whipped cream to which vanilla and sugar has been added; or plain dairy topping mixed with 1 teaspoon of rum flavoring, or 2 to 3 tablespoons of brandy, instead of vanilla. Yield   8 servings.

*   There are 550 milligrams of cholesterol in 100 grams of whole egg, and 30 milligrams of cholesterol in 984 grams of fluid skim milk, for a total of 580 milligrams according to U.S.D.A. Handbook No. 8, pg. 146, items 12 and 29 respectively. Divide 580 milligrams of cholesterol by 8 servings equals 73 average milligrams per serving.

. . . .

CARAMEL PUDDING

F=Fair; G=Good; H=High; L=Low; t or T = trace; n/a = no information available;   dashes = zero or unmeasurable

GRAM WT.	FOOD	VITAMINS	CAL	(mg) SOD	PRO	FAT	CARB	CHOL (mg)*	FATTY ACIDS SAT	UNSAT	CALC	IRON	(mg) POTSM
124	AVERAGE PER SERVING		184	124				67					237
	Ingredients:												
165	3/4 cp brown sugar	B1 B2	615	51	---	---	H	---	---	---	G	G	568
1	dash salt	---	---	196	---	---	---	---	---	---	G	---	---
738	3 cp 2% low-fat milk	A B1 B2 C	435	450	H	F	G	L	L	L	H	L	1292
27	3 tblspn cornstarch	---	102	T	L	T	H	---	---	---	---	---	---
34	2 egg yolks, beaten	A B1 B2	120	18	F	G	L	H	H	T	G	H	33
28	2 tblspn margarine	A D	200	279	L	H	L	---	L	H	L	---	6
n/a	1 tsp vanilla						--- n/a ---						
993	Recipe totals (gms; cal; sod. & potsm.)		1472	994									1899

METHOD

Melt brown sugar and salt in a pan over low heat; brown. Add 2-1/2 cups milk gradually. The sugar may form into hard lumps, but continue heating and stirring until dissolved. Mix cornstarch with remaining milk, add to hot mixture and cook until thickened, stirring constantly. Add beaten egg yolks, cook 2 minutes longer. Add margarine and vanilla; mix well and chill. Yield 8 servings.

*   There are 22 milligrams of cholesterol in 738 grams of fluid skim milk, and 510 milligrams in 34 grams of egg yolk, for a total of 532 milligrams of cholesterol according to U.S.D.A. Handbook No. 8, pg. 146, items 14 and 29 respectively. Divide 532 milligrams of cholesterol by 8 servings equals 67 average milligrams per serving.

. . . .

F=Fair; G=Good; H=High; L=Low; t or T = trace; n/a = no information available; dashes = zero or unmeasurable

GRAM WT.	FOOD	VITAMINS	CAL	(mg) SOD	PRO	FAT	CARB	CHOL	FATTY ACIDS SAT	UNSAT	CALC	IRON	(mg) POTSM
66	AVERAGE PER SERVING		95	123				(mg)* 138					91
	Ingredients:												
150	3 eggs, separated	A B1 B2	225	183	F	F	L	H	H	L	F	F	194
24	2 tblspn granulated sugar	---	96	T	---	---	H	---	---	---	---	L	1
5	1 tsp margarine, melted	A D	34	46	L	H	T	---	L	H	L	---	1
1	1/4 tsp salt	---	---	393	---	---	---	---	---	---	G	---	---
n/a	1/2 tsp vanilla						-n/a-						
28	1/4 cp flour	B1 B2	105	1	F	L	G	---	L	---	L	F	27
185	3/4 cp 2% low-fat milk	A B1 B2 C	110	113	H	F	G	L	L	L	H	L	323
393	Recipe totals (gms; cal; sod. & potsm.)		570	736									546

METHOD

Separate eggs; set whites aside. Beat egg yolks, add sugar and beat again. Stir in melted margarine, salt and vanilla; add flour and milk alternately, then fold in stiffly beaten egg whites. Pour into a well greased mold. Place mold in a pan of water and bake at 350 F. about 1 hour or until firm. Serve hot with your favorite sauce or one of the nutmeg sauces in this chapter. Yield 6 servings.

* There are 825 milligrams of cholesterol in 150 grams of whole egg, and 5 milligrams in 185 grams of fluid skim milk, as calculated from U.S.D.A. Handbook No. 8, pg. 146, items 12 and 29 respectively. Divide 830 milligrams of cholesterol by 6 servings equals 138 average milligrams per serving.

. . . .

PLUM PUDDING

F=Fair; G=Good; H=High; L=Low; t or T = trace; n/a = no information available; dashes = zero or unmeasurable

GRAM WT.	FOOD	VITAMINS	CAL	(mg) SOD	PRO	FAT	CARB	CHOL (mg)*	FATTY ACIDS SAT	UNSAT	CALC	IRON	(mg) POTSM
130	AVERAGE PER SERVING		467	203				55					328
	Ingredients:												
115	1 cp presifted flour	B1 B2	420	2	F	L	G	---	---	---	L	F	109
4	1 tsp baking soda	---		3	407 L	T	G	---	---	---	H	---	---
2	1/2 tsp salt	---	---	785	---	---	---	---	---	---	G	---	---
n/a	1 tsp each nutmeg and cinnamon	--n/a--											
50	2 cp soft breadcrumbs	A^t B1 B2 C^t	140	254	L	L	G	---	---	---	F	F	76
100	2 eggs	A B1 B2	150	122	F	F	L	H	H	L	F	F	129
220	1 cp brown sugar, firmly packed	B1 B2	820	66	---	---	H	---	---	---	G	G	757
113	1/4 lb (1 cp) ground suet	---	969	---	L	H	---	n/a	H	L	---	---	---
248	1-1/2 cp seedless raisins	A B1 B2 C	720	68	L	T	H	---	---	---	G	H	1892
113	4 oz candied cherries	---	383	--	L	L	H	---	---	---	---	---	---
113	4 oz candied pineapple	---	357	---	L	L	H	---	---	---	---	---	---
113	4 oz lemon peel, chopped	---	357	---	L	L	H	---	---	---	---	---	181
113	4 oz citron, chopped	---	355	328	L	L	H	---	---	---	---	L	136
1304	Recipe totals (gms; cal; sod. & potsm.)		4674	2032									3280

METHOD

Sift flour once, measure 1 cup, add soda, salt and spices and sift again. Add bread crumbs and blend. Beat eggs, add brown sugar gradually, pressing out any lumps, and beat until light. Add suet and blend. Add sifted dry ingredients and beat until flour is moistened. Fold in raisins and chopped candied fruits. Mix well. Pour into a 2-quart pudding mold, cover with foil and tie with string to hold tight, unless mold has a tight-fitting cover. Set on a rack in a deep kettle, pour boiling water into kettle to half way up the mold. Cover kettle and steam 2-1/2 to 3 hours. Serve warm with either hard sauce, brandy sauce or nutmeg sauce. Yield 8 to 10 servings.

* There are 550 milligrams of cholesterol in 100 grams of whole egg, per U.S.D.A. Handbook No. 8, pg. 146, item 12. Divide 550 milligrams of cholesterol by 10 servings equals 55 average milligrams per serving.

. . . .

CREOLE YAM PUDDING

F=Fair; G=Good; H=High; L=Low; t or T = trace; n/a = no information available; dashes = zero or unmeasurable

GRAM WT.	FOOD	VITAMINS	CAL	(mg) SOD	PRO	FAT	CARB	CHOL (mg)*	FATTY ACIDS SAT	FATTY ACIDS UNSAT	CALC	IRON	(mg) POTSM
187	AVERAGE PER SERVING		344	178				134					375
	Ingredients:												
908	5 medium sweet potatoes	A B1 B2 C	838	74	L	L	F	---	---	---	L	L	1786
75	1/3 cp margarine	A D	534	740	L	H	L	---	L	H	L	---	17
275	1-1/4 cp brown sugar	B1 B2	1025	83	---	---	H	---	---	---	G	G	946
68	4 egg yolks, beaten	A B1 B2	240	36	F	G	L	H	H	T	H	G	67
102	1/2 cp sherry wine	B1 B2	85	5	T	---	L	---	---	---	L	L	94
n/a	1 tsp nutmeg						--- n/a ---						
66	2 egg whites, beaten stiff	B1 B2	30	96	F	T	L	---	---	---	L	L	92
1	1/4 tsp salt		---	393	---	---	---	---	---	---	-G	---	---
1495	Recipe totals (gms; cal; sod. & potsm.)		2752	1427									3002

METHOD

Boil sweet potatoes until tender. Drain. Peel and mash potatoes while still hot then set aside to cool. Cream margarine and sugar together; add beaten egg yolks and mix well. Combine with potatoes, add sherry and nutmeg. Fold in egg whites and salt. Pour into well greased casserole and bake at 350 F. about 40 minutes. Yield 8 servings.

*   There are 550 milligrams of cholesterol in 100 grams of whole egg, and 510 milligrams in 34 grams of egg yolk, according to U.S.D.A. Handbook No. 8, pg. 146, items 12 and 14 respectively. Divide 1060 milligrams of cholesterol by 8 servings equals 134 average milligrams per serving.

. . . .

SUGARS and SWEETS

SUGARS, SWEETS

F=Fair; G=Good; H=High; L=Low; t or T = trace; n/a = no information available; dashes = zero or unmeasurable

GRAM WT.	FOOD	VITAMINS	CAL	(mg) SOD	PRO	FAT	CARB	CHOL	FATTY ACIDS SAT	UNSAT	CALC	IRON	(mg) POTSM
	Cake Icings (See Chapter Two under Cakes)												
	Candy												
28	Caramels, plain or chocolate, 1 oz.	A^t B1 B2 C^t	115	63	L	F	H	n/a	G	L	G	F	54
28	Chocolate, milk, plain, 1 oz.	A B1 B2 C^t	145	26	L	F	G	n/a	G	L	H	F	108
100	with peanuts	A B1 B2 C^t	543	66	F	F	F	n/a	G	G	H	F	487
28	Fondant mints, uncoated, candy-corn, 1 oz.	A^t B1 B2 C^t	105	59	L	L	H	---	---	---	L	F	25
	Fudge	A B2^t B2^t C	115	53	L	F	H	L	L	L	F	F	1
28	Gum drops, 1 oz.	B1^t B2^t	100	10	T	T	H	---	---	---	L	L	1
28	Hard, 1 oz.	---	110	9	---	L	H	---	---	---	L	F	1
28	Marshmallows, 1 oz.	B1$^{t(N)}$B2^t	90	11	L	T	H	---	---	---	L	F	2
	Mints, uncoated. See Fondant												
100	Peanut brittle (no added salt/soda)	B1 B2	421	31	L	F	H	n/a	L	H	L	F	151
	Chocolate topping												
38	thin type, 1 fluid oz.	A^t B1 B2	90	20	L	L	G	n/a	T	T	L	F	107
38	Fudge type, 1 fluid oz.	A^t B1 B2 C^t	125	34	L	F	G	n/a	L	T	G	F	108
21	Honey, strained or extracted, 1 tb.	B1 B2 C^t	65	1	L	---	H	---	---	---	L	L	11
20	Jams and preserves, 1 tblspn	A^t B1^t B2 C^t	55	2	L	L	G	---	---	---	L	F	18
18	Jellies, 1 tblspn	A^t B1^t B2 C^t	50	3	L	L	H	---	---	---	L	F	14
	Molasses, cane												
20	light, 1 tblspn	B1 B1	50	3	---	---	H	---	---	---	H	G	183
20	Blackstrap, 1 tblspn	B1 B2	45	19	---	---	H	---	---	---	H	H	585
	Sirups												
21	sorghum, 1 tblspn	B1$^{t(N)}$B2	55	--	---	---	H	---	---	---	H	H	---
	Table blends (chiefly corn)												
21	light and dark, 1 tblspn	---	60	14	---	---	H	---	---	---	F	G	1
100	cane and maple	---	252	2	---	---	H	---	---	---	L	T	26
	Sugars												
220	brown, firmly packed, 1 cp	B1 B2	820	66	---	---	H	---	---	---	G	G	757
15	brown, firmly packed, 1 tblspn	B1 B2	54	5	---	---	H	---	---	---	G	G	4
	White (Beet or Cane)												
200	granulated, 1 cp	---	770	2	---	---	H	---	---	---	---	L	6
12	granulated, 1 tblspn	---	48	T	---	---	H	---	---	---	---	T	T

SUGARS, SWEETS

F=Fair; G=Good; H=High; L=Low; t or T = trace; n/a = no information available;   dashes = zero or unmeasurable

GRAM WT.	FOOD	VITAMINS	CAL	(mg) SOD	PRO	FAT	CARB	CHOL	FATTY ACIDS SAT	UNSAT	CALC	IRON	(mg) POTSM
	Sugars continued												
120	powdered, stirred before												
	measuring, 1 cp	---	460	1	---	---	H	---	---	---	---	L	4
	Dextrose													
100	Anhydrous	---	366	---	---	---	H	---------n/a-------		---	---	---
100	Crystallized	---	335	---	---	---	H	---------n/a-------		---	T	---
100	Maple	---	348	---	---	---	H	---	---	---	H	F	242

CANDY

A candy thermometer is probably the most important item in making candy. It eliminates the necessity for manual testing for various stages in cooking the sirup, and is more accurate. The recipes in this chapter give the degrees (or temperatures) to which the sirup must be cooked, and if followed explicitly, should show good results. If you don't have a thermometer, the following tests may help to determine when it's time to stop cooking the sirup.

Half fill a china sauce dish with ice-cold water. Drop a little sirup into the water and pinch it between the thumb and finger.

If sirup forms a soft ball that loses its shape at once when removed from the water, it's at the soft-ball stage. This stage is used for fondant and fudge (thermometer temperature 238 F.).

If sirup forms a stiff ball that retains its shape for a second or two when removed from the water, then flattens out, it's at the stiff-ball stage for caramels and nougats (246 to 250 F. on thermometer).

Hard-ball stage for molasses and taffy, and soft candies to be pulled. The sirup forms a hard ball that will roll on a greased plate when removed from the water (260 F.).

Light to medium-crack stage for toffee and butterscotch and hard candies to be pulled. The sirup forms threads or spirals which are brittle under water, but which soften when removed from the water, and stick to the teeth when chewed (280 F.).

Hard-crack stage for clear brittle candies — sirup threads and spirals are brittle when removed from the water and do not stick to the teeth (300 F.).

. . . .

CHOCOLATE FUDGE

F=Fair; G=Good; H=High; L=Low; t or T = trace; n/a = no information available; dashes = zero or unmeasurable

GRAM WT.	FOOD	VITAMINS	CAL	(mg) SOD	PRO	FAT	CARB	CHOL	FATTY ACIDS SAT	UNSAT	CALC	IRON	(mg) POTSM
								(mg)*					
27	AVERAGE EACH PIECE		89	16				T					32
	Ingredients:												
400	2 cp granulated sugar	---	1540	4	---	---	H	---	---	---	---	L	12
56	2 squares chocolage	A B1 B2	290	2	F	G	F	n/a	F	F	F	G	465
n/a	1/8 tsp cream of tartar						-n/a-						
164	2/3 cp 2% low-fat milk	A B1 B2 C	97	100	H	F	G	L	L	L	H	L	287
28	2 tblspn margarine	A D	200	279	L	H	L	---	L	H	L	---	6
n/a	1 tsp vanilla						-n/a-						
648	Recipe totals (gms; cal; sod. & potsm.)		2127	385									770

METHOD

Mix sugar, grated/finely cut chocolate with the cream of tartar (or 2 tablespoons corn sirup instead), then add milk. Cook rather slowly, stirring until ingredients are well blended. Boil without stirring until thermometer reaches 238 F. Be sure bulb of the thermometer is not touching the botton of the pan. Remove from heat, add margarine but do not stir — wait until sirup is cool (110 F.) then add vanilla and beat sirup until it loses some of its gloss and feels thick, and fudge holds its shape when dropped from the spoon. Spread mixture in a greased pie pan or square baking dish. When cool, cut in squares. Yield About 24 pieces.

. . . .

COCOA FUDGE

F=Fair; G=Good; H=High; L=Low; t or T = trace; n/a = no information available; dashes = zero or unmeasurable

GRAM WT.	FOOD	VITAMINS	CAL	(mg) SOD	PRO	FAT	CARB	CHOL	FATTY ACIDS SAT	UNSAT	CALC	IRON	(mg) POTSM
29	AVERAGE EACH PIECE		82	25				(mg)* T					28
	Ingredients:												
600	3 cp granulated sugar	---	2310	6	---	---	H	---	---	---	---	L	18
64	2/3 cp cocoa	B1 B2	234	182	L	L	H	-------n/a-------			L	F	320
---	dash salt	---	---	196	---	---	---	---			L G	---	---
369	1-1/2 cp 2% low-fat milk	A B1 B2 C	218	225	H	F	G	L	L	L	H	L	646
28	2 tblspn margarine	A D	200	279	L	H	L	---	L	H	L	---	6
n/a	1 tsp vanilla						-------n/a-------						
1061	Recipe totals (gms; cal; sod. & potsm.)		2962	888									990

METHOD

In a medium to large saucepan, mix sugar and cocoa together, pressing out any lumps. Add dash of salt. Gradually add milk until mixture is thoroughly wet. Bring to a boil slowly on medium heat, stirring constantly until mixture bubbles. Reduce heat slightly, continue to boil slowly until mixture reaches the soft-ball stage (238 F.) or until a few drops in cold water forms a soft ball. Do not let bulb of thermometer touch bottom of pan. Remove from heat. Add margarine and vanilla. Do not stir. When sirup cools to 110 F., beat until it thickens and loses gloss. Pour fudge quickly, to prevent hardening, into a greased 8" x 8" x 2" dish or pan. Cool then cut into about 36 squares.

. . . .

BROWN SUGAR FUDGE

F=Fair; G=Good; H=High; L=Low; t or T = trace; n/a = no information available;   dashes = zero or unmeasurable

GRAM WT.	FOOD	VITAMINS	CAL	(mg) SOD	PRO	FAT	CARB	CHOL	FATTY ACIDS SAT	UNSAT	CALC	IRON	(mg) POTSM
31	AVERAGE PER PIECE		104	30									97
	Ingredients:												
28	2 tblspn margarine	A D	200	279	L	H	L	---	L	H	L	---	6
440	2 cp brown sugar	B1 B2	1640	132	---	---	H	---	---	---	H	H	1514
185	3/4 cp 2% low-fat milk	A B1 B2 C	110	113	H	F	G	L	L	L	H	L	324
81	3/4 cp pecans (optional)	A B1 B2 C	555	T	L	H	F	---	---	---	F	F	488
---	dash salt	---	---	196	---	---	---	---	---	---	G	---	---
734	Recipe totals (gms; cal; sod. & potsm.)		2505	720									2332

METHOD

Melt margarine in a saucepan, add sugar and stir until dissolved. Boil without stirring until a soft ball is formed (238 F.). Remove from heat, wait until cool, then beat, or work, until creamy. Add nuts, broken or chopped in pieces; stir, then press into a greased pan and cut into squares. Yield   about 24 pieces.

. . . .

DIVINITY FUDGE

F=Fair; G=Good; H=High; L=Low; t or T = trace; n/a = no information available; dashes = zero or unmeasurable

GRAM WT.	FOOD	VITAMINS	CAL	(mg) SOD	PRO	FAT	CARB	CHOL	FATTY ACIDS SAT	UNSAT	CALC	IRON	(mg) POTSM
38	AVERAGE EACH PIECE		102	11									6
	Ingredients:												
400	2 cp granulated sugar	--	1540	4	---	---	H	---	---	---	---	L	12
168	1/2 cp white corn sirup	---	480	112	---	---	H	---	---	---	F	G	7
118	1/2 cp water							---0---					
66	2 egg whites	B1 B2	30	96	F	T	L	---	---	---	L	L	92
n/a	1 tsp vanilla							---n/a---					
752	Recipe totals (gms; cal; sod. & potsm.)		2050	212									111

METHOD

In a saucepan, mix sugar, corn sirup and water together and cook rather slowly, stirring until sugar dissolves. Then do not stir, but allow sirup to boil at reduced heat until thermometer reaches 260 F. (the hard-ball stage) or until sirup forms a hard ball that rolls around on a greased plate when removed from the ice water. Remove from heat. Beat egg whites with a dash of salt until stiff but not dry. Pour hot sirup slowly, in a thin stream, into the egg whites, beating constantly until it begins to hold its shape. Beat in vanilla (if desired add 1/2 teaspoon almond, too). Beat until candy holds its shape when dropped from a spoon. Drop from teaspoon onto a lightly buttered pan or onto waxed paper. Allow to cool. Yield   about 20 pieces or more, depending on size when dropped.

If candied cherries, pineapple or chopped nuts are added, this should be done just after flavoring is added.

For Seafoam Fudge — Use 1 cup brown sugar, 1 cup granulated sugar, and add 3/4 cup chopped nuts if desired and 1/4 teaspoon maple flavoring instead of almond or vanilla.

. . . .

PENUCHE FUDGE

F=Fair; G=Good; H=High; L=Low; t or T = trace; n/a = no information available; dashes = zero or unmeasurable

GRAM WT.	FOOD	VITAMINS	CAL	(mg) SOD	PRO	FAT	CARB	CHOL (mg)*	FATTY ACIDS SAT	UNSAT	CALC	IRON	(mg) POTSM
29	AVERAGE EACH PIECE		98	17				T					93
	Ingredients:												
660	3 cp brown sugar	B1 B2	2460	198	---	---	H	---	---	---	G·	G	2270
246	1 cp 2% low-fat milk	A B1 B2 C	145	150	H	F	G	L	L	L	H	L	431
28	2 tblspn margarine	A D	200	279	L	H	L	---	L	H	L	---	6
n/a	1 tsp vanilla						--------n/a--------						
108	1 cp chopped pecans	A B1 B2 C	740	T	L	H	F	---	---	---	F	F	651
1042	Recipe totals (gms; cal; sod. & potsm.)		3545	627									3358

METHOD

In a saucepan, mix sugar and milk together, cooking and stirring until it boils. Then do not stir, but cook to the soft ball stage (238 F.). Remove from heat, add margarine and vanilla and stir to blend. Set saucepan in a pan of cold water to cool sirup quickly to 110 F. Beat fudge until it thickens and loses its gloss. Stir in nuts. Pour into a greased pan. When cool, cut into squares. Yield   about 36 pieces.

NOTE   Instead of nuts, add 1 cup shredded coconut.
Instead of pecans, use hickory nuts or walnuts.

*Cholesterol is minimal.

. . . .

PLAIN FONDANT

F=Fair; G=Good; H=High; L=Low; t or T = trace; n/a = no information available; dashes = zero or unmeasurable

GRAM WT.	FOOD	VITAMINS	CAL	(mg) SOD	PRO	FAT	CARB	CHOL	FATTY ACIDS SAT	FATTY ACIDS UNSAT	CALC	IRON	(mg) POTSM
28	AVERAGE PER OUNCE		69	1									1
	Ingredients:												
236	1 cp water	------					--n/a--						-----
400	2 cp granulated sugar	---	1540	4	---	---	H	---	---	---	---	L	12
42	2 tblspn corn sirup	---	120	28	---	---	H	---	---	---	F	G	2
n/a	1 tsp vanilla	------					--n/a--						-----
678	Recipe totals (gms; cal; sod. & potsm.)		1660	32									14

METHOD

Mix sugar, water, and corn sirup together in a saucepan, carefully, to avoid leaving sugar crystals on sides of pan, which could cause fondant to become grainy if left undissolved. Heat very slowly to prevent sirup from boiling before sugar is dissolved, stirring sirup against sides of pan to also dissolve crystals of sugar sticking to it. As soon as the sirup comes to the boiling point, stop stirring. Boil slowly until the soft ball stage (238 F.). While cooking, cover pan a minute or two, which helps to wash crystals down by the steam that forms. As soon as 238 F. is reached, remove pan from the fire and pour at once onto a large platter which has been dipped in cold water, and let stand until it is luke-warm. Add vanilla. Stir with a fork until creamy, then knead with the hands until fondant is firm and smooth, and free of lumps.

If allowed to ripen for several days before using, fondant has a better texture. In any case, it should be stored at least 24 hours, either by wrapping in waxed paper and putting it in a tightly covered jar, or wrapping in a cloth (wrung out in cold water) and storing in a container. Yield   about 1-1/2 pounds.

. . . .

CANDIES FROM FONDANT

Chocolate Creams Use a good quality dipping chocolate, sweet or bitter, and melt in top of double boiler. The water under the boiler should not be allowed to get hotter than 120 F. because overheating spoils chocolate for dipping. While melting, it should be stirred constantly to keep chocolate at an even temperature. After melting, beat chocolate thoroughly. Keep heat very low during the dipping process. To dip fondant centers, use a fork or confectioner's dipper. Dip centers one at a time; when covered, place on oiled paper. The room used for dipping should be cool, so that chocolate may harden quickly.

Wintergreen Flat Creams Melt some fondant in top of a double boiler until soft enough to drop from a spoon. Add a few drops of hot water if necessary. Color with red vegetable coloring to a delicate pink. Flavor with oil of wintergreen. Stir until creamy. Drop from a teaspoon onto oiled paper.

Peppermint Flat Creams Do not color fondant; flavor with oil of peppermint. Follow directions for wintergreen creams.

. . . .

OLD-FASHIONED TAFFY

F=Fair; G=Good; H=High; L=Low; t or T = trace; n/a = no information available; dashes = zero or unmeasurable

GRAM WT.	FOOD	VITAMINS	CAL	(mg) SOD	PRO	FAT	CARB	CHOL	FATTY ACIDS SAT	UNSAT	CALC	IRON	(mg) POTSM
15	AVERAGE EACH PIECE		42	9									1
	Ingredients:												
600	3 cp granulated sugar	---	2310	6	---	--	H	---	---	---	---	L	18
295	1-1/4 cp boiling water						--n/a--						
56	1/2 stick margarine	A D	400	558	L	H	L	---	L	H	L	---	13
30	2 tblspn vinegar	---	4	T	T	---	L	---	---	---	L	L	30
n/a	1 tsp vanilla						--n/a--						
981	Recipe totals (gms; cal; sod. & potsm.)		2714	564									61

METHOD

Mix sugar with boiling water, margarine and vinegar. Bring to a boil slowly, stirring occasionally. Cook without stirring to 260 F., the hard ball stage (see paragraph under Candy in this chapter). Remove from heat and add flavoring. Pour into a greased shallow pan or greased china platter. Let cool. Turn mixture toward center with a spatula as edges become firm.   As soon as taffy is cool enough to handle, grease hands with a little margarine and pull mixture with the tips of the fingers until creamy, and very white. Then stretch (or pull) taffy out into a long, narrow rope and cut into pieces with scissors. Either cool pieces on a lightly buttered platter or wrap them in wax paper or thin plastic, twisting each end of wrap. Yield about 65 pieces.

If colored taffy is desired, use a few drops of food coloring after vanilla is added.

. . . .

610

ELAINE'S SALT WATER TAFFY

F=Fair; G=Good; H=High; L=Low; t or T = trace; n/a = no information available; dashes = zero or unmeasurable

GRAM WT.	FOOD	VITAMINS	CAL	(mg) SOD	PRO	FAT	CARB	CHOL	FATTY ACIDS SAT	UNSAT	CALC	IRON	(mg) POTSM
20	AVERAGE EACH PIECE		59	41									1
	Ingredients:												
200	1 cp sugar	---	770	2	---	---	H	---	---	---	---	L	6
18	2 tblspn cornstarch	---	68	---	L	T	H	---	---	---	---	---	---
2	1/2 tsp salt	---	---	785	---	---	---	---	---	---	G	---	---
240	3/4 cp light corn sirup	---	720	168	---	---	H	---	---	---	F	G	10
118	1/2 cp water	----------	----------	----------	----------	----------	n/a ----------	----------	----------	----------	----------	----------	----------
28	2 tblspn margarine	A D	200	279	L	H	L	---	L	H	L	---	6
606	Recipe totals (gms; cal; sod. & potsm.)		1758	1234									22

METHOD

In a medium, heavy saucepan, mix the sugar, cornstarch and salt together then stir in the corn sirup, water and margarine until thoroughly mixed. Bring to a boil over moderate heat, stirring constantly until sugar dissolves. Continue to cook without stirring until 1/2 teaspoon of sirup dropped in a sauce dish of cold water forms a firm, pliable ball, or cook to the hard-ball stage (260 F.), if a candy thermometer is used. Remove from heat. Add 2 drops red food coloring and 2 teaspoons vanilla. Stir to blend. Pour into a buttered pan or cookie sheet. Let stand until cool enough to handle. Butter the hands so the taffy won't stick to them, gather mixture into a ball and knead on the pan or cookie sheet. Pull and twist until satin-like, and pale in color. Then pull into strands 1/2 to 3/4" thick. Using scissors, cut into pieces 1-1/2" long. Wrap pieces in wax paper, twist ends to seal. Yield   about 30 pieces.

Variations   If pale green taffy is desired, use green food coloring instead of red, also use only 1 teaspoon of vanilla, but add 1 teaspoon of the following flavors; wintergreen, spearmint, mint, etc. For yellow, use 1 teaspoon yellow food coloring instead of red and 1 teaspoon lemon, orange, maple or rum extract. For red taffy, use 1 teaspoon red food coloring and 1 teaspoon strawberry, cherry, respberry, or other flavoring extract.

. . . .

BILOXI PRALINES

F=Fair; G=Good; H=High; L=Low; t or T = trace; n/a = no information available; dashes = zero or unmeasurable

GRAM WT.	FOOD	VITAMINS	CAL	(mg) SOD	PRO	FAT	CARB	CHOL	FATTY ACIDS SAT	FATTY ACIDS UNSAT	CALC	IRON	(mg) POTSM
331	AVERAGE EACH PIECE		106	5				T*					50
	Ingredients:												
400	4 cp granulated sugar	---	1540	4	---	---	H	---	---	---	---	L	12
164	2/3 cp 2% low-fat milk	A B1 B2 C	97	100	H	F	G	L	L	L	H	L	287
320	1 cp maple sirup	---	806	32	---	---	H	---	---	---	F	L	564
108	2 cp pecan halves	A B1 B2 C	740	T	L	H	F	---	---	---	F	F	651
992	Recipe totals (gms; cal; sod. & potsm.)		3183	136									1514

METHOD

In a saucepan, combine sugar, milk, sirup, and stir until well mixed. Boil slowly until sirup reaches the soft ball stage (238 F.). Remove from heat and cool to lukewarm, then beat until smooth and creamy. Add nutmeats, drop from tip of a spoon onto oiled paper (brown paper) making small mounds. Yield about 30 pieces.

....

INDEX

HELPFUL HINTS AND SUGGESTIONS

NEW BOOKS FROM ERMINE PUBLISHERS, INC.

COOKBOOKS

COOKING WITH GOD by Robert L. Robb and Lori David   6.95
Over 275 recipes. Inspirational Biblical quotations

APHRODISIAC COOKBOOK by John Frascone and Mark David   6.95*
Exotic, erotic recipes from around the world

ADULT

WIN WITH GREAT BETTING SYSTEMS by Norman Dash   1.75
Detailed strategy and tactics from an expert

SEX IN THE SUPERMARKET by Lynn Sherwood   2.00
Hilarious expedition into the art of classy seduction

RHEA by Russ Martin   8.95*
Witchcraft and horror from New England to California

BEYOND THE THRESHOLD by Ronald Francis Patrick   8.95*
Horror behind walls of mortuary; industry veteran tells all

WHITE FLESH FOR BLACK MARKETS by John G. Garten   9.95*
Shocking underworld of prostitution-slavery

MASK OF DEATH by Anita Bachelin   3.95
Bizarre murder in a magnificent villa

SONGWRITING Words and Music by Sperry Hunt   3.95
How to write music and lyrics for modern markets

STAR KILLERS by James R. Singleton   2.95
U.S.Air Force Basic Training thriller

RONNIE RUNS WILD - 1980 EDITION by Irwin Zucker and Mark David   1.50
Former California Governor Reagan: up-to-the-minute political satire

ALCOHOLIC'S GUIDE TO SOBRIETY AND RECOVERY by Sandy Beck   2.95
VA-endorsed self-help recovery method, with recovery charts

ESCAPE INTO DANGER by Marguerite S. Gaffney   6.95*
Modern mystery that will keep you suspended

YOUNG ADULT

OVER THE HANDLEBARS by Don Gately   2.95
Short stories about motorcycling

AGAIN I SEE THE MOUNTAINS by Edith Volstad   2.95
Norwegian Youth underground battle Nazi Invasion

THE PRIEST IS AT PEACE by Davida Brouhard   2.95
Inspiring tale of a Priest's love of life and God

GROWING UP by Mark Anthony   1.50
Ageless poetry about growing, feeling and simply being

MISS INDEPENDENCE by Betty L. Gibbs   2.95
Wholesome analysis of crucial career vs. family life

"OUR SNAKE IS GONE AND ONE OF OUR SALAMANDERS   2.95
IS MISSING" by John J. Dalton
Sixth grade action-packed classroom adventure

SEND FOR A FREE CATALOGUE OF ALL EP PUBLICATIONS

*Hardbound

ERMINE PUBLISHERS, INC.
6253 Hollywood Boulevard
Suite 312
Hollywood, California 90028